Applied Linguistics for Teachers of Culturally and Linguistically Diverse Learners

Nabat Erdogan
University of Central Missouri, USA

Michael Wei
University of Missouri–Kansas City, USA

A volume in the Advances in Linguistics and
Communication Studies (ALCS) Book Series

Published in the United States of America by
    IGI Global
    Information Science Reference (an imprint of IGI Global)
    701 E. Chocolate Avenue
    Hershey PA, USA 17033
    Tel: 717-533-8845
    Fax: 717-533-8661
    E-mail: cust@igi-global.com
    Web site: http://www.igi-global.com

Library of Congress Cataloging-in-Publication Data

Names: Erdogan, Nabat, 1979- editor. | Wei, Michael, 1968- editor.
Title: Applied linguistics for teachers of culturally and linguistically
  diverse learners / Nabat Erdogan and Michael Wei, editors.
Description: Hershey, PA : Information Science Reference, [2019]
Identifiers: LCCN 2018054448| ISBN 9781522584674 (hardcover) | ISBN
  9781522584681 (ebook) | ISBN 9781522585022 (softcover)
Subjects: LCSH: English language--Study and teaching. | Applied linguistics.
Classification: LCC PE1066 .A67 2019 | DDC 428.0071--dc23 LC record available at https://lccn.loc.gov/2018054448

This book is published in the IGI Global book series Advances in Linguistics and Communication Studies (ALCS) (ISSN: 2372-109X; eISSN: 2372-1111)

British Cataloguing in Publication Data
A Cataloguing in Publication record for this book is available from the British Library.

All work contributed to this book is new, previously-unpublished material. The views expressed in this book are those of the authors, but not necessarily of the publisher.

For electronic access to this publication, please contact: eresources@igi-global.com.

Advances in Linguistics and Communication Studies (ALCS) Book Series

Abigail G. Scheg
Western Governors University, USA

ISSN:2372-109X
EISSN:2372-1111

MISSION

The scope of language and communication is constantly changing as society evolves, new modes of communication are developed through technological advancement, and novel words enter our lexicon as the result of cultural change. Understanding how we communicate and use language is crucial in all industries and updated research is necessary in order to promote further knowledge in this field.

The **Advances in Linguistics and Communication Studies (ALCS)** book series presents the latest research in diverse topics relating to language and communication. Interdisciplinary in its coverage, ALCS presents comprehensive research on the use of language and communication in various industries including business, education, government, and healthcare.

COVERAGE

- Interpersonal Communication
- Semantics
- Computer-Mediated Communication
- Media and Public Communications
- Discourse Analysis
- Non-Verbal Communication
- Cross-Cultural Communication
- Language in the Media
- Youth Language
- Sociolinguistics

IGI Global is currently accepting manuscripts for publication within this series. To submit a proposal for a volume in this series, please contact our Acquisition Editors at Acquisitions@igi-global.com or visit: http://www.igi-global.com/publish/.

The Advances in Linguistics and Communication Studies (ALCS) Book Series (ISSN 2372-109X) is published by IGI Global, 701 E. Chocolate Avenue, Hershey, PA 17033-1240, USA, www.igi-global.com. This series is composed of titles available for purchase individually; each title is edited to be contextually exclusive from any other title within the series. For pricing and ordering information please visit http://www.igi-global.com/book-series/advances-linguistics-communication-studies/78950. Postmaster: Send all address changes to above address. Copyright © 2019 IGI Global. All rights, including translation in other languages reserved by the publisher. No part of this series may be reproduced or used in any form or by any means – graphics, electronic, or mechanical, including photocopying, recording, taping, or information and retrieval systems – without written permission from the publisher, except for non commercial, educational use, including classroom teaching purposes. The views expressed in this series are those of the authors, but not necessarily of IGI Global.

Titles in this Series

For a list of additional titles in this series, please visit:
https://www.igi-global.com/book-series/advances-linguistics-communication-studies/78950

701 East Chocolate Avenue, Hershey, PA 17033, USA
Tel: 717-533-8845 x100 • Fax: 717-533-8661
E-Mail: cust@igi-global.com • www.igi-global.com

Editorial Advisory Board

Table of Contents

Unit 4
Morpho-Syntax

Unit 5
Semantics

Unit 6
Pragmatics

Unit 7
Phonetics

Unit 8
Phonology

Unit 9
Sociolinguistics

Detailed Table of Contents

Unit 1
What Is Language?

Chapter 1

Patricia A. Kilroe, California College of the Arts, USA

Human beings learn to speak or sign the language or languages they are exposed to as children. To have acquired the language(s) of one's speech community is to have acquired both linguistic and communicative competence. Linguistic competence results from internalizing the knowledge of the basic elements of language (sounds, words, sentences) and the rules for combining these elements into units that enable users to express linguistic meaning. Communicative competence results when learners have acquired knowledge of the appropriate social conventions involved in interpersonal communication. Effective language teaching is enhanced through an understanding of both the structural and social aspects of linguistic communication as well as how these aspects challenge students in the process of second language acquisition.

Unit 2
Morphology

Chapter 2

Nikki Ashcraft, University of Missouri, USA

This chapter introduces basic concepts in the field of morphology. In the first section, a morpheme is defined as the smallest unit of meaning in a language. In the second section, morphemes are divided into free and bound types, with bound morphemes further classified as either affixes (prefixes, infixes, suffixes, or circumfixes) or bound roots. This section additionally distinguishes between the role of function words and content words in a sentence. The third section outlines the nine word classes in English: nouns, pronouns, adjectives, determiners, verbs, adverbs, prepositions, conjunctions, and interjections. The final section of the chapter explains the implications of this information for teaching vocabulary, grammar, and language skills. The chapter concludes with questions for discussion and some practice exercises.

Chapter 3
Howard A. Williams, Teachers College, Columbia University, USA

This chapter presents a basic overview of the formation of words, with special attention to English. It covers the basics of both free and bound morphemes and the manner in which they combine. Productive processes including inflection, derivation, and compounding are examined with regard to their transparency and productivity; less common processes including zero-derivation (conversion) blending, clipping, back-formation are also covered, as are borrowing and coinage. Readers will be provided with guided practice in the analysis of English words into their constituent parts and in the principles of formation.

Unit 3
Syntax

Chapter 4
Howard A. Williams, Teachers College, Columbia University, USA

This chapter surveys the basics of the syntax of main clauses, with special attention to English. Readers are guided through the process of doing syntactic analysis with the aid of syntactic trees that model the properties of linearity, hierarchy, and recursion that characterize the syntax of human languages. The model used is a somewhat simplified version of X-bar syntax, which is currently the best-known and best-tested model of phrase structure within the subfield of syntax and which combines the virtues of simplicity, breadth, and predictive power. There is a section on the theory of grammatical relations and its relationship to phrase structure theory, as well as a section providing an overview of basic world constituent orders.

Chapter 5
Christian Waldmann, Linnaeus University, Sweden
Kirk P. H. Sullivan, Umeå University, Sweden

This chapter deals with syntax rules and grammaticality judgments in the teaching and learning of English as a second and foreign language for linguistically diverse learners. Grammaticality judgment tasks are used in linguistic research to probe speakers' implicit knowledge about the syntactic rules of language. This chapter discusses grammaticality judgment tasks in educational contexts and proposes a method for teaching syntactic rules of English based on the grammaticality judgments of second and foreign language learners of English. The chapter also attempts to raise grammatical consciousness for teaching of English as a second or foreign language as well as illustrating how various media can be used to design and present grammaticality judgment tasks to support language learning and learner engagement, participation, and motivation.

Unit 4
Morpho-Syntax

Chapter 6
Gulsat Aygen, Northern Illinois University, USA

The goal of this chapter is to introduce the connection between morphology and syntax, using inflectional morphemes and functional words that mark specific inflectional categories on the verb. The chapter identifies and discusses four major inflectional categories marked on the verbs, namely, tense, aspect, mood, and voice from a descriptive linguistics approach. This approach provides a much more systematic and simple presentation of how English marks these less-commonly understood and potentially confusing concepts. The chapter first reviews the basic terminology and concepts relevant to the topic and presents a concise survey of both the traditional and the more recent theoretical analyses of English tense, aspect, mood, and voice. Further, it explains and exemplifies the recent analysis of tense, aspect, mood, and voice markers as a demonstration of how they can be taught accurately and in a pedagogically simpler way.

Unit 5
Semantics

Chapter 7
David Stringer, Indiana University, USA

Lexical semantics is concerned with inherent aspects of word meaning and the semantic relations between words, as well as the ways in which word meaning is related to syntactic structure. This chapter provides an introduction to some of the main themes in lexical semantic research, including the nature of the mental lexicon, lexical relations, and the decomposition of words into grammatically relevant semantic features. The mapping between the semantics of verbs and their associated syntax is discussed in terms of thematic roles, semantic structure theory, and feature selection. A review of some of the most influential findings in second language research involving both open-class and closed-class lexical items reveals important implications for classroom pedagogy and syllabus design in the domain of vocabulary instruction.

Unit 6
Pragmatics

Chapter 8
Anna Krulatz, Norwegian University of Science and Technology, Norway

This chapter focuses on the key concepts in the study of pragmatics, including pragmatic competence, different types of meaning (abstract meaning, contextual meaning, and force of an utterance), the cooperative principle and four conversational maxims, as well as politeness and the concept of face (positive and negative). The chapter gives some examples of cross-cultural differences in pragmatic norms to justify the importance of teaching pragmatics in a language classroom, touching briefly on the development of pragmatic skills in a second or foreign language. It then explores different approaches to pragmatics instruction, including raising awareness about pragmatic norms in the target language through deductive and inductive tasks, presenting grammatical structures jointly with their pragmatic functions, and integrating pragmatics with content-based instruction.

Linguistically diverse learners tend to first relate the pragmatic ability they already possess in their first or more dominant language (L1) to act in the L2; as a result, miscommunication and misunderstandings are frequent and common. Teachers can help learners develop awareness about L2 pragmatic norms by making visible how speech acts are performed in the L2 community of speakers while providing opportunities to engage in role-playing or real interactions involving the accomplishment of selected speech acts. This chapter offers an overview of the importance of context in cross-cultural interactions, a brief survey of the theories of speech acts, and concrete pedagogical ideas for teachers to develop linguistically diverse learners' pragmatic awareness and ability while celebrating and promoting linguistic and cultural diversity.

This chapter introduces discourse analysis as a sub-discipline of linguistics. Relevant concepts from pragmatics, another closely-related sub-discipline, are also discussed within the context of discourse analysis. The chapter begins by explaining the relationship between pragmatics and discourse analysis, and key terms such as "text" and "discourse." It then examines the distinctions between linguistic and non-linguistic contexts, and situational and sociocultural contexts. To help readers understand the importance of culture in using language to make meanings, the introduced concepts are illustrated with sample authentic texts as well as examples from English and a few other languages. Placing discourse at the core of language teaching and learning, the chapter recommends a discourse-based approach to help ELLs develop not only communicative competence but also intercultural communicative competence. The chapter provides ESOL teachers with knowledge of discourse analysis and the implications of this knowledge for teaching culturally and linguistically diverse learners of English.

Unit 7
Phonetics

Chapter 11

The main focus of this chapter is to present the articulatory description of English consonants and provide practical guidance on how to teach the consonant phonemes to ELLs. The chapter starts with the introduction of phonetics as a subfield of linguistics. The concepts such as phonemes, contrastive versus non-contrastive sounds, the branches of phonetics that study different aspects of human speech sounds, and two different types of phonemes—consonants and vowels—are introduced in this section. Next, the reader is familiarized with the International Phonetic Alphabet, which is a system of phonetic transcription. The chapter further presents the description of the vocal tract and explores the classification of English consonants according to their place and manner of articulation, and voicing. Some implications from the introduced phonetics theory for teaching phonics, phonemic awareness, and spelling to young ELLs, and pronunciation to adult English learners, as well as a set of recommendations for effective phonetics instruction for ELLs are discussed to conclude the chapter.

Chapter 12

Sofia Alexandrovna Ivanova, University of Georgia, USA
Victoria Hasko, University of Georgia, USA

This chapter focuses on the articulatory phonetics of English vowels; thus, it identifies descriptive parameters for vowel articulation in English, differentiates monophthongs and diphthongs, classifies the vowels of American English using these parameters, and addresses vowel reduction in American English. The theoretical material is followed by a pedagogical consideration of how the specifics of the articulatory characteristics of English vowels can be addressed in the classroom to facilitate comprehension and production of English vowels by English language learners. Supplementary materials are suggested for readers offering sample activities that could be used by language practitioners in ESL classrooms for this goal, as well as for exploring other dialects of English, including specific regional dialects falling under the umbrella of General American English, the variety addressed in this chapter.

Unit 8
Phonology

Chapter 13

Caroline Wiltshire, University of Florida, USA

The chapter takes the reader from the concrete phonetic descriptions of sounds, found in Chapters 11 and 12, to the use of these sounds in English. As in every language, sounds are influenced by their context. A large part of phonological description of a language is an effort to describe how the "same" sound is pronounced differently in different contexts, both phonetic and morphological. The chapter provides the phonemes of English, which are the distinctive units of sound, and examples of how they vary in context. It also illustrates the variation of English morphemes in context, by providing examples of allomorphy. Some implications of variation in context for teaching English are discussed.

Chapter 14

Charles X. Li, Central Washington University, USA

This chapter focuses on formulating North American English (NAE) phonological rules and discussing their pedagogical implications. It begins with a brief account of NAE phonology as a rule-governed system and then outlines feature-based phonology as a theoretical framework in which phonological rules operate. The chapter further defines an inventory of distinctive features for characterizing the NAE phonological system. After discussing rule components and matrix underspecification, the chapter presents phonological rules subsumed under seven categories: deletion, epenthesis, metathesis, reduction, assimilation, dissimilation, and morphophonology. Most rules are couched in three expressions—prose, semi-formal, formal—to meet different needs of readers. Pedagogical implications of phonological rules, discussed in the last section, are explicated in the framework of language transfer and universal grammar. The same section also emphasizes the importance of balancing linguistic analysis and classroom practice.

John Rothgerber, Indiana University, USA

This chapter will provide the language teacher with an introduction to the theory behind the challenges and problems that learners from a variety of language backgrounds face as they learn to pronounce the sounds of English. The primary focus will be on the influence of the first language in second language phonological acquisition. This will include an overview of the role of perception of non-native sounds, as well as a consideration of phonological representation in the mental lexicon and articulatory constraints, all of which can have an effect on difficulties that learners encounter as they learn to pronounce English sounds. Attention will be given to the various components that make up the phonological system, including segmentals, suprasegmentals, phonotactics, and phonological processes. This theoretical understanding will then be applied to pronunciation instruction within the classroom by addressing what teachers can do to maximize the effectiveness of instruction.

Solange Lopes Murphy, The College of New Jersey, USA
Timothy M. Hall, The College of New Jersey, USA
Angelica Lina Vanderbilt, The College of New Jersey, USA

In this chapter, the authors discuss how ESL and general education teachers can judiciously infuse intelligibility-based pronunciation teaching into content-based classrooms. First, within a broad understanding of second language development, they identify various sources of English Language Learners' pronunciation problems, and a rationale for why pronunciation teaching should aim for intelligibility rather than for nativeness. They then present the major pronunciation challenges of the five largest language groups in American schools and offer intelligibility-focused teaching practices to stimulate discussion and evolve teacher practice in harmony with the Common Core State Standards (CCSS). The chapter closes with exercises to further explore implementation of pronunciation teaching practices for ELs' language and academic development.

Unit 9
Sociolinguistics

Jon Bakos, Indiana State University, USA

This chapter examines processes of language variation and change that take place in all languages, with a focus on English. Sociolinguists have observed that demographic and social variables such as where someone is born, their age, gender, and socio-economic status can be relevant to how they speak. However, contemporary work indicates that there is more to how someone speaks than a few checkboxes on a survey. Who does a speaker feel empathy with and want to emulate? How does a multi-faceted sense of personal identity affect how a person speaks? How might a second language (L2) learner's sense of belonging affect their own realization of English? These are some of the questions that this chapter seeks to address.

Foreword

As a native-born Spanish speaker who learned English without the benefit of ESL or bilingual education, in the public schools in the Spanish-speaking border town of Laredo, Texas, I learned that languages—in my case Spanish and English—had value, that each language has its unique qualities and that not everything is translatable, a truism that I continue to confront as I translate my own and other's work. Undoubtedly, it was my early encounters with two language codes and my navigating the multilingual world of the border that led to my intense interest in language and in linguistics, the study of language. I was deep into my graduate program when my interest in semiotics led me to Ferdinand De Saussure's ideas about language; I soon became consumed with Wittgenstein and Vygotsky's notions of language acquisition, with Chomsky's deep structures, and with Pragmatics which at the time in the 1970s was barely making inroads in academic discussions. Later it was Krashen and Zentella and their ideas of second language learning that intrigued me. Because of an unfortunate academic snafu, the seed that would've led me to pursue formal training linguistics beyond my master's degree did not flourish; instead I trained as a literary critic. However, as a professor at a small university back in Laredo in the early 1980s, I taught linguistics classes along with the requisite literature survey courses to future bilingual education teachers. Armed with my meager knowledge of the subject, but with a strong desire to change the way ESL students were taught (or not!), I designed two foundational courses: Introduction to Linguistics and Contrastive Linguistics—Spanish and English.

I found teaching these classes to be fascinating and rewarding for I was training the ESL and bilingual education teachers of my community, changing the way students like me were taught. I was giving them the tools my own teachers so obviously lacked when they punished me—physically with swats and psychologically with fines and assignments—for speaking the only language I knew—Spanish—either in the classroom or in the playground. In retrospect, I realize that my teachers were merely following the pedagogical base for second language learning of the time using Skinnerian reward and punish conditioning as a method to teach a target language and for all practical purposes erase the non-English home language. At least I want to believe this and not that they were blatant racists. Nevertheless, the scars remain over 60 years later, and the feelings of shame and embarrassment surface when I mispronounce a word.

I was in graduate school when the Conference on College Composition and Communication (CCCC) adopted a statement affirming that students had a right to their own language. The statement was quickly adopted by the National Council of Teachers of English. I remember thinking that such a bold move would result in respect for students from cultural and linguistic diverse backgrounds. But that was not to be. Decades later, in the early 2000s, while doing a survey of arts programming in Idaho, a young Latina mother burst into tears as she told the story of how her nine-year old child had been hit for speaking Spanish and was refusing to go to school. I hope that this is an isolated and rare case, but I can't help but feel that the anti-immigrant rhetoric and actions of political leaders have given license to those who are still espousing an English-only mentality and who do not recognize that being linguistically diverse is an asset. Obviously, we still have a lot of work to do as educators.

One of the fundamental markers of identity is language. When we teach English as a second language, we are more than teaching a skill, we are changing lives; we are impacting someone's sense of self, their identity. At one time in my career, I trained adult literacy tutors for Laredo's Literacy Volunteers of America organization. In addition to training tutors, I also tutored adult literacy students seeking to learn English. During the training as well as during my own tutoring classes, I realized that although knowing the formal language of linguistics was unnecessary to teach someone about past tense morphemes, it was a tremendous advantage that I had the language and could discern areas of difficulty so I added units on phonology, morphology and syntax to our training. As I read through the excellent selections in this volume, I am in awe of the rich and varied approaches demonstrated by the authors who are linguists and TESOL professionals. The chapters in *Applied Linguistics for Teachers of Culturally and Linguistically Diverse Learners* are not just for linguistics classes but can help anyone working with second language learners at whatever level. Undoubtedly, the information contained in these chapters will lead to better-trained teachers, and therefore, better teaching as having a broader knowledge of what to do to improve the acquisition of the target language will obviously be more effective in the long run.

Well into the 21st century, the demand for ESL classes is at ever higher levels as non-English speaking immigrants wanting to learn English flock to literacy programs in communities across the United States. Our schools welcome ever higher numbers of students whose native language is not English. The teachers who will teach the children and adults need training in the mechanics of language and must be aware of the approaches to teaching specific items as well as be aware of the larger issues of cultural differences and insensitivity. Not only do the chapters in this book provide invaluable knowledge, strategies, and methods for teaching, but they also offer the analysis, the exploration of certain themes, and the necessary tools for ESOL teachers and teacher trainers to build with. The chapters cover a wide array of linguistics topics, yes, but more importantly, the authors provide practical and applicable techniques; they offer solutions to problems and lay out a template for the kind of teaching we need in our schools today.

Applied Linguistics for Teachers of Culturally and Linguistically Diverse Learners, then, provides a rich source of knowledge and of practical information for anyone engaged with culturally and linguistically diverse students. My wish for you as you read this book is that you will find the treasures it has hidden and that you will share this knowledge, for as a wise person once said, knowledge not lived is sin. Go forward, then. Adelante! Put what is in these pages into practice as you work with those who are learning English as a second, third, or foreign language.

Norma Elia Cantú
Trinity University, USA

Preface

Linguistics is defined as "the scientific study of language" (Lyons, 1968, p. 1). As a scientific study, it has applications in different fields, such as computer science and programming, information technology, medicine, and so on. One of the main applications of linguistics is in the field of education, more specifically, in language learning and teaching. The field that deals with "the theoretical and empirical investigation of real-world problems in which language is a central issue" (Brumfit, 1995, p. 27) and studies the application of linguistics in language teaching and learning is called *applied linguistics*. Irrespective of the language taught, whether first, second, or foreign, knowledge of linguistics and its application is a must for language teachers. It is not coincidental that linguistics is a mandatory component of language teacher education and certification or master's programs in Teaching English to Speakers of Other Languages (TESOL) which intend to prepare effective English for Speakers of Other Languages (ESOL) teachers. Teachers of culturally and linguistically diverse learners, English Language Learners (ELLs) or English Learners (ELs) in our case, need to have a strong understanding of linguistic theory and its application in practice to be able to provide effective and efficient instruction to ELLs. Strong language instruction is especially crucial given the fact that ELLs represent the fastest growing segment of the student population in U.S. schools and fall behind their native English-speaking peers and struggle academically in K-12 (NCES, 2018).

In order to adequately prepare teachers to provide effective language instruction to their culturally and linguistically diverse learners, TESOL programs need to adopt and use textbooks and resources that are designed specifically for this purpose. However, due to the scarcity of resources – lack of comprehensive Applied Linguistics textbooks, many TESOL programs end up using General Linguistics books that are not geared towards ELL education and present only linguistic theory without addressing its application in practice. The incorporation of practical and pedagogical implications from the theory of linguistics into TESOL instruction is left solely to the instructor's discretion, and in the best-case scenario, the instructor tries to find supplemental resources to meet the needs of the course, whereas, in the worst-case scenario, the practical aspect of the TESOL course is completely ignored.

Applied Linguistics for Teachers of Culturally and Linguistically Diverse Learners intends to fix this regrettable divorce between linguistic theory and practice by providing the knowledge of the core subdisciplines of linguistics and their implications for teaching different aspects or domains of English to linguistically and culturally diverse ELLs. Each chapter in the volume introduces different fundamental concepts and theories of linguistics and discusses their application in English language teaching and learning. The main purpose of this publication is to contribute to TESOL and language teacher education programs and improve their overall quality, which, in its turn, will positively impact the education of English learners.

Organization of the Book

Applied Linguistics for Teachers of Culturally and Linguistically Diverse Learners consists of 17 chapters which are organized into the following nine units that provide comprehensive coverage of important sub-disciplines and topics of linguistics:

Unit 1. What Is Language?
Unit 2. Morphology
Unit 3. Syntax
Unit 4. Morpho-Syntax
Unit 5. Semantics
Unit 6. Pragmatics
Unit 7. Phonetics
Unit 8. Phonology
Unit 9. Sociolinguistics

The first unit, *What Is Language?* serves as an introductory unit of the volume. Each of the following eight units represents a different sub-discipline of linguistics and includes its own chapters. All chapters follow the same template; they start with the introduction of the linguistics content – theories and concepts – pertinent to the corresponding sub-discipline and topic, continue with the discussion of the implications from the introduced linguistic theory for teaching English to language learners, and conclude with some discussion questions and exercises. In order to assist the reader with quick access to the linguistic terminology employed in the book, a compiled glossary of terms is supplied at the end of the book. The answers to the exercises included in each chapter are also provided for the reader's reference at the end of the volume.

Chapter 1 defines and makes the distinction between Linguistics and Applied Linguistics, and discusses the concepts of language in general and human language in particular, language use, linguistic knowledge, the theory of Universal Grammar, and language acquisition. It then provides a brief introduction to the linguistic subfields of Phonetics, Phonology, Morphology, Syntax, Semantics, and Pragmatics by discussing the importance of knowledge of sounds, words, sentences, meaning and nonverbal communication in language learning. The chapter concludes with some pedagogical implications and the reiteration of the significance of an understanding of both the structural and social aspects of linguistic communication as well as of basic knowledge of linguistics for effective language learning and teaching.

Chapter 2 introduces the linguistic subfield of Morphology and its unit of study – morphemes. The concepts such as free and bound morphemes, different types of affixes (prefixes, suffixes, infixes, and circumfixes), function words and content words, as well as parts of speech are reviewed within this chapter. Implications from the study of morphology and morphemes for teaching vocabulary, grammar, and language skills such as reading, listening, speaking, writing, and pronunciation to ELLs are discussed, and some practical strategies, techniques, and resources are offered to guide teachers of ELLs on how to use their knowledge of morphology to develop their students' language skills in English.

Chapter 3, after briefly summarizing the notions of word and morpheme, focuses on morphological structures and word formation in English. The chapter discusses etymological versus psychological dimensions of morphological analysis in regard to word meaning, differentiates between productive and non-productive morphemes, examines the hierarchical organization of words, introduces the concepts of inflection and derivation, and lists different processes of word formation, such as compounding, zero-derivation, blending and clipping, coinage, back-formation, and borrowing in English. The implications section of the chapter identifies certain aspects of morphological structure that may pose challenges for language learners and offers some instructional strategies to help students overcome such challenges.

Chapter 4 introduces the linguistic sub-discipline of Syntax and analyzes the basic architecture of English phrases and sentences with the assumption that grammaticality and ungrammaticality judgments are structure-related rather than meaning-related, considering the context of this chapter. It discusses the linear and hierarchical organization of constituents in a sentence, presents syntax tree diagrams, heads and complements, and different types of phrases in an English sentence, uncovers the complex nature of the English predicate, looks into grammatical relations – the spatial-hierarchical relationships among the parts of sentences in English, and explains and demonstrates the application of the X-bar theory on English sentences. Some pedagogical implications from knowledge of syntax are discussed in light of positive and negative linguistic transfer.

Chapter 5 analyzes grammaticality judgments in the framework of Generative Grammar. The chapter explores the concepts and topics such as grammaticality (grammatically well-formedness of a sentence) and ungrammaticality (grammatically ill-formedness of a sentence), acceptability and unacceptability (native speakers' intuitions about the semantic appropriateness of a sentence), language competence and language performance, internal grammar and native speakers' acquisition of syntactic rules. In the implications part of the chapter, the authors discuss the application of the theoretical concepts concerning grammaticality judgments on second and foreign language learning of syntax rules of English by focusing on how L2/FL learners' first language backgrounds can influence their grammaticality judgments and interpretations (positive transfer vs. negative transfer).

Chapter 6 presents the subfield of Morpho-Syntax and focuses on the morpho-syntactic marking of inflectional categories on the English verb. The linguistic concepts such as inflectional and syntactic properties of verbs and the verbal-inflectional categories of tense, aspect, voice, and mood are introduced and analyzed in the chapter. The analysis of linguistic concepts is accompanied by ample sentence examples and modeling of how verb complexes and their inflectional and syntactic properties can be easily identified in an English sentence. The implications from knowledge of morpho-syntactic categories of verbs for teaching English verbs and their inflectional categories of tense, aspect, voice, and mood to language learners are provided within the framework of scientific inquiry – making observations, generalizations, and comparisons. The ultimate goal of the chapter is to help language learners acquire analytical/linguistic skills to improve their language competence and self-monitoring/editing skills to enhance their language performance.

Chapter 7 introduces the linguistic subfield of Semantics and concentrates on lexical semantics or the study of word meaning and how it relates to sentence meaning. The chapter first explores some fundamental concepts of lexical semantics such as reference, sense, mental lexicon, lexical relations (homonymy, polysemy, synonymy, antonymy, hyponymy, and meronymy), subcategorization, feature selection, argument structure, thematic roles, and semantic structure theory. It then introduces the phenomena of lexical relativity and lexical transfer, and discusses how these phenomena are observed in language learning and influence L2 acquisition of lexical semantics and argument structure. The chapter concludes with the summary of pedagogical implications for L2 lexical semantics and vocabulary instruction.

Chapter 8 presents Pragmatics as a sub-discipline of linguistics, defines the concepts of pragmatic knowledge and pragmatic competence, focuses on types of meaning and differentiates between abstract and contextual meaning, introduces the concept of conversational implicature, explains and exemplifies the Gricean Cooperative Principle and conversational maxims, elaborates on the notions of politeness, positive face and negative face, and reveals some important implications from knowledge of pragmatics for second language pedagogy and curriculum design by discussing the importance and the goals of L2 pragmatics instruction and offering some useful pragmatics-focused techniques, tasks, and activities.

Chapter 9 focuses on speech acts and their realization in the cross-cultural pragmatics context. It discusses the relationship between context and language, defines linguistic context and situational context, explores speech act theory and pragmatic concepts such as locutionary, illocutionary, and perlocutionary acts, direct and indirect speech acts, and emphasizes the role of culture in cross-cultural interactions. The notions of pragmatic divergence and pragmatic failure are analyzed in the context of L2 pragmatics acquisition, and the importance of pragmatic competence for communicating in an L2 is reiterated. The chapter offers some practical strategies and tasks to promote L2 learners' speech act awareness and performance as well as some pragmatic considerations for lesson design and implementation.

Chapter 10 examines discourse analysis including the discussion of some relevant concepts from pragmatics. Examples are provided to point out the distinction between discourse analysis and pragmatics in terms of their unit or object of study. The chapter further explores the concepts such as text and discourse, lexical cohesion and grammatical cohesion, and the core term 'context' which is central to the study of both pragmatics and discourse analysis, summarizes and exemplifies descriptive and critical goals of discourse analysis, highlights the importance of the study of discourse analysis not only for linguistics but also for other disciplines, and elaborates on some pedagogical implications from theoretical knowledge of discourse analysis in terms of promoting correct use of cohesive devices and discourse markers by L2 learners, raising English learners' awareness in respect to different types, genres, and social purposes of texts, facilitating L2 learners' intercultural communicative competence, and developing both language learners' and teachers' overall understanding and knowledge of critical discourse analysis.

Chapter 11 describes English consonants from the articulatory aspect and explores the ways this knowledge can inform instructional practices for English learners. The chapter introduces the linguistic subfield of Phonetics, explains the distinction between contrastive and non-contrastive sounds as well as vowels and consonants in a language, presents the International Phonetic Alphabet and the description of the vocal tract, classifies English consonants according to their place and manner of articulation, and voicing, and provides a chart of the English consonant phoneme inventory with the description of articulatory features. Implications from phonetic knowledge of consonants for teaching language and literacy skills to ELLs are discussed, and some recommendations for effective phonetics instruction for young and adult language learners are offered at the end of the chapter.

Chapter 12 explores the articulatory description of vowels according to the height and the backness of the tongue, lip rounding, and tenseness, provides the IPA description of vowels, distinguishes between monophthongs and diphthongs, and focuses on American English vowels. The chapter further classifies and describes English monophthongs with reference to the cardinal vowel system, provides a chart of English vowel sounds with their articulatory description, and discusses some important phenomena, such as the *cot-caught* merger, vowel rhotacization, and vowel reduction, pertinent to American English vowels. Second language classroom implications from knowledge of English vowels are discussed in terms of improving the efficacy and efficiency of L2 perception and pronunciation instruction.

Chapter 13 introduces the linguistic subfield of Phonology, explores the concepts of contrastive (phoneme) and non-contrastive (allophone) sounds, provides the complete phonemic inventory of English consonants and vowels, and focuses on English sounds in context, i.e., the analysis of allophones and allomorphs of English. The discussion of English allophones and allomorphs is supported and enhanced with numerous word examples accompanied by their phonetic transcriptions. The chapter also provides language learners with some concrete strategies for determining phonemes and allophones in a language and differentiating between the two. The chapter concludes with the discussion of some pedagogical implications from knowledge of English phonemes and of allophonic and allomorphic variations for perception, pronunciation, intelligibility, and spelling instruction.

Chapter 14 defines an inventory of distinctive features for describing the North American English (NAE) phonological system, presents about three dozen specific phonological rules in three different expressions, and discusses pedagogical implications for teaching and learning NAE phonological rules in light of interactions between language transfer and language universals so that teachers can predict learners' areas of learning difficulties. In the end, the chapter emphasizes the importance of balancing linguistic explanations and classroom practices couched in the communicative framework for facilitating accuracy, fluency, and automaticity of L2 learner pronunciation.

Chapter 15 refers to phonological theory to explain the causes of pronunciation problems experienced by language learners. It explores the processes of speech perception and production that are central to the acquisition of phonology and pronunciation. The chapter discusses how the perception of segmentals, suprasegmentals, phonotactics, and phonological processes can pose challenges for second language learners, and how such difficulties can be due to the interference from L1 to L2, and influence L2 phonological representations in the mental lexicon. Implications from phonological theory for second language pronunciation instruction point to the importance of facilitating perception practice in L2, enhancing explicit instruction and corrective feedback in pronunciation classes, engaging language learners in communicative activities and promoting the repetition of target phonetic features, and developing an overall awareness of learner pronunciation problems.

Chapter 16 looks at L2 pronunciation problems from a different angle – by focusing on K-12 ESL context. The chapter explores some possible causes of pronunciation problems observed in language learners, tries to identify the primary goal of L2 pronunciation pedagogy by reviewing the two guiding principles – nativeness and intelligibility, analyzes five major language families representing the five largest language groups in U.S. schools and examines their typical pronunciation difficulties in regard to English sounds, and reviews some segmental and suprasegmental features of English speech that contribute to intelligible or unintelligible English pronunciation. The concepts and phenomena discussed in the chapter hold implications for pronunciation instruction, more specifically, for intelligibility-focused pronunciation teaching within academic content instruction.

Chapter 17, the last chapter of the book, presents the linguistic sub-discipline of Sociolinguistics. It defines sociolinguistics, and discusses regional and demographic (age, ethnicity, and gender) variables and their relevant concepts to demonstrate how language use is affected by some sociological factors. The chapter further examines some particular studies to support the argument that regional, demographic, and socio-economic variables indeed affect language use in terms of pronunciation and lexical choice, and to look more closely into what happens when an individual or a community integrates into a different linguistic or cultural society that does not share that person's or community's primary language and culture. Pedagogical implications from knowledge of sociolinguistics urge educators to look at L2 learning as a way of constructing a personal identity in a second language community rather than simply acquiring the linguistic aspects of and carrying out tasks in an L2.

Designed to serve as a textbook or supplementary course material to be used in TESOL programs at colleges and universities both in the U.S. and abroad, we trust that this innovative collection of chapters will bridge the gap between linguistic theory and its application in practice and help to prepare effective ESOL teachers and TESOL professionals by providing deep knowledge of applied linguistics to contribute to the success of linguistically and culturally diverse English learners in school and life.

REFERENCES

Brumfit, C. (1995). Teacher professionalism and research. In G. Cook & B. Seidlhofer (Eds.), *Principle and practice in applied linguistics: Studies in honour of H. G. Widdowson* (pp. 27–41). Oxford, UK: Oxford University Press.

Lyons, J. (1968). *Introduction to theoretical linguistics*. London: Cambridge University Press. doi:10.1017/CBO9781139165570

National Center for Education Statistics. (2018). *The condition of education 2018* (NCES 2018 -144). Retrieved from https://nces.ed.gov/pubs2018/2018144.pdf

Acknowledgment

We are deeply indebted to many people who provided their support and counsel from the inception of this book project to its completion.

First and foremost, we would like to thank all the authors who made their invaluable contribution to this volume both as the authors of the chapters and the reviewers who made the peer review process seamless. We especially thank Dr. Howard Williams, Columbia University – Teachers College, for his contribution of two priceless chapters to this book and for his unparalleled wealth of linguistics knowledge that he shared with us during the development phase of this project.

We are also grateful to our editorial advisory board members, Dr. Norma Elia Cantú, Dr. Loyce Caruthers, Dr. Victoria Hasko, Dr. Hayriye Kayi-Aydar, Dr. Charles Li, Dr. Nihat Polat, and Dr. Anthony Sze-Fai Shiu, for their support of and trust in our project.

Another special thanks goes to the IGI team and our development editors, Maria Rhode and Josephine Dadeboe, for their continuous support and guidance throughout this project.

Lastly, we owe a debt of gratitude to our families who provided their love, support, and belief in this project and its importance for TESOL education, ESOL teacher preparation, and the academic success of English language learners in the United States, without which this volume would not have been possible.

Unit 1
What Is Language?

Chapter 1
Knowledge of Language:
The Sound System, Words, and Sentences

Patricia A. Kilroe
California College of the Arts, USA

ABSTRACT

Human beings learn to speak or sign the language or languages they are exposed to as children. To have acquired the language(s) of one's speech community is to have acquired both linguistic and communicative competence. Linguistic competence results from internalizing the knowledge of the basic elements of language (sounds, words, sentences) and the rules for combining these elements into units that enable users to express linguistic meaning. Communicative competence results when learners have acquired knowledge of the appropriate social conventions involved in interpersonal communication. Effective language teaching is enhanced through an understanding of both the structural and social aspects of linguistic communication as well as how these aspects challenge students in the process of second language acquisition.

LINGUISTICS AND APPLIED LINGUISTICS

Languages are complex systems through which people communicate the full range of human experience. Personal identity is expressed through language, and social interaction without language is almost unimaginable. The scientific study of the structure and use of language is known as **linguistics**, and a *linguist* is someone who engages in such study. (The term *linguist* may also refer to someone who is fluent in more than one language.) Depending on their subfield or specialty, linguists who are engaged in research may pursue the answers to questions pertaining to the nature of language itself, to the relationship of language to the human brain, or to the insights to be gained about society through the study of language use.

The major structural areas of linguistics include the study of speech sounds (the subfields of which are *phonetics* and *phonology*), words (*morphology*), phrases and sentences (*syntax*) and meaning (*semantics* and *pragmatics*). Each of these subfields is introduced in this chapter and explored in detail in the subsequent units of this book. The major subfield of linguistics that explores the systematic study of

DOI: 10.4018/978-1-5225-8467-4.ch001

language use at both an individual and societal level is known *sociolinguistics*; in the final unit (Unit 9, "Sociolinguistics,") this topic is explored in relation to culturally and linguistically diverse (CLD) learners. There are many additional subfields of linguistics, as diverse as how languages change over time (historical linguistics) and how children learn their first language (language acquisition). What linguists working in each of the different subfields of linguistics have in common is their interest in contributing to the collective understanding about language.

In addition to research, there are many ways in which knowledge about language is applied to real-world situations. **Applied linguistics** makes use of linguistic theories and methods in order to address practical questions that are language-related. Language education is one of the major career fields in which applied linguistics is important, and this includes the profession of teaching English to CLD learners. Examples of some of the many additional professionals who make use of applied linguistics include computational linguists, who work in computer science in such areas as speech recognition, machine translation, and grammar checking; speech-language pathologists, who treat people with speech and language disorders; and court interpreters, who interpret for defendants, litigants, and witnesses in courtroom and other legal settings.

WHAT IS LANGUAGE?

Language is a method of human communication consisting of the use of words or signs in a structured way in order to convey meaning. The word *language* is also used to mean the particular system of communication used by a community, such as English, Japanese, or American Sign Language. There are approximately 7,100 languages used in the world today, yet over half the world's population speaks just 23 of those languages, and 86% of people speak an Asian or European language (Simons & Fennig, 2018). Languages change over time to meet the needs of their users, and they also change as groups of speakers come together or become isolated from each other. When a language no longer has any speakers, it is said to be extinct.

A fundamental question in linguistics has to do with how human beings produce and understand language. An early model that proposes how language functions continues to be influential today. This is the speech communication chain, first proposed by Claude Shannon and Warren Weaver in 1949 (cited in Dawson & Phelen, 2016, p.8-9). According to this model, any communication system will include an information source, a transmitter, a signal, a receiver, and a destination. In using language, the speaker/signer/writer is both the information source and transmitter; the signal—speech, signs, or writing—is sent to one or more others, who are both receiver and destination. Essentially, an idea is conceived by a sender, put into words, expressed through a physical medium such as sound or paper, and finally received and decoded in a receiver's mind.

As advances have occurred in psycholinguistics (a subfield concerned with how the mind processes language), more refined models have emerged of speech perception (receiving and interpreting messages) and speech production (formulating and sending messages). In speech perception, for example, psycholinguists have studied how language users can understand utterances despite significant ambient noise or variation in speakers' speech sounds. In speech production, for example, William Levelt (1989; discussed in Dawson & Phelen, 2016, p.374) proposed a model in which three major planning stages of language production happen simultaneously instead of sequentially. These include conceptualization, formulation (which encompasses grammatical and phonological encoding), and articulation.

WHO HAS LANGUAGE?

The human vocal tract is adapted for the production of speech sounds, while specific areas of the human brain are essential for language comprehension and production. Currently it is widely thought that humans have been speaking for about 100,000 years, but there are several contrasting views about how the capacity for language evolved in humans. One view is that language is the result of an evolutionary leap, a single mutation that set human language apart from the communication systems of other species. This is sometimes referred to as the **discontinuity view**. The **continuity view**, in contrast, asserts that the differences between human language and the communication systems of other primates is a matter of degree of complexity, that human communication evolved in stages along with the evolution of the species, from earlier hominids to modern homo sapiens.

Scientific ideas of language evolution are based on evidence from archaeology, paleontology, anatomy, linguistics, and genetics. In recent years, scientists have isolated the gene known as FOXP2 as a possible key to human language ability. While many animal species have the FOXP2 gene, the human version of this gene shows some variation with that of our closest genetic relatives, the great apes. (Specifically, FOXP2 in humans differs in two amino acids from that in gorillas and chimpanzees.) And although many animals have complex systems of communication, none of these systems have the breadth or depth of capacity that human language has.

So what sets human language apart from animal communication systems? One way of addressing this question is by considering the **design features of language**, first proposed by Charles Hockett (1966, standard version discussed in Dawson & Phelen, 2016, pp.20-26). Hockett identified nine characteristics of communication systems, and he noted that all nine are needed in order for a communication system to be considered language. Put another way, only human language exhibits all nine design features, with the final two being the features that distinguish human language from animal communications systems. Very briefly, these are 1) a mode of transmission, such as the voice or hand; 2) the capacity to signal meaning, so that users of the system understand each other; 3) purpose, such as requesting information or issuing a warning; 4) the capacity for each user of the system to both send and receive messages, which not all members of all species can do; 5) cultural transmission, which involves learning through interaction with others of the same species; 6) arbitrariness, which means that the connection between what something is or means and the word or signal for it is purely by convention; 7) the creation of messages out of smaller, discrete units, seen for example in the fact that, in spoken language, sentences are composed of individual words and each word is composed in turn of smaller units of individual sounds; 8) displacement, which involves the ability to communicate about something not present in the space or time of the communication; and 9) productivity, which allows users of the system to create an unlimited number of new messages out of the system's discrete units, as when we express a new idea for the first time using the finite units of sound and grammar contained in our native language.

Although there is still controversy regarding how human language differs from animal communication systems, if language is defined as a communication system that exhibits all nine of the design features, then it is possible to state that only humans have the capacity for language. Research into animal communication systems has revealed that only human language has the characteristic of productivity—the unlimited creation of new messages—and that the capacity to communicate about topics not in the here and now (displacement) is also characteristic only of human language, although proposals have been made that the dance of bees to communicate remote food sources demonstrates displacement. In any event, from the perspective of the current state of research, all animal communication systems are closed systems, that is, they are limited as to the messages that can be conveyed, while only human language allows its users to formulate and convey an unlimited number of novel utterances.

LINGUISTIC KNOWLEDGE

Language users have internalized, largely subconscious linguistic knowledge of the basic elements of language (sound, words, sentences) and the patterns or rules for combining these elements into units that can express well-formed, meaningful utterances (sounds into words, words into messages such as sentences). This knowledge of the elements and rules of language is a user's **mental grammar**. Along with the language user's mental dictionary, which stores words and their meanings, this mental grammar is known as **linguistic competence**, while the actual use of language in spoken, written, or signed form is known as **linguistic performance**. Linguistic performance is observable, while linguistic competence is not; therefore, analysis of linguistic data observed through performance is essential to building an understanding of the mental grammar.

In addition to knowledge of the structural aspects of language, language users demonstrate **communicative competence**, that is, the ability to engage in linguistic interactions with the appropriate social conventions established by their speech community (such as, for example, the rules of conversation: Is it okay to interrupt a conversation partner? How long should the pause be from the end of one person's utterance to the beginning of another's? Is it more appropriate to address a college teacher informally by first name or formally, as Professor So-and-so? etc.).

Another important fact about language users is their **linguistic creativity**. As noted in connection with the design feature of productivity, the discrete units and systematic rules of language allow users to understand and produce original sentences that have never previously been uttered, and each speaker is hypothetically capable of producing infinitely long sentences. For example, the simple sentence *The dog ran after the stick* can be made into an infinitely long sentence just by continuing to add independent clauses to it with the coordinating conjunction *and* between them: *The dog ran after the stick and the squirrel scrambled up the tree and the birds flew away and the lightning flashed and the wind blew across the valley and....*

FUNDAMENTAL PROPERTIES OF HUMAN LANGUAGE

A persistent topic in linguistics has to do with how languages are similar to each other, and how they differ. The field of **linguistic typology** classifies, compares and analyzes languages according to their similarities and differences in structure and organization. All languages, for example, form sentences out of the elements of Subject (S), Verb (V) and Object (O), and the basic order in which these elements function in a particular language allows languages to be classified by one of six possible typologies. (English is classified as SVO, since a basic declarative sentence consists of a subject followed by a verb and then an object: Chris (S) ate (V) breakfast (O).) That is, while all languages contain these basic sentence elements, not all languages order these elements in the same way. Yet the number of possibilities for ordering is not unlimited. In fact, a large majority of the world's languages, over 75%, follow either the pattern of SVO (English, Chinese, etc.) or SOV (Turkish, Korean, etc.). About 10-15% of languages follow the VSO pattern (Welsh, Arabic, etc.). The patterns VOS, OVS, and OSV are rare (Crystal, 2010, p.98). One of the generalizations that can be made from these facts is that, while not universal, there is a strong preference for subjects to precede objects among the world's languages.

Although the basic structural elements of sentences are only three in number, the vocabulary of languages is large and open-ended. There is both great productivity and great variation across languages regarding individual words. Yet here too languages have something in common. A fundamental property of all human languages is that the relation between form and meaning is arbitrary. Words and signs have no necessary relationship to the meaning they express. This was noted in the discussion of the sixth design feature, arbitrariness. That is, words do not resemble the things they are pointing out in the world in any sensory way, the way a drawing of the sun might be thought to resemble the sun itself. For example, the word-form *chair* in English refers to a physical object, typically with four legs and a seat, built for a person to sit on. But word forms for this same object in other languages may bear no resemblance to the spoken or written English form *chair*. For example, *chair* is *silla* in Spanish, *uija* in Korean, *sandalye* in Turkish, and so on. While the word for an object may differ from language to language, however, it is necessarily the case that speakers of the *same* language will use the *same* word for an object, in order for communication to be successful. This tells us that, while words across languages may vary greatly in their structural forms of pronunciation and grammar, when it comes to usage, they function in the same way –through arbitrary convention.

The theory of **Universal Grammar** (UG) proposes that the capacity for human language is innate, and that children are born with a disposition to identify structural patterns in the language(s) to which they are exposed in childhood. UG theorists are interested in establishing **linguistic universals**, the set of features shared by all languages. Evidence for language universals may be found in certain linguistic categories and structural rules. All spoken languages have vowels and consonants, for example, and while the vocabulary of individual languages must be learned, all languages have categories for nouns and verbs. From the perspective of UG, the grammars of individual languages differ because each language employs a somewhat different subset of the totality of structural possibilities.

LANGUAGE ACQUISITION

In addition to investigating the structural properties of languages, linguists who study language universals are interested in understanding how children are able to acquire so complex a communication system as language in just a few short years without explicit instruction. This fact is taken as further evidence that the capacity for human language is innate.

While there are a variety of differing theories of **first language acquisition**, that is, the process through which children acquire their first language, there is widespread agreement about the stages in which children acquire their first language —no matter what the language of their caretakers. (Children learning to sign rather than speak go through parallel stages of acquiring sign language.) These stages include cooing at approximately 2-3 months, followed by babbling at about 4-6 months. By the age of one year babies produce single words, with a two-word phase following several months later. By age two children are able to produce simple sentences, and by age three they can produce several sentences together and use hundreds of words. By age four children are well on the way to adult-like language usage.

While the rapidity with which children acquire their first language offers strong evidence that the capacity for human language is innate, there also may be limits on the window of time within which human beings can acquire a first language. The **critical period hypothesis** suggests that, in order to learn the language of their community completely and fully, children must be exposed to it by the start of adolescence. Note that a critical period has been observed in nonhuman species as well. Many songbirds, for example, must be exposed to their species-specific song when young in order to fully learn it. In fact, the presence of a critical period was identified by biologist Eric Lenneberg as one of the six features of biologically-controlled—that is, innately determined—animal behaviors (Lenneberg 1967, in Dawson & Phelen, 2016, pp.318-319). Two additional features identified by Lenneberg of relevance to first language acquisition are that (1) explicit instruction has little impact on the emergence of the behavior, which has been repeatedly found to be the case by researchers observing children in the process of acquiring their first language, and that (2) there are regular milestones associated with the development of the behavior, which the preceding overview of the stages of first language acquisition has illustrated.

According to the critical period hypothesis, children are innately predisposed to acquire language from birth to the beginning of adolescence, about age thirteen. A child who has not been exposed to language before adolescence will never acquire language completely, because the time period during which the brain structures needed for language can develop ends at adolescence. The critical period hypothesis also has implications for **second language acquisition**, the process through which a language other than one's first language is acquired.

Children who start learning a second language before adolescence are much more likely to achieve native-like competence in the second language than children who begin to learn the second language later on.

Observation of second language learners over many years has confirmed that children seem to be able to achieve competence in a second language more easily than adults. For example, adults and even teens who begin learning a second language in adulthood are likely to speak with an accent as well as to produce sentences that show influence from the grammatical patterns of their first language. But there are exceptions to these general observations, and many people are capable of learning a new language well into adulthood. "Rather than a critical period, there seems to be a steady decline in how well one can learn a second language." (Dawson & Phelen, 2016, pp.320-321). It would also seem that aspects of second language acquisition decline at different rates. The receptive skills of listening and reading comprehension, along with vocabulary acquisition, seem to be more easily mastered by adult language learners than the productive skills of speaking and writing, which are commonly challenged by transfer from the first language.

KNOWLEDGE OF THE SOUNDS OF LANGUAGE

To know the speech sounds of a language is to know, first of all, what sounds can count as speech sounds and what sounds cannot. A person listening to a radio program, for example, is able to distinguish the sounds made by a human voice from, say, static noise carried by radio frequency. Young children acquire the language or languages they are exposed to, and for children learning a spoken language this includes the subset of speech sounds they hear from the set of all possible speech sounds. Each spoken language makes use of between ten and one hundred speech sounds made up of both consonants and vowels; English uses approximately 50 of these sounds (Dawson & Phelan, 2016, p.25). So the speech sounds of whatever language or languages a child learns become the sounds that the child can recognize and produce as familiar units.

Upon hearing the speech of someone who learned English in adulthood, for example, native speakers of English may perceive an "accent" in that person's speech, although the native speakers may not always be able to precisely identify the sounds that seem different from their own spoken English. Likewise, a speaker who is learning English in adulthood may struggle to acquire native-like English pronunciation, particularly of the sounds and sound combinations in English that are not used in the language(s) the learner has already acquired. Many native speakers of Spanish, for example, add a short "e" vowel sound at the beginning of English words that begin with an "s" plus another consonant sound, such as "eSpanish" for "Spanish," because while plenty of words in Spanish begin with an "s" sound, Spanish words do not begin with a combination of "s" plus another consonant. This combination is common at the beginning of English words, however (*Spain, speak, spell,* etc.), so it is easy for native speakers of English to pronounce such words. By comparison, consider how challenging it might be for a native speaker of English to pronounce a word beginning with the combination of sounds "ng." Even though English has many words that end in this combination (*walking, bring, sang,* etc.), English words cannot begin with this sound sequence. Yet it is a common way for words to begin in, for example, Tibetan.

The study and classification of speech sounds is known as **phonetics**. In the 1880s, a group of language teachers formed the International Phonetic Association and created the International Phonetic Alphabet (IPA), a set of written symbols used to represent the individual sounds of human speech (International Phonetic Association). Although the IPA has undergone numerous revisions since it was first published, its essential function continues today: one symbol is assigned to each sound in every human language. For example, the word *knit* in English has four alphabetic letters, but only three sounds, since the "k" is not pronounced: [n] [ɪ] and [t], so we could transcribe this word into IPA as [nɪt]. (In general, IPA transcriptions are enclosed in square brackets.) By establishing a one-to-one correspondence between each of the speech sounds in human language and a designated symbol for that sound, the IPA offers a pathway to the pronunciation of any spoken language.

Individual speech sounds are meaningless, but when combined according to the systematic rules that govern them, the units of speech, in relation to each other, are capable of carrying linguistic meaning. **Phonology** is the branch of linguistics concerned with the rule-governed sound systems of language. Native speakers of any spoken language have internalized the knowledge of which combinations and distributions of sounds are possible in the words of their language, and which are not. *Snag* is a word in English, for example, since English phonology permits the initial consonants [s] + [n] followed by a vowel and ending with another consonant, [g]. But, continuing with the example above contrasting English with Tibetan, because the sound combination "ng" cannot begin a word in English, native speakers of English will recognize that these same four speech sounds cannot make a word when they are reordered as n + g + a + s = *ngas. (An asterisk before a word indicates that it is unacceptable in the context of a given language.)

The minimum unit of speech that can contrast with other units to express differences in meaning is called a *phoneme*. One way that linguists determine the phonemes of an individual language is through *minimal pairs*. Minimal pairs of words help determine if two speech sounds in a given language that differ in only one phonological aspect are—or are not—separate phonemes capable of expressing differences in meaning. For example, despite their four-letter spelling, the English words *reef* and *leaf* each have three sounds. Both words have the same vowel sound (transcribed as /i/) and the same final consonant sound (/f/). They differ only in their initial sounds, /r/ and /l/ respectively. (In contrast to phonetic transcription, phonological transcriptions are generally enclosed in slashes.) Because *reef* /rif/ and *leaf* /lif/ are two separate words in English with two different meanings, differing only in the first sound of each word, they are considered a minimal pair, and /r/ and /l/ are therefore considered separate phonemes. But for Japanese speakers, perception of the difference between the sounds /r/ and /l/ is not great enough for these two sounds to distinguish one word meaning from another, so in Japanese /r/ and /l/ cannot be used to make a minimal pair of words.

Another important aspect of the study of speech sounds concerns how speakers make use of pitch, stress, and intonation to indicate questions, convey emphasis, express emotion, and other meaning-bearing functions. In English, for example, speakers will generally pose a yes/no question by ending it with rising intonation ("Is the cat sitting on the mat?"), while a declarative statement is made by ending a sentence with falling intonation ("The cat is sitting on the mat."). This area of linguistic study, known as *prosody*, plays an important part in both the linguistic and communicative competence of second language learners.

Readers will find detailed information about phonetics and phonology in Units 7 and 8, respectively.

KNOWLEDGE OF WORDS

Words are independent units of language. Because native speakers have internalized both the possible sound combinations and the rules for word formation in their language, they usually know whether a word exists or not in that language. English has the word *great* for example, but for most English language users there is no word *grat* (unless they are familiar with it as an acronym in the jargon of finance), even though *great* and *grat* are similar in structure. Children acquire the words of the language or languages they are exposed to, beginning with simple one-syllable word forms and increasing in complexity with their cognitive development. But unlike other aspects of language acquisition, language users are capable of learning new words throughout their lifetimes. The rules for structuring those words, however, are, like the rules governing speech sounds and sentence structure, largely unconscious.

How do language users determine when something is an acceptable word in their language and when it is not? In the process of acquiring their native language(s), users internalize the rules for structuring words out of component parts, and they also acquire words learned in the course of their experience that are stored in their own mental dictionary. For example, English language users will recognize the word *happy* as an adjective that can be used to modify a noun such as *baby*, as in the phrase *the happy baby*. Similarly, the adjective *unhappy* will be considered acceptable in the phrase *the unhappy baby*, since a word-formation rule allows the prefix *un-* to attach to the beginning of *happy* to create its opposite meaning. English speakers will also know that *un-* can express opposite meaning when it attaches to the beginning of certain verbs, as in *do* and *undo*. But when the *un-* is attached to a noun such as *cat*, the resulting form *uncat* will be considered nonsense. English speakers can make this judgment based on their knowledge of the words stored in their mental dictionary as well as their internalized knowledge of the types of words that *un-* may or may not attach to.

The study of how words are structured and formed is known as **morphology**. Words are made up of units called *morphemes*, which are the smallest segments of language that carry linguistic meaning. Morphemes are of two basic types. A morpheme that can stand alone as a word or act as the base to which other morphemes are attached is called a *free morpheme*. Examples of free morphemes are *bird*, *run*, *sad*, etc. A morpheme that cannot stand alone as a word and must attach to at least one other, free, morpheme in order to function meaningfully is called a *bound morpheme*. For example, the noun *joy* is a free morpheme and can stand alone as a word in a sentence: *The parents felt **joy** upon seeing their baby for the first time.* The suffix *-ful*, on the other hand, cannot function as an independent word. But when *-ful* is attached to the base *joy*, the adjective *joyful* results and can function as a word in a sentence, as in *The **joyful** children built sand castles on the shore.* Free morphemes can also combine with each other to form compound words, as in *bird* + *house* → *birdhouse*.

Language users have internalized knowledge about the meaning and function of free and bound morphemes as well as where in a word a bound morpheme may appear. They know, for example, that the prefix *un-* can attach to the beginning of an adjective and the suffix *–ness* can create a noun by following an adjective, as in *unhappiness*. They also know that *un-* cannot follow the free morpheme to which it is attached and that *–ness* cannot precede it, so that **nesshappyun* would be rejected by users as an English word.

Bound morphemes are actually of two types: *inflectional morphemes* are grammatical in function, and *derivational morphemes* can change the meaning or the word class of the base to which they are attached. The word *unhappiness* mentioned above shows both of the ways that derivational morphemes work: the prefix *un-* changes the meaning of the adjective to its opposite, and the suffix *–ness* changes the adjective *(un)happy* into a noun. Inflectional morphemes, on the other hand, perform grammatical functions, such as the suffix *–ed*, used to mark the simple past of regular verbs, or the suffix *–s*, used to mark the plural of nouns. Both of these inflectional morphemes occur in the sentence *Alex dislik**ed** loud nois**es***. Many languages have a large number of inflectional morphemes, but in English there are only eight, all of which are suffixes.

How do languages add new words? Words are more easily added to open class categories such nouns and verbs than to closed class categories whose words are mostly grammatical in function, such as articles, pronouns, and conjunctions. The following are some of the most common ways that English adds new words: *borrowing* from another language (e.g. *sushi* from Japanese), *coinage*, in which words are simply created from the language's possible sound combinations (e.g. the subatomic particle *quark*), *compounds*, in which two or more free morphemes combine (*laptop* from lap + top), *blends*, which combine the first part of one word with the last part of another (*bromance* from brother + romance), *acronyms*, in which a new word is formed by combining the first letter of a set of words (*SCOTUS*, from Supreme Court of the United States), and *clippings*, which are shorter, often informal, versions of longer words (e.g., *biopic*, which is actually a compound made from two clippings, *biographical* and *picture*). Although language users can acquire new words, store them in their mental dictionaries, and use them appropriately, it is uncommon for users to be aware of how the words came into their language unless they learn about these processes in school or elsewhere.

Much more information about morphology can be found in Unit 2, including the structure of words (Chapter 2) and word formation (Chapter 3).

KNOWLEDGE OF SENTENCES

One of the most familiar forms of human message transmission among language users is the sentence, a rule-governed linguistic unit composed of words that can stand alone in expressing meaning, such as a statement or question. One form of evidence that demonstrates that language users have internalized knowledge of the sentence structure of their native language is that they can produce an unlimited number of new sentences at will. But in order to recognize a sentence as such when it is spoken, a language user must first be able to determine where one word ends and another begins. For, unlike the written form of a sentence in English, for example, which contains spaces between the individual words, spoken utterances typically contain few if any pauses between words.

Sohowdoyouknowwhensomethingisorisnotasentencewhenitisspoken? Native speakers rely on their mental dictionaries and their internalized knowledge of word and sentence formation rules. Then again, how do language users determine whether a group of words does or does not constitute a sentence? Upon hearing the sequence of words *the small tan dog wagged its tail*, for example, a native speaker of English would judge it to be a grammatically well-formed sentence. But if the same words are produced in an unfamiliar order, such as *tail dog tan its small the wagged*, the same speaker will judge the sequence ill-formed and reject its being labeled as a sentence. The speaker is aware, even if unconsciously, that for a sentence in English to be well-formed, the words it is composed of must follow certain rules of order and form.

A native user of a language is also able to recognize when a group of words is a complete sentence and when it is a component of a sentence, a *phrase*. In the example just cited, *the small tan dog* contains no verb and therefore is only part of a sentence –a noun phrase. The phrase contains a subject, but it lacks a predicate, something that is asserted about the subject. And just as in evaluating the grammaticality of sentences, a native speaker is able to determine whether or not a phrase is well-formed according to their internalized knowledge of the rules of word combining. For example, *the happy baby* will be considered a well-formed noun phrase, but *the happily baby* will be considered ill-formed because native English speakers have internalized a rule that says an adjective (*happy*) may modify a noun (*baby*), but an adverb (*happily*) may not.

One way that linguists analyze the internal structure of a sentence is according to its phrases, such as noun phrase and verb phrase. In the simple sentence *The children ate the cake*, the subject *The children* is a noun phrase containing the noun *children* preceded by the article *the*. The verb phrase in the sentence is *ate the cake*, composed of the verb *ate* and the direct-object noun phrase *the cake*, which in turn is made up of the noun *cake* and the article *the*. The system of rules for combining words into phrases and phrases into sentences is known as **syntax**. Just as with other aspects of language, children acquire the syntactic rules of the language or languages they are exposed to in predictable stages that are largely unconscious.

Phrases combine to form *clauses*, which consist of both a subject (noun phrase) and a predicate (verb phrase); therefore, a clause is equivalent to a sentence in its simplest form: *The dog slept*. A clause or sentence that can stand alone to express meaning is an *independent clause*. Sentences can be *simple* (one independent clause), *compound* (two or more independent clauses), or *complex* (one independent clause and one or more *dependent*, or *subordinate*, clauses). For example, *The children ate the cake* is a simple sentence containing one independent clause, while *The children ate the cake and the cats chased the mice* is a compound sentence containing the independent clause *The children ate the cake* and a second independent clause *the cats chased the mice* joined to the first clause by the conjunction *and*. In the sentence *The children ate the cake while the cats chased the mice*, the independent clause is *The children ate the cake*, and the clause *while the cats chased the mice* is considered subordinate since it cannot function meaningfully without being attached to the independent clause. The two clauses are joined together to form one complex sentence by means of the subordinating conjunction *while*. In the production of sentences in their first language, children progress from simple to complex sentences over a time period of about three years, from age two to five (Gotzke & Gosse, 2009).

The topic of syntax is covered fully in Unit 3, "Syntax," which includes Chapters 4 and 5.

KNOWLEDGE OF MEANING

Language users know a lot about language meaning. For example, thanks to their mental dictionaries, native speakers of English will know that the word *roof* means "the external upper covering of a house or other building" and not "the upper interior surface of a room or other compartment." Language users are also able to judge whether or not a sentence has meaning. The sentence *The child studies art*, for example, has the expected subject-verb-object structure of English declarative sentences, and speakers know that *child* refers to an animate, human subject capable of actions such as studying, and that art is a common object of study for human beings. But if confronted with another grammatically well-formed sentence such as *Art ran happily*, English language users would be confused: Art is an inanimate subject, so to suggest that it can move by running or that it can experience an emotion such as happiness may well cause speakers to declare this sentence meaningless. The study of how language conveys meaning is known as **semantics**.

When language users learn words, they learn their *reference*, that is, what they are pointing out in the world. For example, the word *cat* refers to a particular class of domestic feline animal, and the referent of the phrase *my cat* refers to a specific individual member of that class. Language users also know a lot about how pairs of words relate to each other in meaning: *synonyms* have approximately the same meaning (for example, *sofa* and *couch* both refer to an upholstered object of furniture intended to seat several people), while *antonyms* are opposite in meaning (*in* vs. *out*, *up* vs. *down*, etc.). Most native speakers recognize the difference between the literal or *denotative* meaning of a word and a word's *connotative* or associative meaning that may carry an emotional charge. For example, the words *childlike*, *youthful*, *childish*, *young*, *immature*, and *juvenile* all denote more or less the same idea, that is, the relative youthful quality of something or someone. But some of these words carry positive connotations (*childlike*, *youthful*, *young*) while others, depending on the context of their use, evoke negative connotations (*childish*, *immature*, *juvenile*). Readers will find much more information about word meaning in Chapter 7, "Lexical Semantics: Relativity and Transfer."

Language users know when a word or sentence is *ambiguous* (*She visited the bank* could mean someone went either to a financial institution or to a slope bordering a river), and they know when a sentence is true or false. For example, the sentence *The sun is shining* may be true or false depending on the conditions under which it is uttered; the sentence *All children are adults* however, is false under any circumstance, because children by definition are not adults. They also know when the truth of one sentence presupposes the truth of another: *Cindy fed her turtle* presupposes the truth of *Cindy has a turtle*.

Non-literal, figurative uses of words, phrases, and sentences often cause confusion among language learners and need to be explained. *My son is a night owl* does not literally mean that someone's human child looks like a raptor, has wings, and flies around at night, but rather that he shares the property with such birds of prey of being more active at night than during the day. One common form of figurative language is the *idiom*, a group of words whose meaning is independent of the sum of its individual words. The meaning of idioms must be learned similarly to the way individual words are learned. The idiom *I'm all ears*, for example, does not mean that the speaker is constructed solely of multiple human ears, but instead means "I'm listening to what you are going to say." Since the use of idioms is frequent in English, it is important for language educators to be aware of idiomatic meaning as they endeavor to help their students acquire vocabulary and use it in appropriate contexts.

Beyond the meaning of individual sentences, language users understand and convey meaning through connected stretches of context-sensitive language. The study of **pragmatics** examines how various contexts affect the interpretation of linguistic utterances. For example, the meaning of the sentence *Can you help me?* would be quite clear to someone witnessing a person struggling to carry several heavy suitcases all at once, but without this situational context the precise meaning is unclear, including whether the utterance is intended as a request for assistance or simply as a general question. Achieving communicative competence in a speech community involves applying one's knowledge of how linguistic meaning connects to context; it also involves knowledge of the social conventions expected during linguistic interactions, such as appropriate forms of address, rules for turn-taking in conversations, and many other aspects of communication established through cultural norms. The topic of pragmatics is addressed in depth in Chapters 8, 9, and 10, which form Unit 6, "Pragmatics."

KNOWLEDGE OF NONVERBAL COMMUNICATION

In addition to language that is spoken, signed, or written, human beings also engage in **nonverbal communication** in the form of gestures, facial expressions, body posture, and proximity during interactions. Although there are similarities across cultures, nonverbal communication is also significantly impacted by the culture of its language users, a fact which can sometimes result in miscommunication between people of different linguistic and cultural backgrounds. For example, the physical distance between speakers during interaction is culturally determined, yet it is often not consciously recognized. The amount of space that is considered appropriate for interaction between people who don't know each other well may vary considerably across cultures. For a high-contact culture, for example, relative closeness shows friendly interest, while for a low-contact culture that same closeness may be perceived as uncomfortably invasive or aggressive. Conversely, in low-contact cultures where relative distance is expected during interactions, visitors from a high-contact culture may feel as though the people around them are cold and indifferent. The study of this aspect of nonverbal communication is known as *proxemics*. Another example of nonverbal communication concerns eye contact: In some cultures, eye contact is expected during teacher-student interactions, while in other cultures students are expected to show respect by avoiding direct eye contact with their teachers. Having some understanding of culturally-determined differences in nonverbal communication can be helpful to language educators in their efforts to help students achieve communicative competence.

IMPLICATIONS FOR TEACHING ENGLISH LANGUAGE LEARNERS

Benefits of Structural Linguistics for Language Teachers

In addition to the internalized mental grammar that has been in focus in the preceding sections, there are several other uses of the term *grammar* that it will benefit language educators to be aware of. The everyday understanding of grammar views language use as correct if it conforms to the rules of the standard variety of a language, and incorrect if it does not. For linguists, this approach to grammar is known as *prescriptive grammar*, but it is rarely the object of their study. Instead, many linguists focus on a more objective, nonjudgmental account of the rules and patterns of a language or dialect based on observing the linguistic performance of native speakers of the language, including how the sounds of the language combine to produce words, how the words combine to form sentences, and how linguistic meaning is conveyed. This approach to grammar is known as *descriptive grammar*. A third approach, known as *pedagogical grammar*, is concerned with the rules of language applied for the purpose of learning another language. While it is essential for teachers of language to be thoroughly familiar with pedagogical grammar, an understanding of language from the perspective of descriptive grammar is also important in language education. An overly close identification with prescriptive grammar, however, may result in students becoming unmotivated or even demoralized.

In order to facilitate second language acquisition among their students, teachers must have a firm grasp of their subject matter, namely language. It is therefore important for English language teachers to understand language structure and usage. Familiarity with structural linguistics enables teachers to creatively explore methods for effective language instruction and error correction that will benefit their students. Knowledge of phonetics allows teachers to better model, explain, and correct student pronunciation. Knowledge of the grammatical morphemes of English can help teachers become more conscious of how students might achieve grammatically accurate sentences, such as through noun plurals and past-tense verb formation. Knowledge of English word formation enables teachers to acquaint their students with the components of English words, empowering students to identify and analyze word meaning as well as to produce correctly formed words. Teachers who can share with their students a basic understanding of how words are coined in English and how to interpret idioms will also help students in vocabulary building.

A knowledge of the similarities and differences in structure between the source and target languages (differences in speech sounds, word formation, or sentence structure) can help teachers increase their awareness of the role of cross-linguistic influence in language learning and thus enable them to design more effective lessons. Perhaps the simplest level of comparative understanding concerns the basic order of the fundamental sentence elements of subject (S), verb (V), and object (O). If the order of these elements in a student's first language is the same as in that of the target language, the student may initially acquire the target language more quickly than if the order of the basic elements in the source and target languages is different. For example, both English and Mandarin are SVO languages, but the basic pattern of Korean, Tibetan, and Japanese is SOV.

Another easily identifiable aspect of language that may differ markedly from source to target language is the writing system: Students whose first language is written with the Latin alphabet, for example, have less initial learning to do in reading and writing than students whose first language employs a non-Latin alphabet or is written in a non-alphabetic system. It is important for teachers to be aware of the literacy challenges students face in learning a new writing system.

At more advanced levels, with a knowledge of semantics teachers can help students navigate the vast world of linguistic meaning, distinguishing denotative meaning from connotative meaning, or recognizing and producing literary tropes such as metaphor, metonymy, puns, and so on. When their study of linguistics also includes a foundation in pragmatics, teachers become invaluable guides for students in their quest to decipher language whose meaning is heavily dependent on context.

Benefits of Sociolinguistics for Language Teachers

Knowledge of the principles of sociolinguistics, including the role of language in the construction of personal and social identities as well as the role of language variation across users from different regions, socioeconomic classes, genders, and other demographic factors will help language educators plan effective, culturally-sensitive lessons and make informed policy decisions about multilingualism, student attitudes toward standard English, and other socially-based language issues that arise in education.

Learning a second language involves being exposed to the culture of the native users of the target language. So in addition to achieving linguistic competence, language users also need to understand and employ the social conventions woven into the culture of the target speech community, such as appropriate forms of address, how to engage in turn-taking in conversation, and many other aspects of communication. When language learners internalize these social norms along with the structural rules of the target language, they achieve communicative competence. Communicative competence is therefore an important objective in language education.

Approaches to the Teaching of Language

Numerous theories of second language acquisition have been put forward in recent decades, and language educators would do well to become familiar with the most well-known among them. From a practical point of view, however, teachers of English learners will want to adopt and develop an approach or methodology of instruction that takes into account such factors as the level and age of their students as well as the purpose of the course they are teaching. It is also important to note that language education requires an understanding of the principles of learning in addition to knowledge about language. Learning styles of students will differ among students both individually (for example, some students are visual learners while others are more auditory) and demographically (children learn differently from adults, for example).

Language learners commonly exhibit cross-linguistic transfer on their way to becoming fluent in a new language, so that what they produce in the target language contains features of their first language, whether in pronunciation, grammar, or vocabulary. For many students, aspects of this learner language become fossilized, and complete bilingualism may never be achieved. Currently the most prominent second language classroom teaching methodology is the communicative approach. This approach emphasizes the importance of achieving successful communication of messages while decreasing emphasis on grammatical accuracy. As a student-centered method, the communicative approach encourages student interaction through the practice of listening and speaking skills.

The range of pedagogical practices that second language educators participate in is vast, from helping students achieve basic spoken communication to facilitating students' improvement in written academic English. Along with fluency in the target language, a basic knowledge of linguistics is a valuable tool for any language teacher engaged in helping students achieve linguistic and communicative competence.

DISCUSSION QUESTIONS

1. Children who are born deaf and who are exposed to sign language from an early age acquire sign language in stages similar to those of spoken language acquisition among hearing children. What does this suggest about the innateness of language vs. the innateness of speech?
2. The critical period hypothesis holds that, for linguistic competence to be native-like, language must be acquired no later than adolescence. Do you think this holds true for all aspects of language acquisition? What factors might make it difficult to acquire a new language in adulthood, and what aspects of language acquisition might be less problematic for adults?

3. While their innate linguistic creativity allows language users to produce completely new utterances at will, they also make frequent use of familiar expressions. Consider the potential value to second language learners of instruction that includes stretches of language such as idioms and common phrases. How might this be approached?

4. Identify the advantages to language teachers in being trained in the International Phonetic Alphabet as well as in morphology and syntax. Do you perceive any disadvantages to such training in structural linguistics? Explain your response.

5. While second language instruction involves teaching pronunciation, vocabulary, and sentence structure, students are not typically taught structural linguistics (e.g., the IPA, morphology, syntax, and semantics). Discuss your view on whether training language learners in basic linguistics might help or hinder their efforts to increase their proficiency in the target language.

6. In traditional second language teaching of the past, vocabulary was taught through lists of individual words and their definitions, which students were expected to memorize. In more recent decades, the importance of teaching vocabulary in context has been emphasized, including groups of words that commonly go together, known as collocations. Discuss your view on the merits of each approach to teaching vocabulary to second language learners.

7. Discuss your view on the value of instruction in nonverbal communication as an aspect of helping language learners achieve communicative competence in the target language.

8. Traditional language teaching of the past stressed the study of grammar rules for correct sentence formation. In recent decades, the emphasis in second language teaching has shifted to communicative competence, with a greater acceptance of learner language (where the target language shows influences from the source language). Develop a viewpoint regarding these two approaches, including whether or not each may be effective in language education.

9. It is commonly thought that writing is the most difficult language skill to master in second language learning. Consider the factors that might contribute to making writing proficiency more difficult to achieve than other aspects of language, such as fossilization of learner language.

EXERCISES

1. The notion of linguistic creativity asserts that we can create infinitely long sentences. Test this for yourself by chaining independent clauses together with a conjunction such as *and*, *or*, or *but*. Alternately, write a simple sentence composed of one independent clause and then lengthen it with a series of adjective clauses introduced by the subordinating conjunction *that*. (For example, *We noticed the owl that spotted the fox that chased the mouse that ran across the field that bordered the hillside that…*)

2. According to linguistic typology, English is an SVO language, meaning that the basic order of elements in a sentence are subject, verb, object. Can you think of any common types of English utterances where SVO is not the basic word order? What about sentences that seem more complex that simply SVO? Examine a variety of English sentences to inform your response.

3. Select one aspect of English grammar and consider how you would explain it to an English learner, including what forms of practice you would ask the learner to do. Consider as possibilities the plural of nouns, the form and use of the indefinite article, or the structure of information questions.

4. Check your understanding of the phonemes of English by producing a dozen or so minimal pairs. (To keep it simple, identify short words that rhyme, such as *cat* and *sat*.) How many separate phonemes can you identify from among your minimal pairs? Note that identifying minimal pairs with students is one way to help them recognize English phonemes and practice pronunciation.

5. Listen to an audio recording or radio broadcast in a language you don't understand. What can you tell about the language from just listening? Can you tell if the language has a predominance of consonants or vowels, or a predictable stress pattern? Can you discern emotional tone? If so, how did you arrive at your conclusions?

6. Words that could exist within the phonological and morphological systems of a language—but don't—are known as *accidental gaps*. Choose an English word at random, then alter it slightly so that it seems unfamiliar. Now research whether the word exists or not. If it does not, you have produced an accidental gap. What meaning would you assign to it? This is an exercise that students may enjoy as they learn about English speech sounds and vocabulary.

7. Examine a short text written in a writing system you are unfamiliar with (alphabetic or non-alphabetic). Are you able to tell if the text is ordered left to right, right to left, or top to bottom? How many different symbols do you note? Do repeated symbols occur in similar positions, such as at the start or end of a group of symbols? Are you able to tell where one word ends and another begins? If so, what is your evidence? Then reflect on the impact that learning a new writing system may have on reading development among second language learners.

8. Consider the kinds of hand gestures you use to express such functions as greeting, beckoning, refusing, accepting, leave-taking, etc. Then choose a culture you consider significantly different from your own and research how the gestures to express these same functions may be similar or different in that culture from those you would make. As you review your findings, reflect on the potential role of gestures in communicative competence.

9. Consider the facial expressions you use to express emotions such as surprise, pleasure, relief, anger, sadness, puzzlement, and joy. Then choose a culture you consider significantly different from your own and research how the facial expressions that express these same emotions may be similar or different in that culture from those you would make. As you review your findings, reflect on the potential role of facial expressions in communicative competence.

REFERENCES

Crystal, D. (2010). *The Cambridge encyclopedia of language* (3rd ed.). Cambridge, UK: Cambridge University Press.

Dawson, H., & Phelen, M. (Eds.). (2016). *Language files: Materials for an introduction to language and linguistics* (12th ed.). Columbus, OH: The Ohio State University Press.

Gotzke, C., & Gosse, H. S. (2009). Introduction to language 3-5 years: Increasingly adult-like understanding and use. In *Handbook of language and literacy development: A roadmap from 0-60 months*. London, Canada: The Canadian Language & Literacy Research Network. Retrieved from http://www.theroadmap.ualberta.ca/understandings/research/37-60#2

International Phonetic Association. (2019). *History of the IPA*. Retrieved from https://www.internation-alphoneticassociation.org

Shannon, C., & Weaver, W. (1949). *The mathematical theory of communication*. Urbana-Champaign, IL: University of Illinois Press.

Simons, G. F., & Fennig, C. D. (Eds.). (2018). *Ethnologue: Languages of the world* (21st ed.). Dallas, TX: SIL International. Retrieved from https://www.ethnologue.com/guides/how-many-languages

ADDITIONAL READING

Brown, H. D. (2014). *Principles of language learning and teaching* (6th ed.). London, UK: Pearson Education ESL.

Comrie, B., Matthews, S., & Polinsky, M. (2003). *The atlas of languages: The origin and development of languages throughout the world* (2nd ed.). New York, NY: Facts on File.

Denham, K., & Lobeck, A. (2013). *Linguistics for everyone: An introduction* (2nd ed.). Boston, MA: Cengage Learning.

Fromkin, V., Rodman, R., & Hyams, N. (2017). *An introduction to language* (11th ed.). Boston, MA: Cengage Learning.

Harmer, J. (2015). *The practice of English language teaching* (5th ed.). London, UK: Pearson Longman.

Jackendoff, R. (n.d.). *FAQ: How did language begin?* Retrieved September 21, 2018, from https://www.linguisticsociety.org/resource/faq-how-did-language-begin

Lieberman, P. (2007). Tracking the evolution of language and speech. *Expedition Magazine, 49*(2). Retrieved from http://www.penn.museum/sites/expedition/?p=9236

Radford, A., Atkinson, M., Britain, D., Clahsen, H., & Spencer, A. (2009). *Linguistics: An introduction* (2nd ed.). Cambridge, UK: Cambridge University Press. doi:10.1017/CBO9780511841613

Richard-Amato, P. (2010). *Making it happen: From interactive to participatory language teaching— Evolving theory and practice* (4th ed.). London, UK: Pearson Education ESL.

Silva, M. (1995). *Grammar in many voices*. Chicago, IL: NTC Publishing Group.

Silva, M. (1998). *Basic grammar in many voices*. Chicago, IL: NTC Publishing Group.

Tannen, D. (n.d.). *Discourse analysis—What speakers do in conversation*. Retrieved September 27, 2018, from https://www.linguisticsociety.org/resource/discourse-analysis-what-speakers-do-conversation

Yule, G. (2017). *The study of language* (6th ed.). Cambridge, UK: Cambridge University Press.

Unit 2
Morphology

Chapter 2
Morphemes

Nikki Ashcraft
University of Missouri, USA

ABSTRACT

This chapter introduces basic concepts in the field of morphology. In the first section, a morpheme is defined as the smallest unit of meaning in a language. In the second section, morphemes are divided into free and bound types, with bound morphemes further classified as either affixes (prefixes, infixes, suffixes, or circumfixes) or bound roots. This section additionally distinguishes between the role of function words and content words in a sentence. The third section outlines the nine word classes in English: nouns, pronouns, adjectives, determiners, verbs, adverbs, prepositions, conjunctions, and interjections. The final section of the chapter explains the implications of this information for teaching vocabulary, grammar, and language skills. The chapter concludes with questions for discussion and some practice exercises.

WHAT IS MORPHOLOGY?

Morphology is the subfield of linguistics which studies morphemes. Morphemes are the smallest units of meaning in a language. They can consist of only one letter, a group of letters, or an entire word. For instance, the indefinite article *a* and the subject pronoun *I* are single letters which have meaning and which are morphemes.

Morphemes can also be groups of letters which represent a meaning but which are not a complete word. For example, although *uni-* is not a complete word, it has a meaning, which is "one." This meaning is manifested in words like *uniform* (there is only "one form;" i.e., everything is the same) and *unicycle* (a cycle with one wheel). Similarly, *-ness* is not a complete word, yet when we add it to other word parts, it refers to a state of being as in *happiness* or *sickness*.

In addition, a morpheme can be an entire word on its own. To illustrate, *dog*, *book*, and *house* are morphemes, but we would also consider them to be complete words. Some words are made up of a combination of morphemes. Consider the word *autobiography*. This word consists of four morphemes: *auto-* (self), *bio-* (life), *graph-* (write), and *–y* (a noun-forming suffix). If we combine the meaning of these four morphemes, we have a noun that refers to a narrative that a person has written about his or her own life. A word, then, can consist of only one morpheme or multiple morphemes.

DOI: 10.4018/978-1-5225-8467-4.ch002

In all of these cases, whether the morpheme consists of a single letter, a group of letters, or a word, the morpheme represents a minimal unit of meaning. Lexical morphology looks at how morphemes are used to create words and inflectional morphology studies how morphemes add grammatical information to a sentence. You will learn more about these aspects of morphology in the coming chapters.

FREE AND BOUND MORPHEMES

Morphemes can be divided into **free morphemes** and **bound morphemes**. As noted above, there are some morphemes that are complete words (e.g., *desk, him, run,* and *sick*). With these morphemes, it is possible for us to categorize them according to their parts of speech (i.e., **nouns**, **pronouns**, **adjectives**, **determiners**, **verbs**, **adverbs**, **prepositions**, **conjunctions**, and **interjections**). This type of morpheme which is recognized as a complete word is known as a free morpheme. Free morphemes have the potential to serve as the base for the attachment of affixes (see below). For example, *desk* can add *–s* to form *desks*; *sick* can add *–ness* to become *sickness*. Additionally, free morphemes can combine with each other to create compound words. For instance, food that remains after a meal is *left over*. These two words are combined to create the adjective *leftover*, as in *I ate leftover pizza for breakfast*.

Bound morphemes are word parts that cannot stand alone as words, for example, *de-* or *-ly*. They must be connected to another morpheme in order to form a word. *De-*, which means "to remove," attaches to the beginning of words like *motivate* and *frost* to create *demotivate* (to reduce someone's motivation) and *defrost* (to remove ice). *-ly* can be added to the end of words to create adverbs, as in *slow/slowly* and *gradual/gradually*. Bound morphemes can be affixes or bound roots, both of which will be discussed in the coming sections. Notice the use of hyphens (e.g., *de-, -ly*) when these forms are written. The hyphens indicate that these forms are not complete words, and the direction of the hyphen shows where the bound morpheme attaches to other morphemes.

Affixes

Affixes are bound morphemes. As such, they must be connected to other morphemes in the language. Affixes can be derivational, in that they allow us to derive, or create, new words with new meanings from morphemes we already have. For instance, *re-* means to repeat an action. When we add *re-* to an existing base word like *write*, we have a new word, *rewrite*, which means to write something again. Likewise, *-al* represents an adjectival function. When we add *–al* to the noun *nation*, the affix changes the noun to an adjective, *national*, as in *national emergency*.

Affixes can also be inflectional, which means they add grammatical information, such as tense, number, or possession, to a word. For instance, *–s* is a morpheme we add to make a noun plural (e.g., *book/books*). Inflectional affixes do not change the part of speech of the word the way that derivational affixes can. Taking our example above, *book* (singular) and *books* (plural) are both nouns. The distinction between derivational and inflectional affixes will be covered in depth in Chapter 3.

Affixes are divided into four categories according to where the affixes can be attached to words: at the beginning (**prefixes**), in the middle (**infixes**), at the end (**suffixes**), or in two parts surrounding the word (**circumfixes**). Prefixes like *bi-, co-, dis-, re-,* and *semi-* appear at the beginning of a word, before the root, the morpheme which expresses the word's core meaning. Table 1 shows examples of how prefixes attach to words to create new meanings.

Table 1. Prefix examples

Prefix (Meaning)	Root/Base	New Word
bi- (two)	cycle	bicycle (with two wheels)
co- (together)	operate	cooperate (work together)
dis- (not)	like	dislike (not to like)
re- (again)	do	redo (do again)
semi- (half)	annual	semi-annual (half year)

Infixes are affixes which are inserted into the middle of a word. Although infixes are an important part of word formation in some other languages, like Tagalog, which is spoken in the Philippines, infixes are rarely used to create new words in English. One situation in which infixes are used in English is when there is a singular noun consisting of multiple morphemes and that noun needs to be made plural. For example:

(1)   one **brother**-in-law
       two **brothers**-in-law

In this case, the –*s* which makes the noun plural is added in between the first and second morphemes of the word rather than to the end of the word.

Another situation in which infixes are encountered is when speakers insert one morpheme inside another for emphasis. This usually occurs in informal speech and often involves curse words. One of the less offensive examples is *absofreakinlutely*. The speaker has inserted the word *freaking* (shortened as *freakin'*) into the word *absolutely*.

Suffixes are affixes that are attached to the ends of words. The addition of a suffix can change the part of speech of a word or add grammatical information to the sentence that includes the suffixed word. Table 2 illustrates how some common suffixes affect a word's part of speech.

Not all suffixes change a word's part of speech, however. Some suffixes create a word with a slightly different reference than the original. For instance, -*ist*, when added to a noun, creates another noun, like in *art/artist*, *cycle/cyclist*, and *behavior/behaviorist*. In this case, the addition of the suffix creates a noun that refers to a person who engages in a particular activity or who adheres to a certain belief.

Table 2. Suffix examples

Suffix	Word 1 (Without Suffix)	Word 2 (With Suffix)
-ish	fool (noun) child (noun)	foolish (adjective) childish (adjective)
-ly	rapid (adjective) strange (adjective)	rapidly (adverb) strangely (adverb)
-ment	amaze (verb) pay (verb)	amazement (noun) payment (noun)
-en	ripe (adjective) wide (adjective)	ripen (verb) widen (verb)

Finally, circumfixes have two parts, one of which attaches to the beginning of a word and the other which attaches to the end. In other words, they encircle the word. Circumfixes are very rare in English. An example is *em-* and *–en* in the word *embolden*. The addition of the circumfix changes the adjective, *bold*, to a verb, *embolden*, meaning "to make bold."

Bound Roots

Bound roots are another category of bound morphemes. These morphemes came into English through the borrowing of words from Latin and Greek. Some examples of word roots are found in Table 3.

Like affixes, bound roots must be attached to other morphemes to create a word. Unlike affixes, bound roots have a core meaning that can serve as the foundation for a word. As an example, let's compare the prefix *pre-* with the Greek root *psycho-*. *Pre-* means "before" and it can be added to words like *preview* (to see something before others), *preregister* (to register before the main registration period), and *pre-nupital* (describing something that occurs before marriage). Yet *pre-* only adds a layer of meaning to these words. The main idea of these words lies in the verbs and adjectives which form their core (i.e., *view, register*, and *nuptial*). In contrast, the root *psycho-* means "of the mind", and it provides the core meaning of words like *psychic, psychiatry*, and *psychedelic*.

Now that we have learned about free and bound morphemes, we can analyze a few examples of words into their parts (see Table 4).

Table 3. Examples of word roots

Root	Origin	Meaning	English Words
-dur-	Latin	last	durable, duration, endure
-min-	Latin	small	diminish, minimize, miniscule
-nov-	Latin	new	innovate, novelty, novice
-bio-	Greek	life	biology, biography, biopsy
-hydro-	Greek	water	dehydrate, hydrant, hydraulic
-phon-	Greek	sound	phonics, telephone, symphony

Table 4. Word analysis examples

Word	Free Morpheme	Bound Morphemes	Total Number of Morphemes
orange	orange	X	1
oranges	orange	-s (suffix)	2
mistrust	trust	mis- (prefix)	2
driver	drive	-er (suffix)	2
bathtub	bath tub	X	2
interdependent	depend	inter- (prefix); -ent (suffix)	3
abnormally	norm	ab- (prefix); -al (suffix); -ly (suffix)	4
uninhabitable	habit	un- (prefix); in- (prefix); -able (suffix)	4

Function Words and Content Words

Function words and **content words** are free morphemes. Function words represent the grammatical relationships between words in a sentence while content words express the main ideas.

Function words include auxiliary verbs, conjunctions, determiners, modal verbs, prepositions, and pronouns. Each of these word classes will be explained later in the chapter. Because of their grammatical functions, these words occur with high frequency in English. Table 5 gives examples of some function words.

Function words are closed classes of words. This means that the language is no longer adding new function words. Another important characteristic of function words is that bound morphemes (i.e., affixes or roots) cannot attach to them, nor can function words attach to other morphemes to form compound words. Therefore, function words stand alone and cannot be used in the creation of new words.

Content words are nouns, verbs, adjectives, and adverbs. They are open classes in that the language is constantly adding new content words! In fact, dictionaries like the *Oxford English Dictionary* announce each month which new words its lexicographers have added. Content words can combine with other morphemes, both free and bound, to create words to express new ideas in the language. Additionally, entirely new content words can be invented, though most new words incorporate morphemes that already exist.

Because new content words are always being formed, there are many more content words than function words in English. Some content words, like *pizza*, are quite common and occur with high frequency. Others, such as *tracheobronchomalacia*, a medical condition, are rare and used with low frequency. One way to learn about the frequency with which a word is used is to search for a word in a corpus like the Corpus of Contemporary American English (COCA) (https://corpus.byu.edu/coca/) to see how many times it appears.

Let's now analyze an example of how function words and content words work together to express meaning. Here is a sentence with the function words underlined:

(2) *Stars <u>can be</u> classified <u>into</u> seven types based <u>on their</u> temperature <u>and the</u> kinds <u>of</u> elements <u>they</u> absorb.*

Table 5. Examples of function words

Function Word Classes	Examples
auxiliary verbs	*be (am, is, are), do/did, have/has/had* e.g., *We <u>have</u> eaten dinner already.*
conjunctions	*and, but, or, because, although* e.g., *I called her repeatedly, <u>but</u> she didn't answer.*
determiners	*a, an, the, my, your, their, that, those* e.g., *Please pass out <u>these</u> papers.*
modal verbs	*can, could, may, should, would* e.g., *We <u>should</u> try to leave early.*
prepositions	*in, on, at, of, through* e.g., *The books are <u>in</u> the bedroom <u>on</u> the shelf.*
pronouns	*I, me, you, he, him, we, us* e.g., *<u>They</u> took a picture of <u>us</u>.*

The main ideas of the sentence are expressed by the content words (*stars, classified, seven, types, based, temperature, kinds, elements, absorb*). However, the function words link the content words to each other. For instance, the preposition *into* connects the act of classification to the number of types that will be used in that classification. The conjunction *and* indicates that both temperature and absorption of elements are criteria that will be used in the classification process and shows that these two criteria have equal status.

WORD CLASSES

Words can be divided into nine classes or parts of speech. These classes are nouns, pronouns, adjectives, determiners, verbs, adverbs, prepositions, conjunctions, and interjections.

Nouns

Nouns identify people, places, things, and ideas. For example, in the sentence *John ate pancakes for breakfast*, there are three nouns: *John* (the person eating), *pancakes* (the thing he is eating), and *breakfast* (the meal he is eating).

There are several different ways to classify nouns. One way of categorizing nouns is as common nouns or proper nouns. Common nouns are the names we use to identify people, places, things, and ideas more generally by type (e.g., teacher, school, book, theory). In contrast, proper nouns are the actual names of specific people, companies, places, and things (e.g., *Abraham Lincoln, Asia, the Sahara Desert, Kleenex®*). Proper nouns are always capitalized in English. Compare the common nouns and the proper nouns in Table 6.

Another way to categorize nouns is by whether they are concrete or abstract. Concrete nouns are those that we can perceive in the real world. We can physically see, hear, smell, taste, and touch them. Examples of concrete nouns are *chair, music, flower, salt,* and *bunny*. On the other hand, abstract nouns represent feelings, ideas, and principles. For instance, *happiness, compassion, truth, religion,* and *democracy* are all abstract nouns.

A final way to categorize nouns is by countability. Some nouns exist in both singular and plural forms (e.g., *desk/desks, child/children*). We are able to count and quantify these nouns (e.g., *one desk/30 desks, one child/18 children*.) Nouns that can be numbered are called count nouns.

There are, though, other nouns in English which cannot be counted. They are called noncount or uncountable nouns. These nouns represent objects which cannot easily be separated into individual units (e.g., *water, ketchup*) or where the individual units are so small that they are not used individually (e.g., *sand, rice*). Noncount nouns may also represent broader categories of nouns. For instance, the

Table 6. Examples of proper nouns and common nouns

Category	Common Nouns	Proper Nouns
People	man, girl, student, employee, patient	Mr. Smith, Sally, Jack Reynolds
Places	store, park, church	Thrifty Supermarket, Jacksonville Municipal Park, First Baptist Church
Things	book, song, movie	*Little Women, Under Pressure, Star Wars*

Table 7. Noun classification

Noun	Common	Proper	Concrete	Abstract	Count	Noncount
clock/clocks	X		X		X	
Lake Michigan		X	X			X
homework	X		X			X
health	X			X		X
nationalism	X			X		X

word *furniture* is uncountable whereas the different kinds of furniture (e.g., *beds, tables, chairs*) are countable. An additional kind of noncount noun are some of the abstract nouns mentioned previously (e.g., happiness). Noncount nouns are sometimes referred to in grammar books as mass nouns. Table 7 illustrates how some different nouns can be classified.

As noted earlier, nouns are content words and an open word class, which means that new nouns can be created by recombining existing morphemes or inventing entirely new words. For example, the *Oxford English Dictionary* has recently added the nouns *nothingburger*, "a person or thing of no importance, value, or substance" (Martin, 2018, para. 2) and *idiocracy*, "a society consisting of or governed by people characterized as idiots, or a government formed of people considered stupid, ignorant, or idiotic" (Martin, 2018, para. 3).

Pronouns

Pronouns are words that stand in for, or replace, nouns. They may appear almost anywhere in a sentence that a noun might appear. Notice how the nouns in the A sentences are replaced by pronouns in the B sentences.

(3) A. *Sally does not like John.* B. *She does not like him.*
   A. *(The speaker) bought a car.* B. *I bought it.*
   A. *Rick and Audrey got married.* B. *They got married.*

Pronouns take different forms depending on whether they are the subject or an object in a sentence. A special kind of pronoun, a reflexive pronoun, is used when the pronoun refers to the same subject of the sentence, as in *Karen looked at herself in the mirror*. In this case, the subject (*Karen*) and the object (*herself*) are the same person. Possessive pronouns can replace a noun and the possessive determiner (see later in this chapter) which modifies it, as is illustrated by the following sentences.

(4) A. *His car is parked over there.* B. *His is parked over there.*
   A. *This is her book.* B. *This is hers.*
   A. *Your answer is wrong, but my answer is right.* B. *Yours is wrong, but mine is right.*

Table 8 summarizes these pronouns according to their function.

Table 8. Pronouns by function

Subject	Object	Reflexive	Possessive
I	me	myself	mine
We	us	ourselves	ours
You (singular)	you	yourself	yours
You (plural)	you	yourselves	yours
He	him	himself	his
She	her	herself	her
It	it	itself	(no form)
They	them	themselves	theirs

Recall that a pronoun may appear almost anywhere in a sentence that a noun might appear. One situation where a pronoun cannot replace a noun is when that noun functions as an object in a separable phrasal verb, such as *throw away*, that has not been separated. For example, you can say *Throw the trash away* or *Throw it away*. It is possible to substitute the pronoun for the noun when it separates the verb and the particle. However, if you say *Throw away the trash*, it is not possible to substitute *it* for the noun *trash*. It is grammatically incorrect to say **Throw away it*. In other words, if a pronoun is used with a separable phrasal verb, the pronoun must be located between the verb and the particle.

Another form of pronoun refers to people and things, but in a generic way. These are called indefinite pronouns. The following sentences illustrate the use of indefinite pronouns.

(5)   *Does anyone know the answer?*
      Somebody stole my wallet!
      They lost everything in the fire.

There are four demonstrative pronouns: *this* and *that* (for singular) and *these* and *those* (for plural). Normally, *this* and *these* are used to refer to nouns that are closer in space or time, and *that* and *those* are used to refer to nouns that are farther way in space or time. Compare the sentences with nouns in A to the sentences with demonstrative pronouns in B.

(6)   A. *These rings are more expensive.*   B. *These are more expensive.*
        A. *Give me that book.*   B. *Give me that.*

Finally, the relative pronouns (*who, whom, which,* and *that*) appear in adjective clauses. They link the adjective clause to the rest of the sentence by referring to a noun in the independent clause. For example, in the sentence *The police arrested the man who had robbed me*, *who* in the adjective clause refers to *man* in the independent clause.

As function words, pronouns have historically been a closed word class. That is, it has not been possible to add new pronouns to the language. There is a movement, though, to introduce a more gender-neutral pronoun to the set of personal pronouns in English, a pronoun which does not refer to a person as male or female. One suggested subject pronoun is *ze* (Lindqvist, Renström, & Gustafsson Sendén, 2018) as in *Ze finished the exam early*. It remains to be seen whether this pronoun will be accepted into usage by the larger community of English speakers.

Adjectives

Adjectives are words that provide additional information about nouns and pronouns. Adjectives may describe the noun or pronoun's physical characteristics such as size, shape, color, age, or number; its origin or the material from which it is made; the kind of noun of pronoun; the speaker's opinion of it (e.g., *fun, wonderful, disgusting*); or other qualities. Notice the kind of information the adjectives in the following sentences provide about the nouns and pronouns:

(7)   *It is <u>small</u> and <u>round</u>.*
          (size)   (shape)

      <u>*Homemade*</u> *pies are* <u>*delicious*</u>*.*
          (origin)   (opinion)

      The <u>*elderly*</u> *man suffered a* <u>*cardiac*</u> *arrest.*
          (age)   (kind)

      <u>*Plastic*</u> *cups are* <u>*detrimental*</u> *to the environment.*
      (material)   (opinion)

Adjectives also play a role when we wish to compare the qualities of two or more items. Take, for example, the sentence *Water is <u>healthier</u> than soda*. The adjective *healthy* is used in a form, *healthier than*, which compares the two drinks. If we say *Water is <u>the healthiest</u> drink*, we are comparing water to all other drinks that exist. When one item has a quality more than all others, we use the adjective in superlative form (e.g. *the healthiest*).

One source of descriptive adjectives is the present (*-ing*) and past (*-ed*) participles of verbs. As an example, consider the verb *break*. The present participle form, *breaking*, acts as an adjective in the sentence *We heard the sound of <u>breaking</u> glass*. The past participle form, *broken*, functions as an adjective in the sentence <u>*Broken*</u> *glass covered the floor*.

As content words, adjectives are an open word class. Some adjectives which have recently been added to the *Oxford English Dictionary* are *applaudatory*, "expressing approval or praise" ("applaudatory, adj.", 2019), and *jammable*, "that can be jammed or rendered inoperative by jamming" ("jammable, adj.", 2019). These adjectives were created by adding affixes (*-atory* and *-able*) to existing verbs (*applaud* and *jam*).

Determiners

Determiners also modify nouns and help to limit what those nouns refer to. Determiners include possessive determiners, demonstratives, articles, and quantifiers.

Table 9. Possessive determiners

Person	Possessive Determiner	Example Sentence
I	my	I parked <u>my car</u>.
We	our	We protected <u>our homes</u> from the fire.
You (singular & plural)	your	You must do <u>your homework</u>.
He	his	<u>His sister</u> lives in Miami.
She	her	The students in <u>her class</u> are noisy.
It	its	The dog licked <u>its leg</u>.
They	their	<u>Their company</u> is profitable.

Possessive Determiners

Possessive determiners indicate that the noun belongs to someone. Table 9 lists the possessive determiners and shows their usage in sentences.

Demonstratives

Like demonstrative pronouns, there are four demonstrative determiners: *this* and *that* (for singular) and *these* and *those* (for plural). *This* and *these* refer to nouns closer in space or time while *that* and *those* refer to nouns farther way. The difference between a demonstrative pronoun and a demonstrative determiner is that the pronoun can be used to replace the noun whereas the determiner is used before the noun to emphasize it. This is evident from the examples below which were shown earlier. The A sentences have demonstrative determiners while the B sentences have demonstrative pronouns.

(8)   A. *<u>These rings</u> are more expensive.*   B. *<u>These</u> are more expensive.*
       A. *Give me <u>that book</u>.*   B. *Give me <u>that</u>.*

Articles

Articles are another type of determiner. *A* and *an* are indefinite articles which are used with singular count nouns. *A* is used before nouns (or their modifiers) which begin with consonant sounds (e.g., *a car*, *a red umbrella*) while *an* is used before nouns (or their modifiers) which begin with vowel sounds (e.g., *an elephant*, *an orange shirt*).

The is the definite article. One use of the definite article is to indicate that the noun is known to both the speaker and the listener. Notice how *the* is used in the following dialogue:

(9)   *Person A: Where did you put the iron?*
     Person B: It's in the closet.

In this case, Person A expects that Person B is familiar with the iron to which he/she is referring.

Another use of the definite article is to refer to all nouns of a category. For example, *The potato is a misunderstood vegetable.* Here, *the potato* refers to all potatoes rather than to a particular one.

The definite article *the* can be used with singular count nouns (e.g., *the car*), plural count nouns (e.g., *the cars*) as well as noncount nouns (e.g., *the furniture*). *The* also has several special uses such as with superlative adjectives (e.g., *the most delicious*), country names that are plural (e.g., *the United Arab Emirates*), and to identify parts of a whole (e.g., *the dairy section*).

Quantifiers

Quantifiers are the final category of determiner. As you might expect, quantifiers relate to quantity. Words and phrases like *many* and *a few* are used with plural count nouns (e.g., *many flowers*) while words and phrases such as *much* and *a little* are used with noncount nouns (e.g., *a little mayonnaise*).

The determiners presented in this section are closed classes of words. New words are not being added to these categories.

Verbs

The verb class is composed of lexical (or main) verbs, auxiliary verbs, and modals.

Lexical Verbs

Lexical verbs represent actions (e.g., *sleep, eat, walk, study*) and states of being (e.g., *be, have, know, seem*). They can serve as the main verb in a clause. For example, *I slept all night, but I am still tired.*

Lexical verbs are classified as transitive or intransitive. Transitive verbs are always accompanied by objects. Some examples of transitive verbs are *bring*, *carry*, *need*, *offer*, and *put*. Notice in these example sentences how the verb does not express a complete idea without its accompanying object.

(10) *Please bring your textbooks tomorrow.*
      Not **Please bring tomorrow.*

      The server carried the drinks into the dining room.
      Not **The server carried into the dining room.*

      I need some help.
      Not **I need.*

Intransitive verbs, on the other hand, cannot have an object. Some examples of intransitive verbs are *arrive, die, disappear, smile,* and *sleep.* These example sentences show how the verb expresses a complete idea without an object.

(11) *They arrived late.*
      He died last night.
      My jewelry has disappeared!

Table 10. Conjugation of 'go' in simple present tense

Person	Pronouns	Verb
First person singular	I	go
First person plural	We	go
Second person singular	You	go
Second person plural	You	go
Third person singular	He, She, It	goes
Third person plural	They	go

Many verbs can act as either transitive or intransitive verbs. An example is the verb *sing*. In the sentence *Mary sang a song*, the verb is transitive. In the sentence, *Mary sings in the choir*, the same verb is intransitive. Most dictionaries will indicate if a verb is transitive, intransitive, or both.

Verbs can be conjugated by person (first, second, or third) and number (singular or plural). For example, Table 10 presents the conjugation of the verb *go* in simple present tense.

In addition, verbs take different forms to indicate whether the action occurred in the past, present, or future. This is known as the verb tense. Furthermore, the verb form will tell us if the action is ongoing or completed, if the action occurs just once or if it is repeated multiple times, and the temporal relationship between this action and other actions. This kind of information is called aspect. Aspect can be simple (for actions that occur once or routinely), progressive (for continuous actions with no designated beginning or end), perfect (for actions that continue for a set period of time or to show the relationship between one action and other actions), or perfect progressive (for continuous actions with no designated beginning or end that are related to other actions). It is possible in English to have 12 different tense-aspect combinations. These are illustrated in Table 11 with the verb *work*.

A final point to make about lexical verbs is that they can appear in active voice or passive voice. In active voice, the subject of the sentence is the agent who is performing the action. All of the sentences in Table 11 are in active voice. In passive voice, more emphasis is put on the action and the recipient of that action, usually because the agent is less important or unknown. Passive voice verbs consist of a *be*-verb which reflects the tense and aspect while the main verb appears in past participle form. If the agent is known, it can optionally be included at the end of the sentence in a *by*-phrase. Table 12 compares sentences in active and passive voice in all twelve tense-aspect combinations.

As may be gleaned from Table 12, some of the passive voice constructions sound overly formal and downright awkward. Although these sentences are grammatically correct, a writer may prefer to use active voice for stylistic reasons.

Lexical verbs are an open class of words. Some new verbs that have recently been added to the *Oxford English Dictionary* are *destigmatize*, "to make socially acceptable" ("destigmatize, v.", 2019), and *upvote*, "In social media contexts: to register approval of or agreement with something posted by another user" ("upvote, v.", 2019). As with other open classes, we can notice that these new words were created by adding affixes, *de-* and *up-*, to already existing words, *stigmatize* and *vote*.

Table 11. Tense-aspect combinations with the verb 'work'

Tense-Aspect	Verb Form	Meaning
Simple present	I work every day.	Habitual action in the present
Present progressive	I am working now.	Action in progress in the present
Simple past	I worked last week.	Completed action at a specified time in the past
Past progressive	I was working when the lights went out.	Action in progress in the past when another past action interrupted it
Present perfect	I have worked in many jobs over the years.	Action occurred repeatedly at indefinite times in the past, at some time before the present
Present perfect progressive	I have been working in this job for five years.	Action began in the past and is still in progress in the present
Past perfect	I had worked on the project before I typed the report.	One past action was completed before another past action was completed
Past perfect progressive	I had been working at the company for five years when I received a promotion.	One past action was in progress when another past action was completed
Future simple	I will work on Friday. AND I am going to work on Friday.	The action will be completed at a time in the future
Future progressive	At 4 p.m. on Friday, I will be working.	The action will be in progress at a specified time in the future
Future perfect	I will have worked on the project before I type the report.	One future action takes place before another future action takes place
Future perfect progressive	If I receive a promotion in 2025, I will have been working at the company for five years when I receive it.	One future action will be in progress when another future action is completed

Table 12. Comparison of active voice and passive voice

Tense-Aspect	Active Voice	Passive Voice
Simple present	The analyst generates the reports every day.	The reports are generated every day (by the analyst).
Present progressive	The analyst is generating the reports now.	The reports are being generated now (by the analyst).
Simple past	The analyst generated the reports yesterday.	The reports were generated yesterday (by the analyst).
Past progressive	The analyst was generating the reports when the CEO arrived.	The reports were being generated (by the analyst) when the CEO arrived.
Present perfect	The analyst has generated the reports several times this week.	The reports have been generated (by the analyst) several times this week.
Present perfect progressive	The analyst has been generating reports since 1 p.m.	The reports have been being generated (by the analyst) since 1 p.m.
Past perfect	The analyst had generated the reports before the CEO arrived.	The reports had been generated (by the analyst) before the CEO arrived.
Past perfect progressive	The analyst had been generating reports for several hours before the CEO arrived.	The reports had been being generated (by the analyst) for several hours before the CEO arrived.
Future simple	The analyst will generate the reports. OR The analyst is going to generate the reports.	The reports will be generated (by the analyst). OR The reports are going to be generated (by the analyst).
Future progressive	The analyst will be generating reports for several hours.	The reports will be being generated (by the analyst) for several hours.
Future perfect	The analyst will have generated the reports before the CEO arrives.	The reports will have been generated (by the analyst) before the CEO arrives.
Future perfect progressive	The analyst will have been generating reports for several hours before the CEO arrives.	The reports will have been being generated (by the analyst) for several hours before the CEO arrives.

Auxiliary Verbs

As can be seen in the previous Tables 11 and 12, lexical verbs often require assistance to create the wide variety of forms necessary to express the 12 different tense-aspect combinations. They cannot do it on their own! This is where the auxiliary words *be*, *have*, and *do* come in.

As noted earlier, *be*-verbs can serve as lexical verbs when they express a state of being (e.g., *They <u>were</u> happy together*). However, they also have an auxiliary role in expressing verbs in progressive and perfect progressive aspects (e.g., *We <u>are</u> eating*; *I will have <u>been</u> driving for 8 hours by the time night falls*). We see *be*-verbs again as an integral part of forming passive voice (e.g., *The painting <u>was</u> stolen*).

Have can be a lexical verb when it refers to possession (e.g., *I <u>have</u> two brothers*). In addition, it serves a supportive role in expressing verbs in perfect and perfect progressive aspects (e.g., *He <u>has</u> delivered all the packages*).

The verb *do* is a lexical verb when it refers to performing an action, like in the sentence *She never <u>does</u> her homework*. However, it acts as an auxiliary verb in the creation of negative statements (e.g., *I <u>do</u> not like her*) as well as in the formation of yes/no questions (e.g., *<u>Did</u> you see them at the party?*). It can also be added for emphasis as in *I <u>do</u> love you!* Auxiliary verbs are a closed class of words. No new words can be added to this class.

Modals

Modals work closely with the main verb in the sentence to add nuance to the meaning expressed. For instance, take the sentence *I watch TV in the evening*. This is a statement of fact. However, add the modal *might*, and we get the sentence *I might watch TV in the evening*. The word *might* injects a sense of uncertainty. Watching TV is a possibility, but you may decide to do something else instead. Another example is the sentence *You are 16 years of age*. Again, this is a statement of fact. If we add the modal *must*, we have the sentence *You must be 16 years of age (to leave school, to get married, to drive a car)*. The insertion of the modal *must* has created the sense that age is a requirement. Table 13 illustrates the meaning of a range of modal verbs and their use in sentences. Modals are a closed class of words.

An important point to note about modal verbs is that they come before the main verb of the sentence. When modals are used, neither the modal nor the main verb are conjugated. Also, as seen in Table 13, there are several modals which have similar meanings. The choice of which modal to use depends on the context. For example, *Would you hand me that pen?* is more formal and more polite than *Can you hand me that pen?*

Adverbs

Adverbs are words and phrases that tell us how, where, when, how often, and how intensely the action of the sentence occurs. Table 14 gives examples of adverbs in sentences.

Adverbs can also add intensity to an adjective or another adverb. For example, *The girl was <u>too</u> sick to play* (the adverb *too* modifies the adjective *sick*) and *Jason picked up the knife <u>very</u> carefully* (the adverb *very* modifies the adverb *carefully*).

Of the different types of adverbs, adverbs of manner are the type most likely to add new words to the class. This is because new adverbs of manner can be created by adding the suffix –*ly* to any adjective. For example, if a new adjective were invented to describe a person, e.g., **prasty*, someone might later add –*ly* to the word to say that the person walks or dresses **prastily*.

Table 13. Modal verbs

Modal verb	Meaning	Example
can	ability permission request	*He can play trumpet.* *Can we play outside?* *Can you hand me that pen?*
could	past ability possibility suggestion polite request condition	*When I was younger, I could touch my toes.* *Your keys could be in the bedroom.* *We could fly through New York.* *Could you hand me that pen?* *If I were retired, I could travel more.*
had better	warning	*You had better drive the speed limit.*
may	permission possibility	*May we play outside?* *You may want to arrive early.*
might	possibility	*You might want to arrive early.*
must	obligation conclusion	*You must drive the speed limit.* *You stayed up all night; you must be tired.*
ought to/should	advice expectation	*You ought to/should eat more vegetables.* *He left the house at 3 p.m. He ought to/should be here by now.*
will	future polite request	*John will bring the drinks on Saturday.* *Will you hand me that pen?*
would	past habit polite request condition	*When I was a child, we would go camping every summer.* *Would you hand me that pen?* *If he did his homework, he would pass the class.*

Table 14. Adverb examples

Adverb Meaning	Example
How (manner)	Sally drives <u>safely</u>. Jack ate the meat <u>hungrily</u>.
Where (place)	I am going <u>upstairs</u>. You can sit <u>here</u>.
When (time)	He is busy <u>now</u>. Why didn't you tell me <u>before</u>?
How often (frequency)	They <u>always</u> get up at 6 a.m. We <u>rarely</u> cook at home.
How intensely (degree)	The child <u>hardly</u> speaks. He has left; you <u>just</u> missed him!

Prepositions

Prepositions are another closed class of words. Prepositions occur in phrases with nouns and object pronouns (e.g., *on the table, under the ground, before him,* and *in it*). The prepositions link these nouns and pronouns to the rest of a sentence and provide information about time, location, and movement, among other meanings. For example, in the sentence, *We wake up early in the morning,* the preposition *in* connects the noun *morning* to the rest of the sentence and tells us the time when the action occurred.

Conjunctions

Conjunctions are a closed class of words which connect words, phases, and clauses and show the relationship between them. Two important types of conjunctions are coordinating conjunctions and subordinating conjunctions. There are seven coordinating conjunctions: *for, and, nor, but, or, yet*, and *so*. These can be remembered with the acronym FANBOYS. Coordinating conjunctions connect multiple words, phrases, or clauses with equivalent status in a sentence. For instance, in the question, *Would you like coffee or tea?*, *or* connects the two noun objects which make up two equal choices. In the sentence, *He was tall and thin, and* links the two adjectives which describe the man. With *I called her, but she was not at home, but* connects two independent clauses which express contrasting ideas. I called her because I thought that she would be at home. In *We took our umbrellas, for it was raining, for* binds two independent clauses showing a cause and effect relationship. The choice of coordinating conjunction is important, then, to reflect accurately the relationship between the elements being joined. Different conjunctions imply different meanings. For example, *We can eat dinner and see a movie* means that we can do both activities on the same day whereas *We can eat dinner or see a movie* means that we only have time or money to do one of the activities.

Subordinating conjunctions link a dependent adverbial clause to an independent clause creating a complex sentence. Subordinating conjunctions show relationships between the two clauses such as time sequence, cause and effect, opposing ideas, or conditions. For example, with the sentence *Call me when you get there*, the subordinating conjunction *when* indicates that the two clauses are connected through a time relationship. In the sentence, *She wore a sweater although it was sweltering*, we see the fact that the woman wore a sweater is in contrast to the fact that the weather was hot. The subordinating conjunction *although* indicates the relationship between these two clauses which express contradictory ideas. Other subordinating conjunctions are *before, after, while, because, since, even though*, and *if*. Like with coordinating conjunctions, the choice of the appropriate subordinating conjunction is important for expressing your intended meaning. To illustrate, *I washed dishes before I talked to my mother on the phone* shows a different sequence of events than *I washed dishes while I talked to my mother on the phone*.

Interjections

Interjections are the final part of speech. They consist of words that show emotion like *Wow!*, *Ouch!*, and *Fiddlesticks!* as well as many vulgar words. Because they show emotion, they are often written with exclamation marks and given stress in spoken utterances. Interjections are an open word class; however, grammatically, they are not very important as their use is entirely optional.

IMPLICATIONS FOR TEACHING ENGLISH LANGUAGE LEARNERS

Having a strong understanding of morphology, function and content words, and word classes enables teachers to develop instructional practices to build English language learners' vocabulary and develop their grammatical knowledge. Additionally, teachers can use this knowledge to help learners with reading comprehension, expressing their ideas in speech and writing, and having clearer, more natural sounding pronunciation.

Teaching Vocabulary

In their review article on the place of academic vocabulary in the development of academic language, Nagy and Townsend (2012) describe six characteristics of academic language, several of which relate to the present discussion. First, academic language contains large numbers of words with roots of Latin and Greek origin. Some of these words were previously given as examples in Table 3. Second, academic language contains longer words with more word parts. To demonstrate, a word like *intercontinental* is six syllables long and contains both a prefix and a suffix. Finally, academic language contains more content words than conversational language does. Academic language employs more nouns and adjectives and makes greater use of nominalization (i.e., the conversion of verbs to nouns). For example, *destroy*, a verb, and *destruction*, a noun, both have the same core meaning. Yet in academic texts, we are more likely to see a sentence such as *The destruction of the city ended the war* than *The city was destroyed, and the war ended.* This leads to academic language having greater lexical density, a concept that we will return to later.

Teaching learners about affixes and word roots will facilitate their learning of vocabulary, in general, and academic vocabulary, in specific. Teachers can begin to develop learners' morphological awareness as early as the kindergarten years (see, for example, Zoski & Erikson, 2016). Teachers can ask learners to identify words in songs or stories that have the same prefix or suffix and talk about the meaning of that morpheme. As learners begin to engage in reading of a more academic nature, teachers can highlight morphemes that recur in disciplinary texts. For instance, in math, a teacher might focus on the root *-meter*, meaning "to measure," when it occurs in words like *kilometer, thermometer,* and *diameter*, or the root *quad-*, meaning "four," in words such as *quadrant, quadrangle*, and *quadruple*. A science teacher might focus on the adjective suffix *–ic* when teaching a unit on earth science and encountering words like *seismic, volcanic, and metamorphic.* Additionally, there are morphemes that cut across content areas, like the prefix *sub-*, meaning "under," which is found in a wide variety of words like *subatomic, subconscious, subcontinent, subcutaneous, subdue, subheading, submerge, subterranean*, and many others. In other words, no matter the subject, morphology is relevant to vocabulary learning.

Teachers might also offer direct instruction on morphology by explicitly teaching sets of purposefully chosen prefixes, suffixes, or roots. Learners should be shown how a new word can be divided into meaningful parts as well as how the addition of suffixes to a word creates word families, such as *care, careful,* and *carefully.* Connections should be made between words that are composed of the same morpheme, like *transfer, transmit, and transport.* Students can then engage in learning activities such as sorting words by part of speech or related meanings, creating mind maps to show the relationship between words which contain the same morpheme, or going on morpheme scavenger hunts in which they search for morphemes in written text. If students keep a vocabulary notebook, they might designate a separate page for listing affixes and roots. Additionally, teachers may use online flash card applications, like Quizlet (quizlet.com), to provide students with extra practice on the spelling and meaning of the morphemes under study.

Another point to consider when teaching morphology is that the learners' first language (L1) may share some cognates (either free or bound morphemes) with English. A cognate is a morpheme with the same (or similar) pronunciation, spelling, and meaning that occurs across multiple languages. For instance, both English and Spanish make use of the prefixes *bi-, pre-, super-, tele-, trans-*, and many others. Thus, learners may already be familiar with these morphemes and just need their attention drawn to these cognates in order to transfer this knowledge to English.

Not all morphemes that look and sound alike are cognates, though, as their meanings may be very different. Words like *embarrassed* in English and *embarazada* in Spanish are false cognates. *Embarazada* means that a woman is pregnant!

Teaching Grammar

Word classes form the basis of much of grammar teaching. Many language learning curricula, and course textbooks, are organized around the structural elements of language. Even integrated skills courses usually incorporate a thread of grammar learning objectives. It is important, then, for teachers to have a firm grasp of the different classes of words (how they are formed, how they are used, and what they mean), so that teachers can teach these forms to learners and develop appropriate pedagogical tasks for learners to practice the forms in guided, controlled, and communicative situations.

A teacher's understanding of word classes is also integral to his/her ability to assess learners' language development and to provide error correction and feedback. A teacher needs to be able to identify which forms learners are using correctly and incorrectly and explain errors to learners in a way that is comprehensible to them.

Developing Language Skills

Morphology and word classes also have implications for the development of different language skills. In reading, knowledge of morphology and word classes is important for recognizing known words as well as guessing the meaning of new words. Thus, a learner's knowledge of morphology and word classes plays an important role in reading fluency and reading comprehension. Attempting to guess the meaning of a word, or its word class, from its parts is a useful strategy for language learning more generally and for reading in particular. Analyzing word parts to guess meaning and word class is a strategy that teachers can explicitly teach to their learners in language as well as content-area classes. Teachers can model this strategy when new words are introduced during pre-reading or when the words are encountered during reading. Learners can be encouraged to "think-aloud" and explain how they approach analyzing new words as they are reading. For example, if students encounter a sentence about *the dissolution of salt*, they can determine that *dissolution* is a noun from its suffix *–tion*. They can also identify that the word has a prefix *dis-*, which means "apart." Further, they might connect *dissolution* to the verb *dissolve* which they had studied earlier.

Teachers should be aware, though, of the limitations of morphology instruction for guessing the meanings of new words. Not all word parts are morphemes; that is, not all word parts have a meaning. In addition, many words have been borrowed into English from other languages, languages which may have morphological rules and patterns that differ from English. Additionally, the meanings of some words have evolved so much over time that knowledge of the individual morphemes may not help students decipher the word's modern day meaning. For example, the words *conceive*, *perceive*, and *receive* all contain the root *–ceive*, which comes from a Latin word meaning "to take," yet given the way these words are currently used, it may be hard for learners to see a connection between them. It is recommended, then, for morphology instruction to focus on 1) those affixes and roots having explicit meanings that relate to modern usage of the words they form part of, and 2) high frequency affixes and roots which appear in a greater number of words.

Table 15. Word form table

Noun	Verb	Adjective	Adverb
anger	anger	angry	angrily
confusion	confuse	confused/confusing	confusingly
development	develop	developed/developing/developmental	developmentally
economy	economize	economical	economically
receipt	receive	receptive	receptively

Another benefit of morphology and word class instruction is that learners may make errors in word choice when speaking or writing due to a lack of understanding of how suffixes can change a word's class. For instance, a learner may write, "I hope to be *success*" (using the noun form) rather than "I hope to be *successful*" (using the adjective form). When teaching vocabulary, teachers can present the various forms of a word and have students complete a table in which they fill in the noun, verb, adjective, and adverb forms of the word, as applicable, paying attention to the suffixes that are used for each word class. An example of such a table can be seen in Table 15.

The distinction between content words and function words has classroom implications, too, particularly for the selection of reading and listening texts. In the United States, the Common Core State Standards (CCSS) place high importance on exposing students to complex texts (National Governors Association, 2010). In the CCSS, text complexity is defined through an analysis of qualitative dimensions, quantitative dimensions, and reader and task considerations. Among the quantitative dimensions are word length and word frequency. As we have seen in this chapter, content words tend to be longer than function words since content words can support the addition of affixes, and in fact, might contain several of them. This means that content words are often multisyllabic and can be harder than function words for learners to decode, pronounce, and remember. Additionally, we know that function words are high frequency; learners will encounter them over and over again, in both social conversations and academic situations. The frequency of content words, however, depends on the subject matter. The more specialized the topic, the less frequently the words in that domain will be encountered.

One method for determining the complexity of the text that we ask learners to read or listen to is to calculate the text's lexical density. Lexical density is the ratio of content words to the total number of words in the text. A number of websites, such as UsingEnglish.com and analyzemywriting.com, offer useful tools for instantly analyzing the lexical density of a text. These sorts of tools can help teachers select reading and listening texts that are appropriately challenging for their learners and which fulfill the expectation of the CCSS to expose students to complex texts.

Finally, the distinction between function words and content words has relevance for teaching pronunciation. English is a stress-timed language. This means that the stresses in a sentence occur at regular intervals, creating a rhythm. The words that are stressed are the content words, with one syllable in each of those words receiving greater stress (Celce-Murcía, Brinton, & Goodwin, 2010). In the following examples, the dots and underlining indicate the stressed syllables.

(12)
        •   •   •   •

A.   The <u>chem</u>ical is dis<u>sol</u>ved in the <u>wa</u>ter over<u>night</u>.

   •   •   •   •   •   •

B.   <u>Wa</u>ter e<u>va</u>porates from the <u>sur</u>face of the <u>earth</u> and <u>ri</u>ses into the <u>at</u>mosphere.

Given that the stressed syllables occur at regular intervals, speakers have to pronounce the function words more quickly so they can reach the stressed syllable on the beat. The lack of emphasis on the function words causes those words to be reduced and not spoken as clearly. Pronunciation exercises focusing on stress and rhythm can help learners not only speak more clearly, but also distinguish content words more readily during classroom listening. Kinaesthetic activities which involve speaking and clapping on the stressed syllable can aid learners in developing a more natural rhythm when speaking the language.

DISCUSSION QUESTIONS

1. Think of a class that you have taught, observed, or participated in. What were some of the important vocabulary words or grammatical structures that emerged during that lesson? Which morphemes were important for learners to know and understand?

2. Review a list of common prefixes in the English language, such as this one compiled for the Cambridge Dictionary: https://dictionary.cambridge.org/us/grammar/british-grammar/word-formation/prefixes. Which prefixes could be taught to beginning proficiency students? Intermediate? Advanced? Explain your reasoning.

3. Thinking of the classroom implications section of this chapter, what kinds of activities to develop morphological awareness and knowledge could you implement in your classes?

4. Review the tables of contents for two English language textbooks targeted towards the same proficiency level. Compare the word classes that are taught and the order in which they are taught. Present your findings to your classmates. Why do you think these word classes were selected for this proficiency level and sequenced in this order?

5. If you are a content-area teacher (i.e., you teach math, science, social studies, or some other content area), or plan to be one, locate a content-area text that is appropriate for the age of students you teach. Choose one of the paragraphs from this text and calculate the lexical density. Present your findings to your classmates.

EXERCISES

1. How many morphemes are in the following sentences?
   a. Sarah looked at the organisms through a microscope.
   b. We asked the singer for her autograph.
   c. The rebels are fighting for a democratic government.

2. Read each word. Identify whether the underlined section of the word is a free morpheme or a bound morpheme.

   a. work<u>er</u>   f. weak<u>en</u>
   b. <u>hand</u>ful   g. <u>re</u>lapse
   c. <u>im</u>possible   h. <u>cook</u>ed
   d. hung<u>rily</u>   i. cup<u>s</u>ful
   e. re<u>tell</u>   j. <u>fire</u>place

3. In Table 16, match the prefix or word root on the left with its meaning on the right. Two of the answers will not be used.

4. Look at the list of prefixes and roots in the previous exercise (Exercise 3). Generate an example of a word that contains each prefix or root.

   1. _____   6. _____
   2. _____   7. _____
   3. _____   8. _____
   4. _____   9. _____
   5. _____   10. _____

5. In the following quotes, identify the underlined words as a noun, pronoun, adjective, determiner, verb, adverb, preposition, conjunction, or interjection.
   a. When you are (1) <u>discontent,</u> you (2) <u>always</u> want more, more, more. Your desire can never be satisfied. (3) <u>But</u> when you practice (4) <u>contentment</u>, you can say to yourself, "(5) <u>Oh</u> yes, I already have everything that I really (6) <u>need</u>." —— *Dalai Lama*
   b. (7) <u>If</u> you (8) <u>judge</u> people, you have no time to love (9) <u>them</u>. —— *Mother Teresa*
   c. Being (10) <u>deeply</u> loved (11) <u>by</u> someone gives you strength, (12) <u>while</u> loving (13) <u>someone</u> deeply gives you courage. —— *Lao Tzu*
   d. No one can make you feel (14) <u>inferior</u> (15) <u>without</u> your (16) <u>consent</u>. —— *Eleanor Roosevelt*

Table 16. Matching exercise

Prefix/Root	Meaning
_____1. anti-	a. large
_____2. bene-	b. under
_____3. ex-	c. extremely
_____4. hypo-	d. one
_____5. macro-	e. well
_____6. mono-	f. across, through, beyond
_____7. pan-	g. against
_____8. semi-	h. alike
_____9. trans-	i. outside
_____10. ultra-	j. half
	k. not
	l. all, whole, completely

6. Underline the content words in the following sentences.
    a. Mitochondria are organelles which bring nutrients into the cell.
    b. The scientific method starts with a hypothesis that can be tested.
    c. The background of an artwork is the area that seems to be furthest away from the viewer.
    d. In 1606, King James I granted a charter to the Virginia Company to establish a settlement in North America.
    e. Speed can be calculated by dividing the distance traveled by the time it takes to travel that distance.

REFERENCES

applaudatory, adj. (2019). In *OED Online* (3rd ed.). Retrieved from http://www.oed.com/view/Entry/249093

Celce-Murcía, M., Brinton, D., & Goodwin, J. M. (2010). *Teaching pronunciation: A course book and reference guide* (2nd ed.). Cambridge: Cambridge University Press.

destigmatize, v. (2019). In *OED Online* (3rd ed.). Retrieved from http://www.oed.com/view/Entry/68753899

jammable, adj. (2019). In *OED Online* (3rd ed.). Retrieved from http://www.oed.com/view/Entry/73895578

Lindqvist, A., Renström, E. A., & Gustafsson Sendén, M. (2018). Reducing a male bias in language? Establishing the efficiency of three different gender-fair language strategies. *Sex Roles*; Advance online publication. doi:10.100711199-018-0974-9

Martin, K. C. (2018, October 3). New words notes for October 2018 [Web log post]. Retrieved from https://public.oed.com/blog/new-words-notes-september-2018/

Nagy, W., & Townsend, D. (2012). Words as tools: Learning academic vocabulary as language acquisition. *Reading Research Quarterly*, *47*(1), 91–108. doi:10.1002/RRQ.011

National Governors Association Center for Best Practices, Council of Chief State School Officers. (2010). *Common core state standards for English language arts & literacy in history/social studies, and technical subjects, Appendix A: Research supporting key elements of the standards*. Washington, DC: Author.

upvote, v. (2019). In *OED Online* (3rd ed.). Retrieved from http://www.oed.com/view/Entry/74232793

Zoski, J., & Erickson, K. (2016). Morpheme-based instruction in kindergarten. *The Reading Teacher*, *70*(4), 491–496. doi:10.1002/trtr.1542

ADDITIONAL READING

Carstairs-McCarthy, A. (2018). *An introduction to English morphology* (2nd ed.). Edinburgh: Edinburgh University Press.

Celce-Murcia, M., & Larsen-Freeman, D. (1999). *The grammar book: An ESL/EFL teacher's course* (2nd ed.). Boston: Heinle/Cengage.

DeCapua, A. (2008). *Grammar for teachers: A guide to American English for native and non-native speakers*. New York: Springer. doi:10.1007/978-0-387-76332-3

Flanigan, K., Templeton, S., & Hayes, L. (2012). What's in a word? Using content vocabulary to *generate* growth in general academic vocabulary knowledge. *Journal of Adolescent & Adult Literacy*, *56*(2), 132–140. doi:10.1002/JAAL.00114

Folse, K. S. (2016). *KEYS to teaching grammar to English language learners: A practical handbook* (2nd ed.). Ann Arbor, MI: University of Michigan Press. doi:10.3998/mpub.8882354

Green, J. D. (2015). Language detectives: Teaching and learning about suffixes. *The Reading Teacher*, *68*(7), 539–547. doi:10.1002/trtr.1350

Hendrix, R. A., & Griffin, R. A. (2017). Developing enhanced morphological awareness in adolescent learners. *Journal of Adolescent & Adult Literacy*, *61*(1), 55–63. doi:10.1002/jaal.642

Kieffer, M. J., & Lesaux, N. K. (2010). Morphing into adolescents: Active word learning for English-language learners and their classmates in middle school. *Journal of Adolescent & Adult Literacy*, *54*(1), 47–56. doi:10.1598/JAAL.54.1.5

Mountain, L. (2015). Recurrent prefixes, roots, and suffixes: A morphemic approach to disciplinary literacy. *Journal of Adolescent & Adult Literacy*, *58*(7), 561–567. doi:10.1002/jaal.394

Plag, I. (2003). *Word-formation in English*. Cambridge: Cambridge University Press. doi:10.1017/CBO9780511841323

Rasinski, T. V., Padak, N., Newton, J., & Newton, E. (2011). The Latin-Greek connection: Building vocabulary through morphological study. *The Reading Teacher*, *65*(2), 133–141. doi:10.1002/TRTR.01015

Razfar, A., & Rumenapp, J. C. (2014). *Applying linguistics in the classroom: A sociocultural approach*. New York: Routledge.

Stockwell, R. P., & Minkova, D. (2001). *English words: History and structure*. Cambridge, UK: Cambridge University Press. doi:10.1017/CBO9780511791161

Chapter 3
Word Formation

Howard A. Williams
Teachers College, Columbia University, USA

ABSTRACT

This chapter presents a basic overview of the formation of words, with special attention to English. It covers the basics of both free and bound morphemes and the manner in which they combine. Productive processes including inflection, derivation, and compounding are examined with regard to their transparency and productivity; less common processes including zero-derivation (conversion) blending, clipping, back-formation are also covered, as are borrowing and coinage. Readers will be provided with guided practice in the analysis of English words into their constituent parts and in the principles of formation.

MORPHOLOGY, WORDS, AND MORPHEMES

If the components of language are organized in terms of 'smallest to largest', the study of **morphology** is often described as the next level of analysis above phonetics and phonology. At the bottom level one studies, for example, the very basic question of how a set of individual English sounds such as *l*, *i*, and *t* may or may not be sequenced and sound 'native' (e.g., *l+i+t* versus *t+i+l* versus *i+l+t* are possible, while *t+l+i* is not). Morphology is only tangentially concerned with sound. However, calling it 'the next higher level' is a bit misleading. The crucial difference is that while the key terms, concepts, and principles of phonetics and phonology involve sound alone, the study of morphology involves key terms, concepts, and principles built around **meaning**. While the sound system tells us that the sequences *til*, *lit*, and *ilt* are all possible words of English, it tells us nothing about actual words nor about the status of those actual words as meaning-bearing elements in sentences. It might be best to say that the two studies are simply parallel and that they occasionally intersect.

The basic unit of morphology is the **morpheme**, which is thought of as a mental representation of a unit of meaning in a language. These mental representations are constructed by language learners through the language heard around them and are realized in such pronounced forms as *girl*, *tall*, *and*, *fast*, *below*, and *them*. Each counts as an analytically basic structural unit of meaning; in other words, each points to a single real-world 'picture' or visualization. Since each would also be labeled in everyday language as a **word**, it is worth asking why we need to apply the specialized term 'morpheme' to them.

DOI: 10.4018/978-1-5225-8467-4.ch003

The answer is that not every morpheme counts as a word, and not every word consists of a single morpheme. Let us take an example. In a word such as *played*, we are capable of distinguishing two parts to the meaning. The first part is 'play', which denotes a certain activity, and the second part (most often, at least) denotes 'past time'. We process the two parts of the word together to indicate a certain event or activity in the past. The suffix, which is pronounced as a *-d*, has a meaning but unlike 'play', it could not be called a word. We would thus say that the word *played* consists of two morphemes, only one of which could stand on its own as a word. The other morpheme must be attached to a verb like *play* in order to be interpreted at all. The same observation could be made about the word *books*. If one were to enter a room and shout "*Book!*", hearers would be able to associate the utterance with a certain kind of object and, perhaps, respond with "What book?" If, on the other hand, a person were to enter a room and shout "*S!*", hearers would not associate the sound with plurality and respond with, "How many?" Rather, they would have no idea what the speaker was indicating.

The relevant distinction here, then, is between **free** and **bound** morphemes. While all morphemes carry basic elements of meaning, a free morpheme can normally stand on its own as a word while a bound morpheme normally cannot; a test like that above can serve to distinguish them.[1] In English and many other languages, bound morphemes may occur either after a free, root morpheme (in which case it counts as a **suffix**), or before it (in which case it is called a **prefix**).

Consider the following words. How many morphemes make up each word? Which morphemes are bound, and which free?

(a) *button*	(d) *bitterness*	(g) *rabbit*
(b) *lucky*	(e) *later*	(h) *pretest*
(c) *luckily*	(f) *underhanded*	(i) *readability*

If you followed the discussion above, your answers should be as follows: (a) one; (b) two; (c) three (the 'i' in *luck+i+ly* is simply a spelling convention); (d) two; (e) two; (f) three; (g) one; (h) two; (i) three (*read+abil+ity*, again with a spelling variation *abil* rather than *able* that is related to sound rules and not of direct relevance to morphological analysis). In general, the buildup of larger words from individual morphemes operates according to the **principle of compositionality**. This principle states simply that 'larger' parts are built up as a function of the accretion of 'smaller' parts. Consider the word *voters*, in which the meaning 'officially select' (*vote*) combines with the meaning 'person who performs an act' (*-er*) plus 'plural' (*-s*) to build up to the meaning "persons who officially select". The meaning is fully compositional. Likewise, the meaning of the word *readable* may be decomposed to the meanings of *read* and *able* and yield the meaning "able to be read". In the case of the word *button*, we cannot say that it is composed of the two free morphemes *but* and *ton*, since their individual meanings do not build up to the meaning of the small flat disks attached to shirts. Rather, these syllables are only accidental 'sound-alikes' whose similarities are of interest only to the study of phonetics and phonology.

In general, morphemes remain within their separate 'free' versus 'bound' categories in the **lexicon**, i.e., the mental inventory of basic meaning-related forms that resembles a physical dictionary. However, there is occasional category overlap where forms appear to be listed once in each category. The most systematic cases in English involve prepositions versus prefixes. The prepositions *over*, *under*, *in*, *out*, *up*, and *down* clearly stand alone as free morphemes in phrases such as *over the hill*, *up the chimney* and *under the table*. They just as clearly act as bound prefixes in *overpower*, *underrate*, *invasion*, *outstand-*

ing, *upgrade*, and *downcast*. There are less systematic cases of overlap as well. One is the use of *ism* to refer, in general, to a doctrine of beliefs, as in a sentence like "Capitalism, socialism, libertarianism – these are three of the many *isms* in our modern world". Another much more recent case is the free use of the suffix *–ish* (the subject of a recent *Slate* article by McCulloch (2014)), as used in the exchange,

A: Are you hungry?
B: *Ish…*

where the reply is taken to mean "Yes, somewhat". Such examples call attention to themselves as odd departures from the norm.

The distinction between free and bound morphemes seems simple enough, but the issues discussed in the following sections will illustrate how segmenting words into morphemes is not always as straightforward as it first appears.

ETYMOLOGICAL VERSUS PSYCHOLOGICAL REALITY

Linguistic analysis may be motivated by different interests. People interested in **etymology**, or the historical development of word meanings, may look at words in a way different from people addressing the **psychological** question that has dominated linguistics since the Chomskyan revolution – specifically, what does it mean for a native speaker to 'know' his or her native language? Part of the knowledge that enables speakers of English to produce, comprehend, and judge the acceptability of sentences is morphological knowledge. For example, they will clearly enough associate the prefix *de-* with the meaning 'negative, reversive' that when they learn the meaning of a new verb such as *clone*, they will automatically be able to comprehend and produce another new verb *declone* (or the hyphenated *de-clone*) without having to consult a dictionary. For these speakers, the two-part meaning of this new word ('to reverse the act of cloning') has **psychological reality**.

Now compare *declone* with the word *deny*. Historically, this verb consists of the same Latin prefix *de-* combined with a stem that was originally *negy*. A speaker of English normally has no mental access to the history of this word nor even to the identity or existence of its parts; as a result, the word is learned and known as a single unit. One would have to point out to the speaker that a prefix is present and, since the *–ny* part of the word cannot be associated with a meaning, we would say the word has effectively been **lexicalized** as a single morpheme in the mental dictionaries of its users. Though the historical source *de+negy* has **etymological reality**, it has no psychological reality, and a linguist who is not concerned with history will say the word is stored mentally as a single morpheme. While it is sometimes possible to argue about particular cases, in general the distinction is clear enough. Often these two types of 'reality' converge, in which case the word's meaning structure has been well preserved in its morphemic structure over the years (for example, the word *eyebrow* is historically ancient, and it still means the brow above the eye). In general, while linguists have a high regard for the study of word origins and meaning change, this textbook gives special privilege to the psychological point of view on the ground that languages are most commonly studied **synchronically** – that is, as the languages exist at one point in time, such as the current moment – rather than **diachronically**, or as they change over generations or centuries. An infant learning a first language is engaged in synchronic learning.

The issue of etymology versus psychology overlaps heavily with a slightly different issue, that of whether someone is able to identify and assign a clear meaning to a morpheme or not. Consider again the word *voters*. A proficient speaker naturally segments this word into three parts: *vote+er+s*. As evidence that this segmenting takes place, consider that these speakers are freely able to use the verb *vote* ("I voted last week", "Who did you vote for?") as well as the suffix *–er* ("a winner", "a cloner", etc.), and the plural morpheme *–s* ("books", "rates", etc.). Psychologically speaking, then, this word has three morphemes, each with an identifiable or **transparent** meaning. However, what can be said about a word like *shutters*, the decorative wooden boards placed on either side of a window? The plural nature of the word seems clear enough since the utterance "One shutter has fallen off my house" seems comprehensible and normal. However, does a speaker recognize the *-er* syllable as the same suffix found in *voter*? For many, the answer would be clearly 'no'. For them, the meaning of *–er* in *shutter* is not transparent but **opaque**. While a voter is recognized as someone who 'votes', a shutter is not necessarily recognized as something that 'shuts'. That is, the connection between shutters and the act of shutting may not be made. For that person, the word *shutters* consists of two (and only two) morphemes – *shutter+s*.

The difference between opacity versus transparency of meaning plays a role in the pronunciation of a bound morpheme. Consider the sound of the English prefix *re-* in the word *relive* (or *re-live*), as in, 'Would you like to relive your childhood?' Speakers will recognize the meaning 'again' in the prefix, which is pronounced with a stressed high front vowel [i-] (as in *see*). Now compare the word *relax*. This verb contains the same historical prefix, but the word is not processed as 'to make lax again'. Rather, most speakers probably store this word mentally as a unitary form. A result of mono-morphemic storage is that the initial syllable tends to lose stress and be pronounced with a reduced vowel like the *a-* in *allow*, though stress is certainly *possible* (see Chapter 12 for details on stress and English vowels). Additional examples of the stressed vowel coupled with transparent meaning include *rerun*, *refinish*, and *redevelopment*; other examples of the optional unstressed vowel with opaque meaning are *repair*, *return*, and *reduce*.

When the psychological dimension is taken into account, then, it should be clear that the morphological analysis of a particular word will not always be identical from person to person. This does not mean that two people with different psychological analyses of *shutters* will experience misunderstanding in talking about these objects; it simply means that their conceptions of the word's morphemic structure are a bit different even though the end product corresponds semantically to the same object in the real world. For the most part, linguists assume that native speakers of a language do converge on a *more or less* identical morphology, aside from difficult cases like *shutters*.

PRODUCTIVITY VERSUS NON-PRODUCTIVITY

Sometimes the meaning of a bound morpheme may be transparent, but that morpheme cannot be used to form new words. The lexicon may contain many words that make use of that morpheme but in effect, the list is complete. A good example is the negative prefix which is attached to adjectives and realized in multiple forms as *in-*, *il-*, *ir*, and *im-* (think of words such as *inedible, illegal, irrational*, and *immobile*). This prefix was inherited into English from a host of Latin-derived words that are commonly used in everyday English. However, English has not developed the ability to form new words with them. When we wish to negate a new adjective, we use the prefixes *un-* or *non-*. These are **productive** prefixes, while the Latin-derived prefixes are **non-productive**. If we take a relatively new adjective such as *laminated*, we say that an object is ***unlaminated*** or ***non-laminated***, not ****illaminated*** or ****inlaminated***. Likewise, a person who is not 'cool' is ***uncool***, not **incool*. It could be argued that there has been no historical motivation to make the Latin prefixes productive since the lexicon has always had alternative means available to negate adjectives – specifically, the forms ***un-*** and ***non-*** – and new words using the Latin forms have been **blocked**, or prevented from being created, as a result.

There are cases which seem to fall in between. English inherited from Latin another prefix which takes different forms depending on the nature of the initial segment of the root to which it attaches. Before sounds made with the lips (such as ***m*** or ***p***), it is written as ***com-*** (as in ***commit, compose***); before other consonants, it is ***con-*** (***connect, contact***); before vowels, it is ***co-*** (***coalesce, cooperate***). Latin sound rules determined the alternative pronunciations (as also happened with ***in-/il-/ir-/im-***), but English received these words from Latin in more or less their current form. Though many English speakers are at least vaguely aware that the prefixes convey a meaning like 'together' or 'with', for others the meanings of ***con-/com-*** are opaque; that is, we cannot assign a meaning to them. At any rate, we cannot form new words with them. However, the prefix ***co-*** survives as a prefix meaning 'simultaneous and interactive', so that when two people ***co-present*** a talk, they are standing and performing an act of presenting together; if two people were ***co-cloning*** in a laboratory, they would again be understood as engaged in an interactive activity. Thus, while the ***co-*** prefix is productive (and transparent in meaning), its alternative pronunciations ***con-/com-*** are non-productive (and, for many speakers, opaque). For words with the latter prefixes, the process of sound alternation that was familiar to Latin speakers is, for all intents and purposes, dead; learners simply memorize the words as they are learned.

FREE VERSUS BOUND ROOTS

Up to now, every example we have presented of a multi-morphemic word has consisted of one free morpheme plus at least one bound morpheme. We might conclude that words in English include at least one free morpheme. For the vast majority of words, this is the case. We cannot, for example, combine the noun suffix ***–nomy*** (meaning 'study of') with the adjective suffix ***–ical*** (meaning 'like') and expect to derive some word **nomical*. We need a suitable **root** such as ***eco-*** or ***astro-*** in order to create actual words such as ***economical*** and ***astronomical***. In doing this analysis, we identify three parts to the word – a root and two suffixes. However, we encounter a new problem in analyzing such words. While ***eco-*** and ***astro-*** are clearly root forms, they do not constitute words in their own right (one cannot say, "Look at the astros in the sky tonight!"). To the degree that we can assign clear-cut psychological meanings to ***eco-*** or ***astro-***, the assignments take place only in the context of the presence of one or more suffixes. Since we made reference to the required presence of a root in our definition of **bound morpheme**, it seems to follow that ***eco-*** and ***astro-*** are not only roots but also bound forms – in other words, **bound roots**. Another example case often cited is ***cran-*** in the word ***cranberry***. While we have no trouble disassembling ***blueberry*** or ***blackberry*** into clear-cut free morphemes, we have no mental reference for ***cran-*** and as a result, it appears to acquire meaning only once bound with ***berry***. It does not help to cite a frequently-mentioned etymology that connects these berries with ***cranes***, the birds that evidently enjoy them; after all, speakers ordinarily have no access to the history of words and will not compute the meaning of ***cranberry*** in this way.

ROOTS, STEMS, AFFIXES, AND THE HIERARCHICAL ORGANIZATION OF WORDS

Before delving into an examination of affix types, let us point out an obvious fact from examples (a-i) in the first section above. A bound morpheme is not always added to a **root**, strictly speaking. In the case of *lucky*, we can certainly say that the adjective suffix *–y* (meaning 'having the quality of') has been added to a root *luck* meaning 'chance' or 'fortune'. *Luck* is, in an intuitive sense, the 'heart' of the word *lucky*. However, what shall we say about the *-ly* in *luckily*? Linguists distinguish a **root** from a **stem** in the following way:

(a)   A *root* is the structurally indivisible 'meaning center' of a word.

(b)   A *stem* is that portion of a word to which an affix is added.

Following these criteria, we can say that in the case of *lucky*, the free morpheme *luck* counts **both** as a root and a stem when the addition of *–y* is considered. It is a root because of its unitary structure and centrality of meaning; it is also a stem because it is the 'chunk' to which a suffix is added. In the case of *luckily*, we say that *–ly* is added to a stem, but not to a root, since *lucky* is made up of two morphemes and is therefore not a structurally indivisible form. In the words below, which parts count as roots, and which parts count as stems?

(a)   *biological*   (b) *improper*   (c) *unbreakable*

In (a), we identify the root morpheme as *bio-*, a bound root originally meaning 'life'. To that root (which is also a stem) we add the suffix *–logy*, meaning 'the study of'. To the stem *biology-* we add another suffix, *-ical*. For *improper*, we begin with the root *proper*, to which we add the prefix *im-*; the root is again also a stem. In (c), we add the verbal suffix *–able* to the root *break-*; then, to that stem, we add the prefix *un-*. In other words, *breakable* is a stem but not a root.

Examples (a) and (c) are particularly good examples of an additional point – namely, that word morphology is not merely compositional but also **hierarchical**. That is, longer words are built up from roots in a stepwise fashion rather than as simple, linear, necklace-like **concatenations** of *A+B+C* (in the chapter on phrase and sentence structure, we will see that sentences are built up in a similar way). In the case of *biological*, this should be obvious: we add *–ical* to *biolog-*, not to *bio-* (i.e., there is no word **bioical* into the middle of which we insert *-logy-*). We add the suffixes from the root outward. In the case of *unbreakable*, hierarchy is less obvious, but it can be easily shown. We must first add the suffix *–able* to derive *breakable* before we can add the negative prefix *un-*. The reason is that there is no word **unbreak*. If we put brackets around the constituent parts of the word, the result will look like the following:

[un+[break+able]]

Morphology follows a pattern of building larger structures out of smaller ones, and the manner of building will reflect the interpretation of the word. The principle is similar to that involved in mathematical operations. That is, the value (i.e., the meaning or interpretation) of the sequence 7-(4+1) is not the same as the value of the sequence (7-4)+1. In the first case the value is 2, and in the second case it is 4. Likewise, while we can derive an interpretation from the expression [un+[break+able]], we cannot (unfortunately) derive one from the expression [un+break]+able]. How can a person "unbreak" something?

TYPES OF AFFIXATION

Having covered some of the basic vocabulary and some of the tricky issues in morphology, let us zero in on the set of bound morphemes which are not bound roots – specifically, the **affixes**. An affix is the generic term for a bound non-root morpheme. For speakers of the majority of languages, it amounts to the generic term covering **prefixes** and **suffixes**. It may seem to make sense that an affix would attach either to the left or to the right of a root. However, there are languages that split roots in the middle and insert **infixes**, i.e., bound morphemes that are surrounded by root material. An example is the Philippine language Tagalog, where a root such as *kuha* (meaning 'take') is infixed with *mu* to yield *kumuha* to derive the infinitive form (meaning 'to take').[2] There are also argued to be **circumfixes**, which insert two affixes simultaneously, one as a prefix and one as a suffix, where the two affixes are said to specify meaning in a joint fashion. The most well-known example is German, whose verbs have a third principle part – i.e., a past participle – that adds *ge-* before the root and *–t* (or another ending) after the root:

spiel+en 'play'   *spiel+te* 'played'   *ge+spiel+t* '(have) played'

Most often, languages manage as English does with prefixes and suffixes.

Inflection vs. Derivation

Affixes are typically classified according to whether they count as **inflectional** or **derivational**. Since English is likely to be the best-known language for readers of this chapter, our examples will concentrate on English; however, the distinction is well-attested in many other languages.

Linguists have characterized the differences between inflectional and derivational affixes according to the following criteria:

1. A derivational morpheme creates a new word, while an inflectional morpheme does not.
2. A derivational morpheme often changes the part of speech represented by a stem, while an inflectional morpheme always retains the same part of speech.
3. Inflection is a grammatical process, while derivation is a lexical process.

In general, a word created through derivational morphology is the sort of word that is likely to appear in a dictionary with its own definition, or at least with an official 'listing', while a word containing only a root plus an inflection is not. Let us take two examples: the English verbal suffix *–ing* as in *My friend is sleeping*, and the suffix *–ship* as in *membership*.

The root *sleep* is a verb; when the progressive suffix *–ing* is added as above, the result is also a verb. From the point of view of semantics, we can say that the suffix has left the essential meaning alone but added (partial) information about the manner in which the action occurs or is viewed. The inflection is added by a simple rule which applies to virtually every verb – *race*, *eat*, *flow*, and so on – when one wishes to signal the same refinement of meaning. One does not need a dictionary to determine that the progressive form of *sleep* is *sleeping* or to specify the way its meaning differs from *sleep*. In other words, the addition is a fully **grammatical** process.

To create the word *membership*, one adds the suffix *–ship* to the noun *member*. The result is also a noun. However, we can say that the meaning has changed considerably here, because the root typically names a person (e.g., *a member of the wedding party*), while *membership* can never name a person (**My friend is a membership*). Rather, the *-ship* suffix turns a concrete noun into something abstract, something like 'the condition of being an X'. Moreover, the form of this word cannot be determined automatically in the same way that adding *–ing* can do with *sleep*. It is not impossible that English could derive the same meaning through the use of a different noun suffix such as *–ity* or *-hood*. In fact, there are no words **memberity* or **memberhood*, but this knowledge cannot come from the application of a rule. Rather, it is information to be memorized on a case-by-case basis – and it is typical of **lexically**-derived forms that they are simply memorized, while grammatical forms may be automatically generated by grammatical rules. For a learner of English who wants to derive an abstract noun from the root word *member*, it is necessary to check a dictionary -- just as it is necessary to consult a French dictionary to determine that the French word for 'horse' is *cheval*. The information is not predictable by rule.

Inflectional Morphemes

It remains to ask which bound morphemes count as inflectional, and which as derivational. The task is not difficult, since English has a relatively small set of inflections that attach to stems as follows:

noun inflections:	*verb inflections:*	*adjective inflections*:
-(e)s	**-s, -ing, -ed, -en**	**-er, -est**

In the case of nouns, the regular plural *-s* ending is an inflection; in the case of verbs, the third person singular present *–s* ending, the progressive *–ing* suffix, the past tense and past participle *–ed* form, and the past participle *–en* form found on some verbs (*eaten, taken,* etc.) count as inflections. The *–en* suffix is also a fully predictable grammatical inflection in a passive voice sentence such as *The food was eaten quickly.* Finally, for adjectives, the comparative and superlative forms are also inflections.

We have said that none of the inflections above require special mention as part of the lexical entries of words in which they occur, and in that sense they are grammatically-specified endings. However, English does have a number of unpredictable, irregular forms that signal plurality, time, and comparison that would clearly require men tion in the lexicon. For example, the plural form of *criterion* is *criteria*, the plural of *ox* is *oxen*, and we must say *better* rather than **gooder* and *more interesting* rather than **interestinger*. So too, when we specify the four **principal parts** of verbs in Indo-European languages – that is, the simple present, simple past, past participle, and *–ing* participle – we do not always get uniform results:

Part #1	Part #2	Part #3	Part #4
play	*played*	*(have) played*	*playing*
notice	*noticed*	*(have) noticed*	*noticing*
hide	*hid*	*(have) hidden*	*hiding*
shake	*shook*	*(have) shaken*	*shaking*
break	*broke*	*(have) broken*	*breaking*
seek	*sought*	*(have) sought*	*seeking*

We regard verbs like **play** and **notice** as regular verbs with predictable forms. In the case of **hide**, **shake**, **break** and **seek**, there is no added past suffix **-ed**; rather, the present and past are distinguishable by the alternation in their root vowels alone. Nor do we get even this much uniformity with the verb **be**, where there are a multiplicity of forms – **is, am, are, was, were, be, being,** and **been**. We nevertheless traditionally regard all of these as inflected forms, on the model of regular cases such as **book/books** and **play-played**, since the alternations among regular and irregular forms indicate precisely the same predictable changes of meaning in each case. (There remains the problem of specifying precisely what the alternation consists of – should we treat the vowels as affixes in **shake/shook** in a way parallel to our claim that the **–ed** ending is an affix, or should we simply say that the individual forms are lexicalized as given? The topic has been much discussed over the years.)

In many other languages, inflections obligatorily specify grammatical relations (a topic covered in detail in the chapter on phrase and sentence structure). In Indo-European languages such as Russian, Greek, or Latin the suffix that a speaker places on a noun indicates whether that noun functions in the sentence as a subject, direct object, indirect object, or possessive form. Consider the sentence *The boy gives the rose to the girl* in Latin:

puer+$\varnothing$	*puell+ae*	*ros+am*	*dat.*
boy (subject)	girl (indirect object)	rose (direct object)	give (3rd-sing.)

The ending *–ae* on **puell-** tells us that the girl is the beneficiary of the action; the ending *–am* on **ros-** tells us that the rose is the object that is given; the lack of an ending on **puer** tells us that this is the subject of the sentence, i.e., the agent performing the action. The benefit of these inflections is that the speaker may re-order the elements of the sentence and still be understood. Speakers of English, which mostly lacks such inflections, are required to produce the same words in a fairly invariant 'subject-first' order because such inflections are lacking.

The sort of **case marking** illustrated above for Latin is by no means limited to Indo-European languages. Japanese, too, inflects for case. For example, the sentence **Sushi-ga oishi desu**, 'The sushi is delicious', places the suffix *–ga* on the subject. However, the sentence **Yuko-ga sushi-o tabemashita**, 'Yuko ate the sushi', places the *–o* inflection on **sushi** to indicate the direct object. The only remnant of case marking on English nouns is the possessive *–s* marker, as in **the cat's tail**.

Derivational Morphemes

Inflection is a grammatically determined process involving a small set of suffixes. Derivation, which is lexically determined, shows a far different picture. English has a wealth of derivational affixes that include both prefixes and suffixes. A sampling of derivational suffixes, and the nature of the stems to which they attach, is given below:

Stem type+suffix type	Suffix	examples
noun + noun suffix	*-ship, -hood*	*fellowship, neighborhood*
adjective + noun suffix	*-ness, -ity,*	*happiness, sanity*
noun + adjective suffix	*-ous, -ful, -like, -y*	*venomous, helpful, childlike, lucky*
verb + noun suffix	*-er, -ion*	*reader, relation*
verb + adjective suffix	*-ive*	*sedative*
adjective + adverb suffix	*-ly*	*quickly*
noun + verb suffix	*-ify*	*solidify*

Certain suffixes, rather than simply changing one part of speech into another, add highly specialized meanings:

Stem type+suffix type	Suffix	Meaning	examples
noun + noun suffix	*-ette*	'small N'	*cigarette*
noun + adjective suffix	*-ese, -ian*	'from N country'	*Chinese, Canadian*
adjective + verb suffix	*-en*	'to make like Adj'	*whiten, loosen*

In all cases, one generalization should be clear: the character of the suffix will determine the character of the entire word when the suffix is added. That is, the suffix will determine whether the entire word is a noun, verb, adjective, or adverb, regardless of the lexical category of the stem. The last suffix 'rules' the lexical category.

Typically, prefixes (in English and other Indo-European languages, at least) do not change the lexical category[3] but do change the meanings of words significantly, which is typical of derivational morphemes. The prefixes **un-** and **anti-**, in fact, denote the opposite of the stem: a person who is **unable** is not able, and a decision which is **anti-democratic** is not democratic. A **pre-dinner drink** is not drunk at dinner, a **misunderstood order** is not properly understood, and an **undercooked steak** is viewed as not quite 'cooked'. A derivational morpheme thus makes more radical changes than an inflectional one.

One of the features of derivational morphemes is that they differ greatly in their **productivity**, i.e., their ability to create new words that have not existed before. As an example of an almost fully productive suffix, consider *–ness*. A speaker who is used to using the slang term **grody**, if asked to describe the quality of being 'grody', will use **grodiness** rather than *grodity* even though both are noun suffixes that denote qualities. The suffix *–ness* is the productive suffix used to create such meanings; the suffix *–ity*, though it has a transparent meaning and is very common in such words as **vanity**, **insanity**, **humanity**, is not psychologically available as a means to derive new nouns from known adjectives.[4] This represents yet one more type of evidence for our characterization of inflection as a grammatical process, a process by which inflectional endings may be added automatically to any new word that requires them; in contrast, the far more constrained process of derivation takes place in the lexicon.

THE VARIED PROCESSES OF WORD FORMATION

We have already covered in some detail the two principal means by which longer words are formed from roots in everyday speech. We now mention other processes, some of which are quite common and productive while others are much less so. These processes account for most of the genuinely 'new vocabulary' that enters the English lexicon – though as we will see, much of it involves the creative reworking of elements which already exist there.

Compounding

Some writers refer to compounding as a type of derivation, while others place it in a separate category. However one wishes to classify it, the most noticeable feature of compounds is that they are composed of multiple **free morphemes**, as opposed to the combinations of [free+bound] or [bound+free] that characterize inflection and derivation. In English, it is common to contrast many true compounds with similar-looking cases in which an adjective simply modifies a noun:

Adjective+noun	True compound
green *house*	*greenhouse*
free *way*	*freeway*
hot *dog*	hot *dog* or *hotdog*
black *board*	*blackboard*
cold *cream*	*cold* cream

Note that the last expression in the first column refers to a chilled dairy product, while its counterpart in the second column refers to a cosmetic substance that is applied to the skin. Compounds may also be formed from [noun+noun] pairs, as in

Noun+noun	True compound
silver polish	*silver polish*
(i.e., a polish of silver color)	(i.e., a polish to make silver shine)
paper weight	*paperweight*
(i.e., a weight made of paper)	(i.e., a heavy object placed on paper)
toy factory	*toy factory*
(i.e., a child's play object)	(i.e., a factory that makes toys)

Compounds may also be formed from other pairings such as those below:

[noun+verb]: *skydive, color-code, headhunt, break-dance*
[preposition+noun]: *outhouse, undercarriage, overview, afterthought*
[noun+adjective]: *rain-soaked, rat-infested, heat-exposed, death-defying*

Several things may be observed about all such pairs.

(a) One is that the expressions in the left-hand column, where an adjective or noun modifies a noun, are written as two words, while those in the right column may or may not be written as two words. The fact that it is customary to write many compounds as single words with no space between morphemes is evidence that they are, in fact, single mental lexical entries. The fact that they are not *always* written as two words is often difficult to explain. Part of the answer has to do with the age of the expression. For example, in 1900, the name of a favorite summer sport was written as ***base ball***. By 1910, it was written with a hyphen as ***base-ball***, and by 1920 it was simply ***baseball***. The word ***airplane*** underwent exactly the same changes between 1910 and 1930.[5] Age plus frequency probably accounts for the non-hyphenated status of ***housewife*** in contrast to the hyphenated status of ***house-husband***. Once a compound has been truly 'welcomed' into the lexicon as a word, its parts are visually fused.

(b) The fact that many compounds are written as one word reflects a standard assumption about compounds, namely that they are **lexical** and are formed as a result of a lexical process. By contrast, the [adjective+noun] and [noun+noun] pairings in the columns on the left are phrases formed by a grammatical rule – i.e., the same rule that says adjectives modify nouns on their left, as in ***a happy child***. The fact that compounds are lexical does not mean they are all **lexicalized**, or stored as static vocabulary items in the mental lexicon of speakers. This would be too strong a statement, since the process of compound formation is **productive**; that is, we may freely invent new compounds (such as the recently coined term ***cup holder*** in a motor vehicle) that may be brand-new to both speaker and hearer yet are easily comprehended without required explanation.

(c) In a fairly traditional view of compounds, there is a characteristic pattern of **stress** assignment; this pattern can be taken as the most reliable test for the existence of a compound in case the compound is not written as a single word. A noun simply modified grammatically by an adjective takes major stress on the noun, which is the head of its phrase. So,

*On a sweltering summer day, [a hot **dog**] spends a lot of time sleeping.*

In a compound, the stresses are reversed, and their differences are more starkly evident:

*We ordered [**hot** dogs] from the cart in Central Park.*

In other words, the first morpheme in the compound supplies the main stress, and the second morpheme is assigned secondary stress.[6]

There is in principle no limit to the number of free morphemes that can enter into a single compound. When compounds consist of three or more morphemes, the creativity of the lexical compounding process becomes very evident. When English forms such compounds, all morphemes after the first two are written as separate words, with spaces:

*a **hot**dog bun*

However, the primary stress always remains on the first morpheme – in this case, ***hot*** – and ***bun*** receives exactly the same stress as ***dog***. If one wishes to continue lengthening the compound, one may do so by adding another noun and another identical stress, as in

*a **hotdog** bun company*

Such **complex compounds** may be extended indefinitely, with a new noun added in stepwise fashion, as in *a **hot** dog bun company union organizer meeting*, and so on. Each morpheme that is added receives a stress equal to the stresses following the first morpheme. Interestingly, while German has similar methods of compounding, it does not follow the convention of writing the parts of such compounds as separate words or using hyphens. Thus a forest ranger is called a ***Foerster***, the boss of a ***Foerster*** is a ***Foerstermeister***, and the boss of the boss is an ***Oberfoerstermeister***. This convention is responsible for the long words often seen in German written prose.

Zero-Derivation

Zero-derivation, also called **lexical conversion**, takes place when a morpheme of a given lexical category (noun, verb, adjective) is assigned to a different lexical category in its original form, with no affixation at all. The word ***water*** is a typical case. When presented with the word on paper, we normally assume that a noun is intended – i.e., a liquid substance. However, we also use the word as a verb: people ***water*** plants, and rain ***waters*** the landscape. 'To water' means 'to place or pour water on'. Those familiar with American restaurants are certainly aware of the custom of providing each guest with a glass of water at the beginning of a meal. They may not be aware that waiters in many restaurants have created a specialized verb ***water*** to say things such as "You need to ***water*** the table in the corner", meaning that the waiter needs to bring water to the customers at that table. In general, this variety of conversion is highly productive; we are able to take nearly any noun and turn it into a verb, as shown by examples like those below:

paper (n.) → (v.) 'to cover something with paper, such as a wall'
table (n.) → (v.) 'to place something figuratively on a table, such as a proposal'
screen (n.) → (v.) 'to show something on a television or movie screen'
card (n.) → (v.) 'to ask someone for an identification card, e.g., to check age'
glass (n.) → (v.) 'to cover with glass, as a wall'
score (n.) → (v.) 'to tally a score, as in a game'
anchor (n.) → (v.) 'to stabilize movement, as with a ship's anchor'

Many of these conversions may be considered **lexicalized**; that is, they may appear in a (mental or physical) dictionary as both nouns and verbs. Others may be created as needed, and though some may never enter the lexicons of most community speakers, they are at least comprehensible when encountered for the first time. For example, we say in the field of linguistics that the practice of placing a ***star*** (=noun) in front of an unacceptable form is to ***star*** (=verb) that form. If the ***pound*** sign (#) were used instead of a star, could we say that form is ***pounded***? No word currently exists with that meaning, but we could predict its eventual acceptability if it were put to use by a person or book of sufficient influence.

Though noun-to-verb conversions are the most productive, zero-derivation may take place from other forms:

Adj. to verb:	*right* (adj.) → *right* (v.), 'to make right' (e.g., *I righted what was wrong*)
	yellow (adj.) → *yellow* (verb) (e.g., *Age has yellowed the paper*)
Verb to noun:	*make up* (verb) → *makeup* (noun) (e.g., *The actor wore makeup*)
	reach (verb) → *reach* (noun) (e.g., *The company increased its reach.*)
Prep. to verb:	*up* (prep.) → *up* (verb) (e.g., *We upped the number of questions.*)
	down (prep.) → *down* (verb) (e.g., *We downed the whole meal*)

Most of the time it seems easy to determine which form is the 'more basic' or original one. Intuition tells us that *water* and *table*, because of their basic functions in human life, began as nouns and were pressed into service as verbs later. To the degree that these two forms are actually derived psychologically by speakers (rather than simply memorized or **lexicalized** as separate, unrelated forms), it makes sense to think that "noun → verb" is the direction of change. In some recent cases, we have good evidence of the direction of development. One is the computer-related terms ***download/upload***. Both entered public discourse in the 1980s as verbs, and both were quickly converted via zero-derivation into nouns: when a file is ***downloaded***, the result is called a ***download***. Occasionally it may be more difficult to tell what the direction of change has been, and there may be no clear-cut answer; speakers may disagree on which form is more 'basic'.

Beyond derivation, compounding, and zero-derivation, there are a number of lesser-used means by which new lexemes may be formed.

Blending and Clipping

Blends are similar to compounds in that two free morphemes are typically combined into a single word, but they are combined in such a way that one or both are reduced in syllables so that parts of original morphemes are lost. Classic examples are ***smog*** (derived from 'smoke'+'fog') and ***guesstimate*** ('guess'+'estimate').

A word is **clipped** when it loses one or more of its syllables, often as a result of frequent use. One well-documented recent example relates to the portable telephone. In the mid-1980s, these hand-held devices were regularly referred to as ***cellular telephones***. By the 1990s the name was simplified to ***cellular phones*** or ***cell phones***, and nowadays they are simply called ***cells***. Likewise, ***advertisement*** is clipped to ***ad*** in American English and ***advert*** in the U.K.

Evidence that frequency of use plays some role in the creation of clipped forms comes from communities in which certain words or expressions are used far more often than outside those communities. ***Perpetrator*** was clipped to ***perp*** among police detectives. There are many well-attested examples in the restaurant trade that are not always understood to outsiders. Mushrooms may simply be called ***shrooms***; a sandwich may be called a ***san***, and a side order becomes a ***side***. The ultimate 'clipped' form involves the complete deletion of a word, as when the expression ***two eggs over easy*** is rendered in the language produced between waiters and cooks as simply ***two ∅ over easy***.

Coinage

Coinage is the invention of a new word with no necessary cues supplied by the lexical or grammatical processes discussed up to now. A coined word may take almost any form provided it adheres to the sound and grammatical rules of the language in question. Often-cited examples include registered trade names that are invented for their perceived sales potential such as *Lysol*®, *Kleenex*®, and *Band-Aid*® and which later become common nouns written without capitalization. The names that the anatomists of several centuries ago gave to the elaborate range of bones in the human body – *femur*, *tibia*, *fibula*, and *phalanges* can be argued to be coinages even though the scientists who named them were drawing on the ancient Greek and Latin languages for inspiration and partial semantic help.

Coined words may be formed from the initial syllables or sounds of a series of words. It could be argued that the sequence *AMA* (from 'American Medical Association') counts as an **initialism** rather than a word since it is regularly pronounced with the initials themselves: "A-M-A". However, when the sequence of initials forms a unit that can be, and is, pronounced as a syllable, the resulting **acronym** can be regarded as a word in its own right. Thus *NATO*, *TESOL*, and *UNESCO* count as coined acronyms. In older days, it might have been a matter of chance whether such abbreviations supplied pronounceable words. More recently, the acronym may be strategically created first, and the words from which the initials derive are supplied afterward. This may be the origin of such organizations as *MADD* ('Mothers Against Drunk Drivers')[7]. Such coinages have one of the characteristics of **backformation**, which is the next topic to consider.

Back-Formation

A person who entered college in the 1960s was probably familiar with the verb *to orient (oneself)*, meaning 'to find one's way'. The same student also became familiar with the derivational noun *orientation*, which denotes the official introductory meetings held for new students. No doubt the new college student related the noun to the verb. However, as years passed, the verb was evidently not used nearly as commonly as the derived noun. Those perhaps less familiar with it created a new verb, *to orientate (oneself)*. This verb seems to follow a pattern of derivation that already exists (for example, the verb from which *meditation* comes is *meditate*). The term *orientate* is considered a **back-formation**, or a form that is derived 'backwards' from a longer form to a shorter one. It may compete with a word such as *orient* which is already in the lexicon, and older speakers may berate younger speakers for not using the original or 'real' form. Another well-known instance of back-formation is the verb *burgle*, which did not exist prior to the noun *burglar* but was back-formed from it on the mistaken assumption that the final syllable of the noun was an agentive suffix.

Borrowing

It hardly needs pointing out that sometimes words are borrowed directly from other languages and that the pronunciation of these words is often mutated to fit English sound system requirements while the meaning may remain essentially unchanged. Words such as *tsunami* (Japanese), *ketchup* (Malay), *uber* (German), *boutique* (French), *kowtow* (Chinese), *robot* (Czech), *coach* (Hungarian via French), *fiasco* (Italian), *bungalow* (Hindi), *macho* (Spanish), and *muskrat* (Native American) are a small sampling. The largest number of borrowings into English are from Latin through medieval French, a result of the Norman Conquest of 1066 A.D., an event that served to expand the vocabulary of English exponentially by creating a tier of highly literate words to sit atop an already large Old English spoken vocabulary. Some borrowed words are of transparently foreign origin; for example, most speakers are at least vaguely aware of the French source of fairly recent borrowings ending in the *–ique* or *–esque* suffixes. The borrowed status of other words such as *relate* or *condition*, which came into the language a thousand years ago, is not evident to the average speaker, who views them as '100 percent English' words and in general, these are regarded as 'native' words.

One of the hazards of borrowing words is that their original pronunciation may change to accord with the sounds and sound system of the borrowing language. This process of **nativization** of pronunciation may produce words that sound much different from the original. Japanese changed the borrowed English word *television* to *terebi*, since Japanese has no clear *l* or *v* sounds. English, in turn, dropped the *t* sound at the start of the Japanese *tsunami* since English does not permit the *ts* cluster of sounds to begin a word.

MORPHEMES VERSUS ALLOMORPHS

The study of morphology is above all about the relation of individual forms to each other and to real-world interpretations. When we see a minimal, structurally unanalyzable, meaning-transparent, and psychologically real linguistic form that corresponds to a real-world entity or quality, we see a morpheme. What happens, however, when there are multiple forms that denote the same meanings – especially when those forms look very similar?

Let us consider a set of English words that are derived from Latin. Each contains a bound prefix *ex-*. It is important to point out that this prefix has a dubious status in these words with regard to **transparency**. Modern English has retained the prefix to mean "former" (as an *ex-president* is a former president), and speakers may use it productively: one may be an *ex-teacher*, *an ex-sailor*, or an *ex-cloner*. In Latin, however, the prefix meant "out of" or "from", and it prefixed many roots whose meanings are unknown to modern speakers of English.

Latin had a rule about the pronunciation of this prefix, and the rule has carried over to the pronunciation of English words borrowed from Latin that used the prefix. Say each word aloud. Can you identify the pattern that determines the pronunciation? (Hint: It has nothing to do with the meanings of the words.)

ex- pronounced as in "ecks"	*ex-* pronounced as in "eggs"
excite	*example*
extra	*exaggerate*
excellent	*exist*
extinguish	*exact*
expose	*executive*
excursion	*exonerate*

If you look carefully, you will notice that all the instances of *ex-* in the first column are followed by stems beginning with a consonant, while all the stems in the second column begin with vowels. The exact nature of this **phonological** generalization will become clearer in the chapters on sounds and sound patterns. However, the generalization also has something directly to do with **morphemes** – in particular, the fact that the Latin meaning "out of" is being expressed in two ways, depending on the particular sound that follows the prefix. We might propose to state the rule in flow-chart fashion as follows:

/prefix meaning 'out of'/ → "ecks" before a consonant
→ "eggs" before a vowel

This sound alternation can be stated in a more precise way using sound and feature notation that will be introduced in the chapters on phonetics and phonology. For now, however, the important point is that we have identified two versions of the Latin morpheme. These versions are called **allomorphs**, or alternative pronunciations, of the basic morpheme meaning "out of". The rule itself is called a **morphophonemic rule** – that is, a rule which needs to specify information about both meaning and sound.

An example of a morphological rule that is not based on sound alternation is the rule for pluralizing German words. German words may be pluralized in a number of ways. Here, we will focus on the four most common ways – the addition of suffixes *–en*, *-er*, *-e*, or the addition of no suffix. Here are four example words meaning 'cup', 'lamb', 'table', and 'finger', respectively:

Tasse – Tassen lamm – laemmer Tisch - Tische Finger – Finger∅

If we are learning German, is there a way for us to predict which plural suffix to add to a singular noun? Unfortunately, although there are some fairly reliable rules of thumb to follow, they are not foolproof. There are many exceptions. For the most part, German plurals are lexicalized and must simply be memorized, item by item. We might then say that the German plural rule operates as follows:

/plural/ → *-en* in the words *Tasse, ...*
→ *-er* in the words *Lamm, ...*
→ *-e* in the words *Tisch, ...*
→ ∅ in the words *Finger, ...*

In other words, the plural meaning is expressed somewhat idiosyncratically in German, requiring the memorization of lists. Note that the last pluralization marker is denoted as ∅, or zero. For words like **Finger**, we would say that there is a **zero-allomorph** denoting the plural. That is, though the noun is said to be plural, we cannot hear an overt sound corresponding to this zero-allomorph. However, we do make the claim that at the mental level, a German speaker encodes, or registers, the form as plural. Evidence to support this claim is that both singular and plural forms of verbs may be used with **Finger**; moreover, the definite article (the German form of English *the*) that modifies the noun must agree in number with it: **der** (sing.) or **die** (pl.) **Finger**.

The twin concepts of 'morpheme' versus 'allomorph' should be understood as the difference between the mental representation of a meaning – for the Latin and German data here, the ideas "out of" and "plurality" – and the physical realization, or 'heard' versions, of those meanings. The distinction between an underlying, 'mentally real' form and a 'physically real' form underlies much work in modern linguistics. It will be revisited in much greater detail in the concepts 'phoneme' versus 'allophone' in the chapters on sound and sound systems, where morphophonemic rules will make their reappearance.

IMPLICATIONS FOR TEACHING ENGLISH LANGUAGE LEARNERS

From the point of view of **language transfer** – the influence of native languages on learner comprehension and production in the second language – the morphology of English is not especially troublesome for the learners of many languages. On the one hand, speakers of Indo-European languages will find much in English that corresponds closely to the morphology of their own languages. Among these features are noun plurals, possessive suffixes, comparative and superlative suffixes, and tense and aspect marking that uses a combination of free functional morphemes (chiefly, auxiliary verbs) and inflectional suffixes (as in the sentence *She is helping us right now*). Such learners are also likely to speak native languages with a rich variety of derivational suffixes that mark, among other things, the part of speech of the derivation (e.g., *-ness* and *–ity* for nouns, *-ish* and *–y* for adjectives, and so on). If learners of English speak a highly inflected Indo-European language such as Polish, Russian, or German, they will be freed from the task of learning complex paradigms of suffixes that are the bane of any student of Latin or ancient Greek, since English largely eliminated such inflections a millennium ago. However, the historical tradeoff has been that word order is quite strict in English; the endings on words that mark nouns as subjects, direct objects, indirect objects, etc. in languages like Polish permit words to be arranged in a wide variety of orderings that are determined by discourse needs. While Latin permits a sequence like *Puer puellae rosam dat* 'The boy gives the rose to the girl' (see the section on inflectional morphemes above), Latin also permits *Puellae puer rosam dat* and *Rosam puer puellae dat*; all three sentences have the same basic meaning. In English, however, *The boy gives the girl the rose* has a meaning different from *The girl gives the boy the rose*. Word order is important in English in a way that it is not in Latin.

At the other end of the scale, certain language families are known for their lack of rich morphology, or for its complete absence. Many analysts argue, for example, that Mandarin Chinese has no bound morphology at all. The kinds of grammatical-relation meanings that are conveyed by inflections in most Indo-European languages are conveyed by strict word order (mainly subject-verb-object) in Chinese as in English. Other meanings, such as plurality, are not required to be conveyed at all unless there is a need to do so – in which case it is accomplished through number expressions that operate as free morphemes. Likewise, verbs carry no overt tense markings. An important implication for teaching beginner speakers of a language like Mandarin (or Cantonese, or Vietnamese) is that learners must become aware of the importance of inflectional morphology in English – that **two book* is an ungrammatical phrase even though it is 'complete' in the sense that the number *two* already indicates plurality. Bound morphology is not an option to use as one wishes; rather, it is a requirement dictated by the rules of the language itself.

Derivational suffixes are a mixed bag of forms that may signify meaning in a number of ways. Some forms, such as *–ness* and *-ity*, form nouns out of adjectives while *-ship*, *-hood* serve mainly to turn concrete nouns into abstract ones (as *friend-friendship*). Other suffixes convey specific meanings. The suffixes *–like* and *–ish* convey the notion of similarity (*childlike* = 'like a child'); the suffixes *–ful* and *–less* convey relative quantities; *-logy* and *–nomy* may be defined as 'study of'; *-ian* and *–ese* denote nationality or ethnicity (*Romanian*, *Vietnamese*); *-ette* conveys a diminutive meaning. Once learners have familiarity with the forms as they occur in basic vocabulary, they may benefit from form-focused instruction in the suffixes themselves.

Prefixes, as we have seen, do not tend to change the part of speech of the stem; in that respect, they are easier than suffixes. However, we have also noted that issues of **meaning transparency** arise with many prefixes, and an individual prefix may be meaning-transparent in one word but not in another. Books exist, and courses are taught at some universities, that enlighten both native and nonnative students by detailing the history of words, including the history of prefix meanings. However, it may be most worthwhile at the intermediate level to below simply to present the most productive and consistently transparent prefixes first – prefixes such as **un-**, **up-**, **down-**, **out-**, **over-**, **under-**, **re-**, **trans-** and **anti-**, and to teach other prefixed word (such as **con-/com-**, **ab-**, **se-**) as whole lexical items with the same stress patterns characteristic of prefixed words.

Compound words, since they are composed of free morphemes, pose fewer problems for meaning comprehension than do words with bound morphology. Once learners get the general sense of what compounds are, the key issue to address is their unique stress pattern, which may be practiced through the creative formation of complex compounds as detailed in the section on compounds.

Though the learning of inflectional morphology in general cannot be called *inherently* more difficult than other aspects of language learning – Turkish children are claimed to master a native morphology far more complex than that of English by the age of four (Slobin, 1985) – the challenge of English inflections for L2 speakers may come from many convergent facts. Two may be sound-related. Many English inflections end in obstruent consonants such as *–s*, *–t*, or *d* (see Chapter 13 for phonetic details) which may not be permissible ways to end words in the native language; thus, a speaker may tend to pronounce **played** simply as **play** because the native language ends most words in vowel or other non-obstruent sounds. Moreover, for those inflections that form syllables by themselves (such as the *–ed* syllable in *faded* or the *–es* syllable in *pages*) the syllable takes no phonological stress (compare the relative 'sound weights' in the pronunciation of the syllable *pag-* with that of *–es* when the whole word is pronounced). Another challenge exists for those learners whose native languages do not use inflections at all; attaching endings to a stem is simply not part of the L1 word-formation system and is difficult to master in a new language. Another source of difficulty is that unlike a language like Turkish, English has relatively few inflections, which may (perhaps ironically) make them easier to ignore, particularly when the inflectional system is not consistent. In the present tense, only the English third-person singular is marked overtly (**The girl plays tennis**, but **I/You/We/They play tennis**). This *–s* suffix may not be mastered by native children until they are five years old, while Turkish or Polish children, whose corresponding morphology is far more complex, master their inflections earlier (Slobin, 1985). Finally, the meanings carried by English inflections are often semantically redundant in context. For example, a learner may not see the value of the third person singular present *–s* ending in a sentence in which singularity is already expressed in the subject (**The girl plays tennis**) or the need for a plural *–s* when a number is already provided explicitly, as in **two books**, or conveyed implicitly, as in **I bought the beans** (cf. ?**the bean**) **at the market**.

Many factors, then, seem to conspire to make English inflectional morphology onerous for L2 learners. These challenges argue for the value of inducing learners to **notice** inflections through explicit and/or implicit L2 instruction -- that is, to induce a conscious and sustained focus on them as a means to their acquisition. Schmidt's (1990) **Noticing Hypothesis** argues that such a step is a prerequisite to mastery of linguistic form. One obvious way to induce noticing is to give explicit instruction in the need for those inflections. Another way is to provide learners with what is commonly called **enhanced input**. For example, teacher speech could highlight the plural *–s* ending by saying it louder and longer than is normal. A fair amount of research has been conducted on written **textual enhancements** such as boldfacing, italicizing, and font mixing, some of which reports significant long-term acquisition of various grammatical forms. For example, Lee (2007) reports on the effect of boldfacing and increased font size in the presentation of the English passive morphemes (e.g., *The window* **WAS** *brok**EN** on Sunday*). A group of 259 Korean high-school juniors was divided into two groups and instructed either with or without these textual alternations. The group with enhancements later performed significantly better on an error correction task involving passive morphology. Nahavandi & Mukundan (2013) studied three student groups totaling 93 learners who were given one of three treatments in their exposure to the English simple past tense -- either (a) no form-focused instruction at all, or (b) explicit form-focused instruction in that ending, or (c) explicit instruction plus textual enhancement. The authors report that enhancement plus explicit instruction outperforms strategies (a) and (b). Jourdenais, Ota, Stauffer, Boyson, and Doughty (1995) report similar effects on teaching Spanish verbal inflections to native speakers of English. Though findings in such studies are mixed, they do argue on balance for the value of applying noticing strategies in the teaching of morphology.

DISCUSSION QUESTIONS

1. **Prefix types.** All of the words below are prefixed. Classify them according to the presence of (a) *transparent* versus *opaque* prefixes; (b) *productive* versus *nonproductive* prefixes; (c) *free* versus *bound* roots. Do any problems arise in making your classifications?

represent	*absolve*	*protest*
sequester	*subterranean*	*obtain*
overlook	*antiwar*	*become*
misplace	*transportation*	*rework*

2. **The possessive –s in English.** Possessives may be formed in English with –s, as in ***Fred's friend*** or ***my parents' car***. Sometimes this possessive –s is described as derivational, and sometimes it is called inflectional. What arguments could be made for each side?

3. **Three uses of English –ing.** In the section on inflection vs. derivation we identified –ing as a verbal inflection denoting progressive meaning, as in *Jane is sleeping now*. What problems come up in this description when the following boldfaced words are considered?
*The **honking** of horns is disturbing my sleep.*
*The players were greeted by **cheering** crowds.*
Given our classification of affix types, what might be said about the uses of *–ing* above?

4. **Derivations, compounds, and lexical class.** We mentioned that where derivational suffixes attach to stems, the last suffix determines the word's lexical class. Is a similar predictive principle at work in compounds? Make a hypothesis, compile a list of 25 compounds, and test your hypothesis against your knowledge of the part of speech of each word.

5. **Complex Compounds.** Using as a basic compound the word *freeway*, construct a complex compound of any length desired and pronounce it. (Remember, as long as you maintain the compound stress pattern discussed above, your new word will be interpreted as a single unit.)

6. **The Phenomenon of Stress Shift.** A rather special case of zero-derivation is the phenomenon of **stress shift** in English words. When a prefixed English verb is turned into a noun, its stress pattern will change to that of a compound:
*I con**vert**ed my friend. My friend is now a **con**vert.*
*The gun mis**fired**. It was a **mis**fire.*
*I down**load**ed the file. I printed out the **down**load.*

Judging from the list of prefixed verbs below, how productive are such conversions?

produce	*overlook*	*mistake*	*import*	*discharge*
repeat	*override*	*mismatch*	*compress*	*abstract*
outrage	*underrate*	*invade*	*disturb*	*persuade*

EXERCISES

1. ***Over* and *under*.** The English words ***over/under*** have two faces. They may count as prefixes, or they may be free morphemes. When they combine as free morphemes, they have the capability of forming compound words. Which words in the list below are compounds, and which are prefixed words? How can you tell?

underwear	*underestimate*	*overcoat*
overpower	*overtake*	*undercut*
understand	*underbrush*	*underling*

2. **The morpheme *meter*.** From the pronunciation of the words below, it could be argued that the morpheme ***meter*** sometimes behaves as a suffix, and sometimes as a free morpheme. Which words would belong to which class, and what evidence can you cite to support this claim?

perimeter	*thermometer*
voltmeter	*millimeter*
speedometer	*centimeter*

3. **A word-formation puzzle.** When someone brings something to ruin, we say that the person has ***destroyed*** it. Yet when this action is reflexively performed, we say the person or entity has ***self-destructed***, not **self-destroyed*. Formulate an account of why there is a difference here. What is the likely process of development of ***self-destruct***?

4. ***E-lexemes*.** In the last 25 years, the term ***electronic*** has been abbreviated as ***e-****+[noun]. Today we speak of ***e-commerce***, ***e-stores***, and so on. After the ***e-*** has been affixed to a form to make a new word, how could we characterize the result in terms of the word formation processes discussed in this chapter? What process or processes are involved? Can the conventional written forms of any of these new words provide a clue as to the nature of these words?

5. **Word Formation Processes.** What word-formation processes are observable in the following words? Explain how you arrived at your choices, noting the parts of speech involved. Note that multiple processes may take place in a single word.
    *Let me **fax** the form to you.*
    *I'm taking a **makeup** exam*
    *I'll **notate** your request and give it to the loan officer. (heard in a bank)*
    *Your idea is absolutely **fantabulous**!*
    *The workers **plastered** the walls of the living room.*
    *The **cleanup** process will take some time.*

*We attended two **talks** at the public library.*
*There is a **freeway overpass** near my house.*
*This machine has **outlasted** its owner.*
*My **tech** friends were enjoying a **post-blogging** drink at the bar.*

REFERENCES

Jourdenais, R., Ota, M., Stauffer, S., Boyson, B., & Doughty, C. (1995). Does textual enhancement promote noticing? *Attention and Awareness in Foreign Language Learning,* 183-216.

Lee, S.-K. (2007). Effects of textual enhancement and topic familiarity on Korean EFL students' reading comprehension and learning of passive form. *Language Learning*, *57*(1), 87–118. doi:10.1111/j.1467-9922.2007.00400.x

McCulloch, G. (2014, June 9). *Ish: How a suffix became a word*. Retrieved from https://slate.com/human-interest/2014/06/ish-how-a-suffix-became-an-independent-word-even-though-it-s-not-in-all-the-dictionaries-yet.html

Nahavandi, N., & Mukundan, J. (2013). Impact of textual enhancement and explicit rule presentation on Iranian elementary EFL learners' intake of simple past tense. *English Language Teaching*, *6*, 1.

Schmidt, R. (1990). The role of consciousness is second language learning. *Applied Linguistics*, *11*(2), 129–158. doi:10.1093/applin/11.2.129

Slobin, D. I. (Ed.). (1985). *The crosslinguistic study of language acquisition*. Hillsdale, NJ: Lawrence Erlbaum Associates, Inc.

ADDITIONAL READING

Aronoff, M., & Fudeman, K. (2011). *What is morphology?* (2nd ed.). UK: Wiley-Blackwell.

Bauer, L. (1983). *English word formation*. Cambridge, UK: Cambridge University Press. doi:10.1017/CBO9781139165846

Campbell, G. L. (Ed.). (1995). *Concise compendium of the world's languages*. London: Routledge. doi:10.4324/9780203159064

Comrie, B. (Ed.). (1987). *The world's major languages*. New York: Oxford University Press.

Giegerich, H. J. (2004). Compound or phrase? English noun-plus-noun constructions and the stress criterion. *English Language and Linguistics*, *8*(1), 1–24. doi:10.1017/S1360674304001224

Jourdenais, R. (1998). *The effects of textual enhancement on the acquisition of the Spanish preterit and imperfect* (Unpublished doctoral dissertation). Georgetown University, Washington, DC.

Matthews, P. H. (1991). *Morphology* (2nd ed.). Cambridge, UK: Cambridge University Press. doi:10.1017/CBO9781139166485

ENDNOTES

[1] By saying "normally" here, we are hedging somewhat. Occasionally, one hears exchanges between people in which the meaning of a bound morpheme does manage to be conveyed without attachment. Imagine, for example, that someone has borrowed two books from you on Monday and promised to return them on Friday. If the person says to you on Wednesday, "On Friday, I'll give you back your book", you *might* be able to utter a very strident "S" with a wavy finger gesture and an impatient look on your face and get your message across – provided the "S" is uttered just adjacent to the uttering of ***book***. However, cases like these are the exceptions that prove the rule: bound morphemes do not exist in isolation.

[2] Thanks to *Language Files* (8th ed., Department of Linguistics, Ohio State University) for the example.

[3] An exception is ***en-*** used as a prefix, where a verb is created from a converted noun (***encage***) or adjective (***enrich***).

[4] It is always possible to create such a word with humorous intentions, and the result will probably be comprehended. However, the source of the humor lies in the fact that it is perceived to be breaking the rules.

[5] See occupation listings in the *U.S. Census Enumeration* for the years 1900-1930.

[6] Actually, this statement can be stated more precisely as, "The most-stressed syllable in the first free morpheme will be primary-stressed in the compound, while the most-stressed syllable in the second morpheme will receive secondary stress." Thus, in the compound ***yellow jacket*** (i.e., a kind of flying insect), the first syllable of each morpheme pronounced as a separate word would give the pronunciations ***YEL low*** and ***JACK et***. When the two words are combined to form a compound, ***JACK*** would be secondary-stressed within the compound, while ***YEL*** would take the primary stress. Within the word ***jacket***, the first syllable remains more heavily stressed than the second. In other words, we appear to require at least three levels of lexical stress with such examples.

[7] In January 2019, when the U.S. government underwent a partial shutdown, a proposal was made for a new group with the name *Stop Shutdowns Transferring Unnecessary Pain and Inflicting Damage in the Coming Years* – using the acronym STUPIDITY (*New York Times* 1/27/19, p. A16). The awkward phrase was crafted around the desired acronym.

Unit 3
Syntax

Chapter 4
Phrase and Sentence Structure

Howard A. Williams
Teachers College, Columbia University, USA

ABSTRACT

This chapter surveys the basics of the syntax of main clauses, with special attention to English. Readers are guided through the process of doing syntactic analysis with the aid of syntactic trees that model the properties of linearity, hierarchy, and recursion that characterize the syntax of human languages. The model used is a somewhat simplified version of X-bar syntax, which is currently the best-known and best-tested model of phrase structure within the subfield of syntax and which combines the virtues of simplicity, breadth, and predictive power. There is a section on the theory of grammatical relations and its relationship to phrase structure theory, as well as a section providing an overview of basic world constituent orders.

WHAT IS SYNTAX?

No matter how difficult it may be to define a term as basic as 'word' in a precise way, it is taken as assumed that a sentence in any language is a collection of units, most of which are words. Some of these units are verbs, some are nouns, some are adjectives and so on, and some represent larger entities. Languages also differ in certain respects. For example, some languages permit prepositions to stand as free words while others use bound affixes to represent English prepositional meanings; some languages make regular use of pronouns while others avoid them; some languages turn concepts into verbs that English would denote through the use of adjectives. However, no language creates sentences simply by stringing words together without some higher level of organization. This higher level of organization is called a **syntax**. While each language has a syntax that is unique to that language, there are common features that recur across languages, and the observation of these commonalities has led many linguists over the years to seek a 'skeleton key' that will reveal a universal structure common to natural (i.e., human) languages.

In the 1950s and 1960s, the linguist Joseph Greenberg surveyed large numbers of languages with the goal of finding what he called **language universals**, i.e., statistical generalizations that generate predictions about features of the next language we might study, once we learn a few facts about the language (Greenberg, 1966). From the 1960s onward, linguist Noam Chomsky took the idea of universality a step

DOI: 10.4018/978-1-5225-8467-4.ch004

further in attempting to ground human language in cognition with the goal of specifying basic features of syntactic structure that are part of our biological inheritance. The goal has been to characterize a **universal grammar** (UG) that transcends, but is reflected in, the surface-level differences among world languages (Chomsky, 1957, 1968, 1986). In general, the 'core' of UG represents the common platform or matrix of principles upon which language learning takes place; this platform includes language features which are unlikely to be taught explicitly as part of a second-language classroom syllabus because they are already shared by the first language. One key principle is that sentences have organizational **structures** of a type that will be sketched in this chapter, using English as the raw data for analysis; the basic framework is held to be biologically given. However, some structural facts are also highly idiosyncratic to individual languages. To take one example, there seems no reason why the fourth sentence below, which seems organized in a way parallel to the other three, should be unacceptable to those who learned English from an early age:

*I don't know **the place where** she went.*
*I don't know **the time when** she left.*
*I don't know **the reason why** she left.*
I don't know **the way how to find her.*

Yet speakers of most dialects of English do not produce ***the way how***; if they are presented with the last sentence above, they will judge it to be ungrammatical (or at least odd) in a way that the other three sentences are not. In the absence of a better explanation, this 'hole' in the system can only be described as a quasi-random **language-particular** fact that warrants special attention by teachers of English as a second language. It does not seem predictable by any general principles.

In between universal principles and language-specific facts lie what Chomsky (1981, 1986) has called **parameters**, or universal alternations between two basic structural options which tend to split world languages into large, fairly uniform groups. For example, languages tend to branch in two directions where the formation of informational questions is concerned – i.e., questions that use words like *who*, *when*, or *where*. Some languages (such as English, Spanish, and German) place these words at the beginning of questions, as in ***Where are you sitting?*** Other languages (such as Mandarin, Japanese, and Korean) leave these ***wh***-words in the same place in a sentence where the corresponding non-***wh*** nouns or adverbs would appear (as in *I'm sitting **here**. You're sitting **where?***). In general, a learner will not be challenged by universal **principles** in the process of learning a new language since they hold more or less constant across very different languages. However, the learner will be confronted with **parametric** differences from an early stage of learning and be forced to make major shifts in orientation toward such things as ***wh***-questions. As for **language-particular** facts, learners will find them challenging throughout the acquisition process.

THE NATURE OF PHRASES

To say that every language has a syntax is essentially to say that the sentences of each language have a structure. What does this structure look like? This chapter will look in detail at the basic architecture of English sentences on the assumption that readers of this book have sufficient knowledge of English to make judgments of their own about grammatical ("OK") sentences of English and ungrammatical ("not

OK") sentences. In the process we will sidestep the obvious fact that sentences can be unacceptable for reasons other than structural ones; that is, we will assume that the judgments given here are structure-related, rather than meaning- or appropriateness-related. We will not attempt to explain why a hearer would find a senseless sentence like, *Please, my invisible airplane wrote the latitude!* or a rude one like *Hey, dummy!* unacceptable. The problems in such sentences belong more properly to the study of semantics and pragmatics, respectively – essentially, to problems of meaning and use.

First, consider the nouns *squirrel* and *Fred*, and sentences in which both occur:

(1) *Squirrels climb trees.*
(2) *Fred bought books.*

Each (grammatical) sentence consists of three words. We might ask questions about all or part of these sentences. For example, we might ask the questions, "What do squirrels do?" and "Tell me again – Fred did WHAT?" and receive as our answers,

(1a) *Climb trees.*
(2a) *Bought books.*

We might also ask questions like, "What can you tell me about squirrels?" or "What's true about books?" We would be unlikely to receive as responses,

(1b) ?*Squirrels trees.*
(2b) ?*Fred bought.*

There is something clearly unacceptable about both (1b) and (2b), and it is not that they are responses to odd questions. For example, we could respond, *Squirrels climb them* or *Fred bought some.* Both responses would be acceptable in a way that (1b-2b) would not. We could think up other similar examples, and we predict that the judgments of acceptability and unacceptability would parallel those above. The intuitive problem with (1b-2b) is that neither sequence seems to constitute a 'unified whole', while (1a-2a) do seem to constitute unified wholes. Using the relevant terminology from traditional grammar, we would say that sentences are divided into two basic parts – **subjects**, which tell us who or what the sentence is about, and **predicates**, which tell us something about those subjects. It is generally agreed that sentences have subjects and predicates. In the traditional formalization used for generations in middle schools throughout the English-speaking world, sentence (1) was diagrammed as

(3) ___squirrels_____|___climb___|___trees___

The words are written on a horizontal line. A bold vertical line divides subject from predicate. A smaller vertical line separates the predicate into two parts, the **verb** and its **direct object**. The essential idea is that the first division point is more basic or fundamental than the second, since the former splits the entire sentence into two large parts, while the latter division takes place over a smaller domain (i.e., the predicate) that is, in turn, contained within a larger domain – i.e., the sentence itself.

These so-called 'stick diagrams' worked well for the kinds of simple sentence analysis done in old-time grammar classes. Linguists have long since adopted a quasi-mathematical convention using 'trees' for making the same kind of diagram. A preliminary tree for sentence (1) might look like the following:

(4)

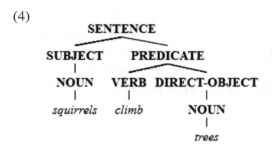

This tree tells us several things. First, the organization of the sentence is **linear** in that one word precedes another. Second, it is **hierarchical**, or tiered into levels. The subject *squirrels* sits on an equal plane with the combined words *climb+trees*, and the latter breaks down into two equal parts which form a second, lower plane. Two of the bedrock principles of syntax are that linguistic structure is both linear and hierarchical. Two elements which sit on the same plane and can be traced back to a common **mother node** in a single step are called **sister nodes**; thus SUBJECT is sister to PREDICATE, and VERB is sister to DIRECT OBJECT. Third, we see that each tree ultimately branches downward into **terminal nodes**, or words that are given category labels such as 'noun' or 'verb'. Fourth, the tree tells us that the 'parts' of this sentence include (a) the subject noun *squirrels*, (b) the verb *climb*, (c) the direct object noun *trees*, and (d) the predicate *climb+trees*. Each of these parts is called a **constituent** of the sentence. A constituent may be informally defined as the full set of nodes and branches that merge upward to a single mother node; that is, a constituent is the sum total of everything that branches under a mother node.

We would like to generalize our claims to sentences that are longer and more complex. Consider another simple sentence, and note that this sentence may be transformed from active voice to passive voice with no loss of meaning:

(5)   *[Squirrels] annoy the cat.* → *The cat is annoyed by [squirrels].*

To say that there is no loss of meaning is to say that if squirrels annoy the cat, then it follows that the cat is annoyed by squirrels, and vice versa. This kind of identity is called **truth-conditional equivalence**: If A entails B and B entails A, then A and B are equivalents.

We have called *squirrels* a noun. Now notice that the same transformation is possible with a longer sentence, and again we see truth-conditional equivalence:

(6)   *[The gray squirrels in the park] annoy the cat.* →
      The cat is annoyed by [the gray squirrels in the park].

Note too, that if we apply the same fragment test that we applied in (1a) and (2a), we get parallel acceptable results:

(7)   *What annoys the cat?* → (a) *Squirrels.*
       (b)   *The gray squirrels in the park.*

We would get no such acceptable results with (6) if we instead chose to reply with, **The gray squirrels in*. The claim is that the sequence *the gray squirrels in the park* behaves as a unit, just as the sequences ***Bought books*** and ***Climb trees*** behaved. We would like to say that ***the gray squirrels in the park*** behaves as a **constituent**, and this constituent is of the same type as the single word *squirrels* in sentence (5). The name given to this constituent type is **noun phrase**, or **NP**. We will further argue that the sequences ***climb trees***, ***bought books***, and ***annoy the cat*** constitute **verb phrases**, or VPs. We now redraw our original tree as follows, using "S" to indicate "sentence":

(8)

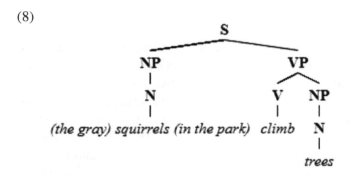

This tree makes the claim that a string of words is a sentence if a tree can be drawn such that S → NP VP, and if there are terminal elements of a type that crucially correspond to the phrasal category (i.e., N for "NP" and V for "VP"). This condition illustrates the key property of **endocentricity**, which simply says that every NP has a **head** that is an N, and every VP has a head that is a V; this property is held to be a universal property of phrases in natural languages.

It will be noticed that we have omitted the labels SUBJECT – PREDICATE in our new tree. We will address the reasoning for this omission in the section on grammatical relations. For now, let us further develop the conception of **phrases** that we have begun. We can apply the same kinds of tests to VPs that we have just applied to NPs, thereby establishing that a VP can consist of one or multiple words, provided only that it have a V as its head. Consider question (9) and its possible responses:

(9)   *What do squirrels do?*
       > *Climb.*
       > *Climb trees.*
       > *Climb trees in the park with great enthusiasm.*
       > *Climb trees energetically.*

Our claim is that each of the possible predicate responses represents a single constituent, as evidenced by the fact that the words 'hang together' as a single unit for processing. As additional evidence, we can note that each of the responses could be placed at the beginning of a sentence, or **fronted**, and serve equally well as a modifier of another sentence if the verb is given an *–ing* suffix:

(10) *Climbing, the squirrel finally reached the top.*
   Climbing trees, squirrels protect themselves from predators.
   Climbing trees in the park with great enthusiasm, squirrels are wonders of nature.
   Climbing trees energetically, squirrels escape cats.

We conclude that predicates, which we have called VPs, are constituents that may consist of one or many words, as long as each predicate contains a V as its **head**, or center.

We can argue the same for Adjective Phrases (**APs**) in (11), where we see fragmented responses:

(11) *How would you describe that tree?*
   > Tall. > Very tall. > Too tall to climb.

We can also use a test that fills a slot in an NP:

(12) *That _____ tree is on my property.*

We could fill the slot with ***tall***, ***very tall***, or even ***too-tall-to-climb*** (though such highly complex APs as the last one sound awkward as pre-noun modifiers and tend to be marked off with hyphens between their parts); our base requirement is that one adjective must serve as head of the AP.

It will be recalled from Chapter 2 that **determiners** include a wide range of function words that are often classified into groups according to the kinds of meaning that they encode – possessive determiners such as ***your/my/her/his/their***, demonstratives such as ***this/that***, and ordinary articles ***a/an/the***, among others. Like nouns, verbs, and adjective, determiners also seem to admit of modification options, given the right context.

(13) *He ate **almost <u>two</u>** pints of ice cream.*
(14) ***Only <u>your</u>** paper (not also my paper) was reviewed.*

A moment's reflection should reveal that the adverb ***almost*** in (13) is not modifying *two pints of ice cream*; it is modifying ***two*** (it is not [almost [two pints of ice cream]], but [[almost two] pints of ice cream]). Likewise, the adverb ***only*** in (14) is intended to modify ***your***, not ***your paper*** (unless the interpretation is 'only your paper, not also your book'). Examples like (13-14) suggest that we also need to speak of determiners as head elements of phrases, which we will refer to as DPs – phrases centered around a head D. Generalizing at this point, we may state a hypothesis widely agreed on in syntactic analysis:

(15) All heads project into endocentric phrasal expansions.

This claim, if true, will simplify our grammar tremendously by setting a basic requirement on heads of any type (including, so far, N, V, Adj, and D): all must originate higher in the tree as phrases of the same type as the head. In other words, if there is a head X, it must project upward into an XP. We will not find an NP, for example, whose head is a V.

We can construct similar arguments in favor of Adverb Phrases (**AdvPs**) (*quickly, very quickly, unbelievably quickly*, etc.) headed by adverbs. We will take a closer look at prepositional phrases (**PPs**) in the next section. Each of these phrasal types will form nodes and branches in trees according to a set of

phrase structure rules that will allow us to create, or **generate**, trees such as the tree in (8) above. A phrase structure rule takes the form X → Y Z and may be read as, "For any X, that X will be rewritten in every case as "Y Z". The X is called the **input**, and the "Y Z" the **output**. Traditional phrase structure rules are an elaborate input-output system. That may sound abstract, but it can be brought down to earth by the paraphrase, "Every X consists of a Y plus a Z". In the case of the English sentence, it may be paraphrased as "Every sentence is composed of an NP followed by a VP". This intuition is captured well in the traditional 'stick' diagram (3) above as well as in tree (8). It then remains to expand, or develop, the input notions 'NP/VP' to determine their own outputs.[1]

A system of phrase structure rules needs to be supplemented with a set of what are called **lexical rules** that specify what items can be placed in the terminal nodes. A lexical rule is simply a statement of what counts as an "N", a "V", an "adjective", and so on in the language that we are studying. For sentences (1) through (8) above, we need to rely on a set of rules that contains at least the following:

(16) N → *squirrel(s), park(s), tree(s), Fred, you, I, he, she*
       V → *climb(s), annoy(s), buy(s)/bought*
       Determiner → *the*
       Adjective → *gray*
       Preposition → *in, by*

Note that pronouns have been included as lexical equivalents to nouns. This set represents only a tiny fraction of the English lexicon and will have to be expanded to yield other sentences, but it is interesting that it is capable of generating quite a large number of sentences as it stands now. It will generate ***Fred climbs trees***, ***Fred bought squirrels***, and ***Squirrels climbed Fred***. It will also generate nonsensical strings like ***Trees bought squirrels*** and ***The park in the squirrel annoys Fred***. We will eventually require some means to exclude these sentences from acceptable English discourse, but we will also claim that the problems with these sentences are essentially **lexical** or **semantic** rather than syntactic; the problems concern our conception of the kinds of things that can or cannot be 'bought' or 'annoyed', for example. The sentence ***Trees bought squirrels*** will be regarded as grammatical, but semantically anomalous; that is, it represents a situation in the world that is in some way impossible or contradictory.

HEADS AND COMPLEMENTS

We will return to drawing trees for entire sentences below, in the section on the English predicate. For now, it is important to make note of a key feature of many **heads** such as N, V, P, and Adj. Heads have the ability to **select** sister constituents called **complements**.

The idea of complements is old, and it has been expressed in different ways by different schools of grammatical analysis. The central intuition is that when a certain head is chosen, it selects or 'goes with' some element that follows it. Importantly, that added element is so strongly associated with the head that the complement is **lexicalized** – i.e., is included as part of the lexical description of the head, even in those cases when the complement is not, strictly speaking, required for the use of the head. When we learn the dictionary meaning of the head, we also learn its (possible or obligatory) association with a complement. Sometimes the association is simply one where a certain **type of phrase**, such as an NP or

PP, must follow the complement; sometimes the association is even more specific in requiring that phrase type to include a certain **lexical item**, or word, in the complement such as the preposition *in* or *with*.

Exactly what does this mean? Let us take a few example types, some of which are likely to be familiar once more traditional terminology is used. We noted in the chapter on morphosyntax that some verbs are transitive, others are intransitive, and still others ditransitive. To use the relevant syntactic term, verbs are classified in terms of the number of **arguments**, or required syntactic positions, they are associated with in the lexicon. Some verbs take a single NP subject argument (e.g., *sleep*, *rain*), others take two NP arguments (e.g., *take*, *make*), while still others take three arguments (e.g., *put*, *give*), the third of which is typically housed in a PP (as in *I put the book on the table*); other three-argument verbs are associated with three NPs (as in *The grocer charged the customer ten dollars*). Sometimes these arguments are required for any use of the verb: we can *make something*, but we cannot simply **make*. In other cases a verb may specify alternative frames. For example, the verb *attach* would be listed as a three-argument verb in sentence (17), but listed as a two-argument verb in (18):

(17)   *Susan attached the poster to the wall.*
(18)   *Susan attached the file.*

Note that *file* in (18) would be interpreted to refer to a computer file. Not surprisingly, the two verbs *attach* have distinctly different but related meanings here (the second being rather metaphorical). In other cases, a verb such as *eat* with more or less stable meaning seems able to appear with either one or two arguments:

(19)   *They ate dinner.*
(20)   *They ate.*

We could claim that in such cases, the lexicon lists two discrete meanings (for *attach*) or a single meaning with two argument frame options (for *eat*).

When looking at examples (17-20), a reader might ask whether we are making anything beyond the generalization from traditional grammar that some verbs are **transitive**, others are **intransitive**, and others **ditransitive**. The answer is that we are indeed saying more, since similar phenomena occur with heads other than verbs where the terms 'transitive', 'intransitive', and 'ditransitive' do not traditionally apply. When these phenomena are considered together with verbs, we see a point of commonality that has larger significance.

Let us then look at adjectives. Certain adjectives such as *nice*, *green*, *hot* seem perfectly acceptable on their own with nothing to follow them:

(21)   (a)   *Our new house is **nice** (now that we've painted it).*
       (b)   *These flowers are **green** (in the spring).*
       (c)   *This curry is overly **hot** (in my opinion).*

While we certainly *could f*ollow the adjectives *nice*, *green*, *hot* with the material in parentheses, we *need n*ot add anything. More to the point, we would not consult our lexicon (whether our mental lexicon or a physical dictionary) and expect to find anything resembling the material in parentheses in the description of the proper use of the adjectives. After all, an almost infinite variety of material could be found after these adjectives, and no efficient storage system (again, whether mental or physical) would contain even a small sampling of them.

The situation is different, however, with certain other adjectives. Consider those in the next set of sentences:

(22) (a) *I am **amazed** at my progress in linguistics.*
  (b) *She is **fond** of white wine.*
  (c) *The umpire was **biased** against the player.*

While the meaning of the boldfaced adjectives may be specified lexically in isolation from the material that comes after them, we can say that each adjective has an organic 'connection' with the prepositional phrases that follow them in a way that the material following the adjectives in (21) does not have. That is, we associate **amazed** with the preposition **at** (as opposed to being **amazed around** or **amazed from** something). We associate *fond* with *of*. We associate **biased** with **against**. Each adjective is listed in the lexicon with a prepositional phrase headed by the respective preposition, together with information about whether this PP is genuinely obligatory or not. For most speakers, it is safe to say that *fond* cannot be used at all without a PP headed by the preposition *of* (e.g., ***Mary is very fond**). In the cases of **amazed** and **biased**, the PPs are optional but still lexicalized; a book can simply be 'biased', and a person can simply be 'amazed', but if a PP specifying the target of bias or amazement follows, it will be headed by a particular preposition. These lexicalized associations are **complements** to the adjectives.

It is important to note that in talking about the relationship between adjectives and prepositions here, we are speaking of something different from mere statistical frequency. There is, no doubt, a strong likelihood that where the word *fish* occurs, the word *water* will occur nearby – much higher than the likelihood of the co-occurrence of *fish* and *desert* – but this reflects only the fact that when we are talking about fish, we are also likely to be talking about water rather than deserts. In the case of the three adjectives in (22), we can go so far as to say that the prepositions that follow them are 'correct' while other prepositions would be 'incorrect' – in other words, that the linguistic relationships involved here go beyond issues of discourse frequency. Though some newly-discovered language very similar to English (call it 'Zinglish') might exist in which a person may be "aware *to* something", the lexical entry for that adjective in English is simply not set up as in the hypothetical Zinglish to include the preposition *to*. While Zinglish uses a PP complement with *to* after the adjective *aware*, English uses a PP with *of*.

Next, consider NPs. When phrasal material is placed before or after certain head nouns, there may be no particular reason to suppose that a lexical association exists between the noun and that material. For example,

(23) (a) *We bought a (new) **house** (in the suburbs).*
  (b) *Juliet made a **plea** (without saying a word).*
  (c) *The lawyer stated her **objections** (with great eloquence).*

No doubt there is a fairly strong statistical co-occurrence among *new*, *house*, *in*, and *suburbs* – suburbs are full of houses, and many are new – but that fact does not bear on the question of whether learning the proper use of the words *new*, *house*, *in*, and *suburbs* crucially involves learning a key **lexical** relationship among any of those four words. Such a connection seems dubious; a speaker may be perfectly 'fluent' in the use of some of the words without knowing a thing about the others. The same holds for the other phrases in parentheses in (23) with respect to their head nouns. The situation is different in the sentences in (24):

(24) (a) *The president made a **decision** (on the proposal).*
   (b) *John made a **plea** (for mercy).*
   (c) *The lawyer stated her **objections** (to the judgment).*

There seems an intuitive connection between the words **decision+on**, **plea+for**, and **objection+to** that does not exist in the corresponding parts of the (23) sentences. Evidence that this is so comes from the ability of speakers to **strand the prepositions** in (24) but not in (23). Stranding prepositions, though frowned on in prescriptive grammar, is done on a regular basis by nearly every native speaker of English:

(23') (a) **?What did you buy a new house in__?*
   (b) **?What did Juliet make a plea without__?*
   (c) **?What did the lawyer state her objections with__?*

Leaving aside the issue of whether the questions in (23') are grammatical, we must regard them as strange; if they are asked, it is unclear what sort of answers would be appropriate. The same is not true of the corresponding transformations of (24) shown in (24'):

(24') (a) *What did the president make a decision on__?*
   (b) *What did John make a plea for__?*
   (c) *Which allegation did the lawyer state her objections to__?*

The ease of comprehension of the (24') questions in comparison with the (23') questions argues for an existing **lexical** relationship between the relevant words in (24'). Part of what is learned in the proper use of the nouns **decision**, **plea**, and **objection** is that they are lexically associated with prepositional phrases headed by specific prepositions. In other words, each of these nouns is lexically listed with a **complement**, though it is in all three cases an **optional** complement.

Finally, let us look at prepositions. The traditional analysis of a prepositional phrase says that prepositions are always followed by NPs. In other words, each instance of use of a preposition requires the presence of a sister NP constituent. Since the head of a PP is a preposition, it follows that its NP sister is also a **complement** to that head, since heads determine the nature of their complements. In traditional grammar, these complements are called **objects of prepositions**, and that label is still appropriate. However, in calling them complements, we are tying together generalizations that we have also made for verbs and adjectives – something that traditional grammar has not done.

At this point we might raise the question, "If some verbs and adjectives take complements while others do not, and if some verbs and adjectives can take optional complements while others take obligatory ones, why would the same not be true for prepositions?" The question is good, and the answer seems to be affirmative – though there may be some resistance from traditionalists on this claim. Consider the points of overlap in the two columns below:

(25)   (a) *She walked **in(to)** the house.*   *She walked **in**.*
        (b) *He came **down** the stairs.*   *He came **down**.*
        (c) *The bird flew **off** the bridge.*   *The bird flew **off**.*
        (d) *We spread mayonnaise **on** it.*   *We put coffee **on (the stove)**.*
        (e) *We bought a box **of** cookies.*   ----
        (f) *I travel **with** my parrot.*   ----
        (g) ----   *The bird flew **away**.*
        (h) ----   *My toy fell **apart**.*

While the boldfaced words in the first column are indisputably traditional prepositions, grammarians have differed in their categorization of those in the second column. They have variously been called 'adverbs' and 'particles'. Often a distinction has been made between those words that are semantically transparent (such as ***walk in***, meaning 'move on foot to the interior of an enclosure') and those that are not (such as the very opaque sequence ***turn in***, meaning 'go to bed at the end of the day'). However, the sheer amount of overlap in the columns strongly suggests that these words are really prepositions and that their behavior is remarkably parallel to verbal and adjectival heads. In the (a-d) examples, we see that ***in***, ***down***, ***off***, and ***on*** are all capable of appearing with or without complements (similar to the behavior of verbs like ***eat*** or adjectives like ***amazed***). In examples (e) and (f), we see that complements are required (as is true with verbs like ***make*** or adjectives like ***fond***). In examples (g) and (h) we witness the opposite situation: ***away*** and ***apart*** seem unable to take complements at all (as is true with verbs like ***sleep*** and adjectives like ***nice***). By assuming that the boldfaced words in the second column are prepositions, we achieve a solid generalization about heads – namely, that they determine their own complements (or lack thereof) – and we incidentally eliminate the need for a special category of words called 'particles' that would have to be listed twice in the lexicon under different category labels. Emonds (1976) has argued that prepositions, like verbs, can be usefully described as 'transitive', 'intransitive', or both, depending on their use.

To sum up this section: we have defined 'complements' as sisters to heads and said that heads bear a special relationship to complements, a relationship that is specified in the lexical entry for the particular head; we have presented data from four different lexical categories V, Adj, N, and P. In the process, we have justified four phrase structure rules that could be written as follows:

(26) VP → V (NP)
     AP → Adj (PP)
     NP → N (PP)
     PP → P (NP)

These rules tell us that each of the four lexical categories V, Adj, N, and P is capable of branching into head and complement. While heads are always required, complements are specified as optional or obligatory on a case-by-case basis, depending on the head. That specification is provided in the lexicon. We can observe the parallelism by showing phrasal expansions in tree form as below:

(26')

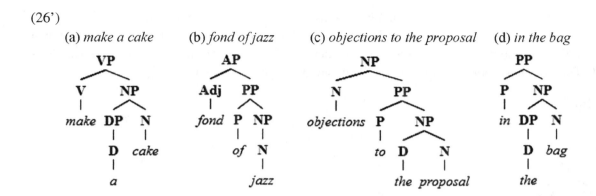

(a) *make a cake* (b) *fond of jazz* (c) *objections to the proposal* (d) *in the bag*

At this point we can address the question, "What is the structure of the English predicate?" As we will see, the relationship between head and complement plays a large role there, as well.

THE STRUCTURE OF THE ENGLISH PREDICATE

So far, we have been working with very simple predicates with verbs that have appeared in their simplest forms. However, a sentence can have two, three, or even four verbs in a complex system, as below:

(27) *Fred bought books.*
(28) *Fred has bought books.*
(29) *Fred is buying books.*
(30) *Fred has been buying books.*

The default assumption is that for each separate word in a sentence, we expect a separate node in the tree. Therefore, we cannot place sets of two, three, or more verbs at a single node. How, then, do we analyze these sequences? We develop below a version of a well-accepted model of syntactic knowledge of English predicates that utilizes the notion of **complements** and thereby simplifies our understanding of the English auxiliary system.

Let us start by contrasting two sentences:

(31) *Fred buys books.*
(32) *Fred can buy books.*

One predicate contains two words, the other three words. Viewing the predicates in another way, however, we can say that they contain an equal number of **morphemes**. The verb ***buys*** comprises a free morpheme (***buy***) plus a bound present tense suffix *–s*. This suffix is required (in dominant dialects, at least); we cannot say ****Fred buy books*** as a normal indicative sentence. In contrast, the verb ***can*** has no such suffix, and the sequence ****Fred cans buy books*** would also count as ungrammatical. ***Can*** and the suffix *–s* are in 'complementary distribution'; that is, where one appears, the other is always absent (the notion of complementary distribution will play a much more prominent role in the Phonology chapters). Complementarity suggests that these two morphemes – the modal verb and the *–s* suffix – are versions of the same essential node type. We will call this node **T**, for 'tense', refer to the predicate as a **T'**, or 'tense-bar', and call the entire sentence a **TP**, or 'tense phrase'. In the upcoming section on modifiers, we will explain the rationale for this move in greater detail, but for now, we are abandoning our original representation of sentences as composed of the sequence NP-VP and deriving from the expansion S → NP VP. The trees now look as below, with VP becoming a right-sister of T:

(31a)   (32a)

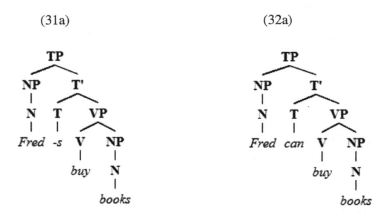

It seems that trees (31a) and (32a) differ in just one small detail. However, it is clear that the two morphemes *can* and *–s* are categorically different from each other. One is a free morpheme, the other a bound morpheme. As evidence, consider that we could say, *John cannot buy books, but Fred <u>can</u>*, while we could not say, **John does not buy books, but Fred <u>–s</u>*. An affix must attach to a 'host', or stem morpheme; it cannot stand alone as a word. To make sentence (31) grammatical, we will have to formulate what looks like a special rule,

(33) Bound affixes must attach to a proper host.

There is nothing startling about principle (33); after all, attachment is what bound morphemes are all about. In the case of a verbal suffix like *-s*, the grammar will look for the closest available verb and attach the suffix to it. Affixation of tensed elements like *–s* is a regular process in English and many other languages. In the case of sentence (32), we need not apply the rule of affixation because there is no overt affix at all. The modal verb is followed by a plain verb stem.

Now let us look at more complex predicates -- those with multiple auxiliary verbs in sequence. There are a number of key generalizations that were first highlighted in Chomsky (1957) in his attempt to formulate a simple statement of what is possible and impossible in English auxiliary-verb combinations. The generalizations may be summarized as below:

(a)   Every predicate has a tense or modal, and at least one (main) verb.
(b)   If a predicate has one verb, the tense will attach to that verb as a suffix.
(c)   If a predicate uses perfect (*have*+V), the verb that follows *have* will be a past participle.
        (E.g., we can say *Summer has gone*, but not **Summer has go/going.*)
(d)   If a predicate uses progressive (*be*+V), the verb that follows *be* will end in *–ing*.
        (E.g., we can say *It is raining*, but not **It is rain/rained.*)
(e)   If a predicate uses a modal verb, the verb that follows the modal will have no suffix.
        (E.g., we can say *Fred can buy books*, but not **Fred can buying/bought books.*)

Two things are important to keep in mind. One is that options (b, c, d, e) are only that – options. While each sentence requires a subject, a tense, and a verb, there is no requirement on the **number** of verbs beyond a main verb (in fact, there can be up to four in active-voice sentences). The other is that we have defined an **ordering** relation among these elements that cannot be altered (thus, **Fred going been have would* is impossible). If we consolidate all this information into a simple statement as in Chomsky (1957), the result looks approximately as follows,

(34) PREDICATE → T/(modal) (*have*+past participle) (*be+-ing*) V

where one may choose between a tense or a modal, but not both. The material in parentheses is optional. Each affix – the T, the past participle, and the *–ing* – is determined by the just-preceding element in the string of morphemes. That is, the tense will attach to whichever verb comes next; the past participle will attach to whichever verb follows *have*; the progressive *–ing* suffix will attach to whichever verb follows *be*; and in the case of modal verbs such as *may/might/must/can/could*, the following verb receives no affix at all – as sentence (32) and its corresponding tree shows.

One last detail needs to be included. We have added a new category to the lexicon – **tense** – and we require a **lexical rule** that tells us how tense is realized in English sentences. In order to do so, we need to address what we mean by 'tense'. We adopt a well-known and fairly uncontroversial definition consistent with that in Comrie (1985) that calls tense a marking (possibly a zero-marking) on a verb that denotes a time relative to the time of speaking. When a speaker says "I am baking cookies", the speaker denotes a time that is contiguous with the time of saying the sentence. We call that **present** tense. When a speaker says, "I baked cookies (yesterday)", the time denoted is (one day) prior to the time of speaking. We call that **past** tense.

What, then, about the 'future', 'present perfect', 'past perfect', present progressive', and other constructions that are frequently referred to as 'tenses'? Such structures, and the meanings they convey, are key parts of a description of English. We will argue (in a way consistent with mainstream linguists) that they are not tenses in the strict sense.

When we refer to future time in English, we typically say "I will bake cookies (tomorrow)"; we also might say, "I am baking cookies (tomorrow)", using the present tense of *be* and leaving part of the intended interpretation up to pragmatic factors, i.e., the context of utterance of the sentence. English does not place affixes on verbs in order to denote future time, as in French:

(35) (a)   *Je joue*. 'I play'; 'I am playing'.
     (b)   *Je jouais*. 'I played'; 'I was playing'.
     (c)   *Je jouerai*. 'I will play'; 'I am going to play'.

Rather, the standard English way of indicating future time is to combine the modal verb *will* with the base form of a verb, as in *will+play*. Such a form, often called 'periphrastic' because it utilizes multiple words to express the idea of futurity, is really better analyzed in terms of modal constructions including the modal auxiliaries *would*, *should*, *shall*, *may*, *might*, *can*, and *could*. We then say that the expression of future time is a function of modal use (or other periphrastic means such as *be going to*) and that English does not have a genuine future 'tense' that is realized morphologically.

What, then, of constructions like those below, together with their traditional names?

(36) (a) *She is playing*   PRESENT PROGRESSIVE (or PRESENT CONTINUOUS)
      (b) *She was playing.*   PAST PROGRESSIVE (or CONTINUOUS)
      (c) *She has played.*   PRESENT PERFECT
      (d) *She had played.*   PAST PERFECT
      (e) *She has been playing.*   PRESENT PERFECT PROGRESSIVE (or PRESENT P. CONTINUOUS)
      (f) *She had been playing*   PAST PERFECT PROGRESSIVE (or PAST PERFECT CONTINUOUS)
      (g) *She will be playing.*   FUTURE PROGRESSIVE (or FUTURE CONTINUOUS)
      (h) *She will have played.*   FUTURE PERFECT
      (i) *She will have been playing.* FUTURE PERFECT PROGRESSIVE (or FUTURE P. CONTINUOUS)

Though traditional grammarians have called each of these a 'tense', linguists generally agree that the labels obscure a key distinction between **time reference** and **aspectual reference** and that each construction (a-i) above, as well as the 'simple present', 'simple past', and 'simple future' combine time marking relative to speaker-time together with a marking of the nature or 'internal consistency' of the event (Comrie, 1976). Thus, for example, a sentence like (36a), ***She is playing***, combines the notion of an event taking place at speaker-time with the notion that this event has some limited duration, or at least is meant to be viewed that way. In contrast, the simple present ***She plays*** is normally taken as the expression of a habit or permanent duration, and ***She has played*** indicates an action that is completed at an unexpressed time prior to speaker-time. These are only rough descriptions of the meaning differences; we do not want to minimize the complexity of meanings expressed through the use of aspect in English. The point here is that all three sentences share a single tense – 'present' -- but indicate different aspects.

The lexical rule for tense, then, simply reads as follows:

(37) tense → present/past

and this is how T, or 'tense', will be represented in trees with **finite**, or time-sensitive, verbs.

Keeping the above picture of auxiliary verbs and tenses in mind, we can now visualize the syntax of complex predicates in terms of the **head-complement** relationship developed in the preceding section. Let us start with a simple example, then try a more complicated one:

(38) *Fred has bought his books.*

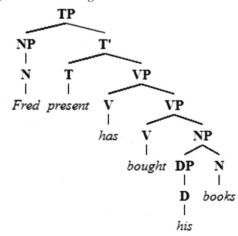

As the tree makes clear, the relation between T and VP is in fact a head-complement relation. Since heads specify complements, we can say that any T consisting of "present" or "past" may lexically specify a complement that is **headed** by a verb ending in *–s* (for third-person present singular forms), ending in a zero-allomorph (for all other persons in the present), or ending in *–ed* (for past forms). In turn, since V *has* is also a head, we can say that *has*, being a perfect form, lexically specifies its own complement – one headed by a past participle form of the verb (*bought*). The verb *bought*, of course, specifies its own complement, a direct object NP.

Tree (39) is more complex, but it follows the same set of rules:

(39) *Fred might be buying books.*

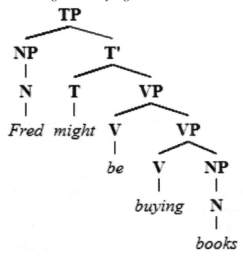

The T node contains the modal verb *might*. Modal verbs select complements that are headed by the base (or 'stem', or 'plain', or affix-less) form of the verb. Since the complement of T is the topmost VP, and since the head of that VP is *be*, we have selected the right complement. Next, the auxiliary verb *be* is a head, and it selects a VP complement headed by an *–ing* form. This requirement is met in the form *buying*, which heads the next lower VP. Finally, the verb *buying* selects a direct object – i.e., an NP complement, in this case *books*.

In making explicit the notion of heads and complements, we have managed to unify the discussion of a number of traditionally separate grammatical phenomena. What, then, do we make of sentential elements that are **not** lexically specified complements? Before pursuing this question, let us first answer an unresolved question from the beginning of this chapter.

GRAMMATICAL RELATIONS

If we reconsider tree (4), the first branching below S indicated that a sentence branches into "SUBJECT… PREDICATE". We might ask what happened to this level of analysis: are we not required to specify subjects and predicate nodes in the tree?

Traditional grammar offers definitions of these two terms approximately as follows:

(40) (a) The **subject** is the *main actor* in a sentence, or at least *what the sentence is about.*

    (b) The **predicate** is *the event performed by the subject,* or at least *what we are saying about the subject.*

    (c) The **direct object** is the *receiver of the action.*

These grade-school definitions may work for a majority of sentences (just as defining nouns as "persons, places, things' and verbs as 'action words' might do), but they do not cover all of them. Compare sentences like:

(41) *The gray squirrels in the park annoy the cat.*
(42) *It is too bad that we lost the election.*
(43) *There's an armchair in the corner.*

We take all three sentences to be grammatical, acceptable and 'complete', as sentences are said to be. In (41), if we were to ask what the sentence is about, the answer would be, "The gray squirrels in the park". That is also the subject NP. If we were to ask what the event performed by that actor is, a reasonable answer would be "the event of annoying the cat". That meaning is covered in the predicate. However, we cannot get such neat results for (42) and (43). No one would say that sentence (42) is 'about' *it,* or that sentence (43) is 'about' **there**. A more plausible reply is that (42) is about our losing the election and (43) is about an armchair. Yet neither ***that we lost the election*** nor ***armchair*** is the subject of (42) or (43). The subjects of (42) and (43) are *it* and **there**. Likewise, it is accurate enough to say that the cat is 'the receiver of the action' of 'annoying' in sentence (41); however, it is less clear that the election is the 'receiver' of the 'loss' in (42) or that we would describe the situation in that way at all. In short, we would like definitions that cover all cases, on the ground that 'exceptions' imply that no real rule exists. A proposed 'rule' defined with exceptions suggests that the actual rule is eluding our grasp.

The general view of syntacticians is that subjects and predicates are formally defined in tree-relational terms, not in terms of meaning – and that these tree relations are represented mentally. A look at **grammatical relations** – the study of the spatial-hierarchical relationships among the various parts of sentences – reveals that subjects and predicates still exist, but the need for labeling them in the tree is rendered unnecessary. How so? We are able with our tree system to specify, for any tree, which NP is the subject simply by tracing a line upward in the tree. If the NP appears in the sequence, TP → NP T', then we can define "subject" as "the first NP under TP and adjacent to (or **sister** to) T'". This definition holds for all three sentences (41-43) above:

(41')

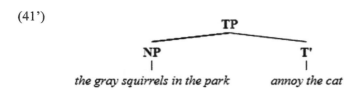

(42')

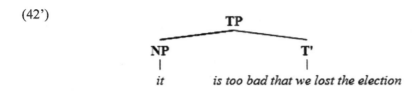

(43')

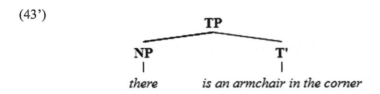

We can extend this line of reasoning to the traditional category **direct object** and say that a direct object is "the first NP under VP that is a right sister to a verb". Thus, for the relevant parts of sentences (41) and (42), we would draw:

(41)   (42)

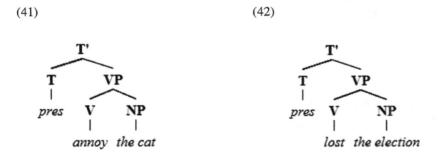

and we now have what looks like an adequate syntactic definition of 'direct object', and it is irrelevant whether that object is the 'receiver' of any action, though of course it often *is* one.

But is this definition adequate? It could be argued that the definition does not take into account traditional **indirect objects**. An indirect object is traditionally said to be the beneficiary or receiver of the event performed, as in *Mary gave John a gift*, or *Can you lend me a hand?* In these sentences, *John* and *me* are the indirect objects, while *a gift* and *a hand* are the direct objects. We expect the tree for the first sentence to look like the following:

(44) *Mary gave John a gift.*

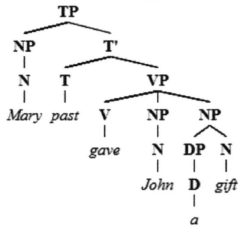

Since we could not say *Mary gave a gift John*, it seems safe to say that the concept **indirect object** can be defined in the following way:

(45) An indirect object is a right sister to V and a left sister to NP.

The implicit assumption here, of course, is that indirect objects cannot exist on their own without the presence of direct objects – at least not in English.

It is worth pointing out that often, grammarians define 'indirect object' in semantic rather than syntactic terms. Some would claim that in the following sentence, *John* is also an indirect object:

(46) *Mary gave a gift to John.*

If John is the recipient or beneficiary of the act of gift giving in (44), surely he is still a recipient or beneficiary in (46). We do not wish to get into unnecessary arguments over the use of terminology, i.e., over who has the better definition of 'indirect object'. We will simply say that if **indirect object** is defined syntactically rather than semantically, only (44) provides an example of one. Sentence (46) does, however, provide a good example of a syntactic **object of a preposition** (or **prepositional object**), of which only a subset contains what could be called 'recipients' or 'beneficiaries'. For example, consider the bracketed PPs below:

(47) *Jack likes roast beef [with **horseradish**].*
(48) *They went home [after **the storm**].*
(49) *We bought a box [of **cookies**].*

Each boldfaced NP is the object of a preposition, but none could be called a recipient or beneficiary of anything. However, we should make note of the (possibly interesting) fact that such meanings can be encoded in two different syntactic positions.

Prepositional objects, then, can be regarded as complements – i.e., right sisters to prepositions – in a class with subjects, direct objects, and indirect objects as categories marking **grammatical relations** that are definable in terms of their positions in trees and relations to other constituents.

MODIFIERS

We have not yet mentioned anything about **modification**. For example, we have said nothing about where we would place adjectives in a tree when they modify nouns.

(50) ***spicy*** *tamales*

And though we have mentioned PPs that are not complements (as in sentences (23a-c) above), we have not said where they would fit into a tree:

(51) *a house **in suburbia***

As a first attempt to draw trees for these NPs, we might try diagrams like the one below:

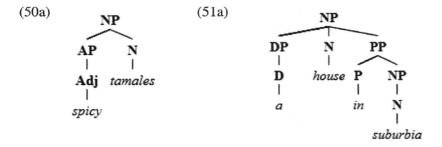

Such representations are fairly traditional (and for those readers who are familiar with the older 'stick diagrams', these trees could be easily converted to the old diagramming system by placing the modifiers on slanted lines below the main line). However, the trees miss an important point. The tree relations above indicate that AP, DP, and PP are complements to the head nouns *tamales* and *house*, since complements are sisters to heads. Yet they do not look like complements. There cannot be anything lexicalized about the relationship between the head noun *tamales* and the AP *spicy*; we do not memorize the preposition *in* as part of an idiomatic syntactic frame for the use of the head noun *house*. Given these facts, we do not want to represent either the AP *spicy* or the PP *in suburbia* as sisters to N in the same way that we would certainly want to represent *money* as a lexicalized sister to *make* in the VP *make money*. Is there a way to show the difference?

The fairly standard solution that has been in use since Chomsky (1970) and was fully developed in Jackendoff (1977) is called the **X' framework**, or **X' theory**. X' (pronounced X-bar) theory argues for an **intermediate** projection between the full phrasal level (NP) and the word level (N). Thus, rather than proceeding directly from NP to N in a word like ***restaurants***, we will require an intermediate step **NP →** **N' → N**. Applied to NPs, the new framework requires a set of phrase structure rules that are presented as follows:

(52) (a) NP → (DP) N'
  (b) (N' → (AP) N' (PP))
  (c) N' → N (NP) (PP)

Let us go through the rules step by step, and then show how the trees for phrases (50) and (51) would be properly drawn. The top line simply repeats our original claim that an NP may begin with a determiner phrase; however, that DP is now paired with an N' rather than an N. This N' then serves as input to the second rule, which introduces modifiers like *spicy* or *in suburbia*. However, as we well know, not every NP contains modifiers, so this second rule is **optional** (note the parentheses around it). We may therefore skip it in simpler phrases (e.g., in NPs such as *tamales* or *a house*) and go directly to the third rule, for which N' will also be the input. The output of the third rule will include the **head** N and any **complements** to N. We then arrive at trees which look like those below:

(50b)   (51b)

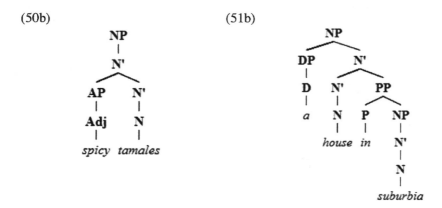

In (50b), there is no determiner because according to the rule, determiners are optional. We therefore go directly to N', which branches into a modifying AP *spicy* and another N'. The N' is not further modified, so it goes directly to N *tamales*. In (51b), we do have a determiner; the N' branches to another N', indicating that there is a modifier to N', which is the PP *in suburbia*. That N' is not further modified, so it branches directly to N *house*. Finally, we see that the NP complement to P, *suburbia*, is not modified at all (e.g., as it might be in *beautiful suburbia*), so NP goes directly to N', and N' goes directly to N.

Is it possible for **two** PPs to follow a head N, one of which is a modifying PP, and the other a complement PP? It certainly is, and use of the three-tiered X' framework will help account for an interpretation puzzle in the process. Consider the three sentences in (53):

(53) (a) *We made a decision on the boat.*
  (b) *We made a decision on the plane.*
  (c) *We made a decision on the boat on the plane.*

The (a) and (b) sentences are ambiguous; it is not clear in (a), for example, whether we decided to make use of a boat (by buying or traveling on one), or whether we made a decision while we were riding on a boat. The same ambiguity holds for (b). For (c), however, there is no such ambiguity: it is clear that we made a decision to buy or travel on a boat while we were riding on a plane. We cannot get the opposite interpretation (i.e., a scenario where we made a decision to travel on a plane while we were riding on a boat), which would make an ungrammatical sentence on that interpretation. If we drew the trees in a two-tiered system as in (50a-51a), we would have no means of capturing these different interpretations, since the two PPs would be treated as equal sisters to N. In the three-tiered X' system, however, we see that the attachments are at different levels:

(53c)

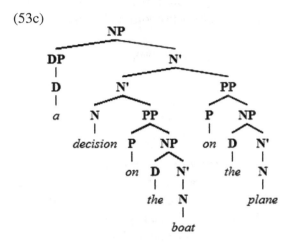

The PP on the right is a sister to N', while the one on the left is a sister to N. This tree captures the idea that the head-complement relationship between ***decision+on (the boat)*** is a closer one than the modifying relationship between ***decision+on (the plane)***. Notice, too, that we could not reverse the order of these two PPs (i.e., ***a decision on the plane on the boat***) and get the same interpretation. The reason is that complements are closer to their heads than modifiers are. Note, too, that we can now also avoid saying that a determiner is a direct modifier of a noun; rather, it is a sister to the higher-level N' (and because a determiner is also a daughter to NP, it is technically called a **specifier** rather than a modifier; a true **modifier** would be a daughter of the higher-level N' and a sister to N'.)

One of the advantages of using this three-tiered system, then, is that it explains ambiguity in a way that earlier syntactic representations could not do. It also explains certain puzzling facts about the **coordination** of phrases. A coordinate structure is a structure utilizing a traditional coordinating conjunction such as ***and, but, so, for*** (meaning 'because'), and ***(either)/or***. It is a commonplace observation that coordination must take place between identical constituent types. Consider the examples in (54):

(54) (a)   *doctors and nurses*
   (b)   *friendly and helpful*
   (c)   **friendly and nurses*
   (d)   *in and out*
   (e)   *ran and jumped*
   (f)   **in and jumped*

If coordination is between pairs of NPs, APs, PPs, or VPs, there is no problem. However, if we propose to coordinate AP+NP, or PP+VP, we get bad results. Coordination requires lexical and grammatical parallelism. The same generalization seems to hold between complement phrases and modifying phrases, as illustrated in the examples below:

(55) *He made pleas for mercy and for reconsideration of his case.*
(56) *He made pleas from the courtyard and from the hallway.*
(57) **He made pleas for mercy and from the courtyard.*

Sentence (57) may be comprehensible with some mental gymnastics, but it is clearly unacceptable. The unacceptability can be accounted for on grounds that there is illegitimate coordination of a complement PP with a modifying PP.

Modifiers within VPs can be treated with the same logic. In sentences (58-60),

(58) *Fred buys tickets **often**.*
(59) *Fred **carefully** read the instructions.*
(60) *Fred has **frequently** landed **in Seattle**.*

traditional grammar would say that **often**, **carefully**, and **frequently** modify the verbs **buys**, **read**, and **landed**. If we were to extend the analysis of NP to VP by assuming a three-tiered level of structure, then we would have to say that these adverbs are sisters of V', just as adjective phrases like **spicy** are sisters to N'. Is it reasonable, however, to draw VPs in an analogous way? The answer seems to be 'yes' if we consider example sentences like (53c), where we saw that the complement PP **on the boat** must be closer to the head N than the modifying PP **on the plane** and that only a single interpretation of that sentence is available while, interestingly, two interpretations each are available for (53a) and (53b). How, then, are those examples relevant? Sentence (58) above contains **ticket**, a direct object, and **often**, a time adverb that modifies **buys**. The sentence would be wholly unacceptable if we reversed the order of those two elements:

(58a) **Fred buys often tickets.*

If we assume that an analogous relationship holds here, i.e., that **often** is a sister to V' and **tickets** is a sister to V, then it seems that the same rule framework we used in (53) for NP can be used for VP, and we can explain the badness of (58a). The tree for (58) would be drawn as below:

(58b)

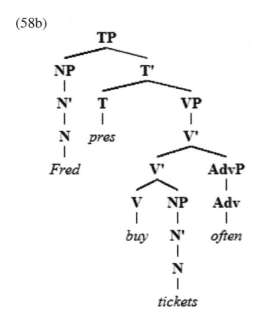

Clearly, *tickets* cannot follow *often* since it is a complement, while *often* is a modifier. What, then, of (59)-(60), where the adverbs appear in different VP positions? Traditional grammar noticed long ago that English adverbs are freer in their positional options than NPs or APs. An adverb may occur on either side of the verb: we can *buy tickets often* or *often buy tickets*, but we cannot have both *a spicy tamale* and **a tamale spicy*. This appears simply to mean that an AdvP can be a right-sister or a left-sister to V'. The VP structure for (59) would simply be that below:

(59a)

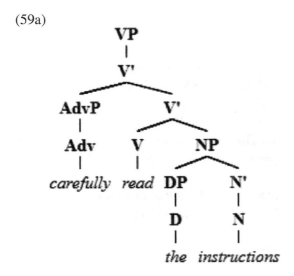

Finally, what about sentence (60), where the adverb appears between two verbs, the auxiliary *has* and the main verb *landed*? We are drawn intuitively to the interpretation that it is the 'landing', not the 'having', that is frequent, and can safely assume that the adverb modifies the V' *landed*. Recall from an earlier section that auxiliary constructions involve **head-complement** relationships, and that if *have* is a head, then *frequently landed in Seattle* would be its complement, a VP. This VP would then be treed as in (59a) above -- but this time we need to **repeat** the modifier rule, since the PP *in Seattle* is also a modifier:

(60a)

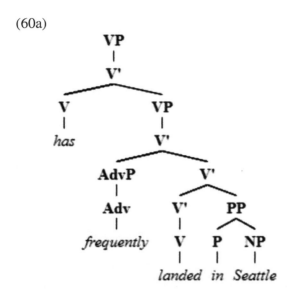

If this line of reasoning is clear, then, we are operating with a set of rules very much like the rules we used for NPs. They may be schematized as in (61):

(61) VP → V'

    (V' → (AdvP) V' (AdvP)(PP))

    V' → V (NP) (PP)

In short, a VP branches to a V', just as an NP branches to an N'. We have no obvious analogue to the **determiners** that we saw with NPs, so the branching with the first rule is only singular or one-way. Using the second rule, we are then free to add modifiers either before, after, or both before and after, V'. Repeated applications of the second rule will permit us as many modifiers as we wish (as in *Fred has frequently reluctantly landed in Seattle in November on Tuesdays with six suitcases*.) Application of the third rule will generate NP objects (as in *landed a plane*) as well as complement PPs (as in the complement interpretation of *decided on the boat*).

To show that the X' framework may be generalized further, we will look at one more phrase type, APs. It is clear from example (26'b), *fond of jazz*, that adjectives may take complements:

(26')(b)

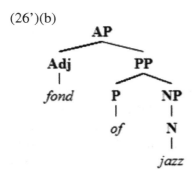

A moment's reflection reveals that *fond* may take a modifier as well as a complement:

(62) *I am especially fond of jazz on Sunday afternoons.*

Since the sentence is technically ambiguous, let us be clear that the reading is, "On Sundays, I especially like jazz" as opposed to "The jazz played on Sundays is what I am fondest of". Notice that reversing the order of the two PPs will not work, nor can the PPs be coordinated:

(63) **I am especially fond on Sunday afternoons of jazz.*
(64) **I am especially fond of jazz and on Sunday afternoons.*

Moreover, the adverb **especially** in (62) seems able to modify the entire sequence **fond of jazz on Sunday afternoons**. It looks, then, as though we are able to expand AP in the same way that we expanded NP and VP. The tree for the AP in (62) would look as follows:

(62')

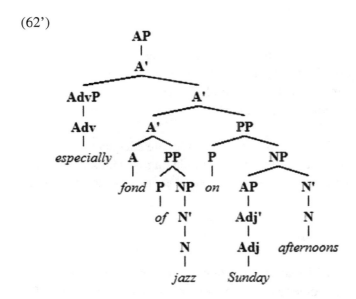

And the expansion for AP, parallel to that of NP and VP, would be the following:

(65) AP → (AdvP) A'
    A' → A' (PP)
    A' → A (PP)

Such a scheme is far superior to one where ***especially***, ***fond***, and ***jazz*** branch directly off the AP node to sit alongside the adjective *fond*, for it makes the right predictions about the behavior of smaller constituents within the larger AP.

The abrupt switch that we made in the section on English predicates from the rule [S → NP VP] to the new rules [TP → NP T'] and [T' → T VP] can hopefully now be placed in a familiar context. We made the switch because the same rationale that applies to other phrases applies to entire clauses. The T node also takes complements, just as smaller phrases do, and in this sense a sentence is much like a phrase. Let us now sum up the rule schemas that we have developed in this chapter:

(66)

TP → NP T'	(= basic subject-predicate rule)
T' → T VP	(= basic predicate rule)
NP → (DP) N'	(= initial NP rule)
N' → (AP) N' (PP)	(= N' modifier rule, optionally applied)
N' → N (NP) (PP)	(= NP complement rule)
VP → V'	(= initial VP rule)
V' → (AdvP) V' (AdvP)	(= V' modifier rule, optionally applied)
V' → V (NP) (PP)	(= VP complement rule)
AP → (AdvP) A'	(= initial AP rule)
A' → A' (PP)	(= A' modifier rule, optionally applied)
A' → A (PP)	(= AP complement rule)
DP → (AdvP) D	(= determiner rule)
AdvP → (AdvP) Adv	(= adverb rule)
PP → P (NP)	(= preposition rule)

Given space, we could pursue the possibility of developing expanded analyses of DPs, AdvPs, and PPs in which these, too, are analyzed into three-level projections. In fact, the relevant literature has done this, with the ultimate goal of illustrating the symmetrical structure of all English phrases. This leads naturally into the intriguing question of whether other languages exhibit the same symmetry – a topic which we cannot pursue here.

Looking at the larger picture, we can say that if these phrase structure rules are adequate and supplemented by a rich set of lexical rules, they will permit the construction of simple English **clauses**, i.e., units comprising TP → NP+T' expansions. While not every clause is a sentence, every sentence comprises at least one clause. For example, the sentence

(67) *Our work will be done when we return from our trip.*

consists of two separate clauses (***Our work will be done*** and ***when we return from our trip***), the second of which is said to be **embedded** inside the other as a 'dependent' or 'subordinate' clause. Together, they create what is traditionally called a 'complex sentence'. While we will not present rules for generating complex sentences in this chapter, the rules that we have developed apply equally to the embedded clause as to the non-embedded, independent, main clause of the sentence.

IMPLICATIONS FOR TEACHING ENGLISH LANGUAGE LEARNERS

Imparting a clear sense of the basic word order of a particular second language is an obvious goal of early second-language instruction. One of the most noticeable features of world languages is that there are strong statistical correlations regarding the feature of **headedness**, or principal branching direction of heads with respect to their mother nodes and their complements. Headedness has been identified as a basic **parameter** that differentiates languages. Pulling together the evidence from the trees in (26') above and elsewhere in the chapter, we notice a striking gross feature of English phrasal expansions – that they have left-branching or **head-first** structures:

(68) $T' \rightarrow T \ VP$ *(can leave, broke the window)*
         $V' \rightarrow V \ (NP)/(PP)$ *(slept, gave Mary a call, put it on the table)*
         $A' \rightarrow Adj \ (PP)$ *(happy, fond of chocolate)*
         $N' \rightarrow N \ (PP)$ *(happiness, bags of groceries)*
         $PP \rightarrow P \ (NP)$ *(away, out, off the table)*

That is, in any expansion of TP, VP, AP, NP, or PP, the head precedes its complements. This generalization does not come without qualifications. For one thing, we have not investigated whether determiners and adverbs can also take complements. For another thing, we have already seen that English is capable of pre-nominal modifiers such as ***happy campers***. If English were consistently head-first, we might expect to hear ****campers happy***, but this is in fact not the way that noun modification works. Moreover, it is possible to argue that NPs can take pre-nominal complements, as in NPs such as (69a):

(69) (a)   *Fred is a pro**fe**ssional student.*
     (b)   *Fred is a professional **stu**dent.*

In the (a) example, with emphasis on the boldfaced syllable, we get the interpretation that Fred is studying to enter one of the professions, such as law or medicine. In (b), we get a much different interpretation, i.e., that Fred is making a career out of being in school. Without the variant emphases as shown, the sentence is ambiguous. As noted in the chapter on word formation, the (a) example exhibits the stress pattern of a **compound**, where the most-stressed syllable in the first free morpheme takes primary stress. Note, too, that if we combine both senses of ***professional*** in a single NP, the interpretation is not at all ambiguous, and we know exactly which instance of the word ***professional*** takes which interpretation:

(70) *Fred is a professional professional student.*

If (70) is sounded out properly, it means that Fred is making a career out of studying (as opposed to actually working in) one of the professions. Further, if we combine the (a) sense of the word with a clear case of another modifier, it is clear that only one ordering is permissible:

(71) (a)   *Fred is a star pro**fe**ssional student.*
     (b)   **Fred is a pro**fe**ssional star student.*

It appears, then, that pre-nominal complements are behaving like post-nominal complements in their requirement to be nearer their heads than modifiers are. Do these facts affect the overall assessment of English as a head-first language? In general, they do not, considering that most complements are **not** of the (69a) type but are rather of the (68) type, and considering that there are few convincing parallel instances of the same phenomenon for other heads; compound nouns are rather 'special'.

How, then, do other languages organize their most basic units? It is useful to contrast English with Japanese here. Japanese represents the other parametric option in that its main branching direction seems in many ways the polar opposite of English:

(72)   Uchi ni inu ga imasu.   Koko ni Suzuki san ga imasu.
              home at dog SUBJ be-PRES   here at Suzuki Mr. SUBJ be-PRES
              'A dog is at home.'   'Mr. Suzuki is here.'

(73)   Soko ni okane ga arimasu.   Koko ni den'wa ga arimasu.
              There at money SUBJ be-PRES   Here at telephone SUBJ be-PRES
              'Over there is some money.'   'Here is a telephone.'

The first, most striking feature of Japanese (for a native English speaker, at least) is that verbs are the final element in a sentence. The second is that their versions of prepositions are generally analyzed as suffixes on a noun (technically making them **postpositions** rather than prepositions). Because Japanese is also a language with tenses, like English, and because tense is realized on its verbs, Japanese tense appears in the opposite part of the TP tree from English. The general consensus on Japanese is that it is a **head-last** language, i.e., one whose principal branching direction is to the right. Japanese trees look approximately as follows:

(74)

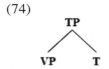

Where modification is concerned, Japanese does place its adjectives before the nouns they modify, as in English. Overall, however, unlike the **SVO** (subject-verb-object) order of English, Japanese exhibits an **SOV** (subject-object-verb) order. While there are six mathematical options for the ordering of S, V, and O, the vast majority of the world's languages may be classified on either the English or the Japanese pattern. In some cases -- such as German, where SVO order is found in main clauses and SOV in dependent clauses – languages are 'mixed'. The study of these inconsistencies, both historically and in a present-day context, has been a topic of fascination for linguists for many years.

It is tempting to ask whether headedness, i.e., principal branching direction, has any effect on the early linguistic production of second language learners. The long tradition of **contrastive analysis** (see, e.g., Lado, 1957; Wardhaugh, 1970) argued that the phenomenon of **negative transfer** of structures of the first or native language will be apparent whenever two languages differ in comparable respects (cf. Odlin, 1989). The proponents of contrastive analysis were careful to undergird their claims in the predominant habit-based, stimulus-and-response-oriented behaviorist learning theory of the time. They also took the trouble to classify levels of difficulty where transfer was predicted to take place. For example, English-speaking learners of Spanish will have to learn that there are two verbs, *ser* and *estar*, corresponding to the English verb *be*, and to use them correctly each time. In contrast, Spanish-speaking learners of English need only learn a form of *be* for both Spanish verbs. The English learners, faced with a 'split' learning task, were argued have a more challenging task than the Spanish learners faced with a case of 'coalescence' of two forms into a single form.

It took more than a decade after the first systematic predictions of contrastive analysis were made for actual empirical studies of transfer phenomena to be carried out, i.e., where large-scale learner production data was collected and examined. One such study was Whitman & Jackson (1972), two researchers working with a population of several thousand Japanese secondary-school students at various levels of attainment in English. The most straightforward predictions of contrastive analysis were that Japanese learners, at least at the early stages of development, would be strongly inclined to reproduce Japanese word order in their English production – e.g., **I my friend the gymnasium in saw* (for *I saw my friend in the gymnasium*). Those learners at the ages of 12-18 could be expected to have produced many thousands of Japanese sentences up to that point in their lives, with the head-last 'habit' well ingrained, and resistance to English SVO could be expected to be strong. In fact, however, the researchers found no replication of Japanese word order in their English learner production data. At most, learners experienced hesitation in producing English sentences. While transfer was indeed observed – the English "r" sound did sound remarkably like the Japanese "r" – the transfer was not at the level of basic constituent order. Data in Rutherford (1983) pointed to a similar conclusion.

The situation is somewhat different where **modifiers** are concerned. Though French is an SVO language like English, French places time adverbs like *souvent* ('often') and *toujours* ('always') in a position just after the verb and before any complements:

(75)   *Ils aiment souvent aller à la plage.*
They like-PRES   often   to-go to the beach
'They like to go to the beach often.'

(76)   *Il fume toujours des Gauloises.*
He smoke-PRES   always   the   Gauloises cigarettes
'He smokes Gauloises all the time.'

We have said that English complements must appear adjacent to their heads, without modifiers intervening.[2] French learners of English do, in fact, often replicate French word order as follows:

(75a)   **They like often to go to the beach.*
(76a)   **He smokes always (the) Gauloises.*

A tentative conclusion might be drawn that where the most basic elements of message communication are concerned, learners are quite sensitive to the code of the new language and will follow it; where 'add-ons' such as adverbial modifiers are involved, learners' attention is less focused (perhaps because they are subconsciously aware that the central message has been successfully transmitted). The conclusion seems *generally* upheld in second-language production research, but it requires much qualification. For example, speakers of SVO languages have been observed to have generalized the SVO order of German main clauses to subordinate clauses as well, where the actual German order is SOV (e.g., Meisel, Clahsen, & Pienemann, 1981). Where such cases of 'overdifferentiation' of base structure exist, the predictions of contrastive analysis seem to have a degree of validity. However, if a researcher hopes to document cases of rich first-language transfer, it seems there are more fruitful places to look than the most basic constituent order.

DISCUSSION QUESTIONS

1. **Simple sentences with copula *be*.** In our discussion of the structure of predicates, we said nothing about what some might imagine as the simplest, 'archetypal' sentence – a sentence such as *Mary is a* doctor or *Don is dishonest*. Such sentences contain a form of the verb *be*. It is important to take note of the fact that English has two different versions of *be*. One is the auxiliary that is associated with progressive predicates such as *Jane's family **is** watching the horse race now*. In that sentence, the word *is* counts as an auxiliary verb. The other, traditionally called "main-verb *be*", may stand on its own with no auxiliaries and is called a **copula**. (Both versions of *be* may appear sequentially in a sentence like *Bob **is being** silly now*.) Though a copula may appear as part of a more complex predicate, its key point of identification is the fact that the copula always comes last in the sequence of verbs and therefore counts as a main verb. When a copula is used, it appears with what is traditionally called either a **predicate adjective** (as in *Don is dishonest*) or a **predicate nominal** (as in *Mary is a doctor*).

Using the X' framework for VPs, draw trees for the sentences below. You will need to decide on the status of predicate adjectives and predicate nouns as either **complements** or **modifiers**. Consider what information you must take into account in making this decision.

> *Mary is a doctor.*   *Don is dishonest.*
> *Mrs. Smith will soon be a mother.*   *Our cat is being very quirky today.*

2. **Determiners.** Grammar books point out that English permits multiple determiners in sequence. As many as three are possible, but notice that some sequences are not possible:

> *our one complaint*   *these two complaints*
> *the two blackbirds*   *that one mistake*
> *my other Mercedes*   *all other comments*
> *half the students*   **the my book*
> *all the other students*   **a one egg*
> *that other guy*   **the this complaint*

It is risky to try to account for the good and the bad cases in terms of **meaning** restrictions alone. After all, if we can say *a single egg*, why not **a one egg*? Also, there are languages (such as Italian) where a sequence translated literally as *the my book* or *a my book* would be acceptable. An account based in **lexical** and/or **syntactic frames** seems the best way to explain the options and prohibitions. How should we proceed? Note the following observations:

(a)   Since each D appears to be a separate word, we want to keep each D in a separate node.

(b)   If possible, we would like to maintain the same phrase structure rules that we have developed without complicating them unnecessarily.

(c)   There are fairly strict **ordering** relations among the D types; not every order is possible.

Keeping (a-c) in mind, what would the dictionary entries for the various determiner types specify, apart from their meaning alone? How could trees be drawn for the good examples? How would the DP rule in (66) have to be revised in order to accommodate the new options? (You can answer these three questions in any order.) In drawing trees, it will be necessary to decide what branching relationships exist among the Ds, and between the Ds and the head N.

3.   **PP 'types'.** In traditional grammar books (such as the *Warriner's* manual used for generations in the U.S.), two types of PPs are often distinguished: an 'adjectival' type and an 'adverbial' type. The first type can be defined in notional terms as answering the questions, "What kind" and "Which one". The second type answers the questions "How", "Where", "When", and Why?" The following sentences illustrate this claim:

Adjectival:
Give me a piece [of the blueberry pie].   (= which?)
Evergreens are trees [with needles].   (= what kind?)
The neighbors [across the street] came to visit.   (= which?)
We saw a movie [about Yosemite Park].   (= what kind?)
Adverbial:
They slept [on the floor].   (= where?)
We'll leave [in two hours].   (= when?)
They play golf [for pleasure].   (= why?)
They removed the nails [with a hammer].   (= how?)

(a)   If it is true that some or all PPs are 'really' adjectival while others are 'really' adverbial, what would the tree structure for such PPs look like? How would that structure prove problematical for the syntactic framework we have presented in this chapter?

(b)   Whether or not we permit trees like those you described in (a), traditional grammarians do seem to agree on what "questions" are answered by these PPs. How, then, can we account for these intuitions within the X' framework? That is, how might we explain, through tree relationships, why some PPs 'feel' adjectival or adverbial?

4.   **Preposition stranding.** The 'stranding' of prepositions as in ***Which clerk did you speak with___?*** has long been regarded as prescriptively wrong, despite the fact that practically every native speaker does it. Stranding involves the fronting of the object of the preposition to the beginning of the sentence, leaving the P alone at the end. One of the features of **complement** PPs is the ability of their objects to detach in this way and produce an acceptable sentence. Modifying PPs are not able to undergo this change. With these facts in mind, test each of the following sentences by manipulating and expanding the sentence in such a way as to force the stranding of the P (e.g., *The cookies that...* or *Which cookies...?*). Which PPs are complements, and which are modifiers?
My friends and I ate a whole box of cookies.

We watched the deer eating our garden flowers on Sunday.
I am appalled at our sales record.
The decision on the plan was difficult to make.
We paid for the sandwich with a ten-dollar bill.
The students hoped for better results.
They met five linguistics students during the conference.
The worst people often lust after power.
Meet me around the corner!
My sister firmly believes in ghosts.

5. **Another property of syntax.** Early in the chapter, we said that two key properties of a syntax are **linearity** and **hierarchy**. A third property that we did not mention is **recursion**. Recursion may be a property of a single rule, or of a rule system. In either case, it exists when at least one **input** term also occurs as an **output** term. Recursion was built into our original rule system for **complements**. To review those rules in (26'), we showed the following four trees:

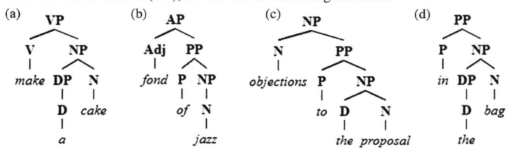

Note, for example, that the output of the PP rule (d) includes an NP. When we expand that NP using rule (c), we see that one of its outputs is PP. That PP will in turn be expanded as P+NP, and the last NP permits branching into another N+PP sequence. In principle, this 'looping' could go on forever, but in the case of complements, it will soon run into a dead end, since complements are lexically specified by heads, and not every head specifies a complement:

*We were not **fond** of the **objections** to the **decision** on the **boat**....?*

Unfortunately, **boat** specifies no obvious complements, and we cannot go further. However, with our improved, final set of rules (62) that permit the inclusion of **modifiers**, the process of recursion becomes more promising since modifiers are adjuncts, and adjuncts may be multiplied as far as desired. Look at (62) and identify points where the system is recursive in the same way as above. Using the lexicon of English and applying modifier rules iteratively, give examples of three long phrases that the system will generate.

EXERCISES

1. **Phrases.** Draw tree representations for the following phrases:
    a. *a foggy day*
    b. *sleepless in Seattle*
    c. *afraid of airplanes*
    d. *a mostly successful attempt*
    e. *having finished our work*
    f. *generally satisfied with her prospects*
    g. *in the box under the table in the kitchen*
    h. *very sick of beans in my salad*

2. **Sentences.** Draw tree representations for the following sentences:
    a. *Their youngest sister has rebelled against her family.*
    b. *Fred wants a new bicycle for his birthday.*
    c. *People in glass houses should take good care of their windows.*
    d. *Joe is building his parents a rustic house in the woods.*
    e. *A question like that really is too difficult.*
    f. *We may have been asking him too many questions.*

3. **Ambiguity.** Linguists often distinguish two types of **ambiguity**. With **lexical** ambiguity, a word may be assigned multiple meanings (such as *right* meaning 'correct' or 'opposite of left') where only the context of utterance may decide the intended meaning. With **structural** ambiguity, the problem is that more than one **tree** may be assigned to a whole sentence. Consider the following NP:

    the man on the house with the shingles

There is potential lexical ambiguity in the word *shingles*, which may refer either to a disease or to a covering for the exterior surface of a house. However, even once we have decided that the second meaning is the correct one, there is additional ambiguity that can be reflected in two possible tree structures. Show, by drawing trees, the syntactic structures of the two interpretations. Which interpretation goes with which tree?

4. **Prenominal adjectives.** We have said that the second line of rule (60), the VP rule, is **iterative**; that is, we may have multiple V' modifiers in a VP that require the repeated application of the second rule to yield V' → V' branching. When discussing NPs, we said nothing about whether the same applies to the second line of the **NP** rule in (52b). We know that the NPs below are possible, which suggests that the second line of the NP rule is also iterative. Draw trees for them in a way parallel to the VP tree for sentence (60):
    a. *hot, spicy tamales with beans*
    b. *a long, happy life with many friendships*

5. **Ungrammaticality.** All of the following sentences are taken from the oral or written production of ESL/EFL learners. Explain, in syntactic and/or lexical terms, the source of the problems.
    a. **I am see him tomorrow night.*
    b. **He visit my best friend every summer.*
    c. **She dislike about what they say.*
    d. **My friend will given me the answers.*
    e. **I don't like too many violent in movies.*
    f. **I want for you a happy life.*

6. **Complements and modifiers.** We have said that complements sit closer to their heads than modifiers and that a modifier cannot intervene between a verb and its direct object. We can use the same test to distinguish complement PPs from modifying PPs. How could relevant modifiers be **added** within the sentences below to test for the syntactic status of the boldfaced PPs below, which are repeated from Discussion Question 3? Do your results ('acceptable' or 'unacceptable') match the same results you found in DQ #3?
    a. *My friends and I ate a whole box **of cookies**.*
    b. *We watched the deer eating our garden flowers **on Sunday**.*
    c. *I am appalled **at our sales record**.*
    d. *The decision **on the plan** was difficult to make.*
    e. *We paid for the sandwich **with a ten-dollar bill**.*
    f. *The students hoped **for better results**.*
    g. *They met five linguistics students **during the conference**.*
    h. *The worst people often lust **after power**.*
    i. *Meet me **around the corner**!*
    j. *My friend firmly believes **in ghosts**.*

7. **A syntactic puzzle.** Note the PPs in the following sentence:
    A stray cat was running [along the top] [of the roof].

    It could be argued that the PP ***along the top*** is a modifier, while ***of the roof*** is a complement. At first glance, this seems to violate the rules for the ordering of complements and modifiers. How, then, is this sentence possible?

8. **A phrase-level puzzle.** Traditional grammar occasionally has trouble categorizing certain English constituents. One problematical type is the time/place expressions in the following sentences:
    *We are going **downtown**.*
    *Let's go **home**.*
    *The package will arrive **next week**.*
    *We ordered pizza **last night**.*

The problem is that the boldfaced expressions seem to be NPs. After all, they behave like NPs in the sentences below:

Downtown *is three miles away.*
Home *is where the heart is.*
Next week *is too late.*
Last night *was great!*

Moreover, the words **next** and **last** are determiners, which are traditionally said to modify nouns. Suggest a way (or ways) in which a syntactic theory could deal with this problem – if it is indeed a problem. If necessary, draw trees to illustrate your solution.

pansion of TP. In the list of rules in (66), you will notice that we did not have a 'middle' rule ptionally expanded T' to include modifiers. Does such an intermediate rule exist? Consider ntences below for hints as to what kinds of sentence might be covered:
She currently has no mailing address.
They inexplicably left town without leaving one.
We have no answer to your question, unfortunately.
You have been looking in the wrong place, obviously.

d the TP rule be modified to permit these sentences? Choose one sentence from (a) and and draw your proposed tree.

10. Exercise 3 in Chapter 3 (Word Formation) asked you to determine whether the part of speech of a compound could be predicted in any way by looking at the free morphemes within a compound. After reviewing your answer, consider whether the discussion of **headedness** in this chapter can throw new light on that answer.

REFERENCES

Chomsky, N. (1957). *Syntactic structures*. The Hague: Mouton.

Chomsky, N. (1968). *Language and mind*. Cambridge, MA: MIT Press.

Chomsky, N. (1970). Remarks on nominalization. In R. A. Jacobs & P. S. Rosenbaum (Eds.), *English transformational grammar* (pp. 184–221). Waltham, MA: Ginn.

Chomsky, N. (1981). *Lectures on government and binding*. Dordrecht: Foris.

Chomsky, N. (1986). *Knowledge of language*. New York: Praeger.

Comrie, B. (1985). *Tense*. Cambridge, UK: Cambridge University Press. doi:10.1017/CBO9781139165815

Comrie, B. (1986). *Aspect*. Cambridge, UK: Cambridge University Press.

Emonds, J. E. (1976). *A transformational approach to English syntax: Root, structure-preserving, and local transformations.* New York: Academic Press.

Greenberg, J. H. (1966). *Universals of language.* Cambridge, MA: MIT Press.

Jackendoff, R. (1977). *X̄ syntax: A study of phrase structure.* Cambridge, MA: MIT Press.

Lado, R. (1957). *Linguistics across cultures.* Ann Arbor, MI: University of Michigan Press.

Meisel, J., Clahsen, H., & Pienemann, M. (1981). On determining developmental stages in natural second language acquisition. *Studies in Second Language Acquisition, 3*(2), 109–135. doi:10.1017/S0272263100004137

Odlin, T. (1989). *Language transfer: Cross-linguistic influence in language learning.* Cambridge, UK: Cambridge University Press. doi:10.1017/CBO9781139524537

Rutherford, W. (1983). Language typology and language transfer. In S. Gass & L. Selinker (Eds.), *Language transfer in language learning* (pp. 358–369). Rowley, MA: Newbury House.

Wardhaugh, R. (1970). The contrastive analysis hypothesis. *TESOL Quarterly, 4*(2), 123–130. doi:10.2307/3586182

Warriner, J. E. (1946). *Warriner's English grammar and composition.* New York: Harcourt.

Whitman, R., & Jackson, K. L. (1972). The unpredictability of contrastive analysis. *Language Learning, 22*(1), 29–41. doi:10.1111/j.1467-1770.1972.tb00071.x

ADDITIONAL READING

Carnie, A. (2013). *Syntax: A generative introduction* (3rd ed.). West Sussex, UK: Wiley-Blackwell.

Radford, A. (1988). *Transformational grammar.* Cambridge, UK: Cambridge University Press. doi:10.1017/CBO9780511840425

ENDNOTES

[1]   Some readers might wonder about subjects in sentences such as ***It** is too bad that we lost the game* or ***There** is a book on the table*. Both sentences contain material in subject position that is generally regarded as 'semantically empty', i.e., meaningless. Though true, we maintain that this meaningless material still falls under the NP node in the trees for these sentences. That is, there is no claim that subjects will be meaningful 100% of the time (though of course they do carry meaning in most instances). See discussion of *it* and *there* subjects after example sentences (42-43).

[2]   The same is claimed to be true for French, but for reasons too complex to explain here, French permits the (70-71) order.

Chapter 5
Syntax Rules and (Un)Grammaticality

Christian Waldmann
Linnaeus University, Sweden

Kirk P. H. Sullivan
Umeå University, Sweden

ABSTRACT

This chapter deals with syntax rules and grammaticality judgments in the teaching and learning of English as a second and foreign language for linguistically diverse learners. Grammaticality judgment tasks are used in linguistic research to probe speakers' implicit knowledge about the syntactic rules of language. This chapter discusses grammaticality judgment tasks in educational contexts and proposes a method for teaching syntactic rules of English based on the grammaticality judgments of second and foreign language learners of English. The chapter also attempts to raise grammatical consciousness for teaching of English as a second or foreign language as well as illustrating how various media can be used to design and present grammaticality judgment tasks to support language learning and learner engagement, participation, and motivation.

WHAT IS (UN)GRAMMATICALITY?

This chapter is framed theoretically within generative grammar, dating back to the early works of Noam Chomsky (see Chomsky 1957, 1965 and later works). Since the first version of generative grammar in the 1950s, the theory has developed and been known as Transformational Grammar, Government and Binding Theory, the Principles and Parameters approach, Minimalism etc. As the proposal is not framed within any specific branch of the theory, the generic term **Generative Grammar** will be used throughout the chapter. The theory presented here is a simplified and slightly adapted version which aims to capture core aspects of generative grammar of relevance to language teaching and learning. For more elaborate descriptions of generative grammar, the reader is referred to Haegeman (1994) for an introduction to

DOI: 10.4018/978-1-5225-8467-4.ch005

Government and Binding Theory, Carnie (2013) for an introduction to the Principles and Parameters approach, and Radford (2004) for an introduction to Minimalism.

An important concept in Generative Grammar that is central to this chapter is **(un)grammaticality**. (Un)Grammaticality refers to the well-formedness of a sentence, that is whether a sentence is constructed according to the grammatical rules of a language. An English sentence that follows the grammatical rules of English is categorized as **grammatical**, whereas a sentence that violates the grammatical rules is categorized as **ungrammatical**. For example, the sentences in (1) are well-formed; they follow the grammatical rules of English and are thus grammatical. By contrast, the sentences in (2) are ill-formed; they are not constructed according to the grammatical rules of English and are thus ungrammatical. In linguistics, an asterisk (*) is used to indicate that a sentence is ungrammatical.

(1)   a.   *Elena bought milk.*
       b.   *The children sleep quietly in their beds.*
       c.   *Do the children sleep quietly in their beds?*
(2)   a.   **Elena bought. / *Bought milk.*
       b.   **The children sleeps quietly in their beds.*
       c.   **Sleep the children quietly in their beds?*

(1a) and (2a) concern rules of argument structure. The verb *buy* is transitive and requires two arguments: a subject (*Elena*) and an object (*milk*). Violating this grammatical rule makes the sentence ungrammatical. (1b) and (2b) illustrate rules of subject-verb agreement. A 3rd person plural subject (*the children*) needs to agree with the verb in number, in this case plural (*sleep*). Incorrect subject-verb agreement, as illustrated by the 3rd person singular *-s* (*sleeps*) in (2b), makes the sentence ungrammatical. (1c) and (2c) illustrate rules of question formation in English. *Yes-/No*-questions are formed with *do*-support. Violating this grammatical rule, for example by trying to form a *yes-/no*-question by fronting the finite verb (which is common in the other Germanic languages), as in (2c), makes the sentence ungrammatical.

(Un)Grammaticality relates to and needs to be contrasted against another important concept in Generative Grammar, **(un)acceptability**. Whereas (un)grammaticality concerns whether a sentence is formed according to the grammar of a particular language, as formulated by linguists, (un)acceptability concerns native speakers' intuitions about a sentence, that is what the speakers find appropriate. As acceptability generally follows from grammaticality, (un)acceptability and (un)grammaticality often, but not always, coincide. The sentences in (1) above are both grammatical and accepted by native speakers of English, whereas the sentences in (2) are both ungrammatical and not accepted by native speakers. However, a sentence can be grammatical but still not be accepted by native speakers. A classic example is shown in (3), taken from Chomsky (1957, p. 17). The sentence is syntactically well-formed but semantically ill-formed. Ideas cannot be green and colorless at the same time, and they cannot sleep. Also, one cannot sleep furiously. Native speakers may thus not accept the sentence due to its strange meaning. Syntactically, however, the sentence is well-formed.

(3)   *Colorless green ideas sleep furiously.*

A sentence can also be ungrammatical and still be accepted by native speakers. For example, sentences involving preposition copying (4) violate the rules of preposition fronting and stranding, but tend to be accepted by native speakers (Radford, Felser, & Boxell, 2012). The grammatical rules of English require that a preposition is either fronted (5a) or stranded (5b), but not both (4).

(4)   *Game developers have created a world **in** which people truly want to lose themselves **in**.*

(5)   a.   *Game developers have created a world **in** which people truly want to lose themselves.*

b.   *Game developers have created a world which people truly want to lose themselves **in**.*

As this chapter does not deal with linguistic theory but with language teaching and learning, it is not necessary to draw a distinct line between (un)grammaticality and (un)acceptability. In this chapter, the term **(un)grammaticality** includes whether native speakers of a language consider sentences to be possible or not. In other words, grammatical refers to sentences that native speakers of English consider to be well-formed and accept, whereas ungrammatical refers to sentences that native speakers consider to be ill-formed and do not accept.

A final aspect that needs to be considered is that (un)grammaticality can be seen as either a dichotomous or gradient phenomenon. The examples in (1)-(5) have been categorized as either grammatical or ungrammatical (*), reflecting a dichotomous view on (un)grammaticality. However, linguists often distinguish between different degrees of (un)grammaticality, such as grammatical, marginally grammatical and ungrammatical. This is also reflected in the different annotations commonly used by linguists, such as *, **, ? and ??. For example, the sentence in (6a) is grammatical, and the sentence in (6b) is ungrammatical. By contrast, it is more difficult to categorize the sentence in (6c) as either grammatical or ungrammatical. Such sentences are often given the annotation ?.

(6)   a.   *Not to be invited is sad.*

b.   **To get not arrested under such circumstances is a miracle.*

c.   *?To be not invited is sad.*

This chapter covers (un)grammaticality in an educational setting, which means that linguistic examples can be chosen to illustrate either dichotomous grammaticality or gradient grammaticality depending on the educational purposes.

LANGUAGE COMPETENCE AND LANGUAGE PERFORMANCE

Generative grammar distinguishes between a speaker's implicit knowledge of their native language(s) and their actual use of this language knowledge in real situations. The term **competence** is used to refer to the speaker's implicit language knowledge, whereas **performance** is used to refer to the speaker's language use. A speaker's use of a language never directly reflects their full implicit knowledge of the language. Factors such as memory limitations, distractions and shifts in attention impact on language performance. Hence, a speaker's knowledge of language is larger than what s/he normally displays in the use of language in real situations. For example, stressful situations, such as talking to a huge crowd of people for the first time, may influence how language is used in several ways. Although a speaker has the language competence to express their thoughts in a particular way, stress may restrain the speaker from accessing and using their full language competence as planned, which may result in an unsatisfactory use of language.

In contrast to traditional grammar with its aim to develop a taxonomy and describe the grammar of a specific language by categorizing words, phrases, sentences etc., generative grammar is a theory that aims to explain the implicit grammatical knowledge that is shared by all native speakers of a language. This grammatical knowledge allows native speakers of a language to judge the (un)grammaticality of sentences with great consistency. A speakers' implicit grammatical knowledge is also referred to as the **internal grammar** of the speaker. A traditional grammar usually takes the form of a grammar book summarizing the grammar of a particular language. An internal grammar is a cognitive ability stored in people's minds, encompassing the syntactic rules of a particular language.

As the focus of this chapter is on knowing grammar (competence) rather than using grammar in authentic communicative situations (performance), it is important to point out that the authors acknowledge the need to consider both language knowledge and use in the teaching and learning of second and foreign languages. However, in order to use language, learners need to develop language knowledge that allows correct, diverse and advanced language use in real situations.

The Acquisition of an Internal Grammar

The internal grammar of a native language is acquired during the first few years of childhood. The acquisition of an internal grammar in childhood is also referred to as first language acquisition (L1 acquisition). It is important to note that a child may acquire several languages as their first languages, in which case the child acquires an internal grammar for each of these languages, and at times they may influence grammar judgments between or across these languages. It is important to remember that although we are talking about the grammar of English, and most English as a foreign or second language courses talk about THE grammar of English, it is actually more correct to speak about the grammars of English. Every child acquires their own grammar of English, although the grammars may be similar. However, there may be some variation, which may be reflected in for example dialectic variation in the production or in more fine-detailed differences in intuition about what is grammatically correct. Sometimes speakers may agree that several structures are grammatically correct but that one is preferred in a particular situation. It is often this preferred grammar that is presented in courses teaching English as a foreign or second language, when acceptance of grammars may be more useful to the learner.

Interestingly, although the acquisition of grammar in childhood follows a similar path irrespective of language (Guasti, 2002, p. 4), the speed with which syntactic rules are acquired may vary between children. It is thus impossible to establish an exact age at which children have acquired an adult-like mature grammar of the language(s) to which they are exposed. However, children have typically acquired the bulk of syntactic rules at 3–4 years of age, such as inflectional morphology (tense, agreement, aspect, case), verb placement and relative clause structure, whereas some less frequently used rules such as certain passive constructions and control constructions are acquired during the next few years following this age (Guasti, 2002; Lust, 2006; O'Grady, 2005). Some syntactic rules dependent on lexical acquisition such as causative and dative alternations, and some rules governing scrambling of objects may not be in place until 8–12 years old (Gropen, Pinker, Hollander, Goldberg, & Wilson, 1989; Pinker, 1989; Unsworth, 2007).

The acquisition of an internal grammar in childhood proceeds automatically and effortlessly when children are exposed to language input through participation in social interactions (Hoff, 2006; Vygotsky, 1986; Waldmann & Sullivan, 2019). Within acquisition research there is a debate concerning what type of evidence in the input children rely on when acquiring the syntactic rules of a language—positive or negative evidence. Positive evidence informs children about what is possible in the language that they are exposed to, i.e. which sentences are grammatically correct and which interpretations are licit. Negative evidence, on the other hand, informs children about what is not possible, i.e. which sentences are ill-formed and which interpretations are illicit. According to generative grammar, children acquire grammar by relying on positive evidence in the input (Marcus, 1993; see also Snyder & Lillo-Martin, 2011). Positive evidence is abundantly available to children—auditively in spoken language and visually in sign language—through their participation in social interactions with adults and other children. By contrast, children are rarely exposed to negative evidence (Morgan & Travis, 1989), and when negative evidence is provided to children, it usually does not focus on the syntactic aspects of an utterance but rather on the semantic content. Experimental research also shows that negative evidence does not effectively lead to changes in children's grammatical knowledge, whereas even very limited exposure to positive evidence does (Kim, O'Grady, Deen, & Kim, 2017). In other words, negative evidence does not seem to assist children in acquiring internal grammars.

Although abundantly available, positive evidence is limited in the sense that children are exposed to a limited amount of utterances while the resulting internal grammar allows them to produce and understand an infinite number of utterances that they have never heard before. Thus, children internalize a grammar that is more comprehensive than their language experiences. Further, in some aspects, children's language experiences cannot explain the full grammatical knowledge that children acquire, i.e. some syntactic aspects of language cannot be acquired solely on the basis of language input. An example that illustrates this concerns the syntactic rules underlying binding of reflexives and pronouns, illustrated in the following sentences:

(7)   a. *Lisa wondered why Elena praised herself.*   (herself = Elena)
       b. *Lisa wondered why Elena praised her.*   (her = Lisa)

Children can acquire syntactic rules stating that reflexives (*herself*) can be bound by a local antecedent (*Elena*), as in (7a), and that pronouns (*her*) can be bound by a nonlocal antecedent (*Lisa*), as in (7b), as they will get exposed to utterances showing that reflexives are locally bound and pronouns nonlocally bound. In (7), a local antecedent is an antecedent occurring in the same clause as the reflexive/pronoun, whereas a nonlocal antecedent is an antecedent occurring outside the same clause. It is, however, not clear how children can acquire syntactic rules specifying that reflexives cannot be nonlocally bound, i.e. *herself* in (7a) cannot refer to *Lisa* (herself ≠ Lisa), and that pronouns cannot be locally bound, i.e. *her* in (7b) cannot refer to *Elena* (her ≠ Elena). In the absence of negative evidence, children are never exposed to utterances showing them that nonlocally bound reflexives and locally bound pronouns are ungrammatical. Yet, from at least age 3, children know that reflexives must be bound by a local antecedent and that pronouns, unlike reflexives, can be bound by a nonlocal antecedent (Guasti, 2002, p. 290).

Despite the abovementioned limitations of positive evidence and the absence of negative evidence in the input, children acquire internal grammars that allow them to identify what sentences are (un)grammatical and what interpretations are (il)licit. Further, although the quantity and quality of the language input may vary greatly between children (Hoff, 2006), children exposed to the same language acquire more or less similar internal grammars of that language (Pullum & Scholz, 2002). Such insights have led generative grammarians to assume that all children must be born with a cognitive predisposition to internalize a grammar of one or more languages in childhood. One central aspect of this predisposition is Universal Grammar (UG), a set of constraints defining what constitutes a possible human language. For example, grammatical categories such as nouns, verbs and adjectives as well as grammatical operations such as the embedding of sentences seem to be universal to all human languages. In generative grammar, it is assumed that such grammatical categories and operations are inborn and provided by UG. This means that children do not have to learn these categories and operations based on language input. As it is not the purpose of this chapter to elaborate on the specific characteristics of UG, it suffices to conclude that UG guides children through the acquisition process by providing a grammatical tool kit that compensates for the limitations in the language input and bridges the gap between children's language experiences and their full grammatical competence.

GRAMMATICALITY JUDGMENTS IN NATIVE SPEAKERS

When acquiring an internal grammar in childhood, speakers achieve a native-like language proficiency. The internal grammar allows speakers not only to produce and understand novel grammatically correct utterances in a language, but also to reliably and with great consensus recognize if an utterance is grammatically correct or if a particular interpretation of an utterance is licit. In other words, speakers with a native-like proficiency in a language have a strong intuition about the grammaticality of utterances in that language. For example, native speakers of English can recognize that the sentence in (8a) is grammatically correct, whereas the sentence in (8b) is ungrammatical:

(8) a. *Who do you think that Lisa praised?*
     b. **Who do you wonder if Lisa praised?*

In both (8a) and (8b), *who* is the object of the embedded verb *praised* (i.e. *who Lisa praised*). Yet, the grammar of English allows *who* to be extracted out of the embedded clause and topicalized (that is, placed at the front of the sentence) in (8a) but not in (8b). This means that native speakers of English have internalized syntactic rules that can generate the sentence in (8a) but not the sentence in (8b).

Native speakers of English also recognize that the complementizer (i.e. the subordinating conjunction) *that* is optional in (8a) and can be omitted without affecting the grammaticality of the sentence, as shown in (9a). By contrast, speakers also recognize that the complementizer must be omitted in the sentence in (9b), and that not omitting *that* would render the sentence ungrammatical, as shown in (9c):

(9) a. *Who do you think Lisa praised?*
     b. *Who do you think praised Elena?*
     c. **Who do you think that praised Elena?*

As in (8a) above, *who* in (9a) is the object of the embedded verb *praised* (i.e. *who Lisa praised*), whereas in the sentence in (9b) and (9c) *who* is the subject of *praised* (i.e. *who praised Elena*). According to the grammar of English, the complementizer *that* is optional if *who* is the object but has to be omitted if *who* is the subject. This means that native speakers of English have acquired syntactic rules that govern the presence and omission of *that* and that depends on the grammatical category of *who* (subject vs. object). These syntactic rules can generate the sentences with omitted *that* in (9a) and (9b) and the sentence with *that* in (8a), but not the sentence with *that* in (9c).

The internal grammar not only regulates syntactic aspects such as word order and the phonological realization of constituents but also how sentences can be interpreted. The sentences in (10) illustrate how the grammar of English constrains the interpretation of the so-called control constructions:

(10) a.   *John tried to go overseas.*
      b.   *John told Lucy to go overseas.*
      c.   *John promised Lucy to go overseas.*
      d.   *John allowed Lucy to go overseas.*

Each sentence in (10) has two verbs: *tried/told/promised/allowed* and *go*. Whereas the superordinate verbs *tried/told/promised/allowed* have an overt subject (*John*), the subordinate infinitive *go* lacks an overt subject. Although an overt subject is missing, native speakers of English intuitively know who is the understood subject of *go*. The internal grammar determines how the understood subject of *go* should be interpreted. In the sentences in (10), the understood subjects are controlled by the superordinate verbs and must be interpreted as being the same as the subject (subject control) or the object (object control) of the superordinate verbs, i.e. either *John* or *Lucy*. Native speakers of English recognize that the subject *John* is the understood subject in (10a) and (10c) (i.e. *John goes overseas*), whereas the object *Lucy* is the understood subject in (10b) and (10d) (i.e. *Lucy goes overseas*). This means that native speakers of English have acquired syntactic rules for subject and object control including the rules that specify verbs as imposing either subject control (such as *try* and *promise*) or object control (such as *tell* and *allow*). These syntactic rules can only generate the interpretations that *John goes overseas* in (10a) and (10c) and that *Lucy goes overseas* in (10b) and (10d). Native speakers of English would, for example, never interpret (10b) as meaning that *John goes overseas* or (10c) as meaning that *Lucy goes overseas*.

Speakers have strong intuitions about the grammaticality of utterances and acceptability of interpretations in their native language(s). Such intuitions come automatically when acquiring the syntactic rules of language(s) in childhood and are independent of formal studies in linguistics. Despite strong intuitions, speakers may not be able to explain why a particular utterance is grammatical/ungrammatical or why a particular interpretation is licit/illicit, unless they have studied linguistics. The intuitions among native speakers are essentially alike for most grammatical constructions, which means that speakers have internalized similar syntactic rules, although all speakers individually acquired their own internal grammar when they were children. This means that native speakers of English would typically not produce the ungrammatical sentences above (or any other ungrammatical utterances for that matter), access the interpretations that are illicit, nor accept them as correct utterances and interpretations when asked to judge them. In other words, an internal grammar for English only generates the grammatically correct utterances in English.

As generative grammarians are interested in modelling the internal grammars of speakers, grammaticality judgment tasks are a widely used method for exploring speakers' internalized syntactic rules and to test theoretical claims. In a grammaticality judgment task, a speaker is exposed to utterances by listening to and/or reading them. The task of the speaker is to assess if and/or to what extent s/he thinks that the utterances are grammatically correct or the interpretations of the utterances are licit (Tremblay, 2005). In this chapter, it is proposed that teachers use simple but well-designed grammaticality judgment tasks for tapping into their students' grammatical knowledge and use the results for introducing and discussing various syntactic phenomena. In other words, students' grammatical knowledge as reflected through their grammaticality judgments forms the starting-point for the teaching of syntax rules. This proposal is further elaborated in the next part of this chapter.

IMPLICATIONS FOR TEACHING ENGLISH LANGUAGE LEARNERS

Second and Foreign Language Learning

Above, we outlined the basic theoretical concepts of the chapter by focusing on the L1 acquisition of syntactic rules. In this part of the chapter, these theoretical concepts are applied on second and foreign language learning of syntax rules of English. From a generative perspective, second and foreign language learning (henceforth L2/FL learning) differs from L1 acquisition concerning, for example, the nature of the initial state, the learning context, the input and the level of ultimate attainment (Bley-Vroman, 1989, 2009; Schwartz & Sprouse, 1996; Slabakova, 2016; White, 2003).

At the initial state of L1 acquisition, children do not have an internal grammar stored in their minds. The only established knowledge about grammar that children have access to is the inborn knowledge provided by UG. By contrast, at the onset of second and foreign language learning, the learner has already internalized the grammar(s) of their first language(s). Existing grammatical knowledge may influence the learning of a new grammar, maybe especially in the early stages of L2/FL learning (Rutherford, 1983). For example, syntactic rules from the first language may be transferred unintentionally to the second or foreign language. Transfer can facilitate the learning of a new grammar if the transferred syntactic rule is also part of the grammar of the new language (positive transfer), or obstruct language learning if the rule is not part of the grammar of the new language (negative transfer). For example, Swedish-speaking learners of English may transfer the syntactic rule that objects follow infinite verbs (VO-order) from Swedish to English. As both Swedish and English has VO-order, such transfer is positive and can facilitate the learning of the grammar of English as in (11a). An example of negative transfer would be if the Swedish-speaking learners transfer verb-second word order (V2-order) and subject-verb inversion in main clauses from Swedish to English as in (11b), in which case, the finite verb will be incorrectly placed in second position, before the subject, in English non-subject-initial declaratives:

(11) a. *Petra ska **köpa mjölk** imorgon.* => *Petra will **buy milk** tomorrow.*
    b. *Igår **köpte han** mjölk.* => **Yesterday **bought he** milk.*

As subjects need to precede finite verbs in English declarative sentences (SV-order), English can be said to have SVO-order.

Transfer is thus an important characteristic of second and foreign language learning as it may reveal how the syntax of the learners' first languages influences the process of learning a new grammar. As first observed by Lado (1957), in an educational context, information about how the syntax of L1s influences the syntax of L2s/FLs may be valuable to teachers as it provides opportunities to illustrate and clarify specific syntactic aspects of the L2/FL against the L1 backgrounds of the learners. Contrasting the syntax of learners' L1s with the syntax of the L2/FL may facilitate learners' understanding and learning of new syntactic rules.

Whether second and foreign language learners also have access to and can make use of the inborn grammatical knowledge provided by UG is, however, debated (see Cook, 1988; Slabakova, 2016; White, 2003). Suggestions range from having full access to UG (Schwartz & Sprouse, 1996), to having partial access to UG via only those features instantiated in the L1 (Hawkins & Chan, 1997; Tsimpli & Dimitra-kopoulou, 2007), to UG not being available to L2/FL learners at all (Bley-Vroman, 1989, 2009; Clahsen & Muysken, 1986). This remains a topic of debate in the field of second language acquisition but will not be discussed further in this chapter.

The acquisition of a grammar in childhood proceeds automatically and effortlessly solely on the basis of positive evidence in the language input, most often in an informal family or family-like setting. L1 acquisition is so automatic that only the absence of exposure to language input can prevent children from acquiring a first language. Second and foreign language learning of grammar in the classroom, on the other hand, largely depends on formal instruction and access to both positive and negative evidence.

The acquisition of a grammar in childhood results in a native-like language proficiency with only minor, if any, individual differences between speakers. Second and foreign language learners, by contrast, typically do not achieve a native-like proficiency. Also, individual variation in proficiency is vast in L2/FL learning (Dornyei, 2006; Skehan, 1989). Factors such as motivation, attitude and learning styles/strategies influence the success of L2/FL learning but not L1 acquisition. Whereas the language knowledge resulting from L1 acquisition is an internal grammar, it is considered more controversial whether the result of L2/FL learning is an internal grammar (see the collected papers in the 2009 special issue of *Studies in Second Language Acquisition*, 31(2)). As access to UG is considered to be a prerequisite for developing an internal grammar, the answer to this question depends on whether one considers L2/FL learners to have access to UG or not. Nevertheless, for the purposes of this chapter, it suffices to conclude that second and foreign language learning will certainly result in the gradual development of a language capacity that provides L2/FL learners with an intuition about the grammaticality of utterances.

Grammaticality Judgments in Second/Foreign Language Learning

This section introduces and exemplifies specific syntactic phenomena and grammaticality judgment task designs and discusses how different first language backgrounds of L2/FL learners may influence judgments and interpretations. The examples have been chosen to illustrate syntactic phenomena suitable for English language learners at various proficiency levels, from basic word order phenomena in declarative and interrogative sentence formation suitable for beginning learners to more advanced phenomena such as forward/backward anaphora and quantification suitable for very advanced learners. The examples are a small selection and not intended to provide a comprehensive picture of the range of syntactic phenomena and designs for grammaticality judgment tasks. Teachers may, of course, choose other syntactic phenomena and task designs suitable to their own and their students' needs. It is important to remember that the learners' first languages may differ from English regarding the selected syntactic phenomena. When referring to learners' L1 backgrounds, the authors predominantly use the frequent languages in the US according to the U.S. Census Bureau, 2017 American Community Survey on language spoken at home (https://factfinder.census.gov/faces/tableservices/jsf/pages/productview. xhtml?pid=ACS_17_1YR_B16001&prodType=table). The section aims to show that teachers can use second and foreign language learners' diverse intuitions about the grammaticality of English utterances as a resource when teaching syntax rules.

Adult second and foreign language learners often do not have the same intuitions about the syntax of the language as native speakers. Yet, grammaticality judgment tasks are also used in linguistic research to tap into the grammatical knowledge of both second and foreign language learners (Ionin & Zyzik, 2014). Second and foreign language learners of English are expected not to show the same uniform agreement on grammaticality as native speakers but provide more variation in their judgments. In educational contexts, grammaticality judgments of linguistically diverse learners of English can uncover the learners' current knowledge about the syntax of English for teachers and potentially also reveal transfer of syntactic rules from the first languages of the learners to English. By drawing on learners' knowledge about the syntax of both English and their first languages, second and foreign language teachers can get a better understanding of the individual needs of the learners and assist learners to a better understanding of the syntactic rules of the target language. Equally, by drawing on learners' own knowledge about the syntax of both English and their first languages, teachers can get a better understanding of where they need to be conscious about their own non-native grammaticality judgments. This will also assist teachers to identify gaps in linguistic understanding and perception of grammatical variation among the learners, to determine the grammatical rules that need to be taught in a particular learner group and to assist learners to a better understanding of the syntactic rules of English.

Grammaticality judgment tasks can be designed to meet the needs of learners at different proficiency levels. The order in which the examples are presented below illustrates an increased complexity of the syntactic constructions. Beginning learners may need to practice more basic syntactic skills than more advanced learners, which means that grammaticality judgment tasks for beginning learners need to target more basic grammatical rules. To give a simple example illustrating word order phenomena, a teacher can present beginning learners of English with the sentences in (12) asking them to assess if the sentences are grammatically correct and why they are grammatically correct/incorrect. Note that in a grammaticality judgment task, the asterisk indicating ungrammaticality should not be used as it reveals the grammaticality of the sentences to the learners. In the examples below, the asterisk is only used for illustrative purposes.

(12) a.   *Petra bought Elena milk yesterday.*
 b.   *Elena bought Petra milk yesterday.*
 c.   *Yesterday Petra bought Elena milk.*
 d.   **Yesterday bought Petra Elena milk.*

Native speakers of English will most likely agree on the grammaticality of the sentences judging (12a), (12b) and (12c) as grammatical and (12d) as ungrammatical, whereas beginning L2/FL learners may not agree on the grammaticality to the same extent. By emphasizing the different meanings of (12a) and (12b), the rules governing the placement of subjects and objects in relation to the finite verb in English can be illustrated. And by contrasting the grammatical sentence in (12c) with the ungrammatical sentence in (12d), the rules governing topicalization can be illustrated.

So what kind of challenges may the sentences in (12) pose for beginning L2/FL learners with different first language backgrounds? As transfer may occur from learners' first languages to English, particularly in the early stages of L2/FL learning, one aspect that could influence learner judgments is whether their internal L1 grammars encompass the grammatical rules of V2-order and subject-verb inversion. In other words, learners whose L1 grammars include V2-order and subject-verb inversion may judge the sentences in (12) differently than learners whose L1 grammars do not include these syntax rules. For example, learners whose first language requires V2-order and allows subject-verb inversion in declarative sentences (for instance, all Germanic languages except English) may consider the sentences in (12a) and (12b) ambiguous. One interpretation, which is also the interpretation preferred by native speakers of English, is that Elena receives milk from Petra in (12a) and that Petra receives milk from Elena in (12b). In this interpretation, which is in line with the SVO-order in English, *Petra* in (12a) and *Elena* in (12b) are assigned the grammatical role of subject, whereas *Elena* in (12a) and *Petra* in (12b) are assigned the role of indirect object.

The other interpretation, which is not accessible to native speakers of English, is that Elena provides Petra with milk in (12a) and that Petra provides Elena with milk in (12b). In this interpretation, which goes against the SVO-order in English, *Petra* in (12a) and *Elena* in (12b) are assigned the grammatical role of indirect object, whereas *Elena* in (12a) and *Petra* in (12b) are assigned the role of subject. This interpretation depends on access to and negative transfer of the rules of V2-order and inversion between subjects and finite verbs. Learners whose first languages require V2-order and allow subject-verb inversion may also incorrectly reject the sentence in (12c) and accept the sentence in (12d), as topicalization of an adverb in their first languages requires subject-verb inversion to establish V2-order.

By contrast, for learners whose first languages do not encompass rules of V2-order and subject-verb inversion but, like English, typically require SVO-order in declaratives (for instance, Chinese, French, Italian, Portuguese, Russian, Spanish, and Vietnamese), the sentences in (12a) and (12b) may be considered unambiguous with *Petra* in (12a) and *Elena* in (12b) being assigned subject roles and *Elena* in (12a) and *Petra* in (12b) being assigned object roles. These learners may also accept the sentence in (12c) and reject the sentence in (12d), as SVO-order should be preserved also in non-subject initial declaratives in their first languages. For these learners, transfer may be positive.

A second example illustrates how a teacher can use grammaticality judgment tasks to introduce word order differences between declaratives and *wh*-questions to beginning L2/FL learners of English. By letting learners assess the grammaticality of the sentences in (13), a teacher can elaborate on the basic SV-order in declaratives and subject-auxiliary inversion in *wh*-questions:

(13) a. *You will buy milk tomorrow.*
     b. *Tomorrow you will buy milk.*
     c. **When you will buy milk?*
     d. *When will you buy milk?*

A comparison of the sentences in (13a) and (13b) with the sentences in (13c) and (13d) can illustrate that the SV-order (i.e. *you will*) in subject-initial declaratives (13a) should be preserved in non-subject-initial declaratives (13b) but not in non-subject-initial *wh*-questions (13c). The sentence in (13d) illustrates that non-subject-initial *wh*-questions require subject-auxiliary inversion (i.e. *will you*).

As *wh*-questions may have different word orders in the L2/FL learners' first languages, transfer from L1 to L2/FL may result in a diversity of judgments of the sentences in (13c) and (13d). Learners whose first language requires non-subject initial *wh*-questions to have SV-order (for instance, Italian and Portuguese) may accept (13c) and reject (13d), as a result of negative transfer. However, learners whose first languages require non-subject-initial *wh*-questions to have V2-order and subject-verb inversion (i.e. all Germanic languages except English) may benefit from transfer and reject (13c) and accept (13d).

A third example illustrates another important syntactic phenomenon concerning the formation of *wh*-questions, namely the placement of *wh*-words. By letting L2/FL learners assess the grammaticality of the sentences in (14), a teacher can introduce and discuss compulsory fronting of *wh*-words in English:

(14) a. *You will buy milk.*
  b. *?You will buy what?*
  c. *What will you buy?*

A comparison of the sentences in (14) illustrates that it does not suffice to replace the direct object (i.e. *milk* in 14a) with a *wh*-word to form a *wh*-question, as in (14b). The *wh*-word also needs to be fronted (14c). Again, L1 transfer may result in a diversity of judgments, as learners whose first languages require *wh*-words to stay in situ (not fronted), such as Chinese (Cheng, 1991), may incorrectly accept (14b) and reject (14c), whereas learners whose first languages typically require fronting of *wh*-words (for instance, Germanic languages, Italian and Portuguese,) may correctly reject (14b) and accept (14c). For more advanced L2/FL learners, a teacher may also consider introducing how *wh*-questions with the *wh*-word in situ, as in (14b), is used correctly in English.

A fourth example illustrates how a teacher can introduce *do*-insertion in the formation of *wh*-questions by asking learners to assess the grammaticality of the sentences in (15):

(15) a. *He bought milk.*
  b. *Who bought milk?*
  c. **What bought he?*
  d. *What did he buy?*

A comparison of the sentences in (15a) and (15b) illustrates that subject-initial *wh*-questions can be formed by replacing the subject (i.e. *he*) with a *wh*-word (i.e. *who*). The sentence in (15c) illustrates that fronting of the object *wh*-word and subject-verb inversion do not suffice to form grammatically correct non-subject-initial *wh*-questions, as lexical main verbs cannot undergo subject-verb inversion. As non-subject-initial *wh*-questions require subject-auxiliary inversion, and an auxiliary is missing in (15c), the insertion of *do* is needed to allow subject-auxiliary inversion, as in (15d).

As regards potential negative transfer effects, learners whose first languages allow lexical main verbs to undergo subject-verb inversion (for instance, Germanic languages except English) may incorrectly accept (15c) and struggle with the rules of *do*-insertion in (15d). By contrast, the subject-initial *wh*-question in (15b) should be less of a problem, as learners whose first languages require SVO-order and *wh*-words to simply replace a constituent may benefit from positive transfer.

A fifth example illustrates how the grammar of English constrains forward and backward anaphoric interpretations (Kennison, Fernandez, & Bowers, 2009; Trnavac & Taboada, 2016). Forward anaphora refers to constructions where the pronoun linearly follows its antecedent, whereas backward anaphora refers to constructions where the pronoun precedes its antecedent. By presenting learners with the sentences in (16) followed by the questions "Who painted the wall?" and "Who cleaned the windows?", a teacher can introduce structural constraints on anaphoric interpretations of the pronoun *he*:

(16)   a. *Before he painted the wall, John cleaned the windows.*   (he = John)
          b. *Before John painted the wall, he cleaned the windows.*   (he = John)
          c. *He cleaned the windows before John painted the wall.*   (he ≠ John)
          d. *John cleaned the windows before he painted the wall.*   (he = John)

To make the task easier for the learners, pictures or photos can be used to illustrate both licit and illicit interpretations of *he*, for example a picture with *John* painting/cleaning and a picture with a third person painting/cleaning. Native speakers of English would agree that *John* and *he* are the same individuals in (16a), (16b) and (16d), but not in (16c). In (16c), *he* and *John* must be different individuals, with *he* referring to a third person. A comparison of the interpretation of *he* in the sentences where *he* follows *John* (16b and 16d) with the interpretations of *he* in the sentences where *he* precedes *John* (16a and 16c) reveals that anaphoric interpretations are not constrained by the linearity between *he* and *John*, but rather by structural aspects. Forward anaphoric interpretations are licit, independent of whether the pronoun is superordinate (16b) or subordinate (16d) to its antecedent. A backward anaphoric interpretation, on the other hand, is only licit when the pronoun is subordinate to its antecedent (16a). In (16c), a backward anaphoric interpretation is not available as the pronoun *he* occurs in the main clause and *John* in the subordinate clause, which means that *John* cannot be the antecedent of *he*. Thus, *he* must refer to a third person.

Regarding potential transfer effects, the interpretations of learners whose first languages does not behave like English with regards to forward and backward anaphora may differ from native speaker interpretations. While Russian typically allows backward anaphora if the pronoun occurs in an embedded clause, as in (16a), backward anaphora is more restricted in Russian than in English (Kazanina & Phillips, 2010). For example, embedded clauses introduced by *poka, while* in English, do not allow backward anaphora if the subject of the main clause is agentive. Such contextual restriction may be incorrectly transferred to English.

A sixth and final example concerns quantification (Aoun & Li, 1989; Cheng, 1991; Huang, 1982). A teacher can present second and foreign language learners with the sentences in (17) to illustrate how quantified expressions are interpreted in English:

(17) a.   *A grammarian fed every cat.*
      b.   *Every grammarian fed a cat.*

Native speakers of English would agree that the sentences in (17) are ambiguous, and that each sentence can have two different interpretations (Fox, 2000; Ionin, Luchkina, & Stoops, 2014). Sentence (17a) can mean either that there is only one grammarian and that they fed every cat (so-called surface scope reading), or that each cat is fed by a different grammarian (so-called inverse scope reading). Sentence (17b) can mean either that each grammarian fed a different cat (surface scope), or that there is only one cat and that every grammarian fed it (inverse scope). To illustrate these interpretations for learners, it is recommended that a teacher uses pictures depicting both licit and illicit interpretations. To illustrate the licit interpretations of the sentence in (17a), pictures depicting the surface reading (for instance, one grammarian feeding three cats) and the inverse reading (for instance, three grammarians each feeding one cat) can be complemented with pictures depicting illicit readings such as three grammarians feeding a single cat or one grammarian feeding one cat. The same pictures can be used to illustrate the surface (three grammarians each feeding one cat) and the inverse (three grammarians feeding the same one cat) readings of the sentence in (17b). By contrasting the licit and illicit interpretations of the sentences in (17), a teacher can illustrate and explain the constraints on the interpretation of quantified expressions for second and foreign language learners. For example, it can be illustrated that the inverse scope reading of (17a) is the same reading as the surface scope reading of (17b). In other words, in a situation where three grammarians are each feeding one cat, both sentences in (17) can be used to describe the situation.

L1 transfer may result in a diversity of judgments among the learners. For learners whose first languages allow both surface and inverse scope readings, for example, Norwegian and Swedish, transfer may be positive and facilitate the learning of English (Bentzen, Merchant, & Svenonius, 2013; Vinka & Waldmann, 2013). By contrast, learners whose first languages do not allow both readings may incorrectly transfer their scope readings to English. For example, it has been observed that languages such as Chinese, German, Japanese and Korean do not allow inverse scope readings of sentences such as in (17a) (Aoun & Li, 1989; Cheng, 1991; Frey, 1993; Huang, 1982). English language learners with these L1 backgrounds may thus not appreciate the ambiguity of (17a) and interpret it as meaning that one and only one grammarian is feeding three cats.

In sum, this section has provided a selection of examples illustrating how grammaticality judgment tasks can be used to address syntactic phenomena in the teaching of English as a second and foreign language. The examples have been discussed in the light of the diverse L1 backgrounds of learners focusing on potential L1 transfer effects. It can be valuable for teachers to understand that certain grammaticality judgments or interpretations can be logically explained by transfer—positive or negative—from the first languages of the learners. However, it is important to note that identifying and addressing instances of L1 transfer in the teaching of syntax rules does not require the teachers to have in-depth cross-linguistic knowledge about various syntactic phenomena. Teachers can address transfer effects by discussing the judgments and interpretations with the learners in order to understand how the learners' L1 background influences their learning of English. Involving the learners' L1 backgrounds in second and foreign language teaching of English may not only facilitate the adaption of the teaching of English syntax rules to learners' needs but also enhance learners' feelings of inclusion and participation. The next section focuses specifically on how the design of grammaticality judgment tasks can facilitate learners' engagement and participation.

Designing Grammaticality Judgment Tasks for Second and Foreign Language Learners

The way grammaticality judgment tasks are designed and presented to second and foreign language learners is central to such tasks achieving their goal of supporting language learners' understanding of their personal grammars and their teachers' understanding of how far the students have come and where their teaching should be directed for maximal affect. In other words, although grammaticality judgment tasks in language teaching have the potential to support both language teaching and language learning, presentation of grammaticality judgment tasks in a less interesting way can result in no benefits for teachers or learners. From the perspective of the teacher, poorly presented grammaticality judgment tasks will not result in important information about the needs of the learners, nor will they foster learner-centered teaching by taking the students' current knowledge about the language as the starting point for the lesson. Thus, presenting grammaticality judgment tasks in interesting and motivating ways will allow the teacher to access learners' grammatical intuitions to make it easier to customize the content of lessons and meet the needs of the students. The detection of where the learner currently is and variance in intuition have driven the use of computer keystroke logging techniques in the use of writing in the classroom (Lindgren & Sullivan, 2019; Sullivan & Lindgren, 2006). The use of grammaticality judgment tasks, however, affords more precise information about grammatical intuitions of interest to the teacher.

Student needs can be highly varied. That is, in addition to being an important source of information for the teacher, we see some further affordances that follow from using grammaticality judgment tasks in language teaching. A key affordance we suggest is that grammaticality judgment tasks have the potential to be an important source of information when teaching a second or foreign language of the multiplicity of intuitions that exist among the learners in a class. In today's increasingly global world with its migratory flows, variety is expected as students potentially come from very many language backgrounds and may transfer very different intuitions into their new language. It is, however, important to remember that grammaticality judgment tasks can reveal that a student has native-like intuitions for a grammatical feature. In other words, grammaticality judgment tasks can reveal both the strengths and the weaknesses of the learners in a particular class.

So how can grammaticality judgment tasks be designed and presented to maximize their potential in the second and foreign language classroom? Grammaticality judgment tasks can be done by simply presenting sentences on PowerPoint, however, we recommended that teachers consider carefully how tasks are designed and presented to learners for clarity. A key aspect here is student exposure and student motivation to rely on their grammaticality intuitions. We propose the use of an interactive presentation quiz software for conducting the grammaticality judgment tasks. By using a quiz software, the learners use their mobile devices (phones, tablets, laptops) to make the grammaticality judgments. The results are automatically summarized and can be presented graphically on a screen using a video projector. Besides the speed and clarity of the presentation of the results, a quiz software ensures that the results of the grammaticality judgments are anonymous which means that the foreign language learners do not have to expose their lack of linguistic knowledge publicly, not need to be stressed that their performance is being judged. The result directs the teaching rather than deciding which students pass and fail.

By using an interactive presentation quiz software, the methods for eliciting intuitions can be very entertaining, inspiring, and fun for the students, and the potential to increase student motivation is large. Motivated students know their strengths and weaknesses, and grammaticality judgment tasks have the potential to continually reveal both strengths and weaknesses to learners – as grammaticality judgment tasks can be made anonymously online, students will only become aware of their own strengths and weaknesses, not other individuals' strengths and weaknesses. These online quiz environments can be used by teachers to present grammaticality judgment tasks every now and then with "simple sentences" that the teacher knows the students will judge correctly. This would result in positive feedback and foster a climate where the students feel a sense of accomplishment, and boost their confidence in the language and their motivation to continue learning the language. As modern technology and online services are ubiquitous in modern student life, by including modern technology such as mobile devices in the teaching and learning of languages, student motivation may increase together with the feeling of participation. It also allows the student to be active and engaged in their learning process and prevent passiveness in the classroom that would negatively affect student learning.

Grammaticality judgment tasks can also be used to strengthen peer and cooperative learning. Learners can work in groups/pairs to discuss and try out their intuitions. It is likely that students feel safer sharing their intuitions in smaller groups than providing intuitions in front of the whole class. This may be beneficial for quieter students who feel safer and more able to express their ideas and thoughts with a single peer or in a small group of peers. When students collaborate around a structured, scaffolding grammar task, they are able to learn from each other as one student's thoughts are noticed by the others and picked up by the others leading to learning that can be transferred into their (un)grammaticality judgments.

Concluding Remarks

Although our proposal deals with the learners' understanding of syntax rules and not with their actual use of these rules in real situations, it is important to point out that we do not suggest that competence is more important in language teaching and learning than performance. They are equally important. However, in order to use language, learners need to know language. Our proposal is thus a way to facilitate learners' understanding of syntax rules in order to create a foundation for correct, varied, and advanced language use. We thus suggest that our proposal is combined with tasks for practicing the syntax rules under discussion in spontaneous speech in real situations.

We do not suggest that teachers build their grammar teaching solely on grammaticality judgment tasks. Rather, we propose that using grammaticality judgment tasks is an approach for introducing, testing and developing various grammatical aspects, and that it be used as a way of introducing new grammatical aspects in order to more easily illustrate syntactic rules. In sum, they are beneficial both for teachers (easy way to illustrate specific syntax rules in a "fun" manner) and for learners (participation and own knowledge may increase engagement and understanding of syntax).

DISCUSSION QUESTIONS

1. **Basic word order phenomena 1**. The following sentences were presented in (12) above to illustrate some basic word order phenomena in English, namely the placement of subjects, finite verbs and objects, and topicalization. We said that the different meanings of (a) and (b) can be used to illustrate the rules governing the placement of subjects and objects in relation to finite verbs, and that contrasting (c) with (d) can illustrate the rules governing topicalization.
   (18) a.   Petra bought Elena milk yesterday.
        b.   Elena bought Petra milk yesterday.
        c.   Yesterday Petra bought Elena milk.
        d.   *Yesterday bought Petra Elena milk.

Discuss how to explain the placement of subjects, objects and finite verbs, and topicalization in English to second and foreign language learners using the examples in (18) and/or your own examples. Also discuss what you think are the main challenges in explaining these grammatical phenomena to second and foreign language learners of English.

2. **Basic word order phenomena 2**. The following sentences were presented in (13) above to illustrate basic SV-order in declaratives and subject-auxiliary inversion in *wh*-questions. We said that comparing the sentences in (a) and (b) with the sentences in (c) and (d) can illustrate the rules governing SV-order in declaratives and the rules governing subject-auxiliary inversion in *wh*-questions.

(19) a.   You will buy milk tomorrow.
     b.   Tomorrow you will buy milk.
     c.   *When you will buy milk?
     d.   When will you buy milk?

Discuss how to explain SV-order in declaratives and subject-auxiliary inversion in *wh*-questions to second and foreign language learners using the examples in (19) and/or your own examples. Also discuss what you think are the main challenges in explaining these grammatical phenomena to second and foreign language learners of English.

3.   **Binding**. In our discussion about the binding domains of pronouns, we said that pronouns must be bound by a nonlocal antecedent. In example (7b) above, this means that the pronoun must be bound by an antecedent occurring in a different clause. However, this is not always true. Consider the examples in (20). Similar to (7b) above, the pronoun *her* in (20a) cannot be bound by *Elena* (her ≠ Elena). Now consider (20b). Who does *her* in (20b) refer to? What does a nonlocal antecedent mean in (20b)?
     (20) a.   Elena praised her.
          b.   Elena praised her cousin.

4.   **Transfer**. L1 transfer is a common feature in second and foreign language learning and can be a valuable resource for second/foreign language teachers. In our discussion about potential transfer effects in grammaticality judgment tasks, we said nothing specific about how teachers can use transfer as a resource in the teaching of the syntax of English. Discuss how positive and negative L1 transfer, both in grammaticality judgment tasks and more generally in the students' oral and written production, can be used by teachers as a resource in the teaching of the syntax of English.

5.   **Grammaticality**. In our description of (un)grammaticality we mentioned that sentences can be semantically or syntactically well-/ill-formed. Come up with your own examples illustrating each of the following:
     a.   a sentence that is semantically ill-formed and syntactically well-formed
     b.   a sentence that is semantically ill-formed and syntactically ill-formed
     c.   a sentence that is semantically well-formed and syntactically well-formed
     d.   a sentence that is semantically well-formed and syntactically ill-formed

EXERCISES

The following exercises aim to increase teachers' understanding of syntactic phenomena, linguistic variation and grammaticality judgments in second and foreign language teaching. All exercises are structured in the same way: the first step is to design a grammaticality judgment task, the second step is to present the task to learners, and the third step is to reflect upon one's own learning. Readers can choose if they want to proceed with the second step after designing the task.

1. **Basic word order phenomena 1**. The sentences in (12) above illustrate the placement of subjects, finite verbs and objects, and topicalization in English.

Step 1

Using these examples as inspiration, create your own examples and design a grammaticality judgment task targeting the placement of subjects, finite verbs and objects in English. Choose between a simple design involving the sentences presented on a paper, or a more advanced design involving the sentences presented through PowerPoint (or a similar program) or an interactive presentation quiz software. Make sure you familiarize yourself with the different options for design and presentation that the chosen program or software offers before deciding on a particular design and presentation.

Step 2

Present the task to a group of 3–5 native speakers of English who are not linguistics students, for example family or friends. Let them collectively assess and discuss the grammaticality and interpretation of the sentences. If needed, provide guidance questions to make sure the discussion focuses on the word order and interpretation of the sentences.

Present the task to a group of 3–5 second or foreign language learners of English. Let them collectively assess and discuss the grammaticality and interpretation of the sentences. If needed, provide guidance questions.

When the discussion has ended, clarify the grammaticality and interpretation of the sentences. Then let the learners discuss what the corresponding sentences to the experimental sentences are in their respective native languages, focusing specifically on the targeted syntactic phenomena (placement of subjects, finite verbs and objects). If needed, provide guidance questions.

Step 3

Reflect upon what you can learn as a teacher from the discussions of the native speakers and the learners regarding (1) how to teach rules governing the placement of subjects, finite verbs and objects, and (2) how to design grammaticality judgment tasks for educational purposes.

2. **Basic word order phenomena 2**.

Step 1

Create your own sentences for a grammaticality judgment task targeting subject-auxiliary inversion in *wh*-questions. If you chose a simple design in the previous exercise it is recommended that you choose a more advanced design including PowerPoint (or a similar program) or an interactive presentation quiz software for this exercise.

Step 2

Follow the instructions in the previous exercise. Ensure that the discussion is focusing on subject-auxiliary inversion in *wh*-questions. Guidance questions: Do their native languages require SV-order in both subject-initial and non-subject-initial declaratives? Do their native languages require subject-auxiliary inversion in subject-auxiliary inversion in non-subject-initial *wh*-questions?

Step 3

Reflect upon what you can learn as a teacher from the discussions of the native speakers and the learners regarding (1) how to teach rules governing subject-auxiliary inversion in *wh*-questions, and (2) how to design grammaticality judgment tasks for educational purposes.

3.   ***Do*-insertion**. The sentences in (15) above illustrate *do*-insertion in the formation of *wh*-questions.

Step 1

Create your own sentences and design a grammaticality judgment task targeting the rules of *do*-insertion. Use PowerPoint (or a similar program) or an interactive presentation quiz software when designing the tasks.

Step 2

Present the task to a group of second or foreign language learners of English and let them assess and discuss the grammaticality of the sentences. Also let the learners discuss what the corresponding sentences are in their respective native languages. Guidance questions: Do their native languages require fronting of object *wh*-words, or do object *wh*-words stay in situ? If fronting is required, does subject-verb inversion apply? Or does fronting of object *wh*-words require the insertion of an auxiliary verb like *do* in English?

Step 3

Reflect upon what you can learn as a teacher from the discussions regarding (1) how to teach rules governing *do*-insertion in *wh*-questions, and (2) how to design grammaticality judgment tasks for educational purposes.

4.   **Binding**. The following sentences can be used to introduce the binding domains of reflexives and pronouns to second/foreign language learners of English:
(21) a.   Peter said that John scratched himself.
       b.   Peter said that John scratched him.

Step 1

Design a grammaticality judgment task that addresses the binding constraints of the reflexive *himself* and the pronoun *him* in (21). It is recommended that you use an interactive presentation software for this exercise to be able to explore different options for designing tasks and visually presenting the results to learners.

Each task should present one of the sentences followed by the following question: "Who is being scratched?" The design should include pictures or photos that illustrate licit and illicit interpretations of the respective sentences. For example, to illustrate different interpretations of the sentence in (21a), three pictures showing John scratching himself, John scratching Peter and John scratching a third person can be used. The task of the learners is to choose the picture/s that they think correctly answer/s the question "Who is being scratched?" The same pictures can be used to illustrate licit and illicit interpretations of the sentence in (21b).

Step 2

Present the task to a group of second or foreign language learners of English. Let them individually interpret *himself* and *him* by taking the quiz on their mobile devices or laptops.

Present the results of the judgments to the learners and discuss their interpretations in order to better understand underlying mechanism such as L1 transfer. When discussion has ended, clarify the interpretation of the sentences and the binding domains of reflexives and pronouns.

Step 3

Reflect upon what you can learn as a teacher from the discussions regarding (1) how to teach rules governing the binding of reflexives and pronouns, and (2) how to design grammaticality judgment tasks for educational purposes.

5. **Control constructions**. The following sentences can be used to illustrate how the understood subject in control constructions is interpreted:
   (22) a. Elena yearned to mow the grass.
        b. Elena begged Petra to mow the grass.
        c. Elena begged Petra to be allowed to mow the grass.

Step 1

Design a grammaticality judgment task for each of the sentences that addresses subject and object control. It is recommended that you use an interactive presentation software for this exercise. The tasks should include pictures or photos to illustrate licit and illicit interpretations of the respective sentences in (22), for example a picture with Elena mowing the grass, a picture with Petra mowing the grass and a picture with a third person mowing the grass. The task of the learners is to choose the picture/s that they think correctly answer/s the question "Who is going to mow the grass?".

Step 2

Present the task to a group of second or foreign language learners of English. Let them individually interpret the understood subject by taking the quiz on their mobile devices or laptops.

Present the results of the judgments to the learners and discuss their interpretations in order to better understand underlying mechanism such as L1 transfer. Let the learners discuss what the corresponding sentences to (22) are in their respective native languages. Guidance questions: Do their native languages allow control constructions of the type in (22), or do the sentences need to be paraphrased? If control constructions are allowed, how are subject and object control manifested in their native languages? If paraphrasing is needed, how are the sentences in (22) paraphrased in their native languages? When discussion has ended, clarify the interpretation of the sentences and the rules for subject and object control.

Step 3

Reflect upon what you can learn as a teacher from the discussions regarding (1) how to teach rules governing subject and object control, and (2) how to design grammaticality judgment tasks for educational purposes.

REFERENCES

Aoun, J., & Li, Y.-A. (1989). Scope and constituency. *Linguistic Inquiry*, *20*, 141–172.

Bentzen, K., Merchant, J., & Svenonius, P. (2013). Deep properties of surface pronouns: Pronominal predicate anaphors in Norwegian and German. *Journal of Comparative Germanic Linguistics*, *16*(2-3), 97–125. doi:10.100710828-013-9057-z

Bley-Vroman, R. (1989). What is the logical problem of foreign language learning? In S. Gass & J. Schachter (Eds.), *Linguistic perspectives on second language acquisition* (pp. 41–68). Cambridge, UK: Cambridge University Press. doi:10.1017/CBO9781139524544.005

Bley-Vroman, R. (2009). The evolving context of the fundamental difference hypothesis. *Studies in Second Language Acquisition*, *31*(2), 175–198. doi:10.1017/S0272263109090275

Cheng, L. L. S. (1991). *On the typology of wh-questions* (Doctoral dissertation). Massachusetts Institute of Technology, Cambridge, MA.

Chomsky, N. (1957). *Syntactic structures*. The Hague: Mouton.

Chomsky, N. (1965). *Aspects of the theory of syntax*. Cambridge, MA: MIT Press.

Clahsen, H., & Muysken, P. (1986). The availability of universal grammar to adult and child learners—a study of the acquisition of German word order. *Second Language Research*, *2*, 93–119.

Cook, V. (1988). *Chomsky's universal grammar*. Oxford, UK: Blackwell.

Dornyei, Z. (2006). *The Psychology of the language learner: Individual differences in second language acquisition*. Lawrence Erlbaum.

Fox, D. (2000). *Economy and semantic interpretation*. Cambridge, MA: MIT Press.

Frey, W. (1993). *Syntaktische Bedingungen für die semantische Repräsentation: Über Bindung, Implizite Argumente und Skopus*. Berlin: Akademie Verlag.

Gropen, J., Pinker, S., Hollander, M., Goldberg, R., & Wilson, R. (1989). The learnability and acquisition of the dative alternation in English. *Language, 65*(2), 203–257. doi:10.2307/415332

Guasti, M.-T. (2002). *Language acquisition: The growth of grammar*. Cambridge, MA: MIT Press.

Hawkins, R., & Chan, C. Y.-H. (1997). The partial availability of universal grammar in second language acquisition: The 'failed functional features hypothesis'. *Second Language Research, 13*(3), 187–226. doi:10.1191/026765897671476153

Hoff, E. (2006). How social contexts support and shape language development. *Developmental Review, 26*(1), 55–88. doi:10.1016/j.dr.2005.11.002

Huang, C.-T. J. (1982). *Logical relation in Chinese and the theory of grammar* (Doctoral dissertation). Massachusetts Institute of Technology, Cambridge, MA.

Ionin, T., Luchkina, T., & Stoops, A. (2014). Quantifier scope and scrambling in the second language acquisition of Russian. In C.-Y. Chu, C. E. Coughlin, B. Lopez Prego, U. Minai & A. Tremblay (Eds.), *Proceedings of the 5th Conference on Generative Approaches to Language Acquisition North America (GALANA 2012)* (pp. 169–180). Somerville, MA: Cascadilla Proceedings Project.

Ionin, T., & Zyzik, E. (2014). Judgment and interpretation tasks in second language research. *Annual Review of Applied Linguistics, 34*, 37–64. doi:10.1017/S0267190514000026

Kazanina, N., & Phillips, C. (2010). Differential effects of constraints in the processing of Russian cataphora. *Quarterly Journal of Experimental Psychology, 63*(2), 371–400. doi:10.1080/17470210902974120 PMID:19585389

Kennison, S. M., Fernandez, E. C., & Bowers, J. M. (2009). Processing differences for anaphoric and cataphoric pronouns: Implications for theories of discourse processing. *Discourse Processes, 46*(1), 25–45. doi:10.1080/01638530802359145

Kim, C.-E., O'Grady, W., Deen, K., & Kim, K. (2017). Syntactic fast mapping: The Korean extrinsic plural marker. *Language Acquisition, 24*(1), 70–79. doi:10.1080/10489223.2016.1187612

Lado, R. (1957). *Linguistics across cultures: Applied linguistics for language teachers*. University of Michigan Press.

Lindgren, E., & Sullivan, K. P. H. (2019). *Observing writing: Insights from keystroke logging and handwriting*. Leiden, The Netherlands: Brill Publishing. doi:10.1163/9789004392526

Lust, B. (2006). *Child language: Acquisition and growth*. Cambridge, UK: Cambridge University Press. doi:10.1017/CBO9780511803413

Marcus, G. F. (1993). Negative evidence in language acquisition. *Cognition, 46*(1), 53–85. doi:10.1016/0010-0277(93)90022-N PMID:8432090

Morgan, J. L., & Travis, L. L. (1989). Limits on negative information in language input. *Journal of Child Language, 16*(3), 531–552. doi:10.1017/S0305000900010709 PMID:2808572

O'Grady, W. (2005). *How children learn language*. Cambridge, UK: Cambridge University Press. doi:10.1017/CBO9780511791192

Pinker, S. (1989). *Learnability and cognition: The acquisition of argument structure*. Cambridge, MA: MIT Press.

Pullum, G. K., & Scholz, B. C. (2002). Empirical assessment of stimulus poverty arguments. *Linguistic Review, 19*, 9–50.

Radford, A., Felser, C., & Boxell, O. (2012). Preposition copying and pruning in present-day English. *English Language and Linguistics, 16*(3), 403–426. doi:10.1017/S1360674312000172

Rutherford, W. (1983). Language typology and language transfer. In S. M. Gass & L. Selinker (Eds.), *Language transfer in language learning*. Powley, MA: Newbury House.

Schwartz, B. D., & Sprouse, R. A. (1996). L2 cognitive states and the full transfer/full access model. *Second Language Research, 12*(1), 40–72. doi:10.1177/026765839601200103

Skehan, P. (1989). *Individual differences in second-language learning*. London: Edward Arnold.

Slabakova, R. (2016). *Second language acquisition*. Oxford, UK: Oxford University Press.

Snyder, W., & Lillo-Marin, D. (2011). Principles and parameters theory and language acquisition. In P. Colm Hogan (Ed.), *The Cambridge encyclopedia of language sciences* (pp. 670–673). Cambridge, UK: Cambridge University Press.

Sullivan, K. P. H., & Lindgren, E. (2006). *Computer keystroke logging: Methods and applications*. Oxford, UK: Elsevier.

Tremblay, A. (2005). Theoretical and methodological perspectives on the use of grammaticality judgment tasks in linguistic theory. *Second Language Studies, 24*, 129–167.

Trnavac, R., & Taboada, M. (2016). Cataphora, backgrounding and accessibility in discourse. *Journal of Pragmatics, 93*, 68–84. doi:10.1016/j.pragma.2015.12.008

Tsimpli, I. M., & Dimitrakopoulou, M. (2007). The Interpretability Hypothesis: Evidence from *wh*-interrogatives in second language acquisition. *Second Language Research, 23*(2), 215–242. doi:10.1177/0267658307076546

Unsworth, S. (2007). L1 and L2 acquisition between sentence and discourse: Comparing production and comprehension in child Dutch. *Lingua, 117*(11), 1930–1958. doi:10.1016/j.lingua.2006.11.009

Vinka, M., & Waldmann, C. (2013). Doing it in Swedish doesn't mean you've done it. In J. Iyer & L. Kusmer (Eds.), *NELS 44: Proceedings of the Forty-Fourth Annual Meeting of the North East Linguistic Society* (pp. 243–254). University of Massachusetts.

Vygotsky, L. (1986). *Thought and language*. Cambridge, MA: MIT Press.

Waldmann, C., & Sullivan, K. P. H. (2019). How the materiality of mobile video chats shapes emergent language learning practices in early childhood. In T. Cerratto Pargman & I. Jahnke (Eds.), *Emergent practices and material conditions in learning and teaching with technologies* (pp. 217–229). Springer. doi:10.1007/978-3-030-10764-2_13

White, L. (2003). *Second language acquisition and universal grammar*. Cambridge, UK: Cambridge University Press. doi:10.1017/CBO9780511815065

ADDITIONAL READING

Carnie, A. (2013). *Syntax: A generative introduction* (3rd ed.). Chichester, UK: Wiley-Blackwell.

Haegeman, L. (1994). *Introduction to government and binding theory* (2nd ed.). Oxford, UK: Blackwell.

Radford, A. (2004). *Minimalist syntax: Exploring the structure of English*. Cambridge, UK: Cambridge University Press. doi:10.1017/CBO9780511811319

Unit 4
Morpho–Syntax

Chapter 6
Morpho–Syntactic Marking of Inflectional Categories in English

Gulsat Aygen
Northern Illinois University, USA

ABSTRACT

The goal of this chapter is to introduce the connection between morphology and syntax, using inflectional morphemes and functional words that mark specific inflectional categories on the verb. The chapter identifies and discusses four major inflectional categories marked on the verbs, namely, tense, aspect, mood, and voice from a descriptive linguistics approach. This approach provides a much more systematic and simple presentation of how English marks these less-commonly understood and potentially confusing concepts. The chapter first reviews the basic terminology and concepts relevant to the topic and presents a concise survey of both the traditional and the more recent theoretical analyses of English tense, aspect, mood, and voice. Further, it explains and exemplifies the recent analysis of tense, aspect, mood, and voice markers as a demonstration of how they can be taught accurately and in a pedagogically simpler way.

WHAT IS MORPHO-SYNTAX?

Morphemes are not a topic of study for only morphology; they are also a topic of syntax. The subfield of linguistics that studies morphemes as the units of both morphology and syntax is called **morpho-syntax** which is also defined as the study of grammatical categories or linguistic units whose properties are definable by both morphological as well as syntactic criteria (Li, 2009, p. 169). Thus, the term *morpho-syntax* is often used to emphasize the sentence-level along with the word-level functions of morphemes.

As we have seen in previous chapters, morphemes may be **derivational** or **inflectional**. Derivational morphemes make new words when they are attached to other words. They change the meaning and sometimes the part of speech of the word. Inflectional morphemes, on the other hand, add grammatical meaning, such as **number**, **tense**, **aspect**, etc. They cannot change the part of speech of the word they are attached to. They are very important in syntax, the study of the structure of phrases and sentences.

DOI: 10.4018/978-1-5225-8467-4.ch006

We call the part of speech of a given word its **syntactic category**. The syntactic category of a word may be a noun, a pronoun, a verb, an adjective, an adverb, a preposition, or a conjunction. These categories may be easily identified using two linguistic criteria: **inflectional properties** and/or **syntactic properties** (Aygen, 2016, pp.13-14). Inflectional properties refer to the inflectional morphemes that can attach to the word, and syntactic properties refer to the location of the word in the sentence, including what can surround it. Here is an example of how we identify the part of speech, that is, the syntactic category of a word, using linguistic criteria:

What is the part of speech/syntactic category of the word *goat*?

- Inflectional properties: *goat* can be pluralized with the inflectional morpheme {-*s*} or the possessive morpheme {'*s*}, both of which can attach only to nouns: *goats, goat's.*
- Syntactic properties: *goat* can appear after an article which flags a noun: *a goat, the goat.*

Based on the above information, the syntactic category of the word *goat* is a noun. We could have thought about the meaning of the word *goat*, yet relying on meaning may not always give us the correct answer. Meaning is useful but not sufficient and not always reliable to identify the syntactic category of a word. Especially for ELLs with diverse linguistic backgrounds, a given word may not be a familiar one. The part of speech is given before the meaning of a word in the dictionary, and one would end up having to memorize the meaning and the part of speech instead of understanding how a part of speech can be identified in linguistic context. Unlike meaning, the syntactic properties or the inflectional properties, however, are always detectable.

INFLECTIONAL AND SYNTACTIC PROPERTIES OF VERBS

As noted, we can identify the part of speech of any word using inflectional and syntactic properties instead of relying on its meaning. With inflectional and syntactic properties, one can identify the verb and its inflectional markers even if one does not know the meaning of the verb. Meaning can be derived within semantic context whereas inflectional morphemes such as **tense, aspect, voice,** or **mood** can be identified within linguistic context. Because verbs mark inflectional categories, we will focus on identifying verbs in this chapter. Verbs have been traditionally defined as expressions of events, states, processes, or actions, but this definition refers only to the meaning of verbs. Linguistically, verbs can be identified by the inflectional morphemes of tense, aspect, and mood. For instance, in the sentence *She has been dancing for hours, has* is a verb because it marks **present tense** and **perfect aspect**[1], *been* is a verb because it marks both **progressive** and **perfect aspect**, and *dancing* is a verb because it marks **progressive aspect**. All three verbs inflected with **present perfect progressive** mark **indicative mood**, as we will see in this chapter. In terms of syntactic properties, verbs appear after the subject of the sentence and within the predicate.

Grammatically, verbs are categorized as **content verbs, linking verbs,** and **function verbs** also known as **helping** or **auxiliary verbs**. Content verbs are those that express a meaning, such as ***dance*** in the example above. Function verbs do not have a specific meaning: they just carry some grammatical information, such as *has* and *been* above. Linking verbs link the subject to the rest of the sentence, which we call the subject complement. Linking verbs, such as [BE], [SEEM], [LOOK], [TASTE], [APPEAR], have some grammatical and some content meaning. Their meaning might be one of *identity* as is the case with the verb [BE]. In the sentence *She is a professor*, the subject and the subject complement refer to the same entity. We could even imagine an equal sign "=" in place of *is* in the sentence. Linking verbs may also connect the subject with its property, relation or position, as in *The students seem confused*, where *confused* is a temporary property, that is, a quality of *the students*. In the **verb complex**, which consists of all the verbs of a given sentence, there must be at least one verb. This main verb is either the content verb, as in *She dances*, or the linking verb, as in *She is a dancer*. However, there may also be auxiliary verbs accompanying the main verb. For instance, in the sentence *She has been dancing for hours*, *has been dancing* is the verb complex. *Has* and *been* are auxiliary verbs and *dancing* is a content verb. Some inflectional morphemes are marked only on verbs; therefore, their presence helps us identify verbs. Tense, aspect, voice, and mood are such inflectional categories marked on verbs.

Tense, aspect, voice and mood are considered inflectional categories in syntax because a complete clause is defined by the existence of a subject and a verb marked with one or more of these categories. To have a complete sentence, some languages require one, others more than one of these categories to be present in the clause.

The sample exercise below includes all four steps involved in the identification of verbs, verb types, and verb complexes (VCs), using linguistic tools:

(1) *My friend bakes cupcakes every Sunday.*
  (i) Find the verb; (ii) explain how you know that it is a verb; (iii) identify the verbs in the verb complex (VC); (iv) identify the type of the verb(s).

A typical answer would be:

i. *bake* is the verb.
ii. It is a verb because of its inflectional and syntactic properties:
  a. Inflectional properties: it is inflected with the third person singular subject agreement morpheme in the present {-s}; it can be marked with the past tense morpheme {-ed}, *baked*, or it can carry the aspect morpheme {-ing}, *baking*. All these morphemes can attach only to verbs.
  b. Syntactic properties: it can appear after the subject and before the object.
      My friend = subject; *bakes* = verb; *cupcakes* = object
iii. *Bake* is the only verb in the verb complex.
iv. *Bake* is a content verb because it has semantic content, i.e. non-grammatical meaning.

Once English learners are equipped with these linguistic tools to identify verbs in verb complexes, they will be ready to identify morpho-syntactic markers of all inflectional categories in English.

Tense

Tense is the grammaticalization of time, or basically, the reference to the time when an **event** happens, or a **state** holds. *She does yoga* includes an event, *She is a yogi* refers to a state, and both are in the present. The syntactic category that marks tense is the verb. The traditional and commonly adopted understanding of tense categorizes it as **absolute** versus **relative** tense. In the traditional approach, absolute tense refers to the evaluation of the **event time**, which is the chronological time an event occurs, with reference to the **speech time**, which is the time of a given utterance. Any event or state preceding the speech time refers to the **past**, those including the speech time refer to the **present**, and those following the speech time refer to the **future**. Relative tense refers to a time in relation to a contextually determined temporal reference point rather than the speech time. It is a concept developed to distinguish present perfect from the past tense: *She has read Shakespeare. vs. She read Shakespeare.*

Under the traditional approach to tense, Reichenbach's (1947) notions of speech time and event time are used to analyze absolute tense, and reference time is used for relative tense. Reference time, also known as relevance time, can be best understood in a sentence with past perfect: *I had washed the dishes when he came.* The dish-washing event is not determined with respect to the speech time; instead, its reference time is the time he came, that is "his arrival." Such a distinction helps to distinguish between past tense and present perfect (Comrie, 1985). In *She has washed the dishes*, the reference time overlaps with the speech time and it is now. In *She washed the dishes*, the relevance time is in the past, that is before the speech time.

However, this traditional approach to tense presents a complicated and conceptually confusing picture of the inflectional system of English because reference/relevance time is more relevant for aspect rather than tense. It also causes most, or almost all, pedagogical material for teaching English to be misleading. English Language Learners (ELLs) get confused with the terminology and never learn the distinction between tense and aspect. Understanding the difference between tense and aspect makes it much easier to see the simple and mathematically elegant tense and aspect system of English. Furthermore, students who speak languages which have much stronger differentials between tense and aspect than in English, or those whose mother tongues have no tense and utilize aspect instead, such as in Mandarin Chinese, can have a harder time adapting to or understanding this type of conflation of tense and aspect.

In the approach adopted in this chapter, there is no need to distinguish between absolute and reference time because what used to be defined as "contextual temporal reference" is, in fact, the inflectional category of aspect, which will be discussed after tense.

The three types of tense are defined with respect to their distance from the speech/utterance time, which is always the present/now. If an event or state refers to a time <u>before</u> the speech time, it is in the **past** and if an event or state refers to a time <u>after</u> the speech time, it is in the **future**, and if an event or state time <u>includes</u> the speech time, it is in the **present**. It is important to understand that the time span for the present is not restricted to the speech time: it may include the day, the week, the month, the year, the century, even the millennium which includes the speech time, as in *We still do not do anything to protect the environment in this millennium.*

If we assume that time is linear, the following diagram (Aygen, 2016) would mark each tense:

(ET= Event Time; ST=Speech Time):
Past _____**ET**_____ST_____
Present _____**ST/ET**_____
Future _____ST_____**ET**_____

An ELL needs to know where to look in the sentence to identify the tense of the sentence. Tense is morphologically marked on the first verb in the verb complex (VC). If there is only one verb in the VC, then it is marked on that verb:

- *She [swam] in the lake yesterday.*   "swam" = past tense

If there are two or more verbs in the verb complex, then tense is marked on the first one:
- *She [has swum] in the lake many times this summer.*   "has" = present tense

The future tense is marked syntactically by the choice of the modal auxiliary verb *will*:[2]
- *I [will swim] in the lake tomorrow.*   "will" = future tense

The complex auxiliary system [BE going to +verb] marks the future only when [BE] is inflected with the present tense:
- *She [is going to swim] in the lake tomorrow.*

There is nothing redundant in language. Whenever we observe two structures seemingly serving the same purpose, there is, in fact, a difference in how they function. In this case, we use [BE+ going to] if we intend to do something, or if we are sure about what is about to happen, based on evidence or other information. We use *will* when we make a decision on the spot: As an answer to the question *What would you like to drink?*, we tend to say, *I will have a cup of coffee*, unless we have been thinking or dreaming about that cup of coffee for a while!

Because it marks intentionality, [BE going to] indicates a stronger probability of the event to take place. For instance, at job interviews, in an answer to the question regarding his/her contributions to the company, the candidate who uses [BE going to] will impress the interviewer more than the candidate who uses [will] simply because, the use of [will] implies a decision made on impulse, whereas, [BE going to] implies contemplation on the topic in advance.

When the auxiliary verb [BE] in [BE going to] is inflected in the past, it implies a past intention to do something which in fact did not happen:

- *She was going to swim in the lake, but it rained, so she couldn't.*

It is important that English language learners practice enough material to acquire the habit of focusing on the very first verb in a verb complex to identify the tense without getting distracted by markers of other inflectional categories, such as aspect. The exercise below demonstrates the steps necessary to identify the tense of a VC in a sentence:

(2)   *I have never had a chocolate soufflé before.*
    (i)   Find the verb complex (VC); (ii) find the verb that marks tense; (iii) identify the tense marked on the verb.

A typical answer would be:

i.   *Have ... had* is the verb complex. *Never* is not part of it because it is not a verb.
ii.   *Have* is the first verb and marks the tense.
iii. *Have* is marked with the present tense.

Sentences in context, such as a paragraph from an article or a story can be used to practice identifying the tense on the verb in each clause.

Aspect

In a traditional approach, aspect is considered a kind of tense as discussed above. Regardless of the closeness of the concepts in terms of referring to the general idea of time, identification of aspect as a separate inflectional category is a more accurate description of how language works. Therefore, the more recent approach to inflectional categories proposes a clausal structure in which inflectional categories tense, aspect, voice and mood are considered as separate **functional heads** in syntax (Aygen, 2004; Chomsky, 2005; Travis, 1991, among others). A functional head such as tense has a syntactic function and contributes to the clause with a grammatical meaning. A **lexical head**, on the other hand, is the word that determines the syntactic category of a phrase, such as the noun *cat* being the head of the noun phrase *the cat*.

Aspect may be **grammatical** or **lexical**. Aspect defined as "the different ways of viewing the internal temporal consistency of a situation" (Comrie, 1976, p. 3), is lexical aspect. Lexical aspect focuses on the different types of aspect that the meaning of a verb indicates and can be learned by understanding the meaning verbs denote. There are four aspectual classes of lexical aspect: states, activities, accomplishments, and achievements (Vendler, 1967). States, also known as statives, are verbs that refer to unchanging states of being, such as *know* or *contain*. Activities, also known as dynamic verbs, express actions, such as *walk* or *give*. Accomplishments refer to verbs that include the beginning of an activity and a result state: *cooking dinner*. Achievement verbs, on the other hand, describe actions that occur instantly, as in *They spotted the car*. These categories of verbs are distinguished with respect to their grammatical behavior. For instance, stative verbs and achievement verbs cannot occur in the progressive aspect and be marked with {-*ing*} in English because they do not have duration; that is, they occur over a period of time: The sentence **He is being tall* (stative) is ungrammatical[3]. However, verbs of activity and verbs of accomplishment can occur in the progressive aspect marked with{-*ing*}: *She is walking* (activity) / *fixing the car* (accomplishment).

Grammatical aspect is categorized as **perfective** and **imperfective**. Languages may mark perfective and imperfective aspect independently of tense. Perfective aspect corresponds to complete actions, states, and events, and the imperfective to progressive nature of actions or events. "Perfectivity indicates the view of the situation as a single whole, without distinction of the various phases that make up that situation, while the imperfective pays essential attention to the internal structure of the situation" (Comrie, 1976, p.16). Both perfective and imperfective aspects are marked on and/or by verbs.

The lack of any aspect marking on the verb is referred to with the term "simple" before the tense of a sentence, such as **simple present**, **simple past** and **simple future**. The term "simple" basically refers to the absence of aspect marking. These events are single, yet they are not perfective because perfective also entails a "perfection" or "completion" of the event. After all, the term "perfect" comes from Latin *perfectus*, and its passive participle form *perficere* which means "completed."

The concept of grammatical aspect that this chapter focuses on refers to the morpho-syntactic marking of aspect on verbs. In English, morpho-syntactic marking consists of the choice of the auxiliary verb [BE] *vs.* [HAVE] and the form of the verb that follows, with the **present participle**{-*ing*} *vs.* the **past participle** marker {-*ed/en*}.

In brief, grammatical aspect in English is analyzed as a grammatical marker of a completed event or action (**perfect**) and or ongoing event or action (**progressive**). Once we know which tense is marked on the first verb of the verb complex, we can move on to identify the three types of aspect English marks morpho-syntactically: progressive, perfect, and perfect progressive. Some examples of these three types of aspect are as follows:

• *They are dancing now.*	progressive
• *They have danced for two hours.*	perfect
• *They have been dancing for a long time.*	perfect progressive

Progressive Aspect

Progressive aspect refers to ongoing events or states. Note that the event or state might be ongoing in any one of the three tense categories: past, present, or future. We represent progressive aspect on a time line with a bold wavy line. Its location depends on the tense marked on the verb complex. What matters for identification of aspect is that it is ongoing, not when or in which tense it is ongoing. ST refers to the speech time, ET event time, and ET2 to the time of the second event.

Progressive (in the past): _____**ET ET2**_____ST _____

- ∘ *They were dancing at 2 o'clock.*
  - ▪ Speech time = now
  - ▪ *at 2 o'clock* = ET2; ET2 is what intersects with an ongoing event at some point. They were dancing before and after 2 o'clock, but when the speaker saw them, it was 2 pm.
  - ▪ Paraphrase: *At the time you saw them, they were dancing.*

Progressive (in the present): _____**ST/ET**_____

- ∘ *They are dancing.*
  - ▪ Speech time/now = or includes ET
  - ▪ Paraphrase: *Right now, they are dancing.*

Progressive (in the future): _____ST_____ **ET**_____

- ∘ *They will be dancing when you see them.*
  - ▪ Speech time = now
  - ▪ Paraphrase: *At the time you see them in the future, they will be dancing.*

If we take a closer look at the verb complexes of the sentences above, we can identify the grammatical marking of progressive aspect in all tenses: *were dancing* (past), *are dancing* (present), *will be dancing* (future). They all have

- the auxiliary verb [BE], which is marked with any tense, and
- followed by the main verb that ends in the morpheme{*-ing*}.

We can combine these two observations into a simple formula for the morpho-syntactic marking of the progressive aspect in English:

- [BE] *verb+ing*

This formula states that

- the progressive aspect requires the auxiliary verb [BE] followed by the main verb carrying the morpheme {*-ing*}in the verb complex.
- Because tense is marked on the first verb, [BE] will carry the tense as the first verb of the verb complex:
    - [BE] in the past = *was/were*; [BE] in the present = *am/is/are*; [BE] in the future = *will be*.

What tense [BE] carries does not depend on aspect. The progressive aspect in English requires two verbs to be present in the verb complex: the auxiliary verb [BE] and the main verb marked with the progressive morpheme {*-ing*}.

ELLs should focus on identifying the morpho-syntactic markings of progressive aspect separate from tense in sentences. Many other languages mark aspect in different ways, requiring students whose L1s mark in such ways to require additional practice. Understanding what tense is and how it works requires a lot of practice with finding the components of the formula [BE] *verb+ing* in VCs. Breaking down the elements of a VC allows us to identify each separate English verb and its inflectional markers. Following is such an exercise:

(3) *They were playing with the therapy dogs when the doctor walked into the therapy room.*
   (i) Find the verb complex marked with the progressive aspect; (ii) identify the progressive aspect formula.

A typical answer would be:

i. *were playing* is the verb complex that is marked with the progressive aspect.
ii. *were* is the [BE] and *playing* is the *verb+ing* component of the progressive aspect formula.

Perfect Aspect

Perfect aspect refers to events or states that are complete. In a verb complex marked with the perfect aspect, the event or state is completed by a given time, which is known as the reference or relevance time. We can paraphrase the meaning of perfect aspect emphasizing the duration and the result or outcome of that duration rather than the event time or the event itself. The outcome depends on the context but it is always a result of the event that is complete. In the perfect aspect, the completion time of an event or state overlaps with one of the three tenses: past, present, or future. On the time line, we represent perfect aspect with a bold, double line. ET2 represents the time by which the event or state is completed. Speech time is always now.

Perfect (in the past): _____**ET2** ____ST_____

- ○ *They had danced for three hours when you arrived.*
  - ▪ *when you arrived* = ET2
  - ▪ Paraphrase: *By the time you arrived, they had danced for three hours.*

A possible outcome: They were tired when you came.

Perfect (in the present): _____ST/**ET2**_____

- ○ *They have danced for three hours.*
  - ▪ Speech time/now = ET2
  - ▪ Paraphrase: *Until now, they have danced for three hours.*

A possible outcome: They are tired now.

Perfect (in the future): _____ST_____**ET2**_____

- ○ *They will have danced for three hours by the time you arrive.*
  - ▪ *The time you arrive* = ET2
  - ▪ Paraphrase: *You will arrive at a specific time in the future and by then, they will have danced for three hours.*

A possible outcome: They will be tired by then.

If we take a closer look at the VCs of the sentences above, we can identify the grammatical marking of perfect aspect in all tenses: *had danced* (past), *have danced* (present), *will have danced* (future). They all have

- the auxiliary verb [HAVE] which marks any tense
- followed by the main verb that ends in the past participle morpheme{*-ed/en*}.

We can combine these two observations into a simple formula for the morpho-syntactic marking of perfect aspect in English:

- [HAVE] *verb+ed/en.*

This formula states that

- the perfect aspect requires the auxiliary verb [HAVE] followed by the main verb carrying the morpheme {*-ed/en*} in the verb complex.
- Because tense is marked on the first verb, obviously, [HAVE] will carry the tense: The auxiliary verb [HAVE] carries the tense markers as the first verb of the verb complex:
  - ○ [HAVE] in the past = *had*; [HAVE] in the present = *have/has*; [HAVE] in the future = *will have.*

However, what tense [HAVE] carries does not depend on aspect, as we noted above. The perfect aspect in English requires <u>two verbs</u> to be present in the verb complex: [HAVE] and the main verb marked with the past participle morpheme {*-ed/en*}.

Perfect aspect is difficult even for native speakers of English, most of whom cannot tell the difference between past tense and perfect aspect without significant training. The reason for this common native-speaker confusion is that both forms would appear with a content verb marked with {-*ed*}. Therefore, additional practice, such as the one below, focusing on complex sentences with both simple past tense and perfect aspect would be useful.

(4)   *They had played with the therapy dogs until the doctor walked into the therapy room.*
     (i)   Find the verb complex marked with the perfect aspect; (ii) identify the perfect aspect formula in that verb complex.

A typical answer would be:

i.   *had played* is the verb complex that is marked with the perfect aspect.
ii. *had* is the [HAVE] and *played* is the *verb+ed/en* component of the perfect aspect formula.

Perfect Progressive Aspect

The perfect and the progressive aspects can combine to form the perfect progressive aspect in English. The perfect progressive refers to the completion of an event or a state that is, was, or will be in progress at the time of another event, ET2 or point in time. The location of the ET2 with respect to the speech time also marks the tense.

The perfect progressive is represented with a bold curly line that includes the ET2 in the following diagrams:

Perfect Progressive (in the past): _____**ET2**____ST_____

  ◦   *They had been working for three hours when you arrived.*
     ▪   When you arrived = ET2
     ▪   Paraphrase: *When you arrived, they had done three hours of work, and they were still working.*
  A possible outcome: They were tired, yet they still continued working.

Perfect Progressive (in the present): _____**ST/ET2**_____

  ◦   *They have been working for three hours.*
     ▪   Speech time = ET2
     ▪   Paraphrase: *They started working three hours ago, and they are still working now.*
  A possible outcome: They are/must be tired, yet they are still working.

Perfect Progressive (in the future): _____ST_____**ET2**_____

  ◦   *They will have been working for three hours by the time you arrive.*
     ▪   *The time you arrive* = ET2
     ▪   Paraphrase: *You will arrive at a specific time in the future and by then, they will have worked for three hours, and they will still be working.*
  A possible outcome: They will be tired, but they will still continue working.

If we take a closer look at the VCs of the sentences above, we can observe that the grammatical marking of the perfect progressive aspect is the result of the combination of the requirements for perfect and progressive aspects: *had been working* (past), *have been working* (present), *will have been working* (future).

Requirements of the perfect aspect are met:

- the auxiliary verb [HAVE]
- followed by the main verb that ends in the past participle morpheme{*-ed/en*}

The verb inflected with the past participle morpheme{*-ed/en*} here is the verb [BE] as *been*. Requirements of the progressive aspect are met as well:

- the auxiliary verb [BE]
- followed by the main verb that ends in the morpheme{*-ing*} as V+ing.

A handy observation that can be used as a linguistic tool to identify perfect progressive is the following:

- the verb [BE] serves two purposes: satisfies the first requirement of progressive aspect and the second requirement of perfect aspect.

Therefore, if a verb complex is in the perfect progressive, the second verb will always be *been*.

Another useful tool is to remember that the perfect progressive aspect in English requires three verbs in the verb complex:

- [HAVE], which carries the tense,
- *been* which satisfies the two requirements observed above, and
- the main verb +{*-ing*}

We can combine these two observations into a simple formula for the morpho-syntactic marking of perfect progressive aspect in English: [HAVE] *been verb+ing*. This formula states that the perfect progressive aspect requires three verbs in the verb complex: the auxiliary verb [HAVE] followed by *been*, and the main verb carrying the morpheme {*-ing*}.

As the first verb in the verb complex, the auxiliary verb [HAVE] carries the tense markers as the first verb of the verb complex:

- [HAVE] in the past = *had*; [HAVE] in the present = *have/has*; [HAVE] in the future = *will have*.

As noted earlier, the tense that [HAVE] carries is completely independent from aspect. To understand this distinction, it is essential that ELLs practice with the components of the formula [HAVE] *been verb+ing* in VCs. The following is such an exercise:

(5) *They had been playing with the therapy dogs when the doctor walked into the therapy room.*
   (i)   Find the verb complex marked with the perfect progressive aspect; (ii) identify the perfect progressive aspect formula in that verb complex.

A typical answer would be:

i. *had been playing* is the verb complex that is marked with the perfect aspect.
ii. *had* is the [HAVE] and *been* is the *verb+ed/en* component of the perfect aspect formula. *been* is the [BE] and *playing* is the *verb+ing* of the perfect aspect formula.

Tense and Aspect Interaction

The following table (Table 1), adapted from Aygen (2016), demonstrates how tense and aspect interact. The aspect column begins with what we call "simple aspect." "Simple" refers to single or recurrent events. It is not a category of grammatical aspect, but we call it simple to express the lack of any aspect marked morpho-syntactically and to distinguish it from overtly marked aspect forms. Some linguists regard this category part of a "habitual" aspect, but the reality of "habitual aspect" is controversial because the habitual nature of some events is not manifested as a grammatical aspect. In English, it is expressed by one of the two modal auxiliaries, namely, "used to" or "would" but it is not an aspect marked morpho-syntactically as an inflectional morpheme.

Table 1, which is a very useful tool to utilize in in-class exercises, as well as take-home assignments, represents both our naming system for inflectional categories tense and aspect, and the formulae that represent the morpho-syntactic markings of these two categories on the verb complex. In this naming system, we go down the left column that represents aspect and then move horizontally to the three corresponding tense types, and we name the tense and aspect of a given verbal complex. The formulae in the aspect column do not include the tense carried by the first verb in the verb complex.

Table 1. Tense/aspect system of English

Aspect	Past	Present	Future
Simple **[V]** Single or recurrent events	__X__Now___ V+ed *It snowed*	_____X/Now_____ V (s) *It snows*	_____Now____X will V *It will snow* or Am/is/are going to +V *It is going to snow*
Progressive **[BE] V+ing** Continuous event	was/were V+ing *It was snowing*	am/is/are V+ing *It is snowing*	will be V+ing *It will be snowing*
Perfect **[HAVE] V+ed (Past participle)** Completed events	had V+ed *It had snowed*	has/have V+ed *It has snowed*	will have V+ed *It will have snowed*
Perfect Progressive **[HAVE] been V+ing (Present participle)** Events that have taken place until a certain time and still goes on during that time	had been V+ing *It had been snowing*	has/have been V+ing *It has been snowing*	will have been V+ing *It will have been snowing*

(adapted from Aygen, 2016)

A sentence with a single verb in the verb complex would be named simple past, simple present, or simple future. Progressive aspect marked with the auxiliary [BE] and *v+ing* may interact with tense horizontally and be named past progressive, present progressive, and future progressive.

Perfect aspect marked with the auxiliary [HAVE] and *v-ed/en* may interact with tense horizontally and be named past perfect, present perfect, and future perfect. Finally, perfect progressive aspect marked with the auxiliary [HAVE], *been*, and *v+ing* may interact with tense horizontally and be named past perfect progressive, present perfect progressive, and future perfect progressive.

A common confusion caused by the traditional approaches to tense and aspect is due to the use of this naming system without distinguishing aspect from tense. This conflation causes an erroneous understanding of the inflectional system in English. This naming system is not only a tense system; it is a combination of tense <u>and</u> aspect. Therefore, the tense of a given sentence can never be "present perfect!" "Present" is the name of the tense, and "perfect" is the name of the aspect. Additionally, L1s of the students may mark tense and/or aspect differently or even not mark them. Therefore, it would be useful to fully understand the system with exercises such as the following:

(6) *When we ask for advice, we are usually looking for an accomplice.*
  (i)   Find the VCs; (ii) identify the tense and aspect formula in each VC.

  A typical answer would be:

i.   *ask* is the verb complex of the subordinate clause and *are ... looking* is the verb complex of the main clause.
ii. *ask* is not marked for aspect; therefore, it is "simple aspect;" *ask* is the first and only verb to mark tense, and since it has no overt marking, it is in the present tense: simple present.

  are is the [BE] and *looking* is the *verb+ing* of the progressive aspect formula; *are* is marked as the present tense form of [BE]: present progressive.

Voice

The third inflectional concept to be discussed is voice. Voice refers to alternations in a verb's argument structure. **Argument structure** is the information carried within the grammatical meaning of a verb regarding what kind of arguments (i.e. subjects and objects) a verb requires and what semantic roles those arguments play in the sentence. Voice is considered a morpho-syntactic category of the verb, just like tense, and aspect.

Active vs. Passive Voice

English marks two basic types of voice: **active voice** and **passive voice** morpho-syntactically.[4] Typically, active and passive voice are defined based on the semantic roles of the subject of a sentence. The semantic role of nominal arguments functioning as subject or object are determined by the verb of the sentence. The subject of a sentence may play many different roles depending on the verb used. As a grammatical category, voice indicates whether the subject has the semantic role of an **agent**, a doer, or a **patient**, the one that is affected by the action denoted in the verb, a **recipient**, the beneficiary from the action,

140

or an **experiencer,** the one who experiences something. Active voice is observed in sentences where the subject is an agent. For instance, in *The carpenter made a bookcase*, the subject of the sentence, *the carpenter*, is the agent because the carpenter is the one enacting the making of the bookcase. Passive voice is observed when the subject of a clause is the patient, not agent. In *A bookcase was made by the carpenter*, the subject of the sentence, *the bookcase*, is the patient, not the agent/doer of the action. The bookcase did not make itself!

In English, the active versus passive voice distinction is relevant only if the verb is a **transitive** verb, that is, if it has at least one object. Remember that we have an agent subject and a patient object in active sentences and a patient subject in passive sentences. When the verb is transitive, it has both an agent subject and a patient object, and this would constitute an active voice, as in *He ate a banana*. The agent/subject, *he*, enacts the action, *ate*, of the object/patient, *banana*.

If the verb loses its subject, then the logical object which serves the semantic role of patient serves as the subject of the sentence and constitutes the passive voice, as in *A banana was eaten*. The subject/patient, *banana*, does not enact the action because it does not *eat* itself. If the verb is **intransitive**, that is, if it does not have any objects, we do not talk about voice because there is only a subject in the sentence, and the subject of intransitives can be neither an agent nor a patient. They can have the semantic role of experiencer. This is the case with the intransitive verb [SLEEP], for instance. In *The guest slept for six hours*, *the guest* is the subject and the experiencer of the act of sleeping at the same time.

The Morpho-Syntactic Markers of Voice

The semantic roles of arguments of a verb, that is, whether it is an agent, a patient, or an experiencer, may be used to teach voice by pairing them with the syntactic role of those arguments: agentive subject and patient object in active voice, patient subject in passive voice, etc. However, semantic roles are only part of what voice is. Voice is an inflectional category, and as such, it is overtly marked morpho-syntactically on the verb complex of a sentence. Secondly, it is much easier to observe and identify voice on overt markers of the verb rather than relying on only semantic roles.

In a passive voice sentence, the transitive verb is morpho-syntactically marked as a passivized one in the verb complex. The morpho-syntactic markers of the passive voice are very well defined. They are different from the typical tense-aspect markers on non-passive verbs, and non-passive verbs include intransitive verbs, verbs without any objects as well as transitive verbs.

Consider the following passive sentences on the left, and compare them with the ones on the right:

- *The topic is discussed (by the participants).*   →   *The topic is being discussed.*
- *The topic was discussed.*   →   *The topic was being discussed.*
- *The topic has been discussed.*   →   *The topic had been discussed.*
- *The topic will be discussed.*   →   *The topic would be discussed.*

The following observations can be made on the passive verb complexes above:

(i) The passive VC appears to begin with the auxiliary verb [BE] in all passive sentences.
(ii) The auxiliary verb [BE] differs only in terms of which tense and aspect it is marked with: is, was, is/was being, has/had been, will/would be.

(iii) The passive VC appears to end with the past participle form of the main verb in all passive sentences: *discussed.*

These observations are formulized as [BE]$^{tense/aspect}$ *v+ed/en* (Aygen, 2016).

Other Indicators of Passive Voice

Outside the VC, there is another indicator of passive voice: the subject of the passive verb is the logical subject of the active verb. For instance, "the topic" in the sentences above is the object of the active verb *discuss* and the subject of the passive verb [BE] *discussed.*

Furthermore, the logical agent of the sentence appears in a *by*-phrase, if it appears at all.

- *The cake was baked <u>by a famous chef</u>.*

The Auxiliary Verb [BE] and Participles

We have already established that the auxiliary verb [BE] is a marker of progressive aspect when it is followed by a verb in the present participle, *verb+ing*; however, it is a marker of the passive voice when followed by the past participle, *verb+ed/en.*

- *The demonstrators are chanting.*   "are chanting" = present tense, progressive aspect
- *The demonstrators are arrested.*   "are arrested" = present tense, passive voice

It is important to know that not all [BE] + past participle (PP) forms are passive voice constructions because the linking verb [BE] may be followed by a past participle verb functioning as an adjective. That is, past or present participles may become independent words that function as adjectives and follow the linking verb [BE]. Consider the examples below on past participles (in the left column) and present participles (in the right column) functioning as adjectives:

- *The singer is excited.*   *The singer is exciting.*
- *The singer seems excited.*   *The singer seems exciting.*
- *He is tired.*   *He is tiring.*
- *He seems tired.*   *He seems tiring.*

The examples above have either the present or the past participle following the linking verb [BE], and the sentence makes sense either way. Secondly, we can use another linking verb [SEEM] interchangeably with [BE]. Thirdly, the present or past participle express a quality of the subject rather than an action.

A property of passive sentences we have noted above is that they allow *by*-phrases to indicate who the agent/doer of the action is, as in *The beach is destroyed [by the storm].* However, the linking verb [BE]+past participle structures do not allow such *by*-phrases, as in *She is married.* We cannot say **She is married by a priest.* This property of passives will help us distinguish them from the linking verb [BE] + past participle structures.

Based on such independent evidence, we know that such participles are now used as adjectives, and they follow the linking verb [BE]. The passive participles follow the auxiliary verb [BE].

Active voice is the default voice marked with the tense-aspect inflectional morphemes represented in the tense-aspect system earlier in this chapter. If a transitive verb in the verb complex exhibits the tense and aspect morphemes in that system, the sentence is in the active voice.

- *The participants <u>have discussed</u> the topic for a long time.*
  - *Have* is an auxiliary verb that marks the present tense and the perfect aspect
  - *discussed* is a transitive verb with the direct object, *the topic*, and it is marked with the second component of perfect aspect, {*-ed/en*} in the sentence.

At this point, it is useful to review the various kinds and functions of [BE] in English:

1. [BE] is a linking verb when it is the main verb. It can be followed by a subject complement that gives information about the subject. *She is a dancer. She is here.*
    Past participles that are lexicalized as adjectives may be subject complements, as well:
    She is tired.
2. [BE] can be a regular auxiliary verb:
    a. It appears as a component of progressive aspect when followed by a *verb+ing*:
        She is washing the dishes.
    b. It appears as a component of passive voice when followed by a *verb+ed/en*:
        She was questioned by the police.

Distinguishing VCs marked with the passive voice formula would help ELLs learn the structure better because the passive voice structure can easily be seen to be violating typical English patterns, not simply modifying them. Following is a sample exercise:

(7) *"Smoking kills you. If you are killed, you have lost a very important part of your life."* (*Brooke Shields*)
    (i) Identify the verb complexes of each clause; (ii) identify the voice of each sentence; (iii) specify how that voice is marked.

A typical answer would include the three verb complexes:

i.   *kills* is the only verb in the VC of the first sentence; *are killed* is the verb complex of the *if*-clause; *have lost* is the VC of the last clause.
ii. The first sentence is in the active voice. The *if*-clause is in the passive voice, and the last clause is in the active voice.
iii. The first sentence is active because (a) the verb is a transitive verb with the object *you*; (b) the verb is marked with the regular simple present tense.
     The verb in the *if*-clause is passive because: (a) the verb does not have an object; (b) the VC manifests the formula of the passive voice: *are* is the present tense form of [BE], and *killed* is the past participle form *v+ed*.

The third VC *have lost* is in the active voice because: (a) the verb is a transitive verb with the object *a very important part of your life*; (b) the verb complex is marked with a regular tense-aspect: present perfect.

Mood

The fourth inflectional category included in this chapter is mood. Mood is also a complex concept discussed by syntacticians, semanticists, and philosophers. Mood is basically the grammaticalization of the general intent of the speaker. In the syntactic literature, there is a functional head, the content of which is semantically defined as mood. Some researchers proposed a specific **imperative mood head** (Rivero & Terzi, 1995); others proposed the highest functional head, the **Complementizer head** (C), in the sentence (Aygen, 2004), or one of the higher heads as the one that represents the mood of the clause (Rizzi & Cinque, 2016). In these contemporary syntactic approaches, mood is represented by a syntactic functional head in syntax and its own morpho-syntactic markers in morphology. English marks three basic mood categories in English: **indicative**, **imperative**, and **subjunctive**.

Indicative Mood

Indicative mood, also known as declarative mood, is used in statements about facts. A fact is generally described as a statement consistent with reality as we perceive it. Reality, or the actual world, is what we believe to be true about the world. The simple reason we expect to be understood when we communicate with others is that we assume that everyone believes in the same reality or world. Because the indicative mood expresses a fact about reality, it is said to refer to the **realis** (Palmer, 1986, pp. 20-27, 70, 83). Consider the sentence below:

- *I will see you in class next Tuesday.*

The speaker of this sentence assumes that the world will remain as we know it until next Tuesday; the class will not be cancelled next Tuesday; both she or he and his/her audience will be alive to meet, and so on.

English language marks such statements that refer to reality, or the actual world, on the verb complex as indicative mood. This sentence and the vast majority of the sentences in this chapter are in the indicative mood. This generalization excludes a few sentences in the subjunctive and imperative mood in the content of the chapter and the example sentences in the sections on imperative or subjunctive mood. The morpho-syntactic markers of the indicative mood are the tense and aspect markers on the verb complex: *She dances/danced/is dancing*.

The VC of statements in the indicative mood is always morpho-syntactically marked with the tense-aspect inflections described in the section above. For instance, in the sentence *I will see you in class next Tuesday*, the VC *will see* is morpho-syntactically marked with the future tense and simple aspect, a tense-aspect combination from the chart above, as expected from a sentence in the indicative mood.

The rule of the thumb to identify the morpho-syntactic marking of indicative mood is to observe a verbal complex (VC) marked with the tense-aspect system in the chart above. Following is an exercise that combines the tense, aspect, and indicative mood exercises:

(8)   *I have had a perfectly wonderful evening, but this is not it.*
      (i)   Find the VCs; (ii) identify the tense, aspect, and (iii) mood marked in each VC.

A typical answer would be:

i.   *have had* is the VC of the first clause and *is* is the VC of the second clause.
ii.   *have* is the first verb, and it is in the present tense. *Have had* is marked with [HAVE] *verb+ed*; therefore, it is in the "perfect aspect." The tense and aspect of the first clause is present perfect. *Is* is the first and only verb to mark tense, and it is the present tense form of the linking verb [BE]. It is not marked for any aspect. Therefore, it is in the simple form. The tense and aspect of the second clause is simple present.
iii. The mood of both clauses is indicative because their VCs are marked with the typical tense-aspect combinations for English.

Imperative Mood

Imperative mood refers to a request or a command. The word "imperative" comes from Latin *imperare* which means "to command." In fact, in most languages, the word for imperative comes from a word that means "to command" in that language: Greek *prostaktiki* from *prostazo*, "to command"; Turkish *emir kipi*, "command mood"; Hebrew *civuy*, "to command." Following Searle (1975), it is commonly accepted that the imperative is used by the speaker to get the hearer to do something. As observed by Wilson and Sperber (1988), when the speaker gives permission or advice, the speaker may not necessarily be getting the hearer to perform an act, just like an imperative not ensuring the act to be carried. For instance, a parent may say,

●   *You may clean your room tomorrow.*

However, this does not mean that the kid will ever clean her or his room. In any case, regardless of the meaning of the sentence above, not every sentence asking the hearer to perform an act is in the imperative mood: the sentence above is in the indicative mood. This is another example of how the meaning of a structure may mislead us in determining the inflectional category of the sentence. The meaning of the sentence may overlap with or be understood as a kind of order or command, but its mood category cannot be determined based on its meaning.

Another example of such contradiction between the meaning of a sentence and its mood is discussed by Birjulin and Xrakovski (2001) who define imperative sentences as semantically conveying the idea that the speaker informs the hearer that s/he wishes some action (by a certain agent) to be caused by this very information. Not all directives are structured as an imperative, either. For instance,

●   *You are going to do as I say.*

The meaning of the sentence above can be interpreted as an order, but its mood is the indicative, not the imperative!

Instead of getting distracted by meaning, it is safer to look at the morpho-syntactic markers of the imperative mood. The imperative is the simplest type of mood in terms of morpho-syntactic marking because the VC of a sentence in the imperative mood is never marked with the tense-aspect system discussed above[5]. Morphologically, the verb does not appear with any morpheme; it appears in its bare form. Syntactically, sentences in the imperative mood allow only the second person "you" as the subject and that subject is usually omitted from the sentence.

- *(You) help yourself/yourselves.*

The subject is not omitted only if it needs to be focused:

- *You do it, not Sarah!*

As argued in Davies (1986), and von Fintel and Iatridou (2017), compound sentences may have an imperative mood marked on the first VC, and an indicative mood marked on the second VC. Consider the compound sentence below:

- *Get a job, and you won't have to live with your parents ever again.*

The first clause *Get a job* exhibits both properties of an imperative: there is no overt subject, and there is a bare verb as would be expected in imperative mood. The second verb complex [*won't have to live*] exhibits properties of an indicative: it has the future tense marker "will," followed by the modal "have to" and the verb. It has an overt subject "you."

The verb in the imperative mood, unlike the indicative mood, has no tense or aspect marker; it appears in its bare form, and the subject is always the second person "you": *Dance* here! The rule of thumb to distinguish imperative mood from indicative mood is to look for tense or aspect markers on the verb complex. If there is any tense or aspect marker involved in the VC, the sentence is in the indicative; if not, the imperative mood. Following is an example with separate sentences marked as indicative or imperative mood:

(9) *"Do not take life seriously. You will never get out of it alive."* (*Elbert Hubbard*)
  (i) Find the VCs; (ii) identify the mood marked in each verb complex.

A typical answer would be:

i. *do...take* is the VC of the first clause and *will ... get out* is the verb complex of the second clause.
ii. *do...take* has no overt tense/aspect marker; there is an implied subject "you", and the [DO] is used for emphasis to accompany the negative "not"; therefore, it is in the imperative mood.
  will ... get out is marked with the future tense marker "will," and the bare form of the verb "get out" and no aspect marker; therefore, it is marked with the simple future tense. Just like any other tense + aspect combination demonstrated in Table 1, this verb complex marked with simple aspect and future tense is in the indicative mood.

In brief, the two morpho-syntactic markers of the imperative mood are (i) the verb in its bare form with no tense-aspect or subject-verb agreement morphology, and (ii) the subject in the second person, whether it is an overt or an understood subject.

Subjunctive Mood

Subjunctive mood refers to events and states out of the real or actual world, and it is considered an **irrealis** mood. Unlike the indicative mood that expresses facts about reality, the subjunctive mood expresses irrealis meanings that are not facts (Crystal, 1985, pp.79-80). Irrealis meanings include uncertainty, prediction, obligation, or desire. Subjunctive mood expresses wishes, suggestions, and contrary-to-fact conditionals. These sentences express hypothetical events or states that are contrary to the factual world. They are expected to be interpreted in a **possible world,** not the actual world in which facts are interpreted. We assume another world among an infinite number of possible worlds in which what we say is true. In those worlds we express **probability**, **improbability**, and **impossibility**. Consider the following sentence:

- *If he has integrity, he will tell the truth.*

We do not know if he has integrity. We assume a possible world in which he has integrity, and if he has it, then we expect him to tell the truth.

In English, subjunctive mood is used in three different types of structures: **wish-constructions**, **counterfactual conditionals**, and structures with **subjunctive verbs** or **adjectives**.

Wish Constructions

Wishes refer to events and states the speaker wants to be true in the present or the past, and it is actually impossible to make them come true. Therefore, the events or states the speaker wishes for are contrary-to fact ones, that is, improbable or impossible ones. English marks the verb complex of such events and states different way than it would mark real or possible events/states.

Present wishes are marked with the <u>past</u> tense:

- *They wish they were young now so that they could run as they used to.*
  - The temporal adverb *now* signals the present, but the verb *were* is marked with the past tense.
  - Meaning: They are not young, and they cannot run as they used to.

Past wishes are marked with the past tense and perfect aspect:

- *She wished she had asked for help at the beginning of the semester when she failed the first quiz.*
  - The temporal phrase *at the beginning of the semester* signals the past, but the verb complex *had asked* is marked with the past perfect.
  - Meaning: She did not ask for help.

It is not only the tense and tense-aspect combinations that flag a subjunctive mood in wish constructions; the subject-verb agreement loses the singular-plural distinction, and it is neutralized as plural. Neutralized means that it will have one form regardless of the number on the subject, and in this case, that form will always be plural:

- *I wish I were an astronomer.*
  - The first-person pronoun *I* is singular, but the verb *were* is in the plural.
  - Meaning: I am not an astronomer.

Understanding how English marks the unreal nature of wishes takes practice with example sentences. Following is such an exercise with a sentence expressing a wish in the subjunctive mood:

(10) *I wish I had answers to all grammar questions now.*
  (i) Identify the VC of each clause; (ii) identify the mood of the sentence; (iii) specify how that mood is marked; (iv) give the meaning of the sentence.

A typical answer would be:

i. *wish* is the only verb in the VC of the main clause; *had* is the only verb in the VC of the subordinate clause.
ii. The complete sentence is in the subjunctive mood.
iii. *wish* is marked in the present tense; *now* is a temporal adverb that marks the present; however, the verb of the subordinate clause *had* is marked in the past tense. The presence of the verb *wish* in the present tense followed by a verb in the past tense in the subordinate clause is a marker of the subjunctive mood.
iv. I do not have answers to all grammar questions.

Counterfactual Conditionals

Conditionals refer to sentences in which there is a condition stated in an *if*-clause for the *then*-clause to be true. Note that *then* need not appear at the beginning of the consequent clause; its use is optional, and we mark this optionality by putting it within parentheses.

- *"If it is far away, (then) it is news. If it is close at home, (then) it is sociology." (James Reston)*

English conditionals have three structures:

(i) Probable condition
(ii) Improbable condition
(iii) Impossible condition

The first type, **probable condition**, refers to possible events:

- *If we take measures, then we will prevent a financial crisis.*
  - In this sentence, if the *if*-clause happens to be true, then the *then*-clause becomes true as well. Because it is still possible for us to take measures, and it is possible to prevent a crisis. This condition is still in the indicative mood, not in the subjunctive mood because it is still possible to prevent the crisis. Probable condition is also called **non-counterfactual** because it is <u>not</u> contrary-to-fact, and there is a possibility for the event *prevent a financial crisis* to be a fact.

In the probable condition, the *if*-clause is always in the present tense, and the *then*-clause is in the future tense. The probable condition may also have modals instead of the future *will*, as in *If we do not want a financial crisis, then we must take measures.*

If we have present tense in both the *if*-clause and the *then*-clause, whenever the event in the *if*-clause happens, the event in the *then*-clause also happens. This type of a probable condition is referred to as **zero conditional**[6]. Zero conditional is usually used for scientific facts as in, *Ice becomes liquid if you heat it.*

The second type of English conditionals, **improbable condition**, refers to improbable events or states:

- *If I were rich, (then) I would help the poor.*
  - Meaning: I am not rich; therefore, I cannot help the poor.

In improbable conditions, the subjunctive is marked with the following:

(i)   The verb in the *if*-clause is marked in the <u>past tense</u> and when the verb is [BE] <u>the subject-verb agreement is neutralized</u> as the plural, just like the present *wish*-constructions discussed above.

(ii) The verb complex in the *then*-clause is marked with a modal implying the past and a bare verb: <u>would/could/should + Verb.</u>

The third type, **impossible condition**, refers to impossible events or states, and is in the subjunctive mood:

- *If they had rejected the project, (then) they would not have invited us to a meeting.*
  - What the impossible condition above states is that they did not reject the project and they invited us to a meeting.

In impossible conditions, the subjunctive is marked with the following:

(i)   The verb in the *if*-clause is marked in the <u>past tense and perfect aspect.</u>

(ii) The verb complex in the *then*-clause is marked with a modal implying the <u>past</u> and a verb in the <u>perfect aspect</u>: *would/could/should have +verb+ed/en*

Mixed conditionals are a subset of the impossible conditions. Mixed conditionals refer to present result of a past condition:

- *If you had called her earlier, (then) she would not be angry with you now.*

In mixed conditionals, the verb complexes are marked as follows:

(i)   The verb in the *if*-clause is marked in the <u>past tense and perfect aspect.</u>
(ii) The verb complex in the *then*-clause is marked with a present conditional such as *would/could* + Verb

In brief, the second and third types of conditionals, namely, the improbable conditions and the impossible conditions including mixed conditionals, are **contrary-to fact conditionals**. They are also called **counterfactuals** because they can no longer be true, and they belong to the subjunctive mood[7].

The following exercise illustrates how counterfactual conditionals are marked as subjunctive mood:

(11) *"If she were right, (then) I would agree with her."* (*Robin Williams*)
    (i)   Identify the VCs of each clause; (ii) identify the type of the conditional and the mood of the complete sentence; (iii) specify how that mood is marked; give the meaning of the sentence.

A typical answer would be:

i.   *Were* is the only verb in the verb complex of the *if*-clause; *would agree* is the VC of the main/ *then*-clause.
ii. The conditional is the improbable condition, and the complete sentence is in the subjunctive mood.
iii. *Were* is marked in the past tense; *would agree* is marked with *would +verb*; both of these are properties of the improbable *if-then* sentences. The subject is in the singular, but the verb *were* is marked with the plural; this is a typical marker of the subjunctive mood.
iv. Meaning: She is not right, and I do not agree with her.

Subjunctive Verbs or Adjectives

English has a set of verbs and adjectives that require a subsequent subordinate/complement clause to be in the subjunctive mood[8]. Some of these verbs are [DEMAND], [REQUIRE], [INSIST], and some adjectives are *important, essential, necessary*.

Subjunctive verbs and adjectives do not allow the verb in the subsequent subordinate/embedded clause to be marked with any "tense, aspect, or subject-verb agreement" marking. The lack of any such inflectional marking is how language flags the **unreal** nature of the content.

- *I <u>insist</u> that she <u>be</u> on time.*   Instead of "she is"
- *It is <u>essential</u> that he <u>come</u> home early.*   Instead of "he comes"

In a declarative sentence with a non-subjunctive verb or a non-subjunctive adjective, the verb in the subsequent subordinate/complement clause would have the relevant tense and subject-verb agreement markers:

- *I hope that she is on time.*

But such inflectional markers make the sentence ungrammatical if the verb is subjunctive such as [DESIRE]:

- Incorrect: **I desire that he will be on time.*
- Correct: *I desire that he be on time.*

It is important to learn the subjunctive verbs and adjectives that forbid the presence of any inflectional morphemes on the verb, at least the most commonly used ones such as the verbs *suggest, demand,* and *insist,* or the adjectives *essential, imperative,* and *important.* Although learning these verbs and adjectives by heart is a possible way to remember them, it is better to understand how they differ from other verbs that require a subjunctive subordinate/complement clause. Why they exhibit this property has been discussed by syntacticians with some convincing arguments although we still do not have definitive answer to that question (Aygen, 2004 & 2006). Another attempt at explaining the difference between subjunctive and non-subjunctive verbs is a conceptual one: verbs that select the indicative mood and those that select the subjunctive mood are different.

For instance, [HOPE], an indicative-selector verb is different from [DESIRE], a subjunctive-selecting one. It is possible to hope as long as one still believes there is a chance of satisfaction. In other words, the domain of *hope* is what is known to be possible in the actual world.

On the other hand, [DESIRE] calls for the subjunctive because one desires for states of affairs that are not only unrealized yet but also not likely to be realized. The domain of *desire* is not what is necessarily possible in the actual world. This also explains why there are no tense markers on the subjunctive because subjunctive events do not occur in real time (Stanescu, 2018). Subjunctives always involve the *ought to* component; that is why, they are commonly verbs of commands or verbs of permission, such as [ASK], [ADVISE], [DECIDE], [DECREE], [FORBID], [PROHIBIT], [ORDER], [SUGGEST], and more. Still, attempts to explain the difference through meaning do not always suffice. Morpho-syntactic markers are still the most reliable tools along with other syntactic accounts of the subjunctive in the linguistic literature.

How Subjunctives Are Marked Morpho-Syntactically: A Summary

English marks subjunctives outside of reality, or outside of the actual world, in three ways morpho-syntactically:

(i) by not using the expected tense-aspect system and the subject-verb agreement on the verb complex. Verbs in the subjunctive mood may lack any tense, aspect, or subject-verb agreement marker, regardless of the person or number properties of the subject: *I insist that she be on time.*

(ii)   by using unexpected tense and subject-verb agreement markings, as is the case in wish-constructions: *I wish I were rich now. Now* refers to the present, but the verb is in the past; furthermore, the subject is in the singular, but the verb is marked with the plural.

(iii)   by using a specific tense+aspect morpho-syntactic marking on the verb complex of the *if*-clause and a modal+aspect marking on the verb complex of the consequent clause to mark the contrary-to-fact or impossible nature of the event in two types of conditionals:

    a.   Improbable condition: *If she were sick, then she would not come to class.*
        The speaker is certain that she is not sick because she is in class.

    b.   Impossible condition: *If she had not rejected the proposal, then someone else would have.*
        The speaker is certain that she rejected the proposal and the *if*-clause is false; that is, she did reject the proposal.

The morpho-syntactic marking of subjunctive mood is an area in which ELLs are particularly vulnerable. After a lot of emphasis on the use of tense and aspect markers for all indicative sentences, it is quite challenging to understand that another mood category requires the lack of them. Additionally, the fact that subjunctive verbs and adverbs are not as commonly used does not help, either. Even native speakers of English speaking any dialect of English are confused with the subjunctive unless they go through extensive formal training or unless they are keen readers. The only way one can fully overcome this challenge is by observing the morpho-syntactic marking of the subjunctive mood in clauses with subjunctive verbs or adjectives. Following is a sample exercise:

(12)   *His mother insisted that he have a normal life.*
    (i)   Identify the VC of each clause; (ii) identify the mood of the complete sentence; (iii) specify how that mood is marked.

A typical answer would be:

i.   *insisted* is the only verb in the VC of the main clause; *have* is the only verb of the VC of the subordinate clause.

ii.   The complete sentence is in the subjunctive mood.

iii.   *insist* is a subjunctive verb; *have* is not marked with tense or subject-verbal agreement morphemes. The subject *he* is in the singular, but the verb *have* is not marked for the singular "has"; both *insist* and the lack of subject-verb agreement on *have* are typical markers of the subjunctive mood.

IMPLICATIONS FOR TEACHING ENGLISH LANGUAGE LEARNERS

This section aims to provide future teachers and learners of English with pedagogical material and linguistic tools to teach the morpho-syntactic markers of tense, aspect, mood, and voice in their classes through the use of the analytical thinking skills rooted in scientific inquiry.

Although the distinction of learners and teachers is made to clarify the roles in this chapter, the learning environment in the classroom includes the teacher not as an omnipotent authority figure but as an obviously more experienced and knowledgeable guide who "teaches" in his/her performance as a fellow-learner while participating in the learning process. Therefore, the use of "we" rather than "you" for all tasks, activities, and discussions in class is recommended.

The model teacher all teachers aspire to would be the one who makes teaching a tool for advanced learning, one who would know how to learn from the students and make what s/he learns from the students obvious by talking about it explicitly. Creating an encouraging learning environment is important for teaching in general, but it is a lot more important when teaching culturally and linguistically diverse students. Those fortunate enough to work with students with diverse backgrounds have an opportunity to learn more from their students, allowing the development and refinement of their own linguistic and teaching skills.

When students observe a teacher as a role model who knows how to learn as well as how to teach, and when the teacher makes use of this unique opportunity of having a class full of students with diverse cultural and linguistic backgrounds by acknowledging it as a privilege and learning from them, students are truly empowered. Empowered students perform and participate more enthusiastically and become better learners themselves.

Teaching Morpho-Syntactic Markers of Tense, Aspect, Mood, and Voice

Adopting a descriptive linguistics approach rather than traditional approaches to grammatical issues as discussed above allows us to observe and identify the systematic and simple way English marks inflectional categories such as tense, aspect, voice, and mood. Application of this linguistics approach to the design of the teaching material and the pedagogical techniques used in classrooms aims to help students acquire two sets of skills: analytical/linguistic skills to improve competence and self-monitoring/editing skills to improve performance. These two skills are interdependent. Improving the performance of ELLs depends on their competence on such topics. In this context, performance includes not only actual language production in speech and writing, but also extends to peer- or self-monitoring, and finally peer- or self-editing. Peer- or self-monitoring and peer- or self-editing skills are particularly important because they allow ELLs to continue to learn/teach themselves and to improve their performance beyond the formal education period. Finally, adopting a linguistic approach will prevent any discrimination against any language that ELLs may speak as L1.

Learner Training

Learner Training refers to analytical/linguistic skills training exercises to teach how to learn from language itself at large, and how to identify inflectional properties of verbs or how such properties are marked on the verb(s) for our purposes. Such skills can easily be acquired by mimicking some basic steps of scientific inquiry:

Begin with a *hypothesis*, that is, a proposed explanation made based on limited evidence. It is a starting point for further evidence. At this point, students make use of what they already know or think they know about the topic. For instance, while identifying verbs, the basic meaning of verbs or anything else students know about verbs may serve the purposes of a hypothesis, such as the traditional definition of verbs as words for actions. This approach does not exclude definitions based on meaning, but it limits the use of such definitions to a basic stepping stone.

Step 1. <u>Making observations</u>: observing patterns of where and how such markers appear and function.

Step 2. <u>Making generalizations</u>: deriving rules or formulae to describe where and how they appear and function.

Step 3. <u>Making comparisons</u>: comparing English to other languages in terms of where or how such markers appear or if they appear at all. When necessary, it involves comparing one structure in English with another one in English.

End with a conclusion, that is, a decision reached by reasoning based on evidence. For instance, the conclusions for the analytical skills exercises in this chapter will include the identification of any morpho-syntactic marker or part of speech by observing its **form**, **location**, and **function**, or FLF. Form refers to what additional endings or different forms a word, or for our purposes, a verb may have; Location refers to where that form appears with respect to other words in a sentence; and Function refers to the purpose the verbs serve in the sentence.

In scientific research, it is essential to test the findings to make sure they are reliable. For our purposes, the conclusion or results of all three steps are tested with new sentences.

Making Observations

We recommend sparing the first week of classes and/or a class each week to demonstrate and practice the process of scientific inquiry so that ELLs acquire and enhance the analytical skills to learn from language itself. These learner-training exercises can be used for any topic in designing curricular activities. We can have ELLs practice the process first in small groups, then as a class. The major goal is to make this process a part of the linguistic skills of learners so that they can keep learning and teaching themselves as they produce language verbally or in written work.

Making Generalizations

In this approach, performance is expected to keep improving through this interaction between conscious efforts of increasing competence as well as performance and making the connection between performance and competence conscious. The secondary goal of these learner training exercises is to give the teacher a chance to observe the weaknesses and strengths of the students and make generalizations in order to fine-tune the syllabus and the curriculum accordingly. Such observations and generalizations also contribute to confirming the language proficiency level of the students.

Making Comparisons

The last step of these analytical-skills exercises includes the comparison of English to different languages. Having a class discussion on these differences is important to raise the consciousness of both teachers and learners regarding the rich linguistic variation observed across languages. Teachers learn what strengths or weaknesses to expect from the negative and positive transfer from L1 of their students, and students are empowered in the process and understand the universal nature of language. In time, with cumulative experience in such comparative discussions in class, a teacher would improve his/her own skills in identifying individual students' problems with certain aspects of English.

ELLs should observe and identify morpho-syntactic markers of inflectional categories in actual sentences in context from reputable sources appropriate for their levels. To meet the needs of specific groups of learners, the source can be determined based on the proficiency levels of learners. One such source for intermediate or advanced learners could be articles from *The New Yorker* magazine, among others. Beginner level sources can be original work written for audiences with limited lexicon, such as paragraphs from age-appropriate short stories, such as Edgar Allan Poe's "The Purloined Letter," or Oscar Wilde's "The Happy Prince." For novice teachers, the internet is a source of many original short stories for FL/L2 students. Using high-interest materials to bridge background knowledge and the new material introduced is recommended.

Once the observations, generalizations, and comparisons are made, it becomes easier to identify not only tense, aspect, voice, and mood but also other inflectional categories, and even other linguistic properties. The inquiry process discussed here can be adapted to any grammatical or linguistic topic to be taught to ELLs.

Teaching material to be used at this point should be designed to help student learn:

(i)   what to look for and where to look to find tense, aspect, voice, or mood;
(ii)   how to compare the observations made with the properties of first language(s);
(iii)   how to monitor peers and oneself in language production; and
(iv)   how to edit others' and/or one's own writing.

Sample Learner Training Case Study: Teaching Verbs

We will first apply this approach to teach/learn verbs as a morpho-syntactic category and move on to teaching/learning morpho-syntactic markers of inflectional categories on verbs. Individual sentences instead of paragraphs will be used in this section. It is important to note that example sentences are selected in such a way that they focus on the specific challenges as well as morpho-syntactic dependencies. We will then illustrate how tasks targeting analytical/linguistic and peer- or self-monitoring/editing skills can be designed for in-class activities.

The analytical exercises are not the only possible ways to present the material. Many other techniques including, but not limited to, flowcharts, word games, puzzles, and competitions would also be very useful at all levels. However, analytical/linguistic exercises are unique in that they will help ELLs acquire the skills "to learn from language itself."

While adopting the material in this chapter for beginners and/or K-12 students, it would be helpful to

- Break down everything into smaller steps:
  ○ Earlier in the chapter, we used the steps that refer to types of that category within each inflectional category. With beginners and K-12 students, one could work with each type of tense without aspect, that is simple tenses, in separate steps while introducing subject-verb agreement markers involved with the present tense. Students can first be asked to identify the tense on the first verb, and then be encouraged to observe the fact that changing the subject may affect the form of the verb. Secondly, it would be easier to study form, location, and function in different steps.

- Prioritize the most crucial to less crucial understandings:
  - For instance, it is crucial to understand that tense is marked on the first verb, not necessarily on the last verb, as is commonly assumed, or that {-*ing*} does not represent tense. However, understanding the contexts in which *will*-future vs. *be going to* future is used is not as crucial for this level since the major goal at this level is to produce language for clear communication rather than mastering nuances, which is part of the goal for intermediate and advanced learners.
- Prioritize the more regularly encountered structures in terms of clear communication to the less regularly encountered:
  - For instance, perfect progressive aspect is not encountered as regularly or often as progressive or perfect, or mixed conditionals are not as common as other types of conditionals.

Furthermore, teachers may choose to start somewhere strategic within each inflectional category rather than following the pattern presented early in the chapter. Almost all example sentences in this chapter are affirmative non-interrogative sentences, but teachers may use interrogative or negative sentences, as well.

For all in-class exercises, small group discussions leading to a class discussion is assumed as the basic model. It is essential that teachers give clear instructions on how a small group operates, including how students within the groups elect:

- A note taker to take notes of the discussion in the group
- A time keeper to make sure the tasks are done in a timely manner
- A discussion leader within the group who also presents the group's findings to the class
- A monitor who observes language use and takes note of shortcomings and/or errors to report to the group and the class.

These roles switch among the members of the group with each exercise. Nobody specializes in any role, and everyone plays each role at different times. The teacher walks around the classroom to monitor and help students as they do group discussions.

We can now proceed with the examples of analytic skills exercises that may be adopted as learner-training or content-training exercises in class.

Teaching Verbs

The major component of teaching material consists of sample sentences and proper tasks assigned to small groups of learners. Depending on the level of proficiency of the learners, simple or more complex sentences may be used. The basic instruction consists of activating what the learners already know about verbs by guiding them through the steps of scientific/linguistic inquiry.

At all levels, it is essential to address the specific challenges that adult second and foreign language learners face when they encounter the linguistic properties of English. These challenges often lie in the differences between the linguistic properties of the learners' L1 and the target language, English. Teachers can specifically make use of the comparison step of the examples given below to increase their own understanding of what transfers from other languages will be brought to class. This step will also make learners conscious of what they are transferring from their L1s.

Grammar terms or linguistic terminology may be introduced to intermediate and advanced students. For beginners and K-12 students, it is essential that we not introduce terminology until they acquire said analytical skills, learn what to look for, and where to look to find them. The next section demonstrates how an analytical approach to identify any object of study, language related or not, can help mimic the basic steps of scientific inquiry and raise consciousness of the similarities and differences between English and other languages.

Analytical Skills Exercise for Beginner/K-12 Students

For beginners and K-12 learners, before getting involved with the metalanguage to discuss these topics, the analytical/linguistic approach can be demonstrated in a context outside language. Paintings or pictures that depict, for example, a variety of birds in their natural habitat can be projected on a screen or distributed to the students. Alternatively, there can be small group discussions followed by a class discussion based on everyone's observations in their lives regarding birds.

The task is to learn how to identify birds and come up with a systematic way to identify them, using their forms, locations, and functions. The students are guided through the thinking process to accomplish this task by asking the relevant questions and inviting them to ask such questions to themselves before attempting to work on any task. Such guidance will help them come up with a hypothesis.

1. *What is to be identified?*
    A: *Birds*
    What kind of birds do we know?
    A: *A sparrow, a dove, a hawk, an eagle, a goose, a chicken, a turkey,* etc.
2. *What are some properties of birds that we know of?* (FORM)
    A: The answers will help construct a "hypothesis" such as *animals with wings, feathers, and only two feet are birds.*
    What are wings for? What are beaks for? In other words, what functions do these overt features serve? (FUNCTION)
    A: *Wings to fly, beaks to feed and eat,* etc.
3. *Based on what we know about them, where should we look for them?* (LOCATION)
    A: *On trees, in bushes, on roofs, in backyards, on electric wires, in or near ponds, on farms, fields,* etc.

Now that everyone knows what to look for and where to look for them, they can formulate a hypothesis and can be guided to mimic the steps of scientific inquiry. At this point, there is no need to use the term "hypothesis", and steps 1 & 2 can be combined as a short cut:

What do we already know? (Hypothesis): Animals that have feathers, beaks and two legs and that can fly are birds, and their most common living habitat consists of trees, roofs, forests, etc.

Step 1: Observe: Observe kinds of birds (form).

Results may include the following or more: chickens, turkeys, ducks, geese, hawks, eagles, sparrows, seagulls, etc. Their colors differ but no observation could be made on what determines their color.

Step 2: Generalize: Where do we look to find them?

> Generalize location: Where do birds live? Identify if there are differences in terms of kinds of birds and where they appear. Look for the smaller birds in bushes, backyards, trees, but for larger domesticated ones on farms, wild ones near ponds, or in forests.
>
> Generalize function: What do birds do? Birds fly. Are there any birds that do not fly? Chickens, or other farm birds?

Step 3. Compare: Compare birds in the U.S. to birds in other parts of the world in terms of where or what kind of birds appear or if they appear at all.

Results may include the following or more: There are birds that do not fly in other parts of the world: Ostriches in Australia, penguins in Antarctica, among others.

Conclusion: *How can we identify and classify birds?*

*Birds can be identified and classified based on their **size** (FORM), their **habitat** (LOCATION), and whether they can **fly or not** (FUNCTION).*

The teacher wraps up the discussion summarizing what the students have done using the first- person plural since the teacher participates in the learning process.

*We have asked ourselves the questions **what**, **where**, and **how**. The answers we have given have taught us how to identify __and__ classify birds using certain criteria: **form**, **location**, and **function**. We can apply the same methods to English sentences and identify verbs.*

The teacher can now introduce basic grammatical terms and ask the students to use their analytical skills to analyze verbs linguistically.

Basic Verb Study Activities for Beginner/K-12 Students

The teacher briefly presents the connection between verbs and actions and states by using pictures or by acting some verbs for the students to identify, as in the game Charades.

Students in small groups are assigned multiple tasks. The goal is to use verbs not in isolation but in a linguistic context as commands or in a non-linguistic context as in acting them:

- Each group prepares a list of verbs to be used as commands. Groups take turns in giving the commands to the rest of the class, and all students have to do whatever command is given. Each group takes turns and each verb can be used only once in a class time.
- Charades for verbs: Each group prepares a second list of verbs which they act for the other students in class to identify which word it is with correct spelling and pronunciation. One group performs, the other groups take a few minutes to discuss the answer and the first group that answers correctly wins.

Analytical/Linguistic Skills Activities for Beginner/K-12 Students

The task is to identify verbs in sentences. Students are asked to underline all verbs in given sentences. In this example, we will use only one sentence. Multiple sentences are necessary for the students to observe the patterns.

Guidance questions and tips may include the following: (i) What do you think is the verb based on all that you know about verbs (hypothesis)? (ii) Now, find further evidence that it is really the verb. Where does the evidence come from? From its appearance (form), where it is located (location), and what it does (function). **Form-location-function**, FLF can be used as an acronym.

We looked for birds in the bushes and forests, and we described what they look like. In brief, **appearance** or **form**, **location**, and **function** were the key elements. These key elements can be used in grammar as well. To identify verbs, we can do the same: we describe them to identify their form and we identify their function by observing the differences in their forms, and we look for their location in the following sentence(s):

- *Her cat ate the fish.*

Hypothesis/the proposed explanation: (students will tend to describe verbs based on their meaning): verbs are words for actions or states; simply put, for things that happen. Therefore, *ate* looks like a verb.

Meaning provides a good hypothesis or a proposed explanation. However, it is not sufficient, and we need more evidence to make sure that the words we guess are verbs are indeed verbs. Look for FLF, which can be used to identify any art of speech or any morpheme.

Form, Location, and Function

Teacher gives guiding questions to help students find the verb in the sentence, observe the differences in its form, and determine the location and function:

(i)   What did her cat do? *Eat the fish*. Which word in the answer is the verb? *Eat*. Which word in the original sentence is the verb? *Ate*. How are they different? *Ate* is the past tense form of *eat* (form); therefore, it marks tense (function).

(ii)   Who ate the fish? *Her cat*. *Her cat* must be the subject, the one who did the eating! *Ate* as the verb follows the subject, *her cat*, (location).

In small groups, she students observe patterns and generalize: verbs appear after the subject and they tell us when that event happened or will happen. That is, they seem to have a job in the sentence: verbs mark the time of the event, namely, tense!

Finally, students compare English verbs to verbs in other languages: e.g., Verbs appear between the subject and the object in English. Japanese verbs appear after the object. Chinese Mandarin verbs are like English in that they appear between subjects and objects, but they do not carry tense.

Conclusion: How can we identify verbs? By their location and function as well as their different forms: In English, verbs are parts of speech that are located after the subject, and they are carriers of tense.

At every step of the exercise, small group representatives report to the class, the class agrees on the answers, and then groups move on to the next tasks.

Analytical Skills Activities for Intermediate/Advanced Students

Multiple sentences with either third person singular or other subjects can be given to help the students observe the subject-verb agreement on verbs when the subject is the third person singular in the simple present.

- *She bakes cookies for her kids every Sunday. /I bake cookies for my kids every Sunday.*
- *She baked chocolate chip cookies last Sunday. / I baked chocolate chip cookies last Sunday.*

Task #1: Observe: (i) the form(s) of the verbs, that is, the endings that appear at the end of verbs, (ii) the location of verbs: with respect to what comes before or after them, and (iii) their function.

Answers: (i) *bakes* and *baked*. They may appear with {-s} or {-ed},{-s};

    (ii) *I* and *she* are subjects; verbs follow subjects, there may be more than one verb in the VC;

    (iii) different endings mark time of the event.

Task #2: Generalize: Verbs follow the subject, they may appear with different endings, which mark tense; verbs carry tense.

Task #3: Compare: Where do verbs occur in your native language? Before the object or after the object?

Some examples from different languages and the English literal translation:

English – SVO language - verbs follow the subject and precede the object: *She loves him.*

Japanese – SOV language – verbs follow the subject and the object: *She him loves.*

Arabic – VSO language – verbs precede the subject and the object: *Loves she him.*

Malagasy – VOS language – verbs precede the object and the subject: *Loves him she.*

Conclusion: Words that follow the subject, and function to carry tense with endings such as {-ed} are verbs in English.

At every step of the exercise, small group representatives report to the class, the class agrees on the answers and then groups move on to the next tasks.

Analytical/ Linguistic Skills Activities on the Structure of the Verb Complex in English – Intermediate or Advanced

The same approach can be used to get advanced students to observe the maximum number and types of verbs and their order English allows in a verb complex.

In English, we find the verb after the subject and before the object. We call all the verbs in a sentence a verb complex (VC). There may be more than one verb in VCs, and the kind(s) of verb we find may be different. Observe all possible variations and describe the different types of verbs in VCs. Finally, describe the maximum number of verbs and the order in which they appear in a VC in English.

After additional instructional activities on types of verbs, sentences would be given to the students to work on as small groups. Depending on what the students already know, such sentences may include some or all possible structures. A sentence with a linking verb illustrates that linking verbs can be the main verb in the VC, just like content verbs:

- *My friend is a good baker.*

Another sentence may have an auxiliary verb in addition to a content verb:

- *My friend is baking cupcakes now.*

The following one would have both modal and regular auxiliary verbs in addition to a content verb:

- *My friend must have baked cupcakes.*

A more challenging sentence could be used to illustrate the maximum complexity English allows with two regular auxiliary verbs, one modal auxiliary and one content verb:

- *My friend must have been baking cupcakes.*

Tasks designed mimic the steps in scientific inquiry:

Task #1: Observe the verbs in each VC in each sentence (FLF).
Task #2: Generalize and classify which verbs can appear in VCs and in which order.

Advanced: Describe the maximum complexity English allows in a VC and the order in which they can occur.

Task #3: Compare what is allowed in a VC in other languages you know.

Conclusion: If there is one verb in the VC, it is either a linking verb or a content verb. These are the main verbs. If there are two, one of them is a modal or regular auxiliary verb. If there are three verbs, either two auxiliaries or one modal and one auxiliary verb accompany the content or linking verb.

Sample Analytical/Linguistic Skills Training Case Study: Teaching Tense

The analytical/linguistic skills acquired while working on the English verb can be transferred to any other topic, including tense. Students can be given the task of identifying the tense in the VC of given sentences. For Beginner and K-12 students, a simplified version of the tense - aspect system given earlier can be used to introduce the concepts with plenty of examples, preferably humorous sentences accompanied by cartoons. Furthermore, using [BE] as a linking verb, [DO], and [HAVE] as content verbs, among the examples of simple present/past/future would lay the grounds for introducing [BE], [DO], and [HAVE] as auxiliary verbs later on.

Analytical/Linguistic Skills Activities on Tense for Beginner/K-12

The teacher presents sentences in which content verbs are inflected in present, past, and future with many verbs. It is advisable to include [BE] as a linking verb, [DO] and [HAVE] as main verbs as well as other content verbs to lay the grounds for the future study of the same verbs used as auxiliary verbs in a follow-up exercise. The sentences exhibit a contrast between the third- person singular subject and other subjects to let the students observe the subject-verb agreement properties of English in the present tense.

For the initial exercise:

- *I walk/She walks to school every day.*
- *The journalist talks to the lawyer every day.*
- *SpongeBob lives in a pineapple all his life.*

For follow-up exercises, we include [BE], [DO], [HAVE] and other tenses:

[DO]
I do/She does nothing every day.
I did/ She did nothing yesterday.
I / She will do nothing today.

[HAVE]
I have/She has two cats.
I had/ She had three cats last year.
I/ She will have three cats again next year.

[BE]
I am / You/We/They are in shape now. Round is a shape!
I/He/She/It was / You/They were not in shape last summer.
I/He/She/It/We/You/They will be in better shape in the summer.

The first activity mimics the steps of scientific inquiry, and the students are asked to observe the sentences given by the teacher to generalize how present tense is marked on verbs.

The guiding questions focusing on FLF, that is, form, location, and function will help students construct a hypothesis:

What are the different forms verbs appear in? What part of the verb changes or has additional form (location)? What endings correspond to present tense (function)? Are they sometimes accompanied by other verbs? Does the form of the verb change when we change the subject?

Tasks designed mimic the steps in scientific inquiry:

Task #1: Observe the verbs and their endings in each sentence (FLF).
Task #2: Generalize and classify the different forms of the verb and their functions.
Task #3: Compare the different forms of verbs that mark tense in other languages you know.

Conclusion: The verb marks the present tense with {-*s*} if the subject is the 3rd person singular; some verbs have different forms, etc. Small group representatives present their observations, generalizations and the results are confirmed with a class discussion.

The students are given a cloze test where the verbs of the sentences are deleted. They are instructed to work in small groups to find the correct answers. The correct verbs with their morpho-syntactic markers are given in a list that includes verbs with incorrect tense of the given sentences. The verbs may be scrambled to challenge the students. A simple version is illustrated below:

The scrambled verb list: ckilde, vlies, blcemi, ilwl, vldie ikcl, lsmcib

- *Squidward _____ in an Easter Island head under the sea.*
- *The puppy _____ the turkey a minute ago.*
- *The doctor _____ the stairs tomorrow.*

There are many cloze test generators on the Internet, including those that would scramble the words to be used as hints.

Analytical/Linguistic Skills Activities on Tense for Intermediate/Advanced

For intermediate and advance learners, working on examples including all auxiliary verbs as well as content and linking verbs would be the target.

The teacher introduces the three types of tense and the irregular verbs that change in form with tense. The example sentences include the forms of verbs marking tense not only with content verbs but also with auxiliary verbs. Some sample sentences are given below:

- *I am not lazy; I am waiting for an inspiration.*
- *Your secret is safe with me because I was not listening to you.*
- *Has she recognized you at the party?*
- *We would have described the scene if she had asked us to.*
- *Nobody will have to die of cancer in 2020.*
- *The first writing system seems to have been invented in 4000 BC in the Middle East.*

Tasks for all levels are the same in that they mimic the steps in scientific inquiry. However, the content material differs. The guiding questions that will help students construct a hypothesis are the following:

How do we identify and classify tense? How is tense marked (form)? Where is tense marked (location)? What kinds of tense are there (function)?

Task #1: Observe the changes on the verb marked with tense in each VC in each sentence (FLF).
Task #2: Generalize and classify tense markers.
　　Advanced: Students are given example sentences and asked to describe and discuss the more complex cases: tense difference between *was going to* vs. *is going to*; lack of tense on modals despite the use of *would* as past, etc.
Task #3: Compare the tense markers in other languages you know.

The conclusion would have to include the observation that tense is always marked on the first verb and the first verb only; regardless of how complex the VC might be! Students may be challenged by including modals and expecting them to observe that modals do not mark tense.

Sample Analytical/Linguistic Skills Training Case Study: Teaching Aspect

The major task is identifying the aspect in the verb complex (VC) of given sentences and using the tense-aspect system efficiently and correctly in speech and writing.

Analytical/Linguistic Skills Activities on Aspect for Beginner/K-12

The teacher presents the progressive aspect first and focuses on it by using the tense-aspect system and other visual material introduced earlier. With the use of level-appropriate sentences, such as those below, the continuous nature of events and states is explained.

- *I am dancing/She is dancing/They are dancing now.*
- *I am cooking/Bob is cooking/Bob and Harry are not cooking dinner.*
- *Many people are playing video games right now.*

The significance of looking for *FLF* is reminded since students need to learn where to look for what and determine its function.

The guiding question to help students construct a hypothesis is the following: Does the event or state denoted by the verb continue or not?

Task #1: Observe what verbs appear, what ending is always observed on the content verb, and what other verb appears in VCs in each sentence. What grammatical meaning do the additional verb and the ending you observe on the content verb seem to add? (the progressive aspect)

Task #2: Generalize and classify progressive markers.

Task #3: Compare the progressive aspect markers in other languages you know.

The conclusion will include the generalization that there is always the auxiliary verb [BE] marked with some tense and a content verb marked with {-ing}.

Additionally, visual material depicting continuous actions may be used to elicit answers that use progressive aspect from the students. Small groups may compose short stories telling a series of continuous actions interrupted by the arrival of other characters in the pictures or video clips with no sound.

Analytical/Linguistic Skills Activities on Aspect for Intermediate/Advanced

The teacher reviews the progressive and presents the perfect aspect as well as the perfect progressive aspect, using the tense – aspect system introduced earlier as well as many sentences similar to the following to include another event that interrupts an ongoing/continuous event:

- *Some dancers were performing on the streets when I was in Paris.*
- *My husband was already washing the dishes when I arrived.*
- *My cats were sleeping when I arrived home.*
- *Many have never gone to school, yet they have managed to live fulfilling lives.*
- *We had been sleeping for hours until we heard the turbulence announcement.*

In small groups, the students are asked to observe the sentences above with the following guiding questions that will help the students construct a hypothesis:

Does the event or state continue or is it over? Or has it been going on until a moment in time? Did it stop or did it not stop and was it continuing at that moment as well? What verbs appear in the VC? What changes in the form of the main verb do you observe? What is the function of the ending and the presence of another verb? (form, location, function)

Task #1: Observe all types of aspect in VCs in each sentence: continuing and complete actions and states.
Task #2: Generalize and classify all aspect markers.
Task #3: Compare what you have observed with the aspect markers in other languages you know.

The conclusion will include the observation that perfect aspect is marked with the auxiliary verb [HAVE] in any tense and the content verb marked with {-ed/-en}, the past participle. As for the perfect progressive, the requirements for both aspect types are met and the result is such that the second auxiliary verb is always in the past participle form "been:" *has been practicing, had been practicing, will have been practicing*, etc.

In terms of comparisons with other languages, observations will differ based on the L1s of participating students. If they do not have aspect marked in their languages, they may be invited to explain how else the continuous nature of events is expressed.

English does not allow all verbs to be marked in the progressive aspect. Corresponding verbs may be elicited from students in their L1s to start the conversation on how some languages may have internal reasons not to mark certain inflectional categories while others may. For instance, the verb *want* is never marked with the progressive aspect in English. Despite all the logical explanations based on the meaning of the verb *want* that English grammarians or linguists have come up with to explain this property of English, the explanations are not universally valid. Many other languages, including Turkish, do mark such verbs with the progressive. It is essential that such properties of English not be assumed to be universal or required properties of human language because it is simply not true, to begin with. Perhaps more importantly, while teaching students with diverse backgrounds, making such incorrect remarks or assumptions would alienate the students, if not insult them. Of course, teachers may and should continue to emphasize the universal nature of language while talking about universal concepts in grammar. However, contrary to general assumptions, some basic concepts such as tense or aspect are not universal, nor are all parts of speech.

As a follow-up exercise, once the perfect aspect is covered, the common mistake of identifying the tense in both sentences as past *tense* has to be addressed. A pair of sentences that would make the difference obvious, such as the ones below, may be used and discussed in class:

- *I walked to school yesterday.*
- *I have walked to school today to get some exercise.*

Sample Analytical/Linguistic Skills Training Case Study: Teaching Voice

Analytical/Linguistic Skills Activities on Voice for Beginner/K-12

The teacher briefly presents the basic concept of voice, providing many examples from both active and passive voice and explaining that the difference can be observed in the answers to these two questions: Who does what? Or what is done by whom? It would be necessary to explain that only verbs with objects may be passivized in English.

The sentences used are restricted in terms of tense and aspect. All tenses in the simple and progressive aspect would be the target at this level. Future progressive may be omitted since it is not as commonly used as others.

Pictures or other visual material may be used to accompany the sentences given:

- *The puppy eats a bone every day. / A bone is eaten (by the puppy) every day.*
- *The puppy ate a bone yesterday. / A bone was eaten (by the puppy) yesterday.*
- *The puppy will eat a bone tomorrow. / A bone will be eaten (by the puppy) tomorrow.*

For follow-up exercises:

- *The cat is eating a fish now. / A fish is being eaten (by the cat) now.*
- *The cat was eating a fish then. / A fish was being eaten (by the cat) then.*

Students are given the task of identifying the voice in the VC of given sentences and then using passive voice correctly in the follow-up tasks. Guiding questions that will help students construct a hypothesis are the following: Who is the doer? Who is the receiver of an action? What is the subject? Is the subject the doer? What auxiliary verb is used in passive sentences? What form of the verb is used in the passive sentences?

Task #1: Observe FLF in VCs in each sentence. Which auxiliary verb appears regularly in the passive VCs? What ending appears where regularly in the passive VC? What seems to be the function of these two constants in passive VCs?

Task #2: Generalize and classify passive voice markers.

Task #3: Compare what you have observed with the passive voice markers in other languages you know.

The conclusion will include observations that can be summed up as [BE] v+{-ed/-en}.

Many languages use different kind of markers for the passive voice. In some languages, including Latin, Swedish, and Turkish, passive voice is marked only on the verb as an ending, and in others, within the verb, as in Austronesian languages.

Secondly, in some languages, passive voice has different functions, and they are named differently, as well. In several Southeast Asian languages, a form of passive voice indicates that an action is undesirable or unpleasant, and it is called the **adversative passive**. In Japanese, it is called the **indirect passive**. If there are students with L1s that have different kinds of passives, they should be encouraged to share that knowledge with the class to emphasize the universal nature of voice changes with language specific variation. For instance, the property of English and many other languages which allows only transitive verbs with objects to be passivized is not a universal property, either. Turkish, among others, allows impersonal passives, which passivize intransitive verbs to function as forbidding actions or imposing rules.

Follow-up task may include pictures, or other visual material may be used to elicit passive voice sentences.

Analytical/Linguistic Skills Activities on Voice for Intermediate/Advanced

The teacher presents many sentences in the active and passive voice, using all tense and aspect combinations with a focus on the most commonly used ones in the verb complexes.

- *The carpenter made a bookcase. / A bookcase was made by the carpenter.*
- *The students have filed a complaint. / A complaint has been filed.*
- *The faculty will discuss the final exam policy. / The final exam policy will be discussed.*

The guiding questions that will help students construct a hypothesis are: What marks passive voice in the verb complex? What else is different in the passive voice when compared to the active voice version of the same sentence? What auxiliary verb is used in passive sentences? What form of the verb is used in the passive sentences? Furthermore, by giving examples of questions asked in the active or passive voice, the students are given a chance to observe if the answer changes based on the voice or not.

Task #1: Observe voice of VCs in each sentence as active, passive, or not relevant.
Task #2: Generalize and classify passive voice markers. What type of verbs can be passivized? What kind of verbs do not interact with voice?
Task #3: Compare what you have observed with the passive voice markers in other languages you know.

The conclusion will include the generalization that the auxiliary [BE] inflected in any tense followed by a past participle marks the passive voice in English.

Follow-up task or assignment: Newspaper headlines are collected and discussed in terms of voice. Are they in the passive or active voice? Does it matter? How does the meaning change if at all?

Small group exercise: Does the answer to the question change if it is in the active or passive voice? Come up with questions and answers, and discuss them.

Sample Analytical/Linguistic Skills Training Case Study: Teaching Mood

Mood is a complicated topic for both native or non-native speakers of English. Therefore, even at the intermediate and advanced level, a lot of time needs to be spent on tasks focusing on each mood type. With the subjunctive mood, each sub-category deserves a separate set of tasks to thoroughly understand the concept and to learn how to use them in speech and writing.

Analytical/Linguistic Skills Activities on Tense for Beginner/K-12

The teacher presents the idea of mood without using the actual terminology unless necessary. A video clip from an animation movie, such as *SpongeBob* may be shown. Follow-up questions would address how real the characters, events, or the settings are in what they watched to introduce the idea of the real-world events and unreal events. A teacher leads a discussion on what type of sentences are used to report or talk about real events, putting example sentences on the board.

A second discussion is done on unreal events. Students contribute to the discussion on wishes, dreams, maybe even conditionals. Examples of each generated by the teacher in collaboration with the students are written on the board.

Finally, the students are asked if commands are real or unreal events, guiding them to see that they belong to a separate category.

Sentences, such as the following in the indicative and imperative moods can be given as examples for the students to observe analytically and look for FLF – form, location, function:

- *Come here! Help me! Have some cake!*
- *I came here last week.*
- *They are helping the students today.*
- *Lucky people will have some cake this afternoon.*

Students are given the task of identifying the tense in the VC of sentences they are given in class or they hear on the video or in any other source provided in class, depending on whether the teacher wants to adopt an integrated-skills approach and incorporate listening among the activities. The example sentences written on the board may serve as a guiding list or may be included in the tasks. The goal is to have students observe that commands are the easiest to identify since the verb does not change its form, and the subject does not appear but it is always "you." The second outcome is to understand that all sentences they have studied so far are in the indicative/declarative or imperative mood.

Guiding questions to help students construct a hypothesis are: Is it real, not real or is it a command? Students use analytical skills and look for FLF:

Task #1: Observe the form of the verbs, what endings appear if any and where, what important component of a sentence seems to be missing in some sentences, and whether you understand what the missing component is even if you do not see/hear it. What grammatical meaning do some sentences seem to add in terms of the attitude or point of view of the speaker? (mood)

Task #2: Generalize and classify the two categories of sentences in terms of what kind of markers they have or do not have in their VC or in the sentence.

Task #3: Compare the progressive aspect markers in other languages you know.

Conclusion will include the generalization that in the first group, there is no subject, the verb has no endings, and this form seems to function as a command (imperative). The second set of sentences are the ones we have been using because they have subjects, and their VCs are marked for tense, or tense and progressive aspect.

As a follow-up exercise, to lay the grounds for the subjunctive mood to be taught in the future, students are given speech context in the form of prompts to decide which type of mood they would be expected to use. For instance, the prompts may include the following:

- *I wish I ...*
- *The other day, something happened.*
- *If it rains, I ...*
- *The house must be clean, and the snacks must be ready before guests arrive for the birthday party. You are in charge. Make your two friends work and help you by telling them what to do.*

Analytical/Linguistic Skills Activities on Tense for Intermediate/Advanced

The teacher introduces the relevant terminology as needed. The basic idea of the three categories of mood are presented with examples, and the students contribute to the discussion by giving examples and contexts in which each mood would be used.

The students are asked to discuss, identify, and classify morpho-syntactic markers of each type of mood separately in different in-class exercises as well as group assignments, mimicking the scientific inquiry steps of observe, generalize, and compare, or simply put, FLF - Form, Location and Function. They are expected to observe and generalize their observations to include the following:

1. The form of the verb is the simplest in the imperative, and the subject is always the second person. It may or may not be overt.
2. All sentences represented on the tense-aspect system presented earlier are in the indicative/declarative mood even when they are interrogatives or negative sentences. These are considered part of the real world.
3. Counterfactual conditionals, wish-constructions, and sentences with subjunctive verbs and adjectives are in the subjunctive mood. These belong to the unreal world/the irrealis. Subjunctives are marked in unexpected ways in the sense that (i) the subject-verb agreement may be what we would consider ungrammatical in declaratives (e.g., *wish* constructions and conditionals), (ii) the verb may carry tense that does not belong to the sentence, (e.g., *wish*) (iii) the verb may lack all tense aspect or subject-verb agreement markers (e.g., subjunctive verbs and adjectives).

Subjunctive verbs and adjectives are often the most difficult ones to understand for students with diverse backgrounds. Knowing how to use them is part of the criteria in classifying an ELL as an advanced speaker in most qualification exams. Subjunctive mood is the most difficult mood to comprehend. Although subjunctive verbs and adjectives belong to a restricted set and one can memorize them all, one cannot actually understand how they work without learning how to identify them in authentic material in English. Therefore, it is essential to have the students mimic the scientific inquiry steps to acquire the analytical/linguistic skills so that they can observe how subjunctive mood can be detected and how this mood affects the morpho-syntactic markers on verbs.

Other tasks, assignments, and assessment models may also be used. For instance, conditional structures need to be understood as a subcategory of the subjunctive. Students may be asked to prepare a group performance or presentation on a given theme such as the environment where they are required to use the conditional structures in their presentations.

Finally, once all inflectional markers are covered, an exercise where students can identify all morpho-syntactic markers on the VC would be very useful. Sentences in context, such as a paragraph from an article or a story rather than isolated sentences can be used for students to identify the verb complex and the tense/aspect/voice/mood marked on the VC in each clause. We cannot overemphasize the significance of comparing how English marks inflectional categories to L1s of students. Many languages from various language families code inflectional categories differently. Some mark the relevant concepts lexically instead of grammatically. Some mark aspect but do not mark tense, as in Mandarin Chinese. Others mark tense but not aspect, as in the case of Khmer. Some others mark neither tense nor aspect, as in Indonesian. Some mark tense on prepositions not on verbs, as is the case in Titan (Aygen & Bowern, 2000). Adopting a linguistic approach that does not discriminate against any language would help contextualize the systematic ways English marks tense, aspect, voice, and mood on the verb complex without alienating or disparaging the different linguistic coding of these concepts in other language families.

Teaching (Self-) Monitoring and (Self-) Editing Skills at all Levels

Training ELLs to learn how to monitor and edit their own language performance takes time as well as a systematic approach. The tasks for all levels are the same, but the content will differ at each level and in each class. The training begins with the teacher as the primary role model. As the teacher continues to monitor the students, students observe how the teacher monitors and provides feedback to them. Then they are asked to start monitoring and editing their peers. Once they acquire the skills for monitoring, they are asked to start self-monitoring. Every phase of training is introduced in addition to the earlier phases. The same process is relevant for editing written work.

Firstly, for every class, the teacher identifies a major grammatical concept, such as an inflectional category of tense, aspect, voice, or mood and posts it on the board at a prominent, regular location reserved for grammar. This topic serves as the area of focus for that class or that week. Students are reminded of these areas of focus and in time, they learn to look at the relevant part of the board to remember what to pay attention to when they speak, write, monitor, or edit. As the primary monitor, the teacher observes students in their small group discussions as well as class discussions in terms of their performance regarding that grammatical concept, takes notes of individual and common problem areas, and provides feedback to the students in the form of written notes to individual students and as part of the class discussion at the end of each class. For editing, the teacher demonstrates how editing is done on sample student writing or any writing done on the board by the students, as well as providing feedback on any written work students submit as an assignment. This practice provides a model for the students.

Secondly, the teacher asks the students to assign one student to monitor the discussions held within small groups every time there is a small group discussion. A different student within each small group takes over this responsibility every time a new task is assigned, allowing each student to take a turn. That student observes all the speech errors related to the a grammatical/linguistic topic of the day in that group and takes notes. At the end of the class, those students are given a chance to report to the whole class the major areas of mistakes they have observed. Then, the teacher writes those areas on the board and reviews, encouraging participation from all students in the class. In small groups, the spokesperson for the group changes with each task as well. In that way, each student gets to present the small group findings to the class and gets a chance to receive feedback on his/her language performance.

Thirdly, in-class writing related tasks include pair-editing before submitting the final version to the teacher. In pairs, students are asked to edit each other's writing samples while communicating with each other. Students are trained to focus on specific grammatical issues as well as other concerns related to writing. Larger writing projects involving individual students, pairs, or groups are presented to the whole class. During those presentations, students listening to the presentations are asked to monitor the performance of the speakers by filling out an evaluation form that includes grammatical performance on specific topics, such as correct use of tense, aspect, voice, or mood, depending on the topic of focus.

Finally, students are asked to monitor themselves, edit their own work, and submit their areas of difficulty to the teacher regularly. Advanced students may also be asked to include a section on how they plan to address their problem areas. This procedure allows teachers to focus on the areas of student confusion.

In conclusion, although the teaching of grammar overtly/directly has long become almost obsolete in L2/FL teaching, as well as in teaching writing at various levels of education, it is possible to incorporate grammatical instruction from a descriptive linguistics perspective in ELL curriculum by incorporating or embedding it in a content-based integrated skills model. Adopting a descriptive linguistics approach does not exclude all traditional approaches, such as defining grammatical concepts with their meaning, but limits their use as a beginning point for further linguistic analysis. In such a model, authentic material and major themes can be used to initiate real-world based language performance in all areas of language skills, namely, speaking, listening, writing, and reading. What is proposed in this chapter is that a linguistic approach to describing how English works morpho-syntactically within such a model would empower ELLs in the following ways:

- This approach would guide learners and teachers alike in the steps of analytical thinking. Such analytical skills adopted to language are in fact linguistic skills in addition to being a type of critical thinking. At any level of education and at any age group, learners are capable of mimicking scientific inquiry and acquiring these skills. What differs is how we design and present tasks to help them acquire these skills across levels. Once acquired, these skills allow ELLs improve their English by themselves beyond formal training.
- These skills would help ELLs establish a connection between competence and performance that cannot be expected to be perfected only through performance.
- Such conscious efforts to analyze and compare morpho-syntactic properties of English with any other language would allow for the speakers to systematically benefit from positive transfer and reduce the effects of negative transfer.
- Being engaged in conversation and discussions with ELLs on such comparisons would help language teachers become better teachers as well. An English teacher who is aware of such comparisons can design better curricula based on all the shortcomings and strengths of students with specific native language backgrounds, providing a student-centered instruction beyond what is generally provided to ELLs.

The linguistic approaches proposed in this chapter may be adopted to teach not only the morpho-syntactic concepts discussed in this chapter, but also the topics related to other areas of applied linguistics that are challenging for language learners (Aygen, 2019).

DISCUSSION QUESTIONS

1. Suppose your curriculum is constrained by time limitations and you need to make a choice between the following options. Which one would you choose, and why? What are some strengths and shortcomings of each? What other options can you think of?
    a. Adopt the traditional approach, such as using "meaning" to teach a part of speech or inflectional categories.
    b. Adopt a descriptive linguistics approach, use "meaning" as a hypothesis building tool, and design tasks on one of these topics to help students acquire analytical skills so that they can learn "to learn from language itself" and utilize those skills to learn the other topics as well.
    c. Other options?

2. One tense may be used to express a time reserved for another time, as may be observed in the examples below:
    a. *We leave for Cancun next week.*
    b. *In the novel, she surprises him with a brand-new car.*

    How would introduction of such uses in addition to the regular uses of tense contribute to the performance of ELLs?

3. Perfect aspect is sometimes simply described as "what happens before another event," and the progressive as "what is/was happening when some other event interrupts or interrupted it." How would such descriptions combine to define the perfect progressive? What are some major shortcomings and strengths of adopting such descriptions to teach aspect to ELLs, as opposed to adopting the linguistic approach of morpho-syntactic markers? In other words, would definitions based on such aspect meanings or morpho-syntactic markers provide a better representation and understanding of aspect for ELLs? Can you think of a hybrid or a different type of approach?

4. Students are commonly encouraged to use the active voice in their writing. This advice is rooted in an article on the relationship between politics and the English language: "Never use the passive where you can use the active" (Orwell, 1946, p. 139). How would you teach the contexts in which passive voice is required vs. contexts in which passive voice usage has discriminatory implications? Make use of the examples below:
    a. Lawyer of the man charged by sexual violence: *I understand that the sweater was removed.*
    b. News headline: *A woman was attacked* vs. *A man attacked a woman.*
    c. *Rules are not made to be broken.*

5. How would the following examples challenge the given instructions regarding passive voice? How can you use these examples to teach active verb's indirect objects becoming the passive verb's subject using analytical/linguistic skills? What new generalizations do you need to make after observing these phenomena about passive voice? How would you revise the given instructions to include the previously overlooked phenomena in the passive voice sentences?

    Instruction 1: To transform an active voice sentence into a passive voice, active subjects and direct objects are reversed.

    Example 1: *The client was given a second package by the manager.*

    Hint 1: What has taken the place of the active subject in Example 1?

    Instruction 2: In passive voice, the subject (S) is the receiver, in active voice, however, S is the doer.

Example 2: *The teacher received the packages.*
Hint 2: Who is the receiver? Who is the doer?

6. How would teaching the concepts "actual world" and "possible world" help learners distinguish indicative mood as opposed to subjunctive mood?

EXERCISES

1. We have discussed helping learners acquire or develop analytical and linguistic skills to identify the verb in given sentences, such as the following:
   a. *"Art is the signature of civilization."* (Beverly Sills)
   b. *The artist is signing the exhibition catalogues.*

Come up with your own sentences in pairs such as the two above to design a task that will focus on the properties of the linking verb [BE] as opposed to the auxiliary verb [BE]. List guiding questions you would use to introduce the task to ELLs. Your guiding questions are expected to help them construct a hypothesis and mimic the steps of scientific inquiry.

Finally, ask your students if their L1s have an equivalent for the linking verb [BE], which is commonly called the *copula* in other Indo-European languages. Inform your students that some dialects of American English, such as most of African American dialects do not use the linking verb [BE] in their grammar, just like some other languages, such as, Japanese, Korean, and Turkish do not have an overt linking verb [BE]. In anticipation of such students omitting the linking verb [BE], design a follow-up task that will include a cloze test where students fill in the blanks with appropriate verbs.

2. Suppose some of your students come from L1s that do not have grammatical tense. Come up with your own sentences such as those below to design tasks to introduce the concept of tense to students.
   a. *I usually play tennis, but I played video games last week.*
   b. *She is here now, but she was in Paris last year.*

Ask your students how they would indicate that the event in a sentence is in fact a past event or a future event in their L1s. Have them give examples to the class and invite others to contribute with their questions or contributions in terms of how their language marks or does not mark tense. To help the students acknowledge the universal nature of this concept, think of additional ways English and many other languages mark the time of an event or a state in ways other than grammatical tense.

3. We have not focused on the syntactic properties of modals in this chapter. Observe the following sentences to compare modals and regular auxiliary verbs, and identify the (ir)relevance of tense with modal verbs:
   a. *Couldn't you have helped your friend?*
   b. *Are some linguists working for Hollywood?*
   c. *I have baked cakes many times, haven't you?*
   d. *I can overcome this challenge, I must overcome it, and I will overcome it.*
   e. *Students can't do better on quizzes unless they have enough time.*

Making use of the sentences above or sentences of your own, design a task that will focus on the differences and similarities between regular auxiliary verbs and modal auxiliary verbs. List guiding questions you would use to introduce the task to ELLs.

4.   The function of the {-*ing*} morpheme in English is often very confusing for ELLs at any level. For beginners, the difference between present tense and progressive aspect is lost due to the incorrect assumption that {-*ing*} marks present. This difference may be observed in the sentences below:
   a.   *I am dancing at the party now.*
   b.   *I was dancing at the party yesterday.*
   c.   *I will be dancing at the party.*

Making use of the sentences above or sentences of your own, design tasks for beginner-level learners that will focus on the difference between present tense and progressive aspect in terms of what they mean and a following one in terms of how they are marked on the verbs. List guiding questions and describe non-linguistic tools, such as visual material you might want to use.

5.   The function of the {-*ing*} morpheme in deriving gerunds and participles in English is very confusing, as well. The terminology used does not help either because a participle with {-*ing*} is called a *present* participle misleadingly implying that {-*ing*} marks the present tense, although it does not. The following pair of sentences illustrate the use of a gerund and a participle:
   a.   *Dancing is so much fun.*
   b.   *She is a true dancing queen!*

Making use of the sentences above or sentences of your own, design a task/tasks for intermediate/advanced students, and focus on the difference between gerunds and participles with {-*ing*}. Try not to use the term "present."

6.   The function of the "past" participle forms of the verb is just as confusing. The {-*ed/-en*} morpheme may appear on verbs to mark the perfect aspect or the passive or even used as an adjective as illustrated below:
   a.   *I have broken my promise.*
   b.   *This vase is broken.*
   c.   *The novel is about broken hearts.*

Making use of the sentences above or sentences of your own, design a task for intermediate or advanced learners that will focus on the difference among these three functions of the {-*ed/-en*} morpheme.

7.   We have seen that the choice of an auxiliary verb determines the aspect of a verb complex although the ending on the content verb also pairs up with a specific auxiliary:
   a.   *I have seen that movie. I am watching another one right now.*

Making use of the sentence above or sentences of your own, design a task/tasks that will address the differences between [BE]/[HAVE] and the auxiliary verb [DO], focusing on aspect.

8.   Passive voice is marked morpho-syntactically on the verb complex: [BE] verb + {-ed/-en} as may be observed below:
     a.   *In this chapter, inflectional categories are explained very well.*

Making use of the sentence above or sentences of your own, design a task/tasks to focus on the seemingly contradictory nature of the auxiliary verb [BE] in the present tense and the "past" ending on the participle in the sentence above.

9.   Mood is a difficult inflectional category to teach. Think of a way to correlate the lexical meaning of the word *mood* and the grammatical meaning of the word *mood* as we have used it in this chapter:
     a.   *I am not in the mood to make the impossible possible.*

A dialogue to use both meanings in the same sentence:

b.   *Wife: Help me reboot this computer!*
c.   *Husband: I am not in the mood to deal with your imperative mood today!*

Design a task/tasks for Beginner or K-12 ELLs to focus on the similarity to help them understand what grammatical mood is and how language marks different kinds of mood.

10.   Almost all sentences in this chapter are in the indicative mood. Excluding the example sentences in the sections on imperative mood and subjunctive mood, there are a few sentences in the subjunctive and in the imperative moods in the content of this chapter. Find those sentences.

REFERENCES

Aygen, G. (2016). *English grammar: A descriptive linguistic approach* (3rd ed.). Dubuque, IA: Kendall Hunt.

Aygen, G. (2019). *Word choice errors: A descriptive linguistics approach (with Sarah Eastlund).* New York, NY: Routledge.

Aygen, G., & Bowern, C. (2000). Titan's tensed prepositions. In A. Okrent, & J.P. Boyle (Eds.), *Proceedings of the Chicago linguistics society* (pp. 35-48). Chicago: Chicago Linguistics Society.

Birjulin, L. A., & Xrakovski, V. S. (2001). Imperative sentences: Theoretical problems. In V. S. Xrakovski (Ed.), *Typology of imperative constructions* (pp. 3–50). Munchen: Lincom Europa.

Comrie, B. (1976). *Aspect.* Cambridge, UK: Cambridge University Press.

Comrie, B. (1985). *Tense.* Cambridge, UK: Cambridge University Press. doi:10.1017/CBO9781139165815

Crystal, D. (1985). *A dictionary of linguistics and phonetics* (2nd ed.). New York: Basil Blackwell.

Davies, E. (1986). *The English imperative*. Beckenham: Croom Helm.

Hamm, F., & Bott, O. (2018). *Tense and aspect. In Stanford encyclopedia of philosophy. Metaphysics Research Lab*. Stanford University.

Li, T. (2009). *The verbal system of the Aramaic of Daniel: An explanation in the context of grammaticalization*. Leiden: Brill. doi:10.1163/ej.9789004175143.i-200

Palmer, F. R. (2012). *Mood and modality*. Cambridge, UK: Cambridge University Press.

Portner, P. (2018). *Mood*. Oxford, UK: Oxford University Press.

Rivero, M. L., & Arhonto, T. (1995). Imperatives, V-movement and logical mood. *Journal of Linguistics*, *31*(2), 301–332. doi:10.1017/S0022226700015620

Searle, J. R. (1975). Indirect speech acts. In P. Cole & J. L. Morgan (Eds.), Syntax and semantics: Vol. 3. *Speech acts* (pp. 59–82). New York: Academic Press.

Stanescu, O. (n.d.). *The subjunctive in that-clauses*. Retrieved from https://www.academia.edu/15279111/THE_SUBJUNCTIVE_IN_THAT_COMPLEMENTS_1._On_the_concept_of_modality

Vendler, Z. (1967). *Linguistics in philosophy*. Ithaca, NY: Cornell University Press.

von Fintel, K., & Iatridou, S. (2017). A modest proposal for the meaning of imperatives. In A. Arregui, M. L. Rivero, & A. Salanova (Eds.), *Modality across syntactic categories* (pp. 288–319). Oxford, UK: Oxford Scholarship Online.

Wilson, D., & Sperber, D. (1988). Mood and the analysis of non-declarative sentences. In J. Dancy, J. M. Moravcsik, & C. C. W. Taylor (Eds.), *Human agency, language, duty and value. Philosophical essays in honor of J.O. Urmson* (pp. 77–101). Stanford, CA: Stanford University Press.

Zanuttini, R., Pak, M., & Portner, P. (2012). A syntactic analysis of interpretive restrictions on imperative, promissive, and exhortative subjects. *Natural Language and Linguistic Theory*, *30*(4), 1231–1274. doi:10.100711049-012-9176-2

ADDITIONAL READING

Alexiadou, A. (2014). Active, middle, and passive: The morpho-syntax of voice. *Catalan Journal of Linguistics*, *13*, 19–40. doi:10.5565/rev/catjl.153

Aygen, G. (2004a). Finiteness, case, and agreement: Clausal architecture. *Occasional Papers in Linguistics, 23*. Cambridge: MIT.

Aygen, G. (2004b). T-to-C and overt marking of counterfactuals: Syntactic and semantic implications. In C. Bowern (Ed.), *Harvard Working Papers in Linguistics 10* (pp. 1–17). Cambridge: Harvard Linguistics Department.

Aygen, G. (2006). Finiteness and the relation between agreement and nominative case. In C. Boeckx (Ed.), *Agreement Systems* (pp. 63–98). Amsterdam: John Benjamins. doi:10.1075/la.92.06ayg

Butt, M. (2003). The light verb jungle. In G. Aygen, C. Bowern, & C. Quinn (Eds.), *Papers from the GSAS/Dudley House workshop on light verbs* (pp. 1-49). Cambridge: Harvard Linguistics Department.

Kemmer, S. (1993). *The middle voice.* Amsterdam: John Benjamins. doi:10.1075/tsl.23

Kitazume, S. (1996). Middles in English. *Word, 47*(2), 161–183. doi:10.1080/00437956.1996.11435951

Levin, B. (1993). *English verb classes and alternation: A preliminary investigation.* Chicago: Chicago University Press.

Orwell, G. (1946). Politics of the English language. *Horizon*: London. Retrieved from https://faculty.washington.edu/rsoder/EDLPS579/HonorsOrwellPoliticsEnglishLanguage.pdf

Reichenbach, H. (1947). *Elements of symbolic logic.* New York: Dover Publications, Inc.

Rizzi, L., & Cinque, G. (2016). Functional categories and syntactic theory. *The Annual Review of Linguistics, 2*(1), 139–163. Retrieved from linguist.annualreviews.org. doi:10.1146/annurev-linguistics-011415-040827

Schafer, F. (2009). The causative alternation. *Language and Linguistics Compass, 3*(2), 641–681. doi:10.1111/j.1749-818X.2009.00127.x

ENDNOTES

[1] Actually, *has* is marked with the third person singular subject-verb agreement in the present tense. Although agreement is another inflectional marker on the verb, it is excluded from this chapter because English does not have a rich morphology of subject-verb agreement.

[2] The properties of modals are beyond the scope of this chapter; however, it is worth noting that other modal auxiliaries, such as "must," "may," or "should" are also used with a bare verb, but they do not belong to a tense category. They do not mark tense and have different grammatical meanings, such as permission, obligation, ability, possibility, and so on.

[3] Ungrammatical sentences or other forms are marked with an asterisk at the beginning of that form.

[4] In English linguistics, there are other manifestations of voice, which we will exclude from the discussion for the purposes of this chapter. For interested readers they are listed here: (i) Causative and anti-causative alternation requires the analysis of transitive verbs as cause + intransitive verbs, and *John broke the vase* is analyzed as causative and *The vase broke* as anti-causative (Levin, 1993; Schafer, 2009). (ii) Reflexive alternation refers to reflexive verbs observed in body-care verbs (Kemmer, 1993): *John washed and combed every morning.* (iii) Middles refer to verbs that do not allow agentive *by*-phrases, such as *This book reads easily* (Alexiadou, 2014; Kitazume, 1991).

5 In appropriate contexts, indicative could also function as an order: *You are doing the dishes tomorrow, not me.*

6 The reason why this sub-type of probable condition is considered a *zero* conditional or almost a non-conditional is because we can replace the *if* with *when* or *whenever*, and the sentence would still be true, and the logical implication between the two clauses is preserved.

7 See Aygen (2004) for a discussion on conditional inversion and how we can only get a counterfactual reading when the auxiliary verb is inverted and *if* is deleted in inverted conditionals. For instance, we can say *If he finished the work on time, we will throw a party for him*, which is not a counterfactual. However, once we invert the conditional as *Should he finish the work on time, we will throw a party for him*, the only available interpretation is that of probable condition.

8 See Aygen (2016) for a complete list of such verbs, adjectives, and even nouns that create sentences in the subjunctive mood.

Unit 5
Semantics

Chapter 7
Lexical Semantics:
Relativity and Transfer

David Stringer
Indiana University, USA

ABSTRACT

Lexical semantics is concerned with inherent aspects of word meaning and the semantic relations between words, as well as the ways in which word meaning is related to syntactic structure. This chapter provides an introduction to some of the main themes in lexical semantic research, including the nature of the mental lexicon, lexical relations, and the decomposition of words into grammatically relevant semantic features. The mapping between the semantics of verbs and their associated syntax is discussed in terms of thematic roles, semantic structure theory, and feature selection. A review of some of the most influential findings in second language research involving both open-class and closed-class lexical items reveals important implications for classroom pedagogy and syllabus design in the domain of vocabulary instruction.

WHAT IS SEMANTICS?

Semantics is the study of how language is used to represent meaning. More precisely, semantics aims to explain how literal meanings are linguistically encoded and decoded by speakers and hearers. Other approaches to meaning include pragmatics, which deals with how meanings are inferred in relation to context, and semiotics, which is a more general study of how we interpret both linguistic and non-linguistic signs. For example, if one person shows a ring to another, saying "Here is the ring", there are several layers of meaning that could be examined. At the level of semantics, the deictic pronoun *here* indicates a proximal location; the verb *be* signifies existence in a location; the determiner *the* shows that both speaker and hearer have previous knowledge of this ring; and the word *ring* picks out a particular type of object in the world. At the level of pragmatics, depending on the context, the hearer might infer that this speech act is a proposal of marriage, or a request for a divorce, or a directive to embark upon a magical quest. In terms of semiotics, the ring itself may be understood as a symbol of a bond, alliance,

DOI: 10.4018/978-1-5225-8467-4.ch007

or vow, which by extension might signify matrimony, allegiance to a college, or religious authority. In comparison with pragmatics and semiotics, semantics has a narrower scope of investigation in that it restricts its concern to linguistic aspects of meaning. Within semantics, there are various theoretical approaches, including formal semantics, which uses propositional logic to capture relations between linguistic expressions and the things to which they refer, and cognitive semantics, which sees meaning in language as emerging from general cognitive principles. These important lines of research are beyond the bounds of the current chapter, which deals with a different aspect of semantics with direct relevance to the language classroom: lexical semantics, the study of how meaning is encoded in words, and how word meaning relates to sentence meaning.

In the following section, fundamental concepts of lexical semantics are introduced, including the traditional distinction between reference and sense, the mental lexicon as a network, and the various types of meaning relations between words. Most modern research in this domain focuses on elements of meaning below the word level, and investigates both features inside words as well as features that words can require in their surrounding linguistic context. An overview is given of the fascinating and ongoing debate among researchers concerning how the meanings of words determine syntactic structure. In the second part of this chapter, several examples of second language (L2) research are presented in order to illuminate how lexical semantics might be relevant for language learning in the classroom. Such research addresses questions of how word meanings in a new language are acquired, given that learners initially assume equivalence between words in translation, even though words rarely have the same meaning in two different languages. It is argued that several findings in L2 lexical semantics are of direct relevance to teaching practice, materials development, and syllabus design.

THE MENTAL LEXICON: A WORLD OF WORDS

Reference, Sense, and Lexical Relations

An important traditional distinction in lexical semantics, as most influentially articulated by Frege (1980 [1892]) and Saussure (1983 [1916]), is between **reference** and **sense**. The reference of a word is the thing, event, or state that it points to in the world. It is what the word denotes, and it is external to the mind. Thus if someone refers to a particular piece of wooden furniture with four legs and a back using the word *chair*, the reference is to that object in the world. In contrast to reference, the sense of a word is its meaning in relation to the linguistic system of which it is a part, and this meaning is internal to the mind. The precise meaning of the word *chair* in English is related to other words such as *beanbag*, *bench*, *pew*, *seat*, *sofa*, *stool,* etc. Translational equivalents of words are rarely completely accurate because the precise set of things a word can denote varies from language to language, in part due to this relational aspect of meaning. In a given language, the translation of the English word *chair* might denote both chairs and stools, or there might be two words corresponding to different types of chair. Moreover, different words or phrases with distinct senses could point to the same individual in the world, for example *Bill, Shakespeare, Ann's husband, the author of Hamlet,* and *the Bard of Avon* might all refer to the same person but they carry different meanings. As Frege (1980 [1892]) observed, using two senses to denote the same referent is quite different from a repetition of terms. The planet Venus may be referred to as the morning star or the evening star, but for someone who is unaware that these terms denote the same object, example (1) carries information, while example (2) does not.

(1) *The morning star is the evening star.*
(2) *Venus is Venus.*

The distinction between reference and sense has led to two distinct research traditions in semantics. Referential (denotational) theories of meaning focus on how words manage to pick out the set of things to which they refer. Formal semantic approaches, such as truth-conditional semantics (e.g., Chierchia & McConnell-Ginet, 2000), as well as Montague Grammar (Montague, 1974), are characterized by their use of logic in semantic analysis, and in such frameworks, whether an expression is meaningful depends on whether it is a logical and truthful expression of external reality. For example, in truth-conditional semantics, nouns and verbs are meaningful because they denote actual entities and situations, respectively. They can either be true or false descriptions of reality. In this tradition, the term *sense* is restricted to an idealistic notion of word meaning, independent of the variation in speakers' minds, such that languages are seen as abstractions over individual differences and the "psychological and sociological" representations "used by a person or population" (Lewis, 1972, p. 170).

In contrast to denotational theories of formal semantics, representational theories of lexical semantics do not consider any aspect of meaning as external to the mind. On this account, one cannot compare a linguistic representation with reality to determine truth, but only check it against other mental representations of the world. The perception of a chair, in terms of its shape, texture, colors, perspective, etc., is created in the mind, and the categorization of this object is likewise a cognitive process. The emphasis in lexical semantic research is on words as concepts, and on the lexicon as a means of relating phonological, syntactic, and conceptual representations. Jackendoff (1989, p. 74) interprets this distinction between (i) meaning in terms of external reality and (ii) meaning in cognition by drawing on Chomsky's (1986) constructs of E-language (external, language as a social abstraction outside the individual mind, out there in the world) and I-language (internal, language as a cognitive system). Denotational theories can be thought of as E-semantics and representational theories as I-semantics, respectively. In this sense, the focus of this chapter is squarely on I-semantics, and on theories of lexical semantics that have arisen in this tradition.

An account of lexical semantics must be somehow embedded in a more general theory of the **mental lexicon**, so let us begin with the question: What is a lexical item? While it is conventional to think of a word as a unitary entity, many researchers in lexical semantics assume some version of Jackendoff's (1997) theory of parallel architecture, according to which a lexical item is a relation, rather than a thing. At a minimum, a word consists of a phonological representation, linked to an independent syntactic representation, linked to an independent conceptual representation. Moreover, the generation of phonological, syntactic, and conceptual forms occurs in modular fashion, so that, for example, only phonological primitives and combinatorial rules are used to create phonological representations. A lexical item is created through correspondences between these distinct representations, as in (3)

(3)

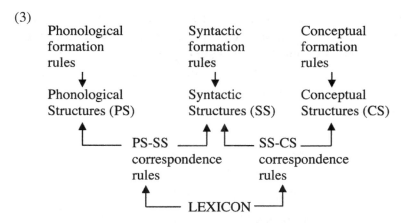

(adapted from Jackendoff, 1997, pp. 39, 100)

This conception of representational modularity at the lexical interface with other cognitive systems is compatible with evidence from speech processing research. When we hear a word, we search to retrieve it from our mental storage system first by paying attention to phonology, not semantics. Words that begin with the same sounds are "primed", that is, they are activated in lexicon so as to enable fast retrieval and integration into syntax. For example, in an early experiment by Swinney (1979), when participants heard the sentence *Because he was afraid of electronic surveillance, the spy carefully searched the room for bugs*, they showed evidence that at least two interpretations of *bugs* ('microphones' and 'insects') were primed, despite only one being pragmatically appropriate.

Just as words stored in the mental lexicon may be phonologically primed in a way unrelated to meaning, they may also be subject to semantic priming, depending on their conceptual relations to other words. For example, in a word recognition task, a response to a target (e.g., *boy*) is faster when it is preceded by a semantically related prime (e.g., *girl*) compared to an unrelated prime (e.g., *telephone*). Evidence from semantic priming, as well as word association tests, slips of the tongue, and lexical recall in cases of aphasia (language deficits following brain damage) makes clear that there are various types of relations between lexical items, and that the organization of the mental lexicon is significantly more complicated than an alphabetically organized dictionary. It makes sense to think of the lexicon as an interactive network with multiple types of connections between elements. In order to develop a theory of how this network might be organized, it is important to understand the various ways in which words can semantically relate to one another.

One of the most important concepts in semantic relations is that of the lexical field, which is a grouping of lexical items that have a general conceptual association, either in terms of an area of knowledge or regular co-occurrence in real-word situations. Modern theories of lexical fields stem from Trier (1931), who built on earlier insights by Saussure (1983 [1916]) to argue that word meaning cannot be understood in isolation from relations with other semantically related words in the same lexicon. Subsequent decades of research have confirmed that words do tend to exhibit strong semantic associations with words in the same semantic domain. This can be effectively demonstrated when two different words have the same phonology or spelling. For example, the word *pole*, meaning a long, thin rod made of wood or metal, is associated with the word *tent*, while another word *pole*, meaning either the northern or southern ends of the rotational axis of the earth (or another celestial body), is associated with the word *north*. These two words (identical phonology, different semantics) sit in distinct lexical fields.

While this general associative concept is useful, more precise **lexical relations** are often identified to clarify the links between particular words, including homonymy, polysemy, synonymy, antonymy, hyponymy, and meronymy, which will be briefly examined in turn. **Homonyms** are unrelated meanings of words that either sound the same (homophones) or are written the same (homographs). Examples of homophones of the word *right* /raɪt/ "correct" are shown below, with links between (simplified) phonological (PS), syntactic (SS), and conceptual structures (CS).

(4)

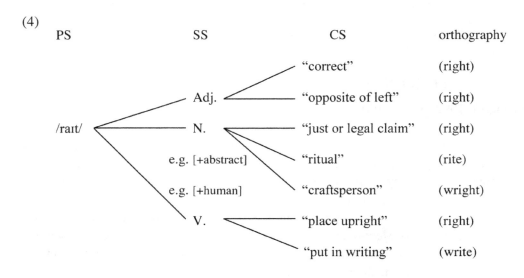

PS	SS	CS	orthography
		"correct"	(right)
	Adj.	"opposite of left"	(right)
/raɪt/	N.	"just or legal claim"	(right)
	e.g. [+abstract]	"ritual"	(rite)
	e.g. [+human]	"craftsperson"	(wright)
	V.	"place upright"	(right)
		"put in writing"	(write)

Dialectal differences in pronunciation mean that not all speakers of English share the same homonyms. For example, *writer* and *rider*, or *caught* and *cot*, may or may not have identical phonology depending on the speech community. Another aspect of homonymy in need of clarification is that true homonyms are perceived as having unrelated semantics (even if there is sometimes a historical connection between meanings), while there often also exist sets of related meanings of a given phonological word.

When different senses of the same phonological word are related in identifiable ways, this is termed **polysemy**. Thus *right* in the sense of *correct* is closely linked to such meanings as *right conduct* (= just, proper), *the right clothes* (= suitable, appropriate), or *the right way round* (= principal side of an object). The distinction between homonymy and polysemy is reflected in many dictionaries, as homonyms usually have separate entries, while polysemous items are listed under a single entry. Thus *bark¹* (the harsh sound made by a dog) is kept distinct from its homonyms, *bark²* (the protective covering of a tree) and *bark³* (a kind of boat). Within these entries, polysemous use is listed in terms of nuances or aspects of meaning, including related shifts in syntactic category. So *bark¹* may cover usages such as (Noun 1) *the bark of a dog*, (Noun 2) similar sounds, such as *coughs* or *gunfire*, (Verb 1) *to make the sound of a bark*, and (Verb 2) *to speak gruffly*, etc. (examples from *The American Heritage Dictionary*).

Polysemy has received significant attention in research on lexical semantics, as aspects of word meaning are often systematically related through **alternations** that shed light on general cognition. Examples of polysemy investigated by Pustejovsky (1995) include the following.

(5) Count / Mass alternations
 a.   *The lamb is running in the field.*
 b.   *John ate lamb for breakfast.*

(6)   Container / Containee alternations
   a.   *Mary broke the bottle.*
   b.   *The baby finished the bottle.*
(7)   Figure / Ground reversals.
   a.   *The window is rotting.*
   b.   *Mary crawled through the window.*
(adapted from: Pustejovsky, 1995, p. 31)

In the case of Figure / Ground reversals, a considerable number of nouns seem to alternate in sense between a physical object used to frame an opening, and the opening itself which is framed by that object (e.g., *window, door, gate, fireplace, hallway, room*). The intended sense is derivable only through linguistic context. That is, in the sentence *John is painting the door*, the door is an object, and in the sentence *John walked through the door*, the door is an opening. Such examples make it clear that a theory of lexical semantic composition has to go beyond simply enumerating meaning components inside words.

Synonymy is in some sense the reverse of homonymy: synonyms are words with different phonology but with the same, or approximately the same, meaning. However, while this is a well-known concept, taught to schoolchildren from a young age, it is rare that two lexical items can be truly interchangeable. The difference between reference and sense is useful to invoke in this case, as more often, supposed synonyms are often two separate senses with a common referent. Pairs such as the nouns *peace* and *calm*, the verbs *enjoy* and *like*, and the adjectives *funny* and *humorous*, can be substituted in some contexts and not others, and word choice is often contextually conditioned. On closer inspection, we find most words are polysemous, and that each sense of a word has different synonyms. The noun *play* may allow *performance* as a synonym in a theatrical context, but *move* or *action* as synonyms in the context of a game. The verb *play* may be close in meaning to *mimic* in the context of imitation, while it could be substituted for *feign* in the context of false emotion or behavior. Apparent synonyms stand apart when polysemy is manipulated; for example, while *big* and *large*, *little* and *small* are often given as classic synonyms, *a big sister* is not the same as *a large sister* (Saeed, 2016, p. 62). Synonyms are sometimes differentiated by dialect and sometimes by register: for example, the choice of *freeway, highway*, or *turnpike* may carry regional dialectal associations, and one would not use *inebriated, drunk*, and *squiffy* interchangeably without consideration of discourse context. As words cannot generally be substituted for one another without some change in interpretation, it is arguable that pure synonyms do not exist.

A related notion is **antonymy**, with refers to the link between words that are considered to be opposites. The semantic assertion of some words implies the negation of others, such that they can form binary pairs. If a book is *open*, this entails that it is not *shut*. If a creature is *alive*, it means that it is not *dead*. Complementary pairs that often work this way include, *day / night, empty / full,* and *on / off.* Another type of antonymy involves so-called relational (or converse) pairs, both of which must exist simultaneously for each to carry a truth value, e.g., *husband / wife, above / below*, and *lend / borrow*. Yet a third type that is commonly identified is gradable (or polar) antonyms, which operate on a scale, and whose truth value is determined by speakers in relation to the scale. Examples include *hot / cold, young / old, happy / sad, long / short*, and *fast / slow*. Subclasses of antonyms are also analyzed in terms of reverse relations. Reverse antonyms include directional terms such as *come / go, enter / exit*, and *up / down*, as well as reversible processes, such as *fill / drain, inflate / deflate*, and *push / pull*. Antonymic relations can be somewhat complex and have engendered considerable research (for more detailed discussion, see Cruse, 1986, pp. 197-262).

The term antonymy is sometimes extended to describe contrasts beyond the binary, especially if words are part of a contrastive taxonomy. Contrastive taxonomies involve "horizontal" relations in a set of terms, in which the elements are neither superordinate nor subordinate to one another. One classic example is that of colors. If a door is described as *red*, this implies that it is not *blue, yellow, green*, etc. This kind of relation also obtains for items at the same level of a hierarchy, such that if something is described as a *duck*, it enters into a contrastive relationship with *goose, swan*, etc. Many taxonomies additionally involve "vertical" relations, such that words are nested in hierarchical structures within the network of the mental lexicon. This type of inclusional relation is known as hyponymy.

Hyponymy may be easily illustrated with either living things or artifacts. For example, a Dalmatian is a type of dog, and a dog is a type of mammal. In this case, the word *Dalmation* is a hyponym of *dog*, and *dog* is a hyponym of *mammal*. The word *armchair* is a hyponym of *chair*, which is a hyponym of *furniture*. Conversely, *mammal* is a hypernym of *dog*, and *dog* is a hypernym of *Dalmatian*, while *furniture* is a hypernym of *chair*, which is a hypernym of *armchair*.

(8)

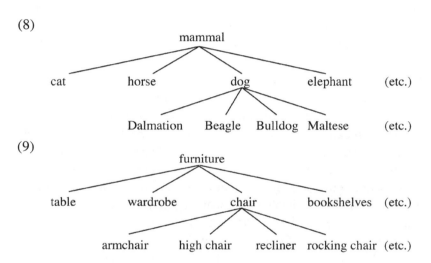

(9)

It is important to remember that we are modelling lexical semantics in terms of the kinds of relations between words in the minds of individuals, and as such these types of hierarchies are not always reflective of scientific taxonomy (or the classification systems of, say, furniture manufacturers). In an individual mind, relations between terms may not accord with prescriptive definitions handed down by academia, governments, or other prestigious social institutions. These are folk taxonomies, which may vary from language to language and even from one individual to another. Thus for some people, a tomato is a fruit, and for others it is a vegetable. For most people, the term *berries* subsumes strawberries, although they are not scientifically classified as such, and the term usually excludes certain botanically defined berries such as watermelons.

In discussing commonalities across cultures in how humans classify the natural world, Atran (1990, 1998) notes the relation between hyponymy and the capacity to make generalizations about the environment. Hyponymies of living things involve strict transitivity; that is, if a relation holds between the first and second level, and between the second and third level, it also holds between the first and third level. All dogs are mammals, and all mammals are animals, therefore all dogs are animals, irrespective of any prototype effects (a dog with three legs would be no less of an animal). Folk taxonomies provide the foundation for systematic reasoning about living kinds relevant to human survival, so that, for example, if a disease is found in one bird species, we know that it is more likely to be found in other bird species than among mammals or reptiles (Atran, 1998). However, the organization of names for artifacts in the lexicon does not exhibit the same rigidity in entailment relations. For example, a dog is an animal, and a chair is furniture. However, while animal is part of the definition of dog, perhaps surprisingly, furniture is not part of a strict definition of chair. Artifacts are more prototypically defined, and cross-cut super-ordinate categories. For example, car-seat is a kind of chair, but not a kind of furniture, and a piano can be both furniture and a musical instrument (Atran, 1990).

If hyponymy describes relations of inclusivity between categories of whole entities, the term **mero-nymy** refers to part-whole relations within entities. The words *hand* and *foot* are meronyms of the word *body*, just as the words *wheel* and *pedal* are meronyms of the word *bicycle*. While meronymy and hyponymy can be represented using similar diagrams (as in examples 8 and 9), meronymy often shows less regularity. Some parts are necessary to the whole (e.g., *seed – apple*, *eye – face*), while others are typical or even occasional but not necessary (*pocket – coat*; *porch – house*). Meronymy is also less likely to exhibit strict transitivity. For example, if a cupboard has a handle, and a kitchen has a cupboard, this does not entail that a kitchen has a handle. The lexical relation of meronymy underlies the linguistic device of synecdoche, used in both literary and everyday language. Thus we can refer to the sea as *the waves*, or a ship as *sails*, or a car as *wheels*.

Lexical relations such as homonymy, polysemy, synonymy, antonymy, hyponymy, and meronymy are well-established semantic links between words in the mental lexicon, but in modern linguistic approaches to lexical semantics, the focus is more often on aspects of meaning below the word level. In particular, much work focuses on those semantic elements that play a role in grammar. The following section presents a brief overview of how this research has developed into a growing and exciting subfield of linguistics.

Features, Subcategorization, Thematic Roles, and Semantic Structures

In one of the most influential research programs attempting to formalize lexical relations, Katz and colleagues (Katz & Fodor, 1963; Katz & Postal, 1964; Katz, 1972) sought to identify semantic components of word meaning that support the kind of inferences we make automatically as we process natural language. On hearing the word *bachelor*, we know that the referent is male, human, animate, and unmarried. Instead of representing such relations in terms of word hierarchies as in examples 8 and 9, Katz posited that the word itself contained these elements as interpretable features. The existence of semantic features within lexical items allows for a reconceptualization of lexical relations. Consider the following examples.

(10) a. *man* [+MALE] [+ADULT] [+HUMAN]
  b. *bachelor* [+MALE] [+ADULT] [+HUMAN] [+UNMARRIED]
  c. *boy* [+MALE] [-ADULT] [+HUMAN]

The relation of hyponymy between (10a) and (10b) is clear because all the features of the word *man* are contained in the feature set of the word *bachelor*. On this account, a lexical item is a hyponym of another term if it contains all of the linguistically relevant features of that term. Similarly, certain types of antonymy can be captured in terms of contrasting features. The word *boy* allows one to infer that the referent is HUMAN, but rules out the interpretation of ADULT and is therefore incompatible with the term *man*.

Early Katzian approaches favored comprehensive semantic definitions, so as to fully explain entailment relations. A word such as *chair* was understood to contain not only grammatically relevant features such as [+OBJECT] and [+CONCRETE (physical)] but also elements to capture a general conceptual definition of the term, such as [+HAS LEGS], [+HAS A BACK], and [+PORTABLE]. Such definitional approaches to word meaning have largely been abandoned, not only in linguistics, but also in philosophy and psychology, following lines of thought that can be traced through Wittgenstein (1958), Putnam (1962), and Rosch (1978) (for an overview and implications for language acquisition, see Stringer, 2012). However, building on Katz's analyses, several researchers developed lexical semantic theories that involved a more restricted subset of meaning components, which included only those semantic components of relevance to grammar. Chomsky (1965) introduced **subcategorization** theory not only to provide an account for how verbs and prepositions select (or subcategorize) for particular syntactic categories in their linguistic environments, but also to explain how certain lexical semantic features might be involved in selectional processes. In other words, the meaning of a verb involves not only inherent semantic features, contained within the verb itself, but contextual features, which it may require of subjects or objects. In the examples in (11), the meaning of the verb constrains the possible semantics of other elements in each sentence.

(11)　a.　　*The boy may frighten sincerity.*
　　　b.　　*John solved the pipe.*
　　　c.　　*The book dispersed.*

Arguably, these examples are not simply semantically incongruous, but involve syntactic violations; they "have a borderline character" (Chomsky, 1965, p. 77), and raise the question of whether this selectional information should be in the syntactic or the semantic component of the grammar. Chomsky (1965) opted for the syntactic solution, proposing interpretable syntactic features such as [+ANIMATE], [+HUMAN], [+ABSTRACT], [+PLURAL], etc. to account for such constraints. However, he maintained a distinction between 'strict subcategorization rules' (category selection) and 'selectional rules' (feature selection), within a general syntactic subcategorization process (Chomsky, 1965, p. 95). In the half-century since Chomsky's (1965) seminal work, while some researchers have continued to analyze such semantic features as part of syntactic selection (e.g., Emonds, 2001), many have taken the alternative option in developing an independent semantic account of how predicates license other elements in their linguistic environment (e.g., Grimshaw, 1979; Jackendoff, 1990; Pinker, 2013 [1989]).

Participants which are integral to the event or state expressed by the predicate are called **arguments**, and the relation between the verb and the participants it selects is termed **argument structure**. Several influential approaches to understanding argument structure have attempted to characterize semantic selection not through features, but through the roles that participants can play in events or states. Lists of the types of roles that arguments can play vary from author to author, and have been termed *participant roles* (Allan, 1986), *deep semantic cases* (Fillmore, 1968), *semantic roles* (Givon, 1990), *thematic roles* (Dowty, 1991; Jackendoff, 1990), and *theta (θ)-roles* (Chomsky, 1981). The term **thematic roles** will be adopted here for subsequent discussion. Drawing on distinctions made in the above works, it is possible to come up with a reasonably standard list of thematic roles, as follows.

(12) AGENT: the initiator of an action, often demonstrating volition, e.g.:

    a. *Harry telephoned Sally.*

    b. *The owl flew out of the tree.*

PATIENT: the entity undergoing the effect of an action, often with a change of state, e.g.:

    a. *Alfred burnt the cakes.*

    b. *The dog chewed the slipper.*

THEME: the entity which is moved by an action, or whose location is described, e.g.:

    a. *Janice put a flower in her hair.*

    b. *The honey is on the table.*

LOCATION: the place in which an action takes place or where something is situated, e.g.:

    a. *They met at the station.*

    b. *The ruin lies under the waves.*

INSTRUMENT: the means, either concrete or abstract, by which an action is carried out or something is made possible, e.g.:

    a. *William split the apple with an arrow.*

    b. *She charmed him with her wit.*

EXPERIENCER: the entity which is aware of the action or state described by the predicate but which is not in control of the action or state, e.g.:

    a. *Helen saw the hawk.*

    b. *Thelma felt good.*

BENEFICIARY: the entity in whose interest an action is performed, e.g.:

    a. *George made some tea for his wife.*

    b. *Ella sung him a song.*

GOAL: the entity towards which something moves, in either (a) a physical or (b) an abstract sense, e.g.:

    a. *Olive gave the spinach to the sailor.*

    b. *Bill tells the same story to everyone he meets.*

SOURCE: the entity from which something moves, in either (a) a physical or (b) an abstract sense, e.g.:

    a. *The package was sent from India.*

    b. *All his ideas come from his teacher.*

On this approach to argument structure, thematic roles are determined by the lexical semantics of the verb, and the mapping to syntax is via a thematic hierarchy (Jackendoff, 1972; Larson, 1988; Speas, 1990), according to which the highest role is linked to the subject position, the next highest to object position, and others to indirect object positions. For example, the verb *put* has the theta-grid <agent, theme, goal>, and the hierarchy specifies Agent > Experiencer > Theme > Source > Goal > Obliques (manner, location, time, etc.), so the canonical mapping of thematic roles will be Agent = subject, Theme = object, and Goal = indirect object (e.g., *Janice put a flower in her hair*). In contrast, the verb *see* lacks an Agent: as the theta-grid is <experiencer, theme>, the mapping will be Experiencer = subject, Theme = object (e.g., *Helen saw the hawk*). The relevance of this for language learning is clear when one considers that translational equivalents in different languages often have different theta-grids. The Spanish verb *gustar* is the most common verb used to translate the English verb *like*, but it patterns thematically like the verb *please*, with an agent in its theta-grid, rather than *like*, which has an experiencer-subject *(Chocolate {pleases / *likes} me; I {like / *please} chocolate)*. This creates a bidirectional learnability problem, such that acquisition is tricky going from English to Spanish as well as from Spanish to English.

Research on thematic roles dominated formal approaches to lexical semantics for the 1980s and much of the 1990s, as researchers attempted to integrate the lexical semantic specifications of verbs with syntactic structure. Chomsky (1981) argued that there cannot be more or fewer NPs in a clause than is required by the verb's argument structure, and stated this in terms of the Theta-Criterion (p. 36):

(13) Each argument bears one and only one θ-role, and each θ-role is assigned to one and only one argument.

Baker (1988) drew on both the Theta-Criterion and on observations by linguists working in the Relational Grammar approach (such as Perlmutter & Postal, 1984), as he formulated the influential Uniformity of Theta Assignment Hypothesis (UTAH). Notably, UTAH claims that thematic roles are assigned via syntactic structure, and that when there is variation in argument structure, identical thematic relationships can be traced to identical structural relationships at the level of deep structure. In this way, the word *boat* in the following examples is a Theme irrespective of whether it surfaces as a subject or an object.

(14)
    a. *Jim sank the boat.*   (*boat* generated in object position, receives Theme interpretation)
    b. *The boat sank ____.*   (*boat* generated in object position, receives Theme interpretation, moves to subject position)

Despite the significant influence and inspiration of research on thematic roles in syntax and psycholinguistics, and despite their continued use as useful descriptive terms, several problems have been identified with this approach. Much current research in lexical semantic theory views thematic roles as epiphenomena whose intuitive appeal belies an underlying inadequacy to fully describe selectional relations.

One criticism has been the lack of evidence for an underlying one-to-one mapping between thematic roles and syntactic structure. In the following sentence, there appear to be at least two types of thematic role assignment.

(15)   *James throws the ball to Sarah.*   (prepositional form)

If understood in terms of conscious actors, volition, and affectedness, the roles are Agent (*James*), Patient (*the ball*), and Beneficiary (*Sarah*). If analyzed in terms of objects, motion, and trajectory, the roles are Source (*James*), Theme (*the ball*), and Goal (*Sarah*) (for an analysis involving two separate tiers of thematic role assignment, see Jackendoff, 1990, pp. 125-129). Another problem for one-to-one mapping is that some verbs allow alternating argument structures. The previous example can be used to illustrate the dative alternation: in the following related structure, on standard accounts, the indirect object is promoted to direct object position.

(16)   *James throws Sarah the ball.*   (double-object dative form)

Approaches that posit one-to-one mapping between thematic roles and syntactic positions would seem to predict that, in cases of alternating argument structure, the basic form should be acquired first, with the more complex, derived form acquired later. However, despite plausible, evolving transformational accounts of this double-object structure (Emonds & Whitney, 2005; Fillmore, 1965; Larson, 1988), the supposedly underlying argument structure is not acquired first for all verbs (Pinker, 1984). That is, the prepositional form does not precede the double-object dative in the spontaneous speech of children, making it likely that it exists as an independent structure (with independent semantics, according to Pinker, 2013 [1989]).

A second general criticism of thematic roles as an account of argument structure is that they lack the fine-grained semantic analysis necessary to explain semantic selection. For example, the English verb *spray*, regardless of context, encodes the interpretation of the moving object in the event as a three-dimensional (3D) aggregate of psychologically dimensionless points (e.g., water, sand, bullets); *smear* requires that the moving object be a 3D semisolid substance (e.g., honey, paint, make-up); and the verb *wrap* specifies that the moving object be a two-dimensional (2D) flexible solid (e.g., paper, foil, a leaf). The verbs *fill*, *cover*, and *coil* require that the entity with the thematic role of location be respectively conceptualized as a volume, a surface or a line. In order to capture this complexity, **Semantic Structure Theory** (Jackendoff, 1990; Pinker, 2013 [1989]) elaborates an independent level of representation, subsuming both lexical and phrasal semantics. While this might seem to be a much more complicated approach to semantic selection than either subcategorization or thematic role assignment, Pinker (2013 [1989], pp. 215-220) argues that the grammatically relevant semantic subsystem is relatively restricted when one considers that it aims to capture the lexical semantics of all verbs in all human languages. This kind of theoretical approach includes conceptual constituents such as EVENT, STATE, THING, etc., basic functional verbs such as GO and BE, a set of subordinating semantic relations, temporal and spatial functions, and the kind of lexical distinctions discussed above, such as animacy, human / nonhuman, dimensionality, count / mass / aggregate, rigidity, and states of matter (solid, liquid, semi-solid, gas). The semantic categories are motivated by descriptive typological surveys of the world's languages and by previous work in the tradition of cognitive linguistics (e.g., Talmy, 1985). The cognitive values of the suggested categories also delimit the kind of inferences that were part of Katz's original feature-based approach to lexical semantics.

Recall that Chomsky (1965) mused on whether semantic selectional information should be in the syntactic or the semantic component of the grammar. While some modern lexical semantic research posits independent semantic structures (Jackendoff, 2010; Levin & Rappaport Hovav, 2011; Pinker, 2013 [1989]), other research opts for conceptual features in syntax (Emonds, 2000; Harley & Ritter, 2002; Lardiere, 2009; Stringer, 2012). However, there is consensus in current work that fine-grained accounts of lexical semantics are an integral part of grammatical description. Moreover, as the acquisition of the lexicon underlies the acquisition of argument structure, and as lexical representations differ across languages, lexical semantics is generally understood to be a core component in the acquisition of L2 syntax.

IMPLICATIONS FOR TEACHING ENGLISH LANGUAGE LEARNERS

Lexical Relativity, Lexical Transfer, and Feature Reassembly

Research into L2 acquisition of lexical semantics has furnished several insights that are directly relevant to the language classroom. One fundamental pair of related observations is that (i) when comparing any two languages, it is apparent that exact lexical equivalence is either rare or nonexistent, such that all words resist precise translation; and (ii) the learner's initial assumptions about word meaning in an L2 stem largely from knowledge of the first language (L1). The first of these observations is termed **Lexical Relativity** (Stringer 2010), and captures the fact that, following the earlier distinction between reference and sense, the meaning of any lexical item is relative to its ambient lexicon. That is, a paired translation may hold for a shared reference in a particular context, but the senses of the two words will necessarily diverge across multiple contexts. Perfect translational equivalence is virtually non-existent due largely to the fact that both the denotational and syntactic properties of words are constrained by those of other words in the same combinatorial system, as famously observed by Saussure (1983 [1916]). Even basic verbs expressing existence or location, equivalent to the English verb *be*, can vary, for example, according to whether the existence is permanent or temporary (Spanish *ser* / *estar*), or whether the entity is animate or inanimate (Japanese *iru* / *aru*). A universal human activity such as drinking does not lead to universal verb semantics. The English verb *drink* is used only of liquids. In Turkish, one can "drink" smoke as well as liquids; in Japanese, one can "drink" medicine, even in solid form; and in Kazak, one can "drink" both liquids and solids, in contexts where English would require the verb *eat*. Young and Morgan (1987) list 15 verbs of consumption in Navajo, corresponding to either *eat* or *drink*, which differ according to such criteria as whether the thing to be consumed is hard, mushy, leafy, liquid, solid but dunked in liquid, or meat, or whether it is consumed from an open or closed container.

Common nouns also splinter in translation: English *rice* corresponds to both Japanese *kome* (uncooked rice) and *gohan* (cooked rice). Sometimes while the referent is ostensibly the same, the grammatical properties vary, shedding light on differences in conceptualization. Thus in English, *grape* is a count noun (and grapes are conceptualized as small bounded objects) while in French, *raisin* 'grape' is a mass noun (and conceptualized as a substance). In French, one must refer to a grain of grape, just as in English one must refer to a grain of rice. The same relativity exists in so-called closed-class categories (word classes that do not regularly admit new coinages), such as prepositions, articles, and quantifiers. For example, crosslinguistic comparisons reveal that the concepts of *"on" a table*, *"on" a wall*, and *"on" a ceiling* are not at all linked to some kind of universal spatial preposition, but involve different lexicalization patterns depending on the language (Bowerman, 1996). In general, assumed equivalence between lexical items falls apart on closer examination.

The second of these insights may be termed **Lexical Transfer**, and was articulated in terms of Full Transfer and Relexification in seminal work by Sprouse (2006). Lexical Transfer builds on what is perhaps the most influential hypothesis of linguistic approaches to L2 grammar, the Full Transfer/Full Access model (Schwarz & Sprouse, 1996), which posits that the initial state of L2 learning corresponds to the L1 grammar, but that learners may nevertheless go beyond their initial assumptions, as their analysis of L2 input is guided by Universal Grammar. Sprouse (2006) extends this approach beyond syntax and phonology to include lexical knowledge. He argues that in L2 acquisition of the lexicon, words initially maintain the syntactic and semantic packaging associated with them in the L1, and are simply relabeled with perceived L2 phonology (Interlanguage (IL) Phonology), as illustrated below.

(17)

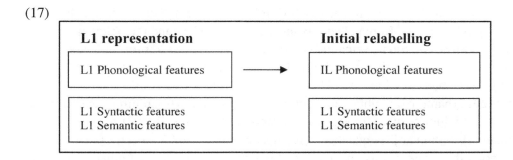

If the learner's initial assumptions about word meaning stem largely from previous linguistic knowledge, then on hearing a new word, such as *gohan* 'rice' in Japanese or *raisin* 'grape' in French, an L1 English-speaking learner will initially assume that the former refers also to uncooked rice, while the latter is a count noun referring to small, bounded objects. Learners of English will experience similar problems in reverse. A shift from one lexicon to another entails thousands of subtle shifts in how we conceptualize the world in order to talk about it.

Taken together, Lexical Relativity and Lexical Transfer imply that standard vocabulary lists with translated word-pairs found in all textbook series, while useful in promoting noticing effects, are also necessarily misleading; that multiple exposure to words in different contexts is a prerequisite for acquisition; that much of lexical learning is bound to be implicit rather than explicit; and that learners from different L1 backgrounds will have different assumptions and paths of acquisition regarding the L2 lexicon.

Not only does Lexical Relativity apply to open-class items (lexical classes that freely admit new members, such as verbs or nouns) but it is also relevant to closed-class items ("functional" classes of grammatical words that do not easily allow new members, such as modals, articles, or quantifiers). The idea that reorganization of functional features is fundamental to L2 acquisition is at the heart of the **Feature Reassembly Hypothesis** (Lardiere, 2009). On this approach, syntactic, phonological, and semantic features constitute the grammatically relevant elements within lexical items, and it is the presence or absence of such features that accounts for language variation (Chomsky, 1995; Travis, 2008). In the course of L2 acquisition, learners must reconfigure syntactically relevant semantic features from functional items in the L1 into new configurations, sometimes on different types of lexical items.

Two examples may be used to illustrate the profound implications of relativity in this domain. Learners of English who are in the process of acquiring the plural morpheme *-s* or the definite article *the* will be quick to realize that the semantics of these elements in the function lexicon do not correspond exactly to analogous items in the L1. In order to explain what the acquisition of plural morphemes entails for English learners of Korean and Korean learners of English, Hwang & Lardiere (2013) provide a comparative analysis of the two languages before reporting their empirical study. Among other things, the plural morpheme in Korean is often optional rather than obligatory. Intrinsic plural marking is, like English, on the noun, and can carry a collective or distributive reading (e.g., *The students read a book* could mean "all together" or "individually"). The intrinsic plural also indicates specificity, ruling out generic readings. It is obligatory with demonstratives, but impossible with numerical classifiers, unless the noun carries the feature [+human], in which case it is optional. Unlike English, extrinsic plural marking in Korean can spread from the noun so that manner adverbs or locative phrases can be marked as plural, in which case the meaning is distributive. There are further specifications for use of these two types of plural marking, but suffice it to say that when faced with the challenge of acquiring the English plural morpheme, a simple dictionary definition equating Korean *–tul* and English *–s* falls far short of a learning strategy. Among other things, Korean learners must come to understand the obligatory nature of plural marking on English count nouns, semantic coercion when it is used to turn mass nouns into count nouns (e.g., *two beers*), and its relation with articles and quantifiers as regards specific count, nonspecific count, or generic interpretation (e.g., *I like {the / some / Ø} tigers*).

Hwang & Lardiere (2013) capture the subtleties of semantic interpretation by splitting the traditional feature of PLURAL and deriving meaning through the interaction of smaller, abstract features such as [±group], [±individuation], [±human], [±quantity], [relative/absolute], and [±specific]. The details of the analysis are beyond the scope of this chapter, but it is important to note that other researchers have arrived at the same conclusion regarding the need for a finer-grained feature analysis of plurality. Harley & Ritter (2002) propose a feature geometry consisting of abstract semantic features in order to produce various categories of plural in languages: plural meaning more than one, dual (only two), plural meaning more than two, paucal (small group), as well as inclusive and exclusive (plurals including or excluding the hearer).

The learning task for plural morphology might seem daunting, but in fact, current theoretical approaches are essentially good news for language teachers. In contrast to previous theories that argued that, depending on the combination of L1 and L2, successful acquisition was difficult or even impossible in this domain, due to an inability to acquire the functional lexicon after a purported critical period (Hawkins, 2005; Hawkins & Hattori, 2006), the Feature Reassembly approach maintains that "any feature contrast that is detectable is, in principle, ultimately acquirable" (Lardiere, 2009, p. 214). And in fact, Hwang and Lardiere (2013) demonstrate in their experimental study that English learners of Korean do converge on nativelike knowledge of the grammar at higher levels of proficiency. One clear implication for the language classroom is that teachers and textbook authors need to be aware of how the target language works in order to provide students with the necessary variety of input, so that students are exposed to lexical items across their full range of distribution. For example, learners of Korean would benefit from juxtaposed examples of [+human] and [–human] numerical classifiers, with optional plural marking only for [+human], while learners of English would benefit from juxtaposed examples of mass nouns and coerced count nouns, so that liquids are identified as countable when in containers.

A second example of relativity in the lexical semantics of functional items involves acquisition of the definite article in English. As argued by Ionin, Ko, & Wexler (2004), the definite article carries a feature [+definite], which means that both speaker and hearer can identify the referent. This is in contrast to other languages, such as Samoan, in which the article carries a feature [+specific], meaning that the speaker (but not necessarily the hearer) can identify the referent. The researchers found that Russian and Korean learners of English, whose L1s lack articles of any kind, fluctuated between definite and specific interpretations. Especially notable was the difficulty learners had in [+specific, -definite] situations, where the speaker, but not the hearer could identify the referent. This finding may help teachers understand why it is that learners of English whose L1s lack articles produce utterances such as *I'm going to meet the friend tonight* when only the speaker knows which friend. In such cases, learners are using a specific rather than a definite article. In their survey of English-language textbooks, Ionin, Ko, & Wexler (2004) note that the relevant data is not sufficiently available as to facilitate acquisition. It seems clear that learners need to be exposed systematically to the article in contexts such as the one given above that clearly distinguish between definite and specific interpretation. Again, the implication for the language classroom is that teachers must provide students with input that covers the full range of contexts in order for the relevant lexical semantics to be learnable.

The Acquisition of Argument Structure

Lexical Relativity and Lexical Transfer are also apparent in research on the L2 acquisition of argument structure, with several implications for instructed language learning. One particular focus in L2 research has been cross-linguistic differences regarding alternations in argument structure. Types of variable argument structure that have been studied include the dative alternation discussed above (examples 15 and 16), the locative alternation (*Mary {sprayed paint onto the car / sprayed the car with paint}*), the benefactive alternation (*Mary {baked a cake for John / baked John a cake}*), the passive alternation (*Mary touched John / John was touched by Mary*), and the causative alternation (*The butter melted / Mary melted the butter*). In each case, some English verbs allow the alternation while others do not, depending at least in part on lexical semantics (for full discussion, see Pinker, 2013 [1989]). Following Lexical Relativity, verbs themselves do not share exact meaning across languages, and moreover, the morphology relevant to the alternations differs cross-linguistically. This means that not only are alternations a problem for all learners, but we expect different sets of issues depending on the L1, even though, if Lardiere (2009) is correct, the necessary evidence for learners is detectable in the input, and therefore ultimately acquirable.

In one pioneering study on the L2 acquisition of causative verbs, Montrul (2000, 2001) examined how the relevant patterns were acquired in three languages, in each case contrasting the performance of learners from the other two languages. In English, many verbs, such as *break* or *sink*, may alternate without any additional morphology, while in Spanish, the basic form of the verb is used in transitive contexts and an anticausative morpheme *se* is required for the intransitive variant (example 18). In Turkish, some verbs exhibit a similar pattern to Spanish, with an anticausative morpheme, while other verbs show the opposite pattern to Spanish, with the basic form of the verb in intransitive contexts and a causative morpheme *ır* being required in transitive contexts (example 19).

(18) a. *María rompió los vasos.*   (causative)
          Mary broke the glasses
          '*Mary broke the glasses.*'
      b. *Los vasos <u>se</u> rompieron.*   (change of state)
          the glasses ANTI-CAUSE *broke*
          '*The glasses broke.*'

(19) a. *Gemi bat-tı.*   (change of state)
          Ship sink-PAST
          '*The ship sank.*'
      b. *Asker-ler gemi-yi   bat-<u>ır</u>-dı.*   (causative)
          Soldier-PL *ship*-ACC *sink*-CAUSE-PAST
          '*The soldiers sank the ship.*'

In the course of a complex battery of tests, Montrul (2000, 2001) found that the L1 did influence learners' assumptions about L2 grammar. For example, Spanish learners of Turkish and Turkish learners of Spanish were facilitated in the recognition of an anticausative morpheme, while English learners of both languages accepted bare intransitive verbs. Moreover, while recognizing the anticausative morpheme in Spanish, Turkish learners nevertheless incorrectly accepted particular intransitive verbs without morphology if these corresponded to bare verbs in the L1. In responses to Turkish stimuli testing causative morphology, both Spanish and English participants often omitted the causative morpheme with transitive verbs, and Spanish speakers had lower accuracy with bare intransitive forms. In the English study, more than 50% of Spanish learners of English rejected the target-like form of the intransitive verb *break*, preferring a form with extra morphology, e.g., *got broken*. Although Montrul (2000) has a more nuanced interpretation of her findings, her results can certainly lend support to the idea that the lexical semantics of predicates in the L1 affects L2 acquisition, and that learners from different L1 backgrounds will have distinct patterns of L2 development. Language teachers can therefore expect the same materials to pose different levels of challenge depending on the L1 backgrounds of learners and can also expect differences at the level of particular verbs, to the extent that not all verbs necessarily pattern the same way in acquisition.

Another common argument structure error familiar to teachers of English involves overpassivization. This term refers to the phenomenon of using passive morphology in cases where a bare intransitive verb would be expected. Research into overpassivization was pioneered by Zobl (1989), who provides L2 writing samples like the following.

(20) a. *The most memorable experience of my life was happened fifteen years ago.* (L1 Arabic)
      b. *My mother was died when I was just a baby.* (L1 Thai)

One productive avenue of L2 research has confirmed that such forms are far from random, as overpassivization occurs with a particular subclass of intransitive verbs. Intransitives may be divided into unergative verbs, whose subject is an Agent generated in subject position, and unaccusative verbs, those whose subject is a Theme, generated in object position before raising to subject position to receive case (Burzio, 1986; Levin & Rappaport, 1995; Perlmutter, 1978). The unaccusative analysis is more intuitive with verbs that have a transitive counterpart (e.g., *John rolled the ball / The ball rolled*; *Mary opened the door / The door opened*), but there is also evidence for underlying object status for the Theme in nonalternating unaccusatives, such as *arrive, fall, and die*. For example, expletive *there* may fill the subject position, or the verb may form a dynamic nominal modifier, as shown below.

(21) a. *There arrived three men* (unaccusative) / **There laughed three men* (unergative)
      b. *the fallen soldiers* (unaccusative) / **the hesitated leader* (unergative)

Tests for **unaccusativity** vary from language to language. For example, in French only unaccusative verbs take the 'be' rather than the 'have' auxiliary in the perfect tense (*Il est arrivé* – he is arrived – "He arrived; *Il a toussé* – he has coughed – "He coughed"). In Turkish, only unergative verbs license the impersonal passive construction (*Burada çalış-ıl-ır-* here work-PASS-PRES – "Here people work"; **Burada öl-ün-ür* - here die-PASS-PRES – "Here people die"). In Japanese, the quantifier *takusan* 'a lot' only modifies objects, so the interpretation differs for unaccusatives (with underlying objects) and unergatives (*Takusan tui-ta* - a lot arrive-PAST - "A lot of people arrived"; *Takusan ason-da* - a lot play-PAST - "Somebody played a lot"). However, despite variation in how the difference is manifested, all languages seem to distinguish the two classes.

There is a consensus in L2 research that learners of English overgeneralize from the passive (in which objects also raise to subject position) in assuming that this subclass of intransitive verbs also needs a morphological reflex (in the form of auxiliary *be*) to license the raising of the Theme to subject position. Interestingly, L2 learners of English demonstrate this kind of abstract analysis of the input irrespective of the L1, clearly revealing a deep knowledge of unaccusativity (Balcom, 1997; Hirakawa, 2001;

Oshita, 2002; Zobl, 1989). However, there are arguably still transfer effects in the case of those verbs that alternate with a transitive variant, depending on how such alternations are morphologically realized in the L1. Kondo (2005) showed that while both Japanese and Spanish learners of English patterned together in overpassivizing unaccusatives in general, they differed in the case of alternating verbs. The Spanish participants only made significant overpassivization errors with unaccusatives that had transitive counterparts (precisely those that would require anticausative morphology in Spanish, as shown earlier in example 18). These findings illuminate not only a universal distinction based on knowledge of unaccusativity, but also argument structure transfer from Spanish.

Lexical Semantics in the Language Classroom

Collectively, the findings on acquisition of the lexical semantics of verbs corroborate research in the domain of functional items such as articles and plural morphology in revealing that learner language is often sophisticated in terms of its lexical architecture. It exhibits both universal aspects of the human language faculty as well as evidence of cross-linguistic influence. Some of the more important implications for language instruction may be summarized as follows.

- The twin observations of (i) Lexical Relativity (which holds that word meaning is relative to particular language systems) and (ii) Lexical Transfer (which argues that L1 lexical semantics constitutes the initial state for the learning of the L2 lexicon) together imply that acquisition of L2 lexical semantics requires multiple exposure to words across a range of semantic and syntactic contexts. Note that this is in tandem with findings in pedagogical research on first language acquisition of vocabulary, which holds that effective teaching must involve multiple exposures in different contexts (Stahl, 2005) and that contextual support greatly enhances acquisition (Nash & Snowling, 2006), with learners ideally engaged in structured read-alouds, discussion sessions, and independent reading experiences (Cunningham, 2005).
- Traditional vocabulary lists are noticing tools, rather than keys to acquisition.
- Successful vocabulary teaching must incorporate systematic recycling of new words with contextual cues.
- In order to provide students with exposure to lexical items across their full range of distribution, teaching, textbook writing, and curriculum development require linguistic awareness of how open- and closed-class items work in the target language.
- Teachers can expect (and can predict) student variation in this domain based on the L1 background of students, as the L1 determines learners' initial assumptions regarding both the syntax and semantics of lexical items.
- Given that acquisition relies on contextual cues, as learners process language input in a range of contexts for communicative purposes, much of lexical learning is bound to be implicit rather than explicit. However, this does not preclude explicit direction of attention to meaning in context.
- Despite the magnitude of the learning task, any contrast in semantic features is acquirable as long as it is detectable in the language to which learners are exposed, so there are no limits on second language learning in this domain.

DISCUSSION QUESTIONS

1. Even though words in two different languages can have the same reference, they almost always differ in the senses that they can have, so that in a different context, reference is no longer shared. For example, the Japanese word *doa* is the translation of English *door*, but only for a Western-style door with hinges and a handle. Other senses have other translations, such as *shoji* for traditional paper sliding doors, or *fusuma* for wooden panel doors. Can you think of other examples in languages that you know of words that do not share senses with their most typical English translation?

2. In classroom contexts, we often assume that learners "know a word" such as *put* if they can match it with a word in another language (as in a vocabulary list), or if they can use it correctly in a particular sentence. Yet the Shorter Oxford English Dictionary (1993) uses over three-and-a half thousand words to define the verb *put*. What does it mean to know a verb? What does it mean to know a noun?

3. Consider the locative verbs *put*, *fill*, *spray*, and *splash*. In syntax, do they all need a direct and an indirect object? What variations are there? In semantics, do they specify particular kinds of direct or indirect objects? How can we state these selectional properties in lexical entries?

4. Textbooks often explain the English passive (e.g., *The garden was painted by Monet*) as a construction derived from an underlying active sentence (e.g., *Monet painted the garden*), following several distinct grammatical operations. Which of these is relevant to overpassivization errors in L2 English? Why might some learners use passive morphology with some intransitive verbs?

5. If you were designing a series of L2 English textbooks, how would you propose to incorporate new vocabulary, whether open-class items, such as verbs and nouns, or closed-class items, such as articles and quantifiers?

EXERCISES

1. In the following sentences, decide which noun phrases might be used by the speaker as referring expressions.
    a. James bought a new bike.
    b. Emily might buy a cake.
    c. My daughter pointed at the dragon.
    d. Who opened the door to find nobody there?

2. Choose two nouns, one animate, one an artifact, and create tree diagrams to illustrate hyponymy. Do you find any differences between the two diagrams?

3. Assign thematic roles to the noun phrases in these sentences. Are there any that could have two different roles?
    a. *Bill* kissed *Jennifer*.
    b. *Maggie* threw the *frisbee* to *Ian*.
    c. *Elliot* baked *Jane a cake*.
    d. *The key* opened the *door*.
    e. *The sun* crosses *the sky* from *east* to *west*.

4.   Using the diagnostics mentioned in the chapter, decide which of these intransitive verbs are unergative (with an underlying subject), and which are unaccusative (with an underlying object):
agree, burn, cough, depart, fall, live, sit, smile, think, yawn
What kind of overpassivization errors might we expect in L2 English with some of these verbs?

5.   In which of the following contexts could we predict overuse of the definite article in L2 English, and why?

   a. Mark wants to buy a book on Saturday.   (He already knows which one)
                                                      (He doesn't know which book yet)
   b. Karen did not want to talk to a reporter.   (She wanted to avoid one reporter in particular)
                                                      (She didn't want to talk to any reporter)

REFERENCES

Allan, K. (1986). *Linguistic meaning*. London: Routledge & Kegan Paul.

Atran, S. (1990). *Cognitive foundations of natural history: Towards an anthropology of science*. Cambridge, UK: Cambridge University Press.

Atran, S. (1998). Folk biology and the anthropology of science: Cognitive universals and cultural particulars. *Behavioral and Brain Sciences, 21*(4), 547–609. doi:10.1017/S0140525X98001277 PMID:10097021

Baker, M. (1988). *Incorporation: A theory of grammatical function changing*. Chicago, IL: University of Chicago Press.

Balcom, P. (1997). Why is this happened? Passive morphology and unaccusativity. *Second Language Research, 13*(1), 1–9. doi:10.1191/026765897670080531

Bowerman, M. (1996). Learning how to structure space for language: A crosslinguistic perspective. In P. Bloom, M. A. Peterson, L. Nadel, & M. F. Garrett (Eds.), *Language and Space* (pp. 385–436). Cambridge, MA: The MIT Press.

Burzio, L. (1986). *Italian syntax: A government-binding approach*. Dordrecht: Reidel. doi:10.1007/978-94-009-4522-7

Chierchia, G., & McConnell-Ginet, S. (2000). *Meaning and grammar: An introduction to semantics* (2nd ed.). Cambridge, MA: MIT Press.

Chomky, N. (1981). *Lectures on government and binding*. Dordrecht: Foris.

Chomsky, N. (1965). *Aspects of the theory of syntax*. Cambridge, MA: MIT Press.

Chomsky, N. (1986). *Knowledge of language*. New York: Praeger.

Chomsky, N. (1995). *The Minimalist Program*. Cambridge, MA: MIT Press.

Cruse, D. A. (1986). *Lexical semantics*. Cambridge, UK: Cambridge University Press.

Cunningham, A. E. (2005). Vocabulary growth through independent reading and reading aloud to children. In E. H. Hiebert & M. L. Kamil (Eds.), *Teaching and learning vocabulary: Bringing research to practice* (pp. 45–68). Mahwah, NJ: Erlbaum.

de Saussure, F. (1983). *Course in general linguistics (translated and annotated by R. Harris)*. London: Duckworth. (Original work published 1916)

Dowty, D. R. (1991). Thematic proto-roles and argument selection. *Language, 67*(3), 547–619. doi:10.1353/lan.1991.0021

Emonds, J. E. (2000). *Lexicon and grammar: The English syntacticon*. New York: Mouton de Gruyter.

Emonds, J. E., & Whitney, R. (2005). Double object constructions. In M. Everaert & H. van Riemsdijk (Eds.), *The Blackwell companion to syntax* (pp. 73–144). Hoboken, NJ: Blackwell.

Fillmore, C. (1968). The case for case. In E. Bach & R. T. Harms (Eds.), *Universals in linguistic theory* (pp. 1–88). New York, NY: Holt, Rinehart, and Winston.

Frege, G. (1980). On sense and reference. In P. Geach & M. Black (Eds.), *Translations from the philosophical writings of Gottlob Frege* (3rd ed.; pp. 56–78). Oxford, UK: Blackwell. (Original work published 1892)

Givon, T. (1990). *Syntax: A functional-typological introduction II*. Amsterdam: Benjamins.

Grimshaw, J. (1979). Complement selection and the lexicon. *Linguistic Inquiry, 10*(2), 279–326.

Harley, H., & Ritter, E. (2002). Person and number in pronouns: A feature-geometric analysis. *Language, 78*(3), 482–526. doi:10.1353/lan.2002.0158

Hawkins, R. 2005. Revisiting *wh*-movement: the availability of an uninterpretable [wh] feature in interlanguage grammars. In L. Dekydtspotter, R. A. Sprouse, & A. Liljestrand (Eds.), *Proceedings of the 7th Generative Approaches to Second Language Acquisition Conference (GASLA 2004)* (pp. 124-137). Somerville, MA: Cascadilla.

Hawkins, R., & Hattori, H. (2006). Interpretation of English multiple *wh*-questions by Japanese speakers: A missing uninterpretable feature account. *Second Language Research, 22*(3), 269–301. doi:10.1191/0267658306sr269oa

Hirakawa, M. (2001). L2 acquistion of Japanese unaccusative verbs. *Studies in Second Language Acquisition, 23*(2), 221–245. doi:10.1017/S0272263101002054

Hwang, S. H., & Lardiere, D. (2013). Plural-marking in L2 Korean: A feature-based approach. *Second Language Research, 29*(1), 57–86. doi:10.1177/0267658312461496

Ionin, T., Ko, H., & Wexler, K. (2004). Article semantics in L2-acquisition: The role of specificity. *Language Acquisition, 12*(1), 3–69. doi:10.1207153278171a1201_2

Jackendoff, R. (1972). *Semantic interpretation in generative grammar*. Cambridge, MA: MIT Press.

Jackendoff, R. (1989). What is a concept, that a person may grasp it? *Mind & Language, 4*(1/2), 68–102. doi:10.1111/j.1468-0017.1989.tb00243.x

Jackendoff, R. (1997). *The architecture of the language faculty*. Cambridge, MA: MIT Press.

Jackendoff, R. (2010). *Meaning and the lexicon: The parallel architecture 1975–2010*. Oxford: Oxford University Press.

Katz, J. J. (1972). *Semantic theory*. New York: Harper and Row.

Katz, J. J., & Fodor, J. A. (1963). The structure of a semantic theory. *Language, 39*(2), 170–210. doi:10.2307/411200

Katz, J. J., & Postal, P. M. (1964). *An integrated theory of linguistic descriptions*. Cambridge, MA: MIT Press.

Kondo, T. (2005). Overpassivization in second language acquisition. *International Review of Applied Linguistics in Language Teaching, 43*(2), 129–161. doi:10.1515/iral.2005.43.2.129

Lardiere, D. (2009). Some thoughts on the contrastive analysis of features in second language acquisition. *Second Language Research, 25*(2), 173–227. doi:10.1177/0267658308100283

Larson, R. K. (1988). On the double object construction. *Linguistic Inquiry, 19*, 335–391.

Levin, B., & Rappaport Hovav, M. (1995). *Unaccusativity: At the syntax-lexical semantics interface*. Cambridge, MA: MIT Press.

Levin, B., & Rappaport Hovav, M. (2011). Lexical conceptual structure. In K. von Heusinger, C. Maienborn, & P. Portner (Eds.), *Semantics: An international handbook of natural language meaning I* (pp. 418–438). Berlin: Mouton de Gruyter. doi:10.1515/9783110226614.420

Lewis, D. (1972). General semantics. In D. Davidson & G. Harman (Eds.), *Semantics of natural language* (pp. 169–218). Dordrecht: Reidel. doi:10.1007/978-94-010-2557-7_7

Montague, R. (1974). *Formal philosophy: Selected papers of Richard Montague* (R. H. Thomason, Ed.). New Haven, CT: Yale University Press.

Montrul, S. (2000). Transitivity alternations in L2 acquisition: Toward a modular view of transfer. *Studies in Second Language Acquisition, 22*(2), 229–273. doi:10.1017/S0272263100002047

Montrul, S. (2001). First-language-constrained variability in the second-language acquisition of argument-structure-changing morphology with causative verbs. *Second Language Research, 17*(2), 144–194. doi:10.1177/026765830101700202

Nash, H., & Snowling, M. (2006). Teaching new words to children with poor existing vocabulary knowledge: A controlled evaluation of the definition and context methods. *International Journal of Language & Communication Disorders, 41*(3), 335–354. doi:10.1080/13682820600602295 PMID:16702097

Oshita, H. (2001). The unaccusative trap in second language acquisition. *Studies in Second Language Acquisition, 23*(2), 279–304. doi:10.1017/S0272263101002078

Perlmutter, D. M. (1978). Impersonal passives and the unaccusative hypothesis. *Proceedings of the 4th Annual Meeting of the Berkeley Linguistics Society*, 157-190.

Perlmutter, D. M., & Postal, P. M. (1984). The 1-Advancement Exclusiveness Law. In D. M. Perlmutter & C. Rosen (Eds.), *Studies in Relational Grammar 2* (pp. 81–125). Chicago, IL: University of Chicago Press.

Pinker, S. (1984). *Language learnability and language development*. Cambridge, MA: Harvard University Press.

Pinker, S. (2013). *Learnability and cognition: The acquisition of argument structure* (2nd ed.). Cambridge, MA: MIT Press. (Original work published 1989) doi:10.7551/mitpress/9700.001.0001

Pustejovsky, J. (1995). *The generative lexicon*. Cambridge, MA: MIT Press.

Putnam, H. (1962). The analytic and the synthetic. In H. Feigh & G. Maxwell (Eds.), Minnesota studies in the philosophy of science, Vol. 3: Scientific explanation, space, and time (pp. 358–397). Minneapolis, MN: University of Minnesota Press.

Rosch, E. (1978). Principles of categorization. In E. Rosch & B. Lloyd (Eds.), *Cognition and categorization* (pp. 27–48). Hillsdale, NJ: Lawrence Erlbaum.

Saeed, J. I. (2016). *Semantics* (4th ed.). Oxford, UK: Wiley Blackwell.

Schwartz, B. D., & Sprouse, R. A. (1996). L2 cognitive states and the Full Transfer / Full Access model. *Second Language Research*, *12*(1), 40–72. doi:10.1177/026765839601200103

Speas, M. (1990). *Phrase structure in natural language*. Dordrecht: Kluwer. doi:10.1007/978-94-009-2045-3

Sprouse, R. A. (2006). Full transfer and relexification: L2 acquisition and creole genesis. In C. Lefebvre, L. White, & C. Jourdan (Eds.), *L2 acquisition and creole genesis: Dialogues* (pp. 169–181). Amsterdam: John Benjamins. doi:10.1075/lald.42.11spr

Stahl, S. (2005). Four problems with teaching word meanings (and what to do to make vocabulary an integral part of instruction). In E. H. Hiebert & M. L. Kamil (Eds.), *Teaching and learning vocabulary: Bringing research to practice* (pp. 95–114). Mahwah, NJ: Lawrence Erlbaum.

Stringer, D. (2010). The gloss trap. In Z.-H. Han & T. Cadierno (Eds.), *Linguistic relativity in SLA: Thinking for speaking* (pp. 102–124). Clevedon, UK: Multilingual Matters. doi:10.21832/9781847692788-007

Stringer, D. (2012). The lexical interface in L1 acquisition: What children have to say about radical concept nativism. *First Language*, *32*(1-2), 116–136. doi:10.1177/0142723711403879

Swinney, D. (1979). Lexical access during sentence comprehension: (Re)consideration of context effects. *Journal of Verbal Learning and Verbal Behavior*, *18*(6), 645–660. doi:10.1016/S0022-5371(79)90355-4

Talmy, L. (1985). Lexicalization patterns: Semantic structure in lexical forms. In T. Shopen (Ed.), Language typology and syntactic description, Vol.3: Grammatical categories and the lexicon (pp. 57-149). Cambridge, UK: Cambridge University Press.

Travis, L. de M. (2008). The role of features in syntactic theory and language variation. In J. M. Liceras, H. Zobl, & H. Goodluck (Eds.), *The role of formal features in second language acquisition* (pp. 22–47). New York: Lawrence Erlbaum Associates.

Trier, J. (1931). *Der deutsche Wortschatz im Sinnbezirk des Verstandes* [German vocabulary in the 'sense district' of the mind]. Heidelberg, Germany: Winter.

Wittgenstein, L. (1958). *Philosophical investigations* (2nd ed.). Oxford, UK: Blackwell.

Young, R., & Morgan, W. Sr. (1987). *The Navajo language: A grammar and colloquial dictionary*. Albuquerque, NM: University of New Mexico Press.

Zobl, H. (1989). Canonical typological structures and ergativity in English L2 acquisition. In S. M. Gass & J. Schachter (Eds.), *Linguistic perspectives on second language acquisition* (pp. 203–221). New York: Cambridge University Press. doi:10.1017/CBO9781139524544.015

ADDITIONAL READING

Levin, B. (1993). *English verb classes and alternations: A preliminary investigation*. Chicago, IL: University of Chicago Press.

Pinker, S. (2013). *Learnability and cognition: The acquisition of argument structure* (2nd ed.). Cambridge, MA: MIT Press. (Original work published 1989) doi:10.7551/mitpress/9700.001.0001

Saeed, J. I. (2016). *Semantics* (4th ed.). Oxford, UK: Wiley Blackwell.

Unit 6
Pragmatics

Chapter 8
Understanding Language in Context:
Key Concepts in Pragmatics

Anna Krulatz
Norwegian University of Science and Technology, Norway

ABSTRACT

This chapter focuses on the key concepts in the study of pragmatics, including pragmatic competence, different types of meaning (abstract meaning, contextual meaning, and force of an utterance), the cooperative principle and four conversational maxims, as well as politeness and the concept of face (positive and negative). The chapter gives some examples of cross-cultural differences in pragmatic norms to justify the importance of teaching pragmatics in a language classroom, touching briefly on the development of pragmatic skills in a second or foreign language. It then explores different approaches to pragmatics instruction, including raising awareness about pragmatic norms in the target language through deductive and inductive tasks, presenting grammatical structures jointly with their pragmatic functions, and integrating pragmatics with content-based instruction.

WHAT IS PRAGMATICS?

Successful communication requires knowledge of not only the lexicon and the rules of phonology, morphology, syntax and semantics, but also the sociocultural rules (also referred to as pragmatic rules), which help interlocutors decide how to interpret what is being said as well as determine what is and is not appropriate in a given situation. Whereas semantics is preoccupied with the conventional meaning of words, phrases, and sentences, the study of **pragmatics** is primarily concerned with how speakers encode and how listeners decode the intended meaning of utterances depending on the situation in which they occur. In other words, pragmatics is preoccupied with the relationship between context and meaning. It can be defined as, "the study of language from the point of view of users, especially the choices they

DOI: 10.4018/978-1-5225-8467-4.ch008

make, the constraints they encounter in using language in social interaction and the effects their use of language has on other participants in the act of communication" (Crystal, 1997, p. 301).

The linguistic choices people make when interacting with each other are affected by cultural norms. Because languages and cultures differ in behavioral expectations that are considered polite or impolite, misunderstandings and clashes can arise in intercultural interactions (House, 2006). For instance, if an American refused an invitation to a dinner party in Mexico by stating the precise reason why they could not attend rather than promising they would try to make it, which is a typical way to refuse invitations in Mexico, their Mexican friend would likely feel offended and upset (Ishihara & Cohen, 2010, p. 79). Cultural conventions underpin pragmatic choices people make when speaking and interpreting messages, and conversely, "linguistic choices in realizing discourse may be taken to reflect deeper differences in cultural preferences and expectation patterns" (House, 2006, p. 264). The study of pragmatics encompasses the area of linguistic enquiry that investigates the interface of language and culture, i.e., language use in a social context. It examines how meaning is constructed and interpreted in a given situation, and how speakers, using their knowledge of social and cultural norms, are able to express more, or something different from what they actually say.

WHAT IS PRAGMATIC KNOWLEDGE?

Pragmatic knowledge or ability is one of the components of communicative competence, a construct introduced by Dell Hymes (1972) in response to Chomsky's (1965) narrow definition of linguistic competence as the speaker's perfect, abstract, and unconscious knowledge of grammar. Hymes (1972) argued that it is problematic to view linguistic competence in isolation from sociocultural factors, and instead proposed that the knowledge of what is contextually appropriate is an integral component of a speaker's knowledge of language. In other words, in addition to knowing how to produce grammatically correct sentences, language users also need to know "when to speak, when not, and … what to talk about with whom, when, where, and in what manner" (Hymes, 1972, p. 277).

In second language acquisition studies, the concept of communicative competence was embraced and further developed by Canale and Swain (1980) and Canale (1983), who understood it as the underlying knowledge required for communication, and who distinguished its four components: grammatical, discourse, strategic, and **pragmatic competence** (sometimes referred to as sociolinguistic competence), arguing that all four are crucial for successful communication. Grammatical competence allows language users to decode and encode literal meaning of utterances (see abstract meaning below), and it is comprised of the knowledge of the lexicon, phonology, morphology, syntax, and semantics. Discourse competence is responsible for creating cohesion and coherence in longer stretches of oral or written text, i.e., it supplements grammatical competence beyond the level of a sentence. Strategic competence enables speakers and listeners to overcome difficulties that arise in communication through both linguistic and non-linguistic means, for example, the use of synonyms, paraphrases, gestures, and visuals to make a message clear. Finally, pragmatic competence is the knowledge of the sociocultural norms and the effect that they have on the selection of appropriate language means to convey a message. It enables speakers to consider factors such as the topic, context, and purpose of an interaction, and the status and roles of the participants.

Other models of communicative competence have been outlined as well, such as the model proposed by Bachman (1990), which situates sociolinguistic skills in a more prominent position. In Bachman's model, language competence is divided into organizational competence, which subsumes grammatical and textual (or discourse) competence, and pragmatic competence, which includes the knowledge of language functions, the ability to use and understand different registers, figurative language, and cultural allusions. For example, pragmatic knowledge enables people to decide when to perform a given speech act (e.g., when it is necessary to apologize), and what linguistic means to select to perform it (e.g., to provide reasons and explanations to support an apology) (see Chapter 9 in this volume for more information on speech acts). In cross-cultural contexts, a lack of pragmatic competence can lead to pragmatic failure (Thomas, 1995), as when a speaker fails to apologize when an apology is expected (also referred to as sociopragmatic failure), or when a speaker provides insufficient reasons and explanations for the offense (also referred to as pragmalinguistic failure). It has been suggested that in a second or foreign language, learning to appropriately produce and understand utterances can pose serious difficulties for language learners. As Ishihara and Cohen succinctly argue, "pragmatic ability is one of the most complex and challenging aspects of communicative competence" (2010, p. 76). In the sections below, we will examine some theoretical concepts that may be useful to language teachers when planning the pragmatics component of their lessons.

TYPES OF MEANING

To successfully participate in communicative actions, the participants have to attend to both the physical context, i.e., where and with whom the interaction takes place, as well as to the linguistic context (also referred to as co-text), i.e., what has been said (or written) prior to their interactional turn (also see Chapter 10 in this volume). Based on this information, the interlocutors construct different levels of meaning: abstract and contextual (Thomas, 1995). Abstract (or literal) meaning is most easily understood as all possible interpretations that words, phrases, and sentences could have independently of the context. For instance, the word "get" has several different meanings, including "to obtain" (as in "He got a new bike") and "to earn" (as in "He gets a lot of money at his new job"). We have all known an English teacher who, upon being confronted with the question "Excuse me, can I use the bathroom?" would invariably respond, "I don't know, can you?," thus indicating that there exist two possible **abstract meanings** of this utterance – one referring to ability (as interpreted by the teacher), and one to permission (as intended by the student). Once a word, a phrase, or a sentence is uttered, its **contextual meaning** is usually immediately obvious to the parties involved in the interaction. Your English teacher clearly understood that you did not question your own ability to go to the bathroom, but rather asked for permission, yet insisted on the prescriptively correct[1] use of the modal verb "can." Sudden changes in topic or a lack of advanced proficiency in a language can, however, make it more difficult to infer the contextual meaning and can potentially cause a misunderstanding.

In addition to distinguishing between abstract meaning and contextual meaning, it is also important to add another level, namely the meaning intended by the speaker (or writer). There is often a discrepancy between what people say literally and what they actually mean. Imagine that you have just colored your hair pink. You meet a friend who exclaims, "Wow, that's different!" The contextual meaning of this sentence depends on the interpretation of the demonstrative pronoun "that" – it could refer to your hair, but it could also refer to something else in the immediate surroundings. Contextual clues such as your friend looking directly at you or pointing towards something else will help you resolve this conundrum. However, their intended meaning remains unclear. Is the reaction positive or critical? Are they saying, "I love your hair," or are they implying that it looks awful? In pragmatics, this communicative intent of the speaker is referred to as **force of an utterance**. In the case above, the contextual meaning of the utterance (how the sentence could be interpreted) is potentially different from its force (the actual meaning intended by the speaker) (Thomas, 1995). Miscommunication is more likely to occur due to a wrong interpretation of the force of an utterance rather than one's inability to assign abstract or contextual meaning.

CONVERSATIONAL IMPLICATURE, THE COOPERATIVE PRINCIPLE, AND THE FOUR MAXIMS

To help explain how listeners deduct what is actually meant from what is said, it is useful to employ the construct of conversational implicature. First proposed by Grice (1975), **conversational implicature** refers to the conclusions made by the recipient of a message when attempting to understand the **force** of the message in a particular context. For instance, when you are walking down the street and a stranger stops you and asks, "Do you know what time it is?" you can infer, with a high degree of likelihood, that they want you to tell them the actual time. However, if you are being slow getting ready to go out, and your friend, who is standing by the door, ready to leave, ask you the same question, the more likely interpretation is, "It is late, and I think we should leave now!" When people communicate with each other, they infer what is meant from what is said based on their knowledge of how conversation works.

To explain how listeners interpret the implied meaning and thus arrive at conversational implicature, Grice proposed the **Cooperative Principle** and four **conversational maxims**. The Cooperative Principle states: "make your conversational contribution such as is required, at the stage at which it occurs, by the accepted purpose or direction to the talk exchange in which you are engaged" (Grice, 1975, p. 78). This means that both the speaker and the listener constantly interpret each other's goals in a conversation and cooperate as they co-construct meaning. Thomas (1995) compared the Cooperative Principle to the assumptions drivers make when entering traffic – namely, that all other drivers will follow the same set of rules. If a driver from South Africa makes an incorrect assumption that traffic runs on the left side of the road in Germany, a sudden disruption on the road or even an accident can occur. Similarly, people follow a set of assumptions when engaging in a conversation, which allows them to convey more than what they actually say. However, if they fail to cooperate, or if they share a different set of values, a conversation may break down.

Grice succinctly summarized the assumptions people make when entering a conversation as four **conversational maxims**. The first maxim, the **maxim of quantity**, states that participants in a conversation should be as informative as required in a given situation. If they provide too little information, they risk not being understood. On the other hand, if they provide too much information, they may bore the listener. How much information is actually needed depends on the context and purpose of the interaction. Suppose that you run into a co-worker in the hallway, and he asks you "Hi, how is your day going?" In this context, a short response such as "Fine, and yours?" will likely suffice. However, when the same question is asked by your parent or partner when you return home from work, you are likely expected to provide more details about your day.

The next maxim, the **maxim of quality** assumes that interlocutors only say what they believe to be true, and for which they have sufficient evidence. For instance, when a stranger asks you what time it is, they expect that you will provide an accurate answer based on what your watch tells you, and that you will give the time for your current location rather than another time zone. Non-observance of the maxim of quality can be used to express sarcasm, such as when, annoyed by the poor taste of food at a restaurant, a customer says to a friend, "Well, that was a rare feast!"

The third maxim, called the **maxim of relation** (also called the maxim of relevance), simply states that the participants in a conversation give responses that are relevant to what has been said before. The interlocutors assume that unexpected, abrupt changes in the topic of a conversation are generally avoided, or else indicated through interceptions such as, "Sorry to change the topic, but we really need to discuss…" It is uncommon for people to tell about a funny incident they had at an amusement park when asked what they would like to have for dinner. The maxim of relevance helps infer contextual from abstract meaning when there is no apparent connection between a question and a received response, as in the following example:

Example 1

    A: Have you seen my gloves?
    B: I haven't folded the laundry yet.

At first sight, B's response does not appear relevant to A's inquiry. However, because A assumes that B knows where the gloves are, she can infer that B put them through a wash, and that they are in the pile of clean, unfolded laundry.

Finally, the **maxim of manner** says that ideas should be expressed in the clearest, briefest, and most orderly manner possible, and that obscure and ambiguous statements should be avoided unless they serve a specific purpose, i.e., they are intended to produce a special implicature. If in response to your colleague's inquiry about your day so far you say, "It's been a splendid and fantastic day, and there are great prospects that it will continue in a similar fashion unless someone does not quit getting on my nerves," the colleague will likely give you a funny look and walk away wondering if you have lost your mind. However, in some situations, such obscurity of expression may be intended on purpose, as when you suspect that the colleague in question is hitting on you and you want to give them a hint that they should stop.

In cases when the speaker is unable to observe one of the maxims, they may explicitly indicate it. For instance, to signal an inability to follow the maxim of relevance, the speaker may say, "I know this is not relevant, but…," while to warn that the maxim of quality is not being observed, they may say "I'm not sure this is correct, but…" There are many reasons why participants in a conversation may decide not to observe a maxim. For example, as we saw above, the maxim of quality may be violated on purpose to express sarcasm. Such instances of non-observance when the speaker purposefully creates an implicature and expects the listener to understand what is implied are referred to as flouting the maxims. Figurative speech, for instance, hyperboles and metaphors, are classic examples of maxim flouting. For example, when someone says, "I have a million things to do today," such a statement clearly flouts the maxim of quality (it cannot possibly be true that they have that many things to do in one day), yet the listener is expected to understand that the speaker simply means that they are very busy. Maxims can also be flouted to obscure the meaning in order to exclude someone else from a conversation. Although my dog does not understand the Cooperative Principle, he does understand the word "cat" and reacts to it with boisterous barking. To avoid embarrassing situations with our neighbors, my husband and I warn each other instantly upon spotting a cat by saying something like, "There's a furry little fellow on the corner ahead." Although clearly, such elaborate descriptions violate the maxim of manner, we never fail to understand the statement as a signal to change the direction of the walk.

Observing or flouting a maxim appropriately requires an advanced level of pragmatic competence. This is because to correctly create and interpret implicatures, interlocutors need to follow sociolinguistic rules and be familiar with the cultural norms of a given speech community, which can be challenging for less proficient language learners. Maxim violations that result from a lack of linguistic or pragmatic competence are referred to as infringing a maxim. Consider a situation when a Norwegian speaker of English, a student, asks a professor to let them borrow a book using the following statement, "Hey Ingrid, I need your book for a minute." Because of the status difference, such a request in English infringes the maxim of quantity. The student should have provided a reason for the request and employed appropriate hedging to soften the request. It is unclear, however, if the maxim was infringed due to an imperfect command of the language or an unwillingness to conform to target language cultural norms. It is highly possible that the Norwegian student knows how to use modal verbs "would" and "could" and realizes that reasons or explanations could be added to mitigate the request. However, their strong egalitarian feelings may have been an underlying factor that impacted their choice of linguistic means. The Norwegian cultural norms do not presuppose a status difference between a student and a professor. Consequently, it may have felt highly unnatural for the student to say, "I'm really sorry to bother you, but do you think I could borrow your book for a few minutes? I have left mine at home, and I really need it to finish this project. I would really appreciate it." As we will see later on in this chapter, pragmatic norms are strongly intertwined with people's personalities, worldviews, and cultures, which may prevent them from acting in a way native speakers would.

It is important to acknowledge that although Grice's theory is helpful in explaining how participants in a conversation are able to convey and infer meanings without being explicit, it has met with a fair amount of criticism. Most importantly, it has been pointed out that the ways in which the maxims are observed or violated vary cross-linguistically and cross-culturally. For instance, Americans tend to be perceived as insincere by people from other cultures because, when they ask, "How are you?" they expect a terse "Fine, thanks" and are uninterested in a genuine response. This phenomenon can be explained by the differences in how various cultures interpret the maxim of quantity and manner – whereas, in the United States, the focus is on brevity, in other cultures, a full report on one's well-being is expected. Another issue with Grice's theory that has been pointed out is that there is often an overlap in the maxims, and it is impossible to pinpoint which one exactly is being followed or violated. For instance, it is almost impossible to find examples of communicative exchanges where the maxim of relevance does not apply (or else we would never be able to make sense out of any conversation that extends beyond abstract meaning of utterances) (Thomas, 1995). For these reasons, Sperber and Wilson (1995) proposed that the four maxims should be conflated into one, which they call the principle of relevance. As Cutting (2008) put it, "conversational implicature is understood by hearers simply by selecting the relevant features of context and recognizing whatever speakers say as relevant of the conversation" (p. 41) (bolding added). Despite these limitations, the Cooperative Principle and the conversational maxims remain influential in the study of pragmatics, and they can be helpful in explaining how people maintain (or breach) politeness when interacting with each other, which is the topic of the next section.

POLITENESS AND THE CONCEPT OF FACE

In pragmatics, **politeness** refers to "the choices that are made in language use, the linguistic expressions that give people space and show a friendly attitude to them" (Cutting, 2008, p. 43). How politeness is performed depends on the social context in which the interaction occurs and the relationship between the interlocutors. In order to maintain politeness, interlocutors attend to their own and other people's **face** defined as positively valued social identity (Goffman, 1967). Most people want to create a self-image that is socially approved, and therefore a lot of care is given in interactions with others to save one's face by conforming to generally accepted social rules. To do so, they can use "verbal and nonverbal strategies … to maintain, defend, or upgrade [their] own social self-image and attack or defend (or "save") the social images of others" (Ting-Toomey & Chung, 2012, p. 190). At times, maintaining one's own or another person's face may require violation of a maxim. For example, if you have just been served fried liver with onions, which you absolutely detest, but you do not want to offend the host, you may choose to eat it and violate the maxim of quality by saying, "Mmmm, this was absolutely delicious." By doing so, you would be attending to the host's **positive face**, i.e., their wish to be a part of a group and to share involvement with others, which is manifested in expressing friendliness or approval (Brown & Levinson, 1987). It is also possible to perform politeness through attending to negative face, which can be defined as a person's right to independence and personal freedom of action (Brown & Levinson, 1987). If a friend who is clearly upset about something chooses not to talk about it and insists that everything is fine, they are flouting the maxim of quality (they are not telling the truth) while at the same time invoking their right to preserve **negative face**.

In some cases, sophisticated interactional turns are required to prevent damaging or threatening a person's face. Speech acts such as invitations, requests, apologies, orders, and insults are examples of face-threatening acts (FTAs) (Brown & Levinson, 1987) (for more on speech acts, see Chapter 9 in this volume). Performing these acts requires interlocutors to select appropriate strategies in order to show respect for each other's expectations regarding the self-image. However, there are many different ways of showing awareness of our own and other people's face, ranging from threatening to preservation-oriented actions. For instance, when asking a friend to lend you some money, you can select one of the following options:

1. Avoid the FTA – choose to wait and save up some money instead of borrowing it.
2. Perform the FTA boldly on record – ask the friend directly, e.g., say, "I would like you to lend me some money."
3. Do the FTA off record – ask the friend indirectly, e.g., say, "I really need to get a new computer, but my savings have completely run out."
4. Do the FTA on record with negative politeness, for example, by including options or using hedges as in, "Would you be able to lend me some money for my new laptop? I can also ask my parents, but I thought I'd check with you first."
5. Do the FTA on record with positive politeness, for example, by appealing to personal values or stressing closeness and solidarity, as in, "I have an emergency expense, and I thought I'd ask you to help me since you are my best friend. Can you lend me some money?"

To determine which of the options to select, the speaker has to consider factors such as the social distance between themselves and the listener, the power they have in this relationship, and the seriousness of the imposition (Brown & Levinson, 1987). For instance, most of us will likely choose not to request money for a new personal laptop from our boss but instead entirely avoid the FTA. On the other hand, when speaking with a life partner, we would probably use a direct statement such as "I need money for a new laptop" rather than employing elaborate off record politeness strategies such as those in option three above. It is also important to acknowledge that cultural differences determine the choice of politeness strategies, something that has not been accounted for by Brown and Levinson (1987), but that is important to consider in the language classroom. For example, when making requests, Polish native speakers tend to use more imperatives in comparison with German native speakers, who tend to opt for interrogatives instead (Ogiermann, 2009). Because politeness norms vary among languages and cultures, being polite in a second or foreign language can be challenging for language learners who may be less familiar with the target language culture in comparison with native speakers for whom deciding what politeness strategy to use (or when to be impolite) is usually unconscious (see also Chapter 9 in this volume).

IMPLICATIONS FOR TEACHING ENGLISH LANGUAGE LEARNERS

Why Is It Important to Teach Pragmatics?

Because pragmatic norms differ among languages and cultures, and because how humans behave and what they say is so strongly rooted in cultural norms, pragmatics is often one of the most challenging areas for foreign and second language learners to grasp. To date, research on how second and foreign language learners develop their pragmatic skills has concluded that language learners take a long time to attain high levels of pragmatic competence, that they go through several developmental stages, and that their pragmatic performance often diverges from that of native speakers (for a summary, see for example Kasper & Rose, 2002). It has been noted that in the early stages of development, learners often rely on unanalyzed language chunks, formulaic expressions, and literal meanings. As their proficiency increases, they start employing more complex syntactic structures as well as more mitigation and elaboration.

However, research suggests that even advanced learners who have a good command of grammar and vocabulary often commit pragmatic fallacies (e.g., Bardovi-Harlig & Hartford, 1990; Taguchi, 2006). These include both sociopragmatic failure, defined as failure to perform the speech act required in a given situation, and pragmalinguistic failure, defined as performance of the required act using inadequate linguistic means (Thomas, 1983). An example of sociopragmatic failure is when one does not apologize in a situation that, in the target language, requires an apology. An example of pragmalinguistic failure is when one provides insufficient reasons or compensation to strengthen the apology.

Pragmatic errors can be caused by limited grammatical competence, as when learners lack the linguistic means to make a polite request and overuse "want" and "need"-statements. Pragmatic errors can also result from the limited noticing of pragmatic norms in the target language and the consequent negative transfer from the first language. For example, a learner of English whose first language is Russian may not realize that the abstract meaning of an English greeting, "How are you?" (an inquiry about one's well-being) does not correspond to the contextual meaning (a greeting). Instead of giving an appropriate brief response such as "Fine, thanks" or "Fine, and you?", the Russian speaker of English may instead offer a long and elaborate description of how their day has been going so far (Kartalova, 1996). Research on pragmatic errors suggests that they can cause miscommunication and might be judged more harshly than grammatical or lexical errors (Biesenbach-Lucas, 2007; Hartford & Bardovi-Harlig, 1996; Hendricks, 2010). To date, however, the teaching of pragmatics has only been given a limited time and space in the language classroom, and findings from research have demonstrated that while learners can achieve some level of pragmatic development in second language settings (Schmidt, 1983), little or no pragmatic development occurs in foreign language settings (Rose, 2000).

Thus, to help prevent negative perceptions and stereotyping of culturally and linguistically diverse learners as unable to communicate in ways that are perceived as appropriate in the target language, language teachers have a particular responsibility to teach pragmatics. As Bardovi-Harlig and Mahan-Taylor affirm, "observation of language learners shows there is a demonstrated need for [teaching pragmatics], and instruction in pragmatics can be successful" (2003, p. 38).

Goals of Pragmatics Instruction

Different approaches to teaching pragmatics have been proposed, but most of the sources recommend various awareness-raising techniques (e.g., Ishihara & Cohen, 2010; Bardovi-Harlig & Mahan-Taylor, 2003), as well as guiding students, modeling of target language practices, and providing feedback on production (e.g., Kasper & Rose, 2002). Whereas few course materials to-date focus on pragmatics, sources of pragmatic data that can be used in the classroom include intuition and retrospection, discourse completion tasks (DTCs), role-plays, and field observations. Researchers and practitioners have suggested that in addition to becoming more aware of target language pragmatic norms, learners need to be given opportunities to practice and to evaluate their own pragmatic performance.

What has been repeatedly stressed, however, is that learners should not be expected to fully conform to the pragmatic norms of the target community but rather be made aware of the differences between their own pragmatic norms and the norms in the target language so that they can make conscious linguistic choices in their pragmatic performance. Likewise, language teachers need to acknowledge the fact that there is no common agreement on pragmatic norms, and that there exists a lot of individual and societal variation, including regional, class, gender, and dialectal differences. For this reason, rather than being prescriptive in nature, pragmatics instruction should focus more generally on increasing learners' sensitivity to how language users make linguistic choices when interacting with others, what constraints they have to take into account when making these choices, and the effect their choices will have on the other participants in the interaction.

Well-developed pragmatic competence is a central component of successful communication. If the participants in a conversation are not able to correctly arrive at implicatures, if they say too much or too little, if they make comments that are not relevant to the topic at hand, or if they make statements that do not conform to the target language rules of politeness, communication may break down. To help language learners adjust their linguistic behavior in a way that is congruent with the target language requirements dictated by the social settings, participants, and goals, language teachers need to spend more time in the classroom focusing explicitly on pragmatics. However, because pragmatic norms are strongly intertwined with culture, teaching pragmatics needs to be delivered in a way that is sensitive to language learners social, cultural, and linguistic identities. Rather than giving learners a recipe for pragmatic performance, the goal of pragmatics in language teaching should be to sensitize them to cross-cultural and cross-linguistic differences in pragmatic norms, and to make them more aware of the consequences their linguistic choices can have on the success (or failure) of interaction. Below, we consider concrete examples of how pragmatics-focused instruction can be implemented in a language classroom and how pragmatics can be integrated into language curricula.

Pragmatics-Focused Tasks and Activities

There has been little or no focus on the development of learners' pragmatic skills in traditional language teaching curricula. At the same time, findings from research suggest that pragmatic competence develops slowly and some aspects of it may never develop without pedagogical intervention (Rose & Kasper, 2001). Consequently, there has been a recent surge in various proposals on how pragmatics could be successfully taught to second and foreign language learners, with most of the approaches focusing on raising awareness of target language pragmatic norms. Bardovi-Harlig and Mahan-Taylor (2002) postulate that pragmatics-focused instruction should expand learner's perceptions of the target language community, provide them with various choices of target language pragmatic devices, and raise their overall pragmatic awareness. In what follows, we are going to take a closer look at various approaches to teaching pragmatics, including **awareness-raising tasks** that can be integrated into any language program, as well as curricular approaches such as integrating pragmatics with grammar teaching and content-based instruction. Although most research on pragmatics learning and resources for pragmatics teaching to-date have targeted adult language learners, a few examples of instructional activities for young learners will also be provided.

Because language learners may not be able to acquire pragmatic norms implicitly (i.e., incidentally) from the **input** they receive, teachers may have to implement explicit instruction approaches, such as awareness-raising, where learners' attention is deliberately focused on target-language pragmatic norms. For instance, rather than exposing learners to a dialog in which the interlocutors disagree about an issue and then prompting the students to perform a similar interaction themselves, the teacher may first provide learners with examples of expressions of disagreement and ask them to compare these with how disagreement is expressed in their first language. The main support for awareness-raising tasks and activities in teaching pragmatics comes from the **noticing hypothesis** (Schmidt, 1990), which states that in order for pragmatic information in the input to be acquired, learners need to pay conscious attention to it. This entails noticing how contextual meaning is derived from abstract meaning under specific contextual conditions. For instance, the teacher can draw the learners' attention to the fact that requests can be made using imperatives (e.g., 'Take out the garbage'), modals ('Could you take out the garbage?') and hints ('Ugh, the garbage stinks!'). The learners first interpret the abstract meaning of each example and then discuss any factors that may impact the choice of form in a specific context (e.g., which form(s) can be used with someone we know vs. a stranger). Once a pragmatic feature is noticed, analyzed, and understood, "the input has the potential to become **intake** and may be stored in long-term memory" (Ishihara & Cohen, 2010, p 101) (bolding added). With younger language learners, teachers can used approaches such as dialogical teaching through visual narratives which entails reading bilingual books and engaging learners in discussions of target pragmatic features (Ishihara, 2013).

Both **deductive** (top-down) and **inductive teaching** (bottom-up) techniques can be used to raise learners' awareness of target-language pragmatic norms. In deductive tasks, learners are first provided with explicit information about a pragmatic feature (or features), and then engage in an analysis of examples and practice. Inductive teaching is based on rule-discovery: learners are presented with examples and prompted to arrive at a rule themselves. McLellan Howard (n.d.) provides a sample lesson plan that focuses on business letters and that combines these two approaches, inductive and deductive, as is often the case in language classrooms. For example, when focusing on how to perform politeness in business letters, the teacher can first present learners with a sample of a typical business letter written in their first language, and a letter written in the target language. The teacher can then point out the differences between the two letters such as forms of address, and lexical and syntactical markers of politeness (deductive teaching). Without necessarily delving into a lecture on positive and negative face, the teacher can then guide the students as they categorize the different strategies used in the two letters as either focusing on establishing rapport and being friendly (positive face) or focusing on one's right to independence (negative face). As a follow-up, the students can be instructed to write two versions of a business letter in the target language, one polite and one impolite. In inductive tasks, on the other hand, learners first analyze examples on their own and are then guided by the teacher in discovery of pragmatic norms. As an additional step, students can first collect pragmatic data themselves and then share and analyze it with classmates. To teach the lesson on politeness in business letters inductively, the teacher could first ask the learners to produce business letters in the target language, and then ask them to explore the differences between the letters they produced and a typical example of a business letter in a target language, providing guidance along the way.

Several other tasks can be implemented to raise learners' awareness of target language pragmatic norms. Ishihara and Cohen (2010) list activities such as collecting second language data in media (for example TV-shows or movies), comparing successful and awkward interactions, conducting role-plays, comparing first language and target language pragmatic norms, sharing and reflecting on personal stories about pragmatic failures, keeping a reflective journal, and responding to discourse completion tasks (DCTs), i.e., incomplete scripted interactions which elicit a particular speech act. When working with beginners, teachers may want to focus on production of commonly used words and expressions in situations such as greetings and good-byes by engaging learners in simple role-plays with a pre-defined status of the participants (e.g., parent/child, boss/employee, customer/shopping assistant), as in the following example:

Example 2 (beginner learners)

> Student A: You are an executive in a big company. Exchange morning greetings with your secretary.
> Student B: You are a secretary. Exchange morning greetings with your boss.

In intermediate classrooms, the role-plays can be expanded to include interactions between participants with different cultural and linguistic backgrounds, and more complex situations such as giving and turning down invitations or compliments (see Example 3). Here the focus could be placed on Grice's maxims, for instance on how to turn down an invitation from a colleague at work as compared to an invitation from a close family member in a way that is clear and unambiguous and that contains the right amount of reasons and explanations.

Example 3 (intermediate learners)

> Scenario A: Your colleague at work, whom you don't know very well, has invited you to a big barbecue party to celebrate his round birthday. Turn down his invitation.
> Scenario B: Your brother has invited you to his daughter's birthday. Turn down his invitation.

Reflection: What reasons and explanations did you use in Scenario A and in Scenario B? Were they the same or different? Was one of the refusals longer/more elaborate than the other? Did you tell the truth or lie? Why?

Young learners can be taught formulaic expressions and routinized greetings, which they can practiced chorally (e.g., at the beginning of each class period or through songs), or with a partner in activities such as inside-outside circle (Vogt & Echevarría, 2008), in which half of the children forms a circle looking out (the inside circle), and the other half forms a circle looking in (the outside circle). Each pair of students facing each other exchange a greeting and then the teacher gives a signal for the outer circle to rotate one person clockwise. The cycle repeats until each student faces their original partner. Young learners readily engage in repetitive activities and routines, and preliminary research suggests that they can be successfully taught such target pragmatic features as directness/indirectness, appropriate and inappropriate behaviors, and pragmatic formulas (Ishihara, 2013).

Teachers working in second language instructional settings, where the target language is also used outside of class, have even more options available to them. For example, they can ask learners to observe native-speaker interactions in the community with a focus on a particular speech act (e.g., ordering food at a restaurant), and then discuss the data students collected together in class. They can also have the learners interview native and non-native speaker informants or ask them to experiment with certain pragmatic behaviors outside of class (e.g., have students respond to abstract instead of contextual meaning of utterances in interactions with others and record how their interlocutors react). Such approaches in which students explore how pragmatic norms operate authentically in the community are referred to as learners as ethnographers (Bardovi-Harlig, 1996) or learners as researchers (Tanaka, 1997). Several advocates of pragmatics-focused instruction point out that it is also important to add a stage in a lesson in which students have opportunities for practice in interaction with others (e.g., Butler, 2012; Usó-Juan & Martínez-Flor, 2008). Finally, it has been pointed out that learners should be prompted to observe and self-evaluate their own pragmatic performance, including comparison of their own pragmatic choices with those of native speaker models (Ishihara & Cohen, 2010).

Integrating Pragmatics Into Language Curricula

Whereas above, we have considered some types and examples of tasks and activities that foster the development of pragmatic competence, it is also important to consider ways in which pragmatics-focused teaching can be integrated into the language classroom at the level of a curriculum. Félix-Brasdefer and Cohen (2012) put forward a proposal for integrating pragmatics with grammar instruction. Rather than presenting grammatical forms in isolation, these authors argue for a presentation of grammatical structures jointly with their pragmatic functions so that the structures become a "communicative resource" allowing language learners to "not only increase their grammatical competence, but [...] also improve their functional knowledge of how to negotiate communicative actions" (p. 664). For instance, when teaching conditional sentences, teachers can target the pragmatic functions of conditionals in constructing polite requests (e.g., 'I was wondering if you could help me with my assignment') or when expressing uncertainty (e.g., 'I am unsure if this is correct'). Rather than focusing solely on the form of conditionals, the teacher instead helps the learners explore communicative functions that conditionals assume in specific communicative contexts.

While traditional grammar textbooks that focus extensively on form rather than on meaning may need special adaptations on part of the teacher, Leech and Svartvik's (2002) volume, *A communicative grammar of English*, is an excellent resource for teaching grammar and pragmatics together. Instead of employing a structural approach, the authors organize the topics based on language functions (e.g., mood, emotion, and attitude; information, reality, and belief). Leech and Svartvik (2002) stress, for example, that "language is more than [a means of giving and receiving information]: it is communication between people. It often expresses the emotions and attitudes of the speaker, and the speaker often uses it to influence the attitudes and behavior of the hearer" (p. 159, original emphasis). While this particular volume is more appropriate for intermediate to advanced language learners, Félix-Brasdefer and Cohen (2012) argue that pragmatics can be a central component of language teaching from beginning levels of instruction as long as selected communicative function corresponds to learners' level of grammatical competence. Whereas teaching contextually appropriate greetings and forms of address can be easily done with beginners, exploring face-preserving strategies when performing refusals should probably be reserved for more advanced learners.

Finally, it has been suggested that the most natural instructional setting where pragmatic competence can be developed along the other components of communicative competence is in content-based programs (Krulatz, 2014). Content-based instruction (CBI) (also referred to as content-based language teaching, or, in European contexts, as content and language integrated learning) is based on a premise that the most efficient way to acquire advanced proficiency in a second or foreign language is when language is combined with meaningful, engaging, non-linguistic content. For example, a social studies class in a German high school can be taught through the medium of English, or a university-level class on French literature can be taught in French. CBI programs range from language-driven, where the main focus is on language and classes are taught by language specialists, to content-driven, where content taken from an academic discipline such as social studies or science is taught in a foreign or a second language.

What CBI programs have in common is that "content and function flow rather smoothly together, being complementary aspects of language as a system for communication" (Eskey, 1997, p. 139). In other words, CBI programs create authentic contexts for language interaction and, as a result, learners have to use language in purposeful and meaningful ways. They cannot do so without employing the pragmatic norms of the target language. For instance, in a natural science class, when participating in a debate concerning the causes of the global warming, the learners can practice how to express agreement, disagreement, and reinforcement in a way that does not pose a threat to the opponent's face. When learning how to write a business letter in an academic writing class, learners can practice how to give constructive peer-feedback through positive politeness strategies. Or, when writing a research paper, they can learn how to appropriately integrate findings from previous research and thus observe the maxim of manner. The types of specific tasks and activities can range from implicit to explicit, both inductive and deductive. The main premise is that since "content and communication are the main focus of [CBI] and guide the selection of activities, students are motivated to raise their [own] pragmatic awareness" (Krulatz, 2014, p. 24).

In all, teaching of second language pragmatics has been gaining attention in the last two decades, and there is now a consensus among second language researchers and practitioners that instruction can contribute to the development of pragmatic competence. While teachers have to make the ultimate decision regarding the optimal instructional practices and materials for their specific teaching contexts, it is hoped that the overview presented in this chapter will aide them in this process.

DISCUSSION QUESTIONS

1. Can you recall a situation when you were interacting with someone from another culture and one of you said something that shocked or surprised the other person, or perhaps even lead to a cul-

tural misunderstanding? Recall as much detail as possible about the situation and analyze what happened using the concepts introduced in this class (e.g., cross-cultural differences, pragmatic transfer, abstract and contextual meaning, face, etc.).

2. Grammatical competence allows language learners to interpret the abstract meaning of an utterance, whereas understanding the contextual meaning is much more complex and requires advanced levels of pragmatic competence. Can you think of examples from your own experience using a foreign language or from observing your students when communication broke down because one of the interlocutors was unable to correctly interpret contextual meaning? Share your example with others.

3. Based on your personal experience as a language learner and/or language teacher, to what extent and how is pragmatics taught in foreign and/or second language courses in your country/at your institution? What strategies/approaches to teaching pragmatics do you think would work best with culturally and linguistically diverse learners?

4. Among the four Gricean maxims, it is perhaps the maxim of relevance that may pose the most challenges for language learners. Can you think of a specific example when a language learner infringed this maxim? What was the possible reason for the maxim violation? Was it a lack of linguistic resources, transfer from the first language, or some other reason? Explain.

5. Think of some linguistic act that makes you particularly uncomfortable (e.g., refusing when a friend invited you to dinner, asking your boss for an extension on a deadline). What face saving-strategies do you use to soften the impact of what you say? Do you tend to appeal to positive or negative face? Would you behave the same when speaking your first language and a foreign/second language you know? Why or why not?

EXERCISES

1. To further explore the distinction between abstract and contextual meaning, think of some examples of figurative language. For instance, what are the different levels of meaning in expressions such as "to be in someone's shoes" or "to be a rolling stone"? Discuss with a partner and add a few more expressions of your own. Note also that how abstract meaning is linked to contextual meaning can differ from culture to culture. If you know people who speak another language than you, ask them to finish the following phrases:
   As tired as a ...
   As happy as a ...
   As heavy as a ...

What kind of knowledge do you think helps speakers and listeners correctly select and interpret figurative language?

2. Think of two different languages or cultures that you know. How would the following actions be appropriately performed in each of those languages/cultures? What could be some potential areas of misunderstanding if these two languages/cultures clashed?
   a. Congratulating someone on a promotion.
   b. Apologizing for spilling the soup.
   c. Firing someone.

3. Discourse Completion Task (DCT) is a common way of data collection in interlanguage pragmatics research. Participants are given short scenarios that elicit various linguistic behaviors and are asked to respond to them orally or in writing. Conduct your own DCT with colleagues/friends/family members who come from other cultures and speak languages other than English. For each scenario, tell them to respond in English and in their other language(s), and then ask them to explain to you how the two responses were similar and/or different and why. For example, you could focus on the speech act of refusal using the following scenarios (borrowed from Stavans & Webman Shafran, 2018):

   a. Your friend invites you to go see a movie, but you don't want to go. What would you say to refuse the invitation?

   b. You are the director of a language institute. One of your teachers asks for a raise but you decide against it. What would you say to refuse his/her request?

   c. Your own scenarios.

   Once you have collected your data, analyze it in terms of maxim violations. For example, you could focus on the maxim of quantity and explain how people from different cultural and linguistic backgrounds either observe or flout this maxim. Is the maxim interpreted in the same way in the different languages/cultures you have examined?

4. Go back to the answer you provided to discussion question 4. Based on what you have learned about teaching pragmatics in this chapter, create an activity or a sequence of activities that focus on the maxim of relevance.

5. Consider the group of learners you are currently working with. If you do not have your own class at present, define a target population you would like to work with (e.g., age, proficiency level, L1 background). Then, select a pragmatic target that you would like to teach (e.g., how to perform invitations, how to save face when refusing, how to express annoyance with different people), and design one deductive and one inductive task to teach it. Share the task with a classmate or classmates and provide each other with feedback (or try it out on each other).

REFERENCES

Bardovi-Harlig, K. (1996). Pragmatics and language teaching: Bridging pragmatics and pedagogy together. In L. F. Bouton (Ed.), *Pragmatics and language learning* (Vol. 7, pp. 21–38). Urbana, IL: Division of English as an International Language, University of Illinois at Urbana-Champaign.

Bardovi-Harlig, K., & Hartford, B. (1990). Congruence in native and nonnative conversations: Status balance in the academic advising session. *Language Learning, 40*(4), 467–501. doi:10.1111/j.1467-1770.1990.tb00603.x

Bardovi-Harlig, K., & Mahan-Taylor, R. (2003, July). Introduction to teaching pragmatics. *English Teaching Forum*, 37-39.

Biesenbach-Lucas, S. (2007). *Students writing emails to faculty: an examination of e-politeness among native and nonnative speakers of English*. Academic Press.

Brown, P., & Levinson, S. (1987). *Politeness. Some universals in language use.* Cambridge, UK: Cambridge University Press. doi:10.1017/CBO9780511813085

Butler, R. E. (2012). Politeness is more than 'please.' Teaching email requests. *ORTESOL Journal, 29,* 12–20.

Canale, M. (1983). From communicative competence to language pedagogy. In Richards & Schmidt (Eds.), Language and communication. London: Longman.

Canale, M., & Swain, M. (1980). Theoretical bases of communicative approaches to second language teaching and testing. *Applied Linguistics, 1*(1), 1–47. doi:10.1093/applin/1.1.1

Chomsky, N. (1965). *Aspects of the theory of syntax.* Cambridge, MA: MIT Press.

Crystal, D. (Ed.). (1997). *The Cambridge encyclopedia of language.* New York: Cambridge University Press.

Cutting, J. (2008). *Pragmatics and discourse. A resource book for students.* London: Routledge.

Eskey, D. (1997). Syllabus design in content-based instruction. In M.A. Snow & D. M. Brinton (Eds.), The Content-based Classroom: Perspectives on Integrating Language and Content. White Plains, NY: Longman.

Félix-Brasdefer, J. C., & Cohen, A. D. (2012). Teaching pragmatics in the foreign language classroom: Grammar as a communicative resource. *Hispania, 95*(4), 650–669. doi:10.1353/hpn.2012.0124

Goffman, E. (1967). *Interactional Ritual: Essays on face-to-face behavior.* Garden City, NY: Anchor Books.

Grice, P. (1975). Logic and conversation. In P. Cole & J. L. Morgan (Eds.), Syntax and semantics (pp. 41–58). New York, NY: Academic Press.

Hartford, B., & Bardovi-Harlig, K. (1996). 'At your earliest convenience': A study of written student requests to faculty. Pragmatics and Language Learning, 7, 55-69.

Hendricks, B. (2010). An experimental study of native speaker perceptions of nonnative request modification in e-mails in English. *Intercultural Pragmatics, 7*(2), 221–255.

House, J. (2006). Communicative styles in English and German. *European Journal of English Studies, 10*(3), 249–267. doi:10.1080/13825570600967721

Hymes, D. (1972). On communicative competence. In J. Pride & J. Holmes (Eds.), *Sociolinguistics* (pp. 269–293). Harmondsworth, UK: Penguin.

Ishihara, N. (2013). Is it rude language? Children learning pragmatics through visual narratives. *TESL Canada Journal/Revue TESL du Canada, 30*(7), 135-149.

Ishihara, N., & Cohen, A. (2010). *Teaching and learning pragmatics. Where language and culture meet.* Longman Applied Linguistics.

Kartalova, Y. (1996). Cross-cultural differences in American and Russian general conventions of communication. Pragmatics and Language Learning, 7, 71-96.

Kasper, G., & Rose, K. (2002). *Pragmatic Development in a Second language.* Oxford, UK: Blackwell Publishing.

Krulatz, A. (2014). Integrating pragmatics instruction in a content-based classroom. *ORTESOL Journal, 31,* 19–25.

McLellan, H. (n.d.). *Politeness is more than "please."* Retrieved from https://americanenglish.state.gov/files/ae/resource_files/howard.pdf

Ogiermann, E. (2009). Politeness and in-directness across cultures: A comparison of English, German, Polish and Russian requests. *Journal of Politeness Research, 5*(2), 189–216. doi:10.1515/JPLR.2009.011

Rose, K. R. (2000). Interlanguage pragmatic development in Hong Kong, phase 2. *Journal of Pragmatics, 41*(11), 2345–2364. doi:10.1016/j.pragma.2009.04.002

Rose, K. R., & Kasper, G. (Eds.). (2001). *Pragmatics in language teaching.* Cambridge, UK: Cambridge University Press. doi:10.1017/CBO9781139524797

Schmidt, R. W. (1983). Interaction, acculturation, and the acquisition of communicative competence: A case study of an adult. In N. Wolfson & E. Judd (Eds.), *Sociolinguistics and language acquisition* (pp. 137–174). Newbury House.

Schmidt, R. W. (1990). The role of consciousness in second language learning. *Applied Linguistics, 11*(2), 129–158. doi:10.1093/applin/11.2.129

Sperber, D., & Wilson, D. (1995). *Relevance: Communication and cognition.* Oxford, UK: Blackwell.

Stavans, A., & Webman Shafran, R. (2018). The pragmatics of requests and refusals in multilingual settings. *International Journal of Multilingualism, 15*(2), 149–168. doi:10.1080/14790718.2017.1338708

Taguchi, N. (2006). Analysis of appropriateness in a speech act of request in L2 English. *Pragmatics, 16*(4), 513–533. doi:10.1075/prag.16.4.05tag

Tanaka, K. (1997). Developing pragmatic competence: A learners-as-researchers approach. *TESOL Journal, 6*(3), 14–18.

Thomas, J. (1995). *Meaning in interaction. An introduction to pragmatics.* London: Longman.

Ting-Toomey, S., & Chung, L. (2012). *Understanding intercultural communication.* New York: Oxford University Press.

Usó-Juan, E., & Martínez-Flor, A. (2008). Teaching learners to appropriately mitigate requests. *ELT Journal, 62*(4), 349–357. doi:10.1093/elt/ccm092

Vogt, M., & Echevarría, J. (2008). *99 Ideas and activities for teaching English learners with the SIOP Model.* Boston: Pearson.

ADDITIONAL READING

Armstrong, S. (2008). "Desperate housewives" in an EFL classroom. *Pragmatic Matters, 9*(1), 4–7.

Bardovi-Harlig, K., & Mahan-Taylor, R. (2002, July). Introduction to teaching pragmatics. *English Teaching Forum, 41*(3), 37-39.

Center for Advanced Research on Language Acquisition. (n.d.). *Pragmatics and Speech Acts.* Retrieved from http://carla.umn.edu/speechacts/index.html

Ishihara, N., & Cohen, A. (2010). *Teaching and learning pragmatics. Where language and culture meet.* Great Britain: Longman Applied Linguistics.

Rose, K. R., & Kasper, G. (Eds.). (2001). *Pragmatics in language teaching.* Cambridge, UK: Cambridge University Press. doi:10.1017/CBO9781139524797

Thomas, J. (1995). *Meaning in interaction. An introduction to pragmatics.* London: Longman.

United States Department of State. (n.d.). *American English for English language teachers around the world. Teaching pragmatics.* Retrieved from https://americanenglish.state.gov/resources/teaching-pragmatics

ENDNOTE

[1] Prescriptivism is preoccupied with the use of language that has been deemed correct based on some arbitrary reasons such as comparisons with grammatical rules of classical languages. It is often contrasted with descriptivism, which focuses not on how language should be used, but on how *it is* used.

Chapter 9
Speech Acts and Cross-Cultural Pragmatics

Clara Bauler
Adelphi University, USA

ABSTRACT

Linguistically diverse learners tend to first relate the pragmatic ability they already possess in their first or more dominant language (L1) to act in the L2; as a result, miscommunication and misunderstandings are frequent and common. Teachers can help learners develop awareness about L2 pragmatic norms by making visible how speech acts are performed in the L2 community of speakers while providing opportunities to engage in role-playing or real interactions involving the accomplishment of selected speech acts. This chapter offers an overview of the importance of context in cross-cultural interactions, a brief survey of the theories of speech acts, and concrete pedagogical ideas for teachers to develop linguistically diverse learners' pragmatic awareness and ability while celebrating and promoting linguistic and cultural diversity.

LINGUISTIC CONTEXT AND SITUATIONAL CONTEXT

One of the main concerns of pragmatics is the relationship between **context** and language, and how this relationship influences the ways we speak. What we say and do with each other, including verbal and non-verbal aspects of communication, is directly affected by the context and situation we are engaged in. Therefore, in order to be able to participate in interactions and communicate successfully, hearers and speakers need to know more than the linguistic features expressed by an **utterance**; they need to know other situational variables that are relevant to the interpretation of these utterances, such as temporal and spatial circumstances, the social identities and status of the participants, the emotions evoked during the interaction, and the social activity that is taking place. All of these variables are shaped by sociocultural values, attitudes, and ways of doing things shared by a community of speakers of a determined language or variety of language.

DOI: 10.4018/978-1-5225-8467-4.ch009

The role of context is crucial for speakers to make interpretations about what is meant in each conversational encounter. Before I came to the U.S. from Brazil to study in California, I learned that a phrase like, *Can I have a cup of coffee?* would suffice to order coffee in a coffee shop in English-speaking countries. Needless to say, I was completely lost when I went to order coffee at my local big coffee shop chain in Los Angeles. On the menu, there were more than 20 options of "a cup of coffee," including size, flavor, and temperature (hot or cold). I had never seen a menu like that in my life! In addition, I did not know whether I should sit or not when I entered the coffee shop, as in Brazil, we usually sit and order a "cafezinho" to drink with friends. So, I suddenly realized that the phrase I had learned, *Can I have a cup of coffee?* was not going to help me to obtain the kind of coffee I wanted. I needed to also consider the place, the people I was ordering coffee from, non-verbal cues, such as waiting in line and sitting after I get my coffee, and the cultural practices and expectations for the situation, such as: Do people order coffee fast? Will people judge me if I take too long to order coffee? What kind of coffee do people usually order when the weather is hot or cold? Do people actually sit and have a conversation at coffee shops or do they just grab the coffee and go? How do these cultural norms work and how do I use language to accomplish those norms? Confronted with these questions, I needed to consider both the **linguistic context** and the **situational context** in order to convey my message accurately.

There are many factors to consider when we speak that go beyond the strict linguistic context, which is limited to words and utterances that surround what has been said or written. Continuing with the same example, as it is the case in most U.S. big coffee shop chains, ordering coffee typically involves the following sequence of events: We get in line, we order the coffee we want really fast (most people already know what they will order), we give out our name, we wait at the counter for the coffee to be ready, we hear our name being called, and then we sit down at a table. Not equipped with all this background knowledge, I kept ordering the same "small cup of coffee," now with the addition to of the adjective "black." For a whole month, I did not know how to order the kind of coffee I really wanted. After living in the U.S. for more than a year, I finally learned that the "cup of coffee" I really liked was a "small latte." It took me some time and a lot of trial and error to acquire that knowledge even though, at the time I moved to California, I had been studying and speaking English for more than 15 years. From this example, we can see how intrinsic the context is to how we communicate. Without contextual knowledge, we might not be able to accomplish our communicative goals.

Making appropriate linguistic choices that take into account the best grammatical forms, vocabulary, and contextual variables to express needs, desires, and feelings in a new or second language (L2) is not an easy task for linguistically diverse learners. Simply memorizing a list of verb conjugations or most frequent words or expressions does not suffice. In order to be successful, linguistically diverse learners also need to acquire **pragmatic ability** which allows speakers and hearers to take into consideration verbal and non-verbal cues, contextual information, including audience and cultural knowledge, and communicative purposes. Every new situation includes specific ways speakers and hearers use language for different social goals. The language used to order a cup of coffee in a big coffee shop chain is different than the language used to participate in a school debate or give a testimony during a trial in the courtroom. There are very conventional and typical ways of acting in these circumstances that require more technical and formal linguistic choices. Furthermore, a trial in a U.S. courtroom or a debate in a U.S. school might be very different from a trial in a Chinese courtroom or a debate in a Finish school. Linguistically diverse learners have to develop the ability to sort out both the background knowledge and linguistic knowledge necessary to understand and participate in new situations.

Because linguistically diverse learners tend to first relate the pragmatic ability they already possess in their first or more dominant language (L1) to act in the L2, miscommunication and misunderstandings are frequent and common. Pragmatic norms are often invisible, so it can be extremely challenging for linguistically diverse learners to truly understand what L2 speakers mean without consciously developing an eye (and ear) towards the many contextual factors that shape conversational encounters in the new language and culture. Developing pragmatic ability can help linguistically diverse learners become aware of otherwise tacit underlying cultural assumptions and social practices that influence ways L2 speakers behave and say things a certain way. By investigating how L2 speakers use their linguistic and contextual knowledge to generate meaning in determined situations for specific purposes, linguistically diverse learners can have the opportunity to make pragmatically appropriate judgments in the course of interactions. One way to do this is by becoming aware of common speech acts performed in the second language and culture.

SPEECH ACT THEORY

Without a doubt, the most researched area of pragmatics is the study of **speech acts**, which refer to how speakers and hearers use language to accomplish social acts, such as apologizing, refusing, thanking, complaining, greeting, and so on. Austin (1962) and Searle (1969) were among the first to explore language beyond the literal meaning of an utterance, considering what people mean when they communicate, how they communicate it, and ways the message is understood in context. Austin (1962) realized that whenever we say something, we accomplish something, and defined language as action. The philosopher started by making a distinction between general statements and utterances that are used to perform an action. He called the first type of statement constatives, which were statements or assertions that could be true or false, such as *My daughter got married yesterday*. The second type of utterance was called **performatives**, which when said, perform an action. Performatives have the verbs in the first person singular and in the present indicative, such as *I pronounce you husband and wife*. When the priest, minister or official utters these words, the act of being married is officiated and completed.

Later on, Austin (1962) abandoned this distinction, realizing that all speech should be considered action. Thus, he proposed a general theory of speech acts that considers constatives and performatives subcases of a general class of performatives that includes explicit and implicit ways of saying and doing things with words. Austin (1962) then offered a distinction based on the **illocutionary force** of the speech act. This comprehensive theory of speech acts entailed three types of acts performed by an utterance: a locutionary act, an illocutionary act, and a perlocutionary act. The **locutionary act** is the actual uttering of words through sounds, grammatical structures, and meaning. The performance of a locutionary act entails an **illocutionary act**, that is, the speaker's intention or purpose, which imposes a force on what is uttered. The **perlocutionary act** is the effect of the utterance on the hearer's feelings, thoughts or actions. In other words, locution is what was said during an interaction, illocution is what was meant by the speaker, and perlocution is the effect of the message on the hearer. To assess for the illocutionary force of an utterance, it is important to identify certain linguistic indicative devices, such as the kind of verb used, word order, stress, intonation, and the mood or tense of the verb.

All utterances exchanged in interaction have an illocutionary force, perlocutionary effect, and propositional content. For instance, when we hear the utterance, *What a great day!*, we have to examine not only the actual phrase or what was said, but also what the speaker meant by uttering this phrase as well as the effect that it had on the hearers. There are a few interpretation options that go beyond the literal meaning of this utterance depending on the context, audience, and purpose of the speaker. If the speaker is being sarcastic, he or she will emphasize the word "great" and pronounce it with a different tone and pitch. This will possibly be accompanied by an inquisitive and somewhat disappointed facial expression. The hearer, in turn, must have experienced the same apparently awful "great" day to understand and feel the effect of what the speaker meant by that specific utterance.

Searle (1969) built upon Austin's ideas and continued to formalize a comprehensive theory of speech acts. For Searle (1976), the basic unit of human communication is the illocutionary act, which is composed by an illocutionary force and a proposition. So, for example, consider the distinction between the way a mother can utter the same proposition with different illocutionary forces. She could choose from a command, *Michael, clean up the room!*, or a request, *Michael, will you clean up the room?*, or a promise, *If you clean the room, Michael, I will buy you a present*. All of these propositions have similar content, but they are uttered differently, both in terms of grammar, intonation, and word order, and in terms of the distinct perlocutionary effects they will have on the hearer. For Searle (1972), it is important that a theory of speech acts captures both the intentional and conventional aspects of the act; that is, the actual words that the speaker is using to convey the act as well as the intended effect that the speaker wishes to impart on the hearer.

Illocutionary acts are rule-governed forms of behavior, and, in most cases, tend to follow regular and predictable patterns within a community of speakers. Searle (1976) provided a classification of illocutionary acts into basic categories or types that take into consideration the point or purpose of the act, the fit or extent to which the words match the actions in the world, and the attitudes and psychological state of the speaker. For example, the utterance *If you do not do your homework, you will not pass the class!* could be interpreted as a threat, a command, or a simple prediction depending on the purpose and psychological state of the reader. For fit, Searle (1976) provided an interesting example using a shopping list to illustrate two different functions for two illocutionary acts. The philosopher asked us to imagine that a wife wrote a shopping list for her husband including the items "bean, butter, bacon, and bread." As the husband goes around the supermarket picking up the items on the list, a detective follows him recording every item he selects in written form. In both cases, the lists will be very similar; however, in the husband's case, the actions match the words, so that is a fit. In contrast, in the detective's case, there is an attempt to get the words to match the actions, going in the opposite direction and, thus, function. In the detective's case, there is no fit between the original function of the list and how the detective is using the list. According to Searle (1976), the different functions of the same list can also be verified by the role of making a mistake in both situations. If, when going around picking up the items, the husband forgets to buy beans and arrives home without them, the wife would be very upset because they would not be able to make their favorite dish for dinner. However, if the husband is being followed by a detective and forgets to buy beans, the detective would not write down the item on the list, with no consequences to dinner. In the case of the detective, the shopping list loses its function to become a piece of evidence instead of a reminder.

Searle (1976) still considered other secondary factors that might impact the illocutionary act, including strength, the status or position of the speaker, interest, relationship to the rest of the discourse in which the act is located, and propositional content determined by indicative devices, such as verb tense, extra linguistic requirements, the presence of performative verbs, and style. These primary and secondary conditions form the basis of a revised taxonomy of speech acts represented in Table 1[1] below:

Table 1. Searle's taxonomy of speech acts

Speech Act	Description	Example
Representatives	The speaker commits him/herself to the truth of the statement.	Stating, suggesting, boasting, complaining, claiming, concluding, deducing
Directives	The speaker attempts to get the hearer to do something.	Asking, ordering, commanding, requesting, begging, pleading, praying, entreating, inviting, permitting, advising
Comissives	The speaker commits him/herself to a future act.	Promises, pledges, vows
Expressives	The speaker expresses a psychological state towards the hearer.	Thanking, congratulating, apologizing, condoling, deploring, welcoming.
Declarations	A socially sanctioned speaker (e.g., a priest, a judge, the boss, etc.) changes the world by uttering an institutionalized act.	Sentencing, baptizing, nominating, marrying, declaring war, firing

Searle (1975) suggested another distinction between speech acts, considering whether they are indirect or direct. **Indirect speech acts** refer to the idea that we do not always mean what we say. Therefore, hearers need to make an inference to understand the message. For example, consider the difference between *Can you please bring your homework tomorrow?* and *Please, bring the homework tomorrow*. The first utterance is an indirect speech act whereas the second would be a direct speech act. In other words, in the first utterance, there is a mismatch between the sentence type (interrogative) and the illocutionary force of the act (command). In the second utterance, there is a conventional or direct match between the sentence type (imperative) and the illocutionary force (command). Particularly, with commands or requests, it is very common for English speakers to realize those speech acts indirectly. Explicit commands or requests in the form of imperatives are rarely used in everyday conversations among English speakers due to socially agreed norms of politeness (Senft, 2014). Exceptions to this social norm are interactions between different ranks in the military, where commands or requests are usually realized directly in the imperative form.

Some indirect forms have become conventions and can be quite commonly found as a type of conversational routine among speakers of a given speech community. In English, requests that start with phrases such as *Could you please...* or *Would you mind...* are examples of polite ways to ask someone to do something indirectly, avoiding the more direct forms that use imperatives. Many of the indirect forms are considered more polite than direct forms as they seem to give the hearer the impression that a choice to perform the request is available to take or not; however, an assessment of the context, the roles of the participants, and the purpose of the speech act is necessary to determine whether the hearer will perceive the request as a routine form or a polite and candid way of asking for something to be done. For instance, when a teacher asks a student, *Would you mind not talking with your partner while I am talking?*, there is not much choice for the student to refuse the request, which still functions as an order or command. In this case, while the speech act is performed indirectly, the message is felt as direct. Thus, to truly assess for politeness, it is important to consider both the power status between hearer and speaker as well as the contextual variables surrounding the utterance. Above all, culture plays a crucial role in how speakers and hearers will interpret the message. The next section will detail the degree to which intercultural interactions are impacted and influenced by cultural norms and expectations.

THE ROLE OF CULTURE IN CROSS-CULTURAL INTERACTIONS

The theories of pragmatics developed by Austin, Searle, and Grice have been written from a Western point of view, especially from an English-speaking perspective. The question of whether these ideas can be universalized or generalized to all conversational situations has been scrutinized by many anthropologists and sociolinguists who found evidence that different conversational norms might apply to non-English speaking cultural practices according to diverse societies. For example, the relationship between politeness and indirectness is not expressed in the same ways in other languages as it is in English. Whereas in English a child is expected to say, *No, thank you,* when asked whether he or she would like to have some juice, in other languages, such as Portuguese or Spanish, a more common way of responding would be the more direct "no." House (1996) found out that German speakers tend to be more direct and self-referenced than English speakers when making requests using expressions such as *Can I...* instead of *Would you like me to...* In a study of Chinese English as a Foreign Language learners' pragmatic competence, Li, Raja, and Sazalie (2015) found out that making apologies and refusals posed the most difficulties for these learners due to cultural differences. Particularly, the use of "maybe" by the learners in utterances such as *I'd like to, but I have some other things today. Maybe I can't take over for you. I'm sorry for that* could cause confusion to English speakers regarding whether the Chinese speaker was refusing or not the request.

As a result of an increase in cross-cultural studies, the field of pragmatics has taken a turn to analyze speech acts from the perspective of language users with special attention to societal and cultural issues, involving the connections between language, ideology, and power (Kasper, Nguyen, & Yoshimi, 2010). Comparisons between speech acts across cultures have provided insight into sources of misunderstanding. Studies have also demonstrated that our linguistic behavior is motivated and shaped by cultural beliefs, values, and attitudes (Archer, Aijmer, & Wichmann, 2012). In this vein, it is important to consider different ways to understand and perform speech acts. To avoid ethnocentric approaches, it is crucial for all of us to reimagine, negotiate, and engage in alternative ways of expressing politeness, requests, thanks, and many other social actions from different cultural perspectives. The ability to perform and judge speech acts in the L2 is heavily influenced by the degree of cultural sensitivity hearers and speakers will have at the moment of the cross-cultural interaction. The next section will expand on the notion of pragmatic ability when learning an L2.

PRAGMATICS AND LANGUAGE LEARNING

Pragmatic ability in an additional language depends on many factors including experiences with speakers and cultural practices of the L2 speech community, linguistic proficiency, gender, age, occupation, and social status. As a starting point, linguistically diverse learners will inevitably, and rightfully, draw on their linguistic repertoires to make sense of what is being conveyed verbally and non-verbally in a conversation with L2 speakers. Often times, the knowledge and cultural background learners bring in their L1 will be very helpful, especially when the pragmatic norms of the L1 match the pragmatic norms of the L2. Learners' linguistic and cultural resources are invaluable assets (García, Johnson, & Seltzer, 2017). Other times, learners will have to acquire new knowledge that will help them sort out implicit and indirect ways L2 speakers use language to perform familiar speech acts. If the cultural norms learners are used to follow do not involve saying "bless you" or something similar when someone sneezes, many

English speakers might find the L2 learner's silence after someone sneezes offensive, rude or impolite. In these situations, it might be important for learners to be aware of pragmatically appropriate ways of acting in the L2 as "unlike the case of grammatical errors, [pragmatic differences] are often interpreted on a social or personal level rather than as a result of the language learning process" (Bardovi-Harlig & Mahan-Taylor, 2003, p. 38).

There are many reasons linguistically diverse learners' pragmatic behaviors or choices might diverge from the typical L2 community of speakers' norms for acting and saying certain things in certain situations. This phenomenon is called **pragmatic divergence**. Ishihara and Cohen (2010) list five reasons pragmatic divergence can happen due to a novice level of pragmatic ability: 1) negative transfer of pragmatic norms, 2) limited grammatical ability in the L2, 3) overgeneralization of perceived L2 pragmatic norms, 4) effect of instruction and/or instructional materials, and 5) learner's choice. The authors point out that the first four types of pragmatic divergence can lead to **pragmatic failure**, that is, a breakdown in communication among the speakers. The fifth type of pragmatic divergence is a unique case in which the learner is both aware of the L2 pragmatic norms and at a high level of linguistic proficiency in the L2, but chooses not to conform or to resist the L2 pragmatic norms. Their choice is driven by a strong sense of identity, which they might feel threatened by following the pragmatic norms of the L2. Figure 1 illustrates the five types of pragmatic divergence.

Negative transfer happens when an L2 learner is unaware of the pragmatic norms of the L2, and uses his or her pragmatic knowledge in their L1 to inform their actions and discourse in the L2. This transfer can impact communication negatively if the pragmatic norms in the L1 are very different from the pragmatic norms in the L2. For example, going back to the way children respond to requests with a simple "no" in Portuguese might lead to a misunderstanding or miscommunication if the child responds to a request in this way when interacting with English speakers. The child's response will seem abrupt and impolite, maybe causing disastrous consequences for the child if he or she is being judged or assessed for their behavior in U.S. schools, for instance. It is important to note, though, that the miscommunication and judgment is not only caused by the child's lack of pragmatic knowledge in the L2, but also for the English speaker's lack of cultural knowledge of how children might interact in Portuguese. Cultural sensitivity and awareness on both sides of the conversation are especially useful in linguistically diverse school contexts. Since conversation operates according to cooperative principles as stipulated by Grice (see Chapter 8), it is crucial in an increasingly diverse world that we consider pragmatic failure as a two-way street. We will discuss this point further when we talk about the role of the teacher in linguistically diverse interactions in the implications for teaching section of the chapter.

Limited grammatical ability in the L2 can lead to pragmatic failure, and that is perhaps the most visible and common interpretation for why L2 learners might not follow certain pragmatic norms when interacting with speakers of the L2 community. For example, L2 learners might not be aware that modal

Figure 1. The five types of pragmatic divergence

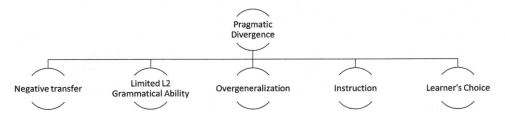

verbs have different levels of strength and cannot be used interchangeably. It is very different to say, *Sara might be getting sick* and *Sara will get sick*. Linguistically diverse learners need to be aware of the difference between "might" and "will" to understand what each utterance is conveying. Being pragmatically proficient in an L2 does not correlate directly with grammatical ability. Some linguistically diverse learners can produce very accurate grammatical sentences; nonetheless, these same learners might not be aware of the nuances and contextual information needed to act in pragmatically appropriate ways. This is also true for different varieties of English. An English learner might know pragmatic norms for how to act in most situations in Los Angeles, California, but when the same learner goes to New York City, London, or Hong Kong, all English-speaking places, the norms might shift and they will have to learn entirely new ways of doing things with words in those new contexts.

Overgeneralization of L2 pragmatic norms most often occurs due to perceived stereotypes about the L2 community of speakers' behaviors. Stereotypes can be diffused through media such as TV or the Internet or through general widespread ideas about what to say and do in certain situations when interacting with speakers of the L2 community. For example, learners might generalize the perceived notion that English-speakers are too direct, and apply that norm to all situations, asking direct and intimate questions such as *What is your religion?* or *What are you doing tonight?* in casual conversations with an English speaker for the first time.Research has demonstrated that American English speakers use the strategy of accepting a compliment only one-third of the time (Center for Advanced Research on Language Acquisition, 2018). Without knowing, learners of American English as an L2 might overgeneralize that response, and accept a compliment by an American English speaker in all situations when other strategies such as mitigating or even refusing the compliment might be perceived as more appropriate.

Another source of pragmatic divergence is the effect of instruction or instructional materials on how L2 learners are supposed to say and act in certain communicative situations. English as a Second Language teachers very frequently ask students to respond in complete sentences in classroom contexts to gauge for how well the students know the language. However, in most everyday situations, answering to a yes or no question using a complete sentence is perceived as out of the ordinary. When asked, *Did you go to the movies yesterday?*, the most typical affirmative answer would be *Yes* or *Yes, I did*, not *Yes, I went to the movies yesterday*. Another example happened to me when I was learning English in Brazil. I learned that when asked, *How are you?*, you had a choice between saying, "fine," "great," "okay," and "well." These choices would be interchangeable, meaning the same - *I am doing well*. When I moved to California, I started having a lot of communication breakdowns because, for some strange reason, my favorite answer was *Okay*. Although I just meant, *I am fine*, people would always respond, *Why okay?* or *What's going on?* After some time, I understood that saying *Okay* meant *So-so* or *I am not doing great* or, indeed, not okay at all. In examining the routines of my L2 community of speakers, I realized that the best response to convey what I meant was *Great!*, which does not prompt any further conversation as it is the most commonly expected response to the question *How are you?* where I lived.

One of the most important sources of pragmatic divergence for speakers of any given language to understand is learner's choice in electing or not certain ways of acting and saying in the L2. Participants of an L2 community should not directly assume that learners are always ignorant of L2 pragmatic behaviors or norms; these learners might be consciously resisting the L2 pragmatic norms as they might feel the new ways of saying and doing in the L2 might conflict with their beliefs or identity (Gomez-Laich, 2016). In a global society, it is crucial that intercultural communication and encounters take into consideration every participant's integrity, respecting and honoring linguistic diversity. Examples of learner's choice might include consciously not choosing to say *I am full* at the end of a deliciously satisfying meal as this linguistic choice might conflict with the learner's own perception of what is polite to say or not to say in those situations, and ethical dilemmas such as the learner choosing to use a high level of honorifics with a much younger speaker in Japanese, as he or she believes in human equality, treating all employees the same (Ishihara & Cohen, 2010).

Pragmatic ability is one of the most complex and challenging aspects of communicating in an L2, taking approximately ten years to be acquired in second language contexts as opposed to foreign language contexts which might involve even more years of intentional study and exposure (Ishihara & Cohen, 2010). An L2 learner can be highly proficient in grammar and vocabulary, but that does not mean that he or she can predict the pragmatics of the L2. Part of the reason pragmatic ability can be so difficult to acquire is the lack of focus this discipline receives in language teaching and learning materials and classes (Bardovi-Harlig & Mahan-Taylor, 2003). Without direct and formal instruction on pragmatics, learners of an L2 are left to their own devices to figure out the often tacit cultural norms that shape how language is used for different purposes and contexts. Fortunately, a range of studies have provided empirical evidence that features of L2 pragmatics are indeed teachable, including speech acts, discourse markers, discourse strategies, and pragmatic comprehension or awareness (Rose, 2005).

IMPLICATIONS FOR TEACHING ENGLISH LANGUAGE LEARNERS

You might be wondering now how pragmatics can help you as a teacher. School interactions also involve unique contexts, audiences, and purposes. There are certain ways of saying things and behaving that are typical of school. Some of these norms and expectations have become so common to us that we even forget they are learned at one point in our lives - for many at kindergarten or pre-school. Consider the norm of raising your hand before you utter the answer to a question the teacher posed to the whole class or having to ask for permission before you go to the bathroom in a certain way at a certain time. Schools, in this sense, can be considered cultures. In school, there are socially constructed norms that require students to learn how to produce, predict and act to participate in culturally appropriate ways (Dixon & Green, 2005).

Often times, especially in school contexts, it is tempting to assume our view of the world applies to everyone; however, as schools become increasingly more linguistically and culturally diverse, teachers need to reflect deeply about how sociocultural and multilingual factors impact teaching and learning contexts (Banks et al., 2005). While it is important for linguistically diverse learners to understand and act in pragmatically appropriate ways in the language most commonly used in schools, it is also equally important for teachers not to impose L2 cultural norms on students, engaging them in awareness raising and cultural comparisons between home or dominant language and new language pragmatic norms. In this process, learner's conscious choice and teacher's sensitivity to diverse ways of using words to act in the world are key to promoting an inclusive and welcoming classroom environment.

The first step into including pragmatics into teaching practices is for teachers to engage in systemic and critical examination of their own and others' assumptions about culture, power, privilege, and difference (Commins & Nguyen, 2015). From this perspective, teachers become language facilitators and cultural mediators of the pragmatic norms commonly practiced in the community of speakers of the school settings they are a part of. Questions teachers should ask entail: How can I help my linguistically diverse learners make inferences? What does it take to be successful at school? What kinds of behaviors and ways of expressing feelings, desires, and needs are necessary to learn to accomplish social tasks in school such as requesting, apologizing, thanking, and explaining? In asking these questions, teachers take the first step into unveiling the pragmatic norms that are shaped by the cultural practices of their classroom and school community.

In order to engage in the deep thinking and reflection necessary to involve linguistically diverse learners in pragmatic awareness and action, teachers need to become aware that the ways of acting and using language at school are not typical or common for everyone. There are many speech acts that can cause confusion for students in school settings. When teachers say, *Can you please sit down?* or *Great job!*, students might answer "no" to the first question or might not understand that "job" means school work in the second utterance. This confusion between what the speaker said, what was meant by it, and how it was understood, that is, the illocutionary force of the speech act, can cause miscommunication among students and teachers. Some forms of teacher-student interactions might also be very unfamiliar to students. Chinese speakers are used to waiting until the end of the class to ask the teacher questions while in most American schools, students are expected to raise their hands and ask questions during class. Some students might be used to hugging each other and the teacher because it provides them with comfort and safety, especially in early elementary grades. In the U.S., touching, kissing, and hugging between teachers and students are not as common as "high fives." In order to fully participate in class and be positively assessed by their behaviors, students need to understand how verbal and non-verbal interactions might differ from the ones they are used to.

Uncovering everyday ways of being and doing in a classroom can be challenging for teachers. It requires a deep examination of emotions, beliefs, and actions that have not been questioned as they represent routine patterns of interactions that are socially well established. Take, for instance, the distinction between *information seeking* and *known information* questions (Mehan, 1979). Known information questions are typically asked in classroom interactions, and constitute a kind of evaluation on the teacher's part. When asking this type of question, the teacher already knows the answer and is usually "testing the knowledge of the respondent" (Mehan, 1979, p. 286). In contrast, information seeking questions are typical of everyday conversations, in which "the first speaker has asked another person for information that the second person presumably has" (Mehan, 1979, p. 285). Known information questions are an integral part of the Initiation-Response-Evaluation (IRE) types of interaction that are so pervasive in U.S. schools. When the teacher asks, *What color is your shirt, Hannah?*, she already knows that the color is green, and wants to evaluate whether Hannah's response would be accurate. If, on the other hand, Hannah is looking for her favorite shirt to go to school and cannot find it, and her mother in order to help her asks the same question, *What color is your shirt, Hannah?*, Hannah's answer will provide her mother with relevant information so that the shirt can be found. When working with linguistically diverse learners, teachers should take into consideration that some students might understand known information questions as information seeking questions and might be confused when they are evaluated on the basis of their response.

Teachers should develop an understanding that their discourse and actions in the classroom are culturally shaped, not givens. As such, these cultural practices need to be made explicit and even questioned in linguistically diverse contexts. Linguistically and culturally diverse learners, as students who are learning new cultural practices in the process of acquiring English as an additional language, need to understand these often implicit norms. For this reason, linguistically and culturally diverse learners need to have access and opportunity to learn the pragmatics of school interactions. Teachers can help make some of these norms and expectations explicit to their linguistically diverse learners. Teachers can also use pragmatics as an opportunity to share different perspectives and promote engaging discussions via cultural comparisons. For example, recent research on second language acquisition has criticized typical U.S. classroom practices where children are mainly providing short answers to evaluative questions posed by the teacher as not being suitable for linguistically diverse learners as these practices do not promote collaborative student talk, which supports learners in expressing their thinking in the L2 (Gibbons, 2015). By deeply reflecting on the pragmatic norms that shape their practices, teachers can also make changes and modify their instruction to include alternative ways of talking and acting that will booster learning outcomes for all students in their classroom. With this knowledge, teachers can empower their linguistically and culturally diverse learners to fully engage in school life socially and academically.

Pragmatic Considerations in Lesson Design and Implementation

After developing awareness through deep reflection about commonly practiced pragmatic norms in their classroom, the second step is for teachers to help learners identify and apply strategies to act in pragmatically appropriate ways in the L2Teachers can help learners develop awareness about pragmatic norms while engaging them in opportunities to practice concrete strategies when performing social actions in the L2 for academic purposes in school settings. One way of doing this is by helping learners become aware of how speech acts are performed in the L2 community of speakers and by providing these learners opportunities to engage in role-playing or real interactions involving the accomplishment of selected speech acts. Ishihara & Cohen (2010) suggest a number of activities for teachers to support learners in learning and performing speech acts. Table 2 illustrates both kinds of strategies with sample tasks.

When designing content lessons, teachers can include a special section on pragmatics that considers verbal and non-verbal cues they or the students might use, relevant contextual information, knowledge about the new culture and students' home cultures, and the communicative purposes of the lesson (*to describe, to compare, to explain…*). The following questions might help teachers consider how pragmatic knowledge can impact students' participation when designing a lesson:

- In what ways can language (verbal and non-verbal) affect the ways students understand content and participate in class?
- What language and behaviors do students need to know to become successful participants in your class?
- What specific cultural norms and expectations do you need to make explicit for your students during that particular lesson or day?

When teaching a content lesson, it is important to help students navigate the classroom norms and expectations for the lesson and not assume they will know all the information they need in advance. For instance, in a Science class that involves a lab, teachers can consider verbal cues, such as questions embedded in step-by-step procedures, non-verbal cues, such as the need to look at the experiment as students follow the procedures, what to write and how to write on lab reports, as well as specific ways to touch or not touch the materials, contextual information, such as when to talk with teacher and partners and what to say during collaboration, and cultural knowledge about techniques and science laboratories. Teachers should also consider the specific speech acts involved in teaching and learning of Science, such as explaining, arguing, and reporting. In some countries, Science classes are entirely theoretical and do not involve labs. Particularly in high school contexts, the knowledge of how to participate in Science labs should not be taken for granted.

Table 2. Strategies to support linguistically diverse learners' speech act awareness and performance

Type of Strategy	Tasks	Examples
Learning Speech Acts	• Interviews • Cross-Cultural Analysis • Modeling • Accessing published materials	Students interview how a speech act such as apologizing or greeting is performed in a given L2 community of speakers noting the language forms they use to convey their message as well as their non-verbal behaviors. Students keep a notebook where they record information about certain speech acts. Information can include what to say, the cultural norms, the strategies speakers use, words and phrases, similarities and differences between home and new language pragmatic norms, and interpretations. A graphic organizer can be provided to learners to help them organize this information. Teachers model different ways to ask questions in the classroom and the various responses students might give. Students can do research on speech acts using the resources, videos, and examples provided in the Center for Advanced Research on Language Acquisition website.
Performing Speech Acts	• Role play • Real play • Asking for feedback • Using communication strategies • Resisting the L2 pragmatic norm	Students engage in pair work to practice different ways of thanking or refusing an invitation in English. Students talk with speakers of the L2 community outside of classroom contexts for authentic purposes. The L2 speaker might be or not aware that the learner is practicing certain speech acts. Students ask for members of the L2 community of speakers for feedback on how they have performed a selected speech act, such as making a request or refusing an invitation. Students can practice using certain conversation starters, such as "I am not sure this will come out right, but I would like to…" or "I am still learning how to…, so I apologize if I say something that might sound abrupt." Teachers can provide learners with conversation starters like these ones to practice during conversations in the classroom. As a fun cross-cultural exercise, learners can engage in discussion about why they might resist some new ways of acting, saying, and being in the new language. This can become an engaging student-led conversation that might raise cultural and linguistic. sensitivity for all students.

Linguistically diverse learners will initially operate under their own assumptions and ideas about the world. Once in school, they need allies who are proficient in the L2 to help them understand and act in pragmatically appropriate ways without risking their own beliefs or negating their own identities. Linguistically diverse learners need to feel they are an integral part of the school culture. Teachers can be the most important ally in this process by being both a cultural mediator, modeling and teaching pragmatic norms in the new language, and a culture enthusiast, embracing diversity and acknowledging that there are many ways of performing different social acts according to different cultural and linguistic practices. In doing so, teachers can facilitate powerful discussions among all students in a class, who, in turn, will appreciate being a part of an inclusive, welcoming, and learning-rich community.

DISCUSSION QUESTIONS

1.   In some classrooms, the teachers might ask, *Do you have any questions?* to gauge students' understanding of subject matter. This is a common indirect way of asking *Do you understand this topic, and if not, please tell me by asking questions* in U.S. schools. However, some students might not understand this cultural practice and answer the question directly saying "no" when they are indeed still confused about the content. Other students might interpret this question as a routine pattern

which is always performed at the end of the class, with no real intention of acknowledging students' concerns. This confusion between what the speaker said, what was meant by it, and the effect on the hearer can lead to miscommunication. Can you think of any more examples of miscommunication or misunderstanding that might happen in your classroom due to lack of pragmatic competence? How would you go about minimizing eventual miscommunication or misunderstanding? What strategies can help linguistically and culturally diverse learners become familiar with such a range of pragmatic norms used in the classroom?

2. In order not to impose the L2 pragmatic norms, it is crucial that teachers foster a community in which learners feel that they can take risks by talking about, reflecting on, and negotiating new cultural practices in the classroom. As an example of an excellent activity to implement, the two teachers in this video provided by the Teaching Channel created a lesson on what it means to be "respectful": https://www.teachingchannel.org/video/social-skills-goals

   In what ways do the two teachers in the lesson featured in the video make visible pragmatic norms, including verbal and non-verbal behaviors, taking into consideration students' input and ideas?

3. How would you teach *politeness* to your linguistically and culturally diverse learners in your classroom? Think of two instances in which students need to use polite requests during a lesson. What linguistic and situational features should the students know to be able to successfully accomplish the requests?

4. Visit the CARLA website: http://carla.umn.edu/speechacts/refusals/index.html, and compare refusals given by speakers of American English, Arabic, British English, Chinese, German, Japanese, and Spanish. What aspects of refusals should teachers of English to Speakers of Other Languages (ESOL) be attentive and sensitive to when working with speakers of Arabic, Chinese, German, Japanese, and Spanish? What are some important distinctions that can be made between American and British ways of refusing that should be highlighted to linguistically diverse learners? How could ESOL teachers foster classroom discussions and cultural comparisons about refusals using these examples?

5. Go to the United States Department of State website on teaching pragmatics: https://americanenglish.state.gov/resources/teaching-pragmatics and choose one of their lesson plans to examine. How would you use those resources? What changes or additions would you make? If you have the opportunity to teach this lesson, how do you think it will support your linguistically and culturally diverse learners?

EXERCISES

1. Describe ways language and context are intrinsically connected using examples from your personal or professional life. Think of one or two examples where simply knowing the linguistic context was not sufficient to accomplish your communicative goals.

2. Provide an example for a speech act, such as apologizing, thanking, accepting an invitation, in the language that you are most comfortable with. Compare how this speech act is typically performed according to the cultural practices you are accustomed to as opposed to another language or a different dialect of English you know.

3. Explain the difference between direct and indirect speech acts.

4. Define pragmatic divergence in your own words.

5. Classify the five different types of pragmatic divergence, providing an example for each one of them from your personal or professional life.

6. Identify the potential reasons for pragmatic divergence in the following interaction: A multilingual undergraduate student of English asks the teacher to provide her with feedback on her writing. The teacher gives her feedback and suggests, "Now I would take it to the Writing Center to get some help with organization and grammar." The student responds, "Oh, okay. I will wait for their feedback."

REFERENCES

Archer, D., Aijmer, K., & Wichmann, A. (2012). *Pragmatics: An advanced resource book for students.* London: Routledge.

Austin, J. (1962). *How to do things with words.* Oxford, UK: Oxford University Press.

Banks, J., Cochran-Smith, M., Moll, L., Richert, A., Zeichner, K., LePage, P., ... McDonald, M. (2005). Teaching diverse learners. In L. Darling-Hammond & J. Bransford (Eds.), *Preparing teachers for a changing world: What teachers should learn and be able to do* (pp. 232–274). San Francisco, CA: Jossey-Bass.

Bardovi-Harlig, K., & Hartford, B. S. (2005). *Interlanguage pragmatics: Exploring institutional talk.* London: Routledge. doi:10.4324/9781410613776

Bardovi-Harlig, K., & Mahan-Taylor, R. (2003). Introduction to teaching pragmatics. *English Teaching Forum, 41*(3), 37-39. Retrieved from https://americanenglish.state.gov/files/ae/resource_files/03-41-3-h.pdf

Center for Advanced Research on Language Acquisition. (2018, October). Retrieved from http://carla.umn.edu/speechacts/index.html

Commins, N., & Nguyen, D. (2015). How should pre-service education programs prepare educators to meet the needs of English language learners/emergent bilinguals relative to Common Core State Standards and Next Generation Science Standards curricula? In G. Valdés, K. Menken, & M. Castro (Eds.), *Common core bilingual and English language learners: A resource for educators* (pp. 231–232). Philadelphia, PA: Caslon.

Dixon, C., & Green, J. L. (2005). Studying the discursive construction of texts in classrooms through interactional ethnography. In R. Beach, J. Green, M. Kamil, & T. Shanahan (Eds.), *Multidisciplinary Perspectives on Literacy Research* (pp. 349–390). Cresskill, NJ: Hampton Press.

García, O., Johnson, S. I., & Seltzer, K. (2017). *The translanguaging classroom: Leveraging student bilingualism for learning.* Philadelphia, PA: Caslon.

Gibbons, P. (2015). *Scaffolding language, scaffolding learning: Teaching English language learners in the mainstream classroom* (2nd ed.). Portsmouth, NH: Heinemann.

Gomez-Laich, M. P. (2016). Second language learners' divergence from target language pragmatic norms. *Studies in Second Language Learning and Teaching, 6*(2), 249. doi:10.14746sllt.2016.6.2.4

Grice, H. P. (1968). Logic and conversation. In H. P. Grice (Ed.), *Studies in the ways with words. Harvard.* Harvard University Press.

House, J. (1996). Contrastive discourse analysis and misunderstanding: The case of German and English. *Contributions to the Sociology of Language, 71*, 345-362.

Ishihara, N., & Cohen, A. D. (2010). *Teaching and learning pragmatics: Where language and culture meet.* London: Longman.

Kasper, G., Nguyen, H. t., Yoshimi, D. R., & Yoshioka, J. K. (Eds.). (2010). *Pragmatics & Language Learning* (Vol. 12). Honolulu, HI: National Foreign Language Resource Center, University of Hawai'i at Manoa.

Li, R., Raja, R., & Sazalie, A. (2015). An investigation into Chinese EFL learners' pragmatic competence. *GEMA Online Journal of Language Studies, 15*(2).

Mehan, H. (1979). "What time is it, Denise?": Asking known information questions in classroom discourse. *Theory into Practice, 18*(4), 285–294. doi:10.1080/00405847909542846

Rose, K. R. (2005). On the effects of instruction in second language pragmatics. *System, 33*(3), 385–399. doi:10.1016/j.system.2005.06.003

Searle, J. (1969). *Speech acts: An essay in the philosophy of language.* Cambridge, UK: Cambridge University Press. doi:10.1017/CBO9781139173438

Searle, J. R. (1975). *A taxonomy of illocutionary acts.* Minneapolis, MN: University of Minnesota Press.

Searle, J. R. (1976). A classification of illocutionary acts. *Language in Society, 5*(1), 1–23. doi:10.1017/S0047404500006837

Senft, G. (2014). *Understanding pragmatics.* London: Routledge. doi:10.4324/9780203776476

United States Department of State. (n.d.). *Teaching pragmatics.* Retrieved from: https://americanenglish.state.gov/resources/teaching-pragmatics

ADDITIONAL READING

Archer, D., Aijmer, K., & Wichmann, A. (2012). *Pragmatics: An advanced resource book for students.* London: Routledge.

Center for Advanced Research on Language Acquisition. (2018, October). Retrieved from http://carla. umn.edu/speechacts/index.html

Ishihara, N., & Cohen, A. D. (2010). *Teaching and learning pragmatics: Where language and culture meet.* London: Longman.

ENDNOTE

[1]   Adapted from Archer, Aijmer, and Wichmann (2012).

Chapter 10
Discourse Analysis

Soe Marlar Lwin
Singapore University of Social Sciences, Singapore

ABSTRACT

This chapter introduces discourse analysis as a sub-discipline of linguistics. Relevant concepts from pragmatics, another closely-related sub-discipline, are also discussed within the context of discourse analysis. The chapter begins by explaining the relationship between pragmatics and discourse analysis, and key terms such as "text" and "discourse." It then examines the distinctions between linguistic and non-linguistic contexts, and situational and sociocultural contexts. To help readers understand the importance of culture in using language to make meanings, the introduced concepts are illustrated with sample authentic texts as well as examples from English and a few other languages. Placing discourse at the core of language teaching and learning, the chapter recommends a discourse-based approach to help ELLs develop not only communicative competence but also intercultural communicative competence. The chapter provides ESOL teachers with knowledge of discourse analysis and the implications of this knowledge for teaching culturally and linguistically diverse learners of English.

PRAGMATICS AND DISCOURSE ANALYSIS

Pragmatics and **discourse analysis** are two closely related fields which examine how language is used to make meanings in actual situations of communication. As sub-disciplines of linguistics, both fields acknowledge that our interpretation of the meaning of a piece of language is based on not only our knowledge of vocabulary and grammar rules, but also our knowledge of the world and the environment in which language is used. Consider the following combinations of words: "canola oil", "olive oil", and "baby oil". All of them are what we call noun phrases and have the same form (Modifier + Noun), but the ways we interpret the first two and the last one are different. For "canola oil" and "olive oil", we interpret them as "oil made from canola" and "oil made from olives" respectively. However, for "baby oil", we interpret it as "oil especially made for using on babies", rather than "oil made from babies" because our knowledge of the world tells us that we do not make oil from babies.

DOI: 10.4018/978-1-5225-8467-4.ch010

What these examples show is that when we put words together to make meanings and when we interpret language in actual situations of communication, we rely on the meanings of individual words and the structures or patterns in which they are combined, as well as what we think is the probable intention of the speaker/writer by drawing on our knowledge of the world and the environment in which the language is used. In other words, to be able to use language adequately and appropriately, we learn more than the speech sounds or phonemes, morphemes, vocabulary and word meanings, and grammatical structures to combine words into phrases, clauses and sentences in the language. We also learn about, for example, how we use language for a purpose, how we convey that purpose to other users of the language, and how we figure out the intended meaning which may not be transparent from the language form itself. As sub-disciplines of linguistics, pragmatics and discourse analysis focus on the latter – i.e., those aspects of meaning that depend on the communicative intentions of language users and the environment in which the language is used.

Specifically, pragmatics studies "the factors that govern our choice of language in social interaction and the effects of our choice on others" (Crystal, 1987, p. 120). Pragmatics can be referred to as the study of "speaker meaning" because it aims to understand how linguistic units relate to the *people* who use them (Morris, 1938) (see Chapters 8 and 9 for the key concepts commonly used in pragmatics). As illustrated in these chapters, pragmatics explains how the choice of language features depends on the communicative intent of the speaker, what he/she considers appropriate for his/her interlocutor(s) in terms of politeness and the kind of force or effect he/she intends to achieve. For example, to ask for help, the speaker may choose to say: "Would you mind helping me?" or "I need your help." or "Help!".

Discourse analysis, on the other hand, deals with the linguistic study of *text*, i.e., how linguistic units are used in actual texts to convey meanings. It focuses on uncovering meanings represented or constructed in texts, and so can be referred to as the study of "text meaning". It points out the choice of language features made in a text and uses the presence (or absence) of certain language features as evidence to make interpretations or comments about the purpose(s) of the text, the target audience(s), the kind of social relationship (e.g., equal or different power or status) suggested between the text producer and audience, the kind of assumptions made in the text about the audience (e.g., their age, gender, ethnicity, social class, preoccupations, aspirations, etc.), the kind of knowledge about the world the audience needs to be able to fill in "what is not being said overtly, but is assumed to be known" (Gee, 2014, p. 18), and so on. In order to uncover meanings represented or constructed in texts, one of the key elements examined in discourse analysis is the social relationship between participants, or the people involved in the process of interaction and production of texts. Therefore, although the two fields are often regarded as two sub-disciplines of linguistics, a solid knowledge of pragmatics is beneficial when doing discourse analysis. In particular, knowledge of pragmatics can be helpful when analysing the choices made by speakers/writers in relation to hearers/readers when producing texts in a specific context. A sound understanding of speakers'/writers' choices in their use of language can then facilitate a discourse analyst in interpreting meanings encoded in the texts that are produced for specific intended audience.

This chapter provides (future) TESOL/ESOL teachers and practitioners with knowledge of key concepts, such as "text", "discourse", and "context", in discourse analysis, as well as their implications for teaching English to culturally and linguistically diverse learners. Since pragmatics and discourse analysis are closely-related and both are concerned with meaning-making in the actual language use, relevant pragmatics concepts will also be referred to when discussing what discourse analysis is.

TEXT AND DISCOURSE

Some linguists (e.g., Carter, Goddard, Reah, Sanger, & Swift, 2008) use the terms "**text**" and "**discourse**" interchangeably to refer to a unit of language above the level of clauses and sentences – i.e., the largest unit of linguistic structure which consists of sentences/clauses. Sentences/clauses are made up of phrases that are formed by combining words. For others (e.g., Widdowson, 2007), "text" refers to the (woven) product or material, as in the original meaning of the word in Latin, whereas "discourse" refers to the (abstract) process leading to the construction of a text. To those linguists who make a distinction between the two terms, discourse means "text in context", and thus includes text (as the resultant material/product) as well as the factors surrounding the production and interpretation of the text, such as the purpose, participants, situation and process of interaction, etc., each of which plays a role in the construction and interpretation of the meanings in the text.

Despite the disparity, a common concern among those who use the terms "text" and "discourse" is to look at language beyond the boundaries of isolated words or sentences. Between the two terms, most of us are more familiar with the term "text" because it is not difficult to find and point to examples of texts. For example, if someone asks, "Show me a text" or "Give me an example of a text", we can easily point to a page or chapter of a book, a notice on the wall, a blog post, a letter or email message, and the list goes on. There is a plethora of texts around us. It should be noted that a text is not defined by its size or form. While some texts contain a long stretch of language (e.g., a journal article), others are made up of a single sentence (e.g., "Handle with care." written on a box) or even a single word (e.g., the word "Cashier" above the counter to make payment at a shopping mall). While some texts are carefully-planned and permanent (e.g., a textbook chapter), others are spontaneously-produced and transient unless they are recorded (e.g., a casual conversation you had with your friends over lunch). While some texts are instances of written language, others are spoken. Then what makes a text? To get some answers to this question, compare the two examples below.

(A) *Soya is a good source of complete protein. Make AAA Travel your first stop. Well, finally, your Year 1 results are here. Even when workers are not paid overtime, they will often work long hours because of job insecurity.*

(B) *Once upon a time there was a mother duck and a father duck who lived in a pond. They had seven baby ducklings. Six of them were beautiful ducklings. The seventh was a really ugly duckling.*

In Example (A), although each word has meaning and each sentence on its own makes sense, we can hardly interpret the four sentences as a meaningful unit on the whole and would find it difficult to identify it as a text. On the other hand, we almost instantly recognize Example (B) as a text and are able to interpret its meaning as a unified whole. A closer look at the two examples shows what distinguishes them. In Example (B), each word has meaning and each sentence makes sense, and there are links/connections among words within a sentence as well as across sentences. A good way to understand the links is to see if you can fill in the blanks:

Once upon a time there was a mother duck and a _____ duck who lived in a pond. ____ had seven baby ducklings. Six of them were beautiful _____. The seventh was a really _____ duckling.

By filling in the blanks, you will see that links are made through the use of words which are related (e.g., **antonyms** – "mother" and "father", "beautiful" and "ugly") or words which are repeated (e.g., "ducklings"). Repetition of words helps to create a sense of continuity of the topic (i.e., this group of sentences is about ducks and ducklings or a duck family). The use of words which are related (e.g., antonyms) helps to create a web or network of key words used in this group of sentences and assists the reader to interpret it as a meaningful unit as a whole. In fact, the use of certain grammatical features like **pronouns** (e.g., "They") also helps to create links by maintaining reference to what is mentioned before or after.

In linguistics, the connections or links that exist in a stretch of language and that help to identify it as a text are called **cohesion**, and the language features that help to establish such links across words and sentences are called **cohesive devices**. Specifically, the links created through the repetition of words or the use of words which are related in meanings (such as **synonyms**, antonyms, etc.) are called **lexical cohesion**. Links established through the use of grammatical features (such as pronouns, **conjunctions**, etc.) are referred to as **grammatical cohesion**. Cohesive relationships occur when we depend on or presuppose the interpretation of another element to interpret some element in a set of sentences, and such cohesive relationships within and between the sentences help us to identify the set of sentences as a text (Halliday & Hasan, 1976).

Cohesion or its absence is crucial in making judgement on whether the stretch of language can be identified as a unified whole or a collection of unrelated sentences. However, it would be insufficient to explain how a text is formed only based on cohesion or internal textual connections created through the use of various cohesive devices. Consider Example (C) below.

(C) *Soya is a good source of protein. The rate of protein synthesis is higher during the day. At night, the temperature is the lowest but it becomes the highest in June. Thus, soya can be part of our diet all year round.*

In Example (C), there are words which are repeated (e.g., "protein", "soya"), words which are related (e.g., antonyms – "day" and "night") and conjunctions (e.g., "Thus"). These seem to create links/connections between words and sentences, but it is hard to arrive at an interpretation and make it fit the situation or purpose for which this group of sentences is produced. In other words, the topic keeps shifting – is it about soya or food digestion process or weather/season? Example (C) shows that cohesion or internal textual connections alone cannot ensure that a piece of language makes sense and can be identified as a text. Other meaningful connections not expressed by words and sentences also need to be achieved by relating the piece of language to the purpose and audience for which it is produced and the situation in which it is produced. In Example (C), it is difficult to make such a connection to the purpose, audience, and situation, and so, it is hard to arrive at an interpretation. This kind of connection, which can be achieved only by relating the piece of language to its purpose, audience, and situation for/in which it is produced, is called **coherence**.

Coherence is the process of filling in a lot of "gaps" which exist in the text, creating meaningful connections which are not actually expressed by the words and sentences as we try to arrive at an interpretation which is in line with our experience of the way the world is (Yule, 2010). For those examples with a single sentence (e.g., "Handle with care." written on a box) or a single word (e.g., the word "Cashier" above the counter to make payment at a shopping mall), we can still identify them as texts because we can relate the particular sentence or word to specific purposes, audiences, and situations for which they are produced, and so, we can make interpretations drawing on our knowledge of the world. Similarly, consider a spoken interaction like this:

Speaker A: Maggie, your dog is scratching the front door.
Speaker B: I have to hand in my assignment by 8 am tomorrow, Paa.

In the above exchange, there are no repeated words or words which are related in meaning (e.g., synonyms, antonyms, etc.). It does not contain such grammatical features as conjunctions to express connections, either. Hence, this stretch of language seems to be lacking cohesive devices and cohesiveness. However, we are able to interpret it as a father asking his daughter to take the dog out for a walk and the daughter's reply to say that she could not because she was busy trying to complete her assignment. We are able to make sense of the exchange because our knowledge of the world (e.g., a dog scratching the front door suggests that it is asking to go for a walk, someone who has to hand in an assignment soon will have little time to spare to do other things than to complete the assignment) helps to draw **inferences** or fill in the gaps and arrive at the interpretation. We can identify the above conversational exchange as a text as we are able to relate it to factors such as the situation, purpose, and participants of the interaction.

In short, to make sense of a stretch of language and call it a text, we do not merely rely on cohesion or the internal links created through language devices. We must also be able to make meaningful connections, e.g., to the purpose, audience, situation, etc., to establish coherence. The presence of cohesive devices in a text facilitates the task of recognizing its coherence. But cohesive devices alone are not sufficient to help readers/listeners to construct the frame of reference and interpret the text. There is an interplay between cohesion and coherence.

Once we pay attention to the factors surrounding the production and interpretation of texts, we are dealing with discourse. As a sub-discipline of linguistics, discourse analysis not only examines language features used in a text, but also relates these choices of language features made by the text producer to the factors surrounding the actual use of the text and makes interpretations about what, who, where, when, and why of the text. Like the linguists who specialize in pragmatics, discourse analysts are interested not only in surface meaning (e.g. what people say) but also in underlying meaning (e.g., what kinds of perspectives on the world the writer/speaker is trying to express, reinforce, or impose on the audience, what kind of social relationship is constructed, etc.). Basic questions a discourse analyst asks include (Johnstone, 2018):

- Why is this stretch of language the way it is?
- Why is it no other way?
- Why are these particular words in this particular order?
- What is the text about?
- Who said or wrote it?
- What motivated the text?
- Who could be the intended audience?
- How does the text fit into the set of things people in its context conventionally do with language?
- What does its medium (or media) of production have to do with what it is like?

Analysis of language features used in a text involves analysis at the word/phrase level, the clause/ sentence level, and the organization of the text as a whole. At the word/phrase level, questions can be asked about lexical choices – e.g., whether the words/phrases used in the text are formal or colloquial expressions, technical terms (jargon) or everyday vocabulary, neutral or evaluative lexis, and with positive or negative **connotations**. Analysis at the clause/sentence level can include questions about types of clause/sentence – e.g., whether they are active or passive, and whether they are declarative, interrogative, imperative or exclamatory. Based on the analysis of language features, interpretations about meanings encoded in the text are made. Discourse analysis pays particular attention to the close relationship or interaction between language features found in a text and the circumstances of producing and interpreting the text. It studies how "contexts shape texts and texts shape contexts" (Johnstone, 2018, p. 8). This brings us to a need to define another important concept – context – in discourse analysis.

CONTEXT

Simply put, **context** refers to the environment or circumstances surrounding the way in which we use language. It is a crucial concept in discourse analysis as it enables us to make inferences. Speakers and writers use language (i.e., they make choices on the organization or structure of a text, and lexical and grammatical features) in relation to their audience and purpose. Likewise, by relating a text to its context we can comment on not only what the text is about, but also who the targeted audience is, what its intended purpose is, what kind of social relationship between writer and reader or speaker and listener is suggested, why the subject/topic is represented in a certain way, etc.

For an understanding of how communication and meaning-making occur through the interaction between language and context, we need to acknowledge that "context" is often used as an umbrella term involving a wide range of elements and that it is multifaceted. For example, Hewings and Hewings (2005) first make a distinction between "linguistic" and "non-linguistic" contexts. The **linguistic context** means the words, phrases, sentences, or paragraphs that surround or co-occur with the particular word, phrase, sentence or paragraph under consideration. For example, the linguistic context of the word "distinction" in the earlier sentence will be all the words, phrases, or sentences that come before or after it. Often the linguistic context is more appropriately referred to as "co-text" or the surrounding text. We draw on such surrounding text to construct meanings about a word, phrase, sentence, or paragraph.

For the **non-linguistic context**, Hewings and Hewings (2005) make another distinction between "local situational context" and "wider sociocultural context". The local situational context includes the physical setting (such as the time and the location), the purpose of communication, and the people (their age, gender, occupation, relative status, etc.) who are involved in the interaction or communication. The wider sociocultural context refers to "the broader background against which communication is interpreted", and it includes "social and political aspects of language or national groups as a whole, and features of institutional domains" (Hewings & Hewings, 2005, p. 22).

When doing discourse analysis, specific language features which can be identified in a text are related to the local situational context by asking questions such as:

- What kind of information/topic(s) about people/events/ideas is represented, from which/whose angle, how much in-depth, and for what purpose?

- What kind of social relationships between the writer/speaker and reader/hearer is constructed (e.g., showing familiarity or creating social distance, little or much expression of the writer/speaker's attitudes and feelings)?
- How are the ideas developed and organized in a text using which mode or channel of communication?

This aspect of discourse analysis is sometimes referred to as the analysis of "**register**" (Painter, 2001). As an example, compare a recipe written in a cookbook and a spoken interaction between friends who were exchanging recipes as they cooked or watched one of them cook. You will find that different language features are used in the two examples, and such differences reflect (i) the different topics or kinds of information covered in each text, (ii) the different types of social relationships between participants, and (iii) different modes of communication.

Similarly, specific language features used in a text can also be related to the wider sociocultural context by asking questions such as:

- What do we know about certain social occasions, cultural ceremonies or beliefs, visions and missions of a particular institution that helps us to interpret the messages in the text?
- What ideologies, worldviews or stereotypes (e.g., about gender, power relation, etc.) are underlying or encoded in the text?

So, in doing discourse analysis, evidence of language features found in a text can be discussed in relation to both the local situational context and the wider sociocultural context. An understanding of the distinctions between the local situational context and the wider sociocultural context can also help us to understand the various goals of discourse analysis.

GOALS OF DISCOURSE ANALYSIS

Discourse analysis is a broad area of inquiry, and the questions discourse analysts ask range from simple ones such as "How are texts structured?" to more complex ones like "How are social actions accomplished?", "How are identities negotiated?", and "How are ideologies constructed?" (Waring, 2018, p. 23). Johnstone (2018) discusses the various aspects of discourse analysis by explaining its "descriptive" and "critical" goals.

Descriptive Goals

For some discourse analysts, the primary goal of discourse analysis is to describe texts and how they work – e.g., the study of what makes English text cohesive. Halliday and Hasan (1976) is often regarded as a classic study in this area. Subsequently, linguists such as Carter et al. (2008) define discourse analysis as an analysis of "the way texts work across the boundaries of single sentences or utterances to form whole stretches of language" (p. 141), and describe in detail how links/connections among words and sentences are made through the use of various cohesive devices. Example (D) below will be used to illustrate this point.

(D) *Rabbit*

Rabbits are gnawing animals, feeding on plants and usually living in groups and sheltering in burrows. When they feed, they do not move far from home, so that a short dash can take them to safety. They rely on their good eyesight and senses of hearing and smell to warn them of enemies. They are hunted by many predators, including human beings.

Most kinds of rabbits produce a large number of young in the course of a year. Even so, only the European rabbit has become widespread and a pest. Most rabbit species are found in pretty restricted areas, and some are endangered.

In some ways rabbits and hares are like rodents, but there are many differences between the two groups. One is that rabbits have four upper incisor teeth. There are two tiny ones behind the big incisors. These are completely covered with enamel, unlike the incisors of rodents, which have enamel only on the outer side.

Source: *Oxford Children's Encyclopedia* (2004)

Those discourse analysts who are interested in describing how links/connections among words and sentences are made through the use of various cohesive devices will identify cohesive devices in Example (D) as in Table 1. Their goal is not to come up with an exhaustive list, but to illuminate how various lexical and grammatical cohesive devices hold different parts of the text together.

Another area of focus in discourse analysis whose primary goal is to describe texts and how they work is the analysis of **text types**. Studies done on this aspect of discourse analysis aim to describe and explain how a group of texts produced for similar social purposes tend to have similar organization or overall structure and lexico-grammatical features (i.e., choices of vocabulary and grammatical patterns). With plethora of texts around us, there have been attempts to categorize them based on certain characteristics shared by a group of texts. Two possible ways (among many) of categorizing texts are (i) based on the mode or channel of communication in which a text is produced and (ii) according to the social purpose for which a text is produced.

Table 1. Cohesive Devices Used in (D)

Lexical Cohesive Devices	Grammatical Cohesive Devices
• Direct repetition of key words: ("rabbit"/ "rabbits") that gives a sense of continuity of the topic. • Meaning relations or structural relations among words used in a sentence or across sentences: e.g., superordinate and **hyponyms** ("rabbits" – "European rabbits"), superordinate and **meronyms** ("rabbit" – "eyesight", "teeth"), **synonyms** ("kinds", "species"), **antonyms** ("tiny", "big"), words from the same lexical field ("rabbits", "plants", "burrows"), words that share the same root/ stem ("feed", "feeding"). • **Collocation**: Words/phrases that collocate ("feeding on plants", "sheltering in burrows", "hunted by predators").	• **Pronouns:** "they" helps to maintain reference to the same thing, makes the reader refer back to the word "rabbits" in the first sentence. • **Ellipsis:** "they rely on their good eyesight, (they rely on their) sense of hearing, (they rely on their) sense of smell" Although these are three different types of senses, the ellipsis helps the reader to see the links that all three senses belong to the rabbits by having to retrieve the information that has been omitted to make sense. • **Conjunctions:** "and" for addition of information, "when" to indicate temporal connection, "so that" to indicate causal connection, etc. • **Determiners:** "many", "most" to help the reader to determine (and the writer to clarify) the quantity of the noun mentioned before.

Based on the mode or channel of communication in which a text is produced, a broad distinction can be made between spoken and written texts. However, such a distinction should be used only as starting points to help us explore the complexities of language use, rather than as straightforward binary categories. Between a typical spoken text, such as a spontaneous conversation among friends, and a typical written text, such as a textbook chapter, there are various other types of spoken and written texts which we produce and interpret in our daily lives and which lie somewhere along the continuum of spoken and written texts. For example, spoken texts such as interviews, announcements, news broadcasts, storytelling and political speeches are produced with different degrees of planning for the speaker and different kinds of listener involvement. Such differences in the degree of planning and listener involvement can result in varying amounts of overlaps, pauses, false start and non-fluency features such as fillers (e.g., "er", "umm") in different types of spoken texts. Similarly, examples of written texts which are produced with little planning (e.g., a note we scribbled for a family member before we leave home in a rush) will show "speech-like" features such as the use of incomplete sentences.

It is also important to note that when we communicate, either in the spoken or written mode, the language we use is typically accompanied by features from other modes of communication – e.g., facial expression, gaze and gestures accompanying our utterances, and images/pictures and different typefaces accompanying and contributing meanings to our writing. Therefore, texts we produce and interpret are more often than not **multimodal** – i.e., more than one mode of communication is used in a single text, and meanings are constructed through interaction between features from different modes. Increasingly, scholars of discourse analysis pay attention to the use of language along with other multimodal resources in their examination of how texts construct meanings.

Whether they are spoken, written, or multimodal, texts can also be categorized according to the social purposes for which they are produced. For example, it is very likely that in your email inbox, you can find considerable variation of language features used in the messages sent by different people for different purposes. Scholars who have attempted to categorize texts in this way often take a functional approach. A functional approach holds the view that the distinctive social purpose of producing a text is what shapes the text's overall structure as well as choices of vocabulary and grammatical patterns. The term "text types" is used to refer to groupings of texts that are similar in terms of co-occurrence of linguistic patterns and share similar social purposes. Some examples of text types include narrative, recounts, instructions, expositions, explanations (Derewianka, 1990; Paltridge, 1996). Referring again to the example (D), the text can be categorized as an information report with the purpose to define, describe, classify, and document a type of animal, or to provide factual information about rabbits in general, about its features, characteristics, etc. Some language features, which can be highlighted to explain how the use of language contributes to achieving the purpose of the text, include the use of

- common nouns (e.g., "rabbits") to give information about rabbits in general;
- present tense (e.g., "are") to provide factual information;
- adjectives that describe features in a relatively factual manner (e.g., "good" eyesight) to provide factual information, rather than "fantastic/wonderful" eyesight;
- complete sentences, making the text sound relatively more serious and authoritative; and
- declarative clauses for giving information.

Table 2 gives an overview of some text types whose social purposes and typical language features have been identified and discussed by scholars interested in this aspect of discourse analysis. Categorizing texts according to the mode or channel of communication in which they are produced and/or their different social purposes is helpful for us to explain (and teach) purposeful use of language in various contexts. It is also helpful for us to understand how a text is constructed by its creator to suit the intended audience and to achieve the intended purpose. However, in the real world, there are very few "pure texts". Most texts are hybrid – i.e., features of more than one mode or one text type can be combined in a single text. Language users often deliberately manipulate the features typical of a mode or a text type in order to achieve certain effects or for a particular purpose. Moreover, some texts may have only one purpose, but texts potentially have more than one purpose, making it problematic to place a text in one of these categories or only in one category. For example, in order to entice the reader to read on, a text about a recipe can begin with a personal recount of the authors preparing and enjoying the meal before giving the instructions on how to make that dish (e.g., see "Lake Breakfast" http://www.sailingbreezes. com/Sailing_Breezes_Current/Other_Reviews/feasts_afloat.htm)

Critical Goals

The aspect of discourse analysis focusing on explaining the text types according to their different social purposes has developed further into what is known as genre analysis. Closely related to the term "text type", but placing the emphasis on the *process* of producing a type of texts and relating such processes to

Table 2. An Overview of Text Types, Their Purposes and Typical Language Features

Text Type	Social Purpose	Typical Overall Structure () Represents an Optional Element	Typical Lexico-Grammatical Features
Narrative	to put together a series of events, which have a twist, to entertain or to teach a moral lesson	(Abstract), Orientation, Complication, Resolution, Evaluation, (Coda)	Past tense, Specific participants, Quotations/dialogues, Words/ expressions showing personal feelings or evaluation
Recount	to record the particulars of an incident, to retell some past events in a chronological sequence	Orientation, Record of events, (Evaluation)	Past tense, (1st person pronoun), Conjunctions to do with time and sequence
Instruction	to tell how to do/make something	Goal, (Material), Method	Imperatives, Base form verbs, No subject, Factual description, Fewer adj/adv that show personal feelings, Words/numbers showing sequence
Information report	to define, describe, classify and document a subject	General statement/classification, Information about a particular aspect of the subject, General statement rounding off the topic	Present tense, Common nouns/ General participants, Factual and formal description
Explanation	to explain how/why something works in a particular way	Opening statement/phenomena, Sequence of statements/explanations	Usually present tense, Generalized non-human participants, Words showing time or cause-effect relationships
Discussion	to analyse and present different points-of-view of an issue; to take a position and justify it	Issue, Argument, Recommendation/ summing up the position	Usually present tense, Personal pronouns, Modals, Logical connectives/ Causal conjunctions

the wider sociocultural context, the term "**genre**" is used instead by those whose goal of doing discourse analysis is not only to describe characteristic features of texts, but also to uncover certain ways of using language to achieve specific sociocultural, institutional, and/or disciplinary purposes (e.g. Painter, 2001; Partridge, 1996; Swales, 1990). In this aspect, producing a type of texts is seen as a process of doing a culture-specific (or institution/discipline-specific) social activity which involves the use of language. Besides explaining how texts of each genre share certain typical overall structure, content, and set of vocabulary and grammatical patterns, studies done on this aspect of discourse analysis have helped to understand how a particular culture (or institution or discipline) uses genres as one of the resources to achieve specific social goals. Accordingly, an analysis of genres is seen as providing a window on the cultural (or institution/discipline-specific) ideologies, values, beliefs, and practices of the people who produced them.

As an example, we can examine wedding invitations from two different cultures. Below (E) is an example of Myanmar wedding invitations, which I have translated into English without altering the format, organization, or the details. (F) is an example of American wedding invitations found online at http://www.czeckitout.com/wedding/american-wedding-invitations-samples

(E)

Wedding Invitation

Grandson of U Bo Thein (Retired Director General, Sweet and Sweet Co. Ltd.) & Daw Shwe Moe, who lived in Yangon, and U Myo Hla (Retired Engineer, Myanma Railway) & Daw Nu Nu, who lived in Pathein; Nephew of Dr Tin Aung (Medical Officer, Mandalay Hospital) & Daw Ma Ma Lay (S.H.B.S No. 2, Mandalay); Youngest son of U Myint Aung (Managing Director, Sweet and Sweet Co. Ltd) & Daw Hla Hla (Director, Sweet and Sweet Co. Ltd.), who live in Yangon, Dagon Township, 50th Street, No. 82

Maung Myo Thein Aung (B.E Mechanical, Yangon Technological University, M.Sc. Mechanical Engineering, Nanyang Technological University, Singapore)

&

Granddaughter of U Ye Yin (Ex-president, Myanmar Sports Council) & (Daw Mya Sein), who lived in Yangon, and U Aung Ko (Aung Ko Construction Co.) & Daw Tin Tin, who lived in Yangon; Sister of Lieutenant Soe Myint Oo and Dr Yadana Khin (temporarily in the USA); Only daughter of Lieutenant Colonel Tin Oo & Dr May Kyi (Medical Officer, Bago Hospital), who live in Bago, Myoma Road, No. 23

Ma Htay Htay Oo (Bachelor of Business Administration, Curtin University, Australia)

Will be holding their wedding reception and would like to cordially invite you to attend as follows.

Wedding Venue: Sedona Hotel, No. 1 Kaba Aye Pagoda Road, Yangon
Wedding Date: 7 November 2018 (Sunday)
Wedding Time: 5 pm to 8 pm

(F)

RACHEL ASHBY KEEFE

&

WILLIAM HANSON WRIGHT II

request the pleasure of your company
at the celebration of their union

sunday, the seventh of may, two thousand and ten
at seven o'clock in the evening
st. john catholic church
321 main street, austin, tx

reception to follow

Comparing (E) and (F), the wedding invitations from two different cultures, what aspects of the content, overall structure, and choice of words and grammatical patters are similar or shared across the wedding invitations from different cultural contexts? What aspects are different or unique for a particular culture? Those aspects which are similar or shared across cultures will explain why they all can be described as belonging to the same genre (i.e., wedding invitation). At the same time, based on those aspects which are different or unique for a particular culture, interpretations can be made about the different values, beliefs, and norms about social relations held by people from different cultures.

It is also important to understand genres as the processes of using language to accomplish social activities which have evolved and will continue to evolve over time. As the society changes, social activities engaged by the people in that society will also change, so will the possibilities and limitations of using language as a resource to accomplish these social activities. As an example, think of how we can book a flight online nowadays and how we had to call or physically visit the airline or travel agent counter to book a flight about 20 or 30 years ago. Then think of the ways language is and was used in each of the two processes.

In a more critical sense, discourse analysis aims to find out more than how we use language to make meaning or what a text refers to and what its purpose is. It views language as an ideological instrument, relates texts to broader ideological issues, and looks at how texts can be used to express, reproduce, and impose certain ways of thinking about the world (Widdowson, 2007). In other words, those discourse analysts who take a critical or political perspective (e.g. Fairclough, 1989; van Dijk, 1993; Gee, 2014) view language not merely as a neutral and objective tool for communication but a means to excerpt power over people and reproduce power relations in society. They examine the use (and abuse) of language in relation to underlying social meanings or worldviews encoded in a text, and aim to uncover broader issues such as ideological biases, political and cultural issues, gender inequality, and social hierarchies (van Dijk, 1993). To them, "language-in-use is always part and parcel of, and partially constitutive of, specific social practices" and "social practices always have implications for inherently political things like status, solidarity, the distribution of social goods, and power" (Gee, 2004, p. 28).

This aspect of discourse analysis is known as **Critical Discourse Analysis**, or **CDA**. CDA can be seen as a departure from the more descriptive goals of discourse analysis, "where the focus has been more on describing and detailing linguistic features than about *why* and *how* these features are produced and what possible ideological goals they might serve" (Machin & Maya, 2012, p. 5). "Basically, people who 'do' CDA are interested in answering the question: How does language express and reinforce power relations between people?" (Lwin & Teo, 2014, p. 61). To answer such questions, detailed and systematic analyses of lexical and grammatical features are conducted on a range of media discourse and political discourse, such as news reports, magazine articles, advertisements, political speeches, etc. For example, through an analysis of quotation patterns, critical discourse analysts reveal bias in news articles and illustrate how "[n]ewspapers have a tendency to quote from authoritative sources in an attempt to make their reports seem credible and reliable" (Lwin & Teo, 2014, p. 61). By interviewing and quoting people in positions of power, such as politicians, CEOs, university professors, and police chiefs, the news reporter can in actual fact be presenting a biased view of the news events and of the world in general. Through a close analysis of who and what is quoted, a critical approach to discourse analysis reveals underlying ideologies of the newspapers and how they enhance the perspectives of the powerful while silencing the voices of the powerless. CDA, as summarized by Fairclough and Wodak (1997), views discourse as a form of social action and addresses social problems.

WHY DISCOURSE ANALYSIS

A text can be analysed in a variety of ways. In fact, the terms "discourse" and "discourse analysis" are used not only by linguists but also by people from other disciplines, such as sociology, history, literary studies, communications studies, political science and several other fields in social sciences. However, discourse analysis from a linguistic perspective (i.e., as a sub-discipline of linguistics) primarily aims to uncover how specific language features – such as vocabulary, grammatical patterns, and overall organization – are used in a particular text for a specific purpose and audience. Claims and interpretations made about the meanings constructed in a text are supported with systematic analyses of language features found in the text, so that features used in different texts (or in different parts of the same text) can be compared in relation to the text's intended purpose and target audience.

A fundamental message of discourse analysis is to look at language beyond the boundaries of isolated words or sentences, and recognize the important roles played by both local situational context and wider socio-cultural context in using language to make meanings. By examining what kind of lexical and grammatical choices are made in a text, for what purpose, by whom, and for whom, and discussing the use/lack of certain language features in relation to the surrounding social, cultural or ideological issues, discourse analysis helps us become sensitive to the language used in the texts around us.

IMPLICATIONS FOR TEACHING ENGLISH LANGUAGE LEARNERS

Applied linguists with a particular interest in language learning and teaching conduct discourse analysis to help find some answers to questions such as what to teach and how to teach (Waring, 2018). Given that developing communicative competence in a language entails more than learning its vocabulary, mastering its grammar, and appropriating its pronunciation, pragmatics and discourse analysis are integral to learning a language as they deal with how the language is actually used by speakers or writers in various social contexts. Especially with regard to culturally and linguistically diverse learners of English, understanding and applying the sets of principles for using the English language appropriately in specific social contexts can be challenging. The set of principles governing how people communicate in social interaction (e.g., how beginnings and endings are signalled, how social status is acknowledged, how politeness and power are conveyed, how the speaker/writer conveys their communicative intent, how the listener/reader has to uncover that intent, etc.) varies from language to language, and from culture to culture.

Use of Cohesive Devices

Waring (2018) points out that **discourse markers** such as "but", "also", "anyway", and "actually" can present grave challenges for English as a Second or Foreign Language (ESL/EFL) learners because they often use these markers literally, overuse or misuse them. Similarly, in their studies of the use of cohesive devices by Chinese EFL learners in their argumentative writing, Yang and Sun (2012) reveal the patterns of incorrect employment of cohesive devices in relation to the learners' proficiency levels and their writing quality. The findings from their study also show that incorrect use of cohesive devices did occur even in advanced learners' writing although the quantity decreased. Some examples of the misuse, improper omission or improper addition of cohesive devices by EFL learners which resulted in meaning ambiguity or hindered the coherence of their written texts include the following (Yang & Sun, 2012, p. 36):

- Reference error: e.g., *Good health is very significant to people. With good health, they can feel happy for you are energetic enough to do a lot of things* (inconsistency of personal reference).
- Conjunction error: e.g., *Wealth can bring us almost everything we want. On the other hand, much of our happiness comes from wealth* (misuse of conjunction).
  We can enjoy material happiness. And moreover we can appreciate spiritual happiness. (overuse/improper addition of conjunction).
  A lot of people no longer feel satisfied with physical contentment, they begin to pursue spiritual happiness (improper omission of conjunction).
- Substitution/ellipsis error: e.g., *He thought that a birthday gift could make his wife happy. He decided to look for an appropriate gift. However, it was an unpleasant experience. He searched from shop to shop. But still he couldn't find an ideal one.* (Readers find it difficult to ascertain for which part "one" substitutes.)
- Lexical cohesion error: e.g., *They are trying their best to preserve their money to become rich. But they don't really know how to prevent their money.* ("Prevent" is misused and should be replaced with "preserve" or "reserve".)

The knowledge learned from discourse analysis as a sub-discipline of linguistics can help teachers better understand ESL/EFL learners' misuse, improper omission or improper addition of features such as discourse markers and cohesive devices. In general, teachers can apply the knowledge learned from discourse analysis to helping their culturally and linguistically diverse learners of English develop discourse competence (Riggenbach, 1999; Wennerstrom, 2003). Discourse competence is a major component of communicative competence referring to the understanding of cohesion and coherence in different types of texts and the ability to produce cohesive and coherent texts (Canale & Swain, 1980). It constitutes knowledge of how to use linguistic resources (i.e., linguistic/grammatical competence) as well as understanding of social and cultural factors for appropriate linguistic choices (sociolinguistic competence) to produce cohesive and coherent texts.

Text Types and Genres

Advocates of a **discourse-based approach** to language teaching (e.g., Celce-Murcia & Olshtian, 2014) argue that "it is discourse (not grammar, vocabulary, speech acts, or strategies) that should function as the core organizer for language teaching and learning" (p. 427). A discourse-based approach places discourse at the core of language teaching and learning. The approach can be viewed as a development from the communicative language teaching (CLT) movement; however, the emphasis is on whole text, cohesion, coherence, context, text types, and communicative goals such as purpose and audience. It aims to help learners develop knowledge of how to use linguistic resources appropriately to produce extended, cohesive and coherent texts to make meaning and achieve a social goal. The approach postulates that learning of English is facilitated by systematically providing learners with exposure to different text types through the use of sample authentic spoken and written texts as teaching materials, and guiding learners to analyze, compare, and evaluate these samples of texts. The aim is to raise learners' awareness that language is used to achieve a social goal and that texts produced for different social purposes and/ or different audiences reflect their particular context of use and have distinctive patterns of organization and distinctive linguistic features. Learners are then given opportunities to apply such awareness to their own use of language.

In teaching language through discourse, learning depends upon the scaffolded support of the teacher who facilitates learners in examining language features used in authentic examples of spoken and written texts, and the specific contexts in which they are used. In this respect, understanding the characteristics of texts and exploring/analyzing them from a discourse perspective is a worthwhile pursuit for language teachers. For example, knowledge of discourse analysis could help teachers become more critical about scripted dialogues, which are largely based on "idealized" spoken texts, commonly used as ESL/EFL materials. While there are pedagogical purposes for using such texts, especially when dealing with lower level students (e.g., scripted dialogues are easier for students to process), the sense of security evaporates when students are faced with the task of interacting in the target language in authentic social contexts outside the classroom since scripted dialogues rarely reflect the unpredictability, dynamism, or the linguistic features and structures of natural spoken discourse. Burns (2001, 2010) illustrates how many of the materials available commercially for the teaching of speaking often fail to equip second language learners with a fundamental understanding of the nature of authentic interaction by comparing two excerpts about asking directions (see Table 3). In the transcript shown in Table 3, the square brackets indicate overlapping speech and dots indicate pauses per second.

Another implication of discourse analysis for teaching ESL/EFL learners is to help them develop an understanding that what is considered to be an obligatory element or a crucial lexical or grammatical feature of a text type or genre produced in English may not be found in a similar text type produced in their first language, and vice versa. For example, just as there are different ways of displaying politeness in different cultures, features which are considered to be crucial to make a narrative good or bad can also be culture- and language-specific. In English narratives, relating a series of events in chronological order is considered necessary but not sufficient. English speakers would expect evaluative comments

Table 3. Scripted vs Authentic Interaction

Scripted Dialogue	Authentic Dialogue
A: Excuse me. How will I get to the North East Shopping Centre? B: Take a number 9 bus to Westmore street. When you reach Westmore Street, transfer to the number 34 bust at the corner of Walton Road. This bus will take you to the North East Shopping Centre. A: How will I know when I have arrived at Westmore Street? B: The bus driver will let you know if you ask him. A: Thank you.	A: Um…give me an idea how to get to your place… I don't cos, I don't um… know it too well round there. I'll probably be, er… coming by bus…so] B: [right, well, going towards… French street, stay on the bus for, oh…about… the trip takes about twenty minutes by bus] A: [right B: now you go… the bus will go out along St Katherine's Road… well you just keep on the bus… A: …. mm … hm… B: and it'll cross over Peters Road which is a fairly major…. A: year, I know Peters….

which convey the storyteller's attitudes about events and his/her interpretations of characters' motives and reactions (Labov & Waletzky, 1967). However, in Japanese, less emphasis is given on evaluative descriptions since omitting the teller's emotion or telling without verbalizing the teller's feelings is preferred (Minami, 2008). Another example of such culture-specific generic feature can be found in Chinese. The discourse patterns of Chinese include explaining the reason why one holds an opinion before stating the opinion, and when making a request, Chinese speakers often give reasons for the request before stating the request itself (Gil & Adamson, 2011). It is, therefore, important for ESL/EFL teachers to have an understanding of cultural differences in the principles and patterns of language use to avoid mistakenly judging a learner from a different cultural or linguistic background as socially, academically or intellectually deficient when the learner's use of language mismatches the principles and patterns expected in English.

Intercultural Communicative Competence

The knowledge of genre can also be applied when conducting a comparative analysis of texts produced for similar social purposes in different cultures or languages. Through such comparative analyses, teachers can help to raise learners' awareness of commonalities as well as differences among texts produced for similar social purposes in different cultures or languages. Commonalities among these texts can be highlighted as the typical features characterizing one particular text type or genre and contributing to achieving the text's social purposes. At the same time, teachers can guide learners to notice those features which are different, and encourage them to reflect on what these differences suggest about the uniqueness, ideology, or value system of a particular culture. For example, Lwin (2010, 2015, 2016) has shown how a comparative analysis of folktales with a similar didactic purpose from different Asian cultures reveals not only their common narrative structures, such as (Tasks → success → reward) and (Tasks → failure → punishment), but also different culture-specific narrative contents, such as characters' names or kinship terms, the types of food, activities, animals, and so on featured in each tale. Through such comparative analyses, teachers can help culturally and linguistically diverse learners of English recognize the close relationship between language and culture, i.e., how the culture of a country emphasizes what is prevalent in that country or what is collectively perceived as important by its people in and through their use of language.

By helping learners develop sensitivity to issues such as social relationship and culture in close connection with using language in a particular context, teachers can help learners to develop not only strategies for effective interpersonal communication but also **intercultural communicative competence**. Intercultural communicative competence involves attitudes of curiosity and openness (to suspend disbelief about other cultures and belief about one's own), knowledge of social groups, their products and practices, skills of interpreting and relating events from another culture, and the ability to critically evaluate perspectives, practices and products of one's own and other cultures (Byram, 2000; Chen & Starosta, 2000). When people from different linguistic and cultural backgrounds communicate through English, they need to have not only communicative competence but intercultural communicative competence to ensure successful interpersonal and intercultural communication.

Developing a Critical Understanding

Last but not least, the knowledge of discourse analysis can also help language teachers to become reflective practitioners who are able to self-evaluate their own use of language in the classroom and examine the implications for teaching and learning (Walsh, 2011). By systematically observing and analyzing the patterns of their own language use in the classroom context (e.g., the ways they use questions, illicit responses, give instructions, provide feedback, etc.), teachers can develop an insight into the classroom as a social event and a better understanding of the important roles language plays for effective teaching and learning. Such an understanding is even more crucial in the TESOL context where English is the subject of study as well as an important tool for teachers to communicate with students about the lesson content, administer discipline, manage interaction, and create opportunities for students' learning. From a more critical perspective, the knowledge of CDA can also help teachers recognize that issues to do with the relationship between language, culture, and power can be found everywhere, including classrooms. Being an expert adult, the teacher is someone who exerts power and authority over the learners, primarily through the use of language – e.g., in controlling the turns for who gets to speak about what for how long in class, what counts as "relevant" and "valued" answers in learners' responses and writing, what questions learners can/should ask in class, and whether they can challenge the contents of the teaching materials used by the teacher and so on (Lwin & Teo, 2014).

To sum up, knowledge of discourse analysis can be useful for both teachers and learners as it can help them see the use of language in its social context, develop sensitivity to issues such as culture and power that are closely related to the use of particular language features, become more critically aware of the ideologies surrounding the production and interpretation of texts, and be competent to make informed choices in their own language use to construct meanings and social relations.

DISCUSSION QUESTIONS

1. View the video available at the following link: https://www.youtube.com/watch?v=dyMSSe7cOvA Describe the contexts in which the word "Dude" is used. What do you think the word "Dude" means in each context? How do you arrive at the meaning for each context?

2. Share an example of text and comment on what sort of knowledge and experiences the text requires on the part of the reader to ascribe meaning to the text. By making the reader fill in such knowledge and experience, how does the text structure the reader's interpretation of the message(s) encoded

in the text? The example text can be in any form – a poster, road sign, shop name, advertisement, announcement, magazine article, newspaper article, invitation card, comic strip, conversation, social media post, web page, etc.

3. The following claims have been made in the studies which support a focus on text in teaching speaking (e.g., Burns & Seidlhofer, 2002; Burns, 2006). Discuss the relevance of each claim to a specific group of learners that you know.

    a. If dialogues are to be used, they should also introduce learners to some features of "real-life" discourse.

    b. Focusing on discourse and text helps students to notice and analyze authentic and appropriate use of language.

    c. Developing awareness of the discourse features of different texts suggests a consciousness-raising approach, rather than implying that students should follow "recipe" type modes in a slavish fashion.

    d. Familiarity with the relevant discourse type can influence speech production. Previous experience of the discourse type makes a critical difference in learners' performance.

    e. The discourse patterns are readily transferable from L1 to L2.

4. Drawing on your understanding of genre-based pedagogy for teaching speaking, examine the speaking activities used for your students (or a group of learners you are familiar with), and discuss the following questions.

    a. Are there any activities that are intended to help the learners develop awareness of text types in spoken or written English?

    b. If yes, in what way(s) do they help the learners to develop this awareness?

    c. If no, how would you use or supplement these materials to focus on developing the learners' awareness of different types of spoken or written texts in English?

5. Examine a classroom TESOL textbook from your own teaching context or a library. Find a few examples of activities which are designed using a text/discourse segment.

    a. Are there any discourse-based activities which you would like to see included in a course you teach? Why or why not?

    b. To what extent or in what ways do you think a discourse-based approach could benefit your teaching context?

    c. How would you go about selecting/sourcing for authentic written and spoken texts?

    d. Do you think there would be any challenges in implementing a discourse-based approach in your teaching context?

    e. What suggestions could you give to make a discourse-based approach work (more) effectively in your teaching context?

EXERCISES

1. Refer to Text A taken from the book *Chimpanzees in the Rain Forest* available at the children's section of a community library. Identify three different types of lexical cohesion and three different types of grammatical cohesion in Text A. Give one example of each of these, and briefly explain how they work as cohesive devices in this text.

Text A: *Chimpanzees in the Rain Forest*

Chimpanzees are mammals. A mammal is a warm-blooded animal with a backbone. Female mammals give birth to live young and feed them with milk from their bodies. Warm-blooded animals have a body temperature that stays the same, no matter what the temperature is outside.

The scientific name for chimpanzees is Pan Troglodytes (PAN TRAH-glow-dite-eez). Pan is the name of a Greek god who was part-man and part-animal. Early travelers to Africa saw wild chimpanzees and thought that this description fit them well.

Chimpanzees belong to the primate family along with monkeys and gorillas. All primates are mammals that have a large brain and hands that can grasp and hold objects.

2. Compare Text A with Text B, which is from the webpage of The Great Ape Trust, an organization advocating the conservation of wild lives and a scientific research facility established with the funds raised from the public. How would you explain to your students that the two texts are about the same topic, but of different text types or genres?

   You may use the following questions to guide your response:

   a. What would you consider to be the purpose of each text?
   b. Who do you think is the target audience?
   c. Identify at least three language features that are used differently in the two texts, and explain how these differences reflect the different purposes or different audiences of the two texts.

Text B

Not long ago, I spent the morning having coffee with Kanzi. It wasn't my idea; Kanzi invited me, though he did so in his customary clipped way. Kanzi is a fellow of few words – 384 of them by formal count, though he probably knows dozens more. He has a perfectly serviceable voice – very clear, very expressive and very, very loud. But it's not especially good for forming words, which is the way of things when you're a bonobo, the close and more peaceable cousin of the chimpanzee.

But Kanzi is talkative all the same. For much of his day, he keeps a sort of glossary close at hand – three laminated, place mat – like sheets filled with hundreds of colorful symbols that represent all the words he's been taught by his minders or picked up on his own. He can build thoughts and sentences, even conjugate, all by pointing. The sheets include not just easy nouns and verbs like ball and Jell-O and run and tickle but also concept words like from and later and grammatical elements like the –ing and –ed endings signifying tense.

3.   John Flowerdew, a renowned scholar in the field of discourse analysis, states:

Identity is important in discourse terms because one's identity is manifested in one's social practice, an important part of which is discursive practice. As well as individuals constructing their own identities, a large part of identity is constructed by others; by how we are perceived. Identity is therefore a binary construction.
Discourse in English Language Education (Flowerdew, 2013, p. 184)

Bearing in mind the above statement, examine how identities of a celebrity are constructed and manifested through discourse. Specifically, choose a celebrity and examine the construction of his/her identities by analysing (a) his/her social media posts and (b) how this celebrity is perceived by others.

For (a), examine what identities the celebrity enacts through his/her social media posts. How does the use of language help to construct those identities? What social values are encoded in the construction of those identities?

For (b), interview at least two people who know the celebrity you have chosen. How is this celebrity perceived by them? What identities do they construct for him/her? What do the identities they construct for this celebrity reveal about the social values they hold?

Finally, reflect on how discourse has the power to present the celebrity with certain identities, thereby shaping the way you view him/her.

4.   Conduct a comparative analysis of texts which have similar purposes but produced in two different cultures or languages, e.g., one in English produced in the North American context and the other in the learners' first language and native culture. Examples of texts can be:

   a.   Birth announcements
   b.   Anniversary well-wishes
   c.   Obituaries
   d.   Recruitment advertisements
   e.   Match-making advertisements

For each text type, examine the overall organization, and specific vocabulary and grammatical patters used in each of the two texts.

Are there features that are common in the two texts? How does the use of these features contribute to achieving the text's social purpose?

Are there features that are different in the two texts? What do these features suggest about the uniqueness of a particular language or culture?

5.   Complete the Table 4 with examples of discourse which the learners in your own teaching context may need to understand, produce or participate in. Consider each of them in relation to their communicative goals (e.g., purposes, audiences, situations).

Table 4.

Spoken discourse	When, Where, With Whom, Why
Written discourse	When, Where, For Whom, Why

Next, consider the text structure, grammatical features and vocabulary typically found in each of them.

Based on such understanding, identify ways to help learners develop strategies for effective interpersonal and intercultural communication, i.e. producing and interpreting texts in various social contexts, with sensitivity to issues such as social relationship, culture, and power.

REFERENCES

Burns, A. (2001). Analysing spoken discourse: Implications for TESOL. In A. Burns & C. Coffin (Eds.), *Analysing English in a global context: A reader* (pp. 123–148). London: Routledge.

Burns, A. (2010). Teaching speaking using genre-based pedagogy. In M. Olafsson (Ed.), *Symposium 2009* (pp. 231-247). Stockholm: National Centre for Swedish as a Second Language, University of Stockholm.

Byram, M. (2000). Assessing intercultural competence in language teaching. *Sprogforum*, *18*(6), 8–13.

Canale, M., & Swan, M. (1980). Theoretical basis of communicative approaches to second language learning and testing. *Applied Linguistics*, *1*(1), 1–47. doi:10.1093/applin/1.1.1

Carter, R., Goddard, A., Reah, D., Sanger, K., & Swift, N. (2008). *Working with texts: A core introduction to language analysis* (3rd ed.). London: Routledge.

Celce-Murcia, M., & Olshtain, E. (2014). Teaching language through discourse. In M. Celce-Murcia, D. M. Brinton, & M. A. Snow (Eds.), *Teaching English as a second or foreign language* (4th ed., pp. 424–437). Boston, MA: National Geographic Learning.

Chen, G. M., & Starosta, W. J. (2000). The development and validation of the intercultural communication sensitivity scale. *Human Communication*, *3*(1), 1–15.

Crystal, D. (1987). *The Cambridge encyclopedia of the English language*. Cambridge, UK: Cambridge University Press.

Derewianka, B. (1990). *Exploring how texts work*. Heinemann Educational Books.

Fairclough, N. L. (1989). *Language and power*. London: Longman.

Fairclough, N. L., & Wodak, R. (1997). Critical discourse analysis. In T. A. van Dijk (Ed.), Discourse studies: A multidisciplinary introduction (Vol. 2, pp. 258-284). London: Sage.

Gee, J. P. (2004). Discourse analysis: What makes it critical? In R. Rogers (Ed.), *An introduction to critical discourse analysis in education* (pp. 23–45). New York, NY: Routledge.

Gee, J. P. (2014). *How to do discourse analysis: A toolkit.* Oxon, UK: Routledge. doi:10.4324/9781315819662

Gil, J., & Adamson, B. (2011). The English language in mainland China: A sociolinguistic profile. In A. Feng (Ed.), *English language education across greater China* (pp. 23–45). Buffalo, NY: Multilingal Matters. doi:10.21832/9781847693518-004

Halliday, M. A. K., & Hasan, R. (1976). *Cohesion in English.* London: Longman.

Hewings, A., & Hewings, M. (2005). *Grammar and context: An advanced resource book.* London: Routledge.

Johnstone, B. (2018). *Discourse analysis* (3rd ed.). Hoboken, NJ: Wiley Blackwell.

Labov, W., & Waletzky, J. (1967). Narrative analysis: Oral versions of personal experience. In J. Helm (Ed.), *Essays on the verbal and visual arts* (pp. 12–44). Seattle, WA: University of Washington Press.

Lwin, S. M. (2010). *Narrative structures in Burmese folk tales.* Amherst, NY: Cambria Press.

Lwin, S. M. (2015). Using folktales for language teaching. *English Teaching, XLIV*(2), 74–83.

Lwin, S. M. (2016). Promoting language learners' cross-cultural awareness through comparative analysis of Asian folktales. *TEFLIN Journal, 27*(2), 166–181.

Lwin, S. M., & Teo, P. (2014). How do we use language to make meaning? In R. E. Silver & S. M. Lwin (Eds.), *Language in education: Social implications* (pp. 45–65). London: Bloomsbury.

Machin, D., & Maya, A. (2012). *How to do critical discourse analysis: A multimodal introduction.* London: Sage.

Minami, M. (2008). Telling good stories in different languages: Bilingual children's styles of story construction and their linguistic and educational implication. *Narrative Inquiry, 18*(1), 83–110. doi:10.1075/ni.18.1.05min

Morris, C. H. (1938). *Foundations of the theory of signs.* Chicago: University of Chicago Press.

Painter, C. (2001). Understanding genre and register: Implications for language teaching. In A. Burns & C. Coffin (Eds.), *Analysing English in a global context: A reader* (pp. 167–180). London: Routledge.

Riggenbach, H. (1999). Discourse analysis in the language classroom: Vol. 1. *The spoken language.* Ann Arbor, MI: University of Michigan Press.

van Dijk, T. A. (1993). Principles of critical discourse analysis. *Discourse & Society, 4*(2), 249–283. doi:10.1177/0957926593004002006

Walsh, S. (2011). *Exploring classroom discourse: Language in action.* London: Routledge. doi:10.4324/9780203827826

Waring, H. Z. (2018). *Discourse analysis: The questions discourse analysts ask and how they answer them.* New York, NY: Routledge.

Wennerstrom, A. (2003). Discourse analysis in the language classroom: Vol. 2. *Genres of writing*. Ann Arbor, MI: University of Michigan Press.

Widdowson, H. G. (2007). *Discourse analysis*. Oxford, UK: Oxford University Press.

Yang, W., & Sun, Y. (2012). The use of cohesive devices in argumentative writing by Chinese EFL learners at different proficiency levels. *Linguistics and Education*, *23*(1), 31–48. doi:10.1016/j.linged.2011.09.004

Yule, G. (2010). *The Study of Language* (4th ed.). Cambridge, UK: Cambridge University Press. doi:10.1017/CBO9780511757754

ADDITIONAL READING

Burns, A. (2006). Teaching speaking: A text-based syllabus approach. In E. Usó-Juan & A. Martinez-Flor (Eds.), *Current trends in the development and teaching of the four language skills* (pp. 235–258). Berlin: Mouton de Gruyter. doi:10.1515/9783110197778.3.235

Burns, A., & Seidlhofer, B. (2002). Speaking and pronunciation. In N. Schmitt (Ed.), *An introduction to applied linguistics* (pp. 211–232). New York: Arnold.

Carter, R., & Goddard, A. (2016). *How to analyse texts: A toolkit for students of English*. London: Routledge.

Flowerdew, J. (2013). *Discourse in English language education*. New York, NY: Routledge.

Gee, J. P. (2018). *Introducing discourse analysis: From grammar to society*. New York, NY: Routledge.

Goatly, A. (2000). *Critical reading and writing: An introductory coursebook*. London: Routledge.

Hyland, K. (2013). *Discourse studies reader: Essential excerpts*. London: Bloomsbury.

Jones, R. H. (2012). *Discourse analysis: A resource book for students*. London: Routledge.

Reaser, J., Adger, C. T., Wolfram, W., & Christian, D. (2017). *Dialects at school: Educating linguistically diverse students*. New York, NY: Routledge. doi:10.4324/9781315772622

Teo, P. (2016). Exploring the dialogic space in teaching: A study of teacher talk in the pre-university classroom in Singapore. *Teaching and Teacher Education*, *56*, 47–60. doi:10.1016/j.tate.2016.01.019

Teo, P., & Ho, C. (2007). *Discourse in the modern world: Perspectives and challenges*. Singapore: McGraw Hill.

Unit 7
Phonetics

Chapter 11
Articulatory Phonetics:
English Consonants

Nabat Erdogan
University of Central Missouri, USA

Michael Wei
University of Missouri – Kansas City, USA

ABSTRACT

The main focus of this chapter is to present the articulatory description of English consonants and provide practical guidance on how to teach the consonant phonemes to ELLs. The chapter starts with the introduction of phonetics as a subfield of linguistics. The concepts such as phonemes, contrastive versus non-contrastive sounds, the branches of phonetics that study different aspects of human speech sounds, and two different types of phonemes—consonants and vowels—are introduced in this section. Next, the reader is familiarized with the International Phonetic Alphabet, which is a system of phonetic transcription. The chapter further presents the description of the vocal tract and explores the classification of English consonants according to their place and manner of articulation, and voicing. Some implications from the introduced phonetics theory for teaching phonics, phonemic awareness, and spelling to young ELLs, and pronunciation to adult English learners, as well as a set of recommendations for effective phonetics instruction for ELLs are discussed to conclude the chapter.

WHAT IS PHONETICS?

Phonetics is a branch of linguistics that studies individual speech sounds in a human language. These speech sounds are also known as **phonemes**. The word *phoneme* is derived from the Greek word *φώνημα* (*phōnēma*), meaning *sound produced*. It is not coincidental that the words *phonetics* and *phoneme* share the same root – *phone* – which means *voice or sound*, as phonetics is the study of minimal units of sound – phonemes.

DOI: 10.4018/978-1-5225-8467-4.ch011

There can be two different types of sounds – **contrastive** and **non-contrastive** sounds – in every language. Phonemes are contrastive or discrete speech sounds which means that they can result in a change in meaning. For example, the words *pat* and *bat* are two discrete words with distinctive meanings because they have different initial phonemes that are included in the phoneme inventory of the English language. While phonemes cause a difference in meaning, non-contrastive sounds, known as **allophones**, do not distinguish meaning of words and are "perceived as the same sound despite the physical difference" (Finegan, 2008, p. 109). Note that a sound perceived as a functionally distinct phoneme in one language can serve as an allophone in another language, or vice versa. For example, the English sound /ð/ represented by the digraph *th* in words such as *then*, *they*, or *those* differs from the sound /d/ as in *den*, *day*, or *doze*. Thus, /ð/ and /d/ function contrastively or occur in **contrastive distribution** in English. However, /d/ and /ð/ are non-contrastive in Spanish since these two sounds occur in **complementary distribution** and serve as the allophones of the same phoneme /d/ in such words like *día* (*day* in English) pronounced like /dia/ and *codo* (*elbow* in English) pronounced like /koðo/. For more information on the pronunciation of allophones, or contrastive as well as complementary distribution, refer to Chapter 13.

Phonetics has three branches each of which concentrates on different aspects of studying speech sounds in human languages. **Articulatory phonetics** is the study of how the speech or vocal organs are used to produce sounds. **Acoustic phonetics** deals with the physical properties of speech sounds. **Auditory phonetics** studies the perception of speech sounds by humans.

This chapter focuses on articulatory phonetics, more precisely, the articulation of English consonants. Contrastive sounds or phonemes of English are divided into two groups – **consonants** and **vowels**. Note that the terms *consonant* and *vowel* do not refer to the letters that represent them, but to the types of *sounds* that are produced (Fromkin, Rodman, & Hyams, 2014). For example, the letter *y* can function as a vowel sound in the words such as *very* /ˈvɛɹi/ or *myth* /mɪθ/, but as a consonant in *yellow* /ˈjɛloʊ/ or *young* [jʌŋ]. The difference between these two fundamental sound types lies in the obstruction involved during the articulation of these sounds. The production of consonants involves some obstruction of the airflow in the vocal tract. Whereas the articulation of vowels, which will be covered in the next chapter, involves little or no obstruction of the airstream in the vocal tract.

In order to acquire the knowledge of English consonants and their adequate pronunciation, it is highly beneficial to recognize and be able to read the phonetic symbols used to represent these phonemes. Moreover, understanding the functions of the articulators involved in the production of consonants as well as knowing the articulatory features of each English consonant will also be helpful in avoiding pronunciation errors and consequently, attaining intelligible English pronunciation. The following sections of this chapter will introduce consonant phonetic symbols and the articulators involved in sound production, present the articulatory aspects of English consonants, and discuss the implications for teaching English consonants to language learners.

THE INTERNATIONAL PHONETIC ALPHABET

Before delving into the articulatory classification of consonants in English, this chapter will introduce **the International Phonetic Alphabet** (IPA) which will assist readers in understanding the symbols used in the Phonetics and the Phonology units of this book. IPA is a system of phonetic transcription that was first published in 1888 by the International Phonetic Association in France (Burleigh & Skandera, 2016), and since then, it has been revised many times, with the most recent version published in

2015 (International Phonetic Association, 2015). The IPA chart introduces a phonetic symbol for each speech sound, which assists with reading languages like English in which letter-sound correspondence is inconsistent and irregular (recall different pronunciations of the -*ough* words such as *cough*, *dough*, *plough*, *rough*, *through*, etc.). Thus, IPA helps to handle the ambiguity caused due to the nature of the grapheme-to-phoneme relationship in English. When reading the chart, one should consider that IPA does not transcribe only English sounds, but is used to transcribe speech sounds from all languages. Therefore, not all the IPA symbols provided in the chart have corresponding sounds in English. Figure 1 provides the consonants portion from the latest re-issue of the IPA chart.

According to the International Phonetic Association, there are two ways of transcribing speech. **Phonemic transcription,** which is also known as 'broad' transcription, uses phonemic notations which include only the distinctive sounds of a language – phonemes. This type of transcription utilizes slashes //. Following are the examples of phonemic transcription:

school   /skul/
team   /tim/

Phonetic transcription, also referred to as 'narrow' transcription, is characterized by phonetic notations which include non-distinctive features of a language or details of the pronunciation that do not distinguish words in a particular language. Square brackets [] are used for phonetic transcription. The same words are transcribed phonetically below:

school   [sku:l]
team   [tʰi:m]

The colon diacritic [:] in the phonetic transcriptions denotes that the preceding vowel is lengthened during articulation. The superscript [ʰ] in the second example indicates that the phoneme /t/ is aspirated which is characteristic of a voiceless stop in the initial position in a stressed syllable. Thus, in phonetic

Figure 1. The International Phonetic Alphabet consonants chart
(IPA, 2015)

CONSONANTS (PULMONIC)   © 2015 IPA

	Bilabial	Labiodental	Dental	Alveolar	Postalveolar	Retroflex	Palatal	Velar	Uvular	Pharyngeal	Glottal
Plosive	p b			t d		ʈ ɖ	c ɟ	k ɡ	q ɢ		ʔ
Nasal	m	ɱ		n		ɳ	ɲ	ŋ	N		
Trill	B			r					R		
Tap or Flap		ⱱ		ɾ		ɽ					
Fricative	ɸ β	f v	θ ð	s z	ʃ ʒ	ʂ ʐ	ç ʝ	x ɣ	χ ʁ	ħ ʕ	h ɦ
Lateral fricative				ɬ ɮ							
Approximant		ʋ		ɹ		ɻ	j	ɰ			
Lateral approximant				l		ɭ	ʎ	L			

Symbols to the right in a cell are voiced, to the left are voiceless. Shaded areas denote articulations judged impossible.

transcription, all the acoustic and articulatory properties of speech sounds are taken into consideration. Chapters 13 and 14 will provide more information about distinctive (phonemic) and non-distinctive (phonetic) features of English, and different phonological rules, including the aspiration rule, that govern English pronunciation.

ARTICULATION OF ENGLISH CONSONANTS

At the beginning of the chapter, we noted that the production of consonants is characterized by the involvement of some obstruction of the airstream in the vocal tract. The articulatory classification of English consonants is directly related to the obstruction of the airstream in one way or another, when pronouncing consonants. English consonants are classified according to place of articulation, manner of articulation, and voicing. The classification of English consonants according to **place of articulation** is based on where in the vocal tract the obstruction of airstream occurs. The classification of consonant sounds according to **manner of articulation** refers to the way or the manner in which the obstruction of airstream occurs. The classification according to **voicing** depends on whether or not the vocal cords vibrate while the airstream makes its way through, during the articulation of consonants.

In order to better understand the articulation of English consonants, one needs to be familiar with the articulators that come into play when producing these sounds. The speech articulators are the parts of the **vocal tract** used in the production of sounds. Structurally, the vocal tract is defined as "the area existing from the superior surface of the vocal folds through to the lips and including coupling of the nasal passages" (Hand & Frank, 2014, p. 266). Put simply, the vocal tract is "the primary region in which speech sounds are formed as recognizable vowels and consonants" with the involvement of articulators (Kent, 1997, p. 143). There are two types of articulators – active and passive. The **active articulators** do most of the moving during the production of a speech sound, while the **passive articulators** are either not movable at all or can move only a little. In other words, the active articulators move towards the passive articulators or the target of the articulation to create a sound (Collins, 2003; Ogden, 2017). The lips and the tongue are active articulators (practice pronouncing the sound /w/ where the lips are rounded, or /n/ for which the tip of the tongue raises and touches the alveolar ridge), while the articulators that are directly connected to the skull, such as teeth, alveolar ridge, hard palate, velum, and so on, are passive articulators. Figure 2 describes the vocal tract and the articulators that participate in the formation of speech sounds.

Familiarity with the active and passive articulators that participate in the production of sounds can assist language learners with correct pronunciation of sounds and words in the target language. It can also help teachers assist their language learners in gaining intelligible speech in an L2. However, only being familiar with the vocal tract and knowing the articulators would not suffice to ensure the correct or intelligible pronunciation in a language. Knowing how those articulators move and act together to produce each sound in the target language can also greatly facilitate the development of intelligible speech in language learners.

Figure 2. The vocal tract

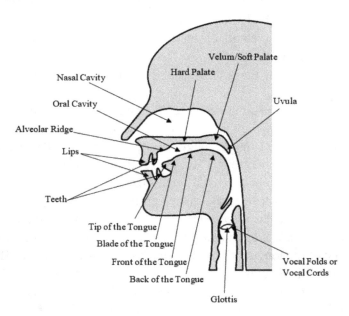

Classification of English Consonants According to Place of Articulation

When pronouncing consonants, the movement of the vocal organs (mostly the lips and the tongue) creates some restriction of airflow. English consonants are classified into the following eight types depending on where the constriction of airflow occurs.

Bilabials. The term *bilabial* comes from the Latin root *labium*, meaning *lip*. The prefix *bi-*, which means *two* or *twice*, is also derived from Latin. Based on this information, we can infer that the word *bilabial* roughly means "two lips". Bilabial sounds are indeed formed by bringing the lower and upper lips together. When the lips touch each other, three bilabial consonants, **/p/**, **/b/**, and **/m/**, are produced. Practice pronouncing the words *party, baby,* and *mother* while also paying attention to the movement of the lips when articulating the initial sounds.

Labiodentals. The term *labiodental* is a compound word that is a combination of Latin words *labium*, the meaning of which is explained above, and *dentalis* or *dent* which means *tooth*. Labiodental consonants are articulated by touching the lower lip to the upper front teeth. The two labiodental consonants in English are **/f/** as in *foot* and **/v/** as in *village*. When pronouncing the initial sounds of these words, you should have your upper teeth against your lower lip, as in the biting position, and feel the air gently blowing out between your teeth and lip. Notice that it is also possible to pronounce labiodentals by touching the upper lip against the lower front teeth. However, it is not a normal or usual way of pronouncing labiodentals. It requires protruding the jaw since most people have their upper teeth that sit in front of their lower teeth, and therefore, it is very difficult to do so (Ogden, 2017).

Interdentals. The prefix *inter-* comes from Latin, meaning *between* or *among*. When we combine the meanings of *inter* and *dental* explained in the previous paragraph, we get a phrase like "between the teeth". As the meaning of the term suggests, interdentals are pronounced by positioning the tip of the tongue between the teeth. Interdentals are sometimes called *dental* consonants because some speakers of English pronounce these sounds by slightly touching the back of the upper teeth with the tip of the tongue. In such a case, it is phonetically more correct to call these consonants **dental** (Fromkin et al., 2014). There are two dental or interdental consonants in English /θ/ and /ð/. The interdental /θ/ is the sound that the *th* digraph gives in words like *think, thunder, healthy, month,* etc. The interdental /ð/ is also orthographically represented by the *th* consonant digraph, however, is pronounced as in the words *they, weather, bathe,* etc.

Alveolars. The Latin term *alveolus* that refers to "the bony structure immediately behind the upper teeth" (Fulk, 2012, p. 22) constitutes the root of the term *alveolar* which is used to describe the English consonants that are pronounced by raising the tongue to approach or touch the *alveolar ridge*, also known as the *tooth ridge*, just behind the upper teeth. There are seven alveolar sounds in English - /t/, /d/, /n/, /s/, /z/, /l/, and /ɹ/. Although these consonants are all categorized as alveolar, they are articulated by raising the tongue to the alveolar ridge in various ways. When pronouncing /t/, /d/, and /n/, the tip of the tongue is raised so that it strikes the alveolar ridge. Try to feel the position of the tongue when pronouncing the initial sounds of the words *till, dill,* and *null*. In the articulation of /s/ and /z/, the tip of the tongue is lowered, while the front of the tongue is raised to create the constriction of airflow, as we experience in the pronunciation of the initial sounds of *sip* and *zip*. The pronunciation of /l/ only slightly differs from the pronunciation of /t/, /d/, or /n/. Pay attention to the articulation of the initial sound in the words *lake* and *late* for which the tip of the tongue is raised to the tooth ridge while the rest of the tongue is lowered. The articulation of /ɹ/ is also very similar to that of /l/ with only a slight difference; when pronouncing the initial sound of such words as *roll, rip,* and *rap*, the tip of the tongue is raised and curled back behind the tooth ridge without touching it[1]. This feature – curling back the tip of the tongue – is a characteristic of **retroflex** articulation. Thus, /ɹ/ is the only retroflex sound in English, which means that no other sound is articulated by curling the tongue tip in English. Note that retroflex articulation is also evident in other languages. For example, there is a retroflex t-sound in Hindi, the IPA symbol for which is /ʈ/, and this sound is contrastive to non-retroflex /t/ which is a different phoneme in Hindi. This means that retroflex articulation is a contrastive feature in Hindi, but not in English. Pronouncing the initial sound of the word *rain* with or without the curled tongue tip would not change the meaning of the word in English but may sound like non-native or accented English. You must have noticed that we have used the IPA symbol /ɹ/ (note that the IPA symbol /ɻ/ could also be used to emphasize retroflexivity of the English r-sound, however, the symbol /ɹ/ is more widely used in English phonetics) to represent the initial sound in such words as *roll, rip,* and *rap*. The IPA symbol /ɹ/ is used for the English r-sound to distinguish it from the Spanish trill /r/ in the articulation of which the tip of the tongue is not curled, but instead, it rapidly vibrates behind the tooth ridge.

Palatals. Also known as alveopalatals, palatal consonants are produced by raising the front of the tongue to the roof of the mouth known as the *palate*. There are five palatal consonants in English - /ʃ/ as in *ship*, /ʒ/ as in *genre*, /tʃ/ as in *chain*, /dʒ/ as in *jet*, and /j/ as in *yard*. Practice pronouncing the words *ship, genre, chain, jet,* and *yard*, and you should feel the front of your tongue raising to the palate when articulating the initial sounds of these words. The pronunciation of the palatal /tʃ/ and /dʒ/ slightly differs from that of the other palatals because /tʃ/ and /dʒ/ are complex sounds. During the production of /tʃ/ and /dʒ/, the tongue first takes the alveolar position for the initial sound /t/ or /d/, and then moves from the alveolar ridge towards the palate to articulate /ʃ/ after /t/ and /ʒ/ after /d/, which is why, some Phonetics or Phonology manuals find it more accurate to call them alveopalatals based on the two stages (first alveolar, then palatal) of tongue movement involved in the production of these sounds.

Note that the palatal consonants /ʃ/, /ʒ/, /ʧ/, and /ʤ/ can occur in every position in words, however, /j/ is only encountered in the initial and middle positions in English. Some may claim that the words *toy* and *soy* end with the consonant /j/ and falsely conclude that the palatal /j/ can also occur in the final position in English. However, when we analyze these words more closely and review their transcriptions, /tɔɪ/ and /sɔɪ/, we can see that the orthographic representation of the words like *toy* and *soy* can easily deceive us. Seeing the letter "y" at the end of the word and hearing a sound like /j/, we can make a false conclusion that it is the consonant /j/. In reality, it is a vowel, more precisely the second segment of the diphthong /ɔɪ/, that ends the words *toy* and *soy* in English. It is also worth mentioning that the palatal /ʒ/ in the initial (as in *genre* or *gendarme*) and final (as in *rouge*, *collage*, or *sabotage*) positions is not quite peculiar to English phonetics and is less common in English; the words with the initial or final /ʒ/ are of French origin borrowed by English. For this reason, you may hear many English speakers alternatively pronounce the words such as *genre*, *beige*, and *prestige* with /ʤ/ instead of /ʒ/ (Carley, Mees, & Collins, 2018). However, this phenomenon never occurs in the opposite direction, i.e., English speakers never replace /ʤ/ with /ʒ/.

Velars. The term *velar* stems from the word *velum* which is another word used for the *soft palate*. English velar consonants **/k/**, **/g/**, and **/ŋ/** are articulated by raising the back of the tongue to the velum. Practice saying the words *coat*, *goat*, and *song* while also paying attention to the position of the tongue when articulating the initial sounds in *coat* and *goat* and the final consonant in *song*. Note that the velar /ŋ/ is the only consonant that never occurs word-initially in English. However, it is widely used in the medial and, especially, final positions in words. One example to the frequent use of the velar sound /ŋ/ in the final position is the *-ing* suffix which is required to form the present participle (*He is swimming in the pool*) and the gerund (*He likes swimming*) in English.

Labiovelars. The term *labiovelar* suggests that the articulation of such sounds should involve the lips (labium) and the soft palate (velum). There is only one labiovelar consonant in English, and that is the sound **/w/**. The labiovelar /w/, as in *wall*, *will*, and *well*, is articulated by rounding the lips and, at the same time, raising the back of the tongue to the velum. Note that some manuals classify /w/ as a bilabial consonant due to the rounded position of the lips during its articulation (Denham & Lobeck, 2010; Rogerson-Revell, 2011). However, we prefer using the term "labiovelar" to also point out the position of the tongue raised to the velum. Practice pronouncing the words starting with /w/, and feel the position of the lips and the tongue while articulating the initial sounds of those words. The labiovelar /w/ can occur only in the initial and medial positions in English, as in *wit* /wɪt/ and *quit* /kwɪt/. As in the case with the palatal /j/, one may falsely think that the words like *low, snow,* and *blow* end with the sound /w/, while what we actually pronounce is the second segment of the diphthong /oʊ/ at the end of all three words.

Glottals. Glottal sounds are formed in the opening between the vocal folds also known as the *glottis* (refer to the illustration of the vocal tract (Figure 2) for the description of the vocal folds and glottis). When the vocal folds approximate, constriction occurs in the glottis, and the glottal **/h/** is formed. The English words *hand*, *hall*, and *hide* start with the glottal consonant /h/. Note that the glottal /h/ occurs only in the initial and medial positions in English words, such as in *home* and *behave*, respectively. It can never occur word-finally in English. One may argue that the exclamation "uh-oh!" includes the glottal /h/ in the final position. However, what is actually pronounced is not the glottal /h/ but the sound phonetically transcribed as [ʔ] and referred to as a **glottal stop** (Fromkin et al., 2014). When pronouncing *uh-oh!*, you should feel the vocal folds completely close and the air stop at the glottis before releasing the air to articulate the glottal stop [ʔ] in English. Note that we have put the glottal stop [ʔ] in the square brackets because we do not refer to this sound as a distinct phoneme in English since it never occurs in contrastive distribution with the glottal /h/ in the English language. Unlike English, in some other languages, /h/ can occur in all positions in words. For example, the Turkish words *hata* (*fault* or *error* in English), *bahar* (*spring*), and *mizah* (*humor*) demonstrate the occurrence of the glottal /h/ in the initial, middle, and final positions respectively, and since there is an almost perfect grapheme-to-phoneme correspondence in Turkish, the pronunciation of these words are exactly the same as their spellings.

Classification of English Consonants According to Manner of Articulation

English consonants are also classified according to the degree or the kind of obstruction of the airflow in the vocal tract when pronouncing the sounds. Based on the degree of obstruction which affects the manner of articulation of the speech sounds, English consonants are divided into six main types which are separately discussed below.

Stops. Consonants the pronunciation of which involves a complete blockage of the airstream in the oral cavity are called stops. There are six stops in English - **/p/, /b/, /t/, /d/, /k/,** and **/g/.** While pronouncing the initial sounds of *pale, bale, tale, dale, kale,* and *gale,* you will notice that the lips cause a complete blockage of the airflow in *pale* and *bale,* the tongue touching the alveolar ridge blocks the airstream in *tale* and *dale,* and the back of the tongue raised to the velum stops the flow of air in *kale* and *gale,* before the air is released to complete the articulation of the sound. Thus, based on this information, we can infer that /p/ and /b/ are bilabial stops, /t/ and /d/ are alveolar stops, and /k/ and /g/ are velar stops in English. Note that some manuals refer to stops as **plosives** or even **stop-plosives** since their articulation requires first the blockage (stage 1) and then the release of the air (stage 2) which results in explosion (stage 3) (Gussmann, 2002; Ogden, 2017; Vennard, 1968). Plosives or stops are further categorized into **aspirated** and **unaspirated** (or non-aspirated), the distinction which depends on whether or not the sound is pronounced with a puff of air (Fromkin et al., 2014; Ogden, 2017). In English, the voiced stops /b/, /d/, and /g/ are unaspirated. However, the voiceless stops /p/, t/, and /k/ can be both aspirated and unaspirated based on their position in words. Although **aspiration** can be a distinctive feature in some other languages (for example, in Thai), it is a non-distinctive feature in English, meaning that it does not result in a meaning change or its presence or absence is predictable in English (Fromkin et al., 2014). Therefore, it is not further discussed in this chapter. For more information on the aspiration feature, what word contexts it occurs in, or how it is phonetically represented in the transcription, refer to Chapters 13 and 14.

Fricatives. While the pronunciation of stops requires a complete closure of the articulators and thus a total blockage of the airflow, the articulation of fricatives involves only a partial obstruction of the airstream, resulting in a narrow constriction formed in the vocal tract. Another way to discriminate between stops and fricatives is to pay attention to the possibility of prolonging the sound; it is almost impossible to prolong stops (for example, try to prolong /d/, and you will see that it is not physically possible, at least in the first stage of articulation – before releasing the air), however, fricatives can be prolonged as much as one's breath allows it. The English language has nine fricatives, **/f/** as in *fan* /fæn/, **/v/** as in *van* /væn/, **/θ/** as in *thin* /θɪn/, **/ð/** as in *than* /ðæn/, **/s/** as in *sip* /sɪp/, **/z/** as in *zip* /zɪp/, **/ʃ/** as in *ship* /ʃɪp/, **/ʒ/** as in *genre* /ˈʒɑnrə/, and **/h/** as in *hand* /hænd/. The friction occurs between the upper front teeth and the lower lip for /f/ and /v/, between the teeth and the tip of the tongue for /θ/ and /ð/, between the front of the tongue and the tooth (or alveolar) ridge for /s/ and /z/, between the front of the tongue and the hard palate for /ʃ/ and /ʒ/, and at the glottis for /h/, thus making /f/ and /v/ labiodental fricatives, /θ/ and /ð/ interdental fricatives, /s/ and /z/ alveolar fricatives, /ʃ/ and /ʒ/ palatal fricatives, and /h/ a glottal fricative. Note that some linguists do not consider /h/ a fricative due to the fact that its articulation does not result in turbulent airflow which, for some, is a strict requirement for fricatives (Yavas, 2011). It is also worth mentioning that the articulation of the alveolar fricatives /s/ and /z/ and the palatal fricatives /ʃ/ and /ʒ/ requires higher frequency and produces more noise, thus categorizing them as **sibilants** which are characterized by intense acoustic energy. The alveolar and palatal fricatives are not the only sibilants in English – there are two other sibilants that are discussed in the next paragraph.

Affricates. The sounds that involve a complete closure (stop) immediately followed by a gradual release (fricative) are called affricates also known as complex consonants since they are a combination of two distinct consonants – a stop (or a plosive) and a fricative. Ogden (2017) defines affricates as "plosives which are released into fricatives" (p. 17). English has two affricates - /tʃ/ as in *choke* and /dʒ/ as in *joke*. The affricates /tʃ/ and /dʒ/ are also produced with more noise and higher frequency and therefore, classified as sibilants. In the pronunciation of these sounds, the tongue first takes the position of the respective stop – /t/ for /tʃ/ and /d/ for /dʒ/, then the closure resulting from the articulation of the stop is immediately released by moving the tongue from the alveolar ridge towards the palate to articulate /ʃ/ after /t/ and /ʒ/ after /d/, which results in producing the palatal affricates /tʃ/ and /dʒ/. Thus, the phonetic symbols representing the affricates include the stops /t/ and /d/ and the fricative consonants /ʃ/ and /ʒ/. If you pay close attention to the IPA consonants chart in Figure 1, you will notice that the affricates /tʃ/ and /dʒ/ are not included in the chart because they can be easily obtained by joining the two symbols together. The reason for not including the complex consonants in the IPA chart is the fact that there are more complex sounds in the world's languages altogether than can be included in one chart. For example, the Russian affricate consonant /ts/ as in *цена* /ˈtsɪˈna/ (*price* in English) and *царь* /ˈtsarʲ/[2] (*king* or *tsar*) is the combination of a stop /t/ and a fricative /s/. As you see in the phonetic transcription, there is a crescent-like line on the symbol /ts/. According to IPA, it is called "a tie bar" which is used to join two symbols to represent affricates or double consonants in all languages (IPA, 2015). Since there already exist the connected symbols for /tʃ/ and /dʒ/ that are widely accepted for the phonetic transcription of English, there is no need to use a tie-bar to join these symbols.

Nasals. In the production of some sounds, the air flows through the nasal cavity instead of the oral cavity. Such sounds are called nasals. There are three nasal consonants – **/m/, /n/,** and **/ŋ/** in English, which constitute the final sounds of *sum*, *sun*, and *sung*, respectively. Thus, based on their place and manner of articulation, /m/ is a bilabial nasal, /n/ is an alveolar nasal, and /ŋ/ is a velar nasal.

Note that some manuals classify nasals as stops or nasal stops since their production, just like that of stops, involves the blockage of the airstream in the vocal tract (Delahunty & Garvey, 2010; Fromkin et al., 2014), while others distinguish the nasals from the stops since the air escapes through the nasal cavity during the articulation of the former and the oral cavity for the production of the latter (Avery & Ehrlich, 1992; Burleigh & Skandera, 2016; Freeman & Freeman, 2004; Ogden, 2017; Radford, Atkinson, Britain, Clahsen, & Spencer, 2009; Thorum, 2013; Yavas, 2011). In this chapter, we have taken the second view and separated the nasals from the stops.

Nasality is a distinctive feature for English consonants, meaning that it is unpredictable whether or not a word will start with a nasal consonant or an oral one (compare *mill* /mɪl/ and *bill* /bɪl/), however, it is a non-distinctive feature for English vowels, which means that the nasalization of English vowels can be predicted, and pronouncing a vowel as oral or nasal will not change the meaning of a word. The articulation of a nasal consonant affects the quality of the preceding vowel, thus making it nasal (refer to Chapters 13 and 14 for more information on the nasalization of English vowels and how the presence or absence of the nasalization feature can lead to the articulation of different allophones of the same phoneme).

Liquids. The production of some English phonemes does not involve much obstruction of the airstream and therefore, does not cause any friction, as a result of which the air flows more fluidly through the mouth. Such consonants are known as liquids. It is worth noting that the term "liquid" comes from the fact that the articulation of these sounds flows freely like water. The two English liquids are **/l/** and **/ɹ/** that begin and end the words *local* and *river*. These sounds are grouped as liquids particularly because of their acoustic similarity due to which some English learners may confuse them (Fromkin et al., 2014). Both liquids are pronounced at the alveolar ridge and therefore, are alveolar liquids.

Glides. Sometimes referred to as semi-vowels (Avery & Ehrlich, 1992; Fromkin et al., 2014) or "moving vowels" (Rogers, 2013, p.30), glides are the consonants the production of which involves little turbulence of the airstream. English has two glides, **/j/** and **/w/**, which represent the initial sounds of *yield* and *wield*, respectively. These sounds are called glides because they are always followed by a vowel, and when articulating these sounds in actual words, the tongue moves quickly towards the neighboring vowel (Fromkin et al., 2014). The glides differ from the liquids in the formation of the obstruction by the tongue as well as in the length of the constriction which is much shorter for the liquids (Stevens, 1998). As mentioned earlier in this chapter, the palatal glide /j/ and the labiovelar glide /w/ can never occur at the end of English words because these sounds become part of diphthongs in the final position.

Many manuals (Burleigh & Skandera, 2016; Collins, 2003; Ogden, 2017; Radford et al., 2009; Yavas, 2011) use a single term – **approximants** – to describe the liquids /l/ and /ɹ/ and the glides /j/ and /w/ in English because during the production of both types of sounds "the articulators approximate a frictional closeness, but no actual friction occurs" (Fromkin et al., 2014, p. 203). In this regard, the articulation of approximants and vowels are very similar since both are produced with a raised velum and no friction noise. However, what distinguishes an approximant from a vowel is the fact that the former is a vocalic sound that functions as a consonant and can never constitute a syllable by itself, while the latter can form a syllable on its own (Ogden, 2017). Note that /l/ is a **lateral** approximant, which means that it is "produced with air flowing past one or both sides of the tongue" (Fromkin et al., 2014, p. 569), while /ɹ/, /j/, and /w/ are **central** approximants because the air flows centrally during their production.

Classification of English Consonants According to Voicing

The classification of English consonants according to voicing depends on the vibration of the vocal cords as a determining feature. The consonants during the production of which the vocal cords vibrate are called **voiced** consonants. Consequently, the consonants the articulation of which does not involve the vibration of the vocal cords are **voiceless** consonants. There are nine voiceless consonants in English – /p/, /t/, /k/, /f/, /θ/, /s/, /ʃ/, /tʃ/, and /h/, which means that all the remaining 15 consonant phonemes (/b/, /d/, /g/, /v/, /ð/, /z/, /ʒ/, /dʒ/, /m/, /n/, /ŋ/, /l/, /ɹ/, /j/, and /w/) are voiced in English. Note that all the voiceless consonants, except /h/, have their voiced counterparts in English. Practice pronouncing the following pairs of words while also paying attention to the articulation of the initial phonemes in each pair, which contrast based only on their voicing feature:

/p/ - *pin*	/b/ - *bin*
/t/ - *tan*	/d/ - *Dan*
/k/ - *coat*	/g/ - *goat*
/f/ - *fan*	/v/ - *van*
/θ/ - *thought*	/ð/ - *though*
/s/ - *seal*	/z/ - *zeal*
/ʃ/ - *sharp*	/ʒ/ - *genre*
/ʧ/ - *chin*	/ʤ/ - *gin*

Notice that the initial sounds in each pair have the same classifications based on their place and manner of articulation. For example, both /p/ and /b/ are bilabial stops, /θ/ and /ð/ are interdental fricatives, /ʧ/ and /ʤ/ are palatal affricates, etc. Therefore, some language learners might find it difficult to detect the only difference – the presence or absence of the voicing feature – between the initial consonants in each pair of the given words. For those who experience such a difficulty, Freeman and Freeman (2004) recommend to close the ears and articulate the contrasting phonemes, which will make it easier to perceive the vibration of the vocal cords.

Voicing is a phonemic or distinctive feature in English. Voicing a consonant can result in articulating a different phoneme and thus, change the meaning of the word. For example, voicing the bilabial stop /p/ in *pill* /pɪl/ can result in pronouncing a totally different word – *bill* /bɪl/ – the initial sound of which differs from that of the previous word by only its voicing feature. Another example can be the words *niece* /nis/ and *knees* /niz/ which differ only in the voicing of their final sounds – the alveolar fricatives /s/ and /z/. Changing the voicing feature of a sound can cause some problems for language learners. Imagine saying *I see her knees every day at work* instead of *I see her niece every day at work*, which may cause confusion, misunderstanding, and even embarrassment if the context does not assist with understanding the intended meaning.

Now, as we have discussed the classification of English consonants according to their place and manner of articulation, and voicing in detail, we will present all English consonant phonemes and summarize their descriptions in a table which will serve as a quick reference for the teachers of English learners. Table 1 provides the consonant inventory of North American English, the symbol for each phoneme, and the classification of English consonants according to their place and manner of articulation as well as voicing. Note that the boldfaced phonetic symbols represent the voiced consonants in English.

When describing English consonants in the chapter, we provided some word examples to demonstrate the articulation of those phonemes in actual words. However, the utilized examples mostly included the described sounds in the word-initial position. In order to fully understand and acquire the articulation of each consonant phoneme, English learners need to be introduced to the distribution of English consonants in word-initial, word-medial, and word-final positions. Table 2 provides examples for each English consonant in different positions in words[3]. As seen in the table, there are no words that start with the consonant /ŋ/ and end with the sounds /h/, /j/, and /w/ in English.

The knowledge of English consonants and their articulatory features is crucial for teachers of culturally and linguistically diverse learners. However, it is equally important to know how to implement this knowledge. The next section will discuss the implications from the articulatory phonetics theory for effective classroom instruction for English language learners.

Table 1. Classification of North American English consonant phonemes

Classification of North American English Consonant Phonemes									
			Place of Articulation							
			Bilabial	Labio dental	Interdental or Dental	Alveolar	Palatal or Alveopalatal	Velar	Labio velar	Glottal
Manner of Articulation / Voicing	Stop	Voiceless	p			t		k		
		Voiced	b			d		g		
	Fricative	Voiceless		f	θ	s	ʃ			h
		Voiced		v	ð	z	ʒ			
	Affricate	Voiceless					ʧ			
		Voiced					ʤ			
	Nasal	Voiced	m			n		ŋ		
	Liquid	Voiced				l ɹ				
	Glide	Voiced					j		w	

IMPLICATIONS FOR TEACHING ENGLISH LANGUAGE LEARNERS

Irrespective of their ages and language proficiency levels, English language learners (ELLs) will benefit from phonetics instruction which is essential for the acquisition of phonics, phonemic awareness, and spelling in elementary grades as well as correct and intelligible pronunciation for all language learners, including adult ELLs. In order to provide effective phonetics instruction, teachers of ELLs should know what to draw from the phonetics theory and how to apply it when teaching. Based on the learner's

Table 2. English consonants in different word positions

Consonant Symbol	Initial Position	Medial Position	Final Position
/p/	pasta	copy	hop
/b/	boy	cabin	club
/t/	table	guitar	cat
/d/	day	window	maid
/k/	cup	baker	trunk
/g/	goal	burger	mug
/f/	fun	coffee	roof
/v/	village	heaven	love
/θ/	thin	author	tooth
/ð/	they	mother	smooth
/s/	salt	classic	miss
/z/	zoo	lizard	buzz
/ʃ/	ship	washer	fish
/ʒ/	genre	casual	beige
/h/	hotel	behind	-----
/tʃ/	chair	pitcher	match
/dʒ/	jacket	pager	pledge
/m/	map	camera	calm
/n/	napkin	manner	woman
/ŋ/	-----	singer	song
/l/	lamp	talent	call
/ɹ/	rabbit	parade	star
/j/	yard	lanyard	-----
/w/	way	away	-----

age, cognitive developmental and English language proficiency levels, and literacy skills, the focus of phonetics instruction can be different, and one aspect of language instruction can be prioritized over the other. For instance, phonics, phonemic awareness, and spelling instruction is the priority in elementary grades, and pronunciation instruction tends to accompany literacy instruction implicitly since it is assumed that young ELLs will "pick up" the native-like English pronunciation easily because they have not reached the critical period yet. However, it is different for adult ELLs, who assumingly[4] already have L1 literacy skills that they can transfer to L2 during literacy acquisition. Adult ELLs are more likely to struggle with English pronunciation. Based on the aforementioned rationale, we further discuss the implications from the phonetics theory for young and adult ELLs separately.

Phonics, Phonemic Awareness, and Spelling Instruction for Young ELLs

Teachers who help their language learners acquire English phonetics or sound systems, consequently support their students' acquisition of phonics and phonemic awareness in English. **Phonics** is described as "a predictable relationship between the sounds (or *phonemes*) in spoken words and their corresponding letters (or *graphemes*) in written words" (Herrera, Perez, & Escamilla, 2015, p. 75), whereas **phonemic awareness** is defined as "the ability to think explicitly about and manipulate the individual sounds or phonemes of spoken language" (Templeton & Bear, 2011, p. 154).

The knowledge of phonics is essential to gaining fundamental literacy skills necessary for the mastery of reading and writing in a language. Phonics instruction teaches students sound-symbol or phoneme-grapheme relationships in a language. In regard to consonants instruction, knowing phonics enables a student to determine one-to-one letter-sound correspondences for individual consonants, spelling and pronunciation of consonant digraphs (such as *th* in *thin* or *than*, *ch* in *chair*, *sh* in *shine*, *tch* in *match* etc.), blends (such as *br* in *brave*, *dr* in *drive*, *cl* in *claim*, *fr* in *friend*, *st* in *stop*, *sp* in *speak*, etc.), and clusters (such as *str* in *street*, *spr* in *spring*, *scr* in *scream*, *spl* in *splash*, etc.), any inconsistencies in regard to the spelling or pronunciation of consonants, and so on. Thus, teachers can implement their knowledge of phonetics theory when teaching individual consonant phonemes, consonant digraphs, blends, and clusters, and the exceptions concerning English consonants.

The process of phonics instruction starts with teaching initial consonants, and continues with the introduction of word families followed by the focus on consonant blends, digraphs, and clusters (Barone, 2010). When teaching initial consonants to English learners, teachers need to be very mindful about the order of the introduced consonants. Teaching consonants haphazardly and unsystematically can hinder English learners' acquisition of those sounds. It is a fact that some consonants, such as /b/, /m/, /d/, or /k/, occur more frequently in the world's languages, whereas some others, like /θ/ or /ð/, are less common (Fromkin et al., 2014). Knowing this, teachers of English learners should purposefully start teaching those consonants that their students are familiar with in their first language. However, sounds cannot and should not be taught in isolation. Phonemes need to be taught in context, and words constitute the smallest context for the phonemes. Templeton and Bear (2011) assert that "when students study phonics, they are learning about spelling, and when they study spelling, they are also learning about phonics and vocabulary" (p. 154). Thus, phonics instruction also involves vocabulary and spelling instruction. In order to teach all these components simultaneously and effectively, teachers of ELLs can use **minimal pairs** defined as "two words in a language which differ from each other by only one distinctive sound (one phoneme) and which also differ in meaning" (Richards & Schmidt, 2013, p. 366). Referring back to the most frequently used consonants in the world's languages (/b/, /m/, /d/, or /k/), we suggest utilizing the minimal pairs containing those commonly known sounds first. For example, to teach the contrast between /b/ and /m/, /m/ and /d/, and /d/ and /k/, teachers can use the minimal pairs *ball* and *mall*, *man* and *Dan*, and *date* and *Kate*, respectively. When teaching these contrastive English consonants, the graphemes representing those sounds in print, the words containing the same sounds, and the pictures illustrating the words including the phonemes would promote language learners' acquisition of phonics, vocabulary, and spelling in English. The example provided in Figure 3 demonstrates one way teachers can present English consonant phonemes to their ELLs.

The teaching of consonant digraphs, blends, and clusters also requires special attention and can be carried out in a similar way (consonant digraph/blend/cluster + minimal pair + pictures). When teaching consonant digraphs to ELLs, teachers need to ensure that their students understand and acquire the

Figure 3.

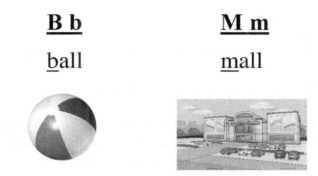

B b   **M m**

b̲all   m̲all

relationship between the spelling and pronunciation of digraphs – two or more consonants that represent one sound (Gunderson, 2009). Some examples of consonant digraphs are *th* in *thin* /θɪn/, *ch* in *chin* /ʧɪn/, or *sh* in *ship* /ʃɪp/. The pronunciation of consonant blends and clusters, which consist of two or more consonants respectively, differs from that of digraphs. Unlike digraphs, the individual consonants constituting consonant blends or clusters can be heard separately, such as *fr* in *friend* /frɛnd/ and *spl* in *splash* /splæʃ/. Modelling the correct pronunciation of consonant digraphs, blends, and clusters as well as providing visual support (words in print and pictures) would facilitate students' understanding, correct pronunciation, and accurate spelling of these phonic elements.

There exist some inconsistencies or exceptions in regard to pronunciation and spelling in English. Therefore, teachers of ELLs need to be careful about overgeneralizing phonics rules when teaching consonants to their students. For example, language learners should be informed that not every *th* consonant digraph is pronounced as an interdental fricative, /θ/ or /ð/. For example, the *th* digraph in such words as *Thomas* and *Thames* is pronounced as the regular alveolar stop /t/ in English. Another example is the consonant digraph *ch* which is not always produced as the palatal affricate /ʧ/, but can be pronounced as /k/ like in *choral* /ˈkɔrəl/ or *character* /ˈkɛrɪktər/.

Effective phonics instruction for ELLs should also involve phonemic awareness instruction which includes tasks such as recognizing individual sounds in words (phoneme isolation), recognizing the common sound in different words (phoneme identity), recognizing the word with the odd sound in a sequence of three or four words (phoneme categorization), combining separately spoken sounds to form a recognizable word (phoneme blending), breaking a word into its sounds (phoneme segmentation), etc. (National Reading Panel & NICHD, 2000). Phonemic awareness, as applied to recognizing and using English consonants, can be established and developed simultaneously with the acquisition of phonics. For example, English learners who have adequate phonics instruction and are familiar with the bilabial stop /b/ should be able to recognize the sound /b/ in the word *bank* (phoneme isolation) and in the set of words *bat*, *boy*, and *bike* (phoneme identity), to detect the word with the odd sound in a sequence such as *bat*, *boy*, and *kite* (phoneme categorization), and so on. To support young English learners' phonemic awareness, teachers can engage them in different activities such as "Picture Sorts" for which, students sort pictures based on the initial consonant sound, "Move It" which requires students to move a chip for each phoneme of the word pronounced by the teacher (for example, for a three-phoneme word, the chip is moved three times), and "Name Comparisons" for which, language learners compare the first sound of their names with those of their peers (Barone, 2010). Language learners can build and improve their phonics and spelling skills as well as phonemic awareness more efficiently if provided with ample language experiences and reading opportunities that are engaging, interesting, and contextually meaningful, and teachers who are knowledgeable about their ELLs' language and literacy needs can accelerate the process of acquisition of phonics, phonemic awareness, spelling, and meaning for their language learners.

Explicit Pronunciation Instruction for Adult ELLs

Learning consonant phonemes and pronouncing them correctly in English can be challenging for some English learners, especially those who have passed the critical period, whose L2 pronunciation has fossilized[5], and who do not have the same sounds in their first language. For example, Arabic learners of English as a second or foreign language may have a difficulty distinguishing between the bilabial stops /b/ and /p/ in English since /p/ does not exist in the Arabic language. Likewise, English learners whose first language is Spanish might be challenged when pronouncing the words starting with the labiodental fricative /v/ in English since the sounds /v/ and /b/ are both pronounced as bilabials in Spanish. In order to help their students with correct pronunciation in English, it is desirable that teachers of English learners should be aware of their students' mother tongues and of how their first language can have an impact on the learners' pronunciation of consonants in English. This awareness can help teachers to take the next step forward and detect the pronunciation challenges of their students and start working towards improving their English learners' pronunciation until optimum speech intelligibility is achieved.

Research shows that explicit pronunciation instruction can be very helpful in improving adult language learners' pronunciation in a second language. To examine the effectiveness of second language explicit pronunciation instruction, Camus (2019) conducted an experimental study with 83 adult learners of Spanish as an L2, for which the experimental group participants received explicit pronunciation instruction on typically difficult segments – the voiceless stops /p, t, k/ in L2 Spanish for twelve weeks. The results of the study revealed that while the control group did not demonstrate any difference in their pronunciation of the voiceless stops, the experimental group improved their ability to produce those sounds and approached very close to native speakers' range in the articulation of all three sounds. The study results encourage language teachers and practitioners to incorporate explicit pronunciation instruction into their teaching.

Explicit pronunciation instruction for adult English learners can be much more specific than that for young ELLs. Adult language learners can be explicitly and directly introduced to English phonemes and their articulatory features. The pronunciation instruction might also require providing specific articulatory techniques (such as "place the tip of your tongue behind your upper front teeth", "raise the back of the tongue to the soft palate", etc.) to help the learners overcome some pronunciation difficulties in English. To support pronunciation instruction and to point out the articulatory differences between distinctive English sounds – consonant phonemes, teachers of adult ELLs can use minimal pairs, as well. The effectiveness of the use of minimal pairs can be maximized if the teacher is knowledgeable about what specific purpose those minimal pairs will serve. For example, if the teacher wants to emphasize the articulatory differences between the alveolar liquids /l/ and /ɹ/ to help some L1 Japanese or Korean learners with their English pronunciation, it would be meaningful to use the minimal pair *late-rate*. If students are experiencing a difficulty differentiating between /f/ and /v/ or /p/ and /b/, there is a great chance that they cannot distinguish between voiceless and voiced consonants. This can be due to their native language background, such as Arabic in which /v/ and /p/ do not exist. For such learners, it is recommended to use the minimal pairs contrasting the voicing feature of labiodental fricatives (/f/ and /v/ as in *fan* and *van*) and bilabial stops (/p/ as in *pin* and /b/ as in *bin*). Making pronunciation instruction purposeful and explicit can help adult ELLs enhance their language learning experiences, and work towards improving their pronunciation for better intelligibility and comprehension in English.

Recommendations for Effective Phonetics Instruction for ELLs

Drawing from and summarizing the information provided in this chapter, we suggest some strategies and techniques that can be employed when teaching English sounds, including English consonants, to culturally and linguistically diverse language learners:

- Start by teaching those English phonemes that are more frequently used in the world's languages. Teaching the phonemes/consonants that have one-to-one letter-to-sound correspondences in English will also facilitate students' acquisition of English pronunciation and spelling. Gradually adding more high-frequency words to learners' word bank will enhance the students' acquisition of English sounds and spelling, and consequently result in expanding their reading experiences in English.

- Use minimal pairs to introduce phonemes to English learners, irrespective of their age or language learning context. An infinite number of minimal pairs can be utilized to highlight different aspects of English phonemes. Make the use of minimal pairs purposeful depending on the phonemic feature you would like to emphasize.

- Incorporate a lot of visuals into your teaching of all English phonemes, including the consonants, to elementary ELLs, which will consequently support the students' acquisition of phonics, phonemic awareness, and spelling in English. Introducing each consonant accompanied by a picture illustrating an item starting (or including) that phoneme and providing the spelling of the word described in the picture would help language learners to establish and develop multi-channel connections among the print, picture, and the sound. Helping ELLs to build such strong associations will assist with retaining the learned information which will further support their overall literacy acquisition. Remember that since elementary ELLs do not usually start school with proficient oral language skills in English, they rely on and need such multi-channel connections more than their native English-speaking peers who come to school with assumingly better developed oral language skills if they do not have any other impairment preventing their oral language acquisition. However, this fact does not mean that native English-speaking students do not benefit from the use of visuals in the classroom. Providing visual support will facilitate and enhance literacy acquisition for all students.

- Teach English phonemes and their pronunciation explicitly. As discussed in the previous section, explicit teaching of English pronunciation will help ELLs reduce their non-native English accent as well as develop intelligible speech in English.

- Phonetics instruction can be incorporated into overall language instruction, the instruction of four language domains – listening, speaking, reading, and writing, or content instruction. Instead of teaching the pronunciation of English phonemes in isolation, consider blending it into language, reading, or other content instruction which will serve as a relatable context for language learners. Remember that English learners learn best in meaningful, interesting, and motivating contexts.

The above recommendations can be expanded and improved to further enhance the effectiveness and efficiency of phonetics instruction for ELLs. Teachers of English learners should know that they can always draw from their students' rich cultural and linguistic backgrounds to enhance their classroom experiences as well as to facilitate student learning, the positive effect of which will be reflected on overall student achievement in school and life.

DISCUSSION QUESTIONS

1.   As discussed in the chapter, some English consonants can cause pronunciation difficulty for learners from certain language backgrounds. Which consonants cause difficulty for you or your students when pronouncing? What are the possible causes of the pronunciation difficulties involving those consonants? Deriving from the information provided in this chapter, discuss some articulation techniques that can be helpful in eliminating such problems.

2.   It was noted in the chapter that some consonants can never occur at the beginning (/ŋ/) or the end (/h/, /j/, and /w/) of words in English. Based on your observation or knowledge of other languages, discuss how this fact can affect English language learning for a person whose first language can have the /ŋ/ sound word-initially (for example, Swahili, Vietnamese, some Siberian languages, etc.), and /h/, /j/, and /w/ word-finally (for example, Arabic). Consider the opposite situation as well, such as when a learner's native language does not have certain consonants word-initially or -finally that normally occur in the initial or final positions in English words. How do you think such facts affect English language learning and pronunciation? If possible, support your answer with some examples from your own language learning or teaching experience.

3.   Some languages do not contain all the sounds that exist in English. For example, Russian, Turkish, German, Chinese, and French do not have interdental consonants. Therefore, it is very common to hear a Russian or a French learner of English to pronounce *them* /ðɛm/ like *zem* /zɛm/, a Turkish speaker to pronounce *three* /θɹi/ as *tree* /tɹi/, and so on. How can you assist your English learners experiencing such difficulties to improve their pronunciation and develop intelligible speech in English? What strategies would you use?

4.   Discuss the ways you can use minimal pairs to teach contrastive English sounds to your English learners as well as to help the students to improve their pronunciation of English consonants.

5.   Teachers of English language learners frequently use strategies like Guided Reading, Read Aloud, etc. during reading instruction in elementary grades. Discuss the ways phonetics, more specifically, consonants instruction can be incorporated into the everyday reading instruction for English learners.

EXERCISES

1.   Provide the phonetic symbol for the initial consonants of the following words, and give the complete description of the consonant. When analyzing each word, make sure to pay attention to the pronunciation of the beginning sound rather than to its orthographic representation (the letter) since the articulated sound and the letter representing that sound do not always overlap in English. Examine the examples carefully before analyzing the following words.

Examples: 1.   ***village*** - /v/ - *voiced labiodental fricative*
          2.   ***philosophy*** - /f/ - *voiceless labiodental fricative*

a.   knight _____

b.   sister _____

c.   comrade _____

d.   physics _____

e.   xylophone _____

f.   chair _____

g.   giant _____

h.   wrong _____

i.   shelter _____

j.   ballet _____

k.   though _____

l.   water _____

2.   Before doing this exercise, review the classification of English consonants according to their place and manner of articulation, and voicing provided in Table 1. Then read the below descriptions, give the phonetic symbol representing each described consonant, and supply English words containing that consonant in the initial, medial, and final positions. Use the example below as a guide.

Example: ***voiceless interdental fricative*** - /θ/ - <u>th</u>ing, au<u>th</u>or, fai<u>th</u>

    a.   voiced alveolar liquid _____

    b.   voiceless glottal fricative _____

    c.   voiced velar stop _____

    d.   voiced bilabial nasal _____

    e.   voiceless alveolar stop _____

3.   Read the following quote from Dr. Martin Luther King, Jr., and underline all the letters representing the alveolar consonants of the English language. Note that you can do this activity on different sentence examples and using different prompts (such as "find all the fricatives", or "find all the voiced consonants", etc.) with your English learners.

I refuse to accept the view that mankind is so tragically bound to the starless midnight of racism and war that the bright daybreak of peace and brotherhood can never become a reality... I believe that unarmed truth and unconditional love will have the final word.

4.   Which of the following pairs of consonants share the same place <u>and</u> manner of articulation? Find those pairs of consonants, indicate what they are called based on their place and manner of articulation (for example, *bilabial stops*, *interdental fricatives*, etc.), and supply a set of minimal pairs for each set of sounds.

After finishing this activity, consider answering the following question.

If the consonants have the same place and manner of articulation, how are they different sounds or distinct phonemes?

    a.   /n/ and /ŋ/ _____

    b.   /k/ and /g/ _____

    c.   /f/ and /v/ _____

d.   /j/ and /h/ _____

e.   /s/ and /z/ _____

f.   /ʃ/ and /ʧ/ _____

g.   /ʧ/ and /ʤ/ _____

h.   /t/ and /d/ _____

i.   /l/ and /ʒ/ _____

j.   /θ/ and /s/ _____

5.   Examine the following words. How can you group them as minimal pairs and utilize them when teaching certain articulatory features of English consonants? The learners of which language backgrounds would benefit from teaching the sounds based on certain minimal pairs? Explain your answers and provide examples.

a. cane   b. Jane   c. gain

d. chain   e. vein   f. bane

g. lane   h. sane   i. Zain

j. pain   k. main   l. rain

m. wain   n. feign   o. Dane

REFERENCES

Avery, P., & Ehrlich, S. (1992). *Teaching American English pronunciation.* Oxford University Press.

Barone, D. (2010). Engaging young ELLs with reading and writing. In G. Li & P. Edwards (Eds.), *Best practices in ELL instruction* (pp. 84–102). New York, NY: Guilford.

Burleigh, P., & Skandera, P. (2016). *A Manual of English phonetics and phonology: Twelve lessons with an integrated course in phonetic transcription.* Tübingen: Narr Francke Attempto.

Camus, P. (2019). The effects of explicit pronunciation instruction on the production of second language Spanish voiceless stops: A classroom study. *Instructed Second Language Acquisition, 3*(1), 81–103.

Carley, P., Mees, I. M., & Collins, B. (2018). *English phonetics and pronunciation practice.* London: Routledge.

Collins, B. (2003). *The phonetics of English and Dutch.* Brill Academic.

Delahunty, G. P., & Garvey, J. J. (2010). *The English language: From sound to sense.* Fort Collins, CO: WAC Clearinghouse.

Denham, K. E., & Lobeck, A. C. (2010). *Linguistics for everyone: An introduction.* Boston, MA: Wadsworth/ Cengage Learning.

Finegan, E. (2008). *Language: Its structure and use.* Boston, MA: Thomson Wadsworth.

Freeman, D. E., & Freeman, Y. S. (2004). *Essential linguistics: What you need to know to teach reading, ESL, spelling, phonics, and grammar*. Portsmouth, NH: Heinemann.

Fromkin, V., Rodman, R., & Hyams, N. (2014). *An introduction to language* (10th ed.). Boston, MA: Wadsworth Cengage Learning.

Fulk, R. D. (2012). *An introduction to Middle English: Grammar, texts*. Buffalo, NY: Broadview Press.

Gunderson, L. (2009). *ESL (ELL) literacy instruction: A guidebook to theory and practice* (2nd ed.). New York, NY: Taylor & Francis.

Gussmann, E. (2002). *Phonology: Analysis and theory*. Cambridge, UK: Cambridge University Press. doi:10.1017/CBO9781139164108

Hand, A. R., & Frank, M. E. (2014). *Fundamentals of oral histology and physiology*. Ames, IA: Wiley Blackwell.

Hazen, K. (2014). *An introduction to language*. Malden, MA: Wiley-Blackwell.

Herrera, S. G., Perez, D. R., & Escamilla, K. (2015). *Teaching reading to English language learners: Differentiated literacies*. Pearson Education.

International Phonetic Association. (2015). *The International Phonetic Alphabet*. Retrieved from https://www.internationalphoneticassociation.org/sites/default/files/IPA_Kiel_2015.pdf

IPA Phonetic Transcription of English Text. (n.d.). Retrieved from https://tophonetics.com/

Kent, R. D. (1997). *The speech sciences*. San Diego, CA: Singular Publishing Group.

National Reading Panel (U.S.) & NICHD (National Institute of Child Health and Human Development). (2000). *Report of the National Reading Panel: Teaching children to read: An evidence-based assessment of the scientific research literature on reading and its implications for reading instruction: Reports of the subgroups*. Washington, DC: National Institute of Child Health and Human Development, National Institutes of Health.

Ogden, R. (2017). *An introduction to English phonetics*. Edinburgh University Press.

Radford, A., Atkinson, M., Britain, D., Clahsen, H., & Spencer, A. (2009). *Linguistics: An introduction*. Cambridge, UK: Cambridge University Press. doi:10.1017/CBO9780511841613

Richards, J. C., & Schmidt, R. (2013). *Longman dictionary of language teaching and applied linguistics*. New York, NY: Routledge. doi:10.4324/9781315833835

Rogers, H. (2013). *The sounds of language: An introduction to phonetics*. New York, NY: Routledge.

Rogerson-Revell, P. (2011). *English phonology and pronunciation teaching*. New York, NY: Continuum.

Stevens, K. N. (1998). *Acoustic phonetics*. Cambridge, MA: MIT Press.

Templeton, S., & Bear, D. R. (2011). Teaching phonemic awareness, spelling, and word recognition. In T. Rasinski (Ed.), *Rebuilding the foundation: Effective reading instruction for 21st century literacy* (pp. 153–178). Bloomington, IN: Solution Tree Press.

Thorum, A. R. (2013). *Phonetics: A contemporary approach*. Burlington, MA: Jones & Bartlett Learning.

Vennard, W. (1968). *Singing, the mechanism and the technic*. New York: Carl Fischer.

Yavas, M. S. (2011). *Applied English phonology*. Oxford, UK: Wiley-Blackwell. doi:10.1002/9781444392623

ADDITIONAL READING

Avery, P., & Ehrlich, S. (1992). *Teaching American English pronunciation*. Oxford University Press.

Fromkin, V., Rodman, R., & Hyams, N. (2014). *An introduction to language* (10th ed.). Boston, MA: Wadsworth Cengage Learning.

Yavas, M. S. (2011). *Applied English phonology*. Oxford, UK: Wiley-Blackwell. doi:10.1002/9781444392623

ENDNOTES

1.   Note that the English /ɹ/ can also be pronounced with bunching up the tongue in the back of the mouth, as a result of which "bunched r" is produced. According to Hazen (2014), "curled Rs are more likely in words like *rat*, *read*, *pry*, or *try*", while "bunched Rs are more likely in words like *bark*, *lager*, *poor*, or *quirk*" (p. 372).

2.   The Russian word *царь* /t͡sarʲ/ includes the letter –ь, known as the "soft sign" (мягкий знак – "my-agkiy znak" in Russian), as the final consonant. This sound is represented by the superscript /ʲ/ in the transcription, the symbol that denotes palatalization in Russian. The presence of this phoneme makes the preceding consonant soft or palatalized.

3.   Notice that the English consonant phonemes are not presented in a haphazard order in Table 2, but are listed according to their manner of articulation (stops, fricatives, affricates, nasals, liquids, and glides).

4.   We use the word "assumingly" for a purpose here since our common sense and generalizations tell us that adults should already have well-established literacy skills in their mother tongue. However, we also recognize the fact that some adult English learners may not have any schooling before immigrating to the United States or any other English-speaking country, or their L1 literacy skills may be insufficient to support their English language acquisition. Teachers of such learners can use the strategies that we have suggested for elementary language learners.

5.   *Fossilization* is a term used in second or foreign language learning. It is a process in which incorrect linguistic features concerning some aspects of pronunciation, vocabulary usage, and grammar become fixed in second or foreign language speech or writing, and "fossilized features of pronunciation contribute to a person's foreign accent" (Richards & Schmidt, 2013, p. 230).

Chapter 12
Articulatory Phonetics:
English Vowels

Sofia Alexandrovna Ivanova
University of Georgia, USA

Victoria Hasko
University of Georgia, USA

ABSTRACT

This chapter focuses on the articulatory phonetics of English vowels; thus, it identifies descriptive parameters for vowel articulation in English, differentiates monophthongs and diphthongs, classifies the vowels of American English using these parameters, and addresses vowel reduction in American English. The theoretical material is followed by a pedagogical consideration of how the specifics of the articulatory characteristics of English vowels can be addressed in the classroom to facilitate comprehension and production of English vowels by English language learners. Supplementary materials are suggested for readers offering sample activities that could be used by language practitioners in ESL classrooms for this goal, as well as for exploring other dialects of English, including specific regional dialects falling under the umbrella of General American English, the variety addressed in this chapter.

ARTICULATORY DESCRIPTION OF VOWELS

This chapter focuses on how the vocal organs are engaged in producing the vowel sounds of American English, including the descriptive parameters of vowel articulation and categorization of American English vowels according to those parameters, an explanation of differences between monophthongs and diphthongs, a brief discussion of vowel reduction, and pedagogical considerations of how these issues can be addressed in an ESL classroom and supplementary materials useful for both teachers and learners. The range of speech sounds utilized by spoken languages are produced in the vocal tract which filters sound produced at the larynx or voice box to create meaningful distinctions between sounds and thus yield the range of sounds of spoken human language (Gick, Wilson, & Derrick, 2013; Zsiga, 2013).

DOI: 10.4018/978-1-5225-8467-4.ch012

Vowels pose an interesting challenge to articulatory description. They are most typically produced with vibrating vocal folds, which limits the utility of the voicing distinction for categorizing vowels (Zsiga, 2013). Since there is little constriction of the vocal tract involved in their production, the place and manner distinctions which can be used to describe the articulatory gestures involved in the production of consonants in rather concrete terms are inadequate for describing the typically open articulations of vowels (Zsiga, 2013). Instead, vowels are most effectively described with reference to the positioning of the tongue body and, to a lesser extent, lips (Gick, Wilson, & Derrick, 2013; Zsiga, 2013). Thus, the four main parameters for describing English vowels are the vertical position of the tongue in the oral cavity during the articulation of the vowel, or tongue *height* (high, mid, or low; in some sources, close, corresponding with high, close-mid, open-mid, and open, corresponding with low), the horizontal position of the tongue in the oral cavity, or tongue *backness* (front, central, or back), lip *rounding* (rounded or unrounded), and *tenseness* (tense or lax) (Shriberg & Kent, 2012; Zsiga, 2013).

Height

The first key difference between vowels refers to the vertical position of the tongue during the articulation of the vowel. Another way to think of tongue height is as the distance between the tongue and the roof of the mouth. There are three values used for describing tongue height: high, mid, and low. Vowels produced with the tongue close to the roof of the mouth (and thus with a nearly closed mouth) are **high** (sometimes referred to as close vowels) – e.g., /i/ as in *beat* and heat; /u/ as in *boot* and *hoot*. Vowels produced with the tongue lowered to the jaw, far from the roof of the mouth (and thus with an open mouth) are **low** (also referred to as open vowels) – e.g., /æ/ as in *bat* and *hat*; /ɑ/ as in *hot* and pot. Vowels produced with the tongue at an intermediate distance between the roof of the mouth and the jaw (such as /ɛ/ in *bet* and *pet*) are **mid**.

The simplest way to feel the difference between high and low vowels is to compare the vowels in a minimal pair like *beat* and *bat*. Both words begin with a *b* sound and end with a *t* sound, and only the vowel is different between the two words. Notice as you pronounce these two words carefully that to produce the high vowel /i/ in *beat*, the tongue is quite high in the mouth, almost touching the roof of the mouth; to produce the low vowel /æ/ in *bat*, the tongue is lowered to the jaw, far from the roof of the mouth. Moving between the words *beat* and *bat* helps to isolate the extreme points of the height continuum for vowels.

Backness

A second key difference between vowels refers to how far forward or back in the mouth the tongue, or, according to some sources, the highest point of the tongue, is positioned during the articulation of the vowel. As with tongue height, there are three values used for describing backness: back, central, and front. Vowels produced with the tongue pushed relatively forward in the mouth are **front** (/i/ as in *beat* and *peel*; /ɪ/ as in *bit* and *pill*; /ɛ/ as in *bet* and *bell*); vowels produced with the tongue bunched up near the back of the mouth are **back** (/u/ as in *boot* and *pool*; /ʊ/ as in *book* and *put*); vowels produced with the tongue in a neutral position, at an intermediate distance between these two values, are **central** (/ʌ/ as in *but* and *hut*). Another way to think of tongue backness is which *part* of the tongue is raised in articulation of the vowel – front, central, or back.

To feel the difference between front and back vowels, try alternating between another minimal pair: *beat* and *boot*. You should feel your tongue move forward in the mouth for the high front vowel /i/ in *beat*, possibly even touching the inside of your lower incisors, and moving back in the mouth for the high back vowel /u/ in *boot*. In addition to backness, these two vowels - /i/ and /u/ - are also different in rounding (see below) - /i/ is unrounded and produced with spread lips, while /u/ is produced with rounded or puckered lips (typical for the high back vowels of English and many other languages); if this additional difference between /i/ and /u/ is distracting to you, try a third minimal pair: *hat* and *hot*. Alternating between the low front vowel /æ/ as in *hat* and the low back vowel /ɑ/ as in *hot*, as with front /i/ and back /u/, you should feel your tongue moving forward in the mouth for /æ/ and moving back in the mouth for /ɑ/, and there is no additional rounding distinction or other articulatory differences between these two vowels.

Rounding

A third key parameter used to describe differences between vowels is lip rounding (also referred to as labialization, particularly when referring to speech sounds in general), which refers to the rounding or puckering of the lips during the articulation of the vowel. With rounding, some accounts use only two values: **rounded** (as in /u/ in *boot* and /o/ in *boat*) and **unrounded** (as in /i/ in *beat*, /ɛ/ in *bet*, and /æ/ in *bat*), while others prefer three: rounded (same as above), spread (as in /i/ in *beat* and /ɛ/ in *bet*), and neutral (as in /æ/ in *bat*).

American English does not have rounded and unrounded vowels in the same part of the vowel space (all four rounded vowels are clustered at the high back corner of the vowel space), so any pair of rounded/unrounded vowels we choose will also differ in either height or backness. Keeping this in mind, try alternating between the minimal pair *beet* and *boot*, then between the minimal pair *loot* and *lot*. Moving between *beet* and *boot*, in addition to a change in vowel backness, you should also observe a considerable difference in rounding of the lips: for the lips are spread for *beet* but rounded, with some forward protrusion, for *boot*. Similarly, moving between *loot* and *lot*, in addition to a change in vowel height, you should also observe a considerable difference in rounding of the lips: rounded for *loot* and neutral for *lot*.

When the lips are rounded, they tend to protrude slightly forward, which has the effect of lengthening the vocal tract, causing the vowel to be slightly more back; this may explain why in many languages, including English, the rounded vowels occur in the high back vowel space, where speakers can most fruitfully exploit this effect, although some languages' inventories (e.g., French and German) feature rounded vowels elsewhere in the vowel space.

Tenseness

A final and perhaps most challenging to define parameter used to describe differences between vowels is tenseness, which refers to whether the tongue and lower face are tense or relatively relaxed during the production of the vowel. In the production of **tense vowels**, speakers make an overall greater muscular effort than in the production of **lax vowels**. Tense vowels are typically higher, less centralized, and longer in duration, than their lax counterparts (see Vowel Reduction below for more on centralization).

To feel the difference between tense and lax vowels, try alternating between the minimal pairs *seat* and *sit*, *beat* and *bit*, *heat* and *hit*. These three pairs contrast the vowels /i/ and /ɪ/, both high front unrounded vowels; the difference between them is that /i/ is tense, and you should feel comparatively more tenseness in the tongue and cheeks as you articulate it, while /ɪ/ is lax, and should not trigger much tenseness in the articulators. Next, try alternating between the high back rounded pair, tense /u/ and lax /ʊ/, with the minimal pairs *Luke* and *look*, *suit* and *soot*, *who'd* and *hood*. You should feel overall more tenseness in the tongue and cheeks for *Luke*, *suit*, and *who'd*, and overall less tenseness for *look*, *soot*, and *hood*.

THE IPA DESCRIPTION OF VOWELS

The acoustic and articulatory properties of the English vowels are represented broadly by the vowel portion of the International Phonetic Association's International Phonetic Alphabet (IPA). Figure 1 introduces the reader to this chart, which attempts to assign a unique symbol to every vowel known to be used contrastively by some languages. Although extra add-on symbols contained in the full IPA chart can be used in combination with vowel symbols to convey information about tone and duration, which are contrastive in some languages, they are not represented by this portion of the chart, which depicts only vowel height, backness, and rounding.

    The IPA vowel chart represents the parameters of vowel height and backness via the vertical and horizontal dimensions of a two-dimensional figure; put simply, it plots vowels according to the position of the tongue during their production. Vowel height and backness correlate with the vertical and horizontal boundaries that subdivide the vowel space into the quadrants of the vowel quadrilateral. Thus, the vowel quadrilateral is a two-dimensional diagram that represents both a theoretical and a real acoustic space in which vowels are positioned according to the relative openness of the mouth and how far forward or back in the mouth the tongue is positioned during their production (imagine the vowel quadrilateral in Figure 1 superimposed over the mouth portion of the vocal tract pictured in the chapter

Figure 1. International Phonetic Alphabet vowel chart
Source: IPA, 2018. Retrieved from https://www.internationalphoneticassociation.org/content/ipa-vowels

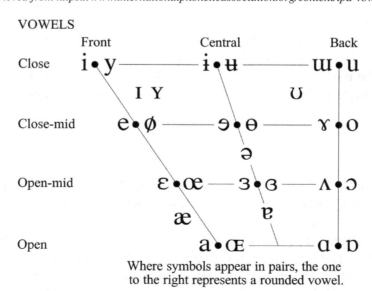

on English Consonants). In this way, the vowel quadrilateral represents the upper and lower extremes of these two physiological parameters of vowel production and, thus, the range of possible vowels, at least in terms of the vertical (openness) and horizontal (backness) dimensions. The upper regions of the vowel quadrilateral represent vowels produced with an almost closed mouth (e.g., /i/ as in *seat*, /ɪ/ as in *sit*, /u/ as in *suit*, and /ʊ/ as in *soot*), while the lower regions represent vowels produced with the mouth wide open (e.g., /æ/ as in *sack* and *hat* and /ɑ/ as in *sock* and *hot*), and the intermediate parts of the vowel quadrilateral represent gradations between the two states. The leftmost regions represent vowels produced with the tongue relatively forward in the mouth, the tongue tip approaching the back of the lower incisors (e.g., /i/ as in *seat*, /ɪ/ as in *sit*, /e/ as in *sate*, /ɛ/ as in *set*, and /æ/ as in *sat*), while the rightmost regions represent vowels produced with the tongue further back in the mouth, the back of the tongue rising slightly toward the velum (e.g., /u/ as in *Luke*, /ʊ/ as in *look*, /o/ as in *low*, /ɔ/ as in *law*, /ɑ/ as in *lock*; refer to the illustration of the Vocal Tract in the Consonants chapter if needed). Height and backness are the most common parameters used to describe the vowel systems of the world's languages and tend to be the first two used by vowel systems which feature relatively fewer vowel contrasts (e.g., five-vowel systems in languages such as Spanish) and thus need fewer parameters to distinguish the distinctive vowel sounds in their inventories (Gick, Wilson & Derrick, 2013; Ladefoged & Disner, 2012).

The additional parameters of rounding and tenseness are less commonly used among the world's languages; however, they are useful in that they allow the vowel space to be further subdivided to accommodate adjacent (that is, very similar in height and backness values) but distinct vowels (Zsiga, 2013). For example, the English pairs /i/ as in *seat* and /ɪ/ as in *sit*, as well as /u/ as in *Luke* and /ʊ/ as in *look*, contrast tense vowels /i/ as in *seat* and /u/ as in *Luke* with their lax counterparts /ɪ/ as in *sit* and /ʊ/ as in *look*, lax vowels in the same (high front for /i/ and /ɪ/ and high back for /u/ and /ʊ/) part of the vowel space and different mostly in their tenseness value. It is unfortunately not possible to compare rounded and unrounded vowels of the same height and backness in American English, as English does not contrast via rounding vowels in the same part of the vowel space; the rounded vowels of American English – /u/ as in *Luke*, /ʊ/ as *look*, /o/ as in *low*, and /ɔ/ as in *law* – are all clustered in the high and mid back part of the vowel space, while the unrounded vowels of American – /i/ as in *leak*, /ɪ/ as in lick, /e/ as in *lake*, /ɛ/ as in *let*, /æ/ as in *lack*, /ʌ/ as in *luck*, /ɑ/ as in *lock* – appear elsewhere. These contrasts do appear in other languages: for example, the French contrast /i/ as in *si* 'if' and /y/ as in *su* 'knew' demonstrates an unrounded and a rounded vowel in the same (high front) part of the vowel space. The English speaker can, however, feel this distinction by starting with a rounded vowel such as /u/ as in *who* and attempting to un-round the lips to a neutral, relaxed position while holding the vowel sound and paying attention to the change in sound quality as a result of this articulatory change; similarly, one could start with an unrounded vowel such as /i/ as in *bee* and attempt to round the lips to a pursed or puckered position while holding the vowel sound and pay attention to the resulting change in sound quality.

While vowel height and backness are represented in the vowel space via horizontal and vertical dimensions respectively, tenseness and rounding – redundant rather than contrastive features in many vowel systems – are not explicitly illustrated in the vowel quadrilateral (Gick, Wilson, & Derrick, 2013). Rounding is demonstrated by the vowel chart in Figure 1 through the positioning of each symbol relative to a neighboring sound: where symbols appear in pairs separated by a dot, the symbol left of the dot represents an unrounded vowel, and the symbol right of the dot represents a rounded sound with the same height and backness. Tenseness, the most challenging to define parameter addressed here, is not explicitly represented by the IPA vowel chart; however, lax vowels tend to be more centralized along the height and backness dimensions than their tense counterparts, and thus both members of the tense/

lax "pairs" can be accurately represented according to height and backness on the vowel quadrilateral. These four parameters are described in greater detail below.

Other ways to describe vowels, not utilized to describe the vowels of American English as they do not generate meaningful vowel contrasts in American English, take advantage of features such as nasality (vowels produced with a lowered velum, which allows air to escape through both the mouth and the nose), duration (a reference to how long the vowel sound is held), and tone (the pitch – stable or changing – at which a vowel sound is produced). As these additional descriptions do not pertain to American English vowels in terms of their contrastive differences, they will not be discussed further in this chapter; see the list of additional readings provided at the conclusion of this chapter for resources that discuss these additional articulatory descriptions in more detail. See also the chapter which follows the present one - "English Sounds in Context: The Pronunciation of Phonemes and Morphemes", which discusses allophones and allomorphs of English, including the nasalization of vowels before the nasal consonants [n, m, ŋ] in the same syllable.

One important note for learners and teachers of English is that the tense/lax distinction in English vowels is often described and perhaps even taught to English learners as a long/short distinction. In some ways, this description is accurate: tense vowels are always longer in duration than lax vowels of the same height and backness in the speech of native speakers of English (Zsiga, 2013). However, native speakers rely considerably more on spectral (height and backness) than duration differences to distinguish the tense/lax pairs of American English (Hillenbrand, Clark, & Houde, 2000), and learners who rely more or exclusively on duration in distinguishing these vowels are likely to encounter problems with comprehensibility (Kondaurova & Francis 2006, 2008; see more on Tenseness below). Similar non-phonemic duration differences may occur due to inherent aspects of vowel articulation: due to the time it takes to open the mouth wide, low vowels tend to be longer than high vowels; additionally, as discussed below, stressed vowels are longer than unstressed vowels, and vowels are longer before voiced than voiceless consonants (Shriberg & Kent, 2012). However, unlike in other languages, duration is not contrastive in English in that no two vowels differ in duration alone, in identical environments (Zsiga, 2013), and thus duration cannot be said to be used to generate meaningful contrasts in American English (Ladefoged & Disner, 2012).

MONOPHTHONGS VS. DIPHTHONGS

Monophthongs are differentiated from diphthongs according to the relative stillness or movement of the articulators throughout the production of the vowel. **Monophthongs**, sometimes referred to as simple or pure vowels, are vowels produced with little movement or change in quality during the vowel's production (Zsiga, 2013), for example, the vowel sound /i/ in *see*. **Diphthongs** are characterized by change in vowel quality resulting from change in tongue position or lip rounding from the beginning to the end of a single vowel (Zsiga, 2013), for example, the vowel sound /aɪ/ in *sigh*.

To represent this change in quality from the beginning to the end of the vowel, diphthongs are typically transcribed with a pair of symbols. In the case of the vowel sound in *sigh*, the beginning of the diphthong is represented by the low central /a/ and the end of the diphthong by the high front /ɪ/, yielding /aɪ/ to accurately transcribe the entire vowel sound in *sigh*.

Note that diphthongs are single two-part vowels that constitute a single syllable, not two separate vowel sounds one after the other separated by a syllable boundary. A word like *sigh* is made up of only one syllable containing as its nucleus a single, two-part vowel (diphthong) /aɪ/, rather than two syllables, the first of which ends in a monophthongal vowel /a/ and the second of which begins with a separate monophthongal vowel /ɪ/.

VOWELS OF AMERICAN ENGLISH

The vowel phonemes of General American English include 12 monophthongs - /i ɪ e ɛ æ ɑ ɔ o ʊ u ʌ ə/ and three diphthongs - /aɪ aʊ ɔɪ/ (Ladefoged, 1999). Figure 2 below demonstrates the Cardinal Vowels, a set of 18 reference vowels, distributed at regular intervals throughout the vowel quadrilateral in rounded/unrounded pairs. These vowels do not represent the vowels of any particular language; rather, they serve as a fixed instrument or system of measurement and comparison (Jones, 1969). There is considerable overlap between the IPA vowel chart and the chart of Cardinal Vowels due to the tendency for real languages to distribute vowels equally throughout the available phonetic space (recall that the vowel space represents two dimensions – the vertical and horizontal space – in which vowels can be produced; see Disner, 1984). Describing the vowels of English with reference to the Cardinal Vowels can facilitate comparison to the vowels of the native languages of English learners. The first 11 English monophthongs correspond generally with Cardinal Vowels 1, 2, 3, 4, 5, 6, 7, 8, and 14, with the addition of high front and high back lax vowels /ɪ/ and /ʊ/.

Note that the schwa (/ə/) is not included in the chart of Cardinal Vowels because it is a neutral sound that occurs only in unstressed syllables and does not have a comparison. If it were included in the chart, it would be located in the center (see Figure 1). Additionally, the American English back vowels /u/, /ʊ/, /o/, and /ɔ/ are generally rounded, as are the Cardinal Vowels 8, 7, and 6 with which they are associated, although in some dialects (e.g., California) the high back vowels may be produced with spread lips (Hagiwara, 1997; Ladefoged, 1999).

Figure 2. Cardinal vowels
Source: Modified from https://commons.wikimedia.org/wiki/File:Cardinal_vowels_on_a_vowel_chart.svg

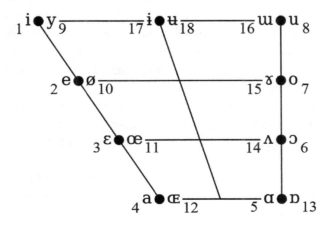

Table 1. Vowel phonemes of American English with articulatory description, example words, and associated cardinal vowels

Vowel	Height	Backness	Rounding	Tenseness	Example Words	Associated Cardinal Vowel
/i/	high	front	unrounded	tense	*beat, seat*	1
/ɪ/	high	front	unrounded	lax	*bit, sit*	N/A
/e/	mid	front	unrounded	tense	*bait, sate*	2
/ɛ/	mid	front	unrounded	lax	*bet, set*	3
/æ/	low	front	unrounded	lax[1]	*bat, sat*	slightly higher than 4
/u/	high	back	rounded	tense	*boot, suit*	8
/ʊ/	high	back	rounded	lax	*book, soot*	N/A
/o/	mid	back	rounded	tense	*boat, soak*	7
/ɔ/	mid	back	rounded	lax/tense[2]	*bought, sought*	6
/ɑ/	low	back	unrounded	lax/tense[3]	*pot, sock*	5
/ʌ/	mid	central	unrounded	lax	*but, suck*	14
/ə/	mid	central	unrounded	lax	*coma, soda*	none; best visualized in center of chart

According to the four parameters outlined above, the monophthong vowel phonemes of American English can be classified as shown in Table 1.

Despite being formally classified as monophthongs, American English /e/ and /o/ are generally slightly diphthongized to [eɪ] and [oʊ], except when they appear before rhyme-/ɹ/, as in *hair* and *short* (Giegerich, 1992; Ladefoged, 1999).

These alternations between [o] and [oʊ] and between [e] and [eɪ] are not **phonemic** (referring to fundamentally different sounds rather than two variants of or two ways of pronouncing a single underlying sound); that is, [o] and [oʊ] are *two context-dependent ways of pronouncing* the same underlying vowel /o/ ([oʊ] in most cases, but [o] before rhyme-/ɹ/, as in *shore*) rather than two fundamentally different vowels. Similarly, [e] and [eɪ] are two possible ways of realizing the phoneme /e/ ([eɪ] in most cases, but [e] before rhyme-/ɹ/, as in *share*). Consider the o-vowel in *show*, *showed*, *shows*, *shoal*, and *shore*; notice that the o-vowel is diphthongized to [oʊ] in the first four instances but remains relatively monophthongal [o] in the last instance, in *shore*, before an r-sound. To hear this with the e-vowel, consider the vowel sound in *hey*, *hate*, *haze*, *hail*, *hair*; notice that in the first four instances, the e-vowel is diphthongized to [eɪ]; however, it remains relatively monophthongal [e] in the last instance, before an r-sound. Attempting to realize /o/ or /e/ before rhyme-/ɹ/ (as in *shore* or *hair*) as diphthongal (or vice versa, as monophthongal before any coda consonant but /ɹ/) may feel and sound strange to native speakers of American English, but it will not generate a new word.

Because these diphthongs are nonphonemic, but rather a matter of pronunciation, swapping [o] for [oʊ], or swapping [e] for [eɪ], in the same phonetic environment (that is, with the same, if any, flanking consonant sounds) may feel and sound unnatural in the context of American English, but the word meaning would not change.

These two nonphonemic diphthongs can be contrasted with three additional diphthongs of American English which are phonemic: /aɪ/ (as in *buy* and *light*), /aʊ/ (as in *cow* and *pout*), and /ɔɪ/ (as in *soy* and *boys*). These three diphthongs are phonemic because alternating between the entire diphthong (e.g., /aɪ/) and just the first part of that diphthong (/ɑ/ in the case of /aɪ/) is ***not*** simply a matter of pronunciation, and ***will*** change the meaning of the word. Consider the minimal pair *light* vs. *lot*: the vowel in *light* is the diphthong /aɪ/, while the vowel in *lot* is the monophthong /ɑ/. Exchanging /aɪ/ for /ɑ/ changes the meaning of the word: it is not simply a context-dependent matter of pronunciation, as we observed with [o] and [oʊ], and with [e] and [eɪ], above. Next, consider the minimal pair *pout* vs. *pot*: as we observed with /aɪ/ and /ɑ/ above, the vowel in *pout* is the diphthong /aʊ/, while the vowel in *pot* is the monophthong /ɑ/, and swapping one for the other changes word's meaning. Similarly, consider the minimal pair *soy* vs. *saw*: as we observed with /aɪ/ and /ɑ/, and with /aʊ/ and /ɑ/, above, the vowel in *soy* is a diphthong /ɔɪ/, while the vowel in *saw* is a monophthong /ɔ/, and swapping one for the other changes the word's meaning.

It is worth noting as part of a discussion of the English tense and lax vowels that in English stressed lax vowels occur only in closed syllables (that is, syllables that end with a consonant - e.g., *bit* and *book*), while stressed tense vowels can occur in either open or closed syllables (e.g., open *bee* and closed *beat*; open *boo* and closed *boot*). Additionally, in English, tense vowels tend to be longer than their lax counterparts of the same height and backness (e.g., /i/ is longer than /ɪ/, /u/ is longer than /ʊ/); thus, many sources characterize the tense/lax contrast as long/short, instead, with /i/ described as the long variant of /ɪ/ and /u/ the long variant of /ʊ/. Finally, there is some debate regarding the tenseness of low vowels. On the one hand, it is posited that low vowels cannot be tense due to articulatory constraints (it is thought to be quite challenging to achieve the tense articulation with the lower jaw in the open position characteristic of low vowels). On the other hand, from a theoretical perspective, it is generally accepted that tense vowels can occur in open syllables in English, while lax vowels cannot, and the low /ɑ/ appears in a variety of open syllables (e.g., *ma, pa, ha, ta-da, la, spa*); additionally, the merging of /ɑ/ and /ɔ/ in some English dialects has yielded additional examples, /ɔ/ in some dialects and /ɑ/ in others (e.g., *maw, paw, caw, thaw, saw, law, raw*).

A Note About /ɔ/

Not all dialects of American English have maintained the phoneme /ɔ/ due to a contemporary and ongoing phenomenon referred to as the *cot-caught* merger, which has caused some native speakers of American English to lose the /ɑ–ɔ/ distinction in their speech. While those who maintain the distinction use /ɑ/ for words like *cot, pod,* and *tot* and /ɔ/ for *caught, pawed,* and *taught*, some speakers produce both words of each set - *cot-caught, pod-pawed, tot-taught* - with the same vowel sound, most like /ɑ/. Some native speakers in many parts of the US clearly demonstrate this merger, while others show no sign of it (Giegerich, 1992; Hillenbrand, 2003; Labov, Ash, & Boberg, 2006; Ladefoged, 1993; Ladefoged & Disner, 2012). The reader should note that, due to the idiosyncratic nature of speech patterns and influence from other dialects, native speakers from similar backgrounds may differ in their use of /ɔ/.

A Note About Rhotacized Vowels

Comparatively rare among the world's languages (Ladefoged & Maddieson, 1996) but common in American English are rhotacized vowels such as [ɚ], as in *bird* and *earth,* and characterized by an 'r'-like quality throughout the entire duration of the vowel (Ladefoged & Disner, 2012). These vowels are not typically seen as phonemic categories in English, but rather analyzed as an underlying vowel influenced by a following consonant [ɹ] (Giegerich, 1992; Ladefoged, 1993). Although they are not seen as phonemic, these vowels are important to mention in a phonetic description of English, since they occur fairly frequently in American English and are often particularly challenging to non-native speakers.

Vowel Reduction

Vowel reduction is often a challenge for ESL learners English language learners. **Lexical stress** (referring to the use of volume, pitch, and vowel duration to emphasize certain syllables and reduce others at the word level) affects the pronunciation of English vowels. While stressed vowels are generally fully articulated, and the syllable in which they appear is louder and higher in pitch than others within the same word, unstressed vowels of English tend to undergo a process of **vowel reduction**, or changes to the quality of the vowel generally including **shortening** (a shorter vowel duration compared to the duration of the same underlying vowel in a stressed position) and **centralization** (a reduction in articulatory effort which has the effect of pushing the vowel toward a mid, central articulation).

In American English, unstressed high tense /i/ and /u/ may reduce to lower, more central /ɪ/ and /ʊ/; many unstressed lax vowels are reduced to a centralized [ə], referred to as schwa (Chomsky & Halle, 1968). Consider the English pronunciation of *banana*: the first and third vowel sounds, each represented by the letter 'a', are reduced to short *uh*-like sounds (schwa), while the second vowel sound, also represented orthographically by the letter 'a', is articulated fully, as [æ], thanks to its stressed status.

In some varieties of English, a high, central [ɨ] occurs as a reduced vowel, in addition to [ə]: in these varieties, [ə] occurs in unstressed word-final positions (e.g., the unstressed vowel in *Rosa*) and inflected forms of such words (e.g., the unstressed vowel in *Rosa's*), while [ɨ] occurs in most other unstressed positions (e.g., the unstressed vowel in *roses*) (Flemming & Johnson, 2007; Ladefoged, 2001; 2005). The reader should note that the amount of reduction in American English may be related to dialect, style, and register, and the same speaker may reduce fewer vowels in careful, formal speech than in casual conversation.

A final note regarding the duration of English vowels concerns the influence of the flanking consonants on vowel duration. English vowels tend to be longer before and after a voiced consonant (b, d, g, v, z, ʒ, dʒ) than its voiceless variant at the same place and manner of articulation (p, t, k, f, s, ʃ, tʃ) - so /i/ is slightly shorter in *seat* than in *seed* - and longer before fricatives (f, v, s, z, ʃ, ʒ) than stops of the same place of articulation and voicing (p, b, t, d, k, g) - so /i/ is slightly shorter in *team* than in *seem*. For more information on this topic, see the next chapter – "English Sounds in Context: The Pronunciation of Phonemes and Morphemes", which explains these issues in detail.

IMPLICATIONS FOR TEACHING ENGLISH LANGUAGE LEARNERS

A review of recent teacher education materials suggests that articulatory phonetics represents a neglected topic. The question of how speech sounds are produced or articulated through the interaction of physiological structures in the vocal tract, as well as the relevance of this question to pronunciation is rarely addressed even in the most popular textbook series (Jones, 2018). It is, therefore, not surprising that second language teachers report being unprepared to address the topic of the sound system of English and its distance from the learners' native languages, let alone translate this theoretical material into effective perception or pronunciation improving classroom activities (Fraser, 2002). Yet, the Teaching English to Speakers of Other Languages (TESOL) / Council for the Accreditation of Educator Preparation (CAEP) PK–12 Teacher Education Program Standards (2009) specify that ESL teachers must understand the rules of the sound system of English, and that they should also be able to recognize and describe similarities and major differences between English and the native languages commonly spoken by their students at different proficiency levels (Standard 1.a.2, in particular).

In relationship to articulatory phonetics, the standards mean that effective ESL teachers are presumed to be able to describe how the target sounds are articulated in the ESL variety they are teaching in accordance with their learners' needs and identity. Thus, when English language learners practice pronouncing an English vowel, the teachers are assumed to be able to utilize their knowledge of articulatory phonetics and compare between the articulatory sound inventories of source and target languages, draw the learner's attention to the contrast, and guide the student's production by explaining how the target sound is produced drawing on the categories on height, backness, rounding, and tenseness, as well as context dependence. Such discussions can be effectively supported with charts, drawings, diagrams or, more recently, multimodal digital imaging of the vocal tract kinematics, as well as waveforms and spectrograms produced with acoustical analysis software tools.

Systematic phonetic instruction would additionally cover articulation of analogous phones, differences between learners' L1 and L2 phonological systems with regards to phonemic inventories, as well as connections with literacy-related activities such as grapheme–phoneme correspondences, and overview of phonological processes and suprasegmental features. The most commonly used and frequently investigated approach to focusing learners' attention on specific articulatory features of analogous phones includes introducing learners to perceptional and production of minimal pairs. A **minimal pair** is a pair of words in a given language which have different meanings in that language and whose realizations are different by only one sound, which serves to demonstrate that the two sounds contrasted by the two words are different phonemes, or meaningfully different sounds in that language (Shriberg & Kent, 2012; Zsiga, 2013). Indeed, the simplest way to feel changes in vowel height, backness, rounding, and tenseness (all of which we will do below) is to pay close attention to the articulators – tongue, lips, teeth, etc. – while pronouncing a minimal pair. The words that language instructors may want to choose to get a feel for vowel parameters will be words that have all the same (if any) consonant sounds flanking their vowel sounds, and only the vowels will differ from one word to the other (e.g., *bed* and *bad*, *pit* and *put*, *hot* and *hut*). It is important to note that minimal pairs are based on the sounds rather than the letters that comprise them, i.e. differences in sound do not always align perfectly with a single difference in spelling. In some cases, there will be more than one difference in the words' spellings, but a pair of words is a true minimal pair if there is only one difference in pronunciation from one word to the other. For example, *phone* and *tone* are a minimal pair even though *phone* has one extra consonant letter at its beginning; in this case, the ***two letters*** *ph* at the start of *phone* represent only ***one sound***, and therefore it is still a minimal pair with *tone*, which is identical with the exception of having a *t* sound (represented orthographically by the letter 't') where *phone* has an *f* sound (represented orthographically by the letters 'ph'). Similarly, with vowels, students should be instructed to pay attention to situations where double letters represent only one sound: *soon* and *sun*, *suit* and *sit*, *sound* and *send* are all minimal pairs even though the first word of each pair has two vowel letters (representing only one vowel sound) while the second word of each pair has only one vowel letter (also representing one vowel sound).

Minimal pairs are useful for isolating speech sounds in order to compare them to and learn to differentiate them from other, similar sounds within the same phonetic environment; maintaining the same phonetic environment outside of the target sound helps reduce the effects of co-articulation on the target sound – for example, if we were comparing the same vowels in *steered* and *caps*, the additional differences between those two words might complicate the task of focusing on the vowel sound. Minimal pairs are, therefore, helpful for isolating articulatory gestures and can be used to create a basis for a focused and systematic articulatory instruction. While explicit articulatory training does not guarantee success in articulation, there is also some encouraging evidence to suggest that it may have a positive impact on adult listeners' ability to produce sounds in their new language more accurately, albeit such an impact may vary depending on learner proficiency (e.g., see Cibelli, 2015).

The TESOL/CAEP P–12 standards specify that the ability to understand and recognize the target language system, in combination with communicative skills, enhances English language learners' oral proficiency development. There is sufficient empirical evidence to argue that explicit phonetics instruction can indeed have a positive impact on English language learners' efforts to improve their pronunciation (Barrera-Pardo, 2004), and that phonetics instruction can both serve as a necessary precursor to target-like production and can also be effective for attuning the perception of learners at multiple stages of development (Golestani & Zatorre, 2009). Explicit articulatory training has been investigated in several recent studies revealing the facilitatory effects of articulatory knowledge on perceptual learning in second language learners through explicit articulatory explanations and exercises (Herd, Jongman, & Sereno, 2013; Hirata, 2004; Lacabex et al., 2008). A considerable number of scholars and studies point to the existence of the production-perception link and have offered empirical evidence of a positive impact of perceptual training on learners' production performance (Flege, Bohn, & Jang, 1997; Sakai & Moorman, 2018) and vice versa (Linebaugh & Roche, 2013). In terms of ESL methodology, it is therefore reasonable to conclude that discriminatory perception training and production may mutually contribute to supporting language acquisition (cf. Hickok & Poeppel, 2007).

It is also important to bear in mind that effective instruction supporting English language learners' communicative skills cannot be limited to a segmental perspective on phonetics instruction which might assist learners in gaining explicit knowledge to support their performance on certain types of tasks (e.g., producing individual sounds or words) but not in the context of authentic open-ended communication. Therefore, while the focus on suprasegmental features such as stress, rhythm, and intonation are beyond the scope of the chapter, they should undoubtedly be integrated with segmental articulatory training as students engage in meaningful communication practice.

DISCUSSION QUESTIONS

1. How are the descriptions of vowels provided in this chapter different from the way vowel sounds are typically described by native speakers or by/to English language learners?

2. How would you explain to an English language learner in plain English (avoiding the specialized terminology you just learned) the difference between the English vowels /i/ and /ɪ/? What about /ɑ/ and /ʌ/? What advice would you give a student struggling to produce these vowels?

3. Why might it be sufficient to describe the American English /ɑ/ as simply low and back? What articulatory information is missing from this description, and why might some sources leave this information out when referring to American English vowels?

4. Which parameter – height, backness, rounding, or tenseness – do you suppose may be the easiest to teach to a non-native learner? Which may be the hardest? Why?

5. Conventional wisdom and anecdotal evidence often suggest that people who already speak several languages are more successful at learning new ones. How might you support or refute this argument using the information introduced in this chapter, particularly in terms of learning new vowel systems?

EXERCISES

Practice Working With Articulatory Description

1. Supply the articulatory description for the following English vowels:
    a)   /i/   b) /æ/   c) /ʊ/   d) /ʌ/   e) /e/

2. Identify the English vowels based on the following articulatory descriptions:
    a.   high, front, lax, unrounded
    b.   high, back, tense, rounded
    c.   low, back, lax, unrounded
    d.   mid, back, tense, rounded
    e.   mid, front, lax, unrounded

Practice Identifying the Vowel Phonemes in Real English Words

3. Supply the IPA symbol for the vowels in the following English words:
    a)   let   b) lot   c) loot   d) late   e) lit

4. Supply a novel minimal pair for each of the following contrasts:
    a)   /i/ - /ɪ/   b) /ɪ/ - /e/   c) /e/ - /ɛ/   d) /ɛ/ - /æ/
    e)   /æ/ - /ɑ/   f) /ɑ/ - /ɔ/   g) /ɔ/ - /o/   h) /o/ - /ʊ/
    i)   /ʊ/ - /u/   j) /ɑ/ - /ʌ/   k) /ʌ/ - /ʊ/   l) /ɔ/ - /ʊ/

Practice Distinguishing Monophthongs and Diphthongs

5. Which of the following words contain diphthongs or diphthongized vowels in American English?
    bee, class, coat, fit, face, hot, how, joy, my, should, spent, stuck, suit,

Practice Identifying Reduced Vowels

6. Identify the letters that represent reduced vowels in the following English words:
    a)   banana   b) comet   c) soda   d) over   e) compare

Pronunciation Practice

7. Identify the word containing the specified vowel in each set of words:
    a)   /ʌ/ duck/look/block   b) /i/ kit/keep/kept   c) /ɛ/ bead/red/vein

8. From each set of three, identify the word that has a different vowel than the other two:
    a)   teach/sit/pier   b) bear/fled/share   c) hook/should/shout

Practice Working With a Vowel Chart

9.   Identify all English vowel phonemes higher than /ɛ/.
10. If you know that a language has only three vowel phonemes, what phonemes are these most likely to be? Sketch this vowel system on a vowel chart and explain your reasoning. (Hint: there are multiple possibilities; consider how vowels are distributed across the vowel space in the English vowel system vs. the five-vowel system of languages like Spanish).

REFERENCES

Barrera-Pardo, D. (2004). Can pronunciation be taught? A review of research and implications for teaching. *Revista Alicantina de Estudios Ingleses: RAEI*, (17), 6-38.

Chomsky, N., & Halle, M. (1968). *The sound pattern of English*. New York, NY: Harper & Row.

Cibelli, E. (2015). *Aspects of articulatory and perceptual learning in novel phoneme acquisition (Doctoral dissertation)*. Berkeley, CA: University of California – Berkeley. Retrieved from https://escholarship.org/uc/item/9tq441d9

Disner, S. F. (1984). Insights on vowel space. In I. Maddieson (Ed.), *Patterns of sounds* (pp. 136–155). Cambridge, UK: Cambridge University Press.

Flege, J. E., Bohn, O. S., & Jang, S. (1997). Effects of experience on non-native speakers' production and perception of English vowels. *Journal of Phonetics*, 25(4), 437–470. doi:10.1006/jpho.1997.0052

Flemming, E., & Johnson, S. (2007). Rosa's roses: Reduced vowels in American English. *Journal of the International Phonetic Association*, 37(1), 83–96. doi:10.1017/S0025100306002817

Fraser, H. (2002, October). *Change, challenge, and opportunity in pronunciation and oral communication*. Paper presented at Plenary Address at English Australia Conference, Canberra, Australia.

Gick, B., Wilson, I., & Derrick, D. (2013). *Articulatory phonetics*. Malden, MA: Wiley-Blackwell.

Giegerich, H. J. (1992). *English phonology*. Cambridge, UK: Cambridge University Press. doi:10.1017/CBO9781139166126

Golestani, N., & Zatorre, R. J. (2009). Individual differences in the acquisition of second language phonology. *Brain and Language*, 109(2-3), 55–67. doi:10.1016/j.bandl.2008.01.005 PMID:18295875

Hagiwara, R. (1997). Dialect variation and formant frequency: The American English vowels revisited. *The Journal of the Acoustical Society of America*, 102(1), 655–658. doi:10.1121/1.419712

Herd, W., Jongman, A., & Sereno, J. (2013). Perceptual and production training of intervocalic /d, ɾ, r/ in American English learners of Spanish. *The Journal of the Acoustical Society of America*, 133(6), 4247–4255. doi:10.1121/1.4802902 PMID:23742375

Hickok, G., & Poeppel, D. (2007). The cortical organization of speech processing. *Nature Reviews. Neuroscience*, *8*(5), 393–402. doi:10.1038/nrn2113 PMID:17431404

Hillenbrand, J. M. (2003). American English: Southern Michigan. *Journal of the International Phonetic Association*, *33*(1), 121–126. doi:10.1017/S0025100303001221

Hillenbrand, J. M., Clark, M. J., & Houde, R. A. (2000). Some effect of duration on vowel recognition. *The Journal of the Acoustical Society of America*, *108*(6), 3013–3022. doi:10.1121/1.1323463 PMID:11144593

Hirata, Y. (2004). Computer assisted pronunciation training for native English speakers learning Japanese pitch and durational contrasts. *Computer Assisted Language Learning*, *17*(3-4), 357–376. doi:10.1080/0958822042000319629

Jones, D. (1969). *An outline of English phonetics* (9th ed.). Cambridge, MA: W. Heffer and Sons.

Jones, T. (2018). Materials Development for Teaching Pronunciation. The TESOL Encyclopedia of English Language Teaching, 1-7.

Kondaurova, M. V., & Francis, A. L. (2006). Russian and Spanish listener's perception of the English tense/lax vowel contrast: Contributions of native language allophony and individual experience. *The Journal of the Acoustical Society of America*, *120*(5), 3293–3293. doi:10.1121/1.4777845

Kondaurova, M. V., & Francis, A. L. (2008). The relationship between native allophonic experience with vowel duration and perception of the English tense/lax vowel contrast by Spanish and Russian listeners. *The Journal of the Acoustical Society of America*, *124*(6), 3959–3971. doi:10.1121/1.2999341 PMID:19206820

Labov, W., Ash, S., & Boberg, C. (2006). *The atlas of North American English*. Berlin: Mouton-de Gruyter. doi:10.1515/9783110167467

Lacabex, E. G., Lecumberri, M. L. G., & Cooke, M. (2008). Identification of the contrast full vowel-schwa: Training effects and generalization to a new perceptual context. *Ilha do Desterro*, *55*, 173–196.

Ladefoged, P. (1993). *A course in phonetics* (3rd ed.). Fort Worth, TX: Harcourt Brace & Company.

Ladefoged, P. (1999). Illustrations of the IPA: American English. In *Handbook of the International Phonetic Association* (pp. 41–44). Cambridge, UK: Cambridge University Press.

Ladefoged, P. (2001). *A course in phonetics* (4th ed.). Boston, MA: Heinle & Heinle.

Ladefoged, P. (2005). *Vowels and consonants: An introduction to the sounds of languages* (2nd ed.). Malden, MA: Blackwell.

Ladefoged, P., & Disner, S. F. (2012). *Vowels and consonants* (3rd ed.). Malden, MA: Wiley-Blackwell.

Ladefoged, P., & Maddieson, I. (1996). *The sounds of the world's languages*. Oxford, UK: Wiley-Blackwell.

Linebaugh, G., & Roche, T. (2013). Learning to hear by learning to speak. *Australian Review of Applied Linguistics*, *36*(2), 146–159. doi:10.1075/aral.36.2.02lin

Sakai, M., & Moorman, C. (2018). Can perception training improve the production of second language phonemes? A meta-analytic review of 25 years of perception training research. *Applied Psycholinguistics*, *39*(1), 187–224. doi:10.1017/S0142716417000418

Shriberg, L. D., & Kent, R. D. (2012). *Clinical phonetics* (4th ed.). Boston, MA: Pearson.

Zsiga, E. C. (2013). *The sounds of language: An introduction to phonetics and phonology*. Malden, MA: Wiley-Blackwell.

ADDITIONAL READING

Ashby, P. (2011). *Understanding phonetics*. New York, NY: Routledge.

Clopper, C. G., Pisoni, D. B., & de Jong, K. (2005). Acoustic characteristics of the vowel systems of six regional varieties of American English. *The Journal of the Acoustical Society of America*, *118*(3), 1661–1676. doi:10.1121/1.2000774 PMID:16240825

Fox, R. A., & Jacewicz, E. (2009). Cross-dialectal variation in formant dynamics of American English vowels. *The Journal of the Acoustical Society of America*, *126*(5), 2603–2618. doi:10.1121/1.3212921 PMID:19894839

Hillenbrand, J. M., Getty, L. A., Clark, M. J., & Wheeler, K. (1995). Acoustic characteristics of American English vowels. *The Journal of the Acoustical Society of America*, *97*(5), 3099–3111. doi:10.1121/1.411872 PMID:7759650

Jacewicz, E., Fox, R. A., & Salmons, J. (2007). Vowel duration in three American English dialects. *American Speech*, *82*(4), 367–385. doi:10.1215/00031283-2007-024 PMID:20198113

Kretzschmar, W. A., Bounds, P., Hettel, J., Pederson, L., Juuso, I., Opas-Hänninen, L. L., & Seppänen, T. (2013). The digital archive of southern speech (DASS). *Southwest Journal of Linguistics*, *27*(2), 17–38.

ENDNOTES

[1]   It is argued to be impossible for low vowels to be tense due to their open articulations; thus, the 'lax' classification of /æ/ has less to do with articulation and more with other considerations, such as its failure to appear in open syllables in English. Although it is relatively long in duration (recall that longer duration is typically associated with the category tense), its open articulation and inability to appear in open syllables are sufficient to definitively motivate its classification as a lax vowel.

[2]   Some accounts describe /ɔ/ as tense, citing this vowel's ability to appear in open syllables (e.g., maw, paw, caw, thaw, saw, law, raw) and its rather long duration (recall that tense vowels are typically longer than lax vowels, an opposition demonstrated by the duration differences in the pairs

/i/ - /ɪ/ and /u/ - /ʊ/); others list it as a lax vowel. There is perhaps somewhat more support overall for the former position; nevertheless, this debate remains unresolved definitively in the literature.

3   Like /ɔ/, the vowel represented by the symbol /ɑ/ is described by some accounts as tense and by others as lax. As for /æ/, it is thought to be impossible to apply the category tense to the low /ɑ/ on a purely articulatory basis; however, /ɑ/ demonstrates the ability to occur in open syllables (e.g., *ma, pa, ha, ta-da, la, spa*), which is atypical for vowels categorized as lax. An additional consideration is that actual realizations of the vowel represented by the symbol /ɑ/ vary somewhat in tenseness: in "pot", /ɑ/ is comparatively more back and lax, while in "father" it is comparatively more central and tense. Thus, as for /ɔ/, there remains some disagreement in the literature about whether /ɑ/ should be classified as tense or lax. An additional consideration is that actual realizations of the vowel represented by the symbol /ɑ/ vary somewhat in tenseness: in "pot", /ɑ/ is comparatively more back and lax, while in "father" it is comparatively more central and tense.

Unit 8
Phonology

Chapter 13
English Sounds in Context:
The Pronunciation of Phonemes and Morphemes

Caroline Wiltshire
University of Florida, USA

ABSTRACT

The chapter takes the reader from the concrete phonetic descriptions of sounds, found in Chapters 11 and 12, to the use of these sounds in English. As in every language, sounds are influenced by their context. A large part of phonological description of a language is an effort to describe how the "same" sound is pronounced differently in different contexts, both phonetic and morphological. The chapter provides the phonemes of English, which are the distinctive units of sound, and examples of how they vary in context. It also illustrates the variation of English morphemes in context, by providing examples of allomorphy. Some implications of variation in context for teaching English are discussed.

WHAT IS PHONOLOGY?

Phonology is the branch of theoretical linguistics which focusses on the sounds of spoken languages, both in specific languages and cross-linguistically. Within a specific language, we seek to explain the system that speakers use to produce and interpret the sounds of that language, while cross-linguistically, we look for patterns that are systematic and shared. These patterns can involve not only individual consonants and vowels, but also larger units, such as syllables, which group both consonants and vowels together, or stress, which affects entire syllables, and smaller characteristics, such as voicing or rounding, which are just one component of the production of an individual consonant or vowel. While phonetics investigates the physical properties of sounds (production, acoustics, perception), phonology considers the use of sounds to encode meaning in a linguistic system. For example, phonology finds that each language organizes a wide variety of phonetic sounds into a smaller system of **phonemes**, the units which are able to make a contrast in meaning in a language; each phoneme may have a range of pronunciations in different phonetic contexts. These phonemes are combined to spell out the **morphemes**, or meaningful

DOI: 10.4018/978-1-5225-8467-4.ch013

units of a language (see Chapters 2 and 3), but phonemes can systematically change when morphemes are added together to build words. Thus, both phonemes and morphemes can be pronounced with a variety of phonetic realizations, depending on context. Phonology seeks to discover the patterns governing these changes.

CONTRAST IN ENGLISH SOUNDS

Increased phonetic sophistication has allowed us to distinguish a vast variety of phonetic sounds used in English. However, not all of these phonetic sounds and distinctions do equal work in English, or in any language. Phonology begins with the study of which sounds are capable of making a meaningful difference between words, and organizing these sounds into distinct **phonemes**. The idea goes back to Saussure (1916/1959), who argued that the role of sounds in language is to make contrasts among words: "Phonemes are characterized…simply by the fact that they are distinct" (p. 119). Changing one phoneme changes the meaning of a word; for example, the words *pat* and *bat* are identical except for the initial sounds, which are therefore responsible for indicating the difference in meaning between the two words. Such pairs of words are called "**minimal pairs**": words that differ in only a single sound but differ in meaning. Thus the definition of the phoneme, as in Swadesh (1934, p. 117) is based on its ability to distinguish meaning in minimal pairs: "the phoneme is the smallest potential unit of difference between similar words recognizable as different to the native [speaker]". Some examples are provided in (1), following the convention that phonemes are provided inside slanted brackets / /, while the phonetics are provided in square brackets [ ]. The appearance of special phonetic diacritics, such as [ʰ] will be explained shortly; none of them is responsible for a contrast in English.

(1)   Some minimal pairs and phonemes of English

	Spelling		Phonetics		Phonemes
Word-initial contrast	*pat*	vs. *bat*	[pʰæt]	vs. [bæt]	/p/ vs. /b/
	could	vs. *good*	[kʰʊd]	vs. [gʊd]	/k/ vs. /g/
Word-final contrast	*sun*	vs. *sum*	[sʌ̃n]	vs. [sʌ̃m]	/n/ vs. /m/
	hiss	vs. *his*	[hɪ̆s]	vs. [hɪz]	/s/ vs. /z/
Word-internal contrast	*pit*	vs. *put*	[pʰɪ̆t]	vs. [pʰʊ̆t]	/ɪ/ vs. /ʊ/
	pat	vs. *pet*	[pʰæt]	vs. [pʰɛ̆t]	/æ/ vs. /ɛ/

Note that both vowels, such as /ɪ, ʊ, æ, ɛ/, and consonants, such as /p, b, m, n/, are phonemes, and furthermore, that a contrast between two words in a minimal pair can be made by the sounds at the beginning (*could* vs. *good*), end (*sun* vs. *sum*) or middle of a word (*pit* vs. *put*); all are equally valid as proof of the phoneme's ability to make a difference between words. Finally, note too that spelling, particularly English spelling, does not always correctly reflect the contrast in sound (as in *hiss* vs. *his*), so minimal pairs are based upon the phonetic transcription rather than the spelling.

THE PHONEME INVENTORY OF ENGLISH

Every language has an inventory of sounds that can make a contrast in meaning (that is, the phonemes), and the Tables 1 and 2 present minimal pairs to show the sounds that make a contrast in English. The sets of phonemes are usually different for different languages, and may even be slightly different in different dialects of the same language. A crucial part of learning a new language is learning which sounds are capable of making differences in meaning.

To show the inventory of consonant phonemes in American English, Table 1 below is organized by the phonetic characteristics of the sounds (this chart follows Hayes 2009). Along with each phoneme is provided a sample word in which that phoneme appears, with the letters used for the phoneme in question underlined.

In most cases, the words form a minimal pair/triplet/etc. with other similar sounds on the chart. There are a few exceptions, however, where a non-identical word is used because a word changed in only the relevant sound does not happen to exist in English; the methods for proving that phonemes are distinct in such cases, using similar words, are discussed in a later section (Methods).

The vowel system of American English can be plotted similarly, as in Table 2 (again based on Hayes 2009). The system includes vowels with a single quality (monophthongs) and vowels that are followed by a high offglide, approximately either [ɪ] or [ʊ] in quality (diphthongs). The diphthongs that begin with an upper mid /e/ or /o/ are included in the table, while the diphthongs that begin with a lower vowel are listed below it, as the two parts of these latter diphthongs differ in both height and front/back.

These tables present a fairly common set of consonant and vowel contrasts used in many varieties of English, although even within American English there are some dialectal differences. For example, the vowel in *bought* is given above as /ɔ/, but for many Americans there is no contrast between this vowel and that of *hot* (Labov, Ash, and Boberg, 2008). In fact, a pair of words that is a minimal pair in some

Table 1. The consonant phoneme contrasts in English

	Bilabial	Labio-Dental	Dental	Alveolar	Post-Alveolar	Palatal	Velar	Labio-Velar	Glottal
stop (-voice)	/p/ *pill*			/t/ *till*			/k/ *kill*		
stop (+voice)	/b/ *bill*			/d/ *dill*			/g/ *gill*		
affricate (-voice)					/tʃ/ *chill*				
affricate (+voice)					/dʒ/ *Jill*				
nasal	/m/ *mill* *sum*			/n/ *nil* *sun*			/ŋ/ *sung*		
fricative (-voice)		/f/ *fill*	/θ/ *thin*[1]	/s/ *sill*	/ʃ/ *shill*				/h/ *hill*
fricative (+voice)		/v/ *villa*	/ð/ *this*	/z/ *Zillow*	/ʒ/ *vision*				
lateral approx..				/l/ *Lynn*					
approx..				/ɹ/ *rill*		/j/ *yell*		/w/ *will*	

Table 2. The vowel phoneme contrasts in English

	Front Unrounded	**Central Unrounded**	**Back Unrounded**	**Back Rounded**
upper high **lower high**	/i/ b<u>ea</u>t /ɪ/ b<u>i</u>t			/u/ b<u>oo</u>t /ʊ/ f<u>oo</u>t
upper mid **lower mid**	/eɪ/ b<u>ai</u>t /ɛ/ b<u>e</u>t	/ɚ/ B<u>er</u>t /ə/ abb<u>o</u>t	/ʌ/ b<u>u</u>t	/oʊ/ b<u>oa</u>t /ɔ/ b<u>ou</u>ght
low	/æ/ b<u>a</u>t	/a/ h<u>o</u>t, f<u>a</u>ther²		
diphthongs:	/aɪ/ b<u>i</u>te, /aʊ/ b<u>ou</u>t, /ɔɪ/ C<u>oi</u>t			

dialects, *cot* vs. *caught,* may have identical pronunciations in others, with both *cot/caught* pronounced as [kʰăt]). For the consonants, some dialects have a distinction (not included above) between the voiced labio-velar approximant /w/ as in <u>w</u>ill or <u>w</u>itch and a voiceless labio-velar fricative /ʍ/ as in <u>wh</u>ich (Hayes, 2009). That is, even within a system like American English, there may be variations; if we look further afield, to British, Irish, Australian, and other varieties of English, we will find other minor points of difference in the inventory of contrasts. However, overall, the system of phonemes for most varieties of English includes about 40 contrasts: 23-24 consonants and 16-17 vowels.

As discussed in the next section, each phoneme is produced in a variety of ways, depending on its phonetic context, so that the number of sounds used in English is much larger. The phonemic system organizes all these sounds into those that are meaningfully distinct vs. those that are merely contextual variants. When transcribing English, the level of detail depends on the purpose. For native speakers of English, a phonemic transcription is enough, as speakers know how to pronounce each phoneme in context. For non-native speakers, or when comparing different varieties of English, more phonetic detail is required to show the specifics of pronunciation for those lacking the phonemic rules or for those with different rules.

NON-CONTRASTIVE SOUNDS IN ENGLISH

How each phoneme is pronounced phonetically often varies depending on the phonetic context in which it is pronounced. Therefore, what we consider to be the same phoneme in a language can be a whole set of phonetically different sounds, in different phonetic contexts. These different pronunciations of the same phoneme are called its "**allophones**", the variant pronunciations of a phoneme in context. Because they are different pronunciations of the same phoneme, they do not make a contrast even though they are phonetically distinct; these phonetic variants cannot be used to make a contrast in a minimal pair.

Generally, each allophone of a phoneme occurs in a different context. This is described as a "**complementary distribution**" because the distribution of the allophones complements each other. For example, the phoneme /t/ in English is pronounced one way word-initially, with a different sound between vowels, and with a third sound word-finally. Each of these pronunciations of /t/ is one of its allophones, and the three allophones are complementary as they each occur in a distinct context (a sound cannot be both word-initial and word-final, for example). Because the sounds are in complementary distribution, they cannot make a contrast in a minimal pair because they cannot appear in the same position in a word. Allophones of the same phoneme are representatives of that same phoneme, and native speakers of a language tend to hear them as the phoneme, rather than hearing the phonetic differences among allophones.

In addition to having its own inventory of phonemes, each language has its own system for pronouncing the allophone in different contexts. These rules are automatic for native speakers of a language, so much so that when learning a new language, speakers tend to follow the allophonic rules of their first language, even though that may not be appropriate in the new language. While replacing one phoneme with a different phoneme results in a different word (or no word at all), using the wrong allophone for the context is more likely to result in a non-native accent. Learners need to be aware of both these possible errors, if they want to avoid them.

EXAMPLES OF ALLOPHONES IN ENGLISH

Allophonic variation is found in both consonants and vowels, and can be caused by the immediate phonetic context (the surrounding consonants or vowels), by a sound's position in the word or syllable, or by whether it is in a stressed or unstressed syllable. This section will provide several examples of allophonic variation that are common in most varieties of English, including the aspiration of voiceless stops (/p t k/), the velarization of /l/ syllable-finally, and shortening and nasalization of vowels.

First, the phonemes /p,t,k/ each have at least two allophones, based on their position in a syllable at the beginning of a word. In absolute word-initial position of a one-syllable word, a /p t k/ phoneme is pronounced with a following puff of air, called aspiration, as [pʰ tʰ kʰ], but after an /s/, these phonemes are pronounced with an unaspirated allophone, as [p t k], as shown in the words in (2).

(2) Two allophones each for /p, t, k/:

Phoneme	Spelling	Sound	Spelling	Sound	Allophones
/p/	*pat*	[pʰæt]	*spat*	[spæt]	[pʰ, p]
	pit	[pʰɪt]	*spit*	[spɪt]	
	pike	[pʰăɪk]	*spike*	[spăɪk]	
	pool	[pʰuɫ]	*spool*	[spuɫ]	
/t/	*tote*	[tʰŏʊt]	*stoat*	[stŏʊt]	[tʰ, t]
	top	[tʰăp]	*stop*	[stăp]	
	take	[tʰĕɪk]	*steak*	[stĕɪk]	
	tone	[tʰõõn]	*stone*	[stõõn]	
/k/	*kale*	[kʰeɪɫ]	*scale*	[skeɪɫ]	[kʰ, k]
	cope	[kʰŏʊp]	*scope*	[skŏʊp]	
	key	[kʰi]	*ski*	[ski]	
	coop	[kʰŭp]	*scoop*	[skŭp]	

In each word pair across a row, the only difference between the word is whether it begins with a /p t k/ or with an /sp st sk/. The two allophones of each voiceless stop are in complementary distribution in these examples. For example, in word-initial position where the aspirated [pʰ] is used), the unaspirated [p] would not be used (*[pæt]),[3] and likewise after /s/, where [p] is appropriate, the [pʰ] allophone would sound wrong to native speakers (*[spʰæt]). These allophones cannot be used to make a contrast or change in meaning, because they both are allophones of the same phoneme /p/. A lack of knowledge of the rules of allophonics leads to speakers mispronouncing words in ways that at best sound like a foreign accent (e.g., [spʰæt]), and at worst can lead to misunderstandings. For example, [pæt] with an unaspirated voiceless [p] sounds more similar to the English word *bat* than to *pat*, since phonetically the [p] sound is closer to the expected allophone of /b/ than of /p/ in word-initial position; in American English, the voiced stop /b/ is unaspirated and weakly voiced in word-initial position in *bat*, while the voiceless stop /p/ is strongly aspirated word-initially in *pat*.

A second example of a phoneme and its allophones is the lateral phoneme /l/, which has different allophones at the beginning and end of syllables. In syllable-initial and word-initial position, the /l/ is pronounced as the alveolar lateral approximant [l], as in the examples on the left below. In syllable and word final position, however, it is pronounced with a secondary velarization, meaning that the back of the tongue is raised towards the velum at the same time as the tongue tip touches the alveolar ridge. This results in the sound transcribed phonetically as [ɫ], as in the examples on the right. Two syllable words appear in the data below with the IPA symbol ['] appearing before the syllable which has main stress.

(3) Two allophones of the phoneme /l/ = [l, ɫ]:

Syllable-initial /l/ = [l]   **Syllable-final /l/ = [ɫ]**

laugh	[læf]	*fall*	[faɫ]	*bale*	[beɪɫ]
loop	[lŭp]	*pool*	[pʰuɫ]	*bell*	[bɛɫ]
listen	['lɪsẽn]	*file*	[faɪɫ]	*feel*	[fiɫ]
lie	[laɪ]	*toll*	[tʰoʊɫ]	*pull*	[pʰʊɫ]
allow	[ə'laʊ]	*ill*	[ɪɫ]	*foul*	[faʊɫ]
blend	[blẽnd]	*wealth*	[wɛɫ̪θ]	*filthy*	['fɪɫ̪θi]

The two environments are complementary, as the /l/ is either syllable-initial or syllable-final, so the two allophones [l] and [ɫ] cannot appear in the same context nor be used to distinguish word meanings. That is, we cannot make a minimal pair contrasting the two sounds in word-initial position, because we find only [l] there; likely we cannot make a minimal pair contrasting the two in word-final position, because there we find only [ɫ]. Complementary distribution of two sounds guarantees that we cannot make the sounds contrast with each other in a minimal pair.

Likewise, consonants may have multiple allophones. In the examples for /l/ above, a closer inspection reveals that the /l/ has a dental place of articulation in *wealth* [wɛɫ̪θ] and *filthy* ['fɪɫ̪θi], where /l/ appears before an interdental fricative /θ/; [ɫ̪] is another allophone of /l/ in a very specific context. The phoneme /l/ has yet another allophone, which occurs when /l/ is pronounced after a voiceless stop in word-initial position. This is the position in which the voiceless stop is usually aspirated. In this case, the aspiration of the initial stop carries over onto the /l/, making it into a voiceless [l̥]; a circle below a normally voiced symbol indicates that it is voiceless. This pattern affects not only the lateral approximant, but the other approximants /w j ɹ/ as well, as shown below. The symbol for the voiceless palatal approximant is [j̊] here, as a circle below the segment would be hard to see.

(4)

After voiceless stops		After voiced stops		Phoneme & Allophones
played	[pl̥eɪd]	*blade*	[bleɪd]	/l/ = [l̥ l]
clay	[kl̥eɪ]	*glade*	[gleɪd]	
pray	[pɹ̥eɪ]	*brain*	[bɹẽɪn]	/ɹ/ = [ɹ̥ ɹ]
train	[tɹ̥ẽɪn]	*drain*	[dɹẽɪn]	
crane	[kɹ̥ẽɪn]	*grain*	[gɹẽɪn]	
tweed	[tw̥id]	*dweeb*	[dwib]	/w/ = [w̥ w]
queen	[kw̥ĩn]	*guacamole*	[gwakə'moʊli]	
pew	[pj̥u]	*beautiful*	['bjutɪfoɫ]	/j/ = [j̥ j]
cute	[kj̥ut]	*argue*	['aɹɡju]	

As seen in these examples, entire groups of phonemes often have allophones following the same pattern. For example, all the approximants (/l, ɹ, j, w/) have voiceless allophones after voiceless stops (/p, t, k/) at the beginnings of syllables, and all the voiceless stops (/p, t, k/) have aspirated allophones initially and unaspirated allophones after /s/. Groups of sounds that share phonetic properties pattern together in having the same kinds of allophones in the same positions. The descriptions of the positions that provide the context for the allophones, such as being before or after voiceless stops, also often refer to groups of sounds that share phonetic properties. These groups provide the basis for writing phonological rules (see Chapter 14).

As mentioned above, not only consonants but also vowels have allophones. In English, vowels are longer before voiced consonants in the same syllable and shorter before voiceless consonants in the same syllable. In the data below, the short version of the vowels is marked with a diacritic mark over the vowel, as in [ĕ] (some of the data is from Hayes, 2009, p. 22).

(5)   Two allophones for each vowel before voiced and voiceless consonants:

Before voiceless		Before voiced		Phoneme & allophones		
wick	[wĭk]	*wig*	[wɪg]	/ɪ/	=	[ĭ, ɪ]
hiss	[hĭs]	*his*	[hɪz]			
hack	[hæ̆k]	*hag*	[hæg]	/æ/	=	[æ̆, æ]
pat	[pʰæ̆t]	*pad*	[pʰæd]			
safe	[sĕɪf]	*save*	[seɪv]	/eɪ/	=	[ĕɪ, eɪ]
fate	[fĕɪt]	*fade*	[feɪd]			
bet	[bĕt]	*bed*	[bɛd]	/ɛ/	=	[ɛ̆, ɛ]
peck	[pʰɛ̆k]	*peg*	[pʰɛg]			
boat	[bŏʊt]	*bode*	[boʊd]	/oʊ/	=	[ŏʊ, oʊ]
lope	[lŏʊp]	*lobe*	[loʊb]			
bite	[băɪt]	*bide*	[baɪd]	/aɪ/	=	[ăɪ, aɪ]
white	[wăɪt]	*wide*	[waɪd]			

Across each row, the word-final consonants in each pair above differ only in voicing, as in the [f] vs. [v] of *safe* vs. *save*, and that difference between consonants results in a predictable difference in the length of the vowels. While examples are provided for only six vowels here, every vowel in English follows this pattern of having two allophones (so far), a shorter and a longer version.

In American English, vowels also show allophonic variation based on whether the following consonant is oral or nasal. Vowels are pronounced with a nasalized allophone when they appear before the nasal consonants [n, m, ŋ] in the same syllable. Thus, for a vowel such as [i], we have three allophones: short [ĭ] before voiceless consonants, [i] before voiced oral consonants, and nasalized [ĩ] before voiced nasal consonants. The data below shows that the same pattern holds for other vowels in English.

(6)   Three allophones of each vowel before voiceless, voiced and nasal consonants:

	Before voiceless		Before voiced		Before Nasal	Phoneme & Allophones
seat	[sĭt]	*seed*	[sid]	*seen*	[sĩn]	/i/ = [ĭ i ĩ]
bit	[bĭt]	*bid*	[bɪd]	*bin*	[bĭn]	/ɪ/ = [ĭ ɪ ĩ]
safe	[sĕɪf]	*save*	[seɪv]	*sane*	[sẽɪn]	/eɪ/ = [ĕɪ eɪ ẽɪ]
bet	[bĕt]	*bed*	[bɛd]	*Ben*	[bẽn]	/ɛ/ = [ĕ ɛ ẽ]
cat	[kʰæ̆t]	*cad*	[kʰæd]	*can*	[kʰæ̃n]	/æ/ = [æ̆ æ æ̃]
lock	[lăk]	*log*	[lag]	*long*	[lãŋ]	/a/ = [ă a ã]
suit	[sŭt]	*sued*	[sud]	*soon*	[sũn]	/u/ = [ŭ u ũ]
cup	[kʰʌ̆p]	*cub*	[kʰʌb]	*come*	[kʰʌ̃m]	/ʌ/ = [ʌ̆ ʌ ʌ̃]
boat	[bŏʊt]	*bode*	[boʊd]	*bone*	[bõʊn]	/oʊ/ = [ŏʊ oʊ õʊ]
Bert	[bɚ̆t]	*bird*	[bɚd]	*burn*	[bɚ̃n]	/ɚ/ = [ɚ̆ ɚ ɚ̃]

In each row, the final consonant differs only in whether it is voiceless, voiced, or a nasal consonant, while each vowel differs in being shortened in the first column, and nasal in the final column. Thus every vowel in English has at least three allophones, shortened, nasalized, and plain, depending on the consonant that follows it syllable-finally.

The realization of a phoneme as a particular allophone depends on phonetic context alone. As we have seen, this context can be the immediate neighboring sound, the consonants or vowels nearby, or the position in the syllable or word. In (7) are provided a summary, with /æ/ standing for any vowel.

(7)   Summary of some examples from English:

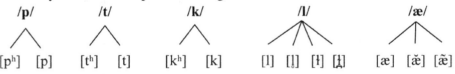

With each phoneme having several allophones, it is clear that a detailed phonetic transcription will include hundreds of sounds. While some differences between sounds are capable of making a contrast between words ([pʰ] vs. [b]), others are predictable variations of the same phoneme in context ([pʰ] vs. [p]).

METHODS FOR FINDING PHONEMES/ALLOPHONES

This section will explain the methods of determining phonemes and allophones from speech data. The examples above have illustrated the primary method for demonstrating that two sounds represent distinct phonemes: the existence of minimal pairs. Such pairs provide immediate confirmation that two sounds are capable of making a difference in meaning, and hence make a contrast between words, which means they must be allophones of distinct phonemes.

Sometimes languages do not provide exact minimal pairs for a contrast. In Table 1, there are a few consonantal phonemes whose example words do not match the general pattern of "__ill" used for most to provide minimal pairs. In the case of the phoneme /ŋ/, the gap results from the systematic absence of this sound from word-initial position in English (and many languages), which means that English speakers would reject a word like *[ŋɪɫ]. To contrast this sound with the other nasal consonants in English, a minimal pair using the word-final position (*sum/sun/sung*) was provided in Table 1 instead. For other sounds, as in the case of the phoneme /j/, the lack of a word "yill" in English is merely an accidental gap, one which might be filled in later if such a word were invented or borrowed. Whether the gap is accidental or motivated by the system, we can instead use a "near-minimal pair" or "analogous pair" as a proof of two sounds being distinct, i.e., allophones of different phonemes. Analogous pairs are two words that contain the suspiciously similar sounds in locally similar contexts, although the entire word may not be otherwise identical. For example, the two sounds [ʒ] and [ʤ] are very similar phonetically, differing only in manner of articulation (fricative vs. affricate), but otherwise both voiced post-alveolars. It is difficult to find a minimal pair in English for the two sounds, partly because the sound [ʒ] is relatively rare, but we can find a near-minimal pair in *pleasure* [ˈpl̥ɛʒɚ] and *ledger* [ˈlɛʤɚ]. The sounds of interest appear in very similar environments, between the same vowels [ɛ__ɚ], and preceded by a lateral, with the only difference being the initial [p]. We can also note that the words sound wrong if we replace one phone with the other: *[ˈpl̥ɛʤɚ] and *[ˈlɛʒɚ] are not possible pronunciations of *pleasure* and *ledger*, supporting the argument that the two sounds belong to distinct phonemes /ʒ/ and /ʤ/, rather than the two sounds being mere allophonic variants of the same phoneme. When there are no minimal pairs, near-minimal pairs can provide evidence of phonemic status.

It is important to be careful that the context is truly analogous, however. While a phonetic transcription of American English reveals that there are different vowels in *cub* [kʰʌb] vs. *come* [kʰʌ̃m], this pair of words cannot be used to argue that there is a phonemic difference between the vowels /ʌ/ and /ʌ̃/, because the words do not provide an analogous context. The difference between the two vowels is that one is oral and one is nasal, and the difference between the two words is also that one ends in an oral consonant /b/, while the other ends in a nasal consonant /m/. The difference in the vowel sounds (oral vs. nasal) might be directly related to the difference in context (oral vs. nasal). A phonemicist should conclude then, that the pair of words is not analogous and the pair of sounds bears further investigation. Only when the context for the sounds is similar, as in *pleasure* and *ledger*, do we feel confident in concluding that the two sounds under examination belong to distinct phonemes, even though the language does not provide minimal pairs.

When we lack both minimal pairs and near-minimal pairs, however, we then investigate whether sounds are allophones of the same phoneme. As in the examples above, cross-linguistic analysis has generally found that allophones of the same phoneme are phonetically similar to each other. For example, the allophones discussed thus far differ in aspiration, nasality, velarization, length, and voicing. Pairs of sounds that are similar to each other and might be allophones of the same phoneme are called "suspicious pairs" (Pike, 1947, p. 75); in the absence of a minimal pair or analogous pairs proving two similar sounds to be distinct, we are suspicious that they may be allophones of the same phoneme. One way to support the conclusion that sounds belong to the same phoneme is by examining the phonetic contexts in which each sound occurs. For example, the [l] occurs at the beginning of syllables and words, while the velarized [ɫ] occurs at the ends of syllables and words. Conversely, the velarized [ɫ] never occurs at the beginning and the plain [l] never at the end. These statements describe a "complementary distribution": where one sound is found, the other is not. When two phonetically similar sounds are in complementary distribution, they are likely allophones of the same phoneme. They cannot be used to make a minimal pair, because the sounds cannot be pronounced in the same context to make a contrast. For example, English cannot make two contrasting words such as [lup] versus [ɫup] meaning something different, because English speakers do not pronounce [ɫ] word-initially and would not allow *[ɫup] at all.

Although the phoneme itself is something more abstract than any of its allophones, which are actual phonetic sounds, we usually name the phoneme with the symbol of its most common allophone, especially if that allophone seems to be the one least affected by its phonetic environment. For example, we consider the vowel phonemes of English to be oral rather than nasal, because the nasalized vowels occur only before nasal consonants in the same syllables, while the oral ones occur when various other sounds, or nothing at all, follows. The context is often responsible in straightforward ways for the allophonic variation, as when vowels are pronounced with nasalization before a nasal consonant; the vowel anticipates the production of the nasal, which involves lowering the velum to allow air out the nose. While the contexts for the nasalized vowel allophone can be simply described, the contexts for the oral allophone cannot; it is often called the "elsewhere" allophone, meaning it occurs wherever the other allophones do not. The name of the phoneme can also be chosen because it is the simpler allophone, either phonetically (plain [l] is a less complex articulation than velarized [ɫ]) or even typographically (/p/ is often used without any examination of whether the [p] allophone is more common or less affected than [pʰ]).

There is one type of allophonic distribution not yet discussed which does not involve complementary distribution, called free variation. The term is used when a phoneme can be pronounced more than one way in the same context, without affecting the meaning. An example would be the pronunciation of word-final voiceless stops in English, illustrated below for the phoneme /p/. The phonetic symbols [p˺] and [p°] indicate an unreleased and released consonant, respectively, and either can be used word-finally for the /p/:

(8)   Word-final /p/

step	[stɛ̆p˺] or [stɛ̆p°]	*loop*	[lŭp˺] or [lŭp°]
keep	[kʰĭp˺] or [kʰĭp°]	*sheep*	[ʃĭp˺] or [ʃĭp°]
tap	[tʰæ̆p˺] or [tʰæ̆p°]	*help*	[hɛɫp˺] or [hɛɫp°]

Note that this is a pattern for any instance of the phoneme /p/, which can always be pronounced as either [p˺] or [p°] word-finally, without changing the meaning. Truly free variation is rare; often the choice of allophone is conditioned by something non-phonological, like wanting to emphasize or disambiguate a word. Free variation is also distinct from the case of a single word having more than one pronunciation, like the word *either*, which may be pronounced as [iðɚ] or [aɪðɚ]. There are two differences that distinguish the two pronunciations of *either* from a case of free variation. The first is that these variant pronunciations are not part of a general pattern (or part of only a very small pattern, including *neither*). The second is that the two vowel sounds that alternate, [i] and [aɪ], are known to occur in minimal pairs (e.g., *beat* vs. *bite*), so that these two vowels belong to two different phonemes and can make a contrast. Sounds in a true free variation, on the other hand, are allophonic and do not contrast. In a case of a word having more than one phonemic pronunciation, such as *either*, we generally consider these two pronunciations to be merely a fact that must be memorized about the individual word.

One final situation that arises in a phonemic analysis is the finding that sometimes two phonemes have the same allophone in a specific phonetic context, which means that in that particular context, there is no contrast between the two phonemes. A commonly cited example is from American English, where the /t/ and /d/ phonemes in intervocalic position are both pronounced in casual speech as the flap [ɾ], when the following syllable does not have stress.

(9) Flapping in American English

	/t/	[t]			[ɾ]
fat	/fæt/	[fæ̆t]	*fatter*	/ˈfætɚ/	[ˈfæɾɚ]
bet	/bɛt/	[bɛ̆t]	*betting*	/ˈbɛtɪŋ/	[ˈbɛɾĩŋ]
beat	/bit/	[bĭt]	*beating/*	ˈbitɪŋ/	[ˈbiɾĩŋ]
	/d/	[d]			[ɾ]
mad	/mæd/	[mæd]	*madder*	/ˈmædɚ/	[ˈmæɾɚ]
bed	/bɛd/	[bɛd]	*bedding*	/ˈbɛdɪŋ/	[ˈbɛɾĩŋ]
bead	/bid/	[bid]	*beating*	/ˈbidɪŋ/	[ˈbiɾĩŋ]

The loss of contrast between two phonemes in a specific environment is called neutralization. Because of this neutralization between /t/ and /d/, we can find that a single pronunciation like [bɛɾĩŋ] can be ambiguous between the words *betting* and *bedding*, which have different phonemic representations /bɛtɪŋ/ and /bɛdɪŋ/.

To summarize the procedures, the investigation of the phonemic system of a language involves first looking for minimal and analogous pairs of words. If such pairs of words can be found, they show that sounds are allophones of distinct phonemes. If such a pair of words cannot be found for a suspicious pair of sounds, then the pattern of distribution for each sound is examined, to determine whether two sounds can be described as being in a complementary distribution, characteristic of allophones of the same phoneme. The exercises will provide a set of data for practice of those methods.

MORPHEMES AND ALLOMORPHS

The second type of variation in context involves **morphemes** (the minimal meaningful unit of language, including roots, prefixes, and suffixes; see Chapters 2 and 3). The pronunciation of a morpheme can also change in the new contexts that result from combining morphemes to make words. Parallel to the term "allophone" for different pronunciations of the same phoneme, different pronunciations of the same morpheme are called its "**allomorphs**". For example, the regular plural suffix, spelled *–s/-es,* is pronounced differently depending on the final sound of the singular word it is added to; after voiceless stops it is [s], after voiceless fricatives it is [əz], and after other sounds, like nasals, voiced stops, or vowels, it is [z], as illustrated in (10).

(10) Allomorphs of plural morpheme

Spelling	Sound	Spelling	Sound	Allomoprh
tip	[tʰɪ̆p]	*tips*	[tʰɪ̆ps]	[-s]
cat	[kʰæ̆t]	*cats*	[kʰæ̆ts]	
pick	[pʰɪ̆k]	*picks*	[pʰɪ̆ks]	
bath	[bæ̆θ]	*baths*	[bæ̆θs]	
bus	[bʌs]	*busses*	[ˈbʌsəz]	[-əz]
bush	[bŏʃ]	*bushes*	[ˈbʊʃəz]	
buzz	[bʌz]	*buzzes*	[ˈbʌzəz]	
hatch	[hæʧ]	*hatches*	[ˈhæʧəz]	
badge	[bædʒ]	*badges*	[ˈbædʒəz]	
tab	[tʰæb]	*tabs*	[tʰæbz]	[-z]
bed	[bɛd]	*beds*	[bɛdz]	
dog	[dɔg]	*dogs*	[dɔgz]	
hive	[haɪv]	*hives*	[haɪvz]	
ball	[baɫ]	*balls*	[baɫz]	
pen	[pʰɛ̃n]	*pens*	[pʰɛ̃nz]	
ear	[iɹ]	*ears*	[iɹz]	
woe	[woʊ]	*woes*	[woʊz]	
fee	[fi]	*fees*	[fiz]	

This allomorphy is based on the phonetic context, as the suffix is pronounced differently after different sounds. As with phonemes and their allophones, we often consider the elsewhere allomorph to be the original form of the morpheme; in this case the plural morpheme would be /-z/, because the allomorph [-z] appears in more kinds of environments, while the other two allomorphs occur in narrowly defined environments.

The same allomorphy is found for other suffixes that are spelled *-s*, such as the third-person singular verb suffix, the possessive, and the contracted form of auxiliary verbs *is* and *has*.

(11) Identical allomorphy for other morphemes

	[s]		**[z]**		**[əz]**	
3rd person	*pats*	[ts]	*wags*	[gz]	*teaches*	[ʧəz]
singular verbs	*tips*	[ps]	*brings*	[ŋz]	*washes*	[ʃəz]
	laughs	[fs]	*sieves*	[vz]	*trudges*	[dʒəz]
possessive	*cat's*	[ts]	*dog's*	[gz]	*witch's*	[ʧəz]
	wife's	[fs]	*bear's*	[ɹz]	*the Bush's*	[ʃəz]

contracted 'is'	*the cat's gone* [ts]	*the dog's playing* [gz]	*my watch's slow* [ʧəz]
	the tap's running [ps]	*the tab's on me* [bz]	*the bus's gone* [səz]

Like the allophonic realizations of a phoneme, this is a regular pattern that is applied by native speakers without conscious awareness. Unlike the allophones, however, morphophonemic alternations typically replace one phoneme with another. That is, /s/ and /z/ are normally separate phonemes, and as we saw above, they can be used to distinguish words with different meanings (e.g., *sip* [sĭp] vs. *zip* [zĭp]). However, in the context of allomorphy, the two sounds are realizations of the same morpheme (the present tense, the possessive, etc.) and indicate the same meaning.

A morpheme may have distinct allomorphs because adding it to a base brings sounds in contact with each other so that they affect each other, as above, or because the resulting word has a new stress pattern, and stressed sounds are pronounced differently. This chapter will discuss several other examples of allomorphy in English, including the past tense suffix *-ed*, vowel laxing (*nation/national, sane/sanity*), and velar softening (*critic/criticize, legal/legislation*).

While there are some exceptions (irregular past tense forms), the usual (regular) past tense in English is formed by adding a suffix spelled *-ed* to a verb form. Although the spelling is consistent, the pronunciation is not. As shown in the data below, the regular past tense is pronounced in three distinct ways: as [t], [d], and as [əd]. Examine the data below to see the distribution of these three allomorphs.

(12) Past tense spelled *-ed*

Allomorph [t]

beeped	[bĭpt]	*soaped*	[sŏʊpt]	*laughed*	[lǽft]
bussed	[bʌ́st]	*washed*	[wɑ̆ʃt]	*biked*	[bă̆ɪkt]
faked	[fĕɪkt]				

Allomorph [d]

ebbed	[ɛbd]	*probed*	[pɹoʊbd]	*waved*	[weɪvd]
mouthed	[maʊðd]	*buzzed*	[bʌzd]	*bagged*[	[bægd]
banned	[bǽnd]	*dimmed*	[dĭmd]	*banged*	[bæŋd]
speared	[spiɹd]	*hoed*	[hoʊd]	*bowed*	[baʊd]
sued	[sud]	*chilled*	[ʧɨɫd]		

Allormorph [əd] in careful speech:

waited	['weɪtəd]	*toted*	['tʰoʊtəd]	*pitted*	['pʰɪtəd]
boarded	['bɔɹdəd]	*waded*	['weɪdəd]	*loaded*	['loʊdəd]

in casual speech:

waited	['weɪɾəd]	*toted*	['tʰoʊɾəd]	*pitted*	['pʰɪɾəd]
boarded	['bɔɹɾəd]	*waded*	['weɪɾəd]	*loaded*	['loʊɾəd]

The forms in casual speech show the results of the allophonic rule of flapping; the careful speech form is also provided to indicate the final phoneme of the verb in order to make the conditioning of the allomorphy clearer. The allomorph [t] appears after voiceless consonants (/p, k, f, θ, s, ʃ, ʧ/), while the allomorph [əd] appears after the alveolar stops (/t/d/) and the flap that is their allophone. The allomorph [d] appears in what we call the elsewhere case. That is, it appears in all other contexts, such as after all of the vowels and after voiced consonants (/b, g, v, ð, z, ʒ, m, n, ŋ, ɹ, l/) except /d/. The allomorphy resembles that of the plural and other suffixes spelled *–s*, which also have three variants: a voiceless one [s] after voiceless consonants, one with a vowel after sibilants [əz], and a voiced one [z] elsewhere. However, in the case of the past tense, which is pronounced with an alveolar stop (t/d), the allomorph with a vowel occurs after verbs ending in an alveolar stop or flap; in the case of the plural suffix which consists of a sibilant (-s), the allomorph with a vowel occurs after forms ending in sibilants.

It is not just suffixes that have allomorphs: prefixes and roots can have them as well. There are many ways to create new words in English by adding various prefixes and suffixes. Some of the suffixes tend to cause a change in the vowel quality of the original word. Consider the data below, in which the addition of various suffixes causes the vowel in the base word to change in quality from [eɪ] to [æ]; the vowels which change are underlined in the spelling of the word. In English, the spelling of the vowels usually stays the same, despite the change in sound to a different phoneme. Note that the longer words are marked not only with ['] before the syllable with primary stress, but also with [ˌ] before a syllable with secondary stress.

(13) Vowel laxing in the base

[eɪ]		**[æ]**	
na̱tion	[ˈneɪʃə̃n]	*na̱tional*	[ˈnæʃənəɫ]
sa̱ne	[sẽɪn]	*sa̱nity*	[ˈsænɪɾi]
opa̱que	[oʊˈpʰĕɪk]	*opa̱city*	[ˌoʊˈpʰæsɪɾi]
volca̱no	[ˌvaɫˈkʰeɪnoʊ]	*volca̱nic*	[ˌvaɫˈkʰænĭk]
sta̱te	[stĕɪt]	*sta̱tic*	[ˈstærĭk]
pa̱le	[pʰeɪɫ]	*pa̱llid*	[ˈpʰælɪd]
ra̱bies	[ˈɹeɪbiz]	*ra̱bid*	[ˈɹæbɪd]
Spa̱in	[spẽɪn]	*Spa̱nish*	[ˈspænĭʃ]
fla̱me	[flẽɪm]	*fla̱mmable*	[ˈflæməbəɫ]
expla̱in	[ĕkˈsplẽɪn]	*expla̱natory*	[ĕkˈsplænəˌtʰoɹi]

This is a case where it is not the suffix that shows allomorphy, but rather the root or base word, where one phoneme is replaced by another in the morpheme. We can prove that [eɪ] and [æ] can make a contrast in English by minimal pairs like *bait* [beɪt] vs. *bat* [bæt], so that they do belong to distinct phonemes, but we see that the vowel [eɪ] in the first column is replaced by the vowel [æ] in the second, where a suffix (-*al, ity, -ic,* etc.) has been added to the stem. Thus, the same morpheme, with the same meaning, has two allomorphs, or two pronunciations (*nation* has [neɪʃə̃n -] and [næʃən-]) depending on whether or not it bears a suffix.

There are a large number of suffixes that can cause allomorphy, although certainly not all do. Yip (1987) discusses cases in which suffixes that begin with *i-* or *a-* cause shortening: -*ic, id, ish, ity, ify, itude, icide, ison, itive, ifer, atory, ative, acy, able.* These suffixes change a variety of vowels in the base, and there are some regular patterns to the changes. As above, if the unsuffixed base word has the vowel [eɪ], the allomorph that appears with the suffix has [æ]. Other pairs include [aɪ]-[ɪ], [oʊ]-[a], [i] - [ɛ] as below (some examples from Yip, 1987, p. 465).

(14) Base allomorphy with suffixation for various vowels in stems

[aɪ]		**[ɪ]**	
mi̱me	[mãɪm]	*mi̱mic*	[ˈmɪmĭk]
fi̱nal	[ˈfaɪnəɫ]	*fi̱nish*	[ˈfɪnĭʃ]
di̱vine	[dɪˈvãɪn]	*di̱vinity*	[dɪˈvɪnɪɾi]
vi̱le	[vaɪɫ]	*vi̱lify*	[ˈvɪlɪfaɪ]
di̱vide	[dɪˈvaɪd]	*di̱visible*	[dɪˈvɪsɪbəɫ]
li̱ne	[lãɪn]	*li̱near*	[ˈlɪniəɹ]
[oʊ]		**[a]**	
co̱ne	[kʰõʊ̃n]	*co̱nic*	[ˈkʰanĭk]
co̱de	[kʰoʊd]	*co̱dify*	[ˈkʰaɾɪˌfaɪ]
so̱le	[soʊɫ]	*so̱litude*	[ˈsalɪˌtʰud]
provo̱ke	[pɹə̥ˈvõʊ̃k]	*provo̱cative*	[pɹə̥ˈvakəɹɪv]
o̱men	[ˈoʊmə̃n]	*o̱minous*	[ˈamənəs]
[i]		**[ɛ]**	
bri̱ef	[bɹif]	*bre̱vity*	[ˈbɹɛvɪɾi]
supre̱me	[səˈpɹĩm]	*supre̱macy*	[səˈpɹɛməsi]
re̱gal	[ˈɹigəɫ]	*re̱gicide*	[ˈɹɛdʒɪˌsaɪd]
le̱gal	[ˈligəɫ]	*le̱gislation*	[ˌlɛdʒɪsˈleɪʃə̃n]
repe̱at	[ɹɪˈpʰĩt]	*repe̱titive*	[ɹəˈpʰɛɾɪˌtɪv]
compe̱te	[kə̃mˈpʰĩt]	*compe̱titive*	[kə̃mˈpʰɛɾɪˌtɪv]

Many phonologically triggered allomorphic variations are very **productive**; that is, if speakers add the morpheme to a new word, they follow the generalizations about which allomorph is appropriate. Linguists have tested this using "wug" tests (Berko, 1958), which present speakers with fictitious words (such as "wug") and ask them to make plurals or past tenses, etc. How speakers produce the new combinations of morphemes gives us evidence about how productive (or not) an allomorphic alternation is. Berko's (1958) research on English speaking children aged 4 to 7 showed they were still learning the plural allomorphy, as they could correctly use the [-s] and [-z] forms most of the time, but did not extend the [-əz] allomorph reliably to new cases like "gutch" or "niz". Adults, on the other hand, predictably and productively used all three allomorphs with the new forms provided.

Not all morphological alternations are equally productive. While the different allomorphs of the past tense and plural suffixes, for example, are extremely productive, the vowel allomorphy in (13) and (14) has some exceptions (e.g., *obesity* keeps the vowel of *obese*), and most speakers do not extend the allomorphy to new words. Another example of allomorphy with limited productivity is traditionally known as "velar softening" (Chomsky & Halle, 1968). In this allomorphy, the two velar stops in English, /k/ and /g/ can alternate due to suffixation; a stem-final /k/ alternates with /s/, while a stem-final /g/ alternates with /dʒ/ before certain suffixes.

(15) Velar softening in base

	[k]		**[s]**
critic	[ˈkɹɪɾɪ̆k]	*criticize*	[ˈkɹɪɾɪˌsaɪz]
electric	[əˈlɛktɹɪ̆k]	*electricity*	[əlĕkˈtɹɪsɪɾi]
opaque	[ˌoʊˈpʰĕɪk]	*opacity*	[ˌoʊˈpʰæsɪɾi]
medical	[ˈmɛɾɪkəɫ]	*medicine*	[ˈmɛɾəsɪ̃n]
classic	[ˈkl̩æsɪ̆k]	*classicist*	[ˈkl̩æsɪsɪ̆st]
public	[ˈpʰʌblɪ̆k]	*publicity*	[pʰəˈblɪsɪɾi]
	[g]		**[dʒ]**
legal	[ˈligəɫ]	*legislation*	[ˌlɛdʒɪsˈleɪʃə̃n]
regal	[ˈɹigəɫ]	*regicide*	[ˈɹɛdʒɪˌsaɪd]
analog	[ˈænəˌlag]	*analogy*	[əˈnælədʒi]
pedagogue	[ˈpʰɛdəgag]	*pedagogic*	[ˌpʰɛdəˈgadʒɪ̆k]
prodigal	[ˈpɹ̥adɪgəɫ]	*prodigy*	[ˈpɹ̥adɪˌdʒi]

The allomorphy of the plural and the past tense was very productive; native speakers of English would follow the generalizations above when making the plural or past of a new word (wugz, wugged). The velar softening allomorphy is partly productive, but only for Latinate words with the suffix –*ity*; Pierrehumbert (2006) found that educated speakers did tend to follow the *electric-electricity* pattern for invented words like *interponic-interponicity*. However, other instances of velar softening were only sporadically productive.

Some allomorphy examples are in between the two extremes, being moderately productive, and possibly applied to new words by native speakers. An example of this is the alternation in the words that end in /–f/ in the singular, changing to a final /–v/ in the plural (Hayes, 2009, p. 193); many very common words show this alternation, as below.

(16) Stem allomorphy in plurals (Hayes, 2009, p. 193)

	[f]		**[v]**
wife	[wăɪf]	*wives*	[waɪvz]
half	[hæf]	*halves*	[hævz]
knife	[năɪf]	*knives*	[naɪvz]
calf	[kʰæ̆f]	*calves*	[kʰævz]
life	[lăɪf]	*lives*	[laɪvz]
elf	[ɛlf]	*elves*	[ɛlvz]
leaf	[lĭf]	*leaves*	[livz]
shelf	[ʃɛlf]	*shelves*	[ʃɛlvz]
thief	[θĭf]	*thieves*	[θivz]
wolf	[wʊlf]	*wolves*	[wʊlvz]
loaf	[lŏʊf]	*loaves*	[loʊvz]
scarf	[skaɹf]	*scarves*	[skaɹvz]
hoof	[hŏf]	*hooves*	[hʊvz]

Note that again the allomorphy is in the base words, not the suffix. The usual result of attaching the plural suffix to a word ending in a voiceless sound like [f], as we saw earlier, would be to use the allomorph [s] for the plural. However, here we see that the base word in the plural has a [v] and attracts the [z] allomorph for the plural, the usual after a voiced consonant. The set of words with this allomorphy seems to be learned, since there are plenty of words ending in [f] which do not follow this pattern, but instead behave normally with no change to the base while taking the [s] plural allomorph.

(17) Plurals for final [f] without allomorphy (Hayes, 2009, p. 194)

trough	[tɹɔf]	*troughs*	[tɹɔfs]	*[tɹɔvz]
oaf	[ŏʊf]	*oafs*	[ŏʊfs]	*[oʊvz]
chief	[ʧĭf]	*chiefs*	[ʧĭfs]	*[ʧivz]
reef	[ɹĭf]	*reefs*	[ɹĭfs]	*[ɹivz]
gaffe	[gæf]	*gaffes*	[gæfs]	*[gævz]
motif	[moʊˈtĭf]	*motifs*	[moʊˈtĭfs]	*[moʊˈtivz]
spoof	[spŭf]	*spoofs*	[spŭfs]	*[spŭvz]

Furthermore, the allomorphy in (16) applies when forming the plurals only, not before other suffixes, even if they sound identical to the plural -*s*. We saw, for example, that the possessive suffix '*s* follows the same pattern of allomorphy as the plural, but the possessive forms of words like *wife* takes the usual allomorph [-s] in the possessive (forming *wife's* [wăɪfs]); in fact, all forms ending in /f/ follow the usual allomorphy in the possessive, even though their plurals end in [vz]. Despite the limitations on the allomorphy of (16), it does still seem to be somewhat productive in the sense of being applied to new words. Berko (1958) found that the adults, tested on the novel form *heaf*, generated two plurals: 58% preferred *heafs*, while 42% said *heaves* (1958, p. 162), which suggests that a good number of speakers apply the allomorphy of *wife/wives* to new forms, while others follow the general pattern.

IMPLICATIONS FOR TEACHING ENGLISH LANGUAGE LEARNERS

Knowledge of the English phonemes and of common allophonic and allomorphic variations can be applied to teaching English learners. In order to teach English pronunciation, comprehension, reading and spelling, it may be helpful for teachers to understand some of the common allophonic and allomorphic variations in English; this section provides some of the applications of the information and concepts above.

For native speakers of English, the allophonic generalizations described in this chapter are below the level of consciousness. This is true of allophonics in general; native speakers have acquired the patterns of their first language through implicit learning, and automatically follow them without being aware of or able to articulate them. When learning a second language, speakers may transfer the patterns of their first language, causing difficulties in learning to perceive or produce the new language. Major (2008) notes that while transfer does not explain all the errors that L2 learners make, knowledge of the differences between the L1 and L2 systems can lead to valid predictions about which sounds and structures are likely to cause problems for learners. For example, it is common for speakers to substitute a sound from their L1 for a similar sound in their L2; Spanish speakers may produce their [r] for English [ɹ], and Hindi speakers tend to use their retroflex [ʈ ɖ] for English alveolar [t d]. The allophonic systems may also play a role; for example, French speakers would use an [l] at the end of words, where English speakers would expect [ɫ], while word-initially, French speakers would tend to use an unaspirated (and dental) [t̪] rather than the expected [tʰ] in English. Learners may also fail to differentiate two sounds that are phonemes in English because those sounds are only allophones in their L1s; for Korean speakers, the /s/ vs. /ʃ/ distinction of English may be difficult because Korean has only an /s/ phoneme with a palatalized allophone. Differences in phonemic systems can also affect comprehension, as they may interfere with accurate perception. Major (2008) points to how perception can interfere in L2 learning, especially for sounds that are similar to but not identical with L1 sounds; L2 sounds that are completely new are easier to learn than L2 sounds that are similar to, and may easily be mistaken for, L1 sounds.

When learning a second language, learners generally use both implicit and explicit learning. Research has shown that explicit teaching of pronunciation can be successful for second language learners (Levis & Wu, 2018). When pronunciation and perception issues result from transfer, a teacher can use an understanding of phonemics to help pinpoint issues causing learners to sound non-native, and to improve their accents. In order to improve intelligibility in English, teachers need to be aware of the phonemic differences, especially those which bear a heavier information load. Some contrasts are very important in making speech intelligible, while others do not bear much information load (Jenkins, 2002); for example, the difference between /p/ and /b/ is used to contrast hundreds of words, while the phonemes /θ/ and /ð/ make very few contrasts. Jenkins argues for perfecting the more important contrasts first, in order to improve intelligibility.

While not all learners of English can or want to acquire a native accent, improving pronunciation can also help learners to avoid judgements associated with non-native accents. Research has shown that speakers with non-native accents may face discrimination or negative judgements; Lev-Ari and Kaysar (2010), for example, found that accented speech was judged less credible than speech with a native accent. For those learners who do want to sound more native-like, control of the allophonic variation is important. Applying knowledge of English allophonics can improve pronunciation teaching, while applying the methods of phonemics to understand the learner's L1 system can help provide teachers with an understanding of the issues their language learners face or the prior knowledge they bring from their L1 phonemics.

Allophonic differences are rarely, if ever, represented in spelling cross-linguistically, so learners need teachers who are able to explain them. Allomorphic differences are represented in some languages, but English generally favors spelling a stem morpheme in the same way in all words despite its distinct pronunciations. For example, in *legal* vs. *legislation*; the *leg-* morpheme has the [l] pronounced the same in both words, but the 'e' and 'g' are pronounced differently in the two words ([lig] vs. [lɛdʒ]), due to the vowel laxing and velar softening mentioned above. For prefixes and suffixes, some allormorphs are spelled differently, but not all. For example, the plural suffix is spelled –*s*, regardless of whether it's pronounced [s] or [z], although the [əz] allomorph is generally represented as –*es*. The possessive morpheme, on the other hand, is always spelled -*'s* despite having the same allomorphy. Understanding how morphemes vary in context can help learners to recognize the same morpheme when it is used with different pronunciations, improving comprehension, and to pronounce a new combination of morphemes correctly when reading it for the first time, improving pronunciation.

DISCUSSION QUESTIONS

1. Which type of change in phonological context are L1 English speakers more likely to notice: allophonic or allomorphic? Why?
2. Is there a need to teach allomorphy that is not very productive? Are there any advantages or disadvantages to doing so?
3. Can a learner's L1 phonemic system (phonemes and allophones) be helpful in learning the system of phonemes and allophones of English as a second language? How?
4. Can a learner's L1 morphemic system be helpful in learning allomorphy in English as a second language? How?
5. What advantages and disadvantages does a teacher who speaks English as a second language have in teaching the allophones and allomorphs of English? How might these advantages or disadvantages affect students who are learning English pronunciation?

EXERCISES

1. **/t/ in American English**
    The description of the three allophones of /t/ in American English in the chapter was not complete. In the data below, you will find three allophones of /t/: [tʰ], [t], and [ɾ]. Note that syllables that have stress are preceded by the symbol [ˈ]. Use the stress information to give a better description of where the [tʰ], [t], and [ɾ] allophones occur (the data is not organized for you).

top	/tap/	[ˈtʰăp]	*spat*	/spæt/	[ˈspæt]
daughter	/datɚ/	[ˈdaɾɚ]	*state*	/steɪt/	[ˈstĕɪt]
city	/sɪti/	[ˈsɪɾi]	*autograph*	/atogɹæf/	[ˈaɾogɹæf]
edit	/ɛdɪt/	[ˈɛɾĭt]	*later*	/leɪtɚ/	[ˈleɪɾɚ]
potato	/pəteɪtoʊ/	[pəˈtʰeɪɾoʊ]	*tomato*	/təmeɪtoʊ/	[təˈmeɪɾoʊ]
stick	/stɪk/	[ˈstĭk]	*sensitive*	/sɛnsɪtɪv/	[ˈsɛnsɪɾɪv]
editorial	/ɛditoɹiəl/	[ɛɾiˈtʰoɹiəɫ]	*tick*	/tɪk/	[ˈtʰĭk]
sensitivity	/sɛnsɪtɪviti/	[ˌsɛnsɪˈtʰɪvɪɾi]	*pot*	/pat/	[ˈpʰăt]
tutor	/tutɚ/	[ˈtʰuɾɚ]	*computer*	/kəmpjuɾɚ/	[kəmˈpjuɾɚ]

2. **_t_ vs _th_ in Indian English**

    Some varieties of Indian English have the following pronunciations:

    a. *taught* [t̪ɔt̪]   *thought* [t̪ʰɔt̪]
    b. *tin*   [t̪ɪn]   *thin*   [t̪ʰɪn]
    c. *team*   [t̪im]   *theme*   [t̪ʰim]

    What do these words prove about their system of phonemes and allophones for the sounds spelled *t* vs *th*? Is their pronunciation likely to cause any difficulties for speakers of American English?

3. **[ð] in Spanish vs. English**

    English has the sound [ð] as a phoneme distinct from similar sounds [d] and [θ], as proven by minimal pairs such as *den* [dɛ̃n] vs. *then* [ðɛ̃n] or *ether* [iθɚ] vs. *either* [iðɚ]. Apply the phonemic methods to determine whether [ð] is an allophone of a distinct phoneme in Spanish, by looking for minimal pairs or complementary distribution with [d̪] in the data below (the ̪ indicates that the sound is dental rather than alveolar).

    Spanish:

	Words with [d̪]		**Words with [ð]**	
where	[d̪onde]	nothing	[naða]
to have to	[d̪eβɛɾ]	spoken	[ablaðo]
giving	[d̪and̪o]	bodega	[boðeɣa]
days	[d̪ias]	you (polite)	[usteð]
ribbon	[band̪a]	side	[laðo]
finger	[d̪eðo]	finger	[d̪eðo]
they give	[d̪an]	wall	[pareð]
store	[tiend̪a]	help	[ajuða]

    Given your findings, does the fact that English and Spanish have some of the same phonetic sounds help your Spanish speakers to learn English as a second language? Can you use your knowledge of the Spanish phonemic system to help?

4. Examine the data below verbs and nouns, and determine the patterns of sound and stress change for each pair.

content_verb	[kə̃n'tʰɛ̃nt]	content_noun	['kʰã̃ntɛ̃nt]
refuse_verb	[ɹə'fjuz]	refuse_noun	['ɹɛfjŭs]
project_verb	[pɹ̥ə'dʒɛ̆kt]	project_noun	['pɹ̥ɑdʒɛ̆kt]
conduct_verb	[kə̃n'dʌkt]	conduct_noun	['kʰã̃ndʌkt]
addict_verb	[ə'dɪ̆kt]	addict_noun	['ædɪ̆kt]
record_verb	[ɹə'kʰoɹd]	record_noun	['ɹɛkɚd]
permit_verb	[pɚ'mɪ̆t]	permit_noun	['pɚmɪ̆t]

5. **//in-//** English has a morpheme //ɪn-// meaning 'not', which can be found in adjective pairs as in the data below (based on the data in Peng, 2013, pp. 101-102).

    a. This morpheme has several allomorphs, and the data is organized based on which allomorph appears in the words. Determine the basis for the different allomorphs: in which context does each allomorph appear?

    b. The spelling of the prefix sometimes changes when added to different roots, making it harder for learners to recognize it as the same prefix or to apply it to new forms without understanding how it changes in new contexts. When does the spelling accurately reflect the allomorphy? When does the spelling differ from the pronunciation?

c. Could an understanding of this allomorphy help you to explain the //in-// prefix to learners of English?

Allomorph /ɪn-/

Adjective		//in-// + Adjective	
attentive	[ə'tʰẽntɪv]	inattentive	[ɪnə'tʰẽntɪv]
offensive	[ə'fẽnsɪv]	inoffensive	[ɪnə'fẽnsɪv]
explicable	[ĕk'splɪkəbəɫ]	inexplicable	[ɪnĕk'splɪkəbəɫ]
humane	[hju'mẽɪn]	inhumane	[ɪ̃nhju'mẽɪn]
tolerable	['tʰaləɹəbəɫ]	intolerable	[ɪ̃n'tʰaləɹəbəɫ]
defensible	[də'fẽnsɪbəɫ]	indefensible	[ɪ̃ndə'fẽnsɪbəɫ]
sensitive	['sẽnsɪɾɪv]	insensitive	[ɪ̃n'sẽnsɪɾɪv]

Allomorph /ɪm-/

perfect	['pʰɚfĕkt]	imperfect	[ɪ̃m'pʰɚfĕkt]
pure	[pju̥ɹ]	impure	[ɪ̃m'pju̥ɹ]
balanced	['bælə̃nst]	imbalanced	[ɪ̃m'bælə̃nst]

Allomorph /ɪŋ-/

considerate	[kə̃n'sɪdəɹə̆t]	inconsiderate	[ɪ̃ŋkə̃n'sɪdəɹə̆t]
correct	['kʰəɹĕkt]	incorrect	[ɪ̃ŋ'kʰəɹĕkt]
glorious	['gloɹiə̃s]	inglorious	[ɪ̃ŋ'gloɹiə̃s]

Allomorph /ɪ-/

legal	['ligəɫ]	illegal	[ɪ'ligəɫ]
literate	['lɪɾəɹə̆t]	illiterate	[ɪ'lɪɾəɹə̆t]
legible	['lɛdʒɪbəɫ]	illegible	[ɪ'lɛdʒɪbəɫ]
relevant	['ɹɛləvæ̃nt]	irrelevant	[ɪ'ɹɛləvæ̃nt]
responsible	[ɹə'spãnsɪbəɫ]	irresponsible	[ɪɹə'spãnsɪbəɫ]
rational	['ɹæʃənəɫ]	irrational	[ɪ'ɹæʃənəɫ]
mature	[mə'ʧu̥ɹ]	immature	[ɪmə'ʧu̥ɹ]
material	[mə'tʰiɹiəɫ]	immaterial	[ɪmə'tʰiɹiəɫ]
numerable	['numɚɹəbəɫ]	innumerable	[ɪ'numɚɹəbəɫ]

REFERENCES

Berko, J. (1958). The child's learning of English morphology. *Word, 14*(2-3), 150–177. doi:10.1080/00437956.1958.11659661

Chomsky, N., & Halle, M. (1968). *The sound pattern of English.* New York: Harper & Row.

De Saussure, F. (1959). *Course in general linguistics [1916]* (C. Bally & A. Sechehaye, Eds., BaskinW., Trans.). New York: McGraw Hill Book Company.

Hayes, B. (2009). *Introducing phonology.* Chichester, UK: Wiley-Blackwell.

Jenkins, J. (2002). A sociolinguistically based, empirically researched pronunciation syllabus for English as an international language. *Applied Linguistics, 23*(1), 83–103. doi:10.1093/applin/23.1.83

Labov, W., Ash, S., & Boberg, C. (2008). *The atlas of North American English: Phonetics, phonology and sound change*. The Hague: Walter de Gruyter.

Lev-Ari, S., & Keysar, B. (2010). Why don't we believe non-native speakers? The influence of accent on credibility. *Journal of Experimental Social Psychology, 46*(6), 1093–1096. doi:10.1016/j.jesp.2010.05.025

Levis, J., & Wu, A. (2018). Pronunciation – Research into practice and practice into research. *The CATESOL Journal, 30*(1), 1–12.

Major, R. C. (2008). Transfer in second language phonology: A review. In J. Hansen Edwards & M. Zampini (Eds.), *Phonology and second language acquisition* (pp. 65–94). Amsterdam: John Benjamins Publishing. doi:10.1075ibil.36.05maj

Peng, L. (2013). *Analyzing sound patterns: An introduction to phonology*. Cambridge, UK: Cambridge University Press. doi:10.1017/CBO9781139043168

Pierrehumbert, J. B. (2006). The statistical basis of an unnatural alternation. *Laboratory Phonology, 8,* 81–107.

Pike, K. L. (1947). *Phonemics*. Ann Arbor, MI: The University of Michigan Press.

Swadesh, M. (1934). The phonemic principle. *Language, 10*(2), 117–129. doi:10.2307/409603

Yip, M. (1987). English vowel epenthesis. *Natural Language and Linguistic Theory, 5*(4), 463–484. doi:10.1007/BF00138986

ADDITIONAL READING

Davidson, L. (2011). Phonetic and phonological factors in the second language production of phonemes and phonotactics. *Language and Linguistics Compass, 5*(3), 126–139. doi:10.1111/j.1749-818X.2010.00266.x

Díaz, B., Baus, C., Escera, C., Costa, A., & Sebastián-Gallés, N. (2008). Brain potentials to native phoneme discrimination reveal the origin of individual differences in learning the sounds of a second language. *Proceedings of the National Academy of Sciences of the United States of America, 105*(42), 16083–16088. doi:10.1073/pnas.0805022105 PMID:18852470

Eckman, F. R. (2004). From phonemic differences to constraint rankings: Research on second language phonology. *Studies in Second Language Acquisition, 26*(4), 513–549. doi:10.1017/S027226310404001X

Gray, S. H., Ehri, L. C., & Locke, J. L. (2018). Morpho-phonemic analysis boosts word reading for adult struggling readers. *Reading and Writing, 31*(1), 75–98. doi:10.100711145-017-9774-9 PMID:29367806

Hillenbrand, J., Getty, L. A., Clark, M. J., & Wheeler, K. (1995). Acoustic characteristics of American English vowels. *The Journal of the Acoustical Society of America, 97*(5), 3099–3111. doi:10.1121/1.411872 PMID:7759650

Jenkins, J. (2000). *The phonology of English as an international language - New models, new norms, new goals*. Oxford, UK: Oxford University Press.

Stuart, M. (1999). Getting ready for reading: Early phoneme awareness and phonics teaching improves reading and spelling in inner-city second language learners. *The British Journal of Educational Psychology*, *69*(4), 587–605. doi:10.1348/000709999157914

ENDNOTES

[1]   The contrast could be illustrated using a word *thill* that fishermen might recognize, but as that is not in common use, the word *thin* appears in Table 1 instead to provide a context that is analogous (see section on Methods).

[2]   The common symbol /a/ is used here for the low non-front unrounded vowel, which in most varieties of American English can vary phonetically from a central unrounded lower-mid vowel (IPA [ɐ]) to a back low vowel (IPA [ɑ]).

[3]   The asterisk before the phonetic data is used to indicate that this form would be ungrammatical or inappropriate.

Chapter 14
The Rules of Phonology

Charles X. Li
Central Washington University, USA

ABSTRACT

This chapter focuses on formulating North American English (NAE) phonological rules and discussing their pedagogical implications. It begins with a brief account of NAE phonology as a rule-governed system and then outlines feature-based phonology as a theoretical framework in which phonological rules operate. The chapter further defines an inventory of distinctive features for characterizing the NAE phonological system. After discussing rule components and matrix underspecification, the chapter presents phonological rules subsumed under seven categories: deletion, epenthesis, metathesis, reduction, assimilation, dissimilation, and morphophonology. Most rules are couched in three expressions—prose, semi-formal, formal—to meet different needs of readers. Pedagogical implications of phonological rules, discussed in the last section, are explicated in the framework of language transfer and universal grammar. The same section also emphasizes the importance of balancing linguistic analysis and classroom practice.

PHONOLOGY AS A RULE-GOVERNED SYSTEM

Phonology is often said to be a rule-governed system. It describes, rather than prescribes, human speech patterns internalized in the brain of the speaker. As a system, phonology consists of segments, and segments in turn consist of smaller building blocks known as **distinctive features** (*df*s) that categorize natural classes of segments. All *df*s stand in relation to one another and alternate along with rapidly changing phonetic environments for oral communication. For example, the word *hand* /hænd/ becomes [hæ̃:m] in *hand me that* if uttered in one breath in which /æ/ is nasalized and lengthened to [æ̃:], /d/ is deleted, and /n/ is assimilated to [m] before *me*. Phonological rules seek to account for triggers and processes of sound alternations such as these.

The feature property of speech sounds has long been recognized at least since the International Phonetic Association (IPA) was established in 1886 but the *df* theory did not appear until 1952 when Jakobson, Frant, and Halle published their book *Preliminaries to Speech Analysis: The Distinctive Features and Their Correlates*. Chomsky and Halle (1968) further developed this theory in *The Sound Patterns of English*. Since then, feature-based phonology has grown steadily and become part of mainstream

DOI: 10.4018/978-1-5225-8467-4.ch014

linguistics. It is now considered an essential part of education for graduate students of linguistics, and it plays an increasingly visible role in the undergraduate classroom of linguistics as well. However, this branch of linguistics, which frequently employs such unusual language and organizational principles that seem to defy non-linguists' understandings and acceptance, has been regrettably brushed away from the English language teaching arena and marginalized in teacher training programs. In the newly published eight-volume *The TESOL Encyclopedia of English Language Teaching* (Liontas, 2018), feature-based phonology does not even earn a single appearance.

This chapter fills this gap by offering an accessible introduction to this challenging subfield of linguistics that will enable ESOL teachers, TESOL graduate students, and teacher candidates to grasp heretofore obscure theoretical concepts and understand precisely the ways in which our own phonological experience is determined by phonological principles. There is no reason for teachers not to benefit from achievements of theoretical linguistics. To that end, this chapter will focus on defining *df*s, describing environment-driven phonological rules, and discussing their implications for teaching NAE as a second or foreign language. These goals assume prior knowledge of articulators in the vocal tract, physical descriptions of sounds, phonemes and allophones, morphemes and allomorphs, IPA symbols, as well as phonemic and phonetic transcriptions. Since these topics are all covered in Chapters 11 through 13, we will turn directly to key topics of feature-based phonology below.

A THEORETICAL FRAMEWORK OF FEATURE-BASED PHONOLOGY

Feature-based phonology posits two levels of sound representation as its theoretical framework. The most basic form, i.e., the phonemic form, of a lexical item, such as /hænd/ for *hand*, is called an **underlying representation** (UR). UR is viewed as what a native speaker knows about the abstract sound image of a word, and by extension, about the underlying sound system of his or her native language. What a word is actually and physically realized as, like [hæ:m] for *hand,* is called its **surface representation** (SR). The process of converting UR to SR is called a **derivation** or a **derivational process**, and can be modeled below:

(1)

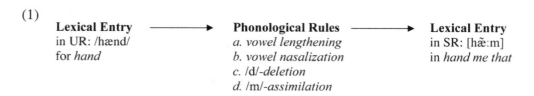

Lexical Entry ⟶	**Phonological Rules** ⟶	**Lexical Entry**
in UR: /hænd/	*a. vowel lengthening*	in SR: [hæ̃:m]
for *hand*	*b. vowel nasalization*	in *hand me that*
	c. /d/-deletion	
	d. /m/-assimilation	

Interestingly, native language speakers have to learn UR sound images of lexical items so as to learn new words, but few speakers learn the derived SR images, so their knowledge of derivational processes remain tacit. Feature-based phonology aims to account for the tacit knowledge that remains subconscious in the mind of native language speakers, and it does so by analyzing components of segments and how the components change from UR to SR so as to account for *how* and *why* segments change in context. If all this is understood, we will be in a better position to explain how and why the four rules in (1) occur, and for that matter, many other rules, too. Nevertheless, the first step in acquiring this branch of linguistics is understanding distinctive features.

DISTINCTIVE FEATURES

Distinctive features refer to physical properties of the vocal tract and constitute the atomic units of segments and phonological structure that can be analyzed in feature-based phonology. They are typically grouped to categories based on the natural classes of segments they describe: *diffuse, manner, place,* and *laryngeal*. By "diffuse" is meant that features under this category spread over a large number of segments also covered in other categories.

Since the inception of feature-based phonology, features have been traditionally specified by binary values to indicate whether a segment is described by the feature. A positive value, written as [+], signifies the presence of a feature, while a negative value, written as [-], denotes its absence. In recent developments of feature phonology, however, phonologists have also proposed the existence of single-valued features known as univalent or privative features or of zero-valued features known as "not to care" features. Since single-valued features can only capture the classes of segments that possess them but not the classes that are without them, we will not include them in this chapter, nor will we include zero-valued features. At least, keeping only binary features in mind eases out memory burdens of those new to phonology.

Depending on purposes, coverage of *df*s varies tremendously from book to book. With reference to multiple sources,[1] this chapter selected 24 features. When assignments of featural values conflict, this chapter followed the majority rule along with the author's own judgement. These selected features are defined one by one in four categories below.

a. Diffuse Features

1. [±**consonantal**] (abbreviated [±**cons**]): Sounds produced with a major obstruction in the oral cavity. All NAE consonants are [+cons] except for glottals /h, ʔ/, glides /j, w/,[2] and vowels. The non-NAE voiceless velar fricative /x/ is also [+cons].
2. [±**sonorant**] ([±**son**]): Singable sounds produced with smooth air flow through the vocal tract, including vowels, nasals, liquids, and glides. Obstruents and glottals are not singable and thus [-son].
3. [±**syllabic**] ([±**syl**]): Sounds that constitute a syllabic nucleus, including vowels and syllabic consonants [l̩], [ɹ̩], [m̩], [n̩], are [+syl], and sounds that do not are [-syl].

b. Manner Features

1. [±**continuant**] ([±**cont**]): Sounds produced with continued air movement through the oral cavity are [+cont], and sounds not produced in this manner are [-cont]. Thus, [+cont] sounds include vowels, fricatives (including /x/), liquids, glides, and the glottal fricative /h/, whereas [-cont] sounds include stops, affricates, nasals, and the glottal stop [ʔ].
2. [±**nasal**] ([±**nas**]): Sounds produced with the opening of the velum to allow air to release through the nasal passage are [+nas]. In NAE, it includes nasals /m, n, ŋ/ and nasalized vowels.
3. [±**delayed release**] ([±**d.r.**]): Sounds produced with a slower tongue drop from the roof of the mouth than oral stops. This feature separates NAE affricates /tʃ, dʒ/ from oral stops /p, b, t, d, k, g/. It also separates the NAE glottal /h/ from the non-NAE fricative /x/.

4. **[±tap]**: All sounds are [-tap] except for the allophone [ɾ] derived from phonemes /t/ and /d/, as in *writer* and *rider*.

5. **[±trill]** (**[±tri]**): All sounds are [-tri] except for the [+tri] [r] in many non-NAE languages and interlanguages that changes the NAE retroflex liquid [ɹ] to the trilled liquid [r].

c. Laryngeal Features

1. **[±voiced]** (**[±vd]**): Sounds produced with vibration of the vocal folds are [+vd]; sounds articulated without the vibration are [-vd]. In NAE, [+vd] specifies vowels, voiced consonants, and glides; [-vd] specifies voiceless obstruents and glottals /h/ and [ʔ].

2. **[±constrained glottis]** (**[±c.g.]**): Sounds articulated with constricted vocal folds. In NAE, it specifies the voiceless allophonic glottal stop [ʔ] only.

3. **[±spread glottis]** (**[±s.g.]**): Sounds articulated with aspiration from open or spread vocal folds that follows the closure of a voiceless oral stop excluding the glottal stop [ʔ]. In NAE, this feature specifies the glottal fricative /h/ and the aspirated allophonic stops [pʰ, tʰ, kʰ].

d. Place Features

1. **[±lateral]** (**[±lat]**): /l/ and its varieties are [+lat], and all other segments are [-lat].

2. **[±labial]** (**[±lab]**): Sounds produced with active movement of one lip or both lips. [+lab] invokes NAE bilabials /p, b, m/ and labiodentals /f, v/, and [-lab] invokes other NAE consonants.

3. **[±round]** (**[±rd]**): Sounds produced with the lips protruding. The [+rd] sounds are simultaneously [+lab], but the opposite is not true. In NAE, [+rd] specifies the labiovelar glide /w/ and back vowels /u, ʊ, o, ɔ/ but not the non-contrastive low central /a/ and low back [ɑ], though /a, ɑ/ can be contrastive in other languages.

4. **[±coronal]** (**[±cor]**): Sounds requiring active raising of the tongue tip or blade. In NAE, it specifies interdentals /θ, ð/, alveolars /t, d, s, z, n, l, ɹ/, alveopalatals /ʃ, ʒ, ʧ, ʤ/, the allophonic flap [ɾ], as well as the trill [r] in many other languages. All other NAE consonants are

5. **[±anterior]** (**[±ant]**): Sounds articulated in front of the alveopalatal area are [+ant]. In NAE, [+ant] includes interdentals /θ, ð/, alveolars /t, d, s, z, n, l/, and the flap [ɾ]; the interlanguage sound [r] is also [+ant]. All sounds articulated at or behind the alveopalatal area are [-ant]. In NAE, [-ant] specifies stops /p, b, k, g/, fricatives /f, v, ʃ, ʒ, x/, affricates /ʧ, ʤ/, nasals /m, ŋ/, the retroflex /ɹ/, glides /j, w/, and glottals /h, ʔ/.

6. **[±distributed]** (**[±dis]**): Sounds produced with the tongue blade being activated to yield more contact (i.e., distribution) between tongue and roof of mouth are [+dis]; sounds produced with the tongue tip being activated to yield less contact or less distribution between tongue and roof of mouth are [-dis]. Thus, in NAE, /θ, ð, ʃ, ʒ, ʧ, ʤ/ and dentalized allophones [t̪, d̪, n̪] are [+dis] while all other segments are [-dis].

7. **[±strident]** (**[±str]**): Sounds articulated with noisy, high-amplitude, hi-pitched friction is [+str]. In NAE, [+str] specifies alveolars /s, z/ and alveopalatals [ʃ, ʒ, ʧ, ʤ/. Other NAE sounds are [+stri].

8. **[±dorsal]** (**[±dor]**): All sounds requiring raising activation of the tongue body. In NAE, [+dor] specifies velars /k, g, ŋ/, glides /j, w/, as well as vowels. This feature also specifies the non-NAE fricative /x/. All other sounds are [-dor].

9. **[±high]** (**[±hi]**): Sounds articulated with a raised tongue body in the oral cavity is [+hi]. In NAE, this feature invokes velars /k, g, ŋ/, glides /j, w/, high front and high back vowels /i, ɪ, u, ʊ/, as well as the non-NAE /x/.
10. **[±back]** (**[±bk]**): Sounds produced with activation of the tongue body behind the palatal area in the oral cavity is [+bk]. In NAE, [+bk] specifies velars /k, g, ŋ/, the glide /w/, and back vowels /ə, ʌ, u, ʊ, o, ɔ, ɑ/.[3] It also specifies the fricative /x/. All other NAE sounds, including the glide /j/, are [-bk].

The next three features are pertinent to NAE vowels only:

1. **[±low]** (**[±lo]**): A sound produced with the tongue body lowed from a neutral position in the oral cavity. NAE has no soft uvulars, so this feature is intended to capture the low front /æ/ and low back /ɑ/.[4]
2. **[±tense]** (**[±tns]**): Vowel sounds articulated with muscles in the oral cavity being stretched tight or rigid. In NAE, [+tns] captures vowels /i, e, u, o/. The back vowel /ɑ/ shows both [+tns] and [-tns] values and is thus assigned the [±tns] value.[5]
3. **[±reduced]** (**[±rdu]**): This feature specifies the schwa /ə/ only; thus, all other vowels are [-rdu]. This feature plays a unique role in producing rhythm, yet it is frequently realized as [-rdu] in inter-language phonology.

Tables 1 and 2 below summarize all the 24 *df*s defined above. Table 1 includes the allophone [ɾ] because it is a hallmark of NAE pronunciation, the allophone /ʔ/ because it frequently appears in native English pronunciation, and two non-NAE phonemes /r/ and /x/ because they often make their way as mispronunciations in learner speech and deserve special attention. Nasals /m, n/ and liquids /l, ɹ/ can serve as syllabic nuclei in unstressed syllables, notated [m̩, n̩] and [l̩, ɹ̩] respectively, so they are assigned [±] values. In addition, /m, n, ŋ] are assigned a [-cont] feature because of total air blockage in the oral cavity even though they are [+son]. Table 2 summarizes 13 features pertinent to NAE vowels. By default, all vowels share features [-cons, +son, +syl, +cont, +vd, +dor], so vowels are differentiated by [lab, rd, hi, lo, bk, tns, rdu] features. Features unrelated with vowels are excluded from this table.

With this inventory of *df*s and their value assignments as summarized in both tables, we are now ready to explicate the inner workings of sound alternations from UR to SR expressed in phonological rules that we will precisely formalize below.

THE RULES OF PHONOLOGY

This section consists of three parts: (1) components of phonological rules, (2) simplification of redundant features, and (3) classified NAE phonological rules. The first two parts are mainly for readers new to rule formation and feature specification.

Table 1. Feature chart for NAE consonants (including two NAE allophones and two non-NAE sounds)

Types	Features	Stops p b t d ɾ k g	Fricatives f v θ ð s z ʃ ʒ x	Affricates tʃ dʒ	Nasals m n ŋ	Liquids l ɹ r	Glides j w	Glottals h ʔ
Diffuse	[cons]	+ + + + + + +	+ + + + + + + + +	+ +	+ + +	+ + +	- -	- -
	[son]	- - - - - - -	- - - - - - - - -	- -	+ + +	+ + +	+ +	- -
	[syl]	- - - - - - -	- - - - - - - - -	- -	± ± -	± ± -	- -	- -
Manner	[cont]	- - - - - - -	+ + + + + + + + +	- -	- - -	+ + +	+ +	+ -
	[nas]	- - - - - - -	- - - - - - - - -	- -	+ + +	- - -	- -	- -
	[d.r.]	- - - - - - -	- - - - - - - - +	+ +	- - -	- - -	- -	- -
	[tap]	- - - + - - -	- - - - - - - - -	- -	- - -	- - -	- -	- -
	[tri]	- - - - - - -	- - - - - - - - -	- -	- - -	- - +	- -	- -
Laryngeal	[vd]	- + - + + - +	- + - + - + - + -	- +	+ + +	+ + +	+ +	- -
	[c.g.]	- - - - - - -	- - - - - - - - -	- -	- - -	- - -	- -	- +
	[s.g.]	- - - - - - -	- - - - - - - - -	- -	- - -	- - -	- -	+ -
Place	[lat]	- - - - - - -	- - - - - - - - -	- -	- - -	+ - -	- -	- -
	[lab]	+ + - - - - -	+ + - - - - - - -	- -	+ - -	- - -	- +	- -
	[rd]	- - - - - - -	- - - - - - - - -	- -	- - -	- - -	- +	- -
	[cor]	- - + + + - -	- - + + + + + + -	+ +	- + -	+ + +	- -	- -
	[ant]	- - + + + - -	- - + + + - - - -	- -	- + -	+ - +	- -	- -
	[dis]	- - - - - - -	- - + + - - + + -	+ +	- - -	- + -	- -	- -
	[stri]	- - - - - - -	- - - - + + + + -	+ +	- - -	- - -	- -	- -
	[dor]	- - - - - + +	- - - - - - - - +	- -	- - +	- - -	+ +	- -
	[hi]	- - - - - + +	- - - - - - - - +	- -	- - +	- - -	+ +	- -
	[bk]	- - - - - + +	- - - - - - - - +	- -	- - +	- - -	- +	- -

Table 2. Feature chart for NAE vowels

Types	Features	Front i ɪ e ɛ æ	Back (including "Central") ə ʌ u ʊ o ɔ a/ɑ
Diffuse	[cons]	- - - - -	- - - - - - -
	[son]	+ + + + +	+ + + + + + +
	[syl]	+ + + + +	+ + + + + + +
Manner	[cont]	+ + + + +	+ + + + + + +
Laryngeal	[vd]	+ + + + +	+ + + + + + +
Place	[lab]	- - - - -	- - + + + + -
	[rd]	- - - - -	- - + + + + -
	[dor]	+ + + + +	+ + + + + + +
	[hi]	+ + - - -	- - + + - - -
	[lo]	- - - - +	- - - - - - +
	[bk]	- - - - -	+ + + + + + +
	[tns]	+ - + - -	- - + - + - ±
	[rdu]	- - - - -	+ - - - - - -

Components of Phonological Rules

There are three components in a phonological rule: the input (UR), the output (SR), and the environment in which the input is realized as the output, as formalized below:

(2)   α -> β / γ____δ

This abstraction has seven signs: α, for the input (a target phoneme or a target natural class of sounds prior to changes); β, for the output derived from α; the arrow, meaning "becomes," so α -> β is read "α becomes β." The slash, the fourth sign, means "in the environment of . . ." and is followed with a specified environment. The fifth sign, the underscore, known as the **environment bar**, indicates where α resides. In (2), α occurs between γ and δ (the sixth and seventh signs), forming a sound string γαδ. Essentially, the rule states that "α becomes β when it occurs in γαδ."

This formalized rule template stands for generalizations that are categorical. An optional generalization is conventionally enclosed in parenthesis, as below, where (β) in parentheses indicates an output that can be realized as an option:

(3)   α -> (β) / γ____δ

Language offers diverse environments, so γ____δ is adapted for environmental or positional changes with the following signs:

(4)

a.	α -> β / #_____	(word-initial, e.g., /p/ in /_æt/ for *pat*)
b.	α -> β / #____#	(word-medial, e.g., /ə/ in /dʒén_ɹəl/ for *general*)
c.	α -> β / ____#	(word-final, e.g., /l/ in /lítə_/ for *little*)
d.	α -> β / ____##	(at the boundary of words, e.g., /t/ in /læs_## tu/ for *last two)*
e.	α -> β / σ_____	(syllable-initial, e.g., /t/ in /ə._ɔp/ for *atop*)
f.	α -> β / ____σ	(syllable-final, e.g., /d/ in /hæn_/ for *hand*)
g.	α -> β / ____σσ	(at the boundary of syllables, e.g. /p/ in /kɔm_fɚt/ for *com(p)fort*)
h.	α -> β / $____	(in the syllabic onset, e.g., /pɹ-/ in /__aɪm/ for *prime*)
i.	α -> β / ____@	(in the syllabic coda, e.g., /-st/ in /fæ__/ for *fast*)
j.	α -> β / ____}	(utterance-final, e.g., /-v/ in /ɪts ðə kɔsts hil seɪ_/ for *It's the costs he'll save.)*
k.	α -> β / {____}	(utterance-medial, e.g., /h/ in /ðæts _ɚ dɹim/ for *That's her dream.)*
l.	α -> α: / γ____δ	(a colon for a lengthened segment when between γ and δ, e.g., /o/ in /h_:m/ for *home*)
m.	α -> ∅ / ____++	(at the boundary of two morphemes, e.g., /k/ in /æs_++t/ for *ask+ed*)

The null sign ∅ in the last rule template expresses a deleted element, so the rule reads: "Sound α (e.g., /k/) is deleted at the end of a morpheme (e.g., /æs_/) when it precedes another morpheme (e.g., /-t/ derived from –*ed*) in the same word," resulting in [æst] instead of [æskt]. Other signs (#, σ, $, @, { }, +) used in the template indicate the boundaries of and various positions in syllables, words, and utterances.

Stress often plays a role. For example, a change can occur between a stressed and an unstressed syllable. In this case, [+stress] or its shorthand form V́ and [-stress] or its shorthand form V are used. Thus, (5a) and (5b) designate the same environment.

(5) a. α -> β / [+stress]_____[-stress]
      b. α -> β / V́_____V

What if two adjacent or distant phonemes are permuted? Numbers can be used under the input and then are permuted in the output:

(6) α β γ ## -> 2 1 3 (adapted from Wolfram & Johnson, 1982, p.131)
     1 2 3

Having familiarized us with these signs and templates, we now turn to two new concepts below in rule formalization to simplify rule writing.

Simplification of Redundant Features

In earlier chapters, we have learned that some sounds are predictable while others are not. Unpredictable ones are underlyingly phonemic and thus meaning-related, while predictable ones do not affect meaning and are phonetic or allophonic. For example, the vowel /æ/ in the context S_m is unpredictable because other vowels can also appear in the same position to make a contrastively different word, as /i/ in *seam*; however, the [+nasal] feature of [æ] in [sæm] and [ī] in *seam* is predictable because each vowel precedes the nasal [m]. As mentioned earlier, speakers learn unpredictable phonemes when they learn new words; dictionaries spell out unpredictable phonemes when they list words, such as *Sam* /sæm/ and *seam* /sim/. These examples show that the feature [nas] is redundant for NAE vowels but non-redundant for NAE nasal consonants because not just /m/, but also /n/ and /ŋ/ can nasalize a preceding vowel. To write a phonological rule, we would not just want to specify a single nasal, for the whole natural class of nasals has the function to nasalize any preceding vowel but not any particular vowel. It is in this sense that we claim that phonological rules make reference to natural classes. Invoking features to get natural classes of sounds in place, redundant (predictable) features are excluded from feature matrixes (i.e., a bundle of features) of the input and output. Technically, exclusion of redundant features is known as **underspecification**, which is the most economical way to call into use relevant segments that undergo changes. Underspecification is usually a learning bottleneck in feature-based phonology, so we will explain it further here. Nasal consonants are by default [+son], so [+son] is redundant if [+nas] is specified; the combination of [+dor, -cons] eliminates all consonants and invokes vowels, so all other features become redundant and can be left out. The examples in (7a) and (7b) show more clearly the differences between the redundant feature matrixes and underspecified distinctive feature matrixes for the three phonemes in the word *seam*:

(7)　a. Redundant feature matrixes for /s/, /i/, /m/:

/s/	/i/	/m/
+cons	−cons	+cons
−son	+son	+son
−syl	+syl	−syl
+cont	+cont	−cont
−nas	+vd	+nas
−d.r.	−lab	−d.r.
−tap	−rd	−tap
−tril	+dor	−tril
−vd	+hi	+vd
−c.g.	−lo	−c.g.
−s.g.	−bk	−s.g.
−lat	+tns	−lat
−lab	−rdu	+lab
−rd		−rd
+cor		−cor
+ant		−ant
−dis		−dis
+stri		−stri
−dor		−dor
−hi		−hi
−bk		−bk

　　b.　Underspecified distinctive feature matrixes (URs) for /s/, /i/, /m/:

/s/	/i/	/m/
−vd	−cons	+cons
+ant	+dor	+lab
−dis	+hi	+nas
+stri	−bk	
	+tns	

The feature theory assumes that words have unique URs of non-redundant *df*s stored in a speaker's mental dictionary, so URs should keep as few features as possible and leave out redundant and predictable features.

In general, to specify a single phoneme, a longer bundle of *df*s is needed, but to specify a natural class of sounds, a shorter bundle of *df*s usually does the work, as shown in (8):

(8)

/s, z/	/i, e, u, o/	/m, n, ŋ/
+ant	+dor	+cons
−dis	+tns	+nas
+stri		

Though underspecification simplifies the selection of distinctive features, placing the specified segments either above or below corresponding feature matrixes is usually a good practice for easier segment-matrix mappings, as also shown in (7) and (8) above.

If finding features just needed for specifying a natural class is still a challenge, readers are advised to follow this three-step elimination method adapted from Hayes (2009, pp. 92-93):

(9)　The Three-step Elimination Method
　　　a.　Be clear about a target segment or a target natural class of sounds to specify;
　　　b.　Start with the complete set of segments in a language;
　　　c.　Use just enough features to eliminate all the segments not wanted and leave the target segment or target natural class in place.

For instance, if we are seeking to describe the natural class of voiceless consonants /p, t, k, f, θ/ that collectively takes the phonetic value [s] derived from the plural morpheme -s, which is also the possessive case ending and the third person singular present tense marker, we can use [+cons] to eliminate glides /j, w/, glottals /h, ʔ/, and all vowels, [-vd] to take away all voiced consonants, and then [-stri] to get rid of all the sibilants. At this point, only our target class remains, i.e., /p, t, k, f, θ, x/. We should disregard the non-NAE phoneme /x/ since we are specifying the natural class of sounds that takes the plural morpheme –s instead of comparing the class with a sound from another language. We will formalize this derivational process when we discuss morphophonemic rules of assimilation that apply only to particular morphemes. The points we are making here have been that, first, we take an elimination method to invoke a target class of sounds and, second, IPA classes of sounds will not serve our purpose because /p, t, k, f, θ/ cross two IPA categories, [+stop] and [+fricative], which are mutually exclusive. Below, we look at general phonological rules that sweepingly apply to various UR-SR derivational processes as categories.

Phonological Rules

In this chapter, we express phonological rules in three formats: prose, semi-formal, and formal so that they complement each other in helping readers gain insights to phonological alternations. In general, prose rules use words for description but do not appeal to *df*s, while formal rules make entire use of *df*s but do not use words and segments, with semi-formal rules using a compromised mixture of segments and features as long as the mixture contributes insight. In most cases, this section provides all three expressions for individual rules, from prose to semi-formal to formal in that order, to meet varying needs of readers. In general, the more formal a rule is, the more precise it becomes in capturing phonological generalizations. Conversely, the less formal a rule is, the more accessible it is to human perusing, though less precise it is. So the whole matter is a trade-off.

Language offers an optimal phonological system with multiple resources which delete, add, reduce, metathesize, assimilate, and dissimilate segments and *df*s for effective oral communication. We will begin with deletion rules below, followed by rules of addition, reduction, metathesis, assimilation, and dissimilation. Roughly, this order reflects phonological rules that operate more at the level of segments toward more at the level of *df*s.

Deletion Rules

Deletion is particularly common when it results in the simplification of a consonant cluster in both tautosyllables (phonemes occurring in one syllable) and heterosyllables (phonemes not occurring in the same syllable): *asked* [æskt] can become [æst], *exactly* [ɪgzǽktli] [ɪgzǽkli], and many more. Since English syllable structure allows both onsets and codas, chances of coda-onset bumping multiply, creating multiple consonant sequences, with the longest being $-C_1C_2C_3C_4\#\#C_1C_2C_3-$, such as [-ksts skj-] as in *These te<u>xts sk</u>ew the facts,* in which the first [-s-] in the left C_2 position is frequently deleted.

Deletion is more common in unstressed than in stressed syllables. Further, unstressed vowels or syllables are often deleted when they occur word-initially known as **aphesis**, as in *'bout* for *about* and *'fend* for *defend,* or in the middle of a word known as **syncope**, as in *cam'ra* for *camera*. **Apocope** is the loss of sounds at the end of a word, as in *chile care* for *child care*. Below we look at several common rules that delete segments. All rules are derived inductively, i.e., examples first, and rules second.

(10) The Medial Schwa Deletion Rule
Examine the sample words uttered in careful and casual speech respectively:

Sample words	Careful speech	Casual speech
operative (adj.)	[ɔ́pəɹətɪv]	[ɔ́pɹətɪv]
operate (v)	[ɔ́pəɹeɪt]	*[ɔ́pɹeɪt]
difference (n)	[dífəɹəns]	[dífɹəns]
devilment (n)	[dɛ́vəlmənt]	[dɛ́vl̩mənt]

These words show that when a stressed syllable is followed with two successive schwas in two unstressed syllables, the first schwa can be deleted but retained if it is followed with a secondary stress, as in the verb *operate* [ɔ́pəɹeɪt] (as compared to *[ɔ́pɹeɪt], the asterisk marks an illicit linguistic form). This rule can be captured in three different expressions:

Prose: A word-medial schwa can be deleted between a stressed syllable
                  and an unstressed syllable in the same word. (Optional)

Semi-formal: ə -> (Ø) / #V́ ____ V#
                ə -> (Ø) / #V́ ____ ə#

Formal: [+rdu] -> (Ø) / #[-rdu] ____ [+rdu]#

Since [rdu] is pertinent to vowels only, it alone makes inclusion of other *df*s redundant. Note that utterance tempo acts as a catalyst for deletion to happen. The faster the tempo is, the more likely a deletion happens.

(11) The /g/-Deletion Rule

When affixations are added, silent letters may sound as the "silent g–articulated /g/" alternation in the following words shows, causing spelling nightmares (Fromkin, Rodman, & Hyams, 2017):

Silent "g"	*Articulated* /g/
gnostic [nástɪk]	a**g**nostic [ægnástɪk]
si**g**n [sãɪn]	si**g**nature [sígnətʃɚ]
mali**g**n [məlãɪn]	mali**g**nant /məlígnənt]
paradi**g**m [pʰæɹədãɪm]	paradi**g**matic [pʰæɹədɪgmǽtɪk]

This phonological alternation can be generalized as the /g/-deletion rule:

Prose: Delete /g/ before /n/ or /m/ in the onset or coda of a syllable.
(Obligatory)

Semi-formal: g /g/ -> Ø / $____/n/
/ _____ /n/ or /m/ @

Formal:

$$\begin{bmatrix} -cont \\ -nas \\ +vd \\ +dor \end{bmatrix} \rightarrow \emptyset \; / \; \$\_\_\_\_ \begin{bmatrix} +nas \\ +cor \end{bmatrix} \; \text{or} \; \_\_\_\_ \begin{bmatrix} +nas \\ +lab \end{bmatrix} @$$

Note that this rule deletes the whole segment /g/. It is obvious that the prose and semi-formal rules work better, making it unnecessary to write an inhumanly formal rule that does not contribute insight. For similar cases below, we will content ourselves to write just a prose or semi-formal rule.

(12) The /h/-Deletion Rule

The pronominal syllable-initial /h/ is frequently deleted, especially in casual speech. Examine the examples below.

a.   /h/ not pronounced in French loans (though not pronouns)
*(**h**)our, (**h**)erb, (**h**)onest, (**h**)onor*

b.   /h/ retained when stressed and sentence-initial:
He likes **h**er.

c.   /h/ frequently deleted elsewhere:
*Did (**h**)e come?* [dɪdi kʌ̃m]
*It's (**h**)er car.* [ɪtsɚ kaɹ]
*What (**h**)ad (**h**)is Dad say?* [wətədiz dæd seɪ]

The /h/-deletion in French loanwords in (a) is unpredictable and thus must be learned from scratch, but the /h/-deletions in (b) and (c) are rule-governed and thus predictable, as generalized below:

Prose: Delete an utterance-medial /h/ in an unstressed pronominal pronoun.

Semi-formal: h -> Ø / {$ _____}
[-stress]

(13) The Postnasal /t/ Deletion Rule

Deletion takes many forms, and the optional deletion of the phoneme /t/ is another example:

	Words/phrases	Careful speech	Casual speech
a.	win.ter	[wín.tɚ]	[wín.ɚ] (c.f. winner)
	ten.ta.tive	[tén.tə.tɪv]	[tén.ə.tɪv]
	want.ed	[wɔ́nt.ɪd], [wán.təd]	[wɔ́n.ɪd], [wán.əd]
	men.tal	[mɛn.təl], [mɛn.tl̩]	[mɛn.əl]
	want to	[wɔ́nt.tə]	[wɔ́n.ə] (spelled wanna)
b.	front	[fɹʌ́nt]	*[fɹʌ́n]
	ant.ler	[ǽnt.lɚ]	*[ǽn.lɚ]
	man.teau	[mǽn.tò]	*[mǽnò]
	men.tal.i.ty	[mɛn.tǽl.ə.ti]	*[mɛn.ǽl.ə.ti]
	pres.en.ta.tion	[pɹɛz.ən.téɪ.ʃən]	*[pɹɛz.ən.éɪ.ʃən]

Analyses of (a) indicate that /t/ can be deleted under two co-occuring constraints: when a syllable boundary exists between the coda /n/ of a preceding syllable that is stressed and the onset /t/ of a following syllable that is stressless. The word *want.ed* is an interesting example because it invokes a **re-syllabification** rule thereby the last consonant in a word-medial or word-final consonant cluster (not just a single word-final consonant), when followed by a word or syllable commencing with a vowel, is pronounced as if it were the onset of the following syllable. As a result, *want.ed* is uttered as if it were *wan.ted*, which satisfies the two co-existing constraints and activates the postnasal /t/ deletion, resulting in [wán.əd].

The phrase *want to* fails to meet the syllable boundary condition. How come that the Postnasal /t/ Deletion Rule is also activated? It turns out that a different rule – the Word-boundary Alveolar Stop Deletion Rule – has to apply first before the Postnasal /t/ Deletion Rule can take effect. This first rule deletes "word-final /t/ or /d/ in cluster of two at a word boundary" prior to a consonant other than /ɹ, y, w, h/, producing *wes*t *side, blin*d *man* (Celce-Murcia et al., 2010, p.172), and *wan*t *to*. Now, *wan.to* meets the two co-occurring conditions and thus activates the Postnasal /t/ Deletion Rule, and ultimately creates [wɔ́n.ə]. Note that the phonological alternations [wán.təd]: [wán.əd] and [wɔ́nt.tə]: [wɔ́n.ə] are examples of **ordered** rule applications, i.e., the activation of the second rule rests on the activation of the first rule, a topic we will return to later in this chapter.

Now, we focus on the examples in (13b), in which the operation of the Postnasal /t/ Deletion Rule generates ungrammatical pronunciations. What blocks this rule from activation? In the first two words *front* and *antler*, the word-final -nt cluster forms a syllabic coda, not meeting the syllable-boundary condition, so /t/ cannot be deleted. The -n.t- sequence in the French loan *man.teau* does cross the syllable boundary, but the second syllable is assigned a secondary stress, so we might say that it is an unstressed syllable that is required for the rule to be active. In the last two examples, *men.tal.i.ty* and *pres.en.ta.tion*, though the cross-syllable boundary condition is met, the syllable with the onset /t/ is assigned stress, and that prevents the rule from functioning.

Now, we are able to generalize this Postnasal /t/ Deletion Rule below:

Prose: Optionally delete the onset /t/ of an unstressed syllable following the coda /n/ of a stressed syllable. (Elsewhere, the /t/ is retained.)

Semi-formal: t -> (∅) / V́n σσ ___V

Formal:

$$\begin{bmatrix} \text{-cont} \\ \text{-nas} \\ \text{+ant} \\ \text{-vd} \end{bmatrix} \rightarrow (\emptyset) \ / \ \acute{V} \begin{bmatrix} \text{+nas} \\ \text{+cor} \end{bmatrix} \sigma\sigma \ \_\_\_V$$

(14) The Adaptive Deletion Rules

Phonological adaptation of loan words often results in various types of deletion as constrained by English syllable structure. Phonotactically, English syllable structure does not permit the onset cluster /hj-/ unless followed by /u/ as in *humor*; thus /j/ is deleted from the Korean automobile name *Hyundai* [hjʌ́ndæ], giving [hʌ́ndeɪ], where the Korean [-tns] /æ/ is replaced with the English [+tns] [e] because English syllables do not end in [-tns] vowels and the [+tns] [e] is the closest available segment to /æ/, both of which share the [-bk] feature. Though /i/ also shares the [-bk] feature, it is a [+hi] tense vowel, further up from the [+lo] /æ/ in Korean, thus not the best candidate for substitution. This example demonstrates that *df*s can account for not only *what* and *how* a phonological change happens but also *why* it happens.

Deletion is omnipresent and heterogeneous, and it cannot be exhausted here. Fortunately, its rule formation is straightforward because it involves deletion of whole segments, so in most cases the prose and semi-formal rules work better than formal rules. Below, we turn to epenthesis.

Epenthesis Rules

Epenthesis, also known as addition or insertion, is a phonological process that adds a whole segment or a *df* not reflected in spelling. This can happen in multiple situations.

When a loanword contains a syllable structure impermissible in English, such as /pf-/ in *Pfenning*, English speakers not knowing German tend to insert [ə] to break up the initial consonant cluster or simply delete the initial /p/, creating an example of either an adaptive epenthesis or an adaptive deletion. Conversely, Korean speakers of English often break up an English monosyllable like *scream* to a four-syllable *secereame* [səkəɹímə].

When loan words are not involved, consonant segments can also be inserted to facilitate the pronunciation of existing clusters in regional dialects. For instance, /t/ is inserted as a transition between /n/ and /s/, forming a [-nts] sequence, as in *fence* [fɛnts] and *prince* [pɹɪnts], and /p/ can be added between /m/ and /f/, as in *com(p)fort*. We hear the same process at work when some English speakers add /ɹ/ between /ɑ/ and /ʃ/ in *Wa(r)shington*. Below, we look at more words with /p/-epenthesis.

(15) The /p/-Epenthesis Rule

Examine the following words, in which /p/ can be optionally inserted in casual speech, creating alternations:

comfort	[kʌ́m(p)fɚt]	flimflam	[flím(p)flæm]
ham fat	[hǽm(p)fæt]	ham fatter	[hǽm(p)fæ̀tɚ]
game fish	[géɪm(p)fɪʃ]	lymphatic	[lɪm(p)fǽtɪk]
Mumford	[mʌ́m(p)fɚd]	tomfool	[tɔ̀m(p)fúl]

These words show that the [p]-insertion is not sensitive to stress location, syllable count, and compounding, although disyllables with initial stress seem to have more triggering power for the epenthesis. This insensitivity makes the rule writing easier:

Prose: Insert /p/ between /m/ and /f/ at the boundary of syllables.

Semi-formal: $\emptyset \rightarrow p \; / \; m \underline{\quad} \sigma\sigma \, f$

Formal: $\emptyset \rightarrow \underset{\begin{bmatrix}-\text{cont}\\-\text{vd}\\+\text{lab}\end{bmatrix}}{p} \Big/ \underset{\begin{bmatrix}-\text{cont}\\+\text{nas}\\+\text{lab}\end{bmatrix}}{m} \underline{\quad} \sigma\sigma \underset{\begin{bmatrix}+\text{cont}\\-\text{vd}\\+\text{lab}\end{bmatrix}}{f}$

The matrix-segment matching reveals that this formal rule captures the shared [+lab] feature in /m-p-f/ that triggers the epenthesis, but this insight is not discernable in the prose and semi-formal rules.

Some dialects do not allow a coda of /l/ to precede a following stop consonant, so [ə] is inserted to break up the cluster, as in *film* [fíləm], *silk* [sílək], *built* [bílət], and *killed* [kíləd]. The last example is reminiscent of a historical pronunciation of schwa in the past tense marker *–ed*, as in Chaucer's familiar examples of *perced* [pɛ̄ɹsəd], *bathed* [bǽðəd], and *engendred* [ɛndʒɛ́ndɹəd] at the beginning lines in *The Canterbury Tales* (Chaucer & Benson, 1987). Below, we formalize this dialectal Schwa-Insertion Rule.

(16) The Dialectal Schwa Epenthesis Rule:

Prose: Insert a schwa between the lateral /l/ and a stop consonant in the coda of a syllable.

Semi-formal: $\emptyset \rightarrow ə \; / \; \underset{[-\text{stress}]}{l} \underline{\quad} C@$ (where C = a [-cont] consonant)

Formal: $\emptyset \rightarrow [+\text{rdu}] \; / \; \underset{[-\text{stress}]}{\begin{bmatrix}+\text{cons}\\+\text{lat}\end{bmatrix}} \underline{\quad} \begin{bmatrix}+\text{cons}\\-\text{cont}\end{bmatrix}@$

All the examples above illustrate that epenthesis occurs at the level of segments. However, epenthesis can also occur at the level of *df*s. The feature [+s.g.] addition rule is such an example, shown in (17) below.

(17) The Feature [+s.g.] Addition Rule
Examine the following sample words:

peak [**pʰ**ik]	but	speak [s**pik**]
team [**tʰ**im]	but	steam [s**tim**]
kill [**kʰ**ɪɫ]	but	skill [s**kɪɫ**]
stupidity [stju.**pʰ**íd.ɹ.ti]	but	replica [ɹɛ́**p**.li.**k**ə]
recount [ɹɪ.**kʰ**áunt]	but	record (n) [ɹɛ́**k**.əɹd]

Oral voiceless stops /p, t, k/ in the left column all aspirate as [pʰ, tʰ, kʰ] when occurring at the beginning of a stressed syllable; those in the right column do not when occurring elsewhere, namely, in a coda, after the initial /s/, or at the beginning of an unstressed syllable. This generalization can be made as follows:

Prose: Voiceless stops become aspirated at the beginning of a stressed syllable.

Semi-formal: p, t, k   ->   pʰ, tʰ, kʰ / σ ___V́

Formal:

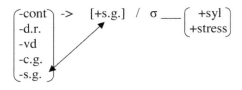

The formal rule explicitly shows that what is added to /p, t, k/ is the [+s.g.] feature. Epenthesis, whether at the level of segment or feature, has significant implications in interphonology, which we discuss in Section V. Below, we turn to metathesis rules.

Metathesis Rules

This phonological process refers to the reordering of sound segments in a word, phrase, or sentence. Thus, *jewelry* becomes *jewlery*, where the [əl] sequence is interchanged to [lə], and *asked* becomes *aksed*, where [s] and [k] are switched. Chaucer freely used both *bird* and *brid* in his Middle English poems for the Modern English word *bird*, where [ɪ] and [ɹ] changed places (Chaucer & Benson, 1987). The author of this chapter sometimes subconsciously switches *relevant* to *revelant*, where [l] and [v] are reordered. Metathesis is especially common with /ɹ/ and a schwa, forming alternations such as *perform~preform, precipitation~percipitation, prepare~perpare*, where *-er-* becomes *–re-* and vice versa.

Spoonerisms are special cases of metathesis,[6] resulting in sound exchanges between words in a phrase or sentence, so the verb phrase *missed my history lecture* becomes *hissed my mystery lecture*, and the sentence *The Lord is a loving shepherd* is metathesized as *The Lord is a shoving leopard* (For more examples, see Wolfram & Johnson, 1982). A metathesis rule can be formulated in a way shown in the *Lord* example, where /l/ alternates with /ʃ/ as below:

(18) The /l ~ ʃ/ Metathesis

    Prose: The word-initial liquid /l/ and word-initial fricative /ʃ/ are switched.

    Semi-formal: /l/ ## /ʃ/ -> [ʃ] ## [l]

    Formal:

$$\# \begin{bmatrix} +\text{cons} \\ +\text{last} \end{bmatrix} \ \# \# \ \begin{bmatrix} -\text{vd} \\ -\text{d.r.} \\ -\text{ant} \\ +\text{stri} \end{bmatrix} \ \text{->} \ \underline{4} \ 2 \ 3 \ \underline{1}$$

$$\underline{1} \qquad\quad 2\ 3 \qquad\quad \underline{4}$$

Of the three versions of the rule, the semi-formal expression is at a glance the clearest.

Reduction Rules

Reduction tones down phonemic contrasts, so that sounds that are normally distinct are sometimes identical in certain environments. For example, most vowels are reduced to /ə/ or /ɪ/ in unstressed syllables, so *CONduct* [kɑ́ndəkt] becomes *conDUCT* [kəndʌ́kt]. Nearly every polysyllable without stress doublets contains one or more reduced vowels, as in *America* [əmɛ́ɹɪkə] and *revolution* [ɹɛvəlúʃən]. Vowel reduction, also known as leveling, can be generalized in the following expressions:

(19) The Vowel Reduction Rule

    Prose: A vowel in unstressed syllables is reduced to schwa (obligatory).

    Semi-formal: [-rdu] -> [+rdu] / σ _____ σ
                                             [-stress]

    Formal:

$$\begin{bmatrix} +\text{dor} \\ -\text{rdu} \end{bmatrix} \ \text{->} \ [+\text{rdu}] \ / \ \underset{[-\text{stress}]}{\sigma \text{_____} \sigma}$$

Not only can vowel contrasts be reduced, but contrasts between consonants can also be reduced. For example, /t/ and /d/, when each directly abuts a preceding stressed vowel and a following unstressed vowels in two syllables, are often neutralized to a flap [ɾ] by many NAE speakers, as in *metal* [mɛ́ɾl̩] and *meddle* [mɛ́.ɾl̩], the two of which can only be differentiated by vowel length, that is, the stressed vowel [ɛ] is shorter in *metal* but longer in *meddle*. We will revisit this consonant reduction or alternation when we discuss assimilation rules below.

Assimilation Rules

Assimilation is a highly productive phonological process in NAE that transfers *df*s of a segment to its neighboring segment so that the two of them sound more alike, thereby smoothening pronunciation. Unlike most phonological processes discussed above that operate largely on the level of segments, almost all assimilations operate on the *df* level.

   Assimilation falls into different yet overlapping categories. In terms of direction, there are *regressive* (or *anticipatory*) and progressive (or *perseverative*) assimilations; in terms of degree, there are *partial* and *total* assimilations. Regressive assimilation refers to the influence that a segment has on its preceding segment (e.g., *pancake* [pæŋkeɪk, *pænkeɪk], where the [+dor] feature in /k/ is assimilated to the [+cor] feature in the preceding /n/ and changes /n/ to [ŋ], so that both [ŋ] and [k] becomes identical in [+dor]). Progressive assimilation refers to the influence that a segment has on its following segment (e.g., *price* [pʰɹ̥aɪs]), where the [-vd] feature in /p/ devoices its following voiced retroflex [ɹ] and alters it to [ɹ̥], rendering [p] and [ɹ] more alike in [-vd]. Both *pancake* and *price* are also examples of partial assimilation because [ŋ: k] and [p: ɹ̥] are still distinct by other features. An example of total assimilation is the alveolar /n/ in *ten* and /t/ in *let* that become [m] when prior to words beginning with the bilabial /m/, as in *ten months* [tɛ́m m-] and *let me do it* [lɛm m-]. These two total assimilations are also regressive assimilations. Total assimilation changes a different segment to a phonetically similar segment, making rule formation plain sailing:

(20) The /n/-Assimilation Rule

   Prose: The alveolar nasal becomes the bilabial nasal before the word-initial
                   bilabial nasal. (optional)

   Semi-formal: n -> m / ___##m

   Formal: $\begin{bmatrix} +nas \\ +cor \end{bmatrix} \longrightarrow \begin{bmatrix} +nas \\ +lab \end{bmatrix} \longleftarrow / \ \_\_\_ \ \#\# \begin{bmatrix} +nas \\ +lab \end{bmatrix}$

   Only the formal rule makes it explicit that it is the [+lab] feature in /m/ that assimilates [+cor] in /n/ to [+lab].

   In addition to regressive, progressive, partial, and complete assimilations, assimilation can also be classified by *place, manner*, and *voicing* (i.e., laryngeal). We will discuss place assimilation first.

   Place assimilation occurs when a phoneme assimilates the place features of adjacent consonants in certain environments. The /-n/ or /-t/ assimilations are classical examples. The alveolar /n/ can be dentalized as [n̪] when prior to the labiodental fricative [θ], as in *tenth* [tɛn̪θ] and *month* [mʌn̪θ]. A [-rd] consonant such as /k, g, s, z, l, ʃ/ acquires [+rd] when prior to the [+rd] glide /w/ or a [+rd] high back vowel /u, ʊ/, as in *quick* [k̹wɪk], *goose* [g̹us], and *zoo* [z̹u] (the crescent sign under the consonants stands for the [+rd] feature). Examples are extensive. Below, we formalize the consonant rounding generalization.

(21) The Consonant Rounding Rule

    Prose: Unrounded consonants become rounded preceding a rounded glide or vowel.

    Semi-formal: unrounded consonants -> [+rd] / σ___ w, u, ʊ

    Formal:

$$\begin{bmatrix} +cons \\ -rd \end{bmatrix} \rightarrow [+rd] \ / \ \sigma\_\_\_ \begin{bmatrix} +son \\ +lab \\ +rd \end{bmatrix}$$

Below, we turn to manner assimilation, which refers to the process in which a sound takes on the same articulation manner as its nearby sound. Vowel nasalization is a good example.

(22) The Vowel Nasalization Rule

In each of the words below, a vowel goes before a nasal sound:

beam [bĩ:m]	ten [tɛ̃:n]	gunman [gʌ̃nmɛ̃n] or [gʌ̃:nmən]
dam [dæ̃:m]	song [sɔ̃:ŋ]	freedom [fɹídəm] or [fɹí:dm̩]

These words show that the vowels pick up the [+nas] feature from the following nasal sounds so that both the vowels and nasals sound alike with reference to nasality, but they also show that vowel nasalization occurs in stressed syllables, including secondary stress (e.g., [-mɛ̃n]). In an unstressed syllable, nasalization is so minimal that it is often ignored. We state this observation below:

    Prose: A vowel in a stressed syllable becomes nasalized before a nasal sound. (obligatory)

    Semi-formal: V́ -> V̋ / _____ [+nas] σ
                      [+stress]

    Formal:

$$\begin{bmatrix} +syl \\ +dor \end{bmatrix} \rightarrow [+nas] \ / \ \underset{[+stress]}{_____} \begin{bmatrix} +cons \\ +nas \end{bmatrix} \sigma$$

(23) The /t/ Tapping Rule

In casual NAE speech, the [-vd] alveolar /t/ often becomes a [+vd] alveolar flap [ɾ] made by rapidly touching the tongue tip against the alveolar ridge and then instantly releasing it. Exam the examples below:

atom [ǽɾəm]	atomic *[əɾɔ́mɪk]
data [dǽɾə]	guilty *[ɡílɾy]
I bought it [aɪ bɔ́ɾɪt]	John lost them [ʤɔn *lɔ́sɾəm]

The examples in the left column show that /t/ becomes [ɾ] when it occurs between two syllabic vowels of which the first is stressed while the second is not. However, the rule is blocked in the examples in the right column, where /t/ occurs either at the beginning of a stressed syllable or after a different consonant. This generalization can be captured below:

Prose: The /t/ phoneme becomes a flap [ɾ] when immediately adjacent to two
vowels of which the first is stressed and the second unstressed. (optional)

Semi-formal: t -> (ɾ) / V́__V

Formal:

$$
\begin{bmatrix} -\text{cont} \\ -\text{nas} \\ +\text{ant} \\ -\text{vd} \\ -\text{tap} \end{bmatrix} \rightarrow \begin{bmatrix} -\text{cont} \\ -\text{nas} \\ +\text{ant} \\ +\text{vd} \\ +\text{tap} \end{bmatrix} / \begin{bmatrix} +\text{syl} \\ +\text{stress} \end{bmatrix} \underline{\hspace{1cm}} \begin{bmatrix} +\text{syl} \\ -\text{stress} \end{bmatrix}
$$

Once more, only the formal rule has the capacity of revealing exactly what features are changed.

(24) The /t, d/ Neutralization Rule

The /t/-tapping rule in (23), however, fails to capture a higher-level generalization because the voiced alveolar /d/ can also be flapped. Consequently, word pairs, *writer* [ɹáɪɾɚ] vs. *rider* [ɹáɪɾɚ], *latter* [lǽɾɚ] vs. *ladder* [lǽɾɚ], sound the same. In other words, /t/ and /d/ are neutralized to [ɾ]. We can capture this generalization as such:

Prose: The phonemes /t, d/ are neutralized to [ɾ] when each is directly flanked by
two vowels the first of which is stressed and the second unstressed.

Semi-formal: t, d -> (ɾ) / V́__V

Formal:

$$
\begin{bmatrix} -\text{cont} \\ -\text{nas} \\ +\text{ant} \\ -\text{tap} \end{bmatrix} \rightarrow \begin{bmatrix} -\text{cont} \\ -\text{nas} \\ +\text{ant} \\ +\text{tap} \end{bmatrix} / \begin{bmatrix} +\text{syl} \\ +\text{stress} \end{bmatrix} \underline{\hspace{1cm}} \begin{bmatrix} +\text{syl} \\ -\text{stress} \end{bmatrix}
$$

Note that the [vd] feature is no longer relevant here.

The phoneme /t/ is phonetically volatile. In addition to deletion and flapping as discussed above, it can also become aspirated as [tʰ], unreleased as [t̚], nasalized as [m], glottalized as [ʔ], velarized as [tˠ], fricated as [ʃ], and affricated as [tʃ], subject to positional restrictions, as shown below:

a.   /t/ -> [tʰ]   team [tʰim]   attack [ətʰǽk]
     /t/ -> [t̚]   debt [dɛt̚]   lost [lɔst̚]
b.   /t/ -> [tˠ]   little [lítˠɬ]   cattle [kʰǽtˠɬ]
     /t/ -> [ʔ]   kitten [kíʔn̩]   bottom [bóʔm̩]
c.   /t/ -> [m]   let me [lɛm mi]   get mixed [gɛm míkst̚]
     /t/ -> [ʃ]   nation [néɪʃən]   position [pəzíʃən]
     /t/ -> [tʃ]   tree [tʃɹi]   meet you [mítʃu]

The examples in (a) show feature-adding alternations that we mentioned earlier, those in (b) show place assimilations, and those in (c) are manner assimilations.

(25) The Onset Liquids-Glides Devoicing Rule

NAE has a devoicing assimilation occurring in the onset of a stressed syllable, where liquids /l, ɹ/ and glides /j, w/ have [-vd] allophones after a [-vd] stop, as illustrated below:

plus [pʰl̥ʌs]	Tlingit [tʰl̥íŋgɪt]	class [kʰl̥æs]
price [pɹ̥aɪs]	tree [ʧɹ̥i]	crisp [kʰɹ̥ɪsp]
pure [pʰj̥uɹ]	tutor [tj̥úɾɚ]	cute [kʰj̥ut]
Pueblo [pw̥éblo]	twist [tʰw̥ɪst]	quick [kʰw̥ɪk]
reply [ɹəpl̥áɪ]	refuse [ɹəfjús]	surplus *[sɚ́pl̥əs]

Though the *tl-* onset is phototactically unwelcome in English, *Tlingit*, as a loanword from Hindi, has nevertheless made its way to English and obeys this devoicing rule, so does the Spanish borrowing *Pueblo*. The last word, *surplus*, shows that devoicing is suspended in the onset of an unstressed syllable.

We could write separate rules for individual devoicing cases, but that would again fly in the face of the very tenet that phonological rules make reference to natural classes. By specifying the natural class with *df*s, we can easily capture this generalization:

Prose: Liquids and glides are devoiced after a voiceless stop or a voiceless affricate in the onset of a stressed syllable.

Semi-formal: l, ɹ, j, w -> [-vd] / $ p, t, k, ʧ _____

Formal:

$$\begin{bmatrix} +\text{cont} \\ +\text{son} \\ -\text{tri} \end{bmatrix} \rightarrow [-\text{vd}] \ / \ \$ \begin{bmatrix} -\text{cont} \\ -\text{vd} \\ -\text{c.g.} \end{bmatrix} \_\_\_\_\_$$

(26) The Coda Fricative Devoicing Rule
NAE has four voiced fricatives /v, ð, z, ʒ/, as shown in the following words:

	careful	**casual**
shave	[ʃeɪv]	[ʃeɪf]
wreathe	[ɹið]	[ɹiθ]
haze	[heɪz]	[heɪs]
luge	[luʒ]	[luʃ]

In careful speech, the [+vd] feature of the fricative in each word is retained, and in casual speech [+vd] is devoiced to [-vd]. Writing four separate rules would miss the point that the four voiced fricatives belong to one natural class and undergo the same devoicing process:

Prose: In NAE, all voiced fricatives can be devoiced at the end of an utterance.

Semi-formal: /v, ð, z, ʒ/ ---> [f, θ, s, ʃ] / _____ }

Formal: $\begin{bmatrix} \text{-son} \\ \text{+cont} \\ \text{+vd} \end{bmatrix}$ ---> $\begin{bmatrix} \text{-son} \\ \text{+cont} \\ \text{-vd} \end{bmatrix}$ / _____ }

Only the formal rule explicitly and precisely reveals the fact that it is the [vd] feature that is changed whereas the [-son, +cont] features are still retained.

(27) The Vowel Length Rule

English vowels each have three values: schwa in unstressed syllables (see Rule 19), plus two full values in stressed syllables, either [+tns] or [-tns], as shown below:

Vowels	**[+tns]**	**Vowels**	**[-tns]**
a, ai, ay, a.C.e	/e/ rain, bay, fake	a	[æ] ran, bat, pack
e, ee, ea, e.C.e	/i/ he, feet, tea, these	e	[ɛ] fetch, tell, set
igh, -i.C.e	/aɪ/ high, ice	i	[ɪ] hit, sip, pick
o, oa, ow, o.C.e	/o/ so, float, slow, phone	o	[ɑ/ɔ][7], hop, slot, fod
oo, u.final -e	/u/ room, blue	u	[ʌ] cup, bus, shut

The [-tns] vowels follow a simple rule throughout the history of English, that is, when they appear in a closed syllable that is stressed. Elsewhere in stressed syllables, vowels acquire the [+tns] feature. This rule is made easy if we focus on the [-tns] feature:

Prose: Stressed vowels acquire the [-tns] feature in a closed syllable. Elsewhere,
       they acquire the [+tns] feature.[8]

Semi-formal: V́ -> [-tns] / _____ C#
         [+stressed]

Formal: $\begin{bmatrix} \text{+syl} \\ \text{+dor} \end{bmatrix}$ -> [-tns] / _____ [+cons]#
             [+stressed]

The [+tns] value, often considered the outcome of the vowel lengthening rule, is also called "alphabet value," and the [-tns] value "relative value" (Gilbert, 2018, pp.1706-1708).[9] In many cases, vowels with alphabet values are written in two vowel letters with the first vowels standing for alphabet values and the second being silent, a Middle English orthographic tradition created by scribes. In general, [-tns] vowels are short and [+tns] vowels are long. Celce-Murcia, et al. (2010, p.126) further classify vowel length into three grades: Vowels are longest in an open syllable or before a sonorant consonant, next longest before a voiced obstruent, and shortest before a voiceless consonant:

Short:	pat [pæt]	clock [kʰlɔk]	safe [seɪf]	bath [bæθ]
Longer:	pad [pæ.d]	clog [kʰlɔ.g]	save [seɪ.v]	bathe [beɪ.ð]
Longest:	pay [peɪː]	clone [kʰloːn]	same [seɪːm]	bale [beɪːɫ]

The [±tns] values are phonemic, but length variations of either [+tns] or [-tns] are allophonic. This vowel length rule, like aspiration, simply adds a new feature and modifies the manner of articulation of the affected vowels.

Next, we look at out last phonological rule, in which alveolars /s, z, t, d/ are palatalized.

(28) The Palatalization Rule

Analyze the following two groups of words:

a. his yelling [hɪs~hɪʃ]   Does your dog bite? [dʌz~dʌʒ]
    last year [læst~læstʃ]   Did you? [dɪd~dɪdʒ]
    He hates your dog. [heɪts~heɪtʃ]   He needs you. [nidz~nidʒ]

b. issue [íʃju]   measure [mɛ́ʒəɹ]
    virtue [vɝ́ɪtʃju]   nature [néɪtʃəɹ]
    arduous [ɑ́ɹdʒjuəs]   procedure [pɹəsídʒəɹ]

These examples differ. First, examples in (a) are across word boundaries, but those in (b) occur word internally; second, items in (a) show that alveolars /s, z, t, d/ and alveolar clusters /ts, dz/ become palatals [ʃ, ʒ, tʃ, dʒ] respectively when followed by an initial palatal glide /j/, while words in (b) shows an "invisible /j/" in spelling (Dickerson, 1985, as cited in Celce-Murcia et al., 2010, p. 434). Palatalization is considered coalescent or reciprocal assimilation whereby two words uttered in sequence without any pause produce a palatal consonant across the word boundary or word-internally. Below, we capture the generalization shown in (a), excluding /ts, dz/ palatalization because they are morphophonemic rules to be discussed further in the chapter:

Prose: Alveolars /s, z, t, d/ become palatals /ʃ, ʒ, tʃ, dʒ/ respectively when
              preceding the glide /j/ at the beginning of a following word.

Semi-formal: s, z, t, d -> ʃ, ʒ, tʃ, dʒ / ____## j

Formal:
$$\begin{bmatrix} -son \\ +ant \\ -dis \\ -tap \end{bmatrix} \rightarrow \begin{bmatrix} -son \\ -ant \\ +dis \\ -tap \end{bmatrix} / \underline{\quad} \#\# \begin{bmatrix} +cons \\ +son \\ +dor \\ -bk \end{bmatrix}$$

The formal expression provides the most explicit information of the three: It is the [+dor] feature of /j/ that causes the features [+ant, -dis] of the input to become [-ant, +dis] of the output because [+dor] requires the tongue body to raise, and this raising activation adds more contact between tongue and roof of mouth. The more such contact there is, the more [+dis] a natural class. The formal expression also shows its charm that all the four rules are collapsed into one to show the precise inner workings of this coalescent assimilation that the prose and semi-formal expressions fail to capture. Below, we move to dissimilation rules.

Dissimilation Rules

Dissimilation, as the opposite of assimilation, renders nearby sounds less alike in terms of *df*s, and it is much less common. Adjacent sounds that resemble each other too closely sometimes dissimilate. For example, *diphthong* [dífθɔŋ] is usually pronounced [dípθɔŋ]. Because the [-fθ-] sequence shares the *df* [+cont] on top of a whole set of redundant features and thus sounds too closely, the [+cont] feature of [f] is dissimilated to the [-cont] feature of [p]. Then why is [p] selected but not a different consonant? That is because the URs of both /f/ and /p/ share the *df*s of [+lab] that is not shared by [θ], which is distinguished by the [-stri] feature. This implicit explanation can in fact be precisely represented in the formal rule below:

(29) The /f/ to /p/ Dissimilation Rule

$$
\begin{bmatrix} +\text{cont} \\ +\text{lab} \\ -\text{vd} \end{bmatrix} \rightarrow \begin{bmatrix} -\text{cont} \\ +\text{lab} \\ -\text{vd} \end{bmatrix} / \underline{\quad\quad} \begin{bmatrix} +\text{ant} \\ +\text{dis} \\ -\text{stri} \\ -\text{vd} \end{bmatrix}
$$

This example illustrates that dissimilation changes just one *df*, that is, from [+cont] to [-cont] of two contrastive sounds /f/ and /p/ in the same position, as is also shown in words such as *fifths* [fɪfθs] dissimilated to [fɪfts]. This [θ~t] alternation also dissimilates the [+cont] feature of [θ] into [-cont] of [t] while the two sounds still share the features [-vd, -stri]. Other times, dissimilation changes more than one feature of two sounds. A good example is the word *chimney* [tʃɪmne]; it is often pronounced as if it were spelled *chimley* [tʃɪmle] because both [m] and [n] share [+nas, -cont] and resemble each other too closely. This [n~l] alternation dissimilates the [+nas, -cont] features of [n] to the [-nas, +cont] features of [l]. Another source of dissimilation is from words containing two nearby [ɹ] sounds, as in *rese(r)voir, southe(r)ner, su(r)prised,* and *Cante(r)bury*. Because these words sound as if (r) were deleted, phonologists often consider them as either dissimilation or deletion. This consideration can be well justified because as a constraint the vowel in the unstressed r-syllable is reduced from [ɚ] to [ə], creating an alternation, and this dissimilated [ə] can be deleted in fast speech, creating a case of deletion.

Morphophonemic Rules

Morphophonemic rules, also known as morphophonological rules, are not general phonological rules because they just describe phonetically conditioned allomorphic variations. Since this topic is covered in detail in Chapter 13, suffice it to say that following cases are all morphophonemic in nature: the prefix *in-* [ɪn] "not" becomes *im-* [ɪm] before bilabials /b, p, m/, *ir-* [ɪɹ] before the retroflex /ɹ/, and *il-* [ɪl] before the lateral /l/. The same applies to other prefixes like *con-* that becomes *-com*, or *en-* that becomes *em-*. All of these are Latin borrowings. Native English *un-* is not assimilated and unpredictable, so this assimilation rule applies only to specific morphemes and thus is not a general phonological rule. Silent-articulated morphological alternations also belong to this area, as attested in word pairs *iamb/iambic* but *climb/climber, sign/signature* but *assign/assignment*. Inflectional morphology also shows a clear morphophonemic nature. Also belonging to this area are the five types of regular morphological inflections that English words can take: the final *–s* as the plural, possessive, third-person singular present tense morpheme, past tense and past participle *-ed*, present participle *–ing*, comparative degree *-er*, and superlative degree *-est*. Take the *–s* form first. After a [+stri] sibilant consonant /s, z, ʃ, ʒ, tʃ, ʤ/, it generates an epenthetic vowel and is realized as unstressed [ɪz] or [əz], as in *roses* and *matches*. After a voiceless nonsibilant consonant, including /p, t, k, θ/ but not /f/ (c.f., *oaf/oafs* but *knife/knives*), it undergoes progressive assimilation and is realized as [s]; after a vowel or a voiced nonsibilant consonant, specifically /b, d, g, l, m, n, ɹ, v, w/, it also undergoes progressive assimilation, takes on the [+vd] feature, and is realized as [z]. Similarly, the regular past tense *–ed* form, when after /t/ or /d/, takes an epenthetic vowel and is realized as [ɪd] or [əd], as in *waited* and *waded*, but when after a voiced segment other than /d/, undergoes progressive assimilation and is realized as /d/, but when after a voiceless consonant other than /t/, undergoes progressive assimilation and is realized as [t]. Unlike phonological rules, which apply automatically whenever their conditions are met, morphophonemic rules apply only to specific morphemes. Compare these two words: *pence* [pɛns] v.s. pens [tɛnz]. In both words, [s] and [z] each follow a voiced nasal [n]. However, only the plural suffix *–s* assimilates in part of its internal structure to the sound /n/ and becomes a voiced [z] because /n/ is a voiced sound. This assimilation does not happen to *pence* because the [s] sound is part of the syllabic coda but not a suffix.

Ordered Rule Application

Earlier, we have mentioned the topic of rule ordering. Now, we look at it in more detail. A rule application is either ordered or unordered. Unordered application refers to cases where the order in which two or more rules apply makes no difference to the output of the derivation, as demonstrated in (30):

(30)

		/tul/ 'tool'	/ɹæm/ 'ram'
UR			
	V-Lengthening	tu:l	ɹæ:m
	Velorization	t̪u:ɫ	--
	Nasalization	--	ɹæ̃:m
	Aspiration	tʰu:l	--
	C-Rounding	tʰuɫ	--
SR		[t̪ʰu:ɫ]	[ɹæ̃:m]

Ordered rule application refers to cases where the application of one rule generates a new environment that renders the application of another rule possible. In (31), the two application orders of the Flapping and Vowel Lengthening Rules result in different outputs:

(31)

a.	UR	/ɹáɪtɚ/ 'writer'	/ɹáɪdɚ/ 'rider'
	V-lengthening	ɹáɪtɚ	ɹáɪ:dɚ
	Flapping	ɹáɪɾɚ	ɹáɪ:ɾɚ
SR		ɹáɪɾɚ	ɹáɪ:ɾɚ

b.	UR	/ɹáɪtɚ/	/ɹáɪdɚ/
	Flapping	ɹáɪɾɚ	ɹáɪɾɚ
	V-lengthening	ɹáɪ:ɾɚ	ɹáɪ:ɾɚ
SR		ɹáɪ:ɾɚ	ɹáɪ:ɾɚ

If the V-Lengthening Rule applies first and the Flapping Rule the second, the vowel length of the output is differentiated; otherwise, the outcome is the same. Since the order in (31a) leads to length difference, it is arguably the proper application order of these two rules.

IMPLICATIONS FOR TEACHING ENGLISH LANGUAGE LEARNERS

The previous section has provided ample NAE phonological rules that guide and support teachers. The three-way rule expressions—prose, semi-formal, and formal—offer convenient options for teachers to choose from and use in the classroom. Experienced teachers may not require further information on pedagogical implications of the rules, but novice teachers and teacher candidates will benefit from further explanations and guidance.

When and How to Choose and Use Different Rule Expressions?

In principle, feature matrixes become longer and more complex when they specify single segments in the input and output but become shorter and less complex when they specify classes of sounds. Rules of deletion, epenthesis, and metathesis often account for UR-SR derivations on the level of segments, so teachers may consider using mainly prose and semi-formal expressions for these rules. However, rules of reduction, assimilation, and dissimilation often operate on the level of *df*s and make reference to natural classes of sounds, so their feature matrixes are generally shorter and less complex. Because formal rules in these UR-SR derivations frequently contribute insights to the inner workings of phonological processes, it is advantageous to use formal expressions that complement prose and semi-formal expressions.

Phonological Rules and Phonological Acquisition

Phonological rules play a major role in shaping learner pronunciation. Second language acquisition (SLA) studies show that acquisition of the phonological system of a target language requires accurate perception of phonemes and phonemic contrasts, but a deeper level of perception does not take place until learners also perceive *df*s and UR-SR derivations. SLA research also shows that although the starting point of children acquiring the L1 is a set of innate principles common to all languages known as universal grammar or UG (Chomsky, 1995), the starting point of acquiring an L2 is much debated. Many researchers now hold that the starting point for SLA is the L1, with full access to UG as a backup. That is, L2 learners start with the L1 and turn to UG when necessary. This view is commonly known as the **Full Transfer/Full Access Hypothesis** (Schwartz & Sprouse, 1996). Briefly, this hypothesis assumes that learners filter the L2 input through the phonological system of their mature native language (Brown, 2000). This chapter integrates these theories into a **Phonological Acquisition Triangle** (PAT) that is actually easier to follow, schematized in (32), where phonological UR-SR derivations are emphasized:

(32) The Phonological Acquisition Triangle
> *Step 1*: Mature L1 UR-SR Derivations

Step 2: Perception of   *Step 3*: Acquisition of
L2 UR-SR Derivations   UG   L2 UR-SR Derivations

In part, the PAT tallies with Flege's Speech Learning Model (SLM, original, 1995; updated, 2007), which hinges on whether a new category can or cannot be established for an L2 sound in the learner's mind. The more similar L2 sounds are to L1 sounds, the more difficult they are established as new categories; conversely, the more distant L2 sounds are from L1 sounds, the more likely they are established as new categories. However, the PAT differs from the SLM in that the PAT admits UG as an important guidance available to learners during their mental processing vacillating between Steps 2 and 3. Furthermore, the SLM leaves an important question unanswered: "How does one define *similar*" between two sounds? (Gass, Behney, & Plonsky, 2013, p.185).

Fortunately, the question can be statistically answered. Because *df*s are countable in number, they lend themselves in calculating similarity rate (*sr*) between any two sounds either in one language or between two languages. Take the glottal /h/ and the non-NAE fricative /x/ for example. A count of the features specified in Table 1 shows that they share 15 redundant features and are differentiated by 6 *df*s, so their *sr* is 0.71 (15/21). Assuming this *sr* is high enough that escapes learner attention, the PAT would predict that learners whose native language has /x/ would more likely to take the short cut from Step 1 directly to Step 3 with little processing when learning the NAE /h/. Now look at a different scenario. Spanish has no phoneme /ʃ/ (though in some dialects), so the *sr* between the NAE /ʃ/ and its zero appearance in Spanish is 0.00. The PAT would predict that Spanish speakers of NAE would more likely take the long route going through all three steps with mental processing.

However, situations are sometimes more complex. For example, /ð/ in English is a phoneme but an allophone of the phoneme /d/ in Spanish because the two sounds are in complementary distribution in the language--[ð] after a vowel and [d] elsewhere (e.g., *dedo* [deðo] 'finger'). To calculate *sr,* which two sounds should we compare? We know that native speakers' mental establishment of new phonemic categories occur at the UR level, and their knowledge about SR is usually subconscious. Based on this reasoning, we should calculate the *sr* between English phoneme /ð/ and Spanish phoneme /d/ but not the English phoneme /ð/ and the Spanish allophone [ð]. A count in Table 1 shows that /ð/ and /d/ share 19 features, with their *sr* being 0.90 (19/21) and are differentiated by only 2 *df*s: [-cont, -dis] for /d/ and [+cont, +dis] for /ð/. With their *sr* being that high, it is not a surprise that Spanish learners of NAE frequently substitute /d/ for English /ð/, without realizing the two sounds are contrastively phonemic in NAE, producing [deɪ] for *they* and confusing it with *day*.

However, language learning is not that straighforward. Language universals, such as typological markedness, also play a role in the acquisition of an L2 sound system. In the world languages, sounds that are common are considered unmarked (e.g., /s, ʃ/), and those that are less common are more marked (e.g., /θ, ð/). Generalizations such as these are logically developed into implicational hierarchies in which the presence of a more marked sound is viewed to imply a less marked sound (Greenburg, 1976). That is, if a language has /θ, ð/, it is predicted that the language also has /s, ʃ/, but the opposite is not true. Eckman (1977) applied implicational hierarchies to second language acquisition and formulated the **Markedness Differential Hypothesis** (MDH), which predicts that linguistic structures are difficult to acquire only when they are more marked in the L2 than in the L1. Thus, unmarked forms are learned before marked forms. Consequently, the **Contrastive Analysis Hypothesis** (Lado, 1957) that L2 sounds absent in the native language are difficult to learn is modified. Under the MDH, sounds not in the L1 may be not difficult to learn unless they are marked. This applies well to the universally unmarked phoneme /ʃ/. Research shows that Spanish speakers learning NAE indeed do not have difficulty pronouncing it even if Spanish does not have this sound (Freeman & Freeman, 2014, p.123). This can be construed that UG backs up Spanish learners when they are processing this new category of sound between steps 2 and 3 in the PAT. If we turn to the concept of *sr* in terms of *dfs*, this complex acquisition process is made even easier to understand.

Take segments /s, ʃ, ʧ/ for example. Depending on which two of them are being compared, in total they share a range of 17 to 19 features and are separated by a range of 2 to 4 *dfs*, as analyzed below:

(33)

$$
\begin{array}{ccc}
/s/ & /\int/ & /\text{ʧ}/ \\[4pt]
\begin{bmatrix} +\text{ant} \\ -\text{dis} \\ +\text{cont} \\ -\text{d.r.} \end{bmatrix} &
\begin{bmatrix} -\text{ant} \\ +\text{dis} \\ +\text{cont} \\ -\text{d.r.} \end{bmatrix} &
\begin{bmatrix} -\text{ant} \\ +\text{dis} \\ -\text{cont} \\ +\text{d.r.} \end{bmatrix}
\end{array}
$$

Close analyses of these feature matrixes reveal that every two of the three sounds differ by two *dfs* and share 19 features save the pair /s, ʧ/, which differs by four *dfs* but share 17 features. Thus, their *srs* are calculated and factored out to demonstrate how similar or different these sounds are, as below:

(34)

Sound pairs	*sr*
a. /s-ʃ/, /ʃ-ʧ/	0.90 (19/21)
b. /s-ʧ/	0.81 (17/21)

Note that 0.90 indicates 90% of similarity between the sounds /s-ʃ/ and /ʃ-ʧ/, and 0.81 shows 81% of similarity between /s-ʧ/ in languages.

English has /s, ʃ, ʧ/, and Spanish has /s, ʧ/. What do the *srs* in (34) inform us of? In light of the PAT, Spanish speakers learning NAE would more likely to substitute /ʃ/ for /ʧ/ than /s/ for /ʧ/ because /ʃ-ʧ/ are more similar (90% similarity) than /s-ʧ/ (81% similarity). The fact that Spanish learners are reported to produce [tíʃɚ] for *teacher* and [ʃɛɹ] for *chair* (Freeman & Freeman, 2014, p.323) supports what *srs* predict.

The *sr* concept informs teachers of targeted pedagogical interventions. That is, when learners substitute /x/ for /h/ or vice versa, teachers should direct their attention to the six *dfs* that separate the two sounds, that is, [-cons, -d.r., +s.g., -dor, -hi, -bk] for /h/ but [+cons, +d.r., -s.g., +dor, +hi, +bk] for /x/. When learners substitute /ð/ for /d/ or vice versa, the pedagogical target should aim at the two *dfs*: [-cont, -dis] for /d/ but [+cont, +dis] for /ð/. When learners substitute /ʃ/ for /ʧ/ or vice versa, instructors should guide them to practising the two *dfs* that differentiate the two similar sounds: [+cont, -d.r.] for /ʃ/ but [-cont, +d.r.] for /ʧ/.

Voicing contrast, pertinent to multiple rules presented above, is yet another difficult feature for learners. It has long been reported that there exists a Voice Contrast Hierarchy in world languages (Dinnsen & Eckman, 1975). English-type languages (the most marked), including Arabic, Hungarian, Swedish, maintain voice contrast in syllable-initial, -medial, and –final positions; German-type languages (the next most marked), including Catalan, Greek, Japanese, Polish, Russian, maintain voice contrast in initial and medial positions, but not in final position; Corsican-type languages (less marked), including Sardinian, only maintain voice contrast in initial position, while Korean (least marked) maintains no voice contrast in all three positions. Predictably, a speaker of English will have the least trouble producing German words, but a German speaker will have a difficult time in producing English words because the learner has to learn to make a voicing contrast in final position.

Syllable structure also plays a role in understanding nearly every phonological rule we generalized above. Interestingly, English learners' emerging acquisition of syllable structure is subject to positional parameters. Much of the studies concerning L2 syllable acquisition is centered on two determinants: the learner's L1 knowledge and the role the universal principles and parameters play. Tarone (1980) claims that learners simplify syllables in English by epenthesis that are permissible in the L1. For example, Korean learners apply epenthesis to word-final sequences as in the English word *sack* [sæ.ke]. In Eckman's 1981 study, Chinese speakers also add a schwa to the end of words with a voiced obstruent coda, such as in the English word *Bob* to produce [bɔ.bə]. Neither Korean nor Chinese has a voice contrast in final position, so these English learners revert to the universal CV syllable structure. Spanish does not have a voice contrast in final position but allows a voiceless consonant in coda, so Spanish speakers choose to devoice a voiced obstruent coda, changing *Bob* to [bɔp]. These examples all support the MDH because a voicing contrast in final position is the most marked and hence the last voicing contrast to be learned.

Based on the MDH and the supporting examples above, it can be generalized that initial position is least marked, medial position more marked, and final position most marked.

Though initial position is typically unmarked, English onset clusters are cross-linguistically marked because many other languages allow only the CV or C+Glide+V structure. How do English learners acquire the Onset Liquids/Glides Devoicing Rule (Rule 25), for example? Research shows that initial C+/j/ clusters (where C stands for a consonant) is less marked (e.g., *few* [fj-]) and the initial C+/ɹ/ cluster is more marked (e.g., *free* [fɹ-]), based on the sonority levels of segments, namely, stops (the least sonorant)-fricatives-nasals-liquids-glides-vowels (the most sonorant). Learners whose first languages do not allow consonant clusters have no problem learning C+/j/ clusters but tend to epenthesize a schwa between C+/ɹ/ clusters, more so with the /fɹ/ cluster, for example, *bride* [bəɹaɪd] and *frog* [fəɹɔg] (Broselow & Finer, 1991).

When comparing errors (deletion and epenthesis) in onset and coda clusters, research has found that error rates in coda clusters far outnumber the onset clusters (Sato, 1984). This once more supports the MDH.

Though adult L2 learners delete unstressed syllables and consonants less frequently than children do (Oller, 1974), they do make deletion errors. When a single coda obstruent precedes an onset obstruent, many learners delete the coda obstruent (e.g., *bad car* [bæ kaɹ]) instead of just unrelease it [bæd˺ kaɹ] as native NAE speakers would do. Conversely, native NAE speakers delete the middle obstruent in the heterosyllabic $-C_1C_2\#\#C_1-$ environment (e.g., [wɛs] for *the west park*), but learners would delete the coda C_1C_2, i.e., [wɛ paɹk] or epenthesize a schwa, i.e., [wɛstə paɹk] to break up the cluster.

Assimilation rules are more subtle. In general, English assimilation rules within words tend to be obligatory, and those between words optional. Regardless, they often require a fast speech tempo or one-breath utterance to get activated. As with other types of rules, assimilation rules are also position-restricted. In fact, nearly every phonological rule delineated above can be classified in terms of positional parameters that constrain UR-SR derivations. Below is a classification of the rules we discussed earlier, where R stands for 'rule" and where some rules are cross-listed because they involve more than one position:

(35)

Initial	Medial	Final
R11	R10	R11
R12, R14	R12, R13	R14, R16
R17, R18, R19	R15, R19	R19
R20, R21	R22, R23	R20, R22
R25, R28	R24, R27, R29	R26, R27, R28

In light of the MDH, these positional classifications should offer teachers insights into prioritizing classroom instruction of the rules.

Some teachers may balk at *df*s and formalized rules. It is probably a good idea for beginning and junior teachers to use just prose and/or semi-formal expressions in the classroom. However, for trainers of teacher candidates, using all three-way rule expressions should work better if descriptive precision is sought for. The traditional intuitive-imitative approach of teaching pronunciation simply poses too much onto learners' shoulders. Take for example the /ɹ/-coloring rule not discussed earlier. Nearly all books explain this rule thusly: Vowels are colored by their immediately following retroflex liquid /ɹ/, and thus the value of the vowels takes on some of the retroflex quality, as in *girl* or *work*. Without a formal phonological analysis, the process of "coloring" remains implicit. The following rule, which applies to all vowels, renders the coloring process explicit:

(36) The /ɹ/-Coloring Rule (formal):

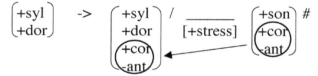

As the arrow shows, the /ɹ/-coloring exactly means the superimposition of the *df* [+cor, -ant] from [ɹ] onto the preceding vowel. It is this superimposition that precisely helps both teachers and learners to understand the colored values of the affected vowel. Then, they can target at these two *df*s for practice rather than just blindly imitate.

Before we move to the following section, a few words about the implication of rule ordering is in order. As we know, different rule orderings result in different outputs. For learners to differentiate the vowel length in [ɹáɪɾɚ] for *writer* and [ɹáɪɾɚ] for *rider*, instructors should teach the V-Lengthening Rule before the Flapping Rule, as shown in (31) above.

Interfaces of Phonological Rules with Other Areas of Language

Phonological rules also play a role in teaching spelling, listening, speaking, and reading. For both naturalistic and classroom-taught English learners, morphological-phonological alternations explicitly help them perceive letter-sound discrepancies and, therefore, have the potential to improve their essential language skills. At the very least, after understanding rule-governed alternations, learners' chances of misspelling words due to various kinds of deletion rules would decrease, including words such as (*a*)*lone* and (*de*)*fend* due to initial schwa deletion; *fed*(*e*)*ral* and *gen*(*e*)*ral* due to word-medial schwa deletion; *iam*(*b*) and *desi*(*g*)*n* due to /b/- and /g/-deletions restored in alternating forms *iambic* and *designation*.

In the nutshell, it would be inconceivable that learners would spell words correctly if they pronounce words incorrectly. It would be unimaginable that learners would improve listening comprehension significantly if they just utter URs of phonological rules while hearing SRs in the input. It would be questionable that learners' reading speed and comprehension would arise effectively if they had not automatized one-breath reading of chunks of sentences that activates SR of phonological rules. The discussion of these topics is outside the scope of this chapter. However, readers who are interested in learning more about these topics are advised to consult Celce-Murcia et al. (2010), an excellent source that devotes three full chapters to these interface areas.

Importance of Balancing Explanations and Practices

Experienced teachers know that merely teaching students how to analyze language parts with little pedagogical interventions usually does not work well. They also know that a good balance between explanations and practice to ensure that sufficient time is devoted to practice is equally important. In addition, they know to recycle material with spaced repetition so as to offer learners opportunities to review aspects of the sound system that they have learned previously.

Table 3, adapted from Celce-Murcia et al. (2010) but with emphasis shifting to *df*s and phonological rules (*PhR*s), provides teachers a communicative framework for teaching pronunciation in order to improve accuracy, fluency, and automaticity of learner pronunciation.

Table 3. A modified communicative framework for teaching pronunciation

Five Steps	Purposes	Activities/Tools	Feedback
1. Description and Analysis of *df*s and *PhR*– oral, written, digital descriptions of *df*s, *PhR*s, articulatory gestures and/acoustic effects	Learner awareness of new *df*s and *PhR*s	Interactive digital sagittal diagrams of the speech organs and lip movements; consonant and vowel charts; teaching aids like rubber bands, kazoos, balloons, teacher modeling, etc. to support imitations	Immediate teacher feedback
2. Listening Discrimination – focused perception of target *df*s and *PhR*s	Learner perception of new *df*s and *PhR*s	Minimal-pair words, phrases, sentences, worksheets, all of which containing target *df*s and *PhR*s	Immediate teacher feedback
3. Controlled Practice – oral reading of minimal-pair sentences and short dialogues to identify target *df*s and *PhR*s	Learner accuracy in producing utterances containing target *df*s and *PhR*s	Repetition practice, oral reading of minimal-pair words, phrases, sentences, worksheets, and short dialogues; proverbs, maxims, tongue twisters, Jazz chants, children's rhymes, short metered poems; pair or small-group work	Timely teacher feedback during individual activities; delayed peer and/or teacher feedback till the end of pair or small-group work
4. Guided Practice – structured communication exercises enabling the learner to monitor for target *df*s and *PhR*s	Learner accuracy and fluency in producing utterances with target *df*s and *PhR*s	Task-based activities such as cued dialogues, gap-filling exercises, story strips; teacher-provided lists of words and phrases containing target *df*s and *PhR*s for student use in and out of class	Delayed peer and/or teacher feedback till the completion of activities to avoid communication disruption
5. Communicative Practice – less structured activities	Meaning-oriented learner fluency in utterances with target *df*s and *PhR*s	Debate, interviews, storytelling, role play, doubt-believe games, clarification of values, problem solving, performance assessment, (dis)agreements, and other speech acts	Delayed peer and/or teacher feedback till the end of activities

L2 pronunciation and speech can hardly become natural and fluent without accurately activating *PhRs*. However, *PhRs* have two contradictory attributes: they are omnipresent, yet they sneakily reside in the subconscious of speakers. These attributes require teachers to understand them, to discover more of them, to introduce them to learners early instead of late so that learners have timely enough chances to become aware of them, perceive them, imitate them, produce them, and eventually automatize them. Accuracy and fluency of natural L2 pronunciation, after all, require teachers' laborious gardening, seeding, watering, weeding, and nurturing to come to fruition. Feature-based phonology ought to become a powerful gardening tool in the hands of teacher-gardeners that enables learners to make predictions of UR-SR derivations themselves leading to independent and automatized pronunciation.

DISCUSSION QUESTIONS

1. Going beyond the information provided in this chapter, further discuss why the *df* theory works better than IPA classes of sounds such as [±stop] and [±fricative]. On the other hand, could the *df* theory work without IPA classifications of sounds?

2. Phonological UR-SR derivations are omnipresent in NAE pronunciation. What would happen to students' pronunciation of NAE as a second or foreign language if only UR forms are taught to them? If UR-SR derivations are taught, when will be the best time to teach them and in what ways?

3. Phonological rules can be stated in prose, semi-formal, and formal expressions to meet various needs of users. Discuss how they are best used to train teacher candidates and how different proficiency levels of your students would dictate your choices of rule formats in classroom instruction

4. One of my international students did not understand why she was slapped with a fine for parking her car in a university parking lot where she said a policeman told her "You can park here." Discuss why this happened by explicitly referring to *df*s in characterizing how native speakers of NAE distinguish the affirmative *can* and the negative *can't* in these two sentences: (a) *You can park here*, and (b) *You can't park here* with /t/ being deleted since the word string *can't park* does meet the deletion condition $-C_1C_2\#\#C_1-$ in hetero-syllables.

5. Use your own examples to discuss the interactions between language transfer and universal grammar. In doing so, make reference to the Phonological Acquisition Triangle and the Markedness Differential Hypothesis.

EXERCISES

1. Give all but only those NAE classes of sounds as specified by the following feature matrixes.

    a. $\begin{bmatrix} +nas \\ +ant \end{bmatrix}$
    b. $\begin{bmatrix} +syl \\ +tns \end{bmatrix}$
    c. $\begin{bmatrix} -d.r. \\ +ant \end{bmatrix}$
    d. $\begin{bmatrix} +son \\ -nas \end{bmatrix}$

    e. $\begin{bmatrix} -son \\ +cont \\ +vd \end{bmatrix}$
    f. $\begin{bmatrix} -cont \\ +ant \\ -nas \end{bmatrix}$
    g. $\begin{bmatrix} +syl \\ +lo \\ -bk \end{bmatrix}$
    h. $\begin{bmatrix} +syl \\ -hi \\ -lo \end{bmatrix}$

2. Build a minimal feature matrix to specify each of the following natural classes of sounds.
   a. /m, n, ŋ/   b. /θ, ð/   c. /l, ɹ, j, w/   d. /u, ʊ, o, ɔ/

3. First, convert each prose interphonological rule below into its semi-formal and formal expressions; then tell which format is preferred and explain why. Finally, tell how each rule deviates from its corresponding NAE phonological rule.
   a. The [-tns] vowel /ɛ/ is epenthesized at the beginning of a word starting with the voiceless fricative /s/.
   b. Voiced obstruents are devoiced at the end of a word.
   c. Stressed tense vowels are realized as stressed lax vowels preceding a coda nasal (disregard /±ɑ/).

4. Specify the phonological environment in which each word below changes its pronunciation from UR to SR. Provide one or two illustrative examples, and then explain what *df or df*s are changed.

	Words	UR	SR	Phonological Environments
a.	best	/bɛst/	[bɛʃ]	_____
b.	attend	/ətɛ́nd/	[ətɛ́m]	_____
c.	they	/ðe/	[neɪ]	_____
d.	your	/jʊɹ/	[dʒɚ]	_____
e.	you're	/juɚ/	[tʃɚ]	_____

5. Use one breath in fast tempo to utter this italicized request so that phonological rules in them are best triggered: *Could you hand Gregory this shutter, please*? Then, do the following operations:
   a. Phonemically transcribe the request as its UR form.
   b. Phonetically transcribe the request as its SR form.
   c. From left to right, carefully compare the UR and SR forms, list and explain as many phonological rules as possible. If necessary, utter the request fast and naturally several more times to reveal rules that might be unnoticed.
   d. Collapse all the rules you have listed into distinct rule categories; that is, if one rule applies more than one time, count them as one rule.
   e. Are there any ordered rule applications? If yes, explain what rules are involved and how they are ordered.

ACKNOWLEDGMENT

Thanks are due to our volume editors, Dr. Nabat Erdogan and Dr. Michael Wei, for their professional guidance; I particularly appreciate Dr. Erdogan's meticulous editing, vital feedback, and great patience during my development of this chapter. Thanks are also due to two anonymous reviewers, whose invaluable feedback helped me improve the quality and readership of this chapter. Errors, however, are my responsibilities.

REFERENCES

Algeo, J., & Butcher, C. A. (2014). *The origins and development of the English language.* Boston, MA: Wadsworth Cengage Learning.

Broselow, E., & Finer, D. (1991). Parameter setting in second language phonology and syntax. *Second Language Research, 7,* 35–59.

Brown, C. (2000). The interrelation between speech perception and phonological acquisition from infant to adult. In J. Archibald (Ed.), *Second language acquisition and linguistic theory* (pp. 4–63). Malden, MA: Blackwell Publishers Inc.

Celce-Murcia, M., Brinton, D. M., Goodwin, J. M., & Griner, B. (2010). *Teaching pronunciation: A course book and reference guide* (2nd ed.). Cambridge, UK: CUP.

Chaucer, G., & Benson, L. D. (1987). *The Riverside Chaucer.* Boston, MA: Houghton Mifflin Co.

Chomsky, N. (1995). *The minimalist program.* Cambridge, MA: MIT Press.

Chomsky, N., & Halle, M. (1968). *The sound pattern of English.* New York: Harper & Row.

Dinnsen, D., & Eckman, F. (1975). In R. E. Grossman, L. J. San, & T. J. Vance (Eds.), *Functionalism* (pp. 126–134). Chicago: Chicago Linguistic Society.

Eckman, F. (1977). Markedness and the contrastive analysis hypothesis. *Language Learning: A Journal of Applied Linguistics, 27,* 315–30.

Eckman, F. (1981). On predicting phonological difficulty in second language acquisition. *Studies in Second Language Acquisition, 4*(1), 18–30. doi:10.1017/S0272263100004253

Flege, J. E. (1995). Second language speech learning: Theory, findings, and problems. In W. Strange (Ed.), *Speech perception and linguistic experience: Issues in cross-linguistic research* (pp. 233–277). Timonium, MD: York Press.

Flege, J. E. (2007). Language contact in bilingualism: Phonetic system interactions. In J. Cole & J. I. Hualde (Eds.), *Laboratory phonology 9.* Berlin: Mouton de Gruyter.

Freeman, D. E., & Freeman, Y. S. (2014). *Essential linguistics: What teachers need to know to teach ESL, reading, spelling, grammar.* Portsmouth, NH: Heinemann.

Fromkin, V., Rodman, R., & Hyams, N. (2017). *An introduction to language* (11th ed.). Boston, MA: Cengage Learning, Inc.

Gass, S. M., Behney, J., & Plonsky, L. (2013). *Second language acquisition: An introductory course* (4th ed.). New York: Routledge Taylor & Francis Group. doi:10.4324/9780203137093

Gilbert, J. B. (2018). Issues in teaching pronunciation: Prosody, intonation, and vowels. In The TESOL encyclopedia of English language teaching (vol. 3, pp. 1701-1709). Hoboken, NJ: TESOL International Association/Wiley Blackwell.

Greenburg, J. H. (1976). *Language universals*. The Hague, The Netherlands: Mouton de Gruyter.

Hayes, B. (2009). *Introductory phonology*. Malden, MA: Wiley-Blackwell.

Jakobson, R., Frant, C. G. M., & Halle, M. (1952). *Preliminaries to speech analysis: The distinctive features and their correlates*. Cambridge, MA: MIT Press.

Lado, R. (1957). *Linguistics across cultures*. Ann Arbor, MI: University of Michigan Press.

Lass, R. (1988). *Phonology: An introduction to basic concepts*. Cambridge, UK: CUP.

Liontas, J. I. (Ed.). (2018). The TESOL encyclopedia of English language teaching. Hoboken, NJ: TESOL International Association/John Wiley & Sons, Inc. doi:10.1002/9781118784235

O'Grady, W., Archibald, J., Aronoff, M., & Rees-Miller, J. (2017). *Contemporary linguistics: An introduction* (7th ed.). Boston: Bedford/St. Martin's Macmillan Learning.

Oller, D. K. (1974). *Towards a general theory of phonological processes in first and second language learning*. Paper presented at the Western Conference on Linguistics, Seattle, WA.

Sato, C. (1984). Phonological process in second language acquisition: Another look at interlanguage syllable structure. *Language Learning, 34*(4), 43–57. doi:10.1111/j.1467-1770.1984.tb00351.x

Schwartz, B., & Sprouse, R. (1996). L2 cognitive states and the full transfer/full access model. *Second Language Research, 12*(1), 40–72. doi:10.1177/026765839601200103

Tarone, E. (1980). Some influence on the syllable structure of interlanguage phonology. *IRAL, 18*, 139–152.

Wolfram, W., & Johnson, R. (1982). *Phonological analysis: Focus on American English*. Englewood Cliffs, NJ: Prentice Hall Regents.

Zsiga, E. C. (2013). *The sounds of language: An introduction to phonetics and phonology*. Malden, MA: Wiley-Blackwell.

ADDITIONAL READING

Brown, J. D. (2012). *New ways in teaching connected speech*. Alexandria, VA: TESOL International Association.

Celce-Murcia, M., Brinton, D. M., Goodwin, J. M., & Griner, B. (2010). *Teaching pronunciation: A course book and reference guide* (2nd ed.). Cambridge, UK: CUP.

Swan, M., & Smith, B. (2001). *Learner English: A teacher's guide to interference and other problems* (2nd ed.). Cambridge, UK: Cambridge University Press. doi:10.1017/CBO9780511667121

ENDNOTES

[1] These sources include: Fromkin et al., 2017 (21 features); Hayes, 2009 (26 features); Lass, 1988 (16 features); O'Grady et al., 2017 (21 features); Wolfram & Johnson, 1982 (16 features); Zsiga, 2013 (22 features).

[2] NAE glides also include the voiceless labial-velar glide /ʍ/ found in dialects.

[3] In the feature system used in this chapter, central vowels are treated as [+bk].

[4] In NAE, [a] and [ɑ] are not contrastive, so they are treated as allophones of the phoneme [ɑ] and has the [+bk] feature.

[5] Phonologists do not agree with each other about which feature, [+tns], [-tns], [0tns], should be assigned to /ɑ/. This chapter assigns [±tns] to it based on the fact that it can end a syllable though frequently it cannot (e.g., *spa* /spɑ/ but *rob* /ɹɑb/).

[6] Spoonerisms are errors resulting in slip of the tongue that switches two sounds or words in a phrase. They are named after the Oxford minister William W. Spooner, who was well-known for deliberately creating such sound rearrangements.

[7] In NAE, /ɑ/ and /ɔ/ are free variations.

[8] Since the early Middle English period, [-tns] vowels have acquired the [+tns] feature in a limited number of closed and stressed syllables ending with *–mb* (e.g., *comb*), *-ld* (e.g., *old*), or *–nd* (e.g., *find*) (Algeo & Butcher, 2014).

[9] Correlations between alphabet values and relative values of vowel letters is not always 100%. Carney (1974) provides correlation percentages based on analyses of a database of 2.5 million words in British English and NAE, as cited in Gilbert, 2018, p.144.

Chapter 15
The Causes of Learner Pronunciation Problems in English

John Rothgerber
Indiana University, USA

ABSTRACT

This chapter will provide the language teacher with an introduction to the theory behind the challenges and problems that learners from a variety of language backgrounds face as they learn to pronounce the sounds of English. The primary focus will be on the influence of the first language in second language phonological acquisition. This will include an overview of the role of perception of non-native sounds, as well as a consideration of phonological representation in the mental lexicon and articulatory constraints, all of which can have an effect on difficulties that learners encounter as they learn to pronounce English sounds. Attention will be given to the various components that make up the phonological system, including segmentals, suprasegmentals, phonotactics, and phonological processes. This theoretical understanding will then be applied to pronunciation instruction within the classroom by addressing what teachers can do to maximize the effectiveness of instruction.

PRONUNCIATION DIFFICULTIES AND PHONOLOGICAL THEORY

Second language (L2) learners face countless challenges in their efforts to acquire a new language, not least of which is the necessity to perceive and produce an entirely new sound system. Through research in the field of L2 phonology, researchers have started to develop an understanding of the causes behind learner pronunciation problems. The way that non-native sounds are perceived, stored in the **mental lexicon**, and articulated can all introduce challenges that learners encounter as they learn to pronounce English sounds. By understanding these challenges and their causes, language instruction can be better guided to help learners succeed.

DOI: 10.4018/978-1-5225-8467-4.ch015

It is first useful to conceptualize the processes by which speech is both perceived and produced. What happens from the time a series of speech sounds is detected by the ear to the time it is recognized as a word with a specific meaning? And, conversely, what happens from the time a word is selected from the mental lexicon to the time it is produced by the vocal apparatus? The following is an adapted information-processing model proposed by Ramus et al. (2010), here reduced in scope to focus on the points relevant for the current chapter.

In perception, speech undergoes several steps of processing which convert it to more abstract levels of representation. First, speech enters the ear and travels to the primary auditory cortex as an acoustic representation. This step of acoustic processing occurs for all sounds, not only speech, and the acoustic representation can be thought of as a way of encoding sound for the brain to understand. Following that, speech then undergoes speech-specific processes that assign it to more abstract levels of representation. For example, a speech segment that has the relevant formant properties (resonance peaks that determine the type of vowel) might be assigned to the phonetic category for the English tense vowel [u], as in *soup* [suːp] or *loop* [luːp]. There may be several such levels of abstraction. As the speech stream continues, the phonological representation is continuously checked for matches against the mental lexicon. The mental lexicon can be thought of as the brain's storehouse of words, and for a particular word it stores information on the sound, meaning, and written form of that word. Once a satisfactory match has been found, then the perception process has finished.

Production occurs in the opposite direction. First, a word is selected from the mental lexicon, usually based on meaning, and its phonological representation is activated. This representation then undergoes processing at several levels to convert it into an articulatory representation. The articulatory representation guides the **articulation** of the vocal apparatus as it produces the speech sounds. For example, the articulatory representation of the English tense vowel [u] determines, among other things, the position of the tongue in the mouth and the shape of the lips.

The relevance of such a model to the current chapter is that pronunciation problems can originate at any step in both the perception and production processes, as well as in representation in the mental lexicon. Each of these areas will be addressed in detail.

Perception

At first thought, it might seem counterintuitive that a problem perceiving a sound could result in a problem pronouncing that sound. However, if a sound cannot be perceived, then its existence might not be evident to a learner. For example, if a learner perceives the phoneme /θ/ as being the same as /s/, such that the words *math* /mæθ/ and *mass* /mæs/ sound the same, then the learner may assume that these are homophones and pronounce them identically. However, taking a step back, we must first address the question of *why* a learner might perceive these different segments as being the same.

In 1957, Liberman, Harris, Hoffman, and Griffith published the findings of an experiment which demonstrated that listeners tend to perceive sounds of the same category as more similar, and those of different categories as more different. In the first part of the experiment, participants were asked to listen to synthetic speech sounds and label them as /b/, /d/, or /g/. Researchers manipulated properties of each sound's formants, which are resonance peaks that occur in human speech and are important for identifying sounds. Specifically, they varied on a continuum each sound's second formant transition, which is one of the primary cues that English listeners use to distinguish /b/, /d/, and /g/. The results showed that, even though the sounds were varied in gradual steps, participants made very abrupt categorization changes, which resulted in three clearly-defined groups with sharp boundaries. In the second part of the experiment, participants completed an ABX discrimination task with the same sounds used in the first part. In a typical ABX discrimination task, three sounds are played in sequence, such that the first sound (A) is different from the second (B), and the third (X) matches either A or B. Participants are required to select which sound X is closest to. If a particular sound pairing is difficult for participants to discriminate, then they should have lower accuracy scores. The results of the second experiment by Liberman et al. showed that participants had more trouble discriminating the target sounds when they were of the same segment category (as measured in the first part of the experiment) than when they were of different categories, even when the second formant transition values were equally spaced. In other words, a good example of /b/ and a bad example of /b/ (where "bad" refers to having second formant transition values quite different from the norm) were more difficult to tell apart than a bad example of /b/ and a bad example of /d/, despite the acoustic differences being the same between them.

The findings by Liberman et al. (1957) led them to propose the concept of **categorical perception**. This describes the phenomenon whereby stimuli are perceived as belonging to distinct categories. Stimuli belonging to one category are perceived as being more similar to each other, and stimuli belonging to separate categories as more different from each other, even though they may be equidistant on a continuum. Categorical perception is not limited to speech sounds. Very young children can readily establish visual categories, such as *dog* or *cat*, after being shown enough stimuli (Harnad, 1987).

This raises the question of how perceptual categories for sounds are formed in the mind. It turns out that segment categories are language-specific; within the first year of life, categories are formed based on the L1 of the infant. In a classic study, Werker and Tees (1984) investigated whether or not infants with English-speaking parents could discriminate stop contrasts which are not contrastive in English. One contrast, from the Interior Salish language of Thompson from British Columbia, was of the glottalized velar and uvular stop phonemes /k'/ and /q'/. English, having only the back stop /k/, lacks this contrast. The second contrast was the Hindi unaspirated retroflex and dental stop contrast /ʈ/ - /t/, which is also absent in English. To measure whether infants could discriminate these sounds, Werker and Tees used a "head turn" experimental paradigm, in which infants were conditioned to turn their heads towards a display when they heard a particular sound being played. The results showed that English infants between six and eight months old could discriminate both contrasts with high accuracy, but from about ten months old, this ability was almost completely lost. Such inability to discriminate these contrasts persists into adulthood for English native speakers. Hindi infants, on the other hand, maintained the ability to discriminate the Hindi stop contrast. By around ten months old, it seems that infants develop perceptual categories based on their L1 and lose the ability to be universal discriminators.

So far, we have seen that listeners of a language perceive speech sounds as belonging to distinct categories. These categories are language-specific and form within the first year of life. Now, to tie this into L2 phonological acquisition, consider the example of an adult native speaker of Japanese who is learning English. Such learners are well-known to have problems pronouncing the English /l/ - /ɹ/ contrast. Where might such problems originate? A body of research has shown that L1 Japanese learners of English actually have great difficulty perceiving the difference between the English phonemes /l/ and /ɹ/ in listening (Goto, 1971; Mochizuki, 1981; Sheldon & Strange, 1982). Japanese has only a single liquid consonant, the tap /ɾ/, which is different from both the English /l/ and /ɹ/. This suggests that learners may be perceiving /l/ and /ɹ/ as members of the same L1 category. Even though /l/ and /ɹ/ have quite different acoustic characteristics and sound noticeably different to English native speakers, they may sound like members of the same category to L1 Japanese learners, albeit poor examples of that category.

Therefore, problems that L1 Japanese learners have pronouncing /l/ and /ɹ/ may be caused by their inability to perceive them in the first place. If words such as *light* and *right* are perceived as being the same, then they may be stored in the mental lexicon as homophones. Cutler and Otake (2004) found evidence in support of this. They tested L1 Japanese learners of English using a lexical decision task with priming. In this task, participants were asked to decide whether a word that they heard was a real English word or not, and the time that it took them to respond was measured. After hearing one word of a /l/ - /ɹ/ minimal pair such as *light - right*, participants were faster to respond to the second word in the pair when it was played. *Light* primed the participants for *right* (and vice versa), even though native speakers did not show such a priming effect. This suggests that learners may have been associating *light* and *right* in their mental lexicons, a conclusion which is supported by further research (Ota, Hartsuiker, & Haywood, 2009). That, in turn, could lead to both words being pronounced the same.

Much research centered on **segmentals** (individual consonants and vowels) has supported the idea that non-native sounds that resemble native phonetic or phonemic categories are difficult to perceive, both for naïve listeners (those not learning the language) and learners. In addition to Japanese, evidence for the difficulty of English /l/ - /ɹ/ has also been gathered for other languages that lack the contrast, such as Korean (Ingram & Park, 1998) and Cantonese (Henly & Sheldon, 1986). Further studies have looked at English voiceless stops for L1 Spanish learners (Flege & Eefting, 1987), the English /m/-/n/ contrast in syllable-final position for L1 Brazilian Portuguese learners (Kluge, Rauber, Reis, & Bion, 2007), and the English /p/-/b/ contrast for L1 Arabic learners (Ota et al., 2009), among many others.

Best (1995) proposed the Perceptual Assimilation Model (PAM) to account for patterns of cross-linguistic speech perception in naïve listeners. The PAM states that non-native segments will be assimilated to the closest native segment categories, although the goodness of fit may vary. When there is a one-to-one mapping of non-native segment to native category, listeners do not have much difficulty in discriminating the non-native segment. However, when two non-native segments are mapped to a single native category, discrimination becomes difficult, as in the case of /l/ and /ɹ/ for L1 Japanese listeners. In addition, when non-native segments do not resemble native segments at all, such as Zulu click contrasts for native English speakers, then discrimination remains strong, since there is no interference from native segment categories (Best, McRoberts, & Sithole, 1988).

Flege (1995) proposed the Speech Learning Model (SLM), in part to account for the role of categorical perception in L2 phonological acquisition. Flege postulated that L2 learners have only a single perceptual space in which phonetic categories are established for both the L1 and L2. That is, learners do not create an entirely new set of perceptual categories when they begin acquiring an L2 in the way that infants do for their L1. Instead, L2 categories have to be fit into the L1 perceptual space as best as possible. The SLM makes predictions for which L2 sounds will be more difficult to acquire. If a learner can distinguish at least some of the phonetic differences between a sound in the L1 and the L2, then it is possible for a new category to be formed. This is not guaranteed, though. The greater the differences are between the L1 and L2 sounds, the more likely it is that a new category will be created. However, if a contrast is not easily discerned, then the L2 sound will be mapped onto an L1 category, even if it is not a good fit. Even if a new category is established for an L2 sound, it might not be the same category as that of a native speaker, since it might be based on different acoustic features. Acquisition proceeds as more input leads to more clearly defined L2 categories. Production, in turn, reflects the properties of the established phonetic categories.

To illustrate, the SLM can be applied to make predictions about the acquisition of the /l/ - /ɹ/ contrast by L1 Japanese learners of English. English /l/ is actually more acoustically similar to Japanese /ɾ/ than is English /ɹ/ (Aoyama, Flege, Guion, Akahane-Yamada, & Yamada, 2004). Therefore, according to the SLM, learners will have more difficulty developing a new category for English /l/ than English /ɹ/. They will tend to map English /l/ onto the L1 category /ɹ/, while for English /ɹ/, since it has more differences from Japanese /ɾ/, they will be more likely to form a new category. In a longitudinal study of Japanese children learning English in the US, Aoyama et al. (2004) found support for this. The learners showed improvement on /l/ - /ɹ/ discrimination over time, and in production, they showed greater improvement on /ɹ/ than on /l/. This suggests that new category development was occurring more for /ɹ/ than /l/; since /l/ resembled the L1 category, it may have been mapped onto that category, even though it represented a poor example of that category.

The focus so far has been on the perception of segmentals. Indeed, much of the research on categorical perception has focused on consonant and vowel segments. The PAM and the SLM, for example, only make explicit mention of segment categories. However, speech perception and production are comprised of much more than just the individual phones that make up the speech sequence. In the following paragraphs, consideration will be given to other aspects of speech perception. As will be seen, problems in L2 perception can develop in relation to any aspect of the perceptual system, and these problems in turn might lead to problems in production.

Suprasegmentals

Suprasegmentals are features of speech which are added over the segment and can exist beyond it at the level of syllable, word, or utterance. They include stress, accent, and tone. As with segmentals, suprasegmentals are language-specific; different languages use different suprasegmental features, often in a way that is contrastive. One common way of classifying languages is on whether they use tone (e.g., Mandarin), stress (e.g., English), or pitch accent (e.g., Japanese). Suprasegmentals can also be used to convey details such as emotional state or pragmatic information. In English, for example, rising intonation can change "open the door for me" from a command into a request. Because suprasegmentals can rely on much different cues than segmentals, such as pitch and duration, it is not immediately clear whether or not learners will demonstrate the same perceptual difficulties as they do with segmentals.

Dupoux, Sebastián-Gallés, Navarette, and Peperkamp (2008) investigated this by looking at how L1 French learners of Spanish perceived stress. In Spanish, stress is lexically contrastive, such that /ˈbebe/ "(s)he drinks" and /beˈbe/ "baby" have different meanings. Stress is indicated on a vowel by higher pitch, longer duration, and higher amplitude. French, however, does not have contrastive stress (nor does it have contrastive tone or pitch accent), and it also does not make use of pitch, duration, or amplitude in a contrastive manner. Therefore, if L1 suprasegmental phonology is constraining perception, L1 French learners of Spanish should have trouble discriminating words that differ only on stress. The results of the study by Dupoux et al. (2008) support that interpretation; L1 French learners seemed to suffer from stress "deafness" which prevented them from accurately discriminating lexical stress contrasts.

The perception of tone by learners from non-tone languages has also been extensively studied. Over 70% of the languages in the world have lexical tone, including languages of Asia, West Africa, and Europe (Yip, 2002). Hallé, Chang, and Best (2004) compared the categorization and discrimination of tones by Mandarin listeners and French listeners. Mandarin is a tone language while French is not. Mandarin listeners performed better in both identification and between-category discrimination of tones than did

French listeners. Hallé et al. concluded that Mandarin listeners treat tones quasi-categorically, much like vowels, while French listeners perceive them simply as nonlinguistic variations in speech melody. Wayland and Guion (2003) similarly investigated the discrimination of Thai tones by both naïve English listeners and L1 English learners of Thai. The learners were better able to discriminate Thai tones than the naïve listeners, but they did not perform as well as native listeners. Furthermore, Eliasson (1997) compared L1 Mandarin and L1 Hindi learners of Swedish in both perception and production. Hindi is not a tone language and uses pitch only for intonation, while Swedish is a tone language, albeit quite different from Mandarin. Swedish has only one tone which conveys information about morphological derivation, rather than being a property of root words as in Mandarin. Overall, L1 Hindi learners had more problems in identification, discrimination, and production of Swedish tone than did L1 Mandarin learners, suggesting that learners from a tone language can more readily acquire tone in a new language. However, L1 Mandarin learners still showed some difficulty, which is likely due to the very different nature of tone in Swedish. Together, these studies show that the perception of tone is influenced by the nature of the L1.

English lexical stress has also received a lot of attention in research. Stressed syllables in English typically have higher pitch, longer duration, and higher amplitude, while unstressed syllables often have reduced vowels. An example is the minimal pair *permit* /pər'mɪt/ (verb) and *permit* /'pɛrmɪt/ (noun). Stress is important for speech segmentation, and trochaic stress patterns (strong – weak) seem to be preferred in English (Yu & Andruski, 2010). Archibald (1992, 1993) investigated the perception and production of English lexical stress by L1 Polish and L1 Spanish learners. Both Polish and Spanish are also stress-based languages, but the rules governing placement of stress are different from English. Archibald found that both groups of learners seemed to transfer stress patterns from their L1. L1 Polish learners, for instance, tended to both produce and perceive stress on the penultimate syllable, such that when they heard the word *maintain* /meɪn'teɪn/ spoken by a native speaker, they incorrectly indicated stress on the first syllable.

As with segmentals, the studies on suprasegmentals presented here again point to the influence of the L1 on the perception of non-native speech. In some cases, as with L1 French learners of Spanish or L1 Hindi learners of Swedish, the absence of the target suprasegmental feature in the L1 seemed to cause severe problems in perception. In cases where the L1 and L2 share the same suprasegmental feature but rely on different cues or rules in realizing it, such as with L1 Polish learners of English, learners showed L1 influences in perception.

Phonotactics

Phonotactic constraints are language-specific constraints that determine where segments can occur within a syllable and which segments can occur together. For example, the Czech composer Antonín Dvořák's last name contains a consonant cluster in the onset of the first syllable that is not allowed by English phonotactics, /dv/, even though each of these phonemes is present in English. Languages vary greatly in syllable structure and the types of consonant clusters that are permitted. English allows certain onset clusters of three consonants, such as in *street*, while Japanese does not allow any complex consonant clusters at all.

The effects of phonotactic constraints on foreign words can be seen through loanword adaptation—the process by which foreign words are adapted into a language. Illicit consonant clusters can be repaired by the insertion of epenthetic vowels, by the deletion of certain consonants, or by the mutation of consonants into allowed clusters. In Japanese, the preferred strategy is vowel epenthesis, so that the Japanese loanword for the English *street* is *sutoriito* /sutoriːto/. The epenthetic vowel used most often in Japanese is /u/, although /o/ is used after alveolar stops /t/ and /d/.

The question arises of where in the phonological system vowel epenthesis is occurring. It is possible, for example, that speakers have difficulty producing illicit consonant clusters as in the name Dvořák, so vowel epenthesis occurs to aid production (in English, a schwa is inserted to form /dəvɔːrʒɑːk/). However, it is also possible that vowel epenthesis is occurring at the perceptual level, such that listeners perceive a vowel even when it is absent in the acoustic input. Dupoux, Kakehi, Hirose, Pallier, and Mehler (1999) investigated this in a series of experiments designed to reveal the perceptual nature of epenthetic vowels. In one experiment using a vowel identification task, Japanese listeners were auditorily presented with non-words that varied in the degree to which a vowel occurred in a consonant cluster. The non-words ranged from no vowel being present in the acoustic signal, as in /ɛbzo/, to a full vowel being present, as in /ɛbuzo/, with four steps in between. Participants were trained in vowel recognition and then asked to listen to each stimulus and respond by indicating whether or not they perceived a vowel in the target position. The results showed that, on average, participants perceived a vowel for all stimuli at a high rate, even when there was no vowel in the acoustic signal (/ɛbzo/). Another experiment using an ABX discrimination task supported these results by showing that Japanese listeners had a high error rate in discriminating pairs of words such as /ɛbzo/ and /ɛbuzo/. Therefore, Dupoux et al. concluded that vowel epenthesis is occurring at the perceptual level, rather than simply being a mechanism to aid articulation of unfamiliar contrasts in production.

Although phonotactic constraints such as vowel epenthesis seem to occur in the perceptual system, it is not clear how they interact with categorical perception. Phonotactics are not addressed in the PAM or the SLM, which are focused only on the categorization of individual segments independent of context. One possibility is that phonotactic constraints apply after segments have been categorized, while another possibility is that they apply concurrently with categorization. Dupoux, Parlato, Frota, Hirose, and Peperkamp (2011) conducted a series of experiments on this topic which compared native speakers of Japanese and Brazilian Portuguese. Similar to Japanese, Brazilian Portuguese does not allow consonant clusters in certain environments, such as in /ɛbzo/. However, while the preferred epenthetic vowel in Japanese is /u/, it is /i/ in Brazilian Portuguese (in each case, the preferred epenthetic vowel is the shortest vowel in the language). Dupoux et al. (2011) created stimuli for a vowel identification task similar to that used in Dupoux et al. (1999) by excising the vowels in steps from pairs of words such as /ɛbuzo/ and /ɛbizo/. If vowel epenthesis occurs after categorization, then coarticulatory effects of the preceding consonant (the way in which a consonant changes to reflect the vowel that follows) should not be relevant, since they will be lost at the categorization stage. However, if Japanese listeners are more likely to perceive a vowel when it has been excised from /ɛbuzo/ and Brazilian Portuguese speakers when it has been excised from /ɛbizo/, this indicates that epenthesis is occurring together with categorization. Results indicated that the latter was occurring: Japanese listeners perceived more /u/ vowels in /ɛbzo/ when the sound had been created from /ɛbuzo/ rather than /ɛbizo/, and Brazilian Portuguese listeners showed the opposite pattern. Overall, the results from Dupoux et al. (2011) suggest that phonotactic constraints apply during categorization. This is not easily compatible with current models of categorization, which focus only on segments in isolation.

Phonological Processes

A **phonological process** (formally represented by a phonological rule) is a language-specific process that causes speech to change in some way as it moves from one level of mental representation to another. For instance, a particular phoneme may systematically change in production when it occurs within a certain context, possibly in order to make articulation easier. One such case is regressive assimilation of place of articulation in English (Darcy, Peperkamp, & Dupoux, 2007). The coronals /t/, /d/, and /n/ typically change their place of articulation in natural speech when followed by a labial or velar segment to match that segment. Therefore, the /t/ in the word *hot* /hɑt/ will assimilate the labial place of articulation if followed by *bread* /brɛd/ to form [hɑp̚brɛd] in production, while the same /t/ in *hot* /hɑt/ will assimilate the velar place of articulation if followed by *glue* /gluː/ to form [hɑk̚gluː]. One task of the listener's phonological system is to reconstruct the underlying segment in order to aid word recognition. However, because phonological processes are language-specific, it is possible that an L2 learner may encounter difficulties in perception due to the influence of L1 phonological processes.

Darcy et al. (2007) addressed the influence of L1 phonological processes on L2 perception by looking at patterns of assimilation in both L1 French learners of English and L1 English learners of French. French differs from English in that it does not have the regressive place assimilation process just described. Instead, it has regressive voicing assimilation, which is a process that occurs within obstruent clusters. When the voicing features (voiced or voiceless) of two obstruents in sequence do not match, the first obstruent will assimilate the voicing feature of the second. For example, the /t/ in *botte* /bot/ (*boot* in English) becomes voiced in production when followed by *grise* /griz/ (*grey* in English) to form [bodgriːz]. If the English regressive place assimilation process were applied to this word pair rather than the French voicing assimilation process, it would result in the illicit *[bokgriːz]. Conversely, if the French voicing assimilation process was applied to the English *hot glue*, it would result in *[hɑdgluː]. The question that Darcy et al. addressed, then, is whether or not learners tended to apply their L1 phonological processes in L2 perception. In the experiment, both L1 French learners of English and L1 English learners of French listened to the same L2 word twice, first in isolation and then followed by another word in the context of a sentence, and had to decide whether or not the words had the same form. The target words in the sentential context were varied to reflect both place assimilation and voicing assimilation. The results showed that lower-proficiency learners from both L1s tended to respond based on the L1 assimilation process. For example, L1 French learners of English tended to respond that a word such as *hot* [hɑt] was of the same form in isolation as in *[hɑdgluː], but was different from the form in [hɑk̚gluː], unlike English native speakers. Higher-proficiency learners, however, tended to respond more based on the L2 process, which suggests that L2 phonological processes can be acquired.

Perception vs. Production

So far, we have focused exclusively on the importance of perception in understanding the difficulties that learners might have in pronouncing the sounds of their L2. Indeed, much of the research on L2 phonological acquisition has focused on the role of perception. One aspect of this that must be addressed, however, is to what extent perception actually relates to production. Is it possible for a learner to produce a sound that cannot be perceived? And, conversely, is it possible that a sound can be perceived but not produced?

A number of studies have addressed the relationship between perception and production (Llisterri, 1995; Peperkamp & Bouchon, 2011; Schmitz, Díaz, Fernández Rubio, & Sebastián-Gallés, 2018; see Flege, 1999 for a review). The general consensus seems to be that there is a relationship between perception and production, but it does not account for all of the observed findings. For example, Sheldon and Strange (1982) reported on the perception and production of the English /l/-/ɹ/ contrast by L1 Japanese learners. While advanced learners still had problems with perception, they were able to produce the contrast quite well. How could they produce a contrast that they could not perceive? Conversely, how might it be possible for a learner to hear a sound that they cannot produce accurately? In the following paragraphs, these points will be addressed through a consideration of both the way that words are encoded in the mental lexicon and how sounds are articulated by the vocal apparatus.

Mental Lexicon

Models of perception such as the PAM and the SLM imply that a distinction cannot be made in the mental lexicon for a contrast that is not perceived. For example, if an L1 Japanese learner of English perceives *light* and *right* as the same, then both words will be represented the same way in the mental lexicon, which will, in turn, cause them to be produced the same. Pallier, Colomé, and Sebastián-Gallés (2001) investigated L1 Spanish L2 Catalan early bilinguals to determine how Catalan minimal pairs were lexically encoded. Catalan contains vowel contrasts, such as /e/-/ɛ/, that are absent in Spanish. Previous research showed that L1 Spanish L2 Catalan early bilinguals have difficulty discriminating this contrast and assimilate both vowels to the Spanish /e/ (Pallier, Bosch, & Sebastián-Gallés, 1997). To investigate underlying lexical representations, Pallier et al. (2001) used a lexical decision task with repetition priming. In this task, participants hear a series of words and non-words and have to decide whether each is a real word or not. There is a repetition effect such that if a participant hears the same word twice in near succession, they will respond more quickly. However, this repetition effect does not occur for minimal pairs. Therefore, if an L1 Catalan speaker hears /netə/ and /nɛtə/ in near succession, there will not be a repetition effect, since these words have different lexical representations. Pallier et al. found, however, that L1 Spanish L2 Catalan bilinguals did have a repetition effect for such minimal pairs, which indicates that they were encoded as homophones in the lexicon. They concluded that a difficulty in perceiving an L2 contrast will lead learners to encode word pairs with that contrast as homophones in their mental lexicons.

However, it does not always seem to be the case that a contrast cannot be represented in the mental lexicon if it cannot be perceived (Cutler, Weber, & Otake, 2006; Darcy, Daidone, & Kojima, 2013; Darcy et al., 2012; Weber & Cutler, 2004). Cutler et al. (2006) investigated the English /l/-/ɹ/ for L1 Japanese learners of English. As previously discussed, this contrast is difficult for this learner group to perceive, even at advanced proficiency levels. In their experiment, Cutler et al. presented participants with a set of pictures and used an eye-tracking device to record which pictures they looked at. Two of the pictures showed objects which started with similar syllables, such as *rocket* and *locker*. Participants were then instructed to look at one of the pictures (e.g., "Look at the rocket.") When told to look at the rocket, participants also had an initial tendency to look at the locker. However, importantly, when instructed to look at the locker, they did not look at the rocket. Cutler et al. interpreted this asymmetry to mean that learners had encoded the /l/-/ɹ/ distinction in the lexicon, but their phonetic processing was unable to discriminate the two sounds; the asymmetry was due to one of the sounds, /l/, being dominant and therefore easier to process.

If some L1 Japanese learners of English have successfully represented the /l/-/ɹ/ contrast in their mental lexicons, that might account for the findings by Sheldon & Strange (1982) that learners could produce the contrast despite not being able to perceive it. However, the question of *how* a contrast could be lexically encoded without being perceived must still be addressed. Weber and Cutler (2004) suggested that metalinguistic or orthographic knowledge might be the mechanism by which perception could essentially be bypassed. In other words, learners might be aware that the first syllables of *rocket* and *locker* must be different because they are written differently, even though they cannot hear the difference. This orthographic knowledge might then be incorporated into the lexical representation of *rocket*. Through articulatory rehearsal, learners might be able to differentiate between the two sounds in production (although not necessarily in a way that is native-like), despite perception still eluding them (Sheldon & Strange, 1982).

Articulation

Articulation refers to how the components of the vocal system, including the lungs, vocal cords, tongue, and so on, physically operate to produce sound. Although much of the recent research on the influence of the L1 phonological system in L2 acquisition has focused on perception, the role of articulation has also received some attention.

Honikman (1964) proposed the articulatory settings theory, which argued that a speaker's articulatory system was defined by the characteristics of sounds in the L1. The theory predicted difficulty in articulating L2 sounds that were absent in the L1. Some evidence in support of articulatory transfer comes from a study by Hurtado and Estrada (2010), who looked at the production of Spanish vibrants—the alveolar tap /ɾ/ and the alveolar trill /r/—by L1 English learners. These two Spanish phonemes are absent in English and are particularly difficult to articulate. The Spanish trill /r/ even presents challenges for L1 Spanish speakers and is one of the last segments to be acquired in L1 acquisition (Hurtado & Estrada, 2010). In their study, Hurtado and Estrada analyzed advanced learners' speech for accurate productions of the vibrants. They found that learners produced both the tap and the trill, but the phonological context played an important role. Accurate vibrants were produced less often when immediately following another alveolar consonant than when following a velar consonant, bilabial consonant, or vowel. This suggests that articulation was easier when the tongue tip—the primary articulator in both the tap and trill—was not involved in the articulation of the previous sound. Such results are not accounted for by purely perceptual models, which do not address such specific differences based on phonological context.

Colantoni and Steele (2008) highlighted the importance of including articulatory constraints in L2 phonological models. They looked at the production of the French uvular fricative /ʁ/ and the Spanish tap /ɾ/ by L1 English intermediate and advanced learners of each language. For each of the target phonemes, they determined through analysis whether learners had mastered features of voice, length, and manner. The phonemes were varied for context: word initial, word final, intervocalic, and preceding a consonant. The results showed a large degree of variation in mastery, depending on both the feature in question and the context. For example, for advanced learners of French, they had mastered manner in intervocalic contexts, but not voice or length, and in word final contexts, they had mastered voice and length, but not manner. Colantoni and Steele concluded that current models of perception are too general to account for such a wide variety of patterns in production. Instead, learners' problems seemed to be due to the inability to coordinate the different articulatory gestures.

The focus throughout this chapter has been on how the phonological system of a learner's L1 can influence the perception and production of the L2. Difficulties in perception can occur in relation to segmentals, suprasegmentals, phonotactics, and phonological processes, and these in turn can cause inaccurate representations in the mental lexicon. Other factors, however, may also affect the way that words are represented in the mental lexicon, such as the orthography of a language or metalinguistic knowledge of phonology. Finally, difficulties in articulating sounds not present in the L1 can also result in production problems. Together, these factors present a picture of the challenges that a learner faces when attempting to learn how to pronounce sounds in an L2.

IMPLICATIONS FOR TEACHING ENGLISH LANGUAGE LEARNERS

This section will address some of the implications that L2 phonological research has for teaching pronunciation to learners. The focus here will be on practical advice that teachers can implement within the pronunciation classroom to enhance instruction. Four main points will be addressed which highlight the importance of perception practice, explicit instruction, communicative production, and understanding learner problems.

Perception Practice

Given our understanding that L2 learners can fail to accurately perceive elements of speech, such as segmentals and suprasegmentals, it is clear that pronunciation instruction should have some focus on improving the perception of difficult sounds. In more traditional pronunciation instruction, learners might practice repeating words after the teacher, but this type of instruction is clearly limited if learners are not accurately hearing the target sounds. By improving perception, the underlying forms of words that learners store in their mental lexicons might become more accurate, and this in turn will lead to improved pronunciation. At least for some contrasts, such as the /l/-/ɹ/ contrast for L1 Japanese learners of English, experimental evidence has shown that training in perception can have a positive effect on pronunciation (Bradlow, Pisoni, Akahane-Yamada, & Tohkura, 1997).

What specifically can teachers do to practice perception? Perhaps the most straight-forward method is the use of minimal pairs that differ only in the target sound; students can practice listening and matching one member of a minimal pair to its corresponding picture. However, minimal pairs are somewhat limited in their use since it can be difficult to find pairs for certain contrasts, such as lexical stress, and because learners may not be familiar with both members of the pair. Darcy (2018) suggests using pairs of words, where one member of the pair is real word and one is a pseudoword, that differ only in the target sound, such as /strit/ and */strɪt/ for *street*. Learners are asked to identify which word in the pair matches a picture. Such an activity can be implemented through a PowerPoint slideshow with audio recordings of the word pairs. Once learners are comfortable with words in isolation, more variety can be introduced by including words within sentences, words spoken by different speakers, or words spoken at a faster rate.

For more advanced practice, and particularly for practice of suprasegmentals such as intonation and sentence stress, learners can listen to recordings of natural speech. They can focus on the rhythmic nature of sentence stress by doing clapping activities while listening, or draw contour lines in the air to match intonation patterns. Shadowing is a good all-purpose activity to help with speaking fluency and also pronunciation. To do shadowing, learners listen and repeat after a recording with a very short delay. Shadowing is particularly effective in pronunciation practice when learners are instructed to focus on one particular feature, such as word stress.

Explicit Instruction and Feedback

Explicit instruction in both segmentals and suprasegmentals has been reported to have a positive effect on pronunciation, particularly comprehensibility (Gordon, Darcy, & Ewert, 2013; Saito, 2011; Thomson & Derwing, 2014). As discussed in regards to the mental lexicon, explicit instruction may help learners bypass limits in perception in order to construct accurate mental representations. Explicit instruction is instruction that focuses the learner's attention on the form of sounds and describes how those sounds are produced in as much detail as is appropriate (this is determined by both the learner population and the degree of phonetics training that the teacher has had). This goes hand-in-hand with perception practice, and the two should be closely linked in the classroom. A resource book such as Celce-Murcia, Brinton, and Goodwin (2010) is invaluable, both because it provides a detailed description of English phonetics in an easy-to-understand way, and because it includes diagrams that can be shown to students to help them visualize the positions of the vocal organs.

For consonants, learners should be taught at least the place and manner of articulation for each sound, and for vowels, the relationship between tongue placement, lip rounding, and vowel sound. For suprasegmentals, learners should be taught at least word stress and vowel reduction (as a pair, given their connected nature), sentence stress, and intonation, preferably in that order. If priority must be given to either segmentals or suprasegmentals, then it is recommended to focus on suprasegmentals (Gordon et al., 2013). Instruction in suprasegmentals seems to have a greater effect on comprehensibility, and in the experiences of this author, many students seem completely unaware of the principles of English suprasegmentals.

English orthography can be both a help and a hindrance in pronunciation instruction. When there is a clear difference in the written alphabet that reflects a sound contrast, such as with the letters *l* and *r*, then this can help students realize that these sounds are not the same. However, there are many sound contrasts in English that are not reflected in orthography. For example, both *bath* /bæθ/ and *bathe* /beɪð/ are written with *th*, but the underlying phoneme is different. At the least, students should be told that the English alphabet does not always offer trustworthy information when it comes to pronunciation. For a highly motivated group of learners, the teacher may find it helpful to introduce the International Phonetic Alphabet (IPA) for English sounds. Even a basic overview of the IPA can be enough to show learners that there are more sounds in English than are indicated via the alphabet.

Finally, explicit corrective feedback is an essential component of pronunciation instruction, especially when paired with explicit instruction (Darcy, 2018). Feedback should be explicit, meaning that the teacher should clearly identify the error and its correction. By doing so, learners understand that their pronunciation is being corrected and not the meaning of what they were saying. Explicit feedback should ideally target problems that learners have already received instruction in, so that learners are able to draw on their own understanding of the error and what should be done to correct it.

Communicative and Repetitive Production

Pronunciation practice that is done only through highly controlled activities may not lead to clear improvements in spontaneous speech (Celce-Murcia et al., 2010). This is evident to any teacher who has given learners a pronunciation drill that seems to lead to improvement, only for learners to immediately revert to their old habits once the drill is finished. Learners may be able to make use of more attentional resources during controlled activities than during spontaneous speech, and controlled activities may not present the same pressure on the articulatory system that highly varied, rapid speech does. Therefore, it is important to also devote practice time to more open, communicative tasks so that learners have an opportunity to put what they have learned into action in a way that reflects actual use.

Celce-Murcia et al. (2010) have developed a communicative framework for pronunciation instruction that aims to integrate communicative activities into instruction. According to the framework, learners first receive explicit instruction in the target feature and do perception practice. Then, learners practice production in a series of activities that gradually become less restrictive. They might begin this with a controlled activity where they ask set questions to a partner and record the answers, and then move on to a less restrictive information gap activity. Eventually, learners engage in open conversation which involves producing the target structure in some way.

One challenge of communicative production activities, however, is that learners might lose focus of the goal of pronunciation and instead focus their attention on meaningful communication alone. To address this, Gatbonton and Segalowitz (2005) proposed the ACCESS methodology, where ACCESS stands for Automatization in Communicative Contexts of Essential Speech Segments. This methodology is not targeted specifically at pronunciation instruction, but it can easily be integrated. While the focus of ACCESS remains on communicative production, it aims for the automatization of the targeted language feature through repetition. Communicative activities should be "genuinely communicative," meaning learners must communicate in order to share information that is used to complete some task. These activities should also feature considerable repetition of the target feature. For example, if learners are practicing question intonation, they might do an interview roleplay where one learner interviews the other about a topic of interest, and later the results of the interview are presented to the class. Such an activity has repetition of the target feature (asking a variety of questions) and a goal (present the findings to the class). Throughout such an activity, the teacher emphasizes to learners that their focus should be on the target feature, and the teacher also provides explicit corrective feedback. In this way, learners stay focused on the goal of pronunciation while also communicating freely.

Understanding Learner Problems

Pronunciation instruction may seem to pose an exceptional challenge for teachers, particularly in contexts where learners are from mixed L1 backgrounds. Each learner may have very different strengths and weaknesses, and this may leave a teacher feeling that they do not know where to begin. Nevertheless, perhaps the most important tool that a teacher can bring to a classroom is the awareness that there are patterns and generalizations to be found in the problems that learners encounter in pronunciation. One goal of this chapter has been to highlight the possible ways that the L1 may influence L2 pronunciation. Using this knowledge, teachers can be better informed about underlying causes of learner problems and how best to overcome them.

It is unreasonable to expect a teacher to learn the phonological system of the L1 of every learner in a class. However, there are several ways that teachers can put to use an understanding of L2 phonology. First, by simply being aware of learners' L1s, teachers can begin to recognize patterns that occur frequently. For example, it probably will not take long in the classroom to realize that low-proficiency L1 Arabic learners of English have problems with the /p/-/b/ contrast, or that L1 Japanese learners of English struggle with vowel reduction. Noticing these patterns and recognizing that they are likely due to L1 influence can greatly assist teachers in targeting areas in need of practice, both for the current group of learners and for future learners. In addition, it can be very helpful to administer diagnostic checks to learners at the beginning of a course. A typical diagnostic involves the learner being recorded as they read a passage (after being given time to practice). One such diagnostic can be found in Celce-Murcia et al. (2010). A perception diagnostic can also be given by having learners listen and match one word from a word/pseudoword pair to a picture for a variety of sounds. Finally, learners themselves can be a great resource in determining problem areas in perception and production. Through experience and self-evaluation, they may have a good sense of their own weaknesses of which they can inform the teacher. Of course, any such self-reports from learners should be verified, since there is a possibility that they have misunderstood some aspect of English pronunciation.

By incorporating perception practice, explicit instruction and feedback, communicative and repetitive production, and an understanding of learner problems, it is possible for teachers to approach pronunciation instruction in a way that is theoretically grounded and best suited to helping learners overcome the particular challenges that they face. The importance of pronunciation instruction in aiding L2 phonological acquisition cannot be overstated, and the overview of research presented in this chapter demonstrates that more so than ever before, teachers have the knowledge at their disposal to target learner problems and maximize the efficiency of instruction.

DISCUSSION QUESTIONS

1. Think back on your own experiences learning an L2. Were you aware of any sounds that were difficult to perceive? If so, what drew your awareness to those sounds?

2. What expectations might the typical L2 learner have for pronunciation instruction? How might these expectations differ from what has been discussed in this chapter?

3. It can be challenging to teach pronunciation to a group of learners from mixed L1 backgrounds, since each learner might have different strengths and weaknesses. However, what advantages might such a situation offer?

4. Learners often have different goals for how they want to sound in an L2. They may want to sound like a native speaker, or simply speak in a way that is comprehensible, or even maintain an accent as part of their identity. How will such differences affect pronunciation instruction?

5. Some teachers report that they do not have enough time to devote to pronunciation instruction in the classroom. How might pronunciation be integrated into other skills to overcome this?

EXERCISES

1. Mandarin does not have a distinction between tense and lax vowels, while English does (/i,e,u/-/ɪ,ɛ,ʊ/). Mandarin vowels more closely resemble English tense vowels. What predictions can you make about how L1 Mandarin learners will perceive such English vowels?

2. Japanese does not have a distinction between tense and lax vowels, but it does have a distinction between long and short vowels. In general, English tense vowels are longer in duration than lax vowels, although this is not the primary cue that native speakers use to distinguish the two. Do you predict that L1 Japanese learners will perceive a difference between English tense and lax vowels?

3. Spanish phonotactics does not allow consonant clusters that begin with /s/ at the beginning of words. For example, the Spanish cognate of the English word *stable* is *estable*. What do you predict that a low proficiency level L1 Spanish learner of English will perceive when they hear the word *strong*, and how will they produce it?

4. Japanese has lexical pitch-accent, which is indicated solely by a change in pitch on a particular syllable. English, on the other hand, has lexical stress, which is indicated by increased pitch, duration, and amplitude on the stressed syllable and vowel reduction on unstressed syllables. What problems do you predict that L1 Japanese learners of English will have with English lexical stress?

5. German has both voiced and voiceless stops, but there is a phonological process that results in stops being devoiced when they occur at the end of a word. For example, the German words *Rad* 'wheel' and *Rat* 'council' are homophones. Do you predict that L1 German learners of English will have difficulty distinguishing between the English words *rod* and *rot*?

REFERENCES

Aoyama, K., Flege, J. E., Guion, S. G., Akahane-Yamada, R., & Yamada, T. (2004). Perceived phonetic dissimilarity and L2 speech learning: The case of Japanese /r/ and English /l/ and /r/. *Journal of Phonetics, 32*(2), 233–250. doi:10.1016/S0095-4470(03)00036-6

Aoyama, K., & Guion, S. G. (2007). Prosody in second language acquisition: Acoustic analyses of duration and F0 range. In O.-S. Bohn & M. Munro (Eds.), *Language experience in second language speech learning* (pp. 281–297). Amsterdam: John Benjamins. doi:10.1075/lllt.17.24aoy

Archibald, J. (1992). Transfer of L1 parameter settings: Some empirical evidence from Polish metrics. *Canadian Journal of Linguistics, 37*(3), 301–340. doi:10.1017/S0008413100019903

Archibald, J. (1993). The learnability of English metrical parameters by adult Spanish speakers. *IRAL: International Review of Applied Linguistics in Language Teaching, 31*(2), 129.

Best, C. T. (1995). A direct realist view of cross-language speech perception. In W. Strange (Ed.), *Speech perception and linguistic experience. Issues in cross-language research* (pp. 171–204). Timonium, MD: York Press.

Best, C. T., McRoberts, G. W., & Sithole, N. M. (1988). Examination of perceptual reorganization for nonnative speech contrasts: Zulu click discrimination by English-speaking adults and infants. *Journal of Experimental Psychology. Human Perception and Performance, 14*(3), 345–360. doi:10.1037/0096-1523.14.3.345 PMID:2971765

Bradlow, A. R., Pisoni, D. B., Akahane-Yamada, R., & Tohkura, Y. I. (1997). Training Japanese listeners to identify English /r/ and /l/: IV. Some effects of perceptual learning on speech production. *The Journal of the Acoustical Society of America, 101*(4), 2299–2310. doi:10.1121/1.418276 PMID:9104031

Celce-Murcia, M., Brinton, D. M., & Goodwin, J. M. (2010). Teaching pronunciation: A course book and reference guide (2nd ed.). New York, NY: Cambridge University Press.

Colantoni, L., & Steele, J. (2008). Integrating articulatory constraints into models of second language phonological acquisition. *Applied Psycholinguistics, 29*(3), 489–534. doi:10.1017/S0142716408080223

Cutler, A., & Otake, T. (2004). Pseudo-homophony in non-native listening. *The Journal of the Acoustical Society of America, 115*(5), 2392. doi:10.1121/1.4780547

Cutler, A., Weber, A., & Otake, T. (2006). Asymmetric mapping from phonetic to lexical representations in second-language listening. *Journal of Phonetics, 34*(2), 269–284. doi:10.1016/j.wocn.2005.06.002

Darcy, I. (2018). Powerful and effective pronunciation instruction: How can we achieve it? *The CATESOL Journal, 30*(1), 13–45.

Darcy, I., Daidone, D., & Kojima, C. (2013). Asymmetric lexical access and fuzzy lexical representations in second language learners. *The Mental Lexicon, 8*(3), 372–420. doi:10.1075/ml.8.3.06dar

Darcy, I., Dekydtspotter, L., Sprouse, R. A., Glover, J., Kaden, C., McGuire, M., & Scott, J. H. G. (2012). Direct mapping of acoustics to phonology: On the lexical encoding of front rounded vowels in L1 English-L2 French acquisition. *Second Language Research, 28*(1), 5–40. doi:10.1177/0267658311423455

Darcy, I., Peperkamp, S., & Dupoux, E. (2007). Bilinguals play by the rules. Perceptual compensation for assimilation in late L2-learners. In J. Cole & J. I. Hualde (Eds.), *Laboratory phonology 9* (pp. 411–442). Berlin: Mouton de Gruyter.

Dupoux, E., Kakehi, K., Hirose, Y., Pallier, C., & Mehler, J. (1999). Epenthetic vowels in Japanese: A perceptual illusion? *Journal of Experimental Psychology. Human Perception and Performance, 25*(6), 1568–1578. doi:10.1037/0096-1523.25.6.1568

Dupoux, E., Parlato, E., Frota, S., Hirose, Y., & Peperkamp, S. (2011). Where do illusory vowels come from? *Journal of Memory and Language, 64*(3), 199–210. doi:10.1016/j.jml.2010.12.004

Dupoux, E., Sebastián-Gallés, N., Navarrete, E., & Peperkamp, S. (2008). Persistent stress 'deafness': The case of French learners of Spanish. *Cognition, 106*(2), 682–706. doi:10.1016/j.cognition.2007.04.001 PMID:17592731

Eliasson, S. (1997). Tone in second language acquisition. In R. Hickey & S. Puppel (Eds.), *Language history and linguistic modeling* (Vol. 2, pp. 1273–1289). Berlin: Mouton de Gruyter.

Flege, J. E. (1995). Second language speech learning. Theory, findings and problems. In W. Strange (Ed.), *Speech perception and linguistic experience. Issues in cross-language research* (pp. 233–277). Timonium, MD: York Press.

Flege, J. E. (1999). The relation between L2 production and perception. In J. J. Ohala, Y. Hasegawa, M. Ohala, D. Granville, & A. C. Bailey (Eds.), *Fifth International Congress of Phonetic Sciences* (vol. 2, pp. 1273-1276). Berkeley, CA.

Flege, J. E., & Eefting, W. (1987). Production and perception of English stops by native Spanish speakers. *Journal of Phonetics, 15*, 67–83.

Freeman, M. R., Blumenfeld, H. K., & Marian, V. (2016). Phonotactic constraints are activated across languages in bilinguals. *Frontiers in Psychology, 7*, 702. doi:10.3389/fpsyg.2016.00702 PMID:27242615

Gatbonton, E., & Segalowitz, N. (2005). Rethinking communicative language teaching: A focus on access to fluency. *Canadian Modern Language Review, 61*(3), 325–353. doi:10.3138/cmlr.61.3.325

Gordon, J., Darcy, I., & Ewert, D. (2013). Pronunciation teaching and learning: Effects of explicit phonetic instruction in the L2 classroom. In J. Levis, & K. LeVelle (Eds.). *Proceedings of the 4th Pronunciation in Second Language Learning and Teaching Conference* (pp. 194-206). Ames, IA: Iowa State University.

Goto, H. (1971). Auditory perception by normal Japanese adults of the sounds "l" and "r.". *Neuropsychologia, 9*(3), 317–323. doi:10.1016/0028-3932(71)90027-3 PMID:5149302

Hallé, P. A., Chang, Y. C., & Best, C. T. (2004). Identification and discrimination of Mandarin Chinese tones by Mandarin Chinese vs. French listeners. *Journal of Phonetics, 32*(3), 395–421. doi:10.1016/S0095-4470(03)00016-0

Harnad, S. (Ed.). (1987). *Categorical perception: The groundwork of cognition.* New York: Cambridge University Press.

Henly, E., & Sheldon, A. (1986). Duration and context effects on the perception of English /r/ and /l/: A comparison of Cantonese and Japanese speakers. *Language Learning, 36*(4), 505–522. doi:10.1111/j.1467-1770.1986.tb01036.x

Honikman, B. (1964). Articulatory settings. In D. Abercrombie, D. Fry, P. MacCarthy, N. C. Scott, & J. Trim (Eds.), *In honour of Daniel Jones* (pp. 73–84). London: Longman.

Hurtado, L. M., & Estrada, C. (2010). Factors influencing the second language acquisition of Spanish vibrants. *Modern Language Journal, 94*(1), 74–86. doi:10.1111/j.1540-4781.2009.00984.x

Ingram, J. C., & Park, S. G. (1998). Language, context, and speaker effects in the identification and discrimination of English /r/ and /l/ by Japanese and Korean listeners. *The Journal of the Acoustical Society of America, 103*(2), 1161–1174. doi:10.1121/1.421225 PMID:9479769

Kluge, D. C., Rauber, A. S., Reis, M. S., & Bion, R. A. H. (2007). The relationship between the perception and production of English nasal codas by Brazilian learners of English. *Proceedings of Interspeech, 2007*, 2297–2300.

Lai, Y. H. (2010). English vowel discrimination and assimilation by Chinese-speaking learners of English. *Concentric: Studies in Linguistics, 36*(2), 157–182.

Liberman, A. M., Harris, K. S., Hoffman, H. S., & Griffith, B. C. (1957). The discrimination of speech sounds within and across phoneme boundaries. *Journal of Experimental Psychology, 54*(5), 358–368. doi:10.1037/h0044417 PMID:13481283

Llisterri, J. (1995). Relationships between speech production and speech perception in a second language. In *Proceedings of the 13th International Congress of Phonetic Sciences* (Vol. 4, pp. 92-99). Stockholm, Sweden: Royal Institute of Technology/Stockholm University.

Mochizuki, M. (1981). The identification of /l/ and /ɹ/ in natural and synthesized speech. *Journal of Phonetics, 9,* 283–303.

Morrison, G. S. (2002). Perception of English /i/ and /ɪ/ by Japanese and Spanish listeners: Longitudinal results. In G. S. Morrison, & L. Zsoldos (Eds.), *Proceedings of the North West Linguistics Conference 2002* (pp. 29-48). Burnaby, Canada: Simon Fraser University Linguistics Graduate Student Association.

O'Dell, M., & Port, R. (1983). Discrimination of word-final voicing in German. *The Journal of the Acoustical Society of America, 73*(S1), S31–S31. doi:10.1121/1.2020331

Ota, M., Hartsuiker, R. J., & Haywood, S. L. (2009). The KEY to the ROCK: Near-homophony in nonnative visual word recognition. *Cognition, 111*(2), 263–269. doi:10.1016/j.cognition.2008.12.007 PMID:19230869

Pallier, C., Bosch, L., & Sebastián-Gallés, N. (1997). A limit on behavioral plasticity in speech. *Cognition, 64*(3), B9–B17. doi:10.1016/S0010-0277(97)00030-9 PMID:9426508

Pallier, C., Colomé, A., & Sebastián-Gallés, N. (2001). The influence of native-language phonology on lexical access: Concrete exemplar-based vs. abstract lexical entries. *Psychological Science, 12*(6), 445–449. doi:10.1111/1467-9280.00383 PMID:11760129

Peperkamp, S., & Bouchon, C. (2011). The relation between perception and production in L2 phonological processing. *Proceedings of Interspeech, 2011,* 161–164.

Ramus, F., Peperkamp, S., Christophe, A., Jacquemot, C., Kouider, S., & Dupoux, E. (2010). A psycholinguistic perspective on the acquisition of phonology. In C. Fougeron, B. Kühnert, M. d'Imperio, & N. Vallée (Eds.), *Laboratory phonology 10: Variation, phonetic detail and phonological representation* (pp. 311–340). Berlin: Mouton de Gruyter.

Saito, K. (2011). Examining the role of explicit phonetic instruction in native-like and comprehensible pronunciation development: An instructed SLA approach to L2 phonology. *Language Awareness, 20*(1), 45–59. doi:10.1080/09658416.2010.540326

Schmitz, J., Díaz, B., Fernández Rubio, K., & Sebastian-Galles, N. (2018). Exploring the relationship between speech perception and production across phonological processes, language familiarity, and sensory modalities. *Language, Cognition and Neuroscience, 33*(5), 527–546. doi:10.1080/23273798.2017.1390142

Sheldon, A., & Strange, W. (1982). The acquisition of /r/ and /l/ by Japanese learners of English: Evidence that speech production can precede speech perception. *Applied Psycholinguistics*, *3*(3), 243–261. doi:10.1017/S0142716400001417

Thomson, R. I., & Derwing, T. M. (2014). The effectiveness of L2 pronunciation instruction: A narrative review. *Applied Linguistics*, *36*(3), 326–344. doi:10.1093/applin/amu076

Wayland, R., & Guion, S. (2003). Perceptual discrimination of Thai tones by naive and experienced learners of Thai. *Applied Psycholinguistics*, *24*(01), 113–129. doi:10.1017/S0142716403000067

Weber, A., & Cutler, A. (2004). Lexical competition in non-native spoken-word recognition. *Journal of Memory and Language*, *50*(1), 1–25. doi:10.1016/S0749-596X(03)00105-0

Werker, J. F., & Tees, R. C. (1984). Cross-language speech perception: Evidence for perceptual reorganization during the first year of life. *Infant Behavior and Development*, *7*(1), 49–63. doi:10.1016/S0163-6383(84)80022-3

Yip, M. (2002). *Tone*. New York: Cambridge University Press. doi:10.1017/CBO9781139164559

Yu, V. Y., & Andruski, J. E. (2010). A cross-language study of perception of lexical stress in English. *Journal of Psycholinguistic Research*, *39*(4), 323–344. doi:10.100710936-009-9142-2 PMID:20033291

ADDITIONAL READING

Bohn, O.-S., & Munro, M. J. (2007). *Language experience in second language speech learning: In honor of James Emil Flege*. Amsterdam, Netherlands: John Benjamins. doi:10.1075/lllt.17

Sebastián-Gallés, N. (2005). Cross-language speech perception. In D. B. Pisoni & R. E. Remez (Eds.), *The handbook of speech perception*. Malden, MA: Blackwell Publishing. doi:10.1002/9780470757024.ch22

Strange, W., & Shafer, V. (2008). Speech perception in second language learners. The re-education of selective perception. In J. G. Hansen Edwards & M. L. Zampini (Eds.), *Phonology and second language acquisition* (pp. 153–191). Philadelphia: John Benjamin. doi:10.1075ibil.36.09str

Chapter 16
Supporting English Learners' Development of Intelligible Speech:
A Focus on the K–12 ESL Context

Solange Lopes Murphy
The College of New Jersey, USA

Timothy M. Hall
The College of New Jersey, USA

Angelica Lina Vanderbilt
The College of New Jersey, USA

ABSTRACT

In this chapter, the authors discuss how ESL and general education teachers can judiciously infuse intelligibility-based pronunciation teaching into content-based classrooms. First, within a broad understanding of second language development, they identify various sources of English Language Learners' pronunciation problems, and a rationale for why pronunciation teaching should aim for intelligibility rather than for nativeness. They then present the major pronunciation challenges of the five largest language groups in American schools and offer intelligibility-focused teaching practices to stimulate discussion and evolve teacher practice in harmony with the Common Core State Standards (CCSS). The chapter closes with exercises to further explore implementation of pronunciation teaching practices for ELs' language and academic development.

DOI: 10.4018/978-1-5225-8467-4.ch016

LINGUISTIC PERSPECTIVES ON PRONUNCIATION AND INTELLIGIBILITY

Schools across the United States are tasked with serving growing populations of English language learners (ELLs). One specific area of concern is how to help ELLs be more readily understood and adept at speaking. Historically, there has been a focus on pronunciation, one's command of second language (L2) phonology, as a means to make learners more intelligible. Relevant methodologies in the service of pronunciation development have, in some cases, been characterized by an interest in how first language pronunciation predicts learner difficulty in a second language, how rote-like drills can be used for remediation, and how expectations of predictable and delineated outcomes can be met. Other methodologies profess that a copious amount of communicative language practice is sufficient to make learners more intelligible. However, the understanding shared by applied linguists and teacher educators working in the field of Second Language Acquisition (SLA) has evolved markedly in recent decades. The essence of our current understanding is that attention to language forms, in this case the phonological system, is helpful, but it should not be divested from the meanings those forms are meant to communicate (Ellis & Shintani, 2014). The understanding we also derive from the field of SLA is that although susceptible to some pedagogical manipulation, the language learning process in general, and by extension the acquisition of intelligible speech, is not always amenable to the ambitious learning timelines to which K-12 institutions and educators strive. Therefore, educators would do well to temper their expectations accordingly and perhaps to set alternative, realizable goals. We address pedagogically motivated concerns about pronunciation development in this chapter by starting with two basic questions: *What constitutes a pronunciation problem?* and *What causes and perpetuates pronunciation problems?* We then settle on the centrality of intelligibility as a guiding principle for teaching practice. Next, we consider pronunciation difficulties that various language groups have when learning English, and we propose intelligibility-oriented solutions for working teachers.

What Constitutes a Pronunciation Problem?

A pronunciation problem might best be understood as some facet of a second language learner's speech that impedes comprehension on the part of a more proficient listener. It is true that speakers around the world perceive varieties of English other than their own to be accented, which can at times pose difficulties for comprehension. A rural South Carolinian speaking to an urban Glaswegian may be one such example. However, both are native speakers of English and if they fail to comprehend each other, their difficulties hardly constitute a pronunciation problem. In fact, due to the sheer variety of world Englishes (inner circle varieties, outer circle varieties, and expanding circle varieties), we can safely say that there are likely to be more comprehension problems than pronunciation problems. And yet speakers of all types, native and non-native alike, manage to make themselves understood despite variations in pronunciation. Skillful communicators make adjustments to various dimensions of language and speech to compensate for and repair communication breakdowns.

Historically, with regards to second language learners, applied linguists working in SLA have distinguished between linguistic **errors** and **mistakes** (Corder, 1967), both of which could precipitate a breakdown in communication, and both were eschewed by educators as barriers to accent-free speech. Errors were systematic deviations from the target-like norms of the second language, whereas mistakes were considered one-off lapses while producing language. As Corder put it, "[m]istakes are of no consequence to the process of language learning" (p.167). Errors, in Corder's view, are significant because their systematicity indicates the current psycholinguistic rules by which learners operate in comprehending and producing language. And so, by this definition, a pronunciation problem "of interest" should be one that systematically appears in the learner's language but somehow fails to serve in the best interests of the learner's communication goals. Examples of errors might include a Japanese learner of English, substituting /l/ for /ɹ/ (e.g., *lice* vs. *rice*). Speakers of Vietnamese or Kayah Li might drop final syllables and consonant clusters at the ends of words. In these cases, the error can cause the listener to fail to comprehend. In sum, **systematicity** and **comprehensibility** are central to our notion of "problem".

What Causes and Perpetuates Pronunciation Problems?

The causes of errors, at the level of pronunciation and indeed in other domains of language such as grammar and vocabulary, can stem from at least three sources: typological relationships, namely the similarities and differences between the speaker's first and second languages, cognitive factors that are universal to language acquisition, and pedagogical effects. It is important to understand that whatever may have been the initial cause of a difficulty may not necessarily be the ongoing reason for perpetuating problems. All three reasons can interact over time.

Linguists and teachers have long and rightly observed that a speaker's first language holds some influence over second language development, especially in pronunciation, through cognitive processes of **linguistic transfer** (Kellerman, 1995; Odlin, 1989; Selinker, 1972). Two types of transfer have been identified: *positive linguistic transfer*, where the first language is usefully relied upon to construct a second language, and *negative linguistic transfer*, where the first language interferes with targetlike development of the second language.

To better understand first language influence, linguists have drawn on findings from linguistic **typology** studies (e.g., Haspelmath, König, Wulf, & Raible, 2001) and conducted contrastive analysis (Lado, 1957) whereby the structural components of each language were identified, categorized, and compared. It was believed that through the identification of similarities and differences, it was possible to predict where second language learners would have difficulty in learning their new language. The starting assumption for inquiry was that difference would predict difficulty in acquiring new language abilities, including pronunciation.

In investigating universals and differences across languages, linguists were able to describe **superset-subset** relationships (e.g., Hale & Reiss, 2003) which can be exemplified in the following way: If language A contains the sounds /f,v,s,z,t,d/ and language B only contains the sounds /f,s,t/, then language B is a subset of language A with respect to that category of sounds (See Figure 1).

However, while it is tempting to claim that learning from subset to superset is the more arduous, it is perhaps best to frame the issue as a learner having one of two types of learning challenges: to add or to subtract. A learner whose first language is a superset, and who is learning a subset must learn to select from a narrower repertoire of already-known structures. In contrast, a learner that is already speaking language B (a subset) and learning language A (a superset) has three new items to learn. In either case, successful learning is contingent on **noticing** the usage, or the absence thereof, of the phonological patterns in question. Brazilian Portuguese and French have nasal vowels and pure vowels, and in this respect, represent a superset to Spanish or Italian, which do not have nasal vowels in standard varieties. Therefore, Spanish learners of Brazilian Portuguese would have to perceive new vowels and learn how to use them. Brazilians learning Spanish would have to learn to restrict their usage of nasal vowels. Each challenge presupposes different cognitive and environmental demands to remediate.

Figure 1. Superset / subset relationship

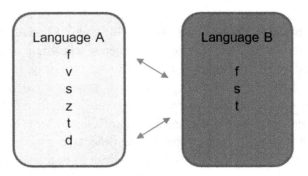

But as intuitively appealing as "difference means difficulty" is, research has concluded that such an axiom is not, in fact, always as reliable as one would hope (Schachter, 1974). Language learning does not seem to be so easily reduced. Difference may predict some initial errors, but it does not always predict difficulty or persistence. The resulting implication for pedagogy is that knowing facts about a learner's first language will not universally or consistently suggest pedagogical interventions *a priori* for a particular second language. Therefore, caution is advised in attempting an approach solely based on this assumption.

Critically, a typological-based view can promote a structural orientation toward language, if care is not taken, that does not take into account the role of meaning. This is problematic if one intends for learners to learn to communicate. For example, Japanese varieties and English varieties may in fact have the same sounds, /r, l/[1]. However, English attributes meaning differences to those sounds when they are contextualized; that is to say, the two sounds are distinct phonemes that help distinguish meanings in the context of a word. In contrast, some speakers of Japanese may not attribute meaning differences to the two sounds necessarily. Therefore, the acquisition challenge for a Japanese learner of English is not to acquire the mechanics of forming the sounds, but rather to acquire how those sounds relate to meaning-making in the new language (McClelland, Fiez & McCandliss, 2002). Equally, while most languages make use of stress across **suprasegmental** sequences of language to convey meaning, a learner's first and second languages might have different stress and intonation patterns, and therefore, the learner must discover how the stress and intonation patterns of the new language relate to the meanings they wish to express. Often times, these form-meaning relationships can be elusive to learners, and this is where teachers can have a positive impact.

There are several cognitive factors that can underlie pronunciation errors. The first, already mentioned, is **linguistic transfer**, whereby the learner transfers first language phonological rules to second language pronunciation. The second is **lack of noticing.** Learners can either fail to notice new forms in the target language input or fail to notice the absence in the target language of forms in their first language. Learners can also fail to notice how they themselves are producing language. Researchers generally agree that noticing that a sound exists in a new language and how a sound or pattern of sounds relates to meaning, on some level, is a necessary step in acquiring that sound for productive purposes in a second language (Ellis, 2006; Schmidt, 1990). A Japanese learner who never had the occasion to notice an important meaning-bearing distinction between /ɹ/ and /l/ in English is less likely to create a record of those sound contrasts in her emerging second language system and, therefore, would not be able to use them purposefully when speaking. Teachers can create opportunities for learners to notice features of the target language, which sets the stage for further learning processes.

The **creative construction process** (Dulay & Burt, 1974; Myles, Mitchell, & Hooper, 1999; Selinker, 1972) is the third factor underlying pronunciation problems. The brain is constantly tinkering with language, creating and re-formulating rules of operation along the way. Each time a learner acquires a new aspect of language, her brain goes through cycles of accommodation and restructuring. It is an error-prone, U-shaped process (i.e., initially correct, then error-prone, then correct again) that ultimately results in errors that are not necessarily induced by L1 influence. An example of a learner developing pronunciation errors due to the creative construction process can be found in Hall (2017) where a 20-year-old Chinese learner of English put /s/ sounds on the ends of many words in the sentence where he had not done previously: *Hes goes tos the stores* (He went to the store). This behavior lasted several months and gradually attenuated without explicit intervention.

Fourth, **item-based learning**, also called exemplar-based learning (Bybee, 2013; Tomasello, 2003), describes how language change happens on an item-by-item basis for a period before the learned phenomenon spreads or generalizes to other contexts. For example, a learner with difficulties with the /l/ sound might correctly pronounce the word "laugh" and "clue", but continues to mispronounce "cluster" or "clever" for a time. In step with item-based learning, several other words involving the "cl-" cluster could be gradually acquired, and eventually, all "cl-" words might become pronounced without difficulty.

The fifth factor is **over-generalization**, somewhat the opposite of the more conservative nature of item-based learning. Over-generalization can be seen where learners extend new knowledge beyond its target-like parameters, for example, a Spanish learner of Brazilian Portuguese over-using nasal vowels.

The sixth factor is **age-related effects**. As articulated through the Critical Period Hypothesis (CPH) and Sensitive Periods Hypothesis (Birdsong, 2006), older learners are less likely than younger learners to attain nativeness in pronunciation due to diminishing plasticity of the brain. The CPH claims that after puberty, a learner's potential to attain native-like language diminishes. Generally, pronunciation, or more precisely *features of pronunciation* are susceptible to such age-related effects. When viewed in the aggregate over the long term, older learners have more variable outcomes than younger learners, some having stronger accents than others. Younger learners tend to converge on target-like pronunciation.

The seventh factor is **fossilization**, which is defined as both a cognitive process and product of language development where the learner ceases to develop in some aspects of one or more domains of language, despite intention to learn and despite adequate exposure (Han, 2004; Selinker, 1972). There is ongoing research into the causes of fossilization, why it affects some domains of language in some learners but not others, even among learners of the same L1, but conclusions remain elusive. Fossilization is argued to result from a convergence of factors that include, but are not necessarily limited to, the learner's diminishing neural plasticity, L1-L2 relationships, the nature of the structure to be acquired, and the learning environment (Han, 2013).

Finally, besides the cognitive factors that motivate pronunciation difficulties, there are also **pedagogical effects**. Each teaching intervention creates a set of language use experiences that differentially engage a learner's cognitive processes described above. Each intervention may have benefits that can help a learner, but also induce trade-offs that perpetuate or create errors. Interventions may cause learners to over-learn in some cases. Pedagogies that are implicit in nature, for example, tend to prioritize communicative modes but do not promote directed noticing and therefore will leave to chance whether a learner engages cognitively with a new facet of the language. Explicit-type interventions may induce knowledge of rules and structures but do not necessarily give practice in communication. Pedagogies that solely engage in rote practice may develop fluency with regards to the linguistic feature of interest but may not help learners when their speech is not monitored or planned.

What conclusions can teachers draw from linguistic perspectives on language learning? First, language is not all about structure. Rather it is about how structures and meanings relate to one another to communicate. Furthermore, language is made up of multiple levels of structure and meaning that are interconnected and, pedagogically speaking, should be treated as such. Second, the learning process is complex, lengthy, unpredictable, and not open to direct manipulation. Teachers can create conditions of learning potential, but they cannot effectuate learning itself. They can provide extensive exposure, interaction, opportunities for noticing, and means for learners to receive feedback about the intelligibility of their utterances that can help the learner's interlanguage perpetuate a state of **self-tuning**. Teachers can anticipate that learning will be a potentially long process with regard to some features, shifting from one error type to the next before stabilizing. They can anticipate that errors are not solely sourced from L1 interference. Third, for older learners in particular, accent-free speech is not realistic, even when there is intention, ample exposure, and effort involved. Finally, teachers should be wary of the trade-offs of single approaches to language teaching, and instead judiciously apply different interventions based on learner need.

Now that the psycho-linguistic landscape of pronunciation development has been described, it is helpful to consider what are realistic goals for learners and teachers. These goals will be discussed according to two principles: nativeness and intelligibility.

Nativeness-Guided Pedagogy vs. Intelligibility: Which Is More Useful?

Two instructional principles have been used to define the goals of pronunciation pedagogy for L2 learners: the nativeness principle and more recently, the intelligibility principle (Levis, 2005). The **nativeness principle** presupposes that there is an ideal native speaker whose language performance represents the desired end-state for learners. Under this principle, a learner would attempt to develop a greatly diminished, perhaps even non-existent accent. However, the construct of a native speaker, especially as the model for a second language learning target, has been found to be highly problematic (Davies, 2003). For one, there are many varieties of "native" English within the inner circle countries of the UK, Canada, the USA, Australia, South Africa, and New Zealand, which raises the question to which variety a language learner should aspire. Next, the nativeness principle presupposes a monolingual speaker. However, multilingualism is actually the norm in many parts of the world, even in the inner circle countries. What is more, the language abilities of multilinguals are psycholinguistically and performatively different from their monolingual counterparts: multilinguals are necessarily multi-competent (Cook, 2008), which makes nativeness an unachievable goal for a second language learner from the outset. It is a foundational observation from the field of SLA that the learning conditions and outcomes of second language are fundamentally different from those of first language acquisition (Bley-Vroman, 1990) as evidenced by inter- and intra-learner differences the world over. Even highly proficient learners exhibit subtle differences in intuition and language use, even if on the surface they appear to be nativelike (Sorace, 2005). Therefore, to compare non-native learners to native speakers in terms of desired outcomes is inevitably a comparative fallacy; multi-competence, not nativeness, is the only outcome for a second language learner.

The arguments against nativeness as the desired end state of second language development have fostered an increasing interest in intelligibility as a guiding principle for pronunciation instruction. The **intelligibility principle** benchmarks success when speakers are understood by listeners who may be either native or non-native speakers themselves (Kennedy & Trofimovich, 2017; Levis, 2005). The intelligibility principle recognizes that phonological ability (i.e., pronunciation) is only one of several resources used to construct meaning. Other dimensions must be considered: morphosyntax, lexicon (including words, collocations, and formulaic sequences), and pragmatics. Intelligibility-guided instruction recognizes that mutual comprehension is strategically and dynamically co-constructed between interlocutors (Ellis & Larsen-Freeman, 2006; Ellis, 2009; Long, 1996; Wray, 2008) and refutes the idea that solutions to pronunciation-initiated communication problems must be met solely with pronunciation-targeted remedies. Therefore, teachers can feel confident that supporting learners across the language dimensions in developing dynamic communication-based abilities will yield more positive results than by supporting pronunciation alone (Kennedy & Trofimovich, 2017).

Language Groups and Their Pronunciation Challenges

As public education in the United States continues to push for standardization, ELs may be falsely regarded as a homogenous group. In reality, ELs make up students who speak hundreds of different native languages, languages which further diversify based on geographic origin, as the proximity produces a variety of dialects and lexicons (Avery & Ehlrich, 2012). This section will focus on the five primary EL groups in the United States, specifically Spanish, Chinese, Vietnamese, French/Haitian Creole, and Arabic (Ruiz-Soto, Hooker, and Batalova, 2015).

The variety of ELs in classrooms and their language needs, in conjunction with a teacher's already demanding schedule, make the very thought of supporting intelligibility development imposing if not unviable. Although decisions about instruction ultimately are based on assessments of individual learners in their specific stage of development, it is helpful for purposes of discussion here to identify common barriers to intelligibility according to language families. Language families are groups of languages with similar ancestral roots that often share places of articulation, phonemes, and stress patterns (Pariona, 2018). Speakers of the same language family have common struggles in English, at least at the beginning of learning due to L1 transfer. For example, many of the errors Spanish speakers make will also be evident in Portuguese speakers' speech because these languages are both categorized as Romance languages (Avery & Ehlrich, 2012; Hocket, 1970). Table 1 presents some typical pronunciation errors in the five largest EL groups in the U.S. schools.

English Features that Contribute to Intelligibility

As stated earlier, intelligibility is not effectuated through a single dimension of language by the speaker alone. Intelligible speakers strategically employ pronunciation, lexicon, morphosyntax, and pragmatics, as well as interactional abilities to communicate effectively. Conversely, no single dimension or language feature poses a barrier to intelligibility alone, which suggests that breakdowns in communication can be prevented or resolved by periphrastic means. Very often, speakers with low intelligibility have cumulative difficulties across several language dimensions. Table 2 presents the dimensions that have the greatest detriment to intelligibility.

Table 1. Major segmental production difficulties in five language families

Language Family	Members	Areas of Shared Difficulty (Segmentals)

Romance	Spanish, French, Italian, Catalan, Portuguese	• -ch- sound substituted for the -sh- sound (vice versa)
		   o E.g., march→ marsh
		 • Use nasal sounds interchangeably
		   o E.g., students may hear "bang" and "ban" as the same
		 • Vowel insertions in words that begin with a consonant cluster and deletions when at the end
		 • /v/ substituted for /b/
		   o E.g., valet→ ballet
		 • /ð/ sound pronounced as /d/ (and vice versa)
		 • Trilled /r/

Sino-Tibetan	Mandarin, Cantonese	• /l/ and /n/ used interchangeably
		 • Omit y when it begins words:
		   o E.g., you→ -oo-
		 • /l/ and /r/ used interchangeably
		 • /p/, /t/, /k/ may be inaudible sounds when at the end of words
		   o E.g., seat→ sea
		 • Uses /p/ and /b/ interchangeably at end of words
		 • Uses /d/ and /t/ interchangeably at end of words
		   o E.g., mad→ mat
		 • Uses /g/ and /k/ interchangeably at end of words
		 • May not associate English intonation and stress with idiomatic meaning.

Austro-Asiatic	Vietnamese	• May not recognize or produce difference between voiced and voiceless consonants o E.g., tab → tap • Phoneme deletions in words with ending consonants • - /tʃ/ substituted for /ʃ/ • /p/ instead sounds like an English /b/ or /f/ at beginnings of words • May not associate English intonation and stress with idiomatic meaning
Semitic	Arabic, Hebrew	• /ɛ/ confused with /ɪ/ • When /θ/ is in a word, learners may insert the /d/, /t/, /s/, or /z/ sounds in its place o E.g., bath→ bat • Insert vowel in the middle a consonant cluster • Use /p/ and /b/ interchangeably • Use /f/ and /v/ interchangeably • Trilled /r/
Indo-Aryan	Hindi, Punjabi, Urdu, Bengali	• /f/ sounds like /p/ and /v/ sounds like /b/ o E.g., leaf→ leap • /v/ sounds like English /w/ • Vowel insertions in words that begin with a consonant cluster and deletions when at the end • May voice, instead of aspirate, the sounds /p/, /t/, /k/ • May not associate English intonation and stress with idiomatic meaning

Adapted from Avery & Ehrlich, 2012; Hocket, 1970; Swan & Smith, 2014

Table 2. Potential behaviors that affect intelligibility

• Misplacement or no indication of prominent information in discourse; absence of discourse structuring devices   • Use of constructions or words that are unfamiliar or unexpected to the listener: non-idiomatic content words, phrases, or formulaic sequences   • Incorrect placement of suprasegmental stress in a sentence (i.e., in unmarked speech, stress is on function words when it should be on content words)   • Omission or addition of entire syllables   • Incorrect syllable timing   • Inappropriate duration between stressed and unstressed syllables   • Unclear production of consonants in clustered positions or at syllable boundaries   • Speed of speech (either too slow or too fast)   • Halting speech or abundant / lengthy pauses during speech

Adapted from Goodwin, 2014

Essentially, intelligibility is derived from a network of form-meaning-use relationships. Although our emphasis in this chapter is pronunciation (phonological form), we are mindful that pronunciation pedagogy should be conducted in the context of meaningful discourse, and so we will necessarily touch to some extent on other language dimensions, specifically content words and formulaic expressions because these carry a significant amount of meaning in discourse and are pedagogically appropriate targets for practicing pronunciation in content classrooms.

Suprasegmentals and Segmentals

The term **suprasegmental** typically refers to speech characteristics such as stress and prosody distributed over words and phrases. The term **segmental** refers to individual phonemes, clusters, or even syllables. Suprasegmental stress patterns are critical for intelligibility in English because they are markers of meaning-bearing content (O'Neal, 2010). For example, content words (nouns, verbs, adjectives, adverbs) are typically stressed more than function words (auxiliary verbs, prepositions, articles). Consider the following examples:

I have to go to the supermarket.
There's no way I'm gonna take you to the movies.

Of course, speakers shift stress according to desired emphasis and learners should become aware of this, but the basic pattern of + stress on content words and - stress on function words in English is a prevailing one. According to Swan and Smith (2014), "stress and rhythm of an English sentence give a lot of acoustic clues to structure and meaning" (p. 95). A speaker who maintains a flat prosodic pattern during speech, even if using appropriate vocabulary, will not indicate what specific information is most salient in the utterance and can potentially lead the English-speaking listener to confusion. Avery & Ehrlich (2012) also caution that sometimes learners who do not yet have a sense of the stress boundaries of English may create choppy speech, yet another barrier to intelligibility, as in the case of Vietnamese speakers, who "may pronounce each word as a separate unit, so that no sentence rhythm emerges" (Swan & Smith, p. 246). Furthermore, ELs from Han and Dravidian language families use pitch to differentiate word boundaries, whereas English speakers use stress (Avery and Ehrlich, 2012).

The notion of suprasegmental stress and prosody, conveniently for teachers, overlays a dimension of language that carries predictable lexical and discourse meaning during communication: formulaic sequences. **Formulaic sequences** are multi-morphemic units (e.g., strong collocations, phrases) that are stored holistically by speakers. Formulaic sequences often have stable prosodic features and phonological forms. They serve as discourse structuring devices and convey content-area-specific concepts in an idiomatic way (Nattinger & DeCarrico, 1992). These can include phrases such as *on the other hand, and that's it, whatever it takes, in conclusion, pass the salt and pepper, economic crisis,* and *at the battle of,* to name a few. When practiced, formulaic sequences afford learners opportunities to produce language with fluency, phonological and lexico-grammatical accuracy, and idiomaticity. From the listener's perspective, formulaic sequences facilitate comprehension because lexical and discourse meanings are conveyed in predictable phonological packaging, thus reducing the decoding burden (Wray, 2000, 2008).

At the word level, of course the selection of appropriate content words in discourse is critical for conveying meaning. However, if learners are unable to correctly integrate the phonological form of the word into an utterance, they may experience a lack of intelligibility.

Within words, articulation of syllables is very important. A learner that omits syllables from particular words altogether greatly interferes with the listeners' capacity to recognize and comprehend that word. When word-appropriate syllables are provided by the speaker, it is also important for recognition purposes that stress is attributed to the correct syllable. This is called **word stress**. Because English is a stress-timed language, the way syllables in words are stressed drives the pace and pronunciation of the dialog. "Stress involves making vowels longer and louder" (Avery & Ehrlich, 2012, p. 64). Word stress can be difficult for learners mainly because the stress patterns in English represent a departure from the L1. Table 3 highlights some of the major patterns for word stress during language production.

Word stress patterns influence how sounds within the syllable are produced. In unstressed syllables of content words, the vowel often defaults to one of three variants of lax vowels: the schwa /ə/, the short-i /ɪ/and the short-e /ɛ/, regardless of how the word is spelled. Linguists call this *vowel reduction*. Stressed syllables can have these vowels (excluding the schwa /ə/), too, but are also open to other vowels that exist in English. Vowel reduction also applies to function words (e.g., prepositions, auxiliary verbs, articles) because due to sentence stress patterns, these words do not receive stress compared to content words. For many Arabic and Chinese speakers, learners often do not successfully produce the stress patterns of a fluent speaker and thus do not reduce vowels, which results in words with full vowels where a fluent speaker would know to shift to a schwa (Swan & Smith, p. 198). In the following sentence, the underlined vowels are reduced.

I had to reduce the quantity of sugar I eat because my doctor needed me to get healthier.

Stress patterns in English exist on a gradient, and the sound of the vowel is adjusted accordingly (Avery and Ehrlich, 2012). A complicating factor from the learner's perspective is that there are a variety of stress patterns in English which poses challenges for learning (Avery & Ehrlich, 2012). Nonetheless, there are general tendencies. According to Avery & Ehrlich (2012), stress "is more likely to fall on the first syllable if the word is a noun, and on the second syllable if the word is a verb" (p. 67). Compound words place the weight of stress on the first word, yet when the words are separated by a space as two distinct nouns, the weight falls on the second word (Avery and Ehrlich, 2012). For example, learners will have to become aware that stress patterns of words like "doghouse" can possibly change when it becomes "dog's house." For native speakers and teachers, these oral cadences may seem intuitive, but for learners these shifts often need to be explicitly taught item by item.

Table 3. Word stress patterns

Stress on 1st Syllable	Stress on 2nd Syllable	Stress on 2nd From Last Syllable	Stress on 3rd From Last Syllable
Two-syllable **nouns** (letter, apple, table)	Two-syllable **verbs** (explain, describe, result)	**Adjectives ending in -ic** (historic, epidemic)	**Nouns ending in -cy, -ty, -phy, -gy** (democracy, photography)
Two-syllable **adjectives** (tricky, handsome)	**Compound adjectives** (run-down, worn-out)*	**Nouns ending in -sion or -tion** (comprehension, distribution)	**Adjectives ending in -cal** (identical, medical)
Compound nouns (telephone, sidewalk, butterfly)	**Compound verbs** (get out, look for, turn in)*		

* In these words, the primary stress is on the second word while the secondary stress is on the first word.

Consonant omission, substitution, or mispronunciation, either in clusters or at syllable boundaries, can pose significant intelligibility problems for learners because they interfere with word recognition on the part of the listener. Consider the following variations on the sentence

"You have to lift it":
You have to lif it.
You have to live it.
You have to lip it.
You have to lib it.

The mispronunciation of the central idea conveyed by the verb *lift* in such a short sentence can cause a significant barrier to intelligibility because a listener may not be able to figure out the intended word from the sounds alone, and in some cases may not be able to rely on speaking context to aid them either. This is particularly a concern in one- and two-syllable words.

Although less of a barrier to intelligibility than sound omission or substitution, mispronunciations due to coarticulation effects in key junctures of talk can make a listener's comprehension effortful. The glottal stop, for example, is very useful in English for conveying negative meaning, but it is difficult for learners to perceive: *I can't get it* /aɪ kæ̃nʔ gɛɾ ɪʔ/. Teachers can sometimes induce mispronunciations in this regard. Teachers trained in phonics methods, for example, should realize that graphic representation of clusters on a page, for example -cl-, -fr-, -nk, str-, do not strictly correspond to how groups of sounds are actually produced, either in timing of movements in the mouth or in actual acoustic realization. This is due to what is termed coarticulation effects, where neighboring phonemes influence each other. For example, in the -cl- cluster, even though the articulatory points of contact for -cl- (actually /kl/ in phonetics) suggests a linear production, first /k/ then /l/, the tongue moves to produce the /l/ sound in the front of the mouth at the same time as it moves to produce the /k/ sound at the back of the mouth. In other words, anticipatory mechanisms shape sounds in clusters in a way that is different from sounds being produced in isolation. The sequence -str- during fluent speech can be akin to /ʃdʒɹ/ in many cases. When /l/ is preceded by short-i /ɪ/ or by the /u/ sound, its quality changes. When /n/ is produced in the context of *I can get you at four o'clock*, it is pronounced in velar position as /ŋ/ instead of the alveolar /n/. The matter of coarticulation effects is relevant to smaller units, that is to say, individual phonemes, which therefore must ultimately be considered in context. A teacher's perception of their own language production and practiced abilities to perceive learner's production are prerequisites for accurate assessment and decisions about remediation. It is helpful that many classroom teachers have already learned about clusters through phonics-based methods as a scaffold towards textual decoding. They can build on that pre-existing knowledge to re-examine more closely their phonics-based knowledge of clusters and determine how sounds are actually produced during fluent oration, thinking about shape, timing, and articulatory points of sounds.

Note that suprasegmentals provide the contexts in which lower-level features like word stress patterns, clusters, and phonemes exist. Therefore, suprasegmental contexts have a significant effect on how segmentals are produced. In many cases, intelligibility issues due to segmental aberrations can be ameliorated by addressing suprasegmental stress first (Orion, 2011). This discloses the shortcomings of just teaching phonemes and other segmental features in an isolated fashion. A "whole-systems" awareness is needed for both the teacher and the learner. Furthermore, when all of these dimensions are learned in relation to their semantic contexts (like specific subject areas or discourse situation), ELs can develop a stronger capacity for linking form to meaning to use and, therefore, intelligibility.

Teachers can play a critical role in helping their ELs become more intelligible by identifying difficulties at the suprasegmental and segmental levels of speech in the context of meaningful lesson structure and content. In doing so, learners can reap the academic and social benefits of being able to interact in the classroom and use their oracy to support literacy development. However, teachers need to be observant, responsive, opportunistic, systematic, and patient. Teachers need to accurately discern where barriers to intelligibility lie for their learners and help them become self-aware. They need to look into their content area materials and classroom discourse for opportunities that will help learners develop intelligibility. Teachers must act consistently and promote opportunities for noticing and recycling. It is critical that teachers act with patience, knowing that interventions do not yield immediate results. By optimizing the conditions for learning, teachers can create conditions where learners can engage their natural learning processes towards becoming more intelligible and therefore more fully participatory in their academic and social contexts.

IMPLICATIONS FOR TEACHING ENGLISH LANGUAGE LEARNERS

In the United States, the number of English learners (ELs) in public schools is currently 4.6 million students (National Center for Education Statistics, 2017) and is projected to grow 5% over the next few years, giving this group a representation of 29% of the total U.S. public-school population by 2024 (National Center for Education Statistics, 2017). These changing demographics suggest that there must be increased, systematic efforts in supporting their language and content area needs.

ELs' ability to express ideas intelligibly and comprehend messages clearly is critical to their academic success. Often times, these learners lack the linguistic means to make themselves understood, struggling with pronunciation as they attempt to express their ideas. These challenges frustrate ELs, stigmatize them vis-à-vis their teachers and English-speaking peers, and hamper their overall academic advancement. Content area teachers often look to English as a Second Language (ESL) teachers to address language challenges, having difficulty seeing past their learners' pronunciation difficulties in particular. However, for many learners, depending on age and learning circumstances, nativelike, accent-free speech is not a realistic goal.

For remediation in K-12 public school settings, the teaching of English pronunciation has historically occurred in ESL classrooms. Realistically, however, given the prevalence of **inclusion** (ELLs and mainstream students reside in the same classroom) and **push-in** models (English language instruction takes place in the mainstream classroom) of instruction, ESL teachers cannot be the only professionals responsible for the work involving ELs, especially considering how fast this population has continuously grown in public schools throughout the U.S. (National Center for Education Statistics, 2017) and how long ELs spend in content-area classrooms throughout the day. The teaching of ELs needs to be the responsibility of all teachers who collaboratively work to support ELs in meeting the required standards to succeed in the academic world. It becomes critical then that training on pronunciation pedagogy be strengthened in teacher preparation programs across the board (Darcy, 2018) to include teachers of grade-level content areas and teachers of ESL.

Attention to pronunciation teaching has increased in the last few decades (Levis & Wu, 2018). Studies in second language (L2) pronunciation have shown that explicit instruction in pronunciation produces greater accuracy, intelligibility, and fewer instances of misunderstanding among ELs (Levis & Wu, 2018; Lee, Jang, & Plonsky, 2015). Because children spend so much time in school, the work a teacher does in the classroom to support ELs' pronunciation development can be important in determining how intelligible a learner will ultimately become. Therefore, a teacher's ability to deliver effective pronunciation teaching is essential for ELs' success in pronunciation learning.

However, studies on the readiness of ESL teachers to deliver pronunciation instruction highlight their insufficient knowledge on phonology and pronunciation teaching strategies (Baker, 2014; Baker & Murphy, 2011). Mainstream teachers are even less well-equipped. Such studies show that teacher training programs often provide future professionals with theoretical knowledge on phonetics and phonology, but once in the classrooms, teachers are challenged to effectively apply such knowledge. Furthermore, to teach pronunciation, it is incumbent upon educators to gain a deeper understanding of 1) how pronunciation relates to communication in general, 2) how pronunciation development is framed in a broader understanding of second language development, and 3) what are relevant and productive intervention strategies given the teaching context.

Speech Intelligibility and the Common Core State Standards

From kindergarten through the 12th grade, the Common Core State Standards for English Language Arts in the Speaking and Listening strand emphasize the need for all learners to develop the level of speech intelligibility that enables them to engage in and benefit from classroom communicative exchanges. Table 4 highlights the specific K-12 standards related to speech intelligibility.

According to the Common Core standards, all teachers, both ESL and non-ESL, are expected to help learners develop the ability to communicate in a mutually comprehensible way. Pronunciation is one essential dimension of one's ability to communicate, besides vocabulary, morphosyntax, and pragmatics. Speaking intelligibly, also expressed as speaking *comprehensibly* or *understandably*, is therefore a fundamental condition for communication that extends beyond simply pronouncing words correctly. To be intelligible from a pronunciation perspective, one needs to make use of proper intonation, stress, and rhythm so that the message becomes understandable to the listener. In the context of classrooms, the lack of ability to speak intelligibly precludes students from participating in classroom discussions successfully, expressing ideas clearly, and engaging the listener in their line of reasoning (Darcy, 2018). Without the ability to participate in collaborative conversations, students are less likely to meet the expectations outlined in the CCSS.

Table 4. CCSS and intelligibility

Grades	Common Core State Standards
K	Speak audibly & express thoughts, feelings, and ideas clearly.
1	Participate in collaborative conversations & express ideas and feelings clearly.
2	Build on others' talk in conversations. Ask and answer questions about what a speaker says.
3-4-5	Engage effectively in collaborative discussions & express ideas clearly. Speak clearly at an understandable pace.
6-7-8	Engage effectively in collaborative discussions & express ideas clearly. Use clear pronunciation.
9-12	Initiate and participate effectively in a range of collaborative discussions and express ideas clearly and persuasively. Present information, findings, and supporting evidence clearly, concisely, and logically such that listeners can follow the line of reasoning.

Ensuring that learners become intelligible is not an easy task, and to infuse pronunciation goals into instruction, teachers must overcome several obstacles. One obstacle to pronunciation instruction is the *recognition of its value*. With the shift away from ESL pull-out classes in American schools toward push-in and inclusion models, language instruction generally, and pronunciation specifically, can often take a conceptual back seat in the list of content-related priorities for teachers (Darcy, 2018). Teachers must begin with the assumption that language ability, and particularly the competencies underpinning intelligibility, are keystones for aural comprehension, oracy, and therefore classroom participation, which in turn make subject area content accessible to the learner. *Instructional time* to devote to pronunciation instruction is a second obstacle. Competing content agendas quickly eat up spare minutes in class periods, leading to lack of treatment on the teacher's part, and even when provided, leading to lack of processing time for the learner. Finally, *teachers' ability* to teach pronunciation represents another obstacle. When teachers are "uncertain about the ways to actually teach pronunciation" (Darcy, 2018, p. 17), they are likely to avoid it, and the prospect of making ELs intelligible users of English and meeting the CCS standards becomes remote.

Studies have shown that the impact of pronunciation instruction goes beyond promoting clear speaking skills and the ability to comprehend fluent and connected speech; it also supports reading and writing development (Gordon & Darcy, 2016; Ranbom & Connine, 2011; Ruellot, 2011), particularly in the areas of sound-spelling correspondence, orthography, sight word recognition, and reading fluency. In the section that follows, we attempt to offer instructional recommendations that consider the existing obstacles and concerns in the infusion of pronunciation instruction in the teaching of language and academic content while capitalizing on the intelligibility model.

Helping ELs With Intelligibility

Addressing an EL's intelligibility difficulties starts with four steps. Step 1 involves identifying a learner's specific communicative patterns that affect intelligibility during speech production and recognition (Munro, 2018). Step 2 focuses on raising the student's awareness of their pronunciation needs through explicit instruction, modeling and practice. Step 3 considers the integration of pronunciation training into the language and content curriculum (Darcy, 2018). Step 4 entails promoting the **transfer of learning** to new linguistic, thematic, and communicative contexts.

Step 1: Identifying ELs' Major Challenges. Selecting the right focus for pronunciation instruction is important, but it is not an easy task. Teachers might be well served by using an assessment checklist (See Table 5) constructed around intelligibility. Teacher efforts would also be supported by collecting audio recordings of learners' speech to facilitate an accurate review of potential concerns (Derwing & Munro, 2015). For elicitation during class time, teachers can implement instructional strategies that involve spontaneous oral communicative exchanges or read-alouds, which facilitate an assessment of the areas affecting intelligibility. The teacher can generate a list of features of pronunciation affecting the learner's production and perception (suprasegmental–word stress, intonation, syllable timing; segmental–vowel reduction, consonant production, phoneme clusters; and fluency) which would later form the basis of practice.

Despite all the factors able to affect an EL's speech intelligibility and the difficulties involved in implementing pronunciation instruction in content classrooms, it is critical that teachers identify the major obstacles to intelligibility and prioritize the focus of their pronunciation instruction **in the context of meaning-bearing formulaic and lexical units.** That is, teachers should focus on the biggest barriers to intelligibility in the following order: **suprasegmentals → missing syllables → clusters → smaller units.**

Table 5. Intelligibility Assessment Rubric

Student Name:			
Lesson Topic:	< -- >		
Holistic impression	Not Intelligible	Somewhat Intelligible	Very Intelligible
Fluency	Fast/Slow		Fluid/Halting
Type of Student Talk	Group Discussion	Read Aloud	Other
Suprasegmental			
Placement of suprasegmental stress in a sentence			
Placement or indication of prominent information in discourse (e.g., appropriate discourse structuring formulaic sequences and content area collocations)			
Segmental			
Omission or addition of entire syllables			
Production of consonants and vowels (e.g., clusters and syllable boundaries)			
Use of constructions or words that are unfamiliar or unexpected to the listener (e.g., appropriate content words for the topic)			
Assessment of progress over time			
Interventions recommended			

Step 2: Raising Student's Awareness of Pronunciation Needs. ELs are not always aware of their pronunciation needs (Dlaska & Krekeler, 2008) and may not feel pronunciation instruction is useful to them. However, students' ability to perceive the features of specific speech sounds will affect their ability to produce intelligible speech. Therefore, raising student self-awareness on their pronunciation needs, combined with explicit instruction of phonological production features, abundant modeling and opportunities for practice, and rich feedback, will likely increase ELs' awareness, perception, and production of sounds towards intelligible speech in English. Through the use of video or audio-recorded read-alouds or speech samples, especially those used during lessons (Derwing & Munro, 2015), teachers can work with learners to raise awareness of whether they are producing the proper stress at the sentence or phrase, word, and segmental (consonants and vowels) levels (McGregor & Reed, 2018) and are perceiving critical characteristics of sounds. The teacher could engage the learner to review and reflect on the recorded samples by following explicit directions on what to listen for. For example, in the case of a student who has difficulty contrasting the sounds /θ/ and /s/, the teacher would explicitly guide the student to reflect on their production of words such as **th**ink /θɪŋk/ and **s**ink /sɪŋk/ in the recorded sample. The teacher could use a mirror or have the student watch a video of themselves producing the sounds.

Step 3: Integrating Intelligibility Instruction in the Language and Content Curriculum. The integration of pronunciation practice through a contextualized approach, as warranted from learner difficulty, in language and content lessons (e.g., mathematics, social studies, science, language arts), is likely to lead ELs towards intelligibility (McGregor & Reed, 2018). For that, the teacher would purposefully select vocabulary items, including academic vocabulary, that are central to their content lesson and that contain the articulatory challenges for the learner. In this way, there is guaranteed practice with authentic, contextualized language, which ensures meaningfulness and relevance to the learner.

Consider the following example which illustrates an activity for a general education sixth-grade science lesson delivered to a group of students comprised of mostly native English speakers and a few English learners who struggle with the distinction between --**sh**- /ʃ/, -**ch**- /tʃ/ and -**th**- /θ, ð/ sounds. The focus of the lesson is on "lionfish" and their characteristics. With the use of a visual representation of a lionfish, the teacher selects descriptors that include sounds that pose challenge to the learner. These words, an average of 5 to 9 vocabulary words, would be emphasized during spontaneous classroom speech and supported by captions. While exploring the characteristics of lionfish, the teacher would purposefully repeat the selected vocabulary items (See Figure 2 below) multiple times, emphasize pronunciation of key sounds to stimulate perception and awareness.

The teacher can exaggerate or clap the stressed syllables during spontaneous speech and provide sufficient modeling to allow the learner to notice the stressed syllables in the utterance. Clapping or tapping activities are helpful for learners to perceive and practice stress patterns at the sentence and word level because they combine stimuli visually, auditorily, and in a tactile manner. Such activities are also helpful for learners who omit or add syllables to words.

The teacher can also use a multimodal approach, that is, expose students to both audio and written modalities to help ELs notice the distinction between the /ʃ/, /tʃ/ and /θ, ð/ sounds. The intentional repetition of targeted sounds followed by opportunities for perception and production of such sounds will help ELs recognize the spoken sound, practice the word in isolation, then in connected utterances (from shorter to longer sentences) with the purpose of enhancing the learner's intelligibility and comprehensibility of those sounds.

Other strategies are also beneficial in this regard. Focusing on high frequency or high communicative value targets such as formulaic sequences or collocations that are important to the classroom task or subject being taught also support the development of intelligible and comprehensible speech. Taking the context of the science lesson previously discussed, examples of formulaic sequences or ready-made chunks would include expressions such as: *on the other hand, in other words, as a result of, during the day*. Instances of collocation would include: *head and body, invasive species, fleshy tentacles, slow-moving*. Therefore, presenting students with meaningful and contextualized chunks of language followed by sufficient modeling of proper stress, rhythm and intonation can enhance ELs' ability to notice the characteristics of particular sounds, offer opportunities for speech production and practice, and affect the learners' intelligibility.

Figure 2. Example activity that integrates pronunciation practice of bolded digraphs through a contextualized approach

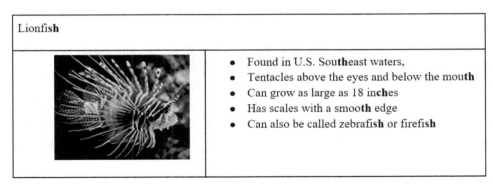

Lionfish	
	• Found in U.S. Sou**th**east waters, • Tentacles above the eyes and below the mou**th** • Can grow as large as 18 in**ch**es • Has scales with a smoo**th** edge • Can also be called zebrafi**sh** or firefi**sh**

Therefore, to help ELs perceive a challenging articulatory feature in English and support their language production towards intelligibility, the teacher should:

1. Promote learners' noticing their own production of the language and contrast it with more target-like speech, in the context of discriminative and productive activities.
2. Provide controlled practice of challenging items with feedback until the learner has developed automaticity of second language phonological processing and production.
3. Emphasize repeated practice and make use of interventions over a period of time to promote transfer between practice done in the classroom and real-life spontaneous communication.
4. Balance form-focused practice with communicative use from practice on all three areas (e.g., suprasegmental, segmental, and fluency) to develop clear and intelligible speech in English.

Step 4: Transfer of Learning to New Contexts. This step often falls casualty to competing priorities of the curriculum. However, the goal of pronunciation instruction is to help the learner transfer learning from the classroom to real-life experiences through meaningful communication. For learners to generalize benefits from one lesson segment, they need opportunities to recycle what they have learned into new contexts, ideally within a day or two of their first exposure and practice.

Teachers should find a way to help learners notice and meaningfully practice previously-learned language patterns in other topics, lesson materials, or classroom talk. Perhaps, for example, the teacher could help learners see similarities between a sound pattern in formulaic sequences in a Monday lesson and a Tuesday lesson. Teachers can also highlight relevant phonological patterns embedded in content on word walls, or in sentence stems often used in writing or speaking. In fact, any classroom routines or regularly used language can provide opportunities for learners to benefit from frequency of meaningful practice under different circumstances of use (Ellis, 2002).

DISCUSSION QUESTIONS

1. In what ways do the sound systems of languages that you know about differ from one another?
2. What are some of the sounds in English that pose difficulty to most language learners despite their language background?
3. In what ways can an English learner's first language not affect their ability to produce intelligible speech in English?
4. What are the implications of students' inability to speak intelligibly for classroom teaching? How should teachers approach those difficulties during classroom instruction?
5. How do the terms "proficiency" and "intelligibility" relate to one another? Can a learner be proficient but not intelligible? What are some instructional strategies to support a proficient language user who is not intelligible?
6. To what extent have you seen evidence of item-based learning, over-generalization, and U-shaped learning in your students? What did it look like?
7. Did you ever interact with a strongly accented person? What aspects of that person's talk helped your comprehension of that person's message?

EXERCISES

1. Underline the stressed syllable in each word and explain which pattern they follow based on Table 3. What word(s) do not follow any of the patterns in the table? Can you think of other words that do not adhere to the patterns in the table?

    a. Photography
    b. Photographic
    c. Possible
    d. Possibility
    e. Informative
    f. Information

    What are the limitations of teaching and learning decontextualized "rules"?

2. Consider an EL who cannot perceive the difference between **bear/pear** and wat**ch**/wa**sh**. Outline at least three instructional strategies that should be emphasized during language and content instruction to help the EL notice these are different words with very different meanings.

3. What intervention sequence would you advise when working with an EL who omits sounds, syllables or clusters in the middle or at the end of words? For instance, an EL who says "*I am going out with my frie (friend)*" or "*I going to vacash (vacation)*."

4. Tap out the entire poem "Mary had a little lamb." Identify the words or parts of words that are stressed. What do the vowels sound like in places where they are not stressed?

5. Watch a YouTube video of a non-native speaker. As you watch it, your tasks are:

    a. Identify stress points
    b. Identify formulaic sequences
    c. Use the rubric provided in Table 5 to make observations of the speaker's level of intelligibility.

REFERENCES

Avery, P., & Ehrlich, S. (2012). *Teaching American English pronunciation*. Oxford, UK: Oxford University Press.

Baker, A. (2014). Exploring teachers' knowledge of second language pronunciation techniques: Teacher cognitions, observed classroom practices, and student perceptions. *TESOL Quarterly*, *48*(1), 136–163. doi:10.1002/tesq.99

Baker, A., & Murphy, J. (2011). Knowledge base of pronunciation teaching: Staking out the territory. *TESL Canada Journal*, *28*(2), 29–50. doi:10.18806/tesl.v28i2.1071

Birdsong, D. (2006). Age and second language acquisition and processing: A selective overview. *Language Learning*, *56*(1), 9–49. doi:10.1111/j.1467-9922.2006.00353.x

Bley-Vroman, R. (1990). The logical problem of foreign language learning. *Linguistic Analysis*, *20*, 3–39.

Bybee, J. (2013). Usage-based theory and exemplar representations of constructions. In T. Hoffmann & G. Trousdale (Eds.), *The Oxford handbook of construction grammar* (pp. 49–69). Oxford, UK: Oxford University Press.

Cook, V. (2008). Multi-competence: Black hole or wormhole for second language acquisition research? In Z. Han (Ed.), *Understanding second language process* (pp. 16–26). Multilingual Matters.

Corder, S. P. (1967). The significance of learner's errors. *International Journal of Applied Linguistics*, 5, 161–170.

Darcy, I. (2018). Powerful and effective pronunciation instruction: How can we achieve it? *The CATESOL Journal*, *30*(1), 13–46.

Davies, A. (2003). *The native speaker: Myth and reality*. Clevedon, UK: Multilingual Matters. doi:10.21832/9781853596247

Derwing, T. M., & Munro, M. J. (2015). *Pronunciation fundamentals: Evidence-based perspectives for L2 teaching and research*. Amsterdam, The Netherlands: Benjamins. doi:10.1075/lllt.42

Dlaska, A. & Krekeler, C. (2008). Self-assessment of pronunciation. *System, 36*(4), 506-516. doi:10.1016/j.system.2008.03.003

Dulay, H., & Burt, M. (1974). A new perspective on the creative construction process in child second language acquisition. *Working Papers on Bilingualism*, *24*(2), 253-278.

Ellis, N. C. (2002). Frequency effects in language processing. *Studies in Second Language Acquisition*, *24*(2), 143–188. doi:10.1017/S0272263102002024

Ellis, N. C. (2006). Selective attention and transfer phenomena in l2 acquisition: Contingency, cue competition, salience, interference, overshadowing, blocking, and perceptual learning. *Applied Linguistics*, *27*(2), 164–194. doi:10.1093/applin/aml015

Ellis, N. C., & Larsen-Freeman, D. (2006). Language emergence: Implications for applied linguistics. *Applied Linguistics*, *27*(4), 558–589. doi:10.1093/applin/aml028

Ellis, R. (2009). *The study of second language acquisition*. Oxford, UK: Oxford University Press.

Ellis, R., & Shintani, N. (2014). *Exploring language pedagogy through second language acquisition research*. New York, NY: Routledge.

Goodwin, J. (2014). Teaching pronunciation. In M. Celce-Murcia, D. M. Brinton, & M. A. Snow (Eds.), *Teaching English as a second or foreign language* (4th ed.; pp. 136–152). Boston, MA: National Geographic Learning/Heinle Cengage Learning.

Gordon, J., & Darcy, I. (2016). The development of comprehensible speech in L2 learners: A classroom study on the effects of short-term pronunciation instruction. *Journal of Second Language Pronunciation*, *2*(1), 56–92. doi:10.1075/jslp.2.1.03gor

Hale, M., & Reiss, C. (2003). The subset principle in phonology: Why the tabula can't be rasa. *Journal of Linguistics*, *39*(2), 219–244. doi:10.1017/S0022226703002019

Hall, T. M. (2017). Learner chunks in second language acquisition. Proquest Dissertations Publishing. (10260547)

Han, Z. (2004). *Fossilization in adult second language acquisition*. Clevedon, UK: Multilingual Matters. doi:10.21832/9781853596889

Han, Z. (2013). Forty years later: Updating the fossilization hypothesis. *Language Teaching*, *46*(2), 133–171. doi:10.1017/S0261444812000511

Haspelmath, M., König, E., Wulf, O., & Raible, W. (Eds.). (2001). *Language typology and language universals: An international handbook* (Vol. 2). Berlin: Walter de Gruyter. doi:10.1515/9783110171549.2

Hocket, C. F. (1970). *A Course in modern linguistics*. New York, NY: The Maemillion Company.

Kellerman, E. (1995). Crosslinguistic influence: Transfer to nowhere? *Annual Review of Applied Linguistics*, *15*, 125–150. doi:10.1017/S0267190500002658

Kennedy, S., & Trofimovich, P. (2017). Pronunciation acquisition. In S. Loewen & M. Sato (Eds.), *The Routledge handbook of instructed second language acquisition* (pp. 260–279). New York, NY: Routledge.

Lado, R. (1957). *Linguistics across cultures: Applied linguistics for language teachers*. Ann Arbor, MI: University of Michigan Press.

Lee, J., Jang, J., & Plonsky, L. (2015). The effectiveness of second language pronunciation instruction: A meta-analysis. *Applied Linguistics*, *36*(3), 345–366. doi:10.1093/applin/amu040

Levis, J. M. (2005). Changing contexts and shifting paradigms in pronunciation teaching. *TESOL Quarterly*, *39*(3), 369–377. doi:10.2307/3588485

Levis, J. M., & Wu, A. (2018). Pronunciation – Research into practice and practice into research. *The CATESOL Journal*, *30*(1), 1–12.

Long, M. (1996). The role of the linguistic environment in second language acquisition. In Handbook of second language acquisition. San Diego, CA: Academic Press. doi:10.1016/B978-012589042-7/50015-3

McClelland, J. L., Fiez, J. A., & McCandliss, B. D. (2002). Teaching the /r/-/l/ discrimination to Japanese adults: Behavioral and neural aspects. *Physiology & Behavior*, *77*(4–5), 657–662. doi:10.1016/S0031-9384(02)00916-2 PMID:12527015

McGregor, A., & Reed, M. (2018). Integrating pronunciation into the English language curriculum: A framework for teachers. *The CATESOL Journal*, *30*(1), 69–94.

Munro, M. J. (2018). How well can we predict second language learner's pronunciation difficulties? *The CATESOL Journal*, *30*(1), 267–282.

Myles, F., Mitchell, R., & Hooper, J. (1999). Interrogative chunks in French L2: A basis for creative construction? *Studies in Second Language Acquisition*, *21*(1), 49–80. doi:10.1017/S0272263199001023

National Center for Education Statistics. (2017). *The condition of education 2017*. Retrieved from https://nces.ed.gov/pubsearch/pubsinfo.asp?pubid=2017144

Nattinger, J. R., & DeCarrico, J. S. (1992). *Lexical phrases and language teaching.* Oxford, UK: Oxford University Press.

O'Neal, G. (2010). The effects of the presence and absence of suprasegmentals on the intelligibility and assessment of an expanding-circle speaker according to other expanding-circle English listeners. *Niigata Studies in Foreign Language and Cultures, 15,* 65–87.

Odlin, T. (1989). *Language transfer.* Cambridge, UK: Cambridge University Press. doi:10.1017/CBO9781139524537

Orion, G. F. (2011). *Pronouncing American English: Sounds, stress, and intonation.* Boston, MA: Heinle Cengage Learning.

Pariona, A. (2018, July 9). *Language families of the world.* Retrieved from www.worldatlas.com/articles/language-families-with-the-highest-number-of-speakers.html

Ranbom, L. J., & Connine, C. M. (2011). Silent letters are activated in spoken word recognition. *Language and Cognitive Processes, 26*(2), 236–261. doi:10.1080/01690965.2010.486578

Ruellot, V. (2011). Computer-assisted pronunciation learning of French /u/ and /y/ at the intermediate level. In J. Levis, & K. Le-Velle (Eds.), *Proceedings of the 2nd pronunciation in second language learning and teaching conference* (pp. 199-213). Ames, IA: Iowa State University.

Ruiz-Soto, A. G., Hooker, S., & Batalova, J. (2015). *Top languages spoken by English language learners nationally and by state.* Migration Policy Institute. Retrieved from https://www.migrationpolicy.org/research/top-languages-spoken-english-language-learners-nationally-and-state

Schachter, J. (1974). An error in error analysis. *Language Learning, 24*(2), 205–214. doi:10.1111/j.1467-1770.1974.tb00502.x

Schmidt, R. (1990). The role of consciousness in second language learning. *Applied Linguistics, 11*(2), 129–158. doi:10.1093/applin/11.2.129

Selinker, L. (1972). Interlanguage. *International Journal of Applied Linguistics, 10,* 209–230.

Sorace, A. (2005). Selective optionality in language development. In L. Cornips & K. P. Corrigan (Eds.), *Syntax and variation: Reconciling the biological and the social* (pp. 55–80). Amsterdam: John Benjamins. doi:10.1075/cilt.265.04sor

Swan, M., & Smith, B. (Eds.). (2014). *Learner English: A teacher's guide to interference and other problems.* Cambridge, UK: Cambridge University Press.

Tomasello, M. (2003). *Constructing a language: A usage-based theory of language acquisition.* Cambridge, MA: Harvard University Press.

Wray, A. (2000). Formulaic sequences in second language teaching: Principle and practice. *Applied Linguistics, 21*(4), 463–489. doi:10.1093/applin/21.4.463

Wray, A. (2008). *Formulaic language: Pushing the boundaries.* Oxford, UK: Oxford University Press.

ADDITIONAL READING

Avery, P., & Ehrlich, S. (2012). *Teaching American English pronunciation.* Oxford, UK: Oxford University Press.

Nattinger, J. R., & DeCarrico, J. S. (1992). *Lexical phrases and language teaching.* Oxford, UK: Oxford University Press.

Orion, G. F. (2011). *Pronouncing American English: Sounds, stress, and intonation.* Boston, MA: Heinle Cengage Learning.

Swan, M., & Smith, B. (Eds.). (2014). *Learner English: A teacher's guide to interference and other problems.* Cambridge, UK: Cambridge University Press.

Wray, A. (2008). *Formulaic language: Pushing the boundaries.* Oxford, UK: Oxford University Press.

ENDNOTE

[1]   Note that we have used the symbol /r/ on purpose since in the mentioned context, it might refer to many allophones of /r/, not just the English retroflex /ɻ/.

Unit 9
Sociolinguistics

Chapter 17
Sociolinguistic Factors Influencing English Language Learning

Jon Bakos
Indiana State University, USA

ABSTRACT

This chapter examines processes of language variation and change that take place in all languages, with a focus on English. Sociolinguists have observed that demographic and social variables such as where someone is born, their age, gender, and socio-economic status can be relevant to how they speak. However, contemporary work indicates that there is more to how someone speaks than a few checkboxes on a survey. Who does a speaker feel empathy with and want to emulate? How does a multi-faceted sense of personal identity affect how a person speaks? How might a second language (L2) learner's sense of belonging affect their own realization of English? These are some of the questions that this chapter seeks to address.

WHAT IS SOCIOLINGUISTICS?

Sociolinguistics is defined as the study of the relationship between language and society. Coulmas (2013, p. 11) claims that "the principal task of Sociolinguistics is to uncover, describe and interpret the socially motivated" choices an individual makes. This inquiry can take many forms, including ethnography, the acoustic examination of dialect features, and pragmatic study of norms, styles, and social dynamics within and between groups.

Sociolinguistics has many areas of interest. One central tenet of language is that for every aspect of it that has been discussed in this book, those elements will undergo variation and change over time. No parts of language are static, and throughout its existence, virtually every part of English has been revised and updated. Phonetically, sounds such as the velar fricative /x/ have been lost, and the entire system of English vowel pronunciation has adjusted through the Great Vowel Shift. Morphologically, English has

DOI: 10.4018/978-1-5225-8467-4.ch017

lost the distinction between strong and weak nouns (as well as most of its case system). Even syntactic variation is possible, with many varieties of Appalachian English allowing double modal forms ("I might could do it."), despite syntactic rules expressly saying that this should not be possible. Changes in language over time and variations between groups have consistently confounded prescriptivists and grammarians, with one of the first known examples by Gerald of Wales, cited in Bailey (1991, p. 19):

...in the southern parts of England ... the speech is nowadays purer than elsewhere. It may be that it retains more of the features of the original language and the old ways of speaking English, whereas the northern regions have been greatly corrupted by the Danish and Norwegian invasions (Gerald of Wales, 1193 [1984]:231).

And yet, despite over 800 years of intervening time since Gerald's complaints over the ailing state of the language, English has soldiered on, continuing to evolve and bifurcate considerably. With the knowledge that variation is inevitable and constant, sociolinguistics thus aims to better understand and describe such changes as best as possible. Further, as English and other languages have grown to have multiple varieties, dialects, and accents, it is vital to observe that these are not simply questions of pronunciation and word formation – an individual's personal identity and sense of self can be connected to their use of dialect. A common stereotype in the United States is that of "Southern hospitality"- that residents of the Southern states are friendly, warm, and inviting. But this can also carry over to a Southern accent itself – simply speaking in this manner can signal someone as friendly, warm, and inviting, even if they are nothing of the sort! This can mean that dialect perceptions and dialect usage can both be a strong part of performing personal identity – directly connecting to someone's mental self-representation.

The chapter will begin by considering isolated variables that have been shown to be relevant in sociolinguistic research, and then focus on a few particular studies that have demonstrated a greater complexity and interconnectedness of factors relating to one's dialect and sense of self. The Labov and Eckert studies are two more groundbreaking works of the 20th Century, while the examination of forms of *like* and of language use by immigrant communities shows more contemporary research that may be more directly relevant to the concerns of L2 English speakers.

REGIONALITY

Where you are from can often be a key factor in how you speak, and this is true the world over. Historically, there have been two elements involved in making groups of people speak differently from one another – isolation and time. Before automobiles and planes, natural barriers such as mountain ranges and bodies of water could effectively separate cities and countries from one another, cutting off communication. Over the course of centuries of separation, even groups that spoke the same language would begin to drift apart linguistically, adapting local norms and customs that were distinct from others. With limited contact from outsiders, dialects and language forms would not mix, and gradually come to have less and less in common with each other. Sometimes the crucial boundaries can be surprising – for example, Sibata (1969) found that decades-old school district boundaries in Japan were having an effect on modern dialect distribution.

Even in the present-day United States with modern transportation and digital communication, most people are still going to spend the majority of their day communicating with the people nearest to them, in the same **speech community**. That is, the other people that live in their city or state, that they see on a day-to-day basis. Members of the same speech community will often share common dialect features, especially in their pronunciations of words. One such example is called *The Northern Cities Shift (NCS)*, which is a way of speaking commonly found in United States cities such as Chicago, Detroit, Cleveland, and Buffalo.

The Northern Cities Shift is a rearrangement of the low and mid vowels in a speaker's system. The NCS is described as a *Chain Shift* (Labov, Ash, & Boberg, 2006) due to the fact that the features of the shift occur in a sequence (or "chain"), as illustrated below in Figure 1. Most typically, the first link of the chain is the tensing and raising of the speaker's /æ/ vowel, moving it more closely into /e/ territory, or even higher, closer to /ɪ/. Sometimes this results in a gliding diphthong, where a word like *dad* might be pronounced closer to /dɪ-æd/.

With /æ/ vacating its position on the vowel chart, the chain typically continues next with the /ɑ/ vowel fronting toward the empty space left by /æ/. This makes words that usually contain /ɑ/ such as *Don* and *hot* start to sound closer to *Dan* and *hat*. As the chain continues, the /ɔ/ vowel moves into /ɑ/ territory, the /ɛ/ vowel moves into /ʌ/ territory, and /ʌ/ can drift toward /ɔ/. The end result is a complete rearrangement of the speaker's low and mid vowels, compared to more standard varieties of American English.

As mentioned, one of the primary impactors of the NCS is where someone is from. The NCS appears most strongly in the largest Northern cities, and is less likely to appear in rural areas of the North (Gordon, 2001). The NCS also has quite definable regional boundaries – not reaching further west than Minneapolis and further east than central New York, and not extending far south below Chicago except for an outpost in St. Louis (Labov, Ash, & Boberg, 2006).

However, there is more to dialect than simply location. The NCS tends to be predominantly used by White Americans, and there is also evidence that its use is stronger in young women than with other speakers (Labov, Ash, & Boberg, 2006). We will see later in the chapter that its usage is affected by a great many things, but for now, we should consider a few factors that have been mainstays of sociolinguistic research.

Figure 1. The Northern Cities Shift

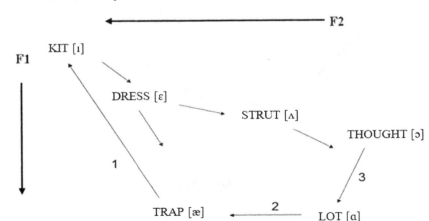

DEMOGRAPHICS

Beyond where someone lives, there are other aspects of identity and personality that will affect how someone speaks, such as their age, ethnicity, gender, and socio-economic status.

Age

Often, speakers of a language will speak differently depending on their age. Reasons for this can easily be interpreted – younger people may want to stand out as different from their parents, while their parents may be focused on sounding professional and adult-like. A frequent pattern related to age is called **age-grading**, a hypothetical distribution of which can be seen in Figure 2.

In Figure 2, we can see what is essentially a reverse-bell curve – a behavior used frequently by younger people in their 20's, that tapers off as they age into their 40's, but then returns as speakers reach their 60's and 70's. Tagliamonte (2012) observes this distribution with behaviors like swearing – adolescents swear liberally so as to earn **covert prestige** with their friends – that is, violating societal rules and norms to build a defiant reputation. However, as the same speaker reaches adulthood, their concerns shift toward raising children, and building professional acclaim in the workplace. As such, these adults are more concerned with acquiring **overt prestige**, that is, building a reputation by obeying social expectations and rules. Toward this end, they stifle usage of curse words and swears. Then, as the speaker reaches retirement age and no longer needs to be concerned with workplace decorum, they return to the speech of their youth and swear much more frequently.

Importantly, age grading is most typically not a factor of a particular generation or group – the expectation would be that with an age graded pattern, most people would follow it and adjust as they age in real time.

Figure 2. Age grading hypothetical example

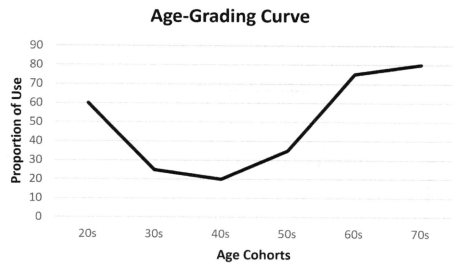

Age-Grading Curve

Ethnicity

Some dialects (and languages) are strongly associated with particular ethnic groups – for example, Yiddish with the Jewish community, Hawaiian and Hawaiian Creole with that Native communities in Hawai'i, and African American English (AAE) with African American communities throughout the United States. Proficiency with these language and dialects can often serve as a strong in-group/out-group marker. AAE, for example, has dozens of systematic features that encompass all levels of language – a few of which are shown below:

(a) habitual *be* + verb-ing
     e.g. *I always be playing ball.*
(b) intensified equative *be*
     e.g. *She be the diva.*
(c) resultative *be done*
     e.g. *She be done had her baby.*
(d) -3rd sg. -s absence
     e.g. *She run everyday.*
(e) ain't for didn't
     e.g. *I ain't go yesterday.*
(Examples from Wolfram, 2004)

Notice that just these five examples encompass alternate uses of the copula, morphological variation, and lexical variation. This level of complexity can serve an important function – no novice could ever hope to imitate the dialect correctly, and would unavoidably make obvious mistakes unless they had spoken it for years. Dialect can thus serve as a litmus test for group membership – without full mastery of its forms, a speaker may only tangentially be considered a member of the local community.

Gender

One formalized effort to describe how women talk differently from men was that of Robin Lakoff's *Language and Woman's Place* in 1975. Lakoff pointed out several features of women's speech, some of which included:

(a) **Hedges:** Phrases such as *sort of, kind of, it seems like*
(b) **Empty adjectives:** *divine, adorable, gorgeous*
(c) **Super-polite forms:** *Would you mind... ...if it's not too much to ask... Is it o.k. if...?*
(d) **Apologize more:** *I'm sorry, but I think that...*
(e) **Speaking less frequently**
(f) **Avoid curse language or expletives**

Lakoff's work has been the subject of criticism in more recent years for being essentialist and framing women's speech as a "gender deficit" or sign of weakness or deference. Eckert (1989) instead argued that differences in speech attributable to gender were like more attributable to differences in power dynamics, with many of the forms that Lakoff observed being more a factor of women being suppressed by society, rather than any sort of innate characteristics. Sex and gender will be a visible factor in the studies later in this chapter.

Other Variables

Depending on the study and the community involved, there may be many other relevant demographic variables to sociolinguistic work. A respondent's occupation, level of education, L1 and L2 background, religion, and cultural heritage may all be relevant to better understanding their speech and identity. To illustrate this, this chapter will now examine individual studies, focusing on the unique composition of each community that was studied.

MARTHA'S VINEYARD

One of the more crucial studies in the present era of Sociolinguistics is William Labov's work in Martha's Vineyard, *The Social Motivation of a Sound Change* (Labov, 1963). Martha's Vineyard is a small island off the Southern coast of Massachusetts, which at the time of his research in 1962 had two main industries: fishing and tourism. Labov's work was an important contribution to the field, because while it was understood that the demographic factors discussed above, like age and gender were important to understanding how people speak, Labov argued in this paper that they were insufficient by themselves to describe speech and identity. He began the paper by considering such factors individually, and used this to show that with just these alone, he had an incomplete picture. He argued that additional elements of islander life and culture had to be taken into account to better describe the relationship of the residents' speech with their local identity.

At the time that Labov conducted his fieldwork on the island, its population was estimated at 5,563. As of 2010, it has roughly tripled to 16,535 (United States Census, 2010). The island had three main ethnic demographics – "Chilmarkers" – White descendants of early colonial settlers on the island, largely concentrated around the Chilmark areas, another group that descended from Portuguese settlers, and a third group of Native Americans.

Dialectally, Labov was interested in a regional pronunciation of the /aɪ/ and /aʊ/ diphthongs, which islanders would commonly produce with a centralized /ə/ onset, making *tide* sound more like /təɪd/ or *toide*, and *loud* sound more like /ləʊd/ or *lowed*. Early in the paper, he notes that there is some phonological conditioning involved in the usage, such that the /əɪ/ and /əʊ/ variants are more likely to appear prior to alveolar stops, so that words like *night* and *out* would have a high likelihood of being pronounced /nəɪt/ and /əʊt/, while words like *five* and *ground* would most likely be said as /faɪv/ and /graʊnd/. It would have been possible to have this be the stopping point in the research – arguing that the variant is the result of a phonological rule that favors particular environments. However, Labov continued to examine the data, looking for finer details.

He found that in addition to phonology, there were relevant demographic variables in play that affected the speech of Islanders. In general, younger people tended to avoid the centralized forms, while older residents used them more strongly. White residents and those of Portuguese descent centralized more than the Native Americans. Fishermen also more commonly had the regional variant than other professions. And as above, any one of these things on its own could have painted a partial picture of speech on Martha's Vineyard.

But Labov observed instead that, more relevant than any of these variables (but derived from them) was a resident's sense of personal investment in the island. Martha's Vineyard in 1962 was at a point of transition – historically, it had been a whaling community, but whaling was extinct as an industry. The island had instead moved to fishing. But the economy was changing again, with the island becoming a tourist destination for the citified well-to-do. As such, residents were feeling pressure. Some felt a desire to identify with the Vineyard's history – especially the Chilmarkers who had been living there for hundreds of years. The Portuguese residents felt a similar pull – for decades they had been marginalized as a minority, but by 1962, they had begun to be accepted and to take on positions of power within the local government. Finally able to assert an Islander identity, they were strongly motivated to do so. By contrast, the Native population was largely restricted to a small region of the Vineyard, and had not been able to become significant players in its politics.

Labov argued that in the past, Islanders had been able to stand out from those on the land by using whaling terminology. This unique jargon served as a means of asserting local identity and setting themselves apart from the mainland. However, as discussed, whaling was no longer a functioning industry, which meant that it could no longer serve as a distinction. So instead, centralizing of /a/ diphthongs rose to take its place, serving as a marker of local membership. Chilmarkers and Portuguese residents were thus able to employ it to show their status, and with fishing as the industry most directly connected to the island's past, fishermen used the accent as well. Labov's finding that older residents centralized more heavily also fit – these were people who were either of working age (as fishermen), or those who had retired from the profession.

However, many younger residents were not yet fishermen, and further, had no desire to be. Instead, they worked in the Vineyard's burgeoning hospitality industry, mingling with affluent mainland guests. These Islanders instead were more interested in the mainland – wanting to move away to major cities. This desire was visible in their speech – the Islander accent was used as a way to stand out from the mainland, which was precisely the opposite of what these young residents wanted. So, rather than embrace the Vineyard's regional speech, they stifled it – aiming to emulate the people they one day hoped to become.

As such, Labov's work in Martha's Vineyard demonstrates important truths about language and sociolinguistic research. Though a respondent's age, ethnicity, and profession were separately a part of how they spoke, the truly relevant variable – personal investment in the island, was built from all of these. Speakers with high investment used their speech to showcase their strong individual connection to the Vineyard, while those with low investment worked to hide this connection and to speak more like those from the mainland.

JOCKS AND BURNOUTS

Another study that showed similar results was that of Penelope Eckert, who studied the speech of high schoolers in Livonia, Michigan during the 1980's. Livonia is a suburb of Detroit, Michigan, which for several decades was a city in decline. During the 1950's and 60's, the city was the seat of the American auto industry, home to "the Big Three" - Ford, General Motors, and Chrysler. The city was home to both automotive manufacturing and supplemental industries such as steel plants, metal stamping companies, and oil refining. Detroit was also a thriving commercial hub, with large department stores such as Hudson's and Crowley's as fixtures of the downtown. In 1967 and beyond, however, the city was shaken by racial tensions and rioting, that led to it being synonymous with "White Flight." Wealthy Whites in the city left it in droves, relocating en masses to the suburbs and leaving much of Detroit abandoned to blight. At its peak at the 1950 census, it had a population of 1.85 million. By 1980, this had dropped to 1.2 million, and as of 2010, was below 700,000 (United States Census, 2010).

Thus, when Eckert began her work in Livonia in the mid-80's, Livonia was a wealthy (and largely White) suburb of deprived (and largely Black) Detroit. Though Livonia is on the southern border of 8 Mile Road that is seen as the boundary with Detroit (and thus the name of the movie by Eminem), the suburb is far enough west to be outside of the city proper, with Redford and Dearborn Heights serving as buffer zones.

Dialectally, Detroit is one of the epicenters of the Northern Cities Shift, discussed above. The NCS has been observed to follow a pattern of **hierarchical diffusion** – that is, it tends to spread outward to the nearest centers of highest population first. Livonia, being only 20 miles away and having a population of over 104,000 as of 1980 (United States Census, 1980), would have been a very likely site to observe the shift. Although her goal was not exclusively to study dialect features, Eckert, similar to Labov, was interested in how high schoolers' use of the NCS was relevant to their presentation of identity.

Eckert conducted her fieldwork over the course of three years of interacting with Michigan high schoolers – observing social interactions and how the students organized themselves. She comments that much of this social structuring is a part of becoming young adults: "As adolescents move away from the family, they seek to replace an ascriptive identity based on place in the family with one based on their characteristics as individuals in relation to a broader society" (Eckert, 1988, p. 187). These young students are thus re-centering their identities beyond simply being their parents' children. Although she describes a great many social groups and cliques such as athletes, socialities, "preppies," she believes that these largely coalesce into two major factions, which the students have labeled "Jocks" and "Burnouts."

In a similar fashion to the islanders on Martha's Vineyard, she describes Jocks as students who have bought into school activities and the promise that high school offers: restricting one's freedom as a youth in order to have greater opportunities as an adult. Although the term "jock" often denotes athleticism, Eckert uses it to describe any sort of student who has chosen to orient their social and personal life around the school. Thus, student council members, athletes, and science club members would all fall under the Jock mantle. She observes that membership in this group is partly a factor of socio-economic status – students who plan to continue on to college or have aspirations of wealth have an incentive to focus on school – good grades, extracurricular activities, and strong letters of recommendation are all strong stepping stones towards a university and a white-collar future (note that this is precisely an example of earning overt prestige, as discussed earlier).

In contrast, students who have chosen not to orient themselves around their high school are labeled as "Burnouts." Eckert again observes that this choice is largely socio-economic – students who do not see themselves going to college in the future do not see the school's bargain as worth their while. This is not to say that they do not envision careers for themselves, but they see themselves working in factories, machine shops, or as tradespeople. For them, being in school is actually a limitation – instead of honing skills and mingling with their potential employers, they are trapped in a place full of people they do not like, learning skills they will never need to pad college applications they will never send. Crucially, the emptying-out of Detroit following the riots meant that the city's affluent managerial class fled, but its industry and blue-collar workers did not. Burnouts, wanting to associate with exactly that group, thus have a much stronger incentive to orient their identities around Detroit, rather than the school, or Livonia at all.

In his 1959 book *The Presentation of Self in Everyday Life*, Goffman describes three main ways that one asserts and performs a personal identity that are relevant to Eckert's work – appearance, setting, and manner (Goffman, 1959). These boil down to how one looks, where one goes, and how one acts. Central to Goffman's thesis is that personal identity requires upkeep – one cannot simply be a Jock by playing one game of football. Instead, being a Jock or Burnout necessitates regular maintenance – and Eckert mentions that there are also "In-betweens" that are not strongly allied to either pole. But for those invested in fully playing the roles, all three elements that Goffman describes are crucial.

For Jocks, they must dress well and groom well, looking clean and professional. Varsity jackets for athletes are a prime way of showing school buy-in. They must regularly attend school functions, which can involve playing on teams, being in band or choir, going to dances and games – and again, doing so consistently to maintain social standing and ties. For Burnouts, similar work is required, but for a different audience. Their upkeep is to associate themselves with Detroit – which obviously necessitates frequent visits. Because the city in the 80's was associated with crime, this also meant that Burnouts needed a harder edge to be taken seriously while in the city (and to not be seen as Jocks). This meant dressing less primly, and could also entail drug and alcohol use (hence, "burning out"). Thinking back to above, Burnouts were thus focused more on *covert prestige* – working to appear hardened and street-smart, rather than proper and bookish.

With these social considerations in mind, it is evident that Jocks and Burnouts had strong incentive to act differently from one another – like the older fishermen compared to the younger service staff on Martha's Vineyard, the two groups of high schoolers had differing aspirations, with different audiences that have contrasting expectations to live up to. In addition to how they dressed (appearance) and where they spent their time (setting), how they acted (manner) was vital in setting themselves apart. And, like in Martha's Vineyard, Eckert found that part of establishing these contrasting identities was accomplished by dialect features, specifically in their usage of the Northern Cities Shift.

Due to Livonia's earlier-mentioned proximity to Detroit, the majority of its residents used some element of the NCS in their speech. However, as described above, the NCS is a **chain shift**, which can happen in stages. The first steps of the shift involve fronting and raising of /æ/ (for example, pronouncing *pan* more like /pɪæn/), but later stages also include the backing and lowering of /ʌ/ (pronouncing *done* more like /dɔn/), which is the variable Eckert focused upon. These later links in the chain allow for gauging the strength of a speaker's accent – someone with raised /æ/ but centralized /ʌ/ would show the NCS, but less intensely than someone who raised /æ/ and *also* backed /ʌ/.

Like in Martha's Vineyard, Eckert observed that single demographic variables did yield information, but incompletely. Historically, the NCS has been found to be most prominent in young women (Labov, Ash, and Boberg, 2006), and overall more so with women than with men. Eckert did indeed conclude that younger women used the backed /ʌ/ variant more frequently than men. However, she found that a better measure was a student's social affiliation. While both Jocks and Burnouts use the NCS form of /ʌ/, she observed that Burnouts of both genders do so more consistently, with girls at the forefront.

Why should this be? The answer can be seen in our discussion of Detroit – for Burnouts, Detroit is their endgame – they are working to build social and professional circles there, and to distance themselves both from their Jock peers and from Livonia itself. Part of how they can construct their identity to signal allegiance with Detroit is to more heavily use the accent associated with it, that of the Northern Cities Shift. Jocks, on the other hand, have the opposite incentive, and show the weakest use of the feature.

Eckert's work illustrates that social identity is conglomeration of many factors, with how one speaks being central. Burnouts put their accent to use as a means of asserting who they are, and to show that being connected to Detroit is a central part of their persona. Just like when we talked of Southern hospitality being internalized with Southern speech, the same effect happens with the high schoolers in Eckert's work – they are associating core personality traits with minor phonetic variations in how someone speaks.

LIKE, LEXICAL ITEMS LIKE "LIKE"

Sociolinguists are interested in more than just pronunciation, however. While accents are a potent means of asserting one's identity, there are other linguistic elements that can make an equally strong statement, with word choice being especially meaningful. Just as with pronunciation, lexical items can vary in their usage by region (pop vs. soda vs. coke), and by age, sex, socio-economic status, and more. And as you have probably guessed by now, any one of those variables on its own is probably not enough to explain the whole story.

One thing that is common for words of English is that they will have multiple meanings and connotations. As we have seen in earlier chapters, words may often function as different parts of speech when modified by morphemes, as with *happy – happiness*. However, morphology may not always be present to signal the different usages, as with the word *well*, which can function as many parts of speech:

(a) Noun: *She threw coins in the **well**.*
(b) Verb: *Water **welled** up from the ground.*
(c) Adjective: *The doctor told him he was **well**, and no longer contagious.*
(d) Adverb: *We are doing **well** at this task.*
(e) Discourse marker: ***Well**, I'm not sure about that.*
(f) Exclamation: ***Well?** When are we going to know?*

In these cases, except for the verb form, there is little morphology to indicate which part of speech is being referred to, and the listener must do so from context. However, most of these usages are part of standard varieties of English, and do not require much nuance to acquire. While the noun and verb forms are fairly infrequent, they are also quite unambiguous, meaning that anyone that needs to learn them should have little difficulty.

However, another word that appears similar is *like*. As an instructor, it is valuable to be aware of some of the many variants of *like*, since many of them are non-standard, and some of them are stigmatized. At the same time, *like* is also extremely frequent in all of its forms, and usages such as the quotative form have been observed in many countries where English is spoken, including the United States, Canada, and the United Kingdom (Tagliamonte & D'Arcy, 2005; Tagliamonte & Hudson, 1999). Some forms are more likely to be used by certain age groups, and other forms depend on particular syntactic constructions in order to function. Looking at some of the scholarship related to the study of *like* can offer insights into possible methods of teaching such a multi-variate word.

In its most basic form, *like* is a transitive verb, describing enjoyment. As a transitive verb it takes a direct object, the thing that the subject likes. Syntactically it thus appears as:

NP **like(s)** NP: *The cat **likes** tuna.*

Like also has other standard uses, such as functioning as a comparative. This takes on a different syntactic structure:

NP VERB(s) **like** NP: *That cloud looks **like** a dog.*

Another comparative form has its own construction:

Like NP, NP: ***Like** the Empire State Building, this building is very tall.*

Like can also be used to frame an example of something, which is again done by using a few possible forms:

NP **like** NP: *Buildings **like** the Empire State Building are very tall.*

Although these versions of *like* can take some time to master, they are largely standardized throughout most varieties of English, and their usage does not vary by age, gender, or any other sociolinguistic variables. However, there are two further uses of *like* that have a more complicated history. These are quotative *like* and discourse marker *like*. The discourse marker form was famously parodied in Frank Zappa's 1982 song *Valley Girl*:

Like, oh my god!
    (Valley girl)
Like, totally!
    (Valley girl)
Encino is, like, so bitchin'
    (Valley girl)
There's, like, the Galleria
    (Valley girl)
And, like
All these, like, really great shoe stores

The discourse marker form came to be stigmatized, seen as bad speech being used by air-headed young women in California ("Valley Girls"), although it is used much more widely in the present day.

Another form of *like* that has received considerable study in Sociolinguistics is the quotative form, which is used to describe what someone else has said. It is often referred to as *quotative be like*, because its usage depends on being paired with the copula:

NP **BE like** [Quotation]: *He was **like** "Why are we leaving so early?"*

Quotative *like* essentially replaces use of verbs like *say* or *tell*, both for direct quotes and paraphrases:

She said "It's time to go."   *She was **like**, "It's time to go."*
She told me it was time to go.   *She was **like**, "Time to go."*

Sometimes it can be used with *all* or *go*:

*She was all **like** "It's time to go."*   *She goes **like** "It's time to go."*

Singler (2001) notes that there are other forms that have served the same function, such as *goes* and *be all,* although *all* has fallen out of more recent usage:

She was all "It's time to go."   *She goes "It's time to go."*

Several sociolinguistic studies have examined quotative *like* as a marker of identity, particularly among young people. One such work was by Cukor-Avila (2002), who was examining the African American population of Springville (a pseudonym), a small town in Texas. She observed that the *be like* form was basically non-existent for adults born before 1970 in the city, but that it was being used more regularly by adolescents, as shown below in Table 1. Based on the interviews with Springville residents speaking African American Vernacular English (AAVE), the table represents the total number of quotative tokens in the data. These were then grouped as either the *say/said* quotative, *be like*, *go*, "Zero" (using nothing to introduce a quote) and "Other."

As can be seen in Table 1, quotative *be like* forms were almost non-existent for speakers born before the 1970's, with Bobby as the only Post-WWII user of the form, but at much lower rates than the Post-1970 group. Further, the *be like* tokens appeared to be coming at the expense of *say/said*, whose rates were decreasing in the younger group to compensate. This trend is even more visible when the data are tracked over time, as shown below in Table 2. Cukor-Avila divided the data into Early, Middle, and Late periods that corresponded to interviews conducted between 1995 and 1999.

The change over time is clearly visible here, with usage of *be like* rising from 7.3% in the Early period to 24.6% in the Late, with an accompanying decline in *say/said*. Cukor-Avila argued that this change was an example of hierarchical diffusion, with the *be like* form spreading from major urban centers of Texas and reaching rural Springville as a prestige variant for younger speakers.

Cukor-Avila observed that the use of quotative *be like* was in this case motivated by a combination of several factors – age, ethnicity, and a distinction between urban and rural communities. The young African-Americans in Springville were drawn to use the quotative form because, like in Martha's Vineyard and in Livonia, they wanted to emulate who they saw as the prestigious group, those in major cities. Since young, urban African Americans were using the form, the youth in Springville were particularly motivated to acquire it, which is part of why Cukor-Avila believed its use was increasing so quickly. Older Springville residents would likely see little incentive to speak like citified youth, and would probably also be having minimal contact with them, and so would not be likely to use quotative *be like*.

Table 1. Overall distribution of dialogue introducers for Springville AAVE speakers

Speaker	Born	Tokens	Say/Said	Be Like	Go	Zero	Other
Post-1970							
Brandy	1982	592	68.6%	14.7%	1.4%	6.8%	8.6%
Samantha	1982	231	61.0%	18.6%	0.4%	10.8%	9.1%
LaShonda	1981	156	66.0%	6.4%	1.3%	17.3%	9.0%
Sheila	1979	256	71.5%	10.2%	2.0%	9.0%	7.4%
Rolanda	1978	25	52.0%	12.0%	4.0%	8.0%	24.0%
Lamar	1976	86	62.8%	none	4.7%	23.3%	9.3%
Post-WWII							
Travis	1965	75	86.7%	none	none	2.7%	10.7%
Vanessa	1961	361	93.4%	none	none	3.6%	2.5%
Bobby	1949	321	75.4%	0.9%	0.6%	20.6%	2.5%
Pre-WWII							
Lois	1941	42	90.5%	none	none	7.1%	2.4%
Slim	1932	100	91.0%	none	1.0%	4.0%	4.0%
Pre-WWI							
Mary	1913	256	69.1%	none	none	26.6%	4.3%
Wallace	1913	653	76.6%	none	0.2%	17.5%	5.8%
Audrey	1907	49	83.7%	none	none	8.2%	8.2%

(from Cukor-Avila, 2002, p. 12)

Table 2. Quotatives over time for three Springville African American teenagers

	Tokens	Say/Said	Be Like	Go	Zero	Other
Early	303	71.9%	7.3%	2.3%	5.9%	12.5%
Middle	434	69.6%	11.5%	0.5%	9.9%	8.5%
Late	342	61.4%	24.6%	1.5%	7.9%	4.7%

(from Cukor-Avila, 2002, p. 14)

MIRPUR PAHARI

Entwined with the discussion of language identity is the study of language attitudes and *language regard*, that is, whether speakers think of how they speak in a positive or negative light. As we have seen in the earlier studies, someone's opinion of dialect can have a strong effect on who they wish to emulate. Other examples of this can easily be found when looking at studies of migration – Evans (2004), for example, observed that Appalachians who relocated to southeastern Michigan were quickly acquiring the dominant NCS form. Although NCS was different from their own dialect, the Appalachians appeared to build rapport with locals in the area due to racial and professional similarities, and were adopting the local speech as well.

These studies, however, have primarily considered migrants who were moving from communities that both shared the same L1. Much more directly related to ESL teaching is, what has tended to happen when someone or a community is integrating into a group that does not share the same language. Work such as Fishman (1972) and Veltman (1983) has often described a three-generation pattern for linguistic assimilation in the United States:

Generation 1: Native speakers of their heritage language, who arrive to the country and learn English
Generation 2: Born in the United States, and very often do not acquire the heritage language
Generation 3: Born in the United States, and basically have no connection to the heritage language and/
    or culture – assimilated to the United States

This is of course oversimplified, but is a useful model to begin with. Possible reasons that the second generation does not acquire the heritage language can include the children having no interest in it, but also their parents not wanting to teach them their native language, fearing it will hold them back from opportunities in the States.

Motivations for preserving or rejecting the language and customs of the family's native country can be many – since language is a crux of personal identity, speakers may wish to maintain their L1 to maintain their sense of who they are, and to preserve relationships. If their native language is a part of their religion, this may be an additional incentive to hold onto it and pass it to their children. And conversely, if the language is stigmatized or outright banned, speakers may be forced to hide their knowledge of it or never speak it in public.

One study that considers these concerns is Lothers and Lothers (2012), which examines the Mirpuri population of England – a group of roughly half a million that has relocated from Pakistani-administered Kashmir to Yorkshire, England. The Mirpuri community arose in the UK following the construction of the Mangla dam in the Mirpur district of Kashmir during the 1960s. The completion of the dam in 1966 and subsequent flooding of much of the region created a diaspora, at the same time as England was having a labor shortage in its textile industry. Many Mirpuri relocated, and while they initially would make frequent return visits to their homeland, British immigration laws became more strict during the 1970's, which prompted the Mirpuri to simply remain in England. This also made it prudent to relocate entire families to the UK, rather than worry about not being able to return.

Lothers and Lothers were working with the Mirpuri community in 2003, roughly 30 years after most of the migration, with an interest in seeing how the Mirpuri language (Mirpur Pahari, a branch of Punjabi) was faring, both in its usage, and in its perception by the community. Did they see speaking the language as an essential part of their culture, or was the community perhaps on the three-generation assimilation pattern? The researchers noted that the Mirpuri maintained connections with their homeland in ways that were unusual for immigrant communities – one of which being arranging marriages between UK-born children and Mirpuri who remained in the homeland. This was seen as a way of maintaining conservative Muslim values, and also served as a means of increasing the size of the UK-based group. Plus, it also meant there was steady influx of new arrivals from the homeland to preserve linguistic and cultural norms. Lothers and Lothers point to earlier research by Reynolds (2002) which suggested that other Punjabi communities in the UK were actively working to promote the use of their language.

The focus of their research was to better understand the Mirpuri community's sense of their language and its future. Before discussing their results, let us first consider some of their questions in detail, as an example of how sociolinguists design and frame ethnographic research (from Lothers & Lothers, 2012, Appendix D.2). They began with the following demographic questions:

Questions About Pothowari/Mirpuri

Name: _____

First language: _____ *Gender:* ☐ *Male* ☐ *Female Age:* _____

Birthplace: _____ *Family:* _____

Marital status: ☐ *Unmarried* ☐ *Married* *Other:* _____ *#of children:* _____

Education: _____ *Can you read?* ☐ *Yes* ☐ *No*

If so, in what language? _____

Where have you lived?

Place(s): _____ _____ _____ _____

Years: _____ _____ _____ _____

Where did your family live in Pakistan? _____

When did your family come to England? _____

Have you returned to Pakistan from England? _____ *For how long?* _____

Such questions allow for sociolinguists to determine if they have balanced, representative sample from the community – ideally one that includes an even balance of gender, age, and other relevant variables. Such questions can also serve as an early warning that a speaker might not be appropriate for the study. For example, if a respondent commented that their family had not lived in Pakistan, they might not actually be Mirpuri. Because some of the later questions ask about printed materials in Mirpuri Pahari, the researchers needed to ask about literacy skills as well, which can be an issue when conducting fieldwork. After asking for demographic information such as the respondents' age and sex, they gave questions that provoked longer responses:

1. *Where else do other Mirpuri speakers live?* _____
2. *Do young people gladly speak Mirpuri?* ☐ *Yes* ☐ *No*
3. *Do you think kids will grow up to speak Mirpuri?* ☐ *Yes* ☐ *No*
4. *Do you want your children to grow up to speak Mirpuri?* ☐ *Yes* ☐ *No*
5. *Do you think it is a good thing to use Mirpuri?* ☐ *Yes* ☐ *No*

These questions focused primarily on the speakers' attitudes toward Mirpuri Pahari, and their opinion of its future. Questions 2-3 ask about the speaker's perceptions – is the language being used by young people, and if so, do they speak it happily? Questions such as 4 and 5 address the speaker's own beliefs – do they think the language should be used, and is it something that should be passed on to the next generation?

6. *In your family, what language do you use with...*
   a. *grandparents* _____
   b. *parents* _____
   c. *brothers/sisters* _____
   d. *children* _____
7. *What language do your children (or children in your family) speak with each other?*
   _____
   a. *If not Mirpuri, can your children understand Mirpuri?*   ☐ *Yes* ☐ *No*
8. *Outside your family, what language do you use with...?*
   a. *neighbors* _____
   b. *shopkeepers* _____
   c. *people at the mosque* _____
   d. *friends* _____
   e. *other* _____

These questions address a few different points, one of which is an attempt to gauge the speaker's **social network**, or group that the speaker interacts with day-to-day. A high *network score* for a speaker would indicate that they had many connections within the local community, including friends, family, and co-workers. If speakers with a high network score were reporting that they regularly used Mirpur Pahari, this would suggest that the language was circulating widely. Conversely, if a speaker were fluent, but isolated, this would mean that their knowledge of Mirpur Pahari was not greatly affecting the larger community (for more on social networks, see Milroy (1980)). Questions 6 and 8 focus on this especially, seeking to know who the speaker interacts with in Mirpur Pahari on a regular basis. This is crucial toward assessing the vitality of the language – if speakers are fluent but never using the language (for example, only speaking English), their fluency is going to fade, and the language will not be an active part of the culture. On the other hand, if it is broadly used in several contexts, the language is likely to continue being spoken. Question 8 looks to see if Mirpur Pahari is being compartmentalized – sometimes multilingual communities will assign languages to specific contexts, such as the workplace or the home. Sanchez (2005) observed this behavior in Aruba, where Spanish, Dutch, and Papiamentu (a local Creole dialect) are spoken. There, Spanish is used in the workplace, Dutch is used in schools, and Papiamentu appears in the home and daily life.

Questions 6 and 7 also assess the longevity of the language within the community – if speakers reported that they only used Mirpuri Pahari with their grandparents and elders, this would suggest that the three-generation pattern described above might be occurring, where the language was not being passed on.

With regard to the questions that Lothers and Lothers classified as Language Vitality, the Mirpuri responses are shown in Table 3.

Table 3. Responses to language vitality questions

Question	Yes	Some	No	NR	Total
2. Do young people gladly speak Mirpuri?	21 (68%)	3 (10%)	7 (22%)	2	33
3. Will children grow up to speak Mirpuri?	22(71%)	1 (3%)	8 (26%)	2	33

(Lothers and Lothers, 2012, p. 6)

Table 4. Responses to attitudes questions

Question	Yes	No	NR	Total
4. Do you want your children to speak Mirpuri?	*28 (90%)*	*3 (10%)*	*2*	*33*
5. Is it a good thing to speak Mirpuri?	*29 (91%)*	*3 (9%)*	*1*	*33*

(Lothers & Lothers, 2012, p. 7)

This suggests that those surveyed were generally optimistic about the future of the language, with the majority of respondents believing that younger people were learning Murpuri Pahari and were generally pleased to use it. As far as the questions about attitudes, the responses toward the language were overwhelmingly positive, as shown in Table 4.

The vast majority of respondents expressed positive attitudes towards using the language, both for themselves and for their children. Later questions asking whether they would be interested in seeing print and other forms of media in Mirpur Pahari were also treated positively.

Table 5 shows the results of questions 6-8 that examined social network. In Table 5, it is visible that usage is skewed toward older generations, but that children are still being regularly engaged in the language by adults. In Question 8, the language does not appear to be isolated to a specific context, used roughly half the time in most contexts (receiving competition from English, Urdu, and other varieties of Punjabi).

Lothers and Lothers (2012) overall found that the Mirpuri were generally enthusiastic about using Mirpur Pahari, although they do comment that the enthusiasm is to some degree stronger than the reality. Nonetheless, they show evidence that a simple three-generation trajectory toward assimilation into a culture is not inevitable. However, they note that the Mirpuri have taken unusual measures that promote the sustainability of their enclave, such as having frequent contact with their homeland, and by employing arranged marriages to maintain a regular population of new arrivals who bring fresh connection to Mirpur, and of course, to Mirpur Pahari.

IMPLICATIONS FOR TEACHING ENGLISH LANGUAGE LEARNERS

A central theme of this chapter is that speakers of a language will seek to emulate the speech of those they admire, and to distance themselves from people they do not want to be like. Or, as with the Native population of Martha's Vineyard, they may feel barred from participating in the community and not believe they are able to emulate another group. These considerations apply both for a speaker's L1 and

Table 5. Language use in the community

	Used MP		Used MP
6a. w/ grandparents	32 (97%)	8a. w/ neighbors	16 (49%)
6b. w/ parents	30 (91%)	8b. w/ shopkeepers	18 (55%)
6c. w/ siblings	23 (70%)	8c. In mosque	18 (55%)
6d. w/ children	18 (55%)	8d. w/ friends	13 (40%)
7a. among children	8 (24%)		

(Lothers and Lothers, 2012, pp. 8-9)

for any other languages they speak. As a learner constructs their linguistic competency in an L2, they are also constructing a personal identity that employs the L2. This may overlap significantly with their personality when speaking their L1, but it may not be identical. Yun (2009) observed that bilingual Korean children who spoke English would apply English for particular situations, like swearing or insulting other children. Abugharsa (2014) had similar findings with bilingual Arabic-speaking children in the United States, where they were more likely to use Arabic in more Arab contexts. Switching between languages in such a fashion (and sometimes even mid-sentence) is referred to as **code-switching**. English language learners (ELLs) may have a strong tendency to code-switch – it can be easier if a learner does not know a particular word, but it can also be a way to maintain identity.

One point for a language teacher to be aware of is that most elements of dialectal pronunciation will be opaque to second language learners. They will almost certainly not recognize subtle changes in phonemes and allophones, which is part of why this chapter did not dwell on them. As an example, many dialects of the United States can be differentiated by their pronunciation of the /ɔ/ and /ɑ/ vowels. Regions such as the Northern Cities and the South tend to produce them distinctly, while much of the rest of the country will say them as a single sound (usually /ɑ/), in what is called the *caught/cot merger*. Again, ELL students will probably not perceive such a minor difference, but it can help their teachers to be knowledgeable of the area's regional pronunciations and local slang. Many dialect features *are* salient to native speakers and learners alike – for example, the tendency in the South to monophthongize /aɪ/ before voiced consonants and word-finally, making a word like "guide" be pronounced closer to [gɑd]. English language learners will be very likely traveling or engaging with media that uses multiple dialects, and teachers can use their knowledge of language to answer these students' questions and help them perceive differences.

It is crucial as an instructor to be aware that as a student is acquiring the elements of language discussed earlier in this book such as vocabulary and grammatical constructions, they are also acquiring a re-evaluation of personal, cultural, and possibly familial identity. ESL materials often describe a learner's motivation in two ways:

- **Instrumental**: a learner is motivated by a specific, functional goal such as getting a job, passing a test, or entering college
- **Integrative**: a learner is motivated by wanting to operate within a culture, with an emphasis on daily life – carrying on conversation, doing business, or running a home.

However, learning a language is about more than simply carrying out tasks. If the learner is an immigrant, when they leave the classroom, they are weighing considerations such as those addressed by the Mirpuri, and deciding how much of an influence they want both English and their native language to continue to have on their own life, and the lives of their children. If they willingly chose to emigrate, they may be eager to allow new elements of speech and culture into their lives. But if they are a refugee, they may perhaps see this decision as forced upon them by their circumstances. They may feel frustrated to be struggling with a new language that their children are acquiring easily, or they may have had a professional identity in their home country that they lack the proficiency to maintain in English.

As teachers of linguistically and culturally diverse learners, our job is to help our students add to themselves without taking away. We should apply our knowledge of language and linguistics to help them acquire a new language, while always remembering the full weight and multiplicity of what they are truly learning.

DISCUSSION QUESTIONS

1. Can you think of other types of language or behaviors that are age-graded? Discuss ways that someone might talk or things they might do that are connected to a particular stage of life.
2. What are some ways that people around you signal their regional identity? How does someone make it obvious that they are a local?
3. In your own academic environment, are there social groups similar to the Jocks and Burnouts described by Eckert? How do people around you signal their social allegiance to a particular group?
4. Who are some celebrities that have built their on-camera personalities around overt prestige? How do they signal this? What about celebrities that have built their reputation upon covert prestige? Can you think of anyone that has changed strategies? Was the change successful?
5. What are some genres of music that depend strongly on use of a particular dialect or regional style? Why is that dialect so crucial to the genre? What tropes or stereotypes is it evoking?

EXERCISES

1. A frequent find on social media are "You Know You're From ..." lists, that will detail all the ways you know that you are from the North, the South, or a particular province or city. Often they will include a mix of local things – landmarks you have visited, meals you have had, oddly-pronounced cities that you know how to say correctly. What would such a list look like for where you are now? Try and identify ten things that are unique to the area (they do not have to all be linguistic).
2. Use the Corpus of Contemporary American English (COCA) to perform some searches.
3. If you use the Chart function when searching for a word, the corpus will display for you which contexts (Spoken, Newspaper, Academic, etc.) it appears in most frequently, and how often it has been used over time. This can show you several things: how commonly-used the word is, if there are certain environments it appears in more frequently, and how its usage is faring over time. For this exercise, search for five words that are synonyms of *good* (awesome, amazing, etc.). For each one, answer the following questions:
    a. How many occurrences (tokens) of it appear in the corpus?
    b. In which context is it used the most?
    c. Is its usage over time rising, falling, or steady?

Word	# of tokens	Most Used Context	Usage
_____	_____	_____	_____
_____	_____	_____	_____
_____	_____	_____	_____
_____	_____	_____	_____
_____	_____	_____	_____

    d. Were you surprised by any of your results?
    e. Did you have cases where your word had another possible meaning?

4. Consider the country that you are in – where are the major regions that you could identify based on their regional accent? For each, describe some characteristics of how the people in that region speak.

    Region   Description

    _____   _____

    _____   _____

    _____   _____

    _____   _____

    _____   _____

    _____   _____

5. Lexical items vary greatly with dialects of English, and especially between countries. Can you match these British and American terms?

    British   **American**

    Aubergine   Diapers

    Draughts   Sneakers

    Lorry   Shopping cart

    Nappies   Checkers

    Queue   Eggplant

    Solicitors   Truck

    Trainers   Lawyers

    Trolley   Line

6. Think about where you live right now and consider the following questions:
    a. Can you tell someone is from here based on how they speak?
    b. How would you describe the way that people here speak?
    c. How would you describe the way that people here act?

    Consider your own answers to these questions, and then ask them to three local people who are from the area. How much agreement is there?

REFERENCES

Abugharsa, A. (2014). *Arabic-English code-switching in young Libyan children in the US* (Doctoral dissertation). Oklahoma State University.

Bailey, R. W. (1991). *Images of English*. Ann Arbor, MI: The University of Michigan Press.

Coulmas, F. (2013). *Sociolinguistics: The study of speakers' choices*. Cambridge, UK: Cambridge University Press. doi:10.1017/CBO9781139794732

Cukor-Avila, P. (2002). She say, she go, she be like: Verbs of quotation over time in African American Vernacular English. *American Speech, 77*(2), 3–31. doi:10.1215/00031283-77-1-3

Eckert, P. (1988). Social structure and the spread of linguistic change. *Language in Society, 17*(2), 183–207. doi:10.1017/S0047404500012756

Eckert, P. (1989). The whole woman: Sex and gender differences in variation. *Language Variation and Change, 1*(3), 245–267. doi:10.1017/S095439450000017X

Evans, B. (2004). The role of social network in the acquisition of local dialect norms by Appalachian migrants in Ypsilanti, Michigan. *Language Variation and Change, 16*(2), 153–167. doi:10.1017/S0954394504162042

Fishman, J. (1972). The Sociology of language. Rowley, MA: Newbury.

Gerald of Wales. (1984). The journey through Wales and the description of Wales (L. Thorpe, Trans.). Harmondsworth, UK: Penguin Books. (Original publication 1193)

Goffman, E. (1959). *The presentation of self in everyday life*. New York, NY: Anchor Books.

Gordon, M. J. (2001). *Small-town values, big-city vowels: A study of the Northern Cities Shift in Michigan*. Durham, NC: Duke University Press.

Labov, W. (1963). The social motivation of a sound change. *Word, 19*(3), 273–209. doi:10.1080/00437956.1963.11659799

Labov, W., Ash, S., & Boberg, C. (2006). *The atlas of North American English: Phonetics, phonology, and sound change*. Berlin: Mouton/de Gruyter. doi:10.1515/9783110167467

Lakoff, R. T. (1975). *Language and woman's place*. New York: Harper & Row.

Lothers, M. & Lothers, L. (2012). Mirpuri immigrants in England: A sociolinguistic survey. *SIL Electronic Survey Report, 2012* (12), 1-33

Milroy, L. (1980). *Language and social networks*. Oxford, UK: Blackwell.

Reynolds, M. (2002). Punjabi/Urdu in Sheffield: Language maintenance and loss and development of a mixed code. In P. Gubbins & M. Holt (Eds.), *Beyond boundaries: Language and identity in contemporary Europe* (pp. 145–162). Clevedon, UK: Multilingual Matters Ltd. doi:10.21832/9781853595578-012

Sanchez, T. (2005). *Constraints on structural borrowing in a multilingual contact situation* (Doctoral dissertation). University of Pennsylvania.

Sibata, T. (1969). *Methods in linguistic geography*. Tokyo: Chikumashobo.

Singler, J. V. (2001). Why you can't do a VARBRUL study of quotatives and what such a study can show us. *University of Pennsylvania Working Papers in Linguistics, 7*, 257–78.

Tagliamonte, S. (2012). *Variationist sociolinguistics: Change, observation, interpretation*. Malden, MA: Wiley-Blackwell.

Tagliamonte, S., & D'Arcy, A. (2005). When people say, "I was like...": The quotative system in Canadian youth. *University of Pennsylvania Working Papers in Linguistics, 10*(2), 257-272.

Tagliamonte, S., & Hudson, R. (1999). Be like et al. beyond America: The quotative system in British and Canadian youth. *Journal of Sociolinguistics, 3*(2), 147–172. doi:10.1111/1467-9481.00070

United States Census. (1980). *General Population Characteristics: Michigan.* Retrieved from https://www2.census.gov/prod2/decennial/documents/1980/1980censusofpopu80124uns_bw.pdf

United States Census. (2010). *Profile of general population and housing characteristics: 2010.* Retrieved from https://factfinder.census.gov/faces/nav/jsf/pages/community_facts.xhtml

Veltman, C. (1983). *Language shift in the United States.* Berlin: Mouton. doi:10.1515/9783110824001

Wolfram, W. (2004). The grammar of urban African American vernacular English. In B. Kormann & E. Schneider (Eds.), *Handbook of Varieties of English* (pp. 111–132). Berlin: Mouton de Gruyter.

Yun, S. (2009). *The socializing role of codes and code-switching among Korean children in the U.S.* (Doctoral dissertation). Oklahoma State University.

Zappa, F. (1982). Valley Girl [Recorded by Frank Zappa]. On Ship Arriving too Late to Save a Drowning Witch. California: Barking Pumpkin Records.

Appendix

ANSWERS TO EXERCISES

Chapter 1

Exercise 1. Answers will vary.
Exercise 2. Answers will vary.
Exercise 3. Answers will vary.
Exercise 4. Answers will vary.
Exercise 5. Answers will vary.
Exercise 6. Answers will vary.
Exercise 7. Answers will vary.
Exercise 8. Answers will vary.
Exercise 9. Answers will vary.

Chapter 2

Exercise 1

a. (12) Sarah/ look/ed/ at/ the/ organ/ism/s/ through/ a/ micro/scope.
Sarah (free morpheme) *look* (free morpheme) *–ed* (suffix) *at* (free morpheme) *the* (free morpheme) *organ* (free morpheme) *–ism* (suffix) *–s* (suffix) *through* (free morpheme) *a* (free morpheme) *micro-* (prefix) *–scope* (root, now used as a free morpheme).

b. (10) We/ ask/ed/ the/ sing/er/ for/ her/ auto/graph.
We (free morpheme) *ask* (free morpheme) *–ed* (suffix) *the* (free morpheme) *sing* (free morpheme) *–er* (suffix) *for* (free morpheme) *her* (free morpheme) *auto-* (prefix) *-graph* (root).

c. (13) The/ rebel/s/ are/ fight/ing/ for/ a/ demo/crat/ic/ govern/ment.
The (free morpheme) *rebel* (free morpheme) *–s* (suffix) *are* (free morpheme) *fight* (free morpheme) *–ing* (suffix) *for* (free morpheme) *a* (free morpheme) *demo-* (root) *–crat* (root) *–ic* (suffix) *govern* (free morpheme) *–ment* (suffix)

Exercise 2

a. bound morpheme   f. bound morpheme
b. free morpheme   g. bound morpheme
c. bound morpheme   h. free morpheme
d. bound morpheme   i. bound morpheme
e. free morpheme   j. free morpheme

Exercise 3

1. g.   6. d.
2. e.   7. l.
3. i.   8. j.
4. b.   9. f.
5. a.   10. c.

Exercise 4

Answers will vary. Some possible answers:

1. antiseptic   6. monolingual
2. benefit   7. pandemic
3. external   8. semicircle
4. hypotension   9. transport
5. macroeconomics   10. ultraviolet

Exercise 5

1. Adjective   5. Interjection   9. Pronoun   13. Pronoun
2. Adverb   6. Verb   10. Adverb   14. Adjective
3. Conjunction   7. Conjunction   11. Preposition 15. Preposition
4. Noun   8. Verb   12. Conjunction 16. Noun

Exercise 6

Content words are underlined.

    a.   <u>Mitochondria</u> are <u>organelles</u> which <u>bring</u> <u>nutrients</u> into the <u>cell.</u>

    b.   The <u>scientific</u> <u>method</u> <u>starts</u> with a <u>hypothesis</u> that can be <u>tested</u>.

    c.   The <u>background</u> of an <u>artwork</u> is the <u>area</u> that <u>seems</u> to be <u>furthest</u> <u>away</u> from the <u>viewer</u>.

    d.   In <u>1606</u>, <u>King James I</u> <u>granted</u> a <u>charter</u> to the <u>Virginia Company</u> to <u>establish</u> a <u>settlement</u> in <u>North America</u>.

    e.   <u>Speed</u> can be <u>calculated</u> by <u>dividing</u> the <u>distance</u> <u>traveled</u> by the <u>time</u> it <u>takes</u> to <u>travel</u> that <u>distance</u>.

Chapter 3

Exercise 1

Based on stress marking, the words *overpower, understand, underestimate, overtake,* and *undercut* contain prefixes, while the words *underwear, underbrush, overcoat,* and *underling* contain **under/over** as free morphemes. Additional evidence is that in the word *underling,* the second syllable *–ling* is a well-attested suffix (as in *yearling*).

Exercise 2

The fact that the pronunciation of the free morpheme **meter** is identical in *voltmeter* and *centimeter* suggests that both are compounds. The lack of stress on the remaining instances of **meter** suggests that the structure in those words is [free morpheme+suffix].

Exercise 3

The example is most likely a case of back-formation. The initial verb is **destroy**. From it comes the derivation **destruction**. From that comes the further derivation **self-destruction**, which is then back-formed to **self-destruct**.

Exercise 4

Two plausible paths to answers exist here. The abbreviation of **electronic** to **e-** looks like a case of clipping. Once **e-** is affixed to any appropriate verb or noun, there is noticeable primary stress on the first syllable (e.g., **e-mail**, **e-store**), which suggests the stress pattern of a compound. Indirect evidence is that the hyphen in **e-mail** that was common use 20 years ago has disappeared. Another way to approach the question is to call the expression **electronic mail** the original source, which was clipped to **e-mail**, which then became a compound.

Exercise 5

    Fax is a **clipped** form of *facsimile*, a noun which has been **converted** to a verb.

    Makeup is a **compound** composed of a verb plus a preposition.

    Notate is a **back-formation** whose most likely path of development was as follows:

    note (n.) → *note* (v.), through conversion; → *notation*, through derivation; → *notate*, through back-formation.

    Fantabulous is a **blend** of *fantastic* and *fabulous*.

    Plaster is a **zero-derivation** that converts a noun to a verb.

    Cleanup is a **compound** made up of [verb+preposition] that is then **converted** to adjective form.

    Talks is a noun **zero-derived** or converted from a verb; it is **inflected** for plural number.

    Freeway overpass is a **complex compound** consisting of two smaller compound words.

    Outlasted is a prefixed verbal **derivation** that has been **inflected** for past tense.

    Tech is a **clipped** form.

    Post-blogging is a prefixed noun **derivation**. *Blog* is a **clipped** form of a **compound** originally consisting of *web+log*. In this sentence, *post-blogging* modifies a noun, so it could be argued that there has been a further **conversion** from noun to adjective status. Note that for those speakers who are familiar with the term *blog* but are not aware of its origin in *web+log*, the clipping process has no psychological reality, as defined in the section on etymological versus psychological reality in Chapter 3.

Chapter 4

Exercise 1

(a)

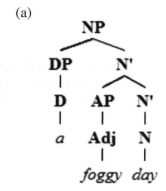

(b)

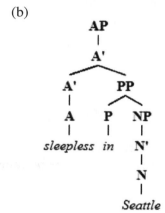

(c)

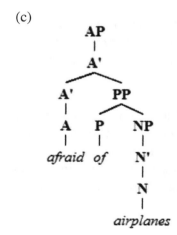

(d)

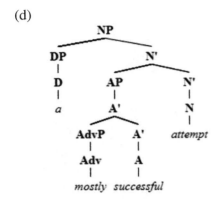

(e)

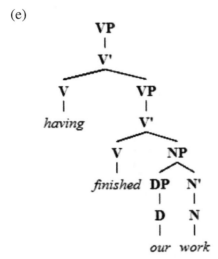

(f)

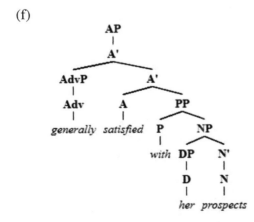

(g)

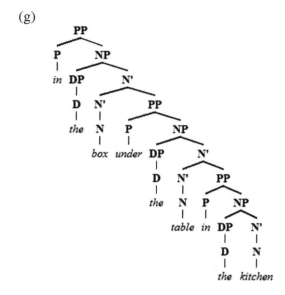

(h)

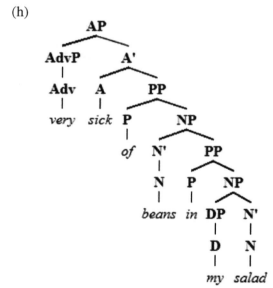

Exercise 2

(a)

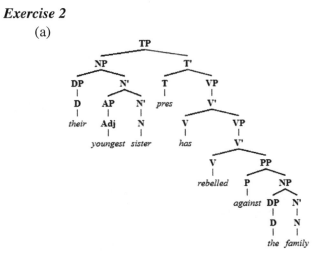

(b)

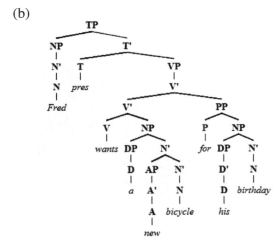

(c)

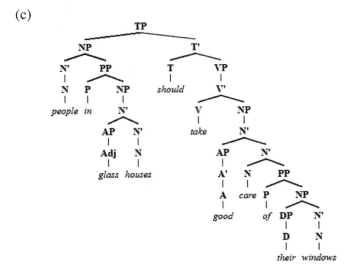

(d)

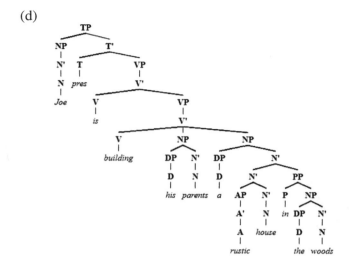

(e)

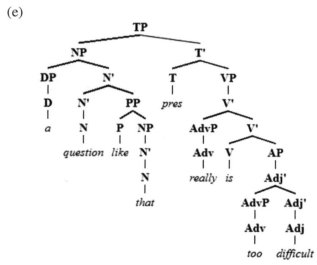

(f)

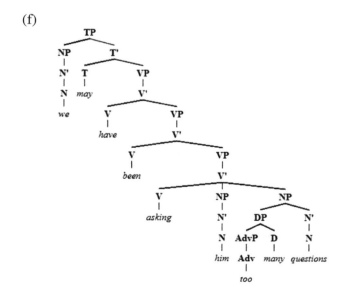

Exercise 3

(a)

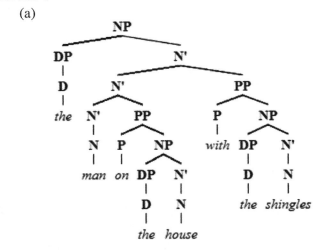

(b)

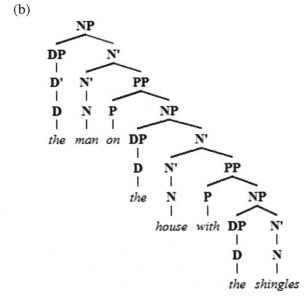

The interpretations: In the top tree, the man is on top of the house and is holding shingles. In the bottom tree, the man is on top of a house which has shingles on its exterior. (There is a third interpretation, in which the man has a certain disease. This involves lexical ambiguity, and the variance in interpretation between it and the first interpretation cannot be captured using tree diagrams.)

Exercise 4

(a)

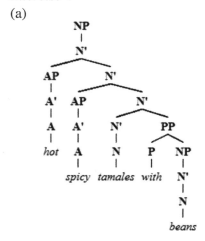

(b)

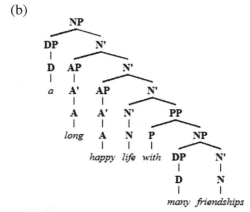

Exercise 5

Note: If these sentences are actually produced, the context of utterance may make the speaker's meaning clear enough that a teacher might call some of them 'acceptable' sentences in a communicative sense. However, the goal in this exercise is to identify syntactic problems.

    a.   The speaker has used the auxiliary *be*, which lexically selects an *–ing* complement rather than a bare verb stem without an affix. On the assumption that the speaker wanted to express a future meaning, the proper formulation was *I am seeing him tomorrow night.*

    b.   The third person singular form of a present-tense verb requires an overt affix *–s*, which is missing. The sentence therefore lacks a tense.

    c.   The verb ***dislike*** selects a direct object NP complement, not a PP headed by ***about***.

    d.   Modal verbs select a plain verb stem as their complement. The speaker has selected a past participle instead.

    e.   The verb like selects an NP complement. The speaker may think that ***violent*** is a lexical noun. Also, ***violence*** is a mass noun, not a count noun, so ***too much*** should replace ***too many***.

    f.   The speaker has separated the complement of ***want*** from its head V with a modifying PP. The order of PPs should be reversed.

Exercise 6

Answers will vary. The strategy would be to insert a PP or AdvP before the boldfaced PP and check the results, which should be approximately as follows and accord with the results in:

a.	*My friends and I ate a whole box [last night]* **of cookies***.*	**UNACCEPTABLE**
b.	*We watched the deer eating our garden flowers [with gusto]* **on Sunday***.*	**ACCEPTABLE**
c.	*I am appalled [often]* **at our sales record***.*	**MARGINAL TO UNACCEPTABLE**
d.	*The decision [yesterday]* **on the plan** *was difficult to make.*	**UNACCEPTABLE**
e.	*We paid for the sandwich [after the meal]* **with a** *ten-**dollar bill***.*	**UNACCEPTABLE**
f.	*The students hoped [with great enthusiasm]* **for better results***.*	**UNACCEPTABLE**
g.	*They met five linguistics students [in Chicago]* **during the conference***.*	**ACCEPTABLE**
h.	*The worst people often lust [with fury]* **after power***.*	**UNACCEPTABLE**
i.	*Meet me [tomorrow night]* **around the corner***!*	**ACCEPTABLE**
j.	*My friend firmly believes [with all her heart]* **in ghosts***.*	**UNACCEPTABLE**

Exercise 7

Although **along the top** is a modifier and **of the roof** is a complement, the latter PP is embedded inside the first PP modifier and is complement to the N **top**. Only the first PP relates directly to the V' **running**.

Exercise 8

The four boldfaced expressions are in fact syntactic NPs. The syntactic theory can deal with them by permitting NPs to be either complements to a word-level constituent or modifiers to a single-bar constituent, just as PPs and APs may be. The phrase structure rules will have to be revised slightly to allow the additions. It will be important to point out that if the NPs are modifiers, they are not direct objects but sisters to single-bar constituents.

Some students may propose an alternative solution that involves creating an underlying PP with either a null preposition or a particular preposition such as **to** (as in [**to downtown**]), followed by a rule that deletes that P. Since the chapter offers no means to delete anything, the solution should be regarded with suspicion.

Exercise 9

TP can be expanded with the middle rule below to accommodate the new sentences:

TP → NP T'

T' → (AdvP) T' (AdvP) (optional rule; may be repeated)

T' → T VP

The tree for the first (a) sentence will therefore look as follows:

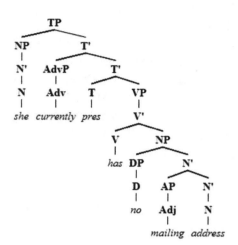

The (b) trees will simply flip AdvP to the right side of V'.

a. *She currently has no mailing address.*
    They inexplicably left town without leaving one.
b. *We have no answer to your question, unfortunately.*
    You have been looking in the wrong place, obviously.

Exercise 10
Compounds such as *greenhouse*, *paperweight*, *ski slope*, *baseball*, *breakwater*, whose part of speech is determined by the last free morpheme, are also **head-last** structures.

Chapter 5

Exercise 1. Answers will vary.
Exercise 2. Answers will vary.
Exercise 3. Answers will vary.
Exercise 4. Answers will vary.
Exercise 5. Answers will vary.

Chapter 6

Exercise 1
Answers may vary. You may review the section on Verbs and the section on Passive Voice to remember the differences between and the uses of the linking verb [BE] and the auxiliary verb [BE].

Exercise 2
Answers may vary depending on the languages chosen. Remember that there are other syntactic units that indicate the time or duration of an event in the sentence, such as adverbs, adverb phrases or adverb clauses of time, and prepositional phrases locating an event in time.

Exercise 3

First, we may add more example sentences such as the following to expand the examples:

> Is she baking a chocolate cake?
>
> He hasn't handed in his assignment yet, has he?
>
> I do not like dishonest people.
>
> Organic farming does not affect climate change as much as animal husbandry.

Some guiding questions may include the following:

(i)   Identify the regular auxiliary verbs and the modal auxiliary verbs in the given sentences as well as those you have added.

    A: Modal auxiliaries: *could, can, must, will*; regular auxiliary verbs: *are, is, have, has, do, does*

(ii) Do you move both modal auxiliaries and regular auxiliaries to make questions?

    A: Yes.

(iii) Do you add "not" to modal auxiliaries to make negative statements?

    A: Yes.

(iv) The first verb in a VC marks the tense. Identify the first verbs in the VCs of the given sentences.

    A: Modal auxiliaries: *could, can, must, will*; regular auxiliary verbs: *are, is, have, has, do, does*

      i.   Do the given forms of the modal verb appear in a sentence that refers to an event in the present as well as the past, or is the use of this form restricted to only one tense?

    A: Add an adverb of time that refers to the present or the past, and see if both work:

      √ Couldn't you have helped your friend yesterday/this evening?

      *Are some linguists working for Hollywood last year?

    Both work with modal auxiliary verbs but not with regular auxiliary verbs.

      ii. Do the verbs change in form when they refer to the past or the present?

    A: Regular auxiliary verbs do, modals do not.

      iii. What forms of the following verbs occur with different forms of the auxiliary verbs?

    A: Verb+ing follows "is/are"; V+ed/en follows "have/has/had".

(v)   Based on your answers above,

    i.   Do you think all auxiliary verbs mark tense?

      A: No. Only regular auxiliaries do.

    ii. What is/are the major difference(s) between a modal verb and a regular auxiliary verb?

      A: Modal verbs are not marked for tense, and they are followed by the base form of another verb, be it an auxiliary verb or a content verb: *could have been, could go*, etc.

Exercise 4

Answers may vary. Review the section on Progressive Aspect as well as the kinds and functions of [BE] within the Passive Voice section of Chapter 6. Adopt the examples in these sections as a model while designing tasks.

Exercise 5

Answers may vary. Review the section on Progressive Aspect in Chapter 6, and consult a reliable grammar book to review what gerunds are. Adopt the examples in Chapter 6 as a model while designing tasks.

Exercise 6

Answers may vary. Review the section on Perfect Aspect in Chapter 6, and consult a reliable grammar book to review participles. Adopt the examples in Chapter 6 as a model while designing tasks.

Exercise 7

Answers may vary. Review the section on Aspect and adopt the examples in Chapter 6 as a model while designing tasks.

Exercise 8

Answers may vary. Review the section on Passive Voice and adopt the examples in Chapter 6 as a model while designing tasks.

Exercise 9

Answers may vary. Review the section on Mood and adopt the examples in Chapter 6 as a model while designing tasks. You may use visual elements, such as cartoons or animations depicting characters in different "moods" uttering sentences in different grammatical moods, or ask students to come up with such characters and utterances, such as Grouchy Smurf complaining and wishing for things to be otherwise, using the subjunctive mood.

Exercise 10

Below are some of the sentences in the subjunctive and the imperative moods in the content of Chapter 6:
(i)   Sentences in the subjunctive mood:
    i.   It is essential that teachers give clear instructions on how a small group operates, including how students within the groups elect ….
    ii.   It is important that English language learners practice enough material to acquire the habit of focusing on the very first verb in a verb complex to identify the tense ….
(ii)   Sentences in the imperative mood:
    i.   Observe all possible variations and describe the different types of verbs in VCs.
    ii.   Finally, describe the maximum number of verbs and the order in which they appear in a VC in English.

Chapter 7

Exercise 1
    a.   James, bike.
    b.   Emily, cake.
        Note that in (a), *bike* refers to is a specific entity in the world, but in (b), reference is to a non-specified *cake*, which presumably exists, or will exist.

    c.   Daughter, dragon.

Note that *daughter* denotes an actual entity in the world, while *dragon* presumably points to a representation of a dragon, such as a picture or a costume. Such cases recall the famous painting by Magritte called the Treachery of Images, showing a pipe with the sentence *Ceci n'est pas une pipe* 'This is not a pipe'. In fact, language can be used to denote representations as well as the objects they depict, as this perfectly normal sentence makes clear.

    d.   door

Note that the *wh*-expression *who* and the quantifier *nobody* are not referential.

Exercise 2: Answers will vary.

Exercise 3

    a.   *Bill* is an AGENT, *Jennifer* is a PATIENT.

    b.   *Maggie* is an AGENT, the *frisbee* is a PATIENT, and *Ian* is a BENEFICIARY. (Agent tier)
Maggie is a SOURCE, the *frisbee* is a THEME, and *Ian* is a GOAL. (Thematic tier)

    c.   *Elliot* is an AGENT, *Jane* is a BENEFICIARY, and the *cake* is a PATIENT.

    d.   The *key* is an INSTRUMENT, and the *door* is a PATIENT.
Note that if an AGENT were present, it would be mapped to the subject position, and the instrument would be in an adjunct phrase.

    e.   The *sun* is a THEME, the *sky* is a LOCATION, the *east* is the SOURCE, and the *west* is the GOAL.

Exercise 4

Expletive *there*:

In the distance, {there burned a straw man / there fell snow from the sky / there lived an ogre in a castle / there sat a fool on a hill / ?there departed the ship from the dock}. (unaccusative)

In the meeting room, there {*agreed / *coughed / *smiled / *thought / *yawned} three men. (unergative)

Dynamic nominal modifiers:

The burned city / The departed guests / The fallen hero / The lived experience / ?The sat dog (unaccusative)

*The agreed people / *The coughed boy / *The smiled girl / *The thought teachers / *The yawned dog (unergative)

Note that not all tests work equally well with all unaccusatives (the question marks in the suggested answers indicate uncertain grammaticality). More fine-grained analyses of different types of unaccustatives can be found in Perlmutter (1978) and Levin & Rappaport Hovav (1995).

Overpassivization errors we expect might include things such as: *My book was fallen down; I was lived there for many years; The plane was departed on time,* etc.

Exercise 5

    a.   *Mark wants to buy a book on Saturday.*
(He already knows which one)
(He doesn't know which book yet)

b.   *Karen did not want to talk to a reporter.*
    (She wanted to avoid one reporter in particular)
    (She didn't want to talk to any reporter)

L2 learners of English overgeneralize the definite article to specific, nondefinite contexts – that is, contexts in which the speaker can identify the thing referred to, but not the hearer. In each of these two sentences, we can predict overgeneralization of *the* in the first case, but not the second.

Chapter 8

Exercise 1: Answers will vary.
Exercise 2: Answers will vary.
Exercise 3: Answers will vary.
Exercise 4: Answers will vary.
Exercise 5: Answers will vary.

Chapter 9

Exercise 1

Answers will vary; however, the response should include the idea that both the linguistic and situational contexts are important for understanding the message the speaker is trying to convey. Situational variables, such as audience, setting, and time of the interaction play a significant role in how messages are delivered and received.

Exercise 2

Answers should include examples for any speech act selected by readers, such as apologizing, refusing an invitation, thanking, greeting, and so on.

Exercise 3

Indirect speech acts refer to the idea that we do not always mean what we say. In indirect speech acts, there is a mismatch between the sentence type and the illocutionary force of the act. In direct speech acts, there is a conventional or direct match between the sentence type and the illocutionary force of the speech act.

Exercise 4

Pragmatic divergence happens when the speaker's and hearer's pragmatic behaviors or choices are dramatically different from each other. Pragmatic divergence often happens among speakers of different languages since cultural norms and expectations shape the ways we speak and hear.

Exercise 5

Examples will vary, but the answers should include the five different types of pragmatic divergence: 1) negative transfer of pragmatic norms, 2) limited grammatical ability in the L2, 3) overgeneralization of perceived L2 pragmatic norms, 4) effect of instruction and/or instructional materials, and 5) learner's choice.

Exercise 6

Pragmatic failure, that is, a breakdown in communication among the speakers might have happened here due to the student's limited grammatical ability in the L2 as the phrase "I would take it to the Writing Center" was understood by the L2 learner as the action being taken by the professor and not herself. The indirect speech act "I would take it…" did not have the intended effect of politeness on the hearer, but of offering direct help as "Now I will help you and I will take it to the Writing Center." Answers might consider other points of view.

Chapter 10

Exercise 1: Answers will vary. Refer to Table 1 as a sample answer.

Exercise 2

a. **Purpose**

Text A: to define, describe, classify and document chimpanzees as a type of animal, to provide factual information about chimpanzees in general, about its features, characteristics, etc.)

Text B: to persuade (to describe one particular chimp and to appeal to prospective donors to donate to the organization)

b. **Audience**

Text A: Children (young students)

Text B: General public (educated adults)

c. **Language features** – examples and how they reflect different purposes/audiences

Nouns: Use of common nouns (e.g. chimpanzees) to give information about chimpanzees in general vs. proper nouns (e.g. kanzi) to describe one particularly famous and intelligent primate

Adjectives: Use of factual adjectives (e.g. warm-blooded, primate, large) to provide factual information vs. (positively) evaluative adjectives (e.g. perfectly serviceable, very clear, very expressive, very very loud) to impress the reader with the positive descriptions of Kanzi

Lexical choice: Use of formal vocabulary (e.g. mammals, young, milk from their bodies, Pan Troglodytes) to provide children (young students) with factual information vs. colloquial vocabulary (e.g. fellow, dozens more, peaceable, sort of) mixed with some formal/technical words (e.g. customary, serviceable, conjugate, grammatical) to persuade the adult, educated readers with a friendly but informative talk

Pronouns: Few 1st or 2nd personal pronouns are used. Mostly 3rd person plural (them) to make the text sound impersonal/ factual vs. the prominent uses of 1st person pronoun (I) to make the text sound personal as if the writer was sharing a personal story as he describes Kanzi as a human being

Types of sentences: Use of complete sentences making the text sound more formal and mainly declarative clauses to give information vs. use of features of spoken language (speech) e.g., asides, afterthoughts and incomplete sentences making the text sound casual and personal.

Discourse structure: Text A represents an information report. It has language features typically found in this text type. It is difficult to categorize Text B into a particular text type. For example, it has some features of a recount or narrative (e.g., use of past tense and a specific participant, Kanzi), but the text also uses present tense to describe Kanzi's characteristics. It is not clearly an information report, an explanation or a discussion either. The text does not have every feature typically found in each of these text types, but a mix of features found in different text types.

Exercise 3

Answers will vary. The aim is to understand the roles played by discourse in constructing identities and influencing someone's perceptions and attitudes towards others.

Exercise 4

Answers will vary. The aim is to raise the awareness that language features usually taught/discussed in an English language classroom to produce or interpret a particular text type or genre may not be the same as those found in the similar text type or genre produced and used in the learners' first language and native culture.

Exercise 5

Answers will vary. The aim is to understand the diverse demands faced by ESL/EFL learners – i.e. different types of talk and text as well as the range of contexts in which learners need to use English.

Chapter 11

Exercise 1

a. knight - /n/ - voiced alveolar nasal
b. sister - /s/ - voiceless alveolar fricative (sibilant)
c. comrade - /k/ - voiceless velar stop
d. physics - /f/ - voiceless labiodental fricative
e. xylophone - /z/ - voiced alveolar fricative (sibilant)
f. chair - /tʃ/ - voiceless palatal affricate (sibilant)
g. giant - /dʒ/ - voiced palatal affricate (sibilant)
h. wrong - /ɹ/ - voiced alveolar liquid (approximant)
i. shelter - /ʃ/ - voiceless palatal fricative (sibilant)
j. ballet - /b/ - voiced bilabial stop
k. though - /ð/ - voiced interdental fricative
l. water - /w/ - voiced labiovelar glide (approximant)

Exercise 2

a. voiced alveolar liquid - /l/ - words will vary
b. voiceless glottal fricative - /h/ - words will vary (note that no word ends in /h/ in English)
c. voiced velar stop - /g/ - words will vary
d. voiced bilabial nasal - /m/ - words will vary
e. voiceless alveolar stop - /t/ - words will vary

Exercise 3

I refuse to accept the view that mankind is so tragically bound to the starless midnight of racism and war that the bright daybreak of peace and brotherhood can never become a reality... I believe that unarmed truth and unconditional love will have the final word.

> aɪ rɪˈfjuz tʊ ækˈsɛpt ðə vju ðət ˈmænˈkaɪnd əz soʊ ˈtræʤɪkli baʊnd tə ðə ˈstɑrləs ˈmɪdˌnaɪt əv
> ˈreɪˌsɪzəm ənd wɔr ðət ðə braɪt ˈdeɪˌbreɪk əv pis ənd ˈbrʌðərˌhʊd kən ˈnɛvər bɪˈkʌm ə ˌriˈæləˌti...
> aɪ bɪˈliv ðət əˈnɑrmd truθ ənd ˌʌnkənˈdɪʃənəl lʌv wɪl həv ðə ˈfaɪnəl wɜrd.

As seen from the provided phonemic transcription, the quote includes all the seven alveolar sounds of English - /t/, /d/, /s/, /z/, /n/, /l/, and /ɹ/.

Exercise 4

a. /n/ and /ŋ/ - No. These sounds do not share the same place and manner of articulation.

b. /k/ and /g/ - Yes. Both are velar stops. Example minimal pair: *coal* and *goal*

c. /f/ and /v/ - Yes. Both are labiodental fricatives. Example minimal pair: *fail* and *veil*

d. /j/ and /h/ - No. These sounds do not share the same place and manner of articulation.

e. /s/ and /z/ - Yes. Both are alveolar fricatives. Example minimal pair: *seal* and *zeal*

f. /ʃ/ and /tʃ/ - No. These sounds do not share the same place and manner of articulation.

g. /tʃ/ and /dʒ/ - Yes. Both are palatal affricates. Example minimal pair: *chain* and *Jane*

h. /t/ and /d/ - Yes. Both are alveolar stops. Example minimal pair: *till* and *dill*

i. /l/ and /ʒ/ - No. These sounds do not share the same place and manner of articulation.

j. /θ/ and /s/ - No. These sounds do not share the same place and manner of articulation.

Despite sharing the same place and manner of articulation, consonants can still be distinct phonemes based on their voicing feature or classification according to voicing. For example, from the above sound pairs that share the same place and manner of articulation (/k/ and /g/, /f/ and /v/, /s/ and /z/, etc.), the first one is voiceless while the second is voiced.

Exercise 5

There can be a limitless number of combinations depending on what articulatory feature you would like to emphasize. For example, in order to demonstrate the contrast of voicing feature, you can pair *cane* and *gain* both of which contain velar stops, *feign* and *vein* that include labiodental fricatives, *chain* and *Jane* that start with palatal affricates, etc. To show the difference based on the place and manner of articulation, you can use the minimal pairs *vein* (labiodental fricative) and *wain* (labiovelar glide), *main* (bilabial nasal) and *rain* (alveolar liquid), etc. Teaching consonants using minimal pairs will benefit students from different language backgrounds. For instance, providing the minimal pair *lane-rain* and explicitly explaining the articulatory differences between /l/ and /ɹ/ would be very beneficial for the Japanese learners of English. Similarly, the Arabic learners of English would greatly benefit from the use of the minimal pairs *pain-bane* and *vein-wain* since these are the consonants that cause problems for the English learners with Arabic as the primary language.

Chapter 12

Exercise 1
    a.   high, front, tense, unrounded
    b.   low, front, lax, unrounded
    c.   high, back, lax, rounded
    d.   mid, central, lax, unrounded
    e.   mid, front, tense, unrounded

Exercise 2
    a)   /ɪ/   b) /u/   c) /ɑ/   d) /o/   e) /ɛ/

Exercise 3
    a)   /ɛ/   b) /ɑ/   c) /u/   d) /e/   e) /ɪ/

Exercise 4: Answers will vary.

Exercise 5
    coat, face, how, joy, my

Exercise 6
    a)   b**a**nana   b) com**e**t   c) sod**a**   d) **o**ver   e) c**o**mpare

Exercise 7
    a)   /ʌ/ - duck   b) /i/ - keep   c) /ɛ/ - red

Exercise 8
    a)   sit   b) fled (recall that /e/ is monophthongal before 'r')   c) shout

Exercise 9
    /i/, /ɪ/, /e/, /u/, /ʊ/, /o/

Exercise 10
While languages with three or fewer vowels are not common, vowel systems tend to distribute vowels as widely and equally as possible across the vowel space in order to maximize the acoustic distinction between those vowels. Therefore, a language with only three vowel phonemes may use high front /i/, high back /u/, and a low vowel such as /a/. Another possibility is a three-vowel system that distinguishes vowels along the height dimension only, yielding the set of high /i/, mid /ə/, and low /a/. Somewhat less likely, since we tend to see more gradations in height distinction than backness distinction, might be a system that takes advantage of backness only, yielding a set like front /i/ or /e/, central /ɨ/ or /ə/, and back /u/ or /o/. Other configurations are possible; the key is maximal dispersion of vowels across the vowel space, utilizing the two most common dimensions of height and backness to denote the contrasts. A three-vowel system is highly unlikely to feature three vowels clustered together in one part of the vowel space and distinguished only by less common features such as rounding or tenseness (e.g., the set /i/, /y/, and /ɪ/).

Chapter 13

Exercise 1

/t/ in American English

From the given data, here are the distributions of the three allophones:

[tʰ]   appears word-initially and word-medially when the following syllable is stressed

[t]   appears after an /s/ in the same syllable, word-initially when the following syllable is not stressed, and word-finally

[ɾ]   appears word-medially when the following syllable is not stressed

Exercise 2

t vs *th* in Indian English

The pairs provided are minimal pairs: words differing in one sound, but with different meanings. While the Indian English speakers are using different initial sounds compared to American English speakers, they are making the same number of distinctions. Their phonemic system contains /ʈ/ and / t̪ʰ/, while American English has /t/ and /θ/.

The Indian English word-initial allophone for /ʈ/ is an unaspirated voiceless retroflex stop [ʈ], while American English has an aspirated [tʰ] in that position. This could cause misunderstandings, as American English listeners tend to hear unaspirated stops as voiced and might mishear *taught* as *dot*. For the *th*, the Indian English speakers' use of the aspirated dental stop [t̪ʰ] in initial position may be confused with American English aspirated alveolar stop [tʰ] used in initial position, and might hear *thought* as *taught*.

Exercise 3

[ð] in Spanish vs. English

The [ð] in Spanish appears in complementary distribution with their [d̪]. In this data, [ð] appears only between vowels and word-finally, while [d̪] appears only word-initially and after the nasal [n]. As these are phonetically similar sounds in complementary distribution, they are allophones of the same phoneme for Spanish speakers.

Using this knowledge, we can predict some of the difficulties Spanish speakers are likely to encounter when learning English, which uses [ð] and [d̪] as allophones of distinct phonemes. In intervocalic position and word-finally, Spanish speakers may have difficulty producing a stop, since in Spanish the fricative allophone [ð] appears there. In word-initial position and after nasals, Spanish speakers may have difficulty producing the fricative [ð], as only the stop appears in those positions. Similarly, perceiving the difference between these sounds in unexpected positions could be more difficult. Pronunciation practice and dictation exercises can focus on words that place these sounds in new positions for Spanish speaking learners of English.

Exercise 4

The nouns in each row are stressed on the first syllable, while the verbs are stressed on the second. Each pair seems to consist of the same phonemes, but the allophones of the vowels are often different due to the differing location of stress. For example, in *project*$_{verb}$ [pɹə'ʤɛ̆kt] vs. *project*$_{noun}$ ['pɹɑ̆ʤɛ̆kt], we see that the first vowel of the verb is phonetically [ə] while the first vowel of the noun is [ɔ]. In other examples as well, the first vowel of the verb, which is unstressed, is some form of [ə], while the first vowel of the noun has various qualities, such as [ɔ], [a], [ɛ], or [æ], suggesting that the schwa is an allophone of all these vowels in unstressed position. You can also observe the aspiration of voiceless stops in stressed position vs. their unaspirated allophones in syllables without stress. In a word pair such as *content*_{verb} [kənˈtʰɛ̃nt] vs. *content*_{noun} [ˈkʰɑ̃ntɛ̃nt], the /k/ and /t/ at the beginning of each syllable have different allophones in each word. At the beginning of a stressed syllable, the allophone of the voiceless stops are aspirated, while at the beginning of an unstressed syllable, the allophones are unaspirated.

Exercise 5

//**in-**//

- a. There are four allomorphs given for this morpheme. In the data, they have the following distributions:

  /ɪn/ appears before words that begin with a vowel, an h, or an alveolar consonant.

  /ɪm/ appears before words beginning with a bilabial stop (/p/, /b/)

  /ɪŋ/ appears before words beginning with a velar stops (/k/, /g/)

  /ɪ/ appears before words beginning with nasal stops (/m/, /n/) or approximants (/l/, /ɹ/)

- b. The spelling does reflect the pronunciation of the /in/ allomorph before vowels, h, and alveolars, and the /im/ allomorph before bilabial stops. The spelling remains *in-*, however, before velars, despite the pronunciation as /ɪŋ/. In the final case, when pronounced as /ɪ/, the spelling does reflect the loss of the nasal from the prefix before /l, ɹ/. In these words, as in the words beginning with nasal stops, the word-initial consonant appears doubled in the spelling, despite the fact that there is only one consonant in the pronunciation. This probably reflects the history of the words, with the prefix final /n/ becoming identical to a following nasal or approximant, and then the sequence of two consonants being simplified to one.

- c. The understanding of the allomorphy might be used in explaining how to pronounce the words based on their spelling. Learners can be warned that the /n/ is pronounced as [ŋ] before velar stops, and that the doubled consonants in the spellings are not pronounced as long consonants. The understanding of the allomorphy might also help in word-recognition and comprehension, as the recognition that the prefix meaning 'not' can have multiple forms may help learners parse out the meanings of new words that begin with one of the allormorphs of /-in/.

Chapter 14

Exercise 1

- a. /n/
- b. /i, e, u, o/ (/ɑ/ may be included)
- c. /t, d, ɾ, θ, ð, s, z, n, l, ɹ/
- d. /l, ɹ, j, w/
- e. /v, ð, z, ʒ /
- f. /t, d, ɾ/
- g. /æ/
- h. /e, ɛ, ə, ʌ, o, ɔ/

Exercise 2

a. $\begin{bmatrix} +cons \\ +nas \end{bmatrix}$ b. $\begin{bmatrix} +cont \\ +cor \\ +ant \\ +dis \end{bmatrix}$ c. $\begin{bmatrix} +cont \\ +son \\ -tri \end{bmatrix}$ d. $\begin{bmatrix} -cons \\ +rd \end{bmatrix}$

/m, n, ŋ/   /θ, ð/   /l, ɹ, j, w/   /u, ʊ, o, ɔ /

Exercise 3

a. Semi-formal: $\emptyset \rightarrow \varepsilon \ / \ \# \, s \underline{\hspace{1cm}}$

Formal:
$$\emptyset \rightarrow \begin{bmatrix} +\text{dor} \\ -\text{hi} \\ -\text{lo} \\ -\text{bk} \\ -\text{tns} \end{bmatrix} / \# \begin{bmatrix} +\text{cont} \\ -\text{vd} \\ +\text{cor} \\ -\text{dis} \end{bmatrix} \underline{\hspace{1cm}}$$

The semi-formal expression is preferred; the complex formal expression does not explain why [ɛ] is epenthesized.

This is a transfer from Spanish. In NAE, /ɛ/ cannot be epenthesized before the initial *s-*.

b. Semi-formal: b, d, g, v, ð, z, ʒ, dʒ -> [-vd] / \underline{\hspace{1cm}}#

Formal:
$$\begin{bmatrix} +\text{cons} \\ +\text{vd} \\ -\text{son} \end{bmatrix} \rightarrow \begin{bmatrix} +\text{cons} \\ -\text{vd} \\ -\text{son} \end{bmatrix} / \underline{\hspace{1cm}}\#$$

(Note: The allophone /ɾ/ is never word-final and should be excluded from consideration.)

The formal expression is preferred; it precisely shows that [+vd] is realized as [-vd].

This rule deviates from the NAE phonological rule because NAE voiced obstruents are devoiced at the end of an utterance but not at the end of a word.

c. Semi-formal: i, e, u, o -> ɪ, ɛ, ʊ, ɔ / \underline{\hspace{1cm}} m, n, ŋ

Formal:
$$\begin{bmatrix} +\text{dor} \\ +\text{tns} \end{bmatrix} \rightarrow \begin{bmatrix} +\text{dor} \\ -\text{tns} \end{bmatrix} / \underset{[+\text{stress}]}{\underline{\hspace{1cm}}} \begin{bmatrix} +\text{cons} \\ +\text{nas} \end{bmatrix} \sigma$$

The formal expression is preferred; it captures the generalization more precisely in terms of tenseness.

This is an interlanguage rule by speakers whose native language does not lengthen vowels before a coda nasal. It deviates from the NAE vowel lengthening rule.

Exercise 4

a. */-st/ ## /ʃ-/: the best shank; the best shoe.* In both examples, /t/ is deleted first and then the [-ant, +dis] features of /ʃ/ are regressively assimilated into /s/ and change /s/ to [ʃ].

b. */-nd/ ## /m-/: They'll atten̲d m̲y tea ceremony,* or *We'll atten̲d m̲ore conferences.* In both utterances, /d/ is deleted first and then the [+lab] feature of /m/ is regressively assimilated into /n/ and changes /n/ to [m].

c. */-n/ ## /ð-/: Ca̲n̲ t̲h̲ey come?* In this example, the features [+son, -cont, +nas, -stri] of /n/ are progressively assimilated to /ð-/ with features [-son, +cont, -nas, +stri] and changes /ð-/ to [n].

d.   /-d/ ## /j-/: <u>Did your</u> *dog run away?* In this example, the [+dor] feature of /j/ causes the [+ant, -dis] features of /d/ to become [-ant, +dis] of [ʤ], thus [ʤɚ].

e.   /-t/ ## /j-/: *Please tell him that you're here.* In this example, the [+dor] feature of /j/ causes the [+ant, -dis] features of /t/ to become [-ant, +dis] of [ʧ], thus, [ʧɚ].

Exercise 5

		Could	you	hand	Gregogy	this	shutter,	please?	
a. Phonemic (UR):	/	kʊd	ju	hænd	ɡɹégɑɹi	ðɪs	ʃʌ́təɹ	pliz	/
b. Phonetic (SR):	[	kʰʊ ʤ ə	hæ̃ːŋØ	ɡɹéɡɹi	ðɪʃ	ʃʌ́ɾɚ	pʰʎí:s	]

c.   From left to right:
1.   Aspiration in *could* and *please*
2.   Coalescent assimilation between /d/ in *could* and /j/ in *you*, resulting in [ʤ]
3.   Vowel reduction of /u/ to /ə/ in *you*
4.   Vowel nasalization in *hand* influenced by /n/
5.   Vowel lengthening in *hand* influenced by /n/
6.   Consonant /d/ deletion in *hand*
7.   Regressive partial assimilation of /n/ to [ŋ] conditioned by the following initial [g]
8.   Medial schwa deletion in *Gregory*
9.   Regressive total assimilation of /s/ to [ʃ] in *this* conditioned by the following initial /ʃ/
10.   /t/ realized as a flap ɾ in *shutter*
11.   /ə/ colored by the following /ɹ/ in *shutter*, resulting in ɚ
12.   Aspiration in *please*
13.   /l/ devoiced to [l̥] after the voiceless stop /p/
14.   Vowel lengthening in in *please* influenced by the voiced /z/
15.   /z/ devoiced to /s/ at the end of the utterance

d.   Categories of phonological rules activated:
1.   Aspiration (activated twice)
2.   Assimilation (thrice)
3.   Vowel reduction (once)
4.   Vowel nasalization (once)
5.   Vowel lengthening (twice)
6.   Deletion (twice: consonant and schwa)
7.   Flapping (once)
8.   /ɹ/-coloring (once)
9.   Devoicing (twice, in onset and coda)

e.   Ordered Rule Applications
1.   The stop /d/ in *hand* is deleted first in the context of –CC + C- so that /n/ abuts /g/; then the [+dor] feature in /g/ erases the [-dor] feature in /n/ and assimilates /n/ to [ŋ] so that both [ŋ] and [g] share the [+dor] feature, easing pronunciation.
2.   The vowel lengthening rule in *please* occurs first to show the effect of the voiced /z/ before /z/ is devoiced since it is utterance-final.

Chapter 15

Exercise 1
L1 Mandarin learners have trouble discriminating tense-lax vowel pairs (Lai, 2010). They tend to perceive both tense and lax vowels as being tense, reflecting their L1 perceptual category.

Exercise 2
L1 Japanese learners seem to rely primarily on duration to distinguish tense and lax vowels (Morrison, 2002). Because this is not the primary difference between the two types of vowels, however, this may lead to an inability to distinguish the two in certain contexts.

Exercise 3
The epenthetic vowel /e/ will likely be inserted at the beginning of the word in perception to form /estrɔŋ/, and this will be reflected in production (Freeman, Blumenfeld, & Marian, 2016).

Exercise 4
L1 Japanese learners of English tend to rely more on pitch changes to show lexical stress (Aoyama & Guion, 2007). Duration, amplitude, and vowel reduction, which are not part of Japanese pitch-accent, are not used to the same extent as by English native speakers.

Exercise 5
There is evidence that L1 German learners do have difficulty distinguishing between such words (O'Dell & Port, 1983), even though voiced and voiceless stops are present in German. The L1 phonological process responsible may remain active in L2 perception.

Chapter 16

Exercise 1
All words follow patterns in the table.
  a. Photography: Stress on 3rd syllable from last
  b. Photographic: Stress on 2nd syllable from last
  c. Possible: Stress on first syllable
  d. Possibility: Stress on 3rd syllable from last
  e. Informative: Stress on 3rd syllable from last
  f. Information: Stress on 2nd syllable from last

First, we think of rules basically as statements of patterns. Although words that share a common suffix, such as -tion, -ity and other Latin derivations tend to share similar stress patterns, it is nonetheless up to the learner to learn the form of the word, its meaning, and its use on an item-by-item basis, and associate it with an already known rule. Second, words that do not fall into common, Latin-derived patterns are highly problematic and necessarily must be learned on an item-by-item basis. There may some groups of words that can be grouped under one rule or another, but at some point, there are too many rules to manage declaratively (focus on form) when learners are focused on communication (focus on meaning).

Exercise 2
1. For voiced-voiceless contrasts, learners can put their fingers on their or the teacher's vocal chords while the words are being pronounced. Do this first while isolating the phoneme and then do it in the context of the syllable and then the word.
2. For affricate-fricative contrasts, learners can use their hand or tissue paper to demonstrate airflow visually, first while isolating the phoneme and then in the context of the syllable and then the word.
3. Words selected for practice should ideally be linked to the content area.

Exercise 3
Answers will vary. One suggestion would be isolation, followed by backward build-up.

Practice the troublesome sequence at the syllable or even the blend level. Then practice the full word in isolation. Then increasingly add words in front of the target word, and ultimately after the target word, ideally working toward some idiomatic sequence: my friend, with my friend, out with my friend, going out with my friend, going out with my friend tomorrow, etc.

Exercise 4
> *Mary, had, little, lamb, fleece, white, snow*
> *Every-where, Mary, went, lamb, sure, go.*

When unstressed, English vowels tend to reduce to schwa.

Exercise 5: Answers will vary.

Chapter 17

Exercise 1: Answers will vary.
Exercise 2: Answers will vary.
Exercise 3: Answers will vary.

Exercise 4

British	**American**
Aubergine	Eggplant
Draughts	Checkers
Lorry	Truck
Nappies	Diapers
Queue	Line
Solicitors	Lawyers
Trainers	Sneakers
Trolley	Shopping cart

Exercise 5: Answers will vary.

Glossary

Abstract Meaning: Literal or dictionary meaning; what a word, a phrase, or a sentence could mean independently of the context.

Acoustic Phonetics: The study of the physical properties of speech sounds.

Active Articulator: The speech organ that actively moves during the production of a speech sound, such as the lips and the tongue.

Active Voice: The voice that indicates the subject is the actor of the action denoted by the verb.

Adjective: A class of words that describes a noun or a pronoun.

Adverb: A class of words that indicate manner, location, time frequency, and intensity. Adverbs can modify verbs, adjectives, or other adverbs.

Affix: A bound morpheme that is added to a stem or root either at the beginning, the end, or at a predictable place in the middle. When attached to a word, affixes add a new meaning or grammatical function to that word (see circumfix, infix, prefix, and suffix).

Age Grading: A linguistic pattern that is marked by visible differences in usage depending on the speaker's age.

Allomorph: An alternative pronunciation of a single morpheme in context; typically referring to differences that are phonemic.

Allophone: The pronunciation of a phoneme in a specific context.

Alternations: Variations in syntactic structure theoretically linked to the lexical semantics of a verb, as related semantic interpretations map onto distinct syntactic structures. Examples include the dative alternation (e.g., *give X to Y / give YX*), the locative alternation (e.g., *spray X onto Y / spray Y with X*), and the causative alternation (e.g., *X breaks Y / Y breaks*).

Ambiguity: The property of being capable of multiple clear-cut interpretations (as opposed to 'vagueness', where no clear-cut interpretation is possible). Linguists distinguish lexical ambiguity, where words such as *bank* may have multiple meanings, from structural ambiguity, where phrases or sentences may be assigned two or more tree structures yielding different meanings.

Antonyms: Words with opposite meanings.

Aphesis: The loss of a sound at the beginning of a word.

Apocope: The loss of a sound at the end of a word.

Applied Linguistics: The field that uses linguistic theories and methods in order to address practical questions that are language-related.

Argument (of a verb): A syntactic position that is lexically associated with the proper use of a particular verb. English verbs generally require a subject argument; transitive verbs require both subject and object arguments; ditransitive verbs are associated with three arguments, one of which is housed in either an NP or PP (e.g., *Mary gave John the ball* vs. *Mary gave the ball to John*).

Argument Structure: The lexical semantic representation of a predicate (e.g., verb, preposition) containing information about the types of elements with it must typically appear (e.g., subject, object, indirect object) such that the semantic representation can determine possible syntactic structures.

Articulation: The physical operation of the components of the vocal system, including the lungs, vocal cords, tongue, and so on, to produce speech sounds.

Articulatory Phonetics: Subfield of phonetics, concerned primarily with aspects related to the articulation and categorization of speech sounds, including the speech organs and their use in the production of speech sounds in the vocal tract.

Aspect: Grammaticalized form of the temporal view of the event or state, marked on or by the verb. The status of whether an action is ongoing or completed, whether it occurs just once or repeatedly, and how this action relates to other actions.

Auditory Phonetics: The study of the perception of speech sounds by humans.

Auxiliary Verb: A verb that accompanies a content verb and carries inflectional morphology such as tense and aspect.

Awareness-Raising Tasks: Tasks based on the noticing hypothesis and intended to help learners notice and understand the relationship between a grammatical form and its contextual meaning.

Back Vowel: Vowel produced with the tongue bunched up near the back of the mouth.

Back-Formation: A process of derivation in which a shorter form is derived from a longer form in such a way as to make the shorter form appear to be the origin of the longer one. The noun ***emotion*** predated the recently back-formed verb *to emote*.

Binary Feature: A distinctive feature whose positive and negative values are both made use of in phonological structure.

Binding: The syntactic relationship between a pronoun/noun and its antecedent. In the sentence *Elena asked Petra to give her more water*, the pronoun *her* refers to *Elena*, which means *Elena* is the antecedent of *her*. *Elena* binds *her*, which is indicated by the coindexation of *Elena* and *her*. By contrast, in the sentence *Elena gave her more water*, the pronoun *her* cannot refer to *Elena*, which means *Elena* cannot bind *her*.

Blending: The combining of two words into one, accompanied by the loss of syllables in one or both original words; cf. *brunch* originating as a blend of *breakfast* and *lunch*.

Borrowing: The process of adopting a word from the vocabulary of one language into the vocabulary of another, either consciously or accidentally through trade or other linguistic interaction between cultural groups.

Bound Morpheme: A morpheme which cannot exist on its own as a word; a morpheme which requires attachment to a root or stem for its proper use and interpretation.

Bound Root: A root which cannot stand on its own as a free morpheme but requires an affix for interpretation.

Branch: A vertical or diagonal line drawn between two nodes that represents the hierarchical relationship between the nodes.

Case Marking: The process of adding an affix to a noun to indicate grammatical relations (such as subject, direct object, or indirect object). Also called *declension.*

Categorical Perception: The mental phenomenon whereby stimuli are perceived as belonging to distinct categories.

Central Vowel: Vowel produced with the tongue in a neutral position, at an intermediate distance between the front and central tongue positions

Chain Shift: A shift of dialect features that occurs in a predictable order, where the movement of each "link" in the chain causes the movement of later links to follow it.

Circumfix: A type of affix which consists of both a prefix and a suffix.

Clause: A pairing of subject and predicate, where the predicate and subject share a mother node.

Clipping: The process of reducing the number of syllables of a word to create a shortened form that is more convenient to use.

Code-Switching: Moving back and forth between two languages throughout the course of a conversation.

Cognate: A morpheme that shares a similar form and meaning between two languages.

Coherence: Connection achieved by relating a stretch of language to the context when interpreting it as a text that makes sense.

Cohesion: Connections or links that exist in a stretch of language and hold the stretch of language together. Cohesion helps to identify a stretch of language as a text.

Cohesive Devices: Language features that help to establish links across words and sentences

Coinage: The creative formation of an entirely new free morpheme (=word) subject only to the requirements of the sound system of a language.

Collocation: The way certain words frequently appear together, often in a certain order, e.g., the word "unforeseen" regularly collocates with the word "circumstances"

Communicative Competence: A language user's ability to engage in linguistic interactions with the appropriate social conventions established by their speech community.

Competence: A speaker's implicit knowledge of their native language(s).

Complement: A phrase which is the lexically specified sister to a syntactic head; traditionally, a constituent that 'completes the meaning' of a verb by adding necessary material after the verb such as a direct object.

Complementary Distribution: In phonology, a distribution of sounds in distinct sets of environments, so that where one appears, the other does not; sounds never appear in contrast in the same position. In morphology and syntax, two elements that are of the same general type but that never occur together in precisely the same place in a word or sentence (for example, *can* and the suffix *–s* are in 'complementary distribution'; i.e., where one appears, the other is always absent).

Compositionality: The principle of meaning buildup that says that smaller meanings combine to create more specialized meanings.

Compound: A combination of two or more free morphemes that combine to create a single word. When the number of free morphemes exceeds two, it may be called a *complex compound*.

Comprehensibility: "Perception of the interlocutor as to how easy or difficult the speaker is to understand" (O'Neal, 2010, p. 70).

Concatenation: The sequential placement of items adjacent to each other, with no regard to any hierarchical relationships among them.

Conditionals: Structures in which the truth value of a clause depends on the truth of the clause that states the condition, i.e., the *if*-clause.

Conjunction: A closed class of words which connect words, phrases, and clauses.

Connotation: Suggestive meaning, the associations that are called up by a word, e.g., *lion* suggests bravery in many people's mind, but connotation can be cultural

Consonant: A phoneme the production of which involves some obstruction of the airflow in the vocal tract.

Constituent: A node, together with all branches and nodes which stem from it, taken as a unit.

Content Verb: A verb with semantic content that belongs to an open class.

Content Words: An open class of free morphemes consisting of nouns, verbs, adjectives, and adverbs.

Context: A concept that involves verbal and non-verbal cues, audience, cultural knowledge, and communicative purposes. In pragmatics, a distinction is made between *linguistic context*, which encompasses the actual sounds and words uttered by speakers and hearers, and *situational context*, which involves extralinguistic aspects of the conversation, including setting, place, persons, and activity. In other words, context refers to the linguistic and non-linguistic environments in which a piece of language occurs, or to circumstances which affect the production of the text by a writer/speaker and the reception of the text by reader/listener.

Contextual Meaning: A possible interpretation (or interpretations) of a word, a phrase, or a sentence in a given physical and linguistic context.

Continuity View of Language Evolution: It asserts that the differences between human language and the communication systems of other primates are a matter of degree of complexity. The continuity view stands in contrast to the discontinuity view, which considers the capacity for human language to have occurred in a qualitative evolutionary leap.

Contrastive Analysis Hypothesis: A prediction that only differences between the L1 and the L2 need to be learned because they are what cause learning difficulties.

Contrastive Analysis: The systematic comparison of languages with regard to structurally comparable features of those languages. Also refers (usually in caps) to a program of research in the 1950s and 1960s in which the identification of differences and similarities between languages was believed capable of predicting the ease or difficulty of learning of foreign or second languages.

Control Constructions: Constructions where a subordinate syntactic argument is missing and needs to be interpreted as being the same as a superordinate argument. A typical example of a control construction is that a superordinate verb—a so-called control verb—determines the understood subject of a subordinate verb. Control verbs can be divided into subject control verbs and object control verbs. Subject control verbs determine that the subject of the control verb is interpreted as the subject of the subordinate verb. For example, in the sentence *Gary promised Steven to wash the car*, the subject of *promised* (*Gary*) is the subject of *wash*. Object control verbs determine that the object of the control verb is interpreted as the subject of the subordinate verb. For example, in the sentence *Gary persuaded Steven to wash the car*, the object of *persuaded* (*Steven*) is the subject of *wash*.

Conversational Implicature: The meaning of an utterance as interpreted by a listener (or reader).

Conversion: A change in part of speech of a lexical item that is not accompanied by the addition or deletion of any part of that item, as the verb *clone* might be adopted as a new noun *(a) clone.*

Cooperative Principle: An assumption first proposed by Grice (1975) that when engaging in a conversation, humans work together to construct meaning and to avoid misunderstanding.

Coordination: The process of sister-adjoining two constituents of identical phrase type with a coordinating conjunction such as *and* between them, as *bread and cheese.*

Copula: The verb *be* in any of its forms when that verb links a subject with a predicate adjective or predicate nominal that refers to the subject.

Other verbs often called 'copular' include *become*, *turn out* (as in "the weather turned out sunny'), *end up* (as in 'Our plan ended up a failure'). In traditional grammar, referred to as linking verbs.

Count Noun: A noun which can be counted and which exists in both singular and plural forms.

Counterfactual: The form of expression of the antecedent and consequent marks them as imagined, nonfactual states or events.

Covert Prestige: Earning acclaim by flaunting societal norms – for example, swearing and being intimidating to appear powerful and confident.

Creative Construction Process: The error-prone process underlying the acquisition of new form-meaning-use connections (e.g., words, morphosyntactic patterns and their situations of use)

Critical Discourse Analysis (CDA): Discourse analysis with critical goals to examine why and how certain language features are used in a text, and what possible ideologies and power relations in a society they express, reinforce or challenge.

Critical Period Hypothesis: It suggests that full native competence in a language is only achievable if the language is acquired by the age of adolescence.

Deductive Teaching: A form of explicit instruction in which the teacher presents some target language rules or norms and then creates opportunities for learners to practice. Deductive teaching is often associated with traditional, teacher-centered teaching practices.

Derivation: The creation of a new word through the attachment of a derivational affix to a stem.

Design Features of Language: Nine characteristics of communication systems first identified by Charles Hockett, who proposed that all nine are needed in order for a communication system to be considered language.

Determiner: A closed class of words which modify nouns and help to limit what those nouns refer to. Determiners consist of possessive determiners, demonstratives, articles, and quantifiers.

Diachronic: Literally, 'through time'; any study involving the development of words, sounds, or grammatical constructions over time.

Diphthong: Vowels characterized by change in quality resulting from change in tongue position or lip rounding from the beginning to the end of a single vowel.

Direct Object: An NP, the right sister of V and NP daughter of V'.

Discontinuity View of Language Evolution: It asserts that human language is the result of an evolutionary leap, a single mutation that set human language apart from the communication systems of other species. The discontinuity view stands in contrast to the continuity view, which proposes that the differences between human language and the communication systems of other primates are quantitative, a matter of degree of complexity.

Discourse Analysis: The systematic study of language in context.

Discourse Markers: Words such as *well, so, anyway* that signal links or boundaries between parts of a text.

Discourse: A term used to describe language in use and how the purposes, participants, environments, processes, etc. of interactions play a role in the construction of texts.

Discourse-Based Approach: A language teaching and learning approach that aims to help learners develop knowledge of how to use linguistic resources appropriately to produce extended, cohesive and coherent texts to make meaning and achieve a social goal.

Distinctive Feature: An articulatory or acoustic property as a building block of segments that specifies a natural class of sounds.

Ditransitive: The lexical property of verbs that are lexically specified to take two complements.

Ellipsis: Leaving out certain words of a sentence but the sentence can still be understood

Elsewhere Allophone: A term used to describe an allophone which appears in the default contexts, those contexts not attributed to other allophones.

Embedded Clause: A subordinate clause within another clause as a constituent of that clause that functions as a noun, adjective, or an adverb.

Endocentricity: The syntactic requirement that every phrase XP have a head X that is of the same category as XP.

Enhanced Input: Linguistic material to which learners are exposed in which certain forms are given non-natural prominence as through bold-facing, italicizing (for written texts) or increased loudness, added length, or raised pitch (for oral production), where the purpose of the added prominence is to promote language acquisition through noticing.

Environment Bar: A line in a specified environment that locates a segment undergoing an alternation.

Environment: A phonetic context that triggers phonological alternations.

Error: Systematic deviations from the target-like norms of the second language.

Etymology: The study of the history and development of individual words.

Event Time: Time that the event denoted by the verb happens.

Face: One's public self-image and how it is maintained in interaction with others.

Feature Reassembly: The hypothesis that the acquisition of L2 grammar involves reorganizing syntactically relevant features from items in the L1 into new configurations, sometimes on different types of lexical items. This account stems from the assumption in linguistic theory that much of language variation can be explained by the presence or absence of syntactic, phonological and semantic features in lexical items.

First Language Acquisition: The process through which children acquire the rules and vocabulary of their native language.

Force of an Utterance: The meaning of a word, a phrase, or a sentence as intended by the speaker (or writer).

Fossilization: Cessation of development in some or all linguistic subsystems despite adequate exposure or intention to learn.

Free Morpheme: A morpheme which could, on its own, constitute an individual word.

Free Variation: Variant pronunciations of a phoneme in the same context, not capable of changing meaning.

Front Vowel: Vowel produced with the tongue pushed relatively forward in the mouth.

Full Transfer/Full Access Hypothesis: A position that holds that the starting point for learning a L2 is the L1; when the L1 does not help, learners' innate university grammar comes to assistance.

Function Words: A closed class of free morphemes which represent grammatical relationships in a sentence. They include auxiliary verbs, conjunctions, determiners, modals, prepositions, and pronouns.

Future Tense: The tense that refers to a time after the moment of utterance.

Genres: Ways of achieving distinct social purposes through the use of particular language forms.

Grammatical Cohesion: Links established through the use of grammatical features such as pronouns and conjunctions.

Habitual Aspect: Grammatical expression of repeated events.

Head: A word-level element that represents the center of a phrase and is placed in a terminal node.

Head-First, Head-Last: The predominant direction of branching in a language. If heads are on the left, the language is 'head-first'; if heads are on the right, the language is 'head-last'.

Hierarchical Diffusion: The spread of a dialect feature by moving from large cities to other nearby, highly populated areas.

Hierarchical Organization: Organization according to the principle that larger units are built up from smaller units which may include intermediate units as well; the result is a top-to-bottom organizational scheme. In syntax, this organization is realized as a tree.

Hierarchy: The property of trees that involves branching into nodes; lower nodes are said to be hierarchically below higher nodes.

High Vowel: Vowel produced with the tongue close to the roof of the mouth.

Hyponyms: Words which have a "type-of" relationship. The meaning of one word represents a member of a class represented by the meaning of the other word.

Illocutionary Force: The speaker's intention and its effect on the hearer when producing an utterance during interaction in context.

Imperative Mood: Mood that expresses orders, commands, or permissions.

Imperfective Aspect: Grammaticalization of an ongoing event or state. It expresses the internal structure of an event or state.

Implicature: The speaker's act of meaning or implicating one thing by saying something else.

Impossible Condition: An event or state that is dependent on a condition that is not impossible; that is, it is not possible for that state or event to be true.

Improbable Condition: An event or state that is dependent on a condition that is not probable; that is, it is not probable for that state or event to be true.

Indicative Mood: Mood that expresses factual events or states possible in the actual world.

Inductive Teaching: Discovery-based explicit teaching in which learners analyze input and attempt to formulate some generalizations about the target language.

Inference: Knowledge and information about the world drawn on by the listener or reader to create connections and arrive at interpretations which are not actually expressed by the words.

Infix: A type of affix which is inserted into the middle of a word.

Inflection: The formation of a word by the addition of an inflectional affix to a stem.

Input: Any target language, both spoken and written, that learners are exposed to.

Input-Output Rule: A formal rule written with an input on the left, an output on the right, and an arrow pointing from left to right, that represents the breakdown of constituents in a sentence.

Instrumental Motivation: An L2 learner's motivation by a specific, functional goal such as getting a job, passing a test, or entering college.

Intake: Language that becomes internalized by a learner based on the available input.

Integrative Motivation: A learner's motivation by wanting to operate within a culture, with an emphasis on daily life – carrying on conversation, doing business, running a home, etc.

Intelligibility: A measure of speaking ability that considers the extent to which another listener can understand. Contrasts with nativeness.

Intercultural Communicative Competence: Knowledge of social products and practices from another culture and ability to critically evaluate and negotiate perspectives of one's own and other cultures.

Interjection: An open class of words which express emotion.

Internal Grammar: A speakers' implicit grammatical knowledge of their native language(s). It is a cognitive ability acquired in childhood and stored in people's minds, encompassing syntactic rules.

International Phonetic Alphabet (IPA): A system of phonetic transcription published in 1888 by the International Phonetic Association in France.

Intransitive Verb: A verb which does not take an object.

Item-Based Learning: Learning proceeds conservatively on an item-by-item basis, rather than in an all-or-nothing rule-based manner.

Language Universal: A common structural or lexical feature of a statistically significant sample of languages.

Language: A method of human communication consisting of the use of words or signs in a structured way in order to convey meaning. The word *language* is also used to mean the particular system of communication used by a community, such as English or American Sign Language.

Lax Vowel: Vowels produced with an overall lesser muscular effort; often more centralized, and shorter in duration, than their tense counterparts.

Lexical Cohesion: Links created through the repetition of words or the use of words which are related in meanings in a stretch of language.

Lexical Item: Words stored in the mental lexicon are termed lexical items. In linguistic theory, lexical items include not only words in a traditional sense, but also lexical items below the word-level (e.g., morphemes) and above the word-level (e.g., idioms) that are stored in long-term memory.

Lexical Meaning: Referring to the meaning that has content and that refers to things, as opposed to grammatical meaning.

Lexical Relations: The types of semantic relationship between lexical items, e.g., homonymy, polysemy, synonymy, antonymy, hyponymy, meronymy, etc.

Lexical Rule: A rule whose input is a terminal node and whose output is an actual lexical morpheme such as a noun, verb, or adjective.

Lexical Stress: The use of volume, pitch, and vowel duration to emphasize certain syllables and reduce others at the word level.

Lexicalization: (1) The state of being confined to, or formed in, the lexicon as opposed to existing in, or being formed through, grammatical processes. (2) The process by which a head becomes so closely associated with another phrase that the association is listed in the lexical entry for that head, as with the association of *make* with a direct object, or the association of *surprised* with a prepositional phrase headed by *at*.

Lexicon: The mental 'storage-chest' of morphemes, or basic forms of a language that go to make up words (and ultimately, phrases and sentences). The information provided in the lexicon approximates that found in a physical dictionary in including pronunciation, part-of-speech class, and meaning characteristics, together with any idiosyncratic restrictions on use.

Linearity: That property of syntax which specifies that one element follows another element in a syntactic representation.

Linguistic Competence: The internalized knowledge that language users have of the basic elements of language (sound, words, sentences) and the rules for combining these elements into units that enable users to express linguistic meaning. Competence can be contrasted with linguistic performance, which refers to the actual use of language in spoken, written, or signed form.

Linguistic Context: The linguistic environment such as the surrounding words, utterances, and sentences.

Linguistic Creativity: The capacity that enables language users to understand and produce original sentences that have never previously been uttered, as well as to potentially produce infinitely long sentences.

Linguistic Performance: The actual use of language in spoken, written, or signed form. Performance can be contrasted with linguistic competence, which is a language user's internalized linguistic knowledge.

Linguistic Transfer: Transfer is an interlanguage process that entails the use of L1 patterns (e.g., phonological, morphosyntactic, semantic) to communicate in the L2. There are two types: *positive transfer*, where the first language patterns are fruitfully engaged for L2 purposes, and n*egative transfer*, where the first language patterns interfere with L2 development and communication.

Linguistic Typology: A field of study that classifies and analyzes languages according to their similarities and differences in structure and organization.

Linguistic Universals: The set of features shared by all languages.

Linguistics: The scientific study of the structure and use of language.

Linking Verb: A verb that connects the subject to a subject complement, traditionally defined as a predicate adjective or noun.

Low Vowel: Vowel produced with the tongue lowered to the jaw, far from the roof of the mouth.

Markedness Differential Hypothesis: A position that claims that unmarked linguistic forms are learned before marked ones.

Mental Grammar: The internalized knowledge language users have about the units and rules of their language, including the rules for combining sounds into words (phonology), the rules of word formation (morphology), the rules for combining words into phrases and phrases into sentences (syntax), and the rules for assigning meaning (semantics).

Mental Lexicon: The system of organization of lexical items in the mind, or the mental storehouse or dictionary of words that contains information on pronunciation, meaning, written form, and so on.

Meronyms: Words which have a "part-of" relationship. The meaning of one word denotes a constituent part of something denoted by the meaning of the other word.

Mid Vowel: Vowel produced with the tongue at an intermediate distance between the roof of the mouth and the jaw

Minimal Pair: A pair of words which have different meanings in their source language and whose realization is different by only one sound.

Mistake: One-off lapses while producing language.

Mixed Conditionals: A subcategory of impossible conditions in which neither the present event or a state in the consequent clause nor the nonfactual state or event in the antecedent clause are true.

Modal: A type of verb that highlights the communicative function of a sentence such as advising, expressing ability, or requesting.

Modifier: A non-lexicalized relationship between a single-bar projection X' and another phrase. Traditionally, any expression which delimits the meaning of another expression, as in the way that *tall* might delimit the general meaning of *tree*.

Modularity: Modularity of mind is the idea that the brain contains distinct modules, with dedicated neural structures for particular functions, such as vision, hearing, and language. Each module has its own set of mental operations that are particular to the domain, and communication between modules is only at higher levels of computation. Linguistic modularity assumes distinct rules and representations for subdomains of the language faculty, such as phonology, syntax, and semantics.

Monophthong: A vowel produced with little movement or change in quality during the vowel's production.

Mood: Grammaticalization of the intent of the speaker as well as the commitment of the speaker to the truth of the proposition.

Morpheme: A basic, structurally unanalyzable linguistic form that is associated with a particular interpretation or meaning. As the smallest unit of meaning in a language, a morpheme can consist of a single letter, a group of letters, or an entire word.

Morphology: The study of morphemes and how they are used to create words and provide grammatical information.

Morphophonemic Rule: A rule focused on sound alternations that cannot be fully explained except by reference to the lexical class or morphological status of a morpheme or word.

Morpho-Syntax: The linguistic field that studies topics that involve both morphology and syntax.

Mother Node: In relation to any node, the node that is reached by tracing the path of a branch one step to the next node above it.

Multimodal: More than one mode or channel of communication used in a single text.

Nativeness: A level of pronunciation ability where a learner can produce the L2 with a natural, fluid, fluent delivery that makes pronunciation sound like s/he was born in a country where the L2 was an official language; an unrealistic bar to set for learners, because mimicking native speakers is not the sole path to intelligible speech.

Nativization: The conscious or unconscious altering of a form borrowed from another language or dialect to accord more closely with the rules or structure of the native language.

Natural Class: A class of sounds that is specified by one or more distinctive features and that undergoes phonological alternations.

Negative Evidence: The grammatically ill-formed sentences in children's input. Negative evidence informs children about what is not possible in the language that they are acquiring.

Negative Face: The need for personal freedom and detachment from others, which is accomplished through giving options and stressing the importance of one's values.

Neutralization: A loss of phonemic contrast in some phonetic contexts.

Node: The endpoint of a tree branch.

Noncount Noun: A noun which cannot be counted; a mass noun.

Non-Counterfactual: The form of expression of the antecedent and consequent marks them as possible or probable states or events.

Non-Linguistic Context: The non-linguistic environment referring to the real-world situation in which the piece of language occurs

Nonverbal Communication: A form of communication in which meaning is expressed in the form of gestures, facial expressions, body posture, and proximity during interactions.

Noticing Hypothesis: Proposed by Schmidt (1990), this hypothesis claims that acquisition of any language feature is preceded by the learner noticing this feature in the available input.

Noticing: Paying attention to a particular aspect of the language, having awareness.

Noun: An open class of words which represent people, places, things, and ideas.

Overpassivization: The phenomenon in L2 English of using passive morphology in cases where a bare intransitive verb would be expected.

Overt Prestige: Earning acclaim by following societal norms – for example, getting high grades and obeying laws.

Parameter: A major identifiable variation in structural orientation between sets of languages that represents a quasi-universal pattern of alternation. For example, the majority of languages seem to place complements either before or after their heads.

Passive Articulator: The articulator that is either not movable or can move only slightly during the production of a speech sound, such as teeth, alveolar ridge, hard palate, velum, etc.

Passive Voice: A sentence in which the recipient of the action is the subject. The verb consists of a *be*-verb and a past participle. The agent can optionally be included at the end of the sentence in a *by*-phrase.

Passive Voice: The voice that indicates the subject is the patient or the experiencer of the action denoted by the verb.

Past Tense: The tense that refers to a time before the moment of utterance.

Perfect Aspect: Grammaticalization of the completion of an event or state. It expresses the event or state as a whole.

Performance: A speaker's use of their language knowledge in real situations.

Performative: A verb that when uttered carries out the action of the speech act being performed; these verbs need to be in the first person and present tense infinitive (e.g., I declare, I sentence, I fire, etc.).

Phoneme: The minimal unit of speech sound in a language; a contrastive speech sound that can result in a meaning change.

Phonemic Transcription: A 'broad' transcription that uses phonemic notations which include only the distinctive sounds of a language – phonemes; /slashes/ are used for phonemic transcription.

Phonemic: Sounds which are fundamentally different from one another rather than two variants of or two ways of pronouncing a single underlying sound.

Phonetic Transcription: A 'narrow' transcription that is characterized by phonetic notations which include non-distinctive features of a language or details of the pronunciation that do not distinguish words in a particular language; [square brackets] are used for phonetic transcription.

Phonetics: A branch of linguistics that studies individual speech sounds in a human language.

Phonological Acquisition Triangle: A proposal that acquisition of similar segments and distinctive features between the L1 and L2 takes a short cut from the L1 to L2 with little learner processing; otherwise, acquisition would take a long route from the L1 to L2 filtered through learner processing with the support of universal grammar.

Phonological Process: A language-specific process that causes speech to change in some way as it moves from one level of mental representation to another. Examples include assimilation and deletion.

Phonology: The branch of linguistics concerned with the rule-governed sound systems of language.

Phonotactics: Language-specific constraints that determine where segments can occur within a syllable and which segments can occur together.

Phrase Structure Rule: Any rule that specifies the structure of a phrase by means of an input-output rule.

Phrase: The maximal projection of a head; may consist of one or many words.

Politeness: Conversational strategies employed by a speaker to maintain positive relations with others.

Positive Evidence: The grammatically correct sentences in children's input. Positive evidence informs children about what is possible in the language that they are acquiring.

Positive Face: The need to belong to a group and share involvement with others, which is manifested through expressing friendliness and seeking approval.

Pragmatic Ability: The language learner's capacity to understand and use grammatical forms and the full range of context variables to convey meaning during a conversation in the L2.

Pragmatic Divergence: A phenomenon in which learners' pragmatic behaviors or choices do not match typical L2 community of speakers' pragmatic norms.

Pragmatic Failure: Communication breakdown between speakers of an L2 community and L2 learners caused by misunderstanding of pragmatic norms either by the speaker or the hearer.

Pragmatics: The study of how context affects the interpretation of linguistic utterances.

Predicate Adjective: Traditionally, an adjective or AP whose meaning is applied to the subject, as *rainy* applies to *weather* in the sentence *The weather is rainy.*

Predicate Nominal (or predicate noun): Traditionally, a noun or NP whose meaning identifies the subject as a member of that set of beings, as *John* in the sentence *John is a doctor* identifies John as a member of the set of all doctors.

Predicate: In syntactic terms, the TP that is the daughter of S and the sister of the subject NP.

Prefix: A type of affix which is attached to the beginning of a word.

Preposition: A closed class of words which join nouns to the other elements of a sentence. They indicate information such as time, location, and movement.

Present Tense: The tense that refers to or includes the moment of utterance.

Principal Parts: In Indo-European languages, the basic forms for verbs including simple present tense, simple past, past participle, and present (*-ing*) participle (if a language has the last of these). Principal parts are often part of lexical learning since many verbs make unpredictable changes in stem vowels that must be memorized (such as *sing/sang/sung*).

Principle: In the theory of Universal Grammar, a universally recurrent feature of human grammars that is held to be given by biological necessity. The principle called "structure-dependence" holds that human languages are governed by the properties of linearity, hierarchy, and recursion and that these properties are available to children learning their first languages as part of the human bioprogram.

Probable/Possible Condition: An event or state that is dependent on a condition that may be true or that may be realized; that is, it is probable for that state or event to be true.

Productivity: The ability of a rule or generalization to be applied to new cases.

Productivity: The degree to which a form such as a prefix or suffix is capable of being used for the creation of new forms.

Progressive aspect: Continuous aspect that expresses ongoing events.

Pronoun: A grammatical term for words which replace nouns or noun phrases.

Psychological Reality: A form is psychologically real to users of a language if they are aware of that form and able to put that form to use without special instruction. While the prefix *anti-* is psychologically real insofar as users may use it to create new words, the prefix *be-* has little to no psychological reality since its original meaning is inaccessible to speakers.

Realis vs. Irrealis: Realis refers to factuality of events or states, whereas irrealis to the non-factual, that is, unreal nature of events or states.

Recursion: That *property of a rule* where at least one of whose input terms is also present in the output, as term A is repeated in the rule A → (A) B, or that *property of a rule system* where at least one input term in a rule is also present in the output of a rule, as a system with one rule A → B C and another rule B → A D will permit the infinite expansion of expressions by means of the recycling of terms A and B.

Redundant Feature: An articulatory or acoustic property that cannot distinguish a sound from another.

Reference/Relevance Time: The time when the state or event is completed. It may be the moment of utterance, the time before or after the moment of utterance, depending on the tense of the verb complex.

Reference: The reference of a word is the thing, event, or state that it points to, or denotes, in the world.

Reflexive Pronoun: An object pronoun that refers to the same person as the subject of a sentence.

Register: Immediate context of situation described in terms of three aspects – the kind of activity or subject matter communicated in the text, the relationship between the writer and the reader or the speaker and the hearer, and the mode or channel of communication through which the text is produced

Relative Pronoun: A type of pronoun used in adjective clauses which refers to a noun in the independent clause.

Root: That part of a word which remains after all affixes have been removed.

Rounded Vowel: Vowel produced with rounding and/or puckering of the lips

Second Language Acquisition: The process through which a language other than one's first language is acquired.

Segmentals: Individual units of speech, typically classified as consonants or vowels.

Self-Tuning: When learners develop a kind of pronunciation awareness that allows them to self-correct without instructor feedback and prompts.

Semantic Structure Theory: An approach to semantics that attempts to capture the complexity of predicate-argument structure in an independent level of linguistic representation, using universal semantic elements that are relevant to grammar.

Semantics: The study of how language conveys meaning.

Sense: The sense of a word is its meaning in relation to the linguistic system of which it is a part. It is the concept associated with a linguistic expression. (In addition to the intended interpretation this chapter, the term 'sense' is also used in semantics to indicate different meanings in cases of homonymy – *bank* in the sense of slope and *bank* in the sense of the institution; as well as related meanings in cases of polysemy – *wood* in the sense of an area covered with trees and *wood* in the sense of the material that comes from trees).

Sentence: A pairing of subject and predicate, when the predicate and subject share a mother node, when the predicate contains a tense, and when the resulting string is given a characteristic intonation pattern.

Sister Node: A node that shares with another node a common mother node. In the rule A → BC, nodes B and C are sister nodes.

Social Network: the people a speaker interacts with directly on a daily basis, such as family, friends, and co-workers.

Specifier (of an NP): A determiner; more generally, a specifier is the daughter of any phrasal projection and a sister of a single-bar (X') projection.

Speech Act: A general act that a speaker performs that includes the uttering of words, a particular intention in making the utterance (illocutionary force), and the production of a particular effect in the hearer.

Speech Community: A more extended community of speakers whose main similarity may be geographic proximity to one another, such as being in the same city or county, rather than other demographic variables.

Speech Time/Utterance Time: Time in which a sentence is uttered.

Stem: That part of a word to which an affix is attached.

Stranding (of a preposition): The resulting condition when the object of a preposition is moved, usually to the first position in the sentence, leaving the preposition alone or 'stranded' in its original position (as in *the train* that I traveled *on __*).

Stress Shift: Where different forms of a word exist, the phenomenon of moving major stress to a different syllable when a new affix is added or when the word's part of speech is changed.

Subject: The first NP branching under S; sister to TP. (Note: in current generative theory, this definition requires some refinement, but the relationship remains the same.)

Subjunctive Mood: Mood that signals counterfactual events or states not possible in the actual world.

Subset: When two languages are being compared, the subset is the language that completely overlaps with the other in terms of shared segmentals and/or suprasegmentals. This means that the other language will have pronunciation attributes that are not present in the subset language.

Suffix: A type of affix which is attached to the end of a word. The addition of a suffix can change a word's part of speech.

Superset: When two languages are being compared, the superset is the language that not only has overlaps with the other language but has additional segmentals and/or suprasegmentals not found in the other language.

Suprasegmentals: Features of speech, such as stress and intonation, which are added over the level of the segment.

Suspicious Pairs: Two sounds that are phonetically similar and may be suspected to be allophones of the same phoneme.

Synchronic: Any linguistic study concerned with a language, or a part of a language, as it exists in one age or at one point in time.

Syncope: The loss of a sound in the middle of a word.

Synonyms: Words with similar meanings.

Syntax: The branch of linguistics concerned with the rules for combining words into phrases and phrases into sentences.

Tense Vowel: Vowels produced with an overall greater muscular effort; often higher, less centralized, and longer in duration, than their lax counterparts.

Tense: Grammatical category marked on the verb; refers to the grammaticalization of the time of an event or state denoted by the verb.

Terminal Node: A tree node that represents word-level constituents, as N, V, Adj, D.

Text: The largest unit of linguistic structure which is above the level of clause and sentence.

Thematic Roles: The roles that participants can play in events or states, as specified by the verb, e.g., Agent, Patient, Theme, etc.

Time: The continuous progress of states or events that occur in succession from past, through present, to future.

Transfer of Learning: Extending language knowledge and ability beyond the original learning conditions to other conditions and contexts of use. Generalization.

Transfer: The application of linguistic features (whether lexical, syntactic, morphological, or sound-related) from one language to another language. L1 transfer refers to when a speaker applies linguistic features from their first language in their second/foreign language. Transfer can facilitate the learning of a second/foreign language if the transferred linguistic feature is shared by both languages (positive transfer) or obstruct language learning if the feature is not shared by both languages (negative transfer).

Transitive Verb: A verb which requires an object.

Transparency Versus Opacity: In morphology, a morpheme is transparent if its meaning is clear when it appears in use, and opaque if its meaning is unclear, or if no issue of meaning is perceived because no separate morpheme is recognized.

Truth-Conditional Equivalence: X is truth-conditionally equivalent to Y if X entails Y and Y entails X.

Typology: The study of the structural and meaning-making characteristics of languages to see what is universal and what is distinct about languages.

Unaccusativity: Unaccusative verbs are a subclass of intransitive verbs whose subject is assumed to be generated in direct object position before raising to subject position.

Unary Feature: An articulatory property the negative value of which does not play a role in phonological structure.

Underspecification: A phonological representation in which predictable features are ruled out.

Universal Grammar (UG): The theory of biologically determined properties common to all human languages, developed by Noam Chomsky and his associates since the 1960s, that proposes that all human languages share a set of fundamental grammatical categories and rules, and that each particular language makes use of a subset of these categories and rules. UG also refers to an inborn capacity that provides children with the universal properties of human languages, such as grammatical categories (nouns, verbs, adjectives, etc.) and grammatical operations (embedding, etc.).

Unrounded Vowel: Vowel produced without rounding and/or puckering of the lips.

Utterance: A unit of speech.

Verb Complex: All the verbs in the predicate of a clause.

Verb: A member of the syntactic class of words that signals events and actions and marks tense, aspect, voice, and mood in inflectional languages.

Vocal Tract: The cavity in humans where speech sounds – vowels and consonants – are formed.

Voice: A grammatical category that expresses the semantic functions the verb assigns to its arguments, i.e. agent, patient, or experiencer.

Vowel Backness: The horizontal position of the tongue during the production of a vowel.

Vowel Centralization: A reduction in articulatory effort, typically associated with vowel reduction, which has the effect of pushing the vowel toward a mid, central articulation.

Vowel Height: The vertical position of the tongue during the production of a vowel.

Vowel Reduction: Changes in the quality of an unstressed vowel, generally including shortening and centralization.

Vowel Rounding: Rounding or puckering of the lips during the production of a vowel.

Vowel Shortening: A shorter vowel duration, typically associated with vowel reduction, compared to the duration of the same underlying vowel in a stressed position.

Vowel Tenseness: Amount of tension in the tongue and lower face during the production of a vowel.

Vowel: Speech sound produced without an appreciable constriction in the vocal tract or contact of the articulators and able to function as the nucleus of a syllable.

X' Theory: A theory of syntactic structure characterized by hierarchical relationships based on endocentric projections of a head X into a higher-level XP (or X").

X': In English, the intermediate projection between a head X and a phrasal-level XP.

Zero Conditionals: A category of probable/possible conditions in which an event or a state is always true whenever the state or an event in the condition is true.

Zero-Allomorph: An allomorph which has no overt pronunciation and is recognizable precisely because no overt form is available to be pronounced. Thus, while the plural of *cart* has the suffix –*s*, the plural of *fish* is notable for being null; its plural is a zero-allomorph.

Compilation of References

Abugharsa, A. (2014). *Arabic-English code-switching in young Libyan children in the US* (Doctoral dissertation). Oklahoma State University.

Algeo, J., & Butcher, C. A. (2014). *The origins and development of the English language.* Boston, MA: Wadsworth Cengage Learning.

Allan, K. (1986). *Linguistic meaning.* London: Routledge & Kegan Paul.

Aoun, J., & Li, Y.-A. (1989). Scope and constituency. *Linguistic Inquiry, 20,* 141–172.

Aoyama, K., Flege, J. E., Guion, S. G., Akahane-Yamada, R., & Yamada, T. (2004). Perceived phonetic dissimilarity and L2 speech learning: The case of Japanese /r/ and English /l/ and /r/. *Journal of Phonetics, 32*(2), 233–250. doi:10.1016/S0095-4470(03)00036-6

Aoyama, K., & Guion, S. G. (2007). Prosody in second language acquisition: Acoustic analyses of duration and F0 range. In O.-S. Bohn & M. Munro (Eds.), *Language experience in second language speech learning* (pp. 281–297). Amsterdam: John Benjamins. doi:10.1075/lllt.17.24aoy

applaudatory, adj. (2019). In *OED Online* (3rd ed.). Retrieved from http://www.oed.com/view/Entry/249093

Archer, D., Aijmer, K., & Wichmann, A. (2012). *Pragmatics: An advanced resource book for students.* London: Routledge.

Archibald, J. (1992). Transfer of L1 parameter settings: Some empirical evidence from Polish metrics. *Canadian Journal of Linguistics, 37*(3), 301–340. doi:10.1017/S0008413100019903

Archibald, J. (1993). The learnability of English metrical parameters by adult Spanish speakers. *IRAL: International Review of Applied Linguistics in Language Teaching, 31*(2), 129.

Atran, S. (1990). *Cognitive foundations of natural history: Towards an anthropology of science.* Cambridge, UK: Cambridge University Press.

Atran, S. (1998). Folk biology and the anthropology of science: Cognitive universals and cultural particulars. *Behavioral and Brain Sciences, 21*(4), 547–609. doi:10.1017/S0140525X98001277 PMID:10097021

Austin, J. (1962). *How to do things with words.* Oxford, UK: Oxford University Press.

Avery, P., & Ehrlich, S. (1992). *Teaching American English pronunciation.* Oxford University Press.

Aygen, G. (2016). *English grammar: A descriptive linguistic approach* (3rd ed.). Dubuque, IA: Kendall Hunt.

Aygen, G. (2019). *Word choice errors: A descriptive linguistics approach (with Sarah Eastlund).* New York, NY: Routledge.

Aygen, G., & Bowern, C. (2000). Titan's tensed prepositions. In A. Okrent, & J.P. Boyle (Eds.), *Proceedings of the Chicago linguistics society* (pp. 35-48). Chicago: Chicago Linguistics Society.

Bailey, R. W. (1991). *Images of English*. Ann Arbor, MI: The University of Michigan Press.

Baker, A. (2014). Exploring teachers' knowledge of second language pronunciation techniques: Teacher cognitions, observed classroom practices, and student perceptions. *TESOL Quarterly, 48*(1), 136–163. doi:10.1002/tesq.99

Baker, A., & Murphy, J. (2011). Knowledge base of pronunciation teaching: Staking out the territory. *TESL Canada Journal, 28*(2), 29–50. doi:10.18806/tesl.v28i2.1071

Baker, M. (1988). *Incorporation: A theory of grammatical function changing*. Chicago, IL: University of Chicago Press.

Balcom, P. (1997). Why is this happened? Passive morphology and unaccusativity. *Second Language Research, 13*(1), 1–9. doi:10.1191/026765897670080531

Banks, J., Cochran-Smith, M., Moll, L., Richert, A., Zeichner, K., LePage, P., ... McDonald, M. (2005). Teaching diverse learners. In L. Darling-Hammond & J. Bransford (Eds.), *Preparing teachers for a changing world: What teachers should learn and be able to do* (pp. 232–274). San Francisco, CA: Jossey-Bass.

Bardovi-Harlig, K., & Mahan-Taylor, R. (2003). Introduction to teaching pragmatics. *English Teaching Forum, 41*(3), 37-39. Retrieved from https://americanenglish.state.gov/files/ae/resource_files/03-41-3-h.pdf

Bardovi-Harlig, K., & Mahan-Taylor, R. (2003, July). Introduction to teaching pragmatics. *English Teaching Forum*, 37-39.

Bardovi-Harlig, K. (1996). Pragmatics and language teaching: Bridging pragmatics and pedagogy together. In L. F. Bouton (Ed.), *Pragmatics and language learning* (Vol. 7, pp. 21–38). Urbana, IL: Division of English as an International Language, University of Illinois at Urbana-Champaign.

Bardovi-Harlig, K., & Hartford, B. (1990). Congruence in native and nonnative conversations: Status balance in the academic advising session. *Language Learning, 40*(4), 467–501. doi:10.1111/j.1467-1770.1990.tb00603.x

Bardovi-Harlig, K., & Hartford, B. S. (2005). *Interlanguage pragmatics: Exploring institutional talk*. London: Routledge. doi:10.4324/9781410613776

Barone, D. (2010). Engaging young ELLs with reading and writing. In G. Li & P. Edwards (Eds.), *Best practices in ELL instruction* (pp. 84–102). New York, NY: Guilford.

Barrera-Pardo, D. (2004). Can pronunciation be taught? A review of research and implications for teaching. *Revista Alicantina de Estudios Ingleses: RAEI*, (17), 6-38.

Bentzen, K., Merchant, J., & Svenonius, P. (2013). Deep properties of surface pronouns: Pronominal predicate anaphors in Norwegian and German. *Journal of Comparative Germanic Linguistics, 16*(2-3), 97–125. doi:10.100710828-013-9057-z

Berko, J. (1958). The child's learning of English morphology. *Word, 14*(2-3), 150–177. doi:10.1080/00437956.1958.11659661

Best, C. T. (1995). A direct realist view of cross-language speech perception. In W. Strange (Ed.), *Speech perception and linguistic experience. Issues in cross-language research* (pp. 171–204). Timonium, MD: York Press.

Best, C. T., McRoberts, G. W., & Sithole, N. M. (1988). Examination of perceptual reorganization for nonnative speech contrasts: Zulu click discrimination by English-speaking adults and infants. *Journal of Experimental Psychology. Human Perception and Performance, 14*(3), 345–360. doi:10.1037/0096-1523.14.3.345 PMID:2971765

Biesenbach-Lucas, S. (2007). *Students writing emails to faculty: an examination of e-politeness among native and non-native speakers of English.* Academic Press.

Birdsong, D. (2006). Age and second language acquisition and processing: A selective overview. *Language Learning, 56*(1), 9–49. doi:10.1111/j.1467-9922.2006.00353.x

Birjulin, L. A., & Xrakovski, V. S. (2001). Imperative sentences: Theoretical problems. In V. S. Xrakovski (Ed.), *Typology of imperative constructions* (pp. 3–50). Munchen: Lincom Europa.

Bley-Vroman, R. (1989). What is the logical problem of foreign language learning? In S. Gass & J. Schachter (Eds.), *Linguistic perspectives on second language acquisition* (pp. 41–68). Cambridge, UK: Cambridge University Press. doi:10.1017/CBO9781139524544.005

Bley-Vroman, R. (1990). The logical problem of foreign language learning. *Linguistic Analysis, 20,* 3–39.

Bley-Vroman, R. (2009). The evolving context of the fundamental difference hypothesis. *Studies in Second Language Acquisition, 31*(2), 175–198. doi:10.1017/S0272263109090275

Bowerman, M. (1996). Learning how to structure space for language: A crosslinguistic perspective. In P. Bloom, M. A. Peterson, L. Nadel, & M. F. Garrett (Eds.), *Language and Space* (pp. 385–436). Cambridge, MA: The MIT Press.

Bradlow, A. R., Pisoni, D. B., Akahane-Yamada, R., & Tohkura, Y. I. (1997). Training Japanese listeners to identify English /r/ and /l/: IV. Some effects of perceptual learning on speech production. *The Journal of the Acoustical Society of America, 101*(4), 2299–2310. doi:10.1121/1.418276 PMID:9104031

Broselow, E., & Finer, D. (1991). Parameter setting in second language phonology and syntax. *Second Language Research, 7,* 35–59.

Brown, C. (2000). The interrelation between speech perception and phonological acquisition from infant to adult. In J. Archibald (Ed.), *Second language acquisition and linguistic theory* (pp. 4–63). Malden, MA: Blackwell Publishers Inc.

Brown, P., & Levinson, S. (1987). *Politeness. Some universals in language use.* Cambridge, UK: Cambridge University Press. doi:10.1017/CBO9780511813085

Burleigh, P., & Skandera, P. (2016). *A Manual of English phonetics and phonology: Twelve lessons with an integrated course in phonetic transcription.* Tübingen: Narr Francke Attempto.

Burns, A. (2001). Analysing spoken discourse: Implications for TESOL. In A. Burns & C. Coffin (Eds.), *Analysing English in a global context: A reader* (pp. 123–148). London: Routledge.

Burns, A. (2010). Teaching speaking using genre-based pedagogy. In M. Olafsson (Ed.), *Symposium 2009* (pp. 231-247). Stockholm: National Centre for Swedish as a Second Language, University of Stockholm.

Burzio, L. (1986). *Italian syntax: A government-binding approach.* Dordrecht: Reidel. doi:10.1007/978-94-009-4522-7

Butler, R. E. (2012). Politeness is more than 'please.' Teaching email requests. *ORTESOL Journal, 29,* 12–20.

Bybee, J. (2013). Usage-based theory and exemplar representations of constructions. In T. Hoffmann & G. Trousdale (Eds.), *The Oxford handbook of construction grammar* (pp. 49–69). Oxford, UK: Oxford University Press.

Byram, M. (2000). Assessing intercultural competence in language teaching. *Sprogforum, 18*(6), 8–13.

Camus, P. (2019). The effects of explicit pronunciation instruction on the production of second language Spanish voiceless stops: A classroom study. *Instructed Second Language Acquisition, 3*(1), 81–103.

Canale, M. (1983). From communicative competence to language pedagogy. In Richards & Schmidt (Eds.), Language and communication. London: Longman.

Canale, M., & Swain, M. (1980). Theoretical bases of communicative approaches to second language teaching and testing. *Applied Linguistics*, *1*(1), 1–47. doi:10.1093/applin/1.1.1

Carley, P., Mees, I. M., & Collins, B. (2018). *English phonetics and pronunciation practice*. London: Routledge.

Carter, R., Goddard, A., Reah, D., Sanger, K., & Swift, N. (2008). *Working with texts: A core introduction to language analysis* (3rd ed.). London: Routledge.

Celce-Murcia, M., Brinton, D. M., & Goodwin, J. M. (2010). Teaching pronunciation: A course book and reference guide (2nd ed.). New York, NY: Cambridge University Press.

Celce-Murcía, M., Brinton, D., & Goodwin, J. M. (2010). *Teaching pronunciation: A course book and reference guide* (2nd ed.). Cambridge: Cambridge University Press.

Celce-Murcia, M., & Olshtain, E. (2014). Teaching language through discourse. In M. Celce-Murcia, D. M. Brinton, & M. A. Snow (Eds.), *Teaching English as a second or foreign language* (4th ed., pp. 424–437). Boston, MA: National Geographic Learning.

Center for Advanced Research on Language Acquisition. (2018, October). Retrieved from http://carla.umn.edu/speechacts/index.html

Chaucer, G., & Benson, L. D. (1987). *The Riverside Chaucer*. Boston, MA: Houghton Mifflin Co.

Cheng, L. L. S. (1991). *On the typology of wh-questions* (Doctoral dissertation). Massachusetts Institute of Technology, Cambridge, MA.

Chen, G. M., & Starosta, W. J. (2000). The development and validation of the intercultural communication sensitivity scale. *Human Communication*, *3*(1), 1–15.

Chierchia, G., & McConnell-Ginet, S. (2000). *Meaning and grammar: An introduction to semantics* (2nd ed.). Cambridge, MA: MIT Press.

Chomsky, N. (1957). *Syntactic structures*. The Hague: Mouton.

Chomsky, N. (1965). *Aspects of the theory of syntax*. Cambridge, MA: MIT Press.

Chomsky, N. (1968). *Language and mind*. Cambridge, MA: MIT Press.

Chomsky, N. (1970). Remarks on nominalization. In R. A. Jacobs & P. S. Rosenbaum (Eds.), *English transformational grammar* (pp. 184–221). Waltham, MA: Ginn.

Chomsky, N. (1981). *Lectures on government and binding*. Dordrecht: Foris.

Chomsky, N. (1986). *Knowledge of language*. New York: Praeger.

Chomsky, N. (1995). *The minimalist program*. Cambridge, MA: MIT Press.

Chomsky, N. (1995). *The Minimalist Program*. Cambridge, MA: MIT Press.

Chomsky, N., & Halle, M. (1968). *The sound pattern of English*. New York, NY: Harper & Row.

Cibelli, E. (2015). *Aspects of articulatory and perceptual learning in novel phoneme acquisition (Doctoral dissertation)*. Berkeley, CA: University of California – Berkeley. Retrieved from https://escholarship.org/uc/item/9tq441d9

Clahsen, H., & Muysken, P. (1986). The availability of universal grammar to adult and child learners—a study of the acquisition of German word order. *Second Language Research, 2*, 93–119.

Colantoni, L., & Steele, J. (2008). Integrating articulatory constraints into models of second language phonological acquisition. *Applied Psycholinguistics, 29*(3), 489–534. doi:10.1017/S0142716408080223

Collins, B. (2003). *The phonetics of English and Dutch*. Brill Academic.

Commins, N., & Nguyen, D. (2015). How should pre-service education programs prepare educators to meet the needs of English language learners/emergent bilinguals relative to Common Core State Standards and Next Generation Science Standards curricula? In G. Valdés, K. Menken, & M. Castro (Eds.), *Common core bilingual and English language learners: A resource for educators* (pp. 231–232). Philadelphia, PA: Caslon.

Comrie, B. (1985). *Tense*. Cambridge, UK: Cambridge University Press. doi:10.1017/CBO9781139165815

Comrie, B. (1986). *Aspect*. Cambridge, UK: Cambridge University Press.

Cook, V. (1988). *Chomsky's universal grammar*. Oxford, UK: Blackwell.

Cook, V. (2008). Multi-competence: Black hole or wormhole for second language acquisition research? In Z. Han (Ed.), *Understanding second language process* (pp. 16–26). Multilingual Matters.

Corder, S. P. (1967). The significance of learner's errors. *International Journal of Applied Linguistics, 5*, 161–170.

Coulmas, F. (2013). *Sociolinguistics: The study of speakers' choices*. Cambridge, UK: Cambridge University Press. doi:10.1017/CBO9781139794732

Cruse, D. A. (1986). *Lexical semantics*. Cambridge, UK: Cambridge University Press.

Crystal, D. (1985). *A dictionary of linguistics and phonetics* (2nd ed.). New York: Basil Blackwell.

Crystal, D. (1987). *The Cambridge encyclopedia of the English language*. Cambridge, UK: Cambridge University Press.

Crystal, D. (2010). *The Cambridge encyclopedia of language* (3rd ed.). Cambridge, UK: Cambridge University Press.

Cukor-Avila, P. (2002). She say, she go, she be like: Verbs of quotation over time in African American Vernacular English. *American Speech, 77*(2), 3–31. doi:10.1215/00031283-77-1-3

Cunningham, A. E. (2005). Vocabulary growth through independent reading and reading aloud to children. In E. H. Hiebert & M. L. Kamil (Eds.), *Teaching and learning vocabulary: Bringing research to practice* (pp. 45–68). Mahwah, NJ: Erlbaum.

Cutler, A., & Otake, T. (2004). Pseudo-homophony in non-native listening. *The Journal of the Acoustical Society of America, 115*(5), 2392. doi:10.1121/1.4780547

Cutler, A., Weber, A., & Otake, T. (2006). Asymmetric mapping from phonetic to lexical representations in second-language listening. *Journal of Phonetics, 34*(2), 269–284. doi:10.1016/j.wocn.2005.06.002

Cutting, J. (2008). *Pragmatics and discourse. A resource book for students*. London: Routledge.

Darcy, I. (2018). Powerful and effective pronunciation instruction: How can we achieve it? *The CATESOL Journal, 30*(1), 13–45.

Darcy, I., Daidone, D., & Kojima, C. (2013). Asymmetric lexical access and fuzzy lexical representations in second language learners. *The Mental Lexicon, 8*(3), 372–420. doi:10.1075/ml.8.3.06dar

Darcy, I., Dekydtspotter, L., Sprouse, R. A., Glover, J., Kaden, C., McGuire, M., & Scott, J. H. G. (2012). Direct mapping of acoustics to phonology: On the lexical encoding of front rounded vowels in L1 English-L2 French acquisition. *Second Language Research*, *28*(1), 5–40. doi:10.1177/0267658311423455

Darcy, I., Peperkamp, S., & Dupoux, E. (2007). Bilinguals play by the rules. Perceptual compensation for assimilation in late L2-learners. In J. Cole & J. I. Hualde (Eds.), *Laboratory phonology 9* (pp. 411–442). Berlin: Mouton de Gruyter.

Davies, A. (2003). *The native speaker: Myth and reality.* Clevedon, UK: Multilingual Matters. doi:10.21832/9781853596247

Davies, E. (1986). *The English imperative.* Beckenham: Croom Helm.

Dawson, H., & Phelen, M. (Eds.). (2016). *Language files: Materials for an introduction to language and linguistics* (12th ed.). Columbus, OH: The Ohio State University Press.

De Saussure, F. (1959). *Course in general linguistics [1916]* (C. Bally & A. Sechehaye, Eds., Baskin W., Trans.). New York: McGraw Hill Book Company.

de Saussure, F. (1983). *Course in general linguistics (translated and annotated by R. Harris).* London: Duckworth. (Original work published 1916)

Delahunty, G. P., & Garvey, J. J. (2010). *The English language: From sound to sense.* Fort Collins, CO: WAC Clearinghouse.

Denham, K. E., & Lobeck, A. C. (2010). *Linguistics for everyone: An introduction.* Boston, MA: Wadsworth/ Cengage Learning.

Derewianka, B. (1990). *Exploring how texts work.* Heinemann Educational Books.

Derwing, T. M., & Munro, M. J. (2015). *Pronunciation fundamentals: Evidence-based perspectives for L2 teaching and research.* Amsterdam, The Netherlands: Benjamins. doi:10.1075/lllt.42

destigmatize, v. (2019). In *OED Online* (3rd ed.). Retrieved from http://www.oed.com/view/Entry/68753899

Dinnsen, D., & Eckman, F. (1975). In R. E. Grossman, L. J. San, & T. J. Vance (Eds.), *Functionalism* (pp. 126–134). Chicago: Chicago Linguistic Society.

Disner, S. F. (1984). Insights on vowel space. In I. Maddieson (Ed.), *Patterns of sounds* (pp. 136–155). Cambridge, UK: Cambridge University Press.

Dixon, C., & Green, J. L. (2005). Studying the discursive construction of texts in classrooms through interactional ethnography. In R. Beach, J. Green, M. Kamil, & T. Shanahan (Eds.), *Multidisciplinary Perspectives on Literacy Research* (pp. 349–390). Cresskill, NJ: Hampton Press.

Dlaska, A. & Krekeler, C. (2008). Self-assessment of pronunciation. *System*, *36*(4), 506-516. doi:10.1016/j.system.2008.03.003

Dornyei, Z. (2006). *The Psychology of the language learner: Individual differences in second language acquisition.* Lawrence Erlbaum.

Dowty, D. R. (1991). Thematic proto-roles and argument selection. *Language*, *67*(3), 547–619. doi:10.1353/lan.1991.0021

Dulay, H., & Burt, M. (1974). A new perspective on the creative construction process in child second language acquisition. *Working Papers on Bilingualism*, *24*(2), 253-278.

Dupoux, E., Kakehi, K., Hirose, Y., Pallier, C., & Mehler, J. (1999). Epenthetic vowels in Japanese: A perceptual illusion? *Journal of Experimental Psychology. Human Perception and Performance*, *25*(6), 1568–1578. doi:10.1037/0096-1523.25.6.1568

Dupoux, E., Parlato, E., Frota, S., Hirose, Y., & Peperkamp, S. (2011). Where do illusory vowels come from? *Journal of Memory and Language, 64*(3), 199–210. doi:10.1016/j.jml.2010.12.004

Dupoux, E., Sebastián-Gallés, N., Navarrete, E., & Peperkamp, S. (2008). Persistent stress 'deafness': The case of French learners of Spanish. *Cognition, 106*(2), 682–706. doi:10.1016/j.cognition.2007.04.001 PMID:17592731

Eckert, P. (1988). Social structure and the spread of linguistic change. *Language in Society, 17*(2), 183–207. doi:10.1017/S0047404500012756

Eckert, P. (1989). The whole woman: Sex and gender differences in variation. *Language Variation and Change, 1*(3), 245–267. doi:10.1017/S095439450000017X

Eckman, F. (1977). Markedness and the contrastive analysis hypothesis. *Language Learning: A Journal of Applied Linguistics, 27*, 315–30.

Eckman, F. (1981). On predicting phonological difficulty in second language acquisition. *Studies in Second Language Acquisition, 4*(1), 18–30. doi:10.1017/S0272263100004253

Eliasson, S. (1997). Tone in second language acquisition. In R. Hickey & S. Puppel (Eds.), *Language history and linguistic modeling* (Vol. 2, pp. 1273–1289). Berlin: Mouton de Gruyter.

Ellis, N. C. (2002). Frequency effects in language processing. *Studies in Second Language Acquisition, 24*(2), 143–188. doi:10.1017/S0272263102002024

Ellis, N. C. (2006). Selective attention and transfer phenomena in l2 acquisition: Contingency, cue competition, salience, interference, overshadowing, blocking, and perceptual learning. *Applied Linguistics, 27*(2), 164–194. doi:10.1093/applin/aml015

Ellis, N. C., & Larsen-Freeman, D. (2006). Language emergence: Implications for applied linguistics. *Applied Linguistics, 27*(4), 558–589. doi:10.1093/applin/aml028

Ellis, R. (2009). *The study of second language acquisition.* Oxford, UK: Oxford University Press.

Ellis, R., & Shintani, N. (2014). *Exploring language pedagogy through second language acquisition research.* New York, NY: Routledge.

Emonds, J. E. (1976). *A transformational approach to English syntax: Root, structure-preserving, and local transformations.* New York: Academic Press.

Emonds, J. E. (2000). *Lexicon and grammar: The English syntacticon.* New York: Mouton de Gruyter.

Emonds, J. E., & Whitney, R. (2005). Double object constructions. In M. Everaert & H. van Riemsdijk (Eds.), *The Blackwell companion to syntax* (pp. 73–144). Hoboken, NJ: Blackwell.

Eskey, D. (1997). Syllabus design in content-based instruction. In M.A. Snow & D. M. Brinton (Eds.), The Content-based Classroom: Perspectives on Integrating Language and Content. White Plains, NY: Longman.

Evans, B. (2004). The role of social network in the acquisition of local dialect norms by Appalachian migrants in Ypsilanti, Michigan. *Language Variation and Change, 16*(2), 153–167. doi:10.1017/S0954394504162042

Fairclough, N. L., & Wodak, R. (1997). Critical discourse analysis. In T. A. van Dijk (Ed.), Discourse studies: A multidisciplinary introduction (Vol. 2, pp. 258-284). London: Sage.

Fairclough, N. L. (1989). *Language and power.* London: Longman.

Félix-Brasdefer, J. C., & Cohen, A. D. (2012). Teaching pragmatics in the foreign language classroom: Grammar as a communicative resource. *Hispania*, *95*(4), 650–669. doi:10.1353/hpn.2012.0124

Fillmore, C. (1968). The case for case. In E. Bach & R. T. Harms (Eds.), *Universals in linguistic theory* (pp. 1–88). New York, NY: Holt, Rinehart, and Winston.

Finegan, E. (2008). *Language: Its structure and use*. Boston, MA: Thomson Wadsworth.

Fishman, J. (1972). The Sociology of language. Rowley, MA: Newbury.

Flege, J. E. (1995). Second language speech learning. Theory, findings and problems. In W. Strange (Ed.), *Speech perception and linguistic experience. Issues in cross-language research* (pp. 233–277). Timonium, MD: York Press.

Flege, J. E. (1995). Second language speech learning: Theory, findings, and problems. In W. Strange (Ed.), *Speech perception and linguistic experience: Issues in cross-linguistic research* (pp. 233–277). Timonium, MD: York Press.

Flege, J. E. (1999). The relation between L2 production and perception. In J. J. Ohala, Y. Hasegawa, M. Ohala, D. Granville, & A. C. Bailey (Eds.), *Fifth International Congress of Phonetic Sciences* (vol. 2, pp. 1273-1276). Berkeley, CA.

Flege, J. E. (2007). Language contact in bilingualism: Phonetic system interactions. In J. Cole & J. I. Hualde (Eds.), *Laboratory phonology 9*. Berlin: Mouton de Gruyter.

Flege, J. E., Bohn, O. S., & Jang, S. (1997). Effects of experience on non-native speakers' production and perception of English vowels. *Journal of Phonetics*, *25*(4), 437–470. doi:10.1006/jpho.1997.0052

Flege, J. E., & Eefting, W. (1987). Production and perception of English stops by native Spanish speakers. *Journal of Phonetics*, *15*, 67–83.

Flemming, E., & Johnson, S. (2007). Rosa's roses: Reduced vowels in American English. *Journal of the International Phonetic Association*, *37*(1), 83–96. doi:10.1017/S0025100306002817

Fox, D. (2000). *Economy and semantic interpretation*. Cambridge, MA: MIT Press.

Fraser, H. (2002, October). *Change, challenge, and opportunity in pronunciation and oral communication*. Paper presented at Plenary Address at English Australia Conference, Canberra, Australia.

Freeman, D. E., & Freeman, Y. S. (2004). *Essential linguistics: What you need to know to teach reading, ESL, spelling, phonics, and grammar*. Portsmouth, NH: Heinemann.

Freeman, D. E., & Freeman, Y. S. (2014). *Essential linguistics: What teachers need to know to teach ESL, reading, spelling, grammar*. Portsmouth, NH: Heinemann.

Freeman, M. R., Blumenfeld, H. K., & Marian, V. (2016). Phonotactic constraints are activated across languages in bilinguals. *Frontiers in Psychology*, *7*, 702. doi:10.3389/fpsyg.2016.00702 PMID:27242615

Frege, G. (1980). On sense and reference. In P. Geach & M. Black (Eds.), *Translations from the philosophical writings of Gottlob Frege* (3rd ed.; pp. 56–78). Oxford, UK: Blackwell. (Original work published 1892)

Frey, W. (1993). *Syntaktische Bedingungen für die semantische Repräsentation: Über Bindung, Implizite Argumente und Skopus*. Berlin: Akademie Verlag.

Fromkin, V., Rodman, R., & Hyams, N. (2014). *An introduction to language* (10th ed.). Boston, MA: Wadsworth Cengage Learning.

Fulk, R. D. (2012). *An introduction to Middle English: Grammar, texts*. Buffalo, NY: Broadview Press.

García, O., Johnson, S. I., & Seltzer, K. (2017). *The translanguaging classroom: Leveraging student bilingualism for learning*. Philadelphia, PA: Caslon.

Gass, S. M., Behney, J., & Plonsky, L. (2013). *Second language acquisition: An introductory course* (4th ed.). New York: Routledge Taylor & Francis Group. doi:10.4324/9780203137093

Gatbonton, E., & Segalowitz, N. (2005). Rethinking communicative language teaching: A focus on access to fluency. *Canadian Modern Language Review*, *61*(3), 325–353. doi:10.3138/cmlr.61.3.325

Gee, J. P. (2004). Discourse analysis: What makes it critical? In R. Rogers (Ed.), *An introduction to critical discourse analysis in education* (pp. 23–45). New York, NY: Routledge.

Gee, J. P. (2014). *How to do discourse analysis: A toolkit*. Oxon, UK: Routledge. doi:10.4324/9781315819662

Gerald of Wales. (1984). The journey through Wales and the description of Wales (L. Thorpe, Trans.). Harmondsworth, UK: Penguin Books. (Original publication 1193)

Gibbons, P. (2015). *Scaffolding language, scaffolding learning: Teaching English language learners in the mainstream classroom* (2nd ed.). Portsmouth, NH: Heinemann.

Gick, B., Wilson, I., & Derrick, D. (2013). *Articulatory phonetics*. Malden, MA: Wiley-Blackwell.

Giegerich, H. J. (1992). *English phonology*. Cambridge, UK: Cambridge University Press. doi:10.1017/CBO9781139166126

Gilbert, J. B. (2018). Issues in teaching pronunciation: Prosody, intonation, and vowels. In The TESOL encyclopedia of English language teaching (vol. 3, pp. 1701-1709). Hoboken, NJ: TESOL International Association/Wiley Blackwell.

Gil, J., & Adamson, B. (2011). The English language in mainland China: A sociolinguistic profile. In A. Feng (Ed.), *English language education across greater China* (pp. 23–45). Buffalo, NY: Multilingal Matters. doi:10.21832/9781847693518-004

Givon, T. (1990). *Syntax: A functional-typological introduction II*. Amsterdam: Benjamins.

Goffman, E. (1959). *The presentation of self in everyday life*. New York, NY: Anchor Books.

Goffman, E. (1967). *Interactional Ritual: Essays on face-to-face behavior*. Garden City, NY: Anchor Books.

Golestani, N., & Zatorre, R. J. (2009). Individual differences in the acquisition of second language phonology. *Brain and Language*, *109*(2-3), 55–67. doi:10.1016/j.bandl.2008.01.005 PMID:18295875

Gomez-Laich, M. P. (2016). Second language learners' divergence from target language pragmatic norms. *Studies in Second Language Learning and Teaching*, *6*(2), 249. doi:10.14746sllt.2016.6.2.4

Goodwin, J. (2014). Teaching pronunciation. In M. Celce-Murcia, D. M. Brinton, & M. A. Snow (Eds.), *Teaching English as a second or foreign language* (4th ed.; pp. 136–152). Boston, MA: National Geographic Learning/Heinle Cengage Learning.

Gordon, J., & Darcy, I. (2016). The development of comprehensible speech in L2 learners: A classroom study on the effects of short-term pronunciation instruction. *Journal of Second Language Pronunciation*, *2*(1), 56–92. doi:10.1075/jslp.2.1.03gor

Gordon, J., Darcy, I., & Ewert, D. (2013). Pronunciation teaching and learning: Effects of explicit phonetic instruction in the L2 classroom. In J. Levis, & K. LeVelle (Eds.). *Proceedings of the 4th Pronunciation in Second Language Learning and Teaching Conference* (pp. 194-206). Ames, IA: Iowa State University.

Gordon, M. J. (2001). *Small-town values, big-city vowels: A study of the Northern Cities Shift in Michigan*. Durham, NC: Duke University Press.

Goto, H. (1971). Auditory perception by normal Japanese adults of the sounds "l" and "r.". *Neuropsychologia, 9*(3), 317–323. doi:10.1016/0028-3932(71)90027-3 PMID:5149302

Gotzke, C., & Gosse, H. S. (2009). Introduction to language 3-5 years: Increasingly adult-like understanding and use. In *Handbook of language and literacy development: A roadmap from 0-60 months*. London, Canada: The Canadian Language & Literacy Research Network. Retrieved from http://www.theroadmap.ualberta.ca/understandings/research/37-60#2

Greenberg, J. H. (1966). *Universals of language*. Cambridge, MA: MIT Press.

Greenburg, J. H. (1976). *Language universals*. The Hague, The Netherlands: Mouton de Gruyter.

Grice, H. P. (1968). Logic and conversation. In H. P. Grice (Ed.), *Studies in the ways with words. Harvard*. Harvard University Press.

Grice, P. (1975). Logic and conversation. In P. Cole & J. L. Morgan (Eds.), Syntax and semantics (pp. 41–58). New York, NY: Academic Press.

Grimshaw, J. (1979). Complement selection and the lexicon. *Linguistic Inquiry, 10*(2), 279–326.

Gropen, J., Pinker, S., Hollander, M., Goldberg, R., & Wilson, R. (1989). The learnability and acquisition of the dative alternation in English. *Language, 65*(2), 203–257. doi:10.2307/415332

Guasti, M.-T. (2002). *Language acquisition: The growth of grammar*. Cambridge, MA: MIT Press.

Gunderson, L. (2009). *ESL (ELL) literacy instruction: A guidebook to theory and practice* (2nd ed.). New York, NY: Taylor & Francis.

Gussmann, E. (2002). *Phonology: Analysis and theory*. Cambridge, UK: Cambridge University Press. doi:10.1017/CBO9781139164108

Hagiwara, R. (1997). Dialect variation and formant frequency: The American English vowels revisited. *The Journal of the Acoustical Society of America, 102*(1), 655–658. doi:10.1121/1.419712

Hale, M., & Reiss, C. (2003). The subset principle in phonology: Why the tabula can't be rasa. *Journal of Linguistics, 39*(2), 219–244. doi:10.1017/S0022226703002019

Hall, T. M. (2017). Learner chunks in second language acquisition. Proquest Dissertations Publishing. (10260547)

Hallé, P. A., Chang, Y. C., & Best, C. T. (2004). Identification and discrimination of Mandarin Chinese tones by Mandarin Chinese vs. French listeners. *Journal of Phonetics, 32*(3), 395–421. doi:10.1016/S0095-4470(03)00016-0

Halliday, M. A. K., & Hasan, R. (1976). *Cohesion in English*. London: Longman.

Hamm, F., & Bott, O. (2018). *Tense and aspect. In Stanford encyclopedia of philosophy. Metaphysics Research Lab*. Stanford University.

Hand, A. R., & Frank, M. E. (2014). *Fundamentals of oral histology and physiology*. Ames, IA: Wiley Blackwell.

Han, Z. (2004). *Fossilization in adult second language acquisition*. Clevedon, UK: Multilingual Matters. doi:10.21832/9781853596889

Han, Z. (2013). Forty years later: Updating the fossilization hypothesis. *Language Teaching, 46*(2), 133–171. doi:10.1017/S0261444812000511

Harley, H., & Ritter, E. (2002). Person and number in pronouns: A feature-geometric analysis. *Language, 78*(3), 482–526. doi:10.1353/lan.2002.0158

Harnad, S. (Ed.). (1987). *Categorical perception: The groundwork of cognition*. New York: Cambridge University Press.

Hartford, B., & Bardovi-Harlig, K. (1996). 'At your earliest convenience': A study of written student requests to faculty. Pragmatics and Language Learning, 7, 55-69.

Haspelmath, M., König, E., Wulf, O., & Raible, W. (Eds.). (2001). *Language typology and language universals: An international handbook* (Vol. 2). Berlin: Walter de Gruyter. doi:10.1515/9783110171549.2

Hawkins, R. 2005. Revisiting *wh*-movement: the availability of an uninterpretable [wh] feature in interlanguage grammars. In L. Dekydtspotter, R. A. Sprouse, & A. Liljestrand (Eds.), *Proceedings of the 7th Generative Approaches to Second Language Acquisition Conference (GASLA 2004)* (pp. 124-137). Somerville, MA: Cascadilla.

Hawkins, R., & Chan, C. Y.-H. (1997). The partial availability of universal grammar in second language acquisition: The 'failed functional features hypothesis'. *Second Language Research*, *13*(3), 187–226. doi:10.1191/026765897671476153

Hawkins, R., & Hattori, H. (2006). Interpretation of English multiple *wh*-questions by Japanese speakers: A missing uninterpretable feature account. *Second Language Research*, *22*(3), 269–301. doi:10.1191/0267658306sr269oa

Hayes, B. (2009). *Introducing phonology*. Chichester, UK: Wiley-Blackwell.

Hayes, B. (2009). *Introductory phonology*. Malden, MA: Wiley-Blackwell.

Hendricks, B. (2010). An experimental study of native speaker perceptions of nonnative request modification in e-mails in English. *Intercultural Pragmatics*, *7*(2), 221–255.

Henly, E., & Sheldon, A. (1986). Duration and context effects on the perception of English /r/ and /l/: A comparison of Cantonese and Japanese speakers. *Language Learning*, *36*(4), 505–522. doi:10.1111/j.1467-1770.1986.tb01036.x

Herd, W., Jongman, A., & Sereno, J. (2013). Perceptual and production training of intervocalic/d, ɾ, r/in American English learners of Spanish. *The Journal of the Acoustical Society of America*, *133*(6), 4247–4255. doi:10.1121/1.4802902 PMID:23742375

Herrera, S. G., Perez, D. R., & Escamilla, K. (2015). *Teaching reading to English language learners: Differentiated literacies*. Pearson Education.

Hewings, A., & Hewings, M. (2005). *Grammar and context: An advanced resource book*. London: Routledge.

Hickok, G., & Poeppel, D. (2007). The cortical organization of speech processing. *Nature Reviews. Neuroscience*, *8*(5), 393–402. doi:10.1038/nrn2113 PMID:17431404

Hillenbrand, J. M. (2003). American English: Southern Michigan. *Journal of the International Phonetic Association*, *33*(1), 121–126. doi:10.1017/S0025100303001221

Hillenbrand, J. M., Clark, M. J., & Houde, R. A. (2000). Some effect of duration on vowel recognition. *The Journal of the Acoustical Society of America*, *108*(6), 3013–3022. doi:10.1121/1.1323463 PMID:11144593

Hirakawa, M. (2001). L2 acquistion of Japanese unaccusative verbs. *Studies in Second Language Acquisition*, *23*(2), 221–245. doi:10.1017/S0272263101002054

Hirata, Y. (2004). Computer assisted pronunciation training for native English speakers learning Japanese pitch and durational contrasts. *Computer Assisted Language Learning*, *17*(3-4), 357–376. doi:10.1080/0958822042000319629

Hocket, C. F. (1970). *A Course in modern linguistics*. New York, NY: The Maemillion Company.

Hoff, E. (2006). How social contexts support and shape language development. *Developmental Review*, *26*(1), 55–88. doi:10.1016/j.dr.2005.11.002

Honikman, B. (1964). Articulatory settings. In D. Abercrombie, D. Fry, P. MacCarthy, N. C. Scott, & J. Trim (Eds.), *In honour of Daniel Jones* (pp. 73–84). London: Longman.

House, J. (1996). Contrastive discourse analysis and misunderstanding: The case of German and English. *Contributions to the Sociology of Language, 71*, 345-362.

House, J. (2006). Communicative styles in English and German. *European Journal of English Studies, 10*(3), 249–267. doi:10.1080/13825570600967721

Huang, C.-T. J. (1982). *Logical relation in Chinese and the theory of grammar* (Doctoral dissertation). Massachusetts Institute of Technology, Cambridge, MA.

Hurtado, L. M., & Estrada, C. (2010). Factors influencing the second language acquisition of Spanish vibrants. *Modern Language Journal, 94*(1), 74–86. doi:10.1111/j.1540-4781.2009.00984.x

Hwang, S. H., & Lardiere, D. (2013). Plural-marking in L2 Korean: A feature-based approach. *Second Language Research, 29*(1), 57–86. doi:10.1177/0267658312461496

Hymes, D. (1972). On communicative competence. In J. Pride & J. Holmes (Eds.), *Sociolinguistics* (pp. 269–293). Harmondsworth, UK: Penguin.

Ingram, J. C., & Park, S. G. (1998). Language, context, and speaker effects in the identification and discrimination of English /r/ and /l/ by Japanese and Korean listeners. *The Journal of the Acoustical Society of America, 103*(2), 1161–1174. doi:10.1121/1.421225 PMID:9479769

International Phonetic Association. (2015). *The International Phonetic Alphabet.* Retrieved from https://www.internationalphoneticassociation.org/sites/default/files/IPA_Kiel_2015.pdf

International Phonetic Association. (2019). *History of the IPA.* Retrieved from https://www.internationalphoneticassociation.org

Ionin, T., Luchkina, T., & Stoops, A. (2014). Quantifier scope and scrambling in the second language acquisition of Russian. In C.-Y. Chu, C. E. Coughlin, B. Lopez Prego, U. Minai & A. Tremblay (Eds.), *Proceedings of the 5th Conference on Generative Approaches to Language Acquisition North America (GALANA 2012)* (pp. 169–180). Somerville, MA: Cascadilla Proceedings Project.

Ionin, T., Ko, H., & Wexler, K. (2004). Article semantics in L2-acquisition: The role of specificity. *Language Acquisition, 12*(1), 3–69. doi:10.120715327817la1201_2

Ionin, T., & Zyzik, E. (2014). Judgment and interpretation tasks in second language research. *Annual Review of Applied Linguistics, 34*, 37–64. doi:10.1017/S0267190514000026

IPA Phonetic Transcription of English Text. (n.d.). Retrieved from https://tophonetics.com/

Ishihara, N. (2013). Is it rude language? Children learning pragmatics through visual narratives. *TESL Canada Journal/ Revue TESL du Canada, 30*(7), 135-149.

Ishihara, N., & Cohen, A. (2010). *Teaching and learning pragmatics. Where language and culture meet.* Longman Applied Linguistics.

Ishihara, N., & Cohen, A. D. (2010). *Teaching and learning pragmatics: Where language and culture meet.* London: Longman.

Jackendoff, R. (1972). *Semantic interpretation in generative grammar.* Cambridge, MA: MIT Press.

Jackendoff, R. (1977). *X̄ syntax: A study of phrase structure*. Cambridge, MA: MIT Press.

Jackendoff, R. (1989). What is a concept, that a person may grasp it? *Mind & Language, 4*(1/2), 68–102. doi:10.1111/j.1468-0017.1989.tb00243.x

Jackendoff, R. (1997). *The architecture of the language faculty*. Cambridge, MA: MIT Press.

Jackendoff, R. (2010). *Meaning and the lexicon: The parallel architecture 1975–2010*. Oxford: Oxford University Press.

Jakobson, R., Frant, C. G. M., & Halle, M. (1952). *Preliminaries to speech analysis: The distinctive features and their correlates*. Cambridge, MA: MIT Press.

jammable, adj. (2019). In *OED Online* (3rd ed.). Retrieved from http://www.oed.com/view/Entry/73895578

Jenkins, J. (2002). A sociolinguistically based, empirically researched pronunciation syllabus for English as an international language. *Applied Linguistics, 23*(1), 83–103. doi:10.1093/applin/23.1.83

Johnstone, B. (2018). *Discourse analysis* (3rd ed.). Hoboken, NJ: Wiley Blackwell.

Jones, T. (2018). Materials Development for Teaching Pronunciation. The TESOL Encyclopedia of English Language Teaching, 1-7.

Jones, D. (1969). *An outline of English phonetics* (9th ed.). Cambridge, MA: W. Heffer and Sons.

Jourdenais, R., Ota, M., Stauffer, S., Boyson, B., & Doughty, C. (1995). Does textual enhancement promote noticing? *Attention and Awareness in Foreign Language Learning,* 183-216.

Kartalova, Y. (1996). Cross-cultural differences in American and Russian general conventions of communication. Pragmatics and Language Learning, 7, 71-96.

Kasper, G., Nguyen, H. t., Yoshimi, D. R., & Yoshioka, J. K. (Eds.). (2010). *Pragmatics & Language Learning* (Vol. 12). Honolulu, HI: National Foreign Language Resource Center, University of Hawai'i at Manoa.

Kasper, G., & Rose, K. (2002). *Pragmatic Development in a Second language*. Oxford, UK: Blackwell Publishing.

Katz, J. J. (1972). *Semantic theory*. New York: Harper and Row.

Katz, J. J., & Fodor, J. A. (1963). The structure of a semantic theory. *Language, 39*(2), 170–210. doi:10.2307/411200

Katz, J. J., & Postal, P. M. (1964). *An integrated theory of linguistic descriptions*. Cambridge, MA: MIT Press.

Kazanina, N., & Phillips, C. (2010). Differential effects of constraints in the processing of Russian cataphora. *Quarterly Journal of Experimental Psychology, 63*(2), 371–400. doi:10.1080/17470210902974120 PMID:19585389

Kellerman, E. (1995). Crosslinguistic influence: Transfer to nowhere? *Annual Review of Applied Linguistics, 15*, 125–150. doi:10.1017/S0267190500002658

Kennedy, S., & Trofimovich, P. (2017). Pronunciation acquisition. In S. Loewen & M. Sato (Eds.), *The Routledge handbook of instructed second language acquisition* (pp. 260–279). New York, NY: Routledge.

Kennison, S. M., Fernandez, E. C., & Bowers, J. M. (2009). Processing differences for anaphoric and cataphoric pronouns: Implications for theories of discourse processing. *Discourse Processes, 46*(1), 25–45. doi:10.1080/01638530802359145

Kent, R. D. (1997). *The speech sciences*. San Diego, CA: Singular Publishing Group.

Kim, C.-E., O'Grady, W., Deen, K., & Kim, K. (2017). Syntactic fast mapping: The Korean extrinsic plural marker. *Language Acquisition, 24*(1), 70–79. doi:10.1080/10489223.2016.1187612

Kluge, D. C., Rauber, A. S., Reis, M. S., & Bion, R. A. H. (2007). The relationship between the perception and production of English nasal codas by Brazilian learners of English. *Proceedings of Interspeech, 2007*, 2297–2300.

Kondaurova, M. V., & Francis, A. L. (2006). Russian and Spanish listener's perception of the English tense/lax vowel contrast: Contributions of native language allophony and individual experience. *The Journal of the Acoustical Society of America, 120*(5), 3293–3293. doi:10.1121/1.4777845

Kondaurova, M. V., & Francis, A. L. (2008). The relationship between native allophonic experience with vowel duration and perception of the English tense/lax vowel contrast by Spanish and Russian listeners. *The Journal of the Acoustical Society of America, 124*(6), 3959–3971. doi:10.1121/1.2999341 PMID:19206820

Kondo, T. (2005). Overpassivization in second language acquisition. *International Review of Applied Linguistics in Language Teaching, 43*(2), 129–161. doi:10.1515/iral.2005.43.2.129

Krulatz, A. (2014). Integrating pragmatics instruction in a content-based classroom. *ORTESOL Journal, 31*, 19–25.

Labov, W. (1963). The social motivation of a sound change. *Word, 19*(3), 273–209. doi:10.1080/00437956.1963.11659799

Labov, W., Ash, S., & Boberg, C. (2006). *The atlas of North American English*. Berlin: Mouton-de Gruyter. doi:10.1515/9783110167467

Labov, W., Ash, S., & Boberg, C. (2008). *The atlas of North American English: Phonetics, phonology and sound change*. The Hague: Walter de Gruyter.

Labov, W., & Waletzky, J. (1967). Narrative analysis: Oral versions of personal experience. In J. Helm (Ed.), *Essays on the verbal and visual arts* (pp. 12–44). Seattle, WA: University of Washington Press.

Lacabex, E. G., Lecumberri, M. L. G., & Cooke, M. (2008). Identification of the contrast full vowel-schwa: Training effects and generalization to a new perceptual context. *Ilha do Desterro, 55*, 173–196.

Ladefoged, P. (1993). *A course in phonetics* (3rd ed.). Fort Worth, TX: Harcourt Brace & Company.

Ladefoged, P. (1999). Illustrations of the IPA: American English. In *Handbook of the International Phonetic Association* (pp. 41–44). Cambridge, UK: Cambridge University Press.

Ladefoged, P. (2005). *Vowels and consonants: An introduction to the sounds of languages* (2nd ed.). Malden, MA: Blackwell.

Ladefoged, P., & Disner, S. F. (2012). *Vowels and consonants* (3rd ed.). Malden, MA: Wiley-Blackwell.

Ladefoged, P., & Maddieson, I. (1996). *The sounds of the world's languages*. Oxford, UK: Wiley-Blackwell.

Lado, R. (1957). *Linguistics across cultures*. Ann Arbor, MI: University of Michigan Press.

Lado, R. (1957). *Linguistics across cultures: Applied linguistics for language teachers*. University of Michigan Press.

Lai, Y. H. (2010). English vowel discrimination and assimilation by Chinese-speaking learners of English. *Concentric: Studies in Linguistics, 36*(2), 157–182.

Lakoff, R. T. (1975). *Language and woman's place*. New York: Harper & Row.

Lardiere, D. (2009). Some thoughts on the contrastive analysis of features in second language acquisition. *Second Language Research, 25*(2), 173–227. doi:10.1177/0267658308100283

Larson, R. K. (1988). On the double object construction. *Linguistic Inquiry, 19*, 335–391.

Lass, R. (1988). *Phonology: An introduction to basic concepts*. Cambridge, UK: CUP.

Lee, J., Jang, J., & Plonsky, L. (2015). The effectiveness of second language pronunciation instruction: A meta-analysis. *Applied Linguistics*, *36*(3), 345–366. doi:10.1093/applin/amu040

Lee, S.-K. (2007). Effects of textual enhancement and topic familiarity on Korean EFL students' reading comprehension and learning of passive form. *Language Learning*, *57*(1), 87–118. doi:10.1111/j.1467-9922.2007.00400.x

Lev-Ari, S., & Keysar, B. (2010). Why don't we believe non-native speakers? The influence of accent on credibility. *Journal of Experimental Social Psychology*, *46*(6), 1093–1096. doi:10.1016/j.jesp.2010.05.025

Levin, B., & Rappaport Hovav, M. (1995). *Unaccusativity: At the syntax-lexical semantics interface*. Cambridge, MA: MIT Press.

Levin, B., & Rappaport Hovav, M. (2011). Lexical conceptual structure. In K. von Heusinger, C. Maienborn, & P. Portner (Eds.), *Semantics: An international handbook of natural language meaning I* (pp. 418–438). Berlin: Mouton de Gruyter. doi:10.1515/9783110226614.420

Levis, J. M. (2005). Changing contexts and shifting paradigms in pronunciation teaching. *TESOL Quarterly*, *39*(3), 369–377. doi:10.2307/3588485

Levis, J., & Wu, A. (2018). Pronunciation – Research into practice and practice into research. *The CATESOL Journal*, *30*(1), 1–12.

Lewis, D. (1972). General semantics. In D. Davidson & G. Harman (Eds.), *Semantics of natural language* (pp. 169–218). Dordrecht: Reidel. doi:10.1007/978-94-010-2557-7_7

Li, R., Raja, R., & Sazalie, A. (2015). An investigation into Chinese EFL learners' pragmatic competence. *GEMA Online Journal of Language Studies, 15*(2).

Liberman, A. M., Harris, K. S., Hoffman, H. S., & Griffith, B. C. (1957). The discrimination of speech sounds within and across phoneme boundaries. *Journal of Experimental Psychology*, *54*(5), 358–368. doi:10.1037/h0044417 PMID:13481283

Lindgren, E., & Sullivan, K. P. H. (2019). *Observing writing: Insights from keystroke logging and handwriting*. Leiden, The Netherlands: Brill Publishing. doi:10.1163/9789004392526

Lindqvist, A., Renström, E. A., & Gustafsson Sendén, M. (2018). Reducing a male bias in language? Establishing the efficiency of three different gender-fair language strategies. *Sex Roles*; Advance online publication. doi:10.100711199-018-0974-9

Linebaugh, G., & Roche, T. (2013). Learning to hear by learning to speak. *Australian Review of Applied Linguistics*, *36*(2), 146–159. doi:10.1075/aral.36.2.02lin

Liontas, J. I. (Ed.). (2018). The TESOL encyclopedia of English language teaching. Hoboken, NJ: TESOL International Association/John Wiley & Sons, Inc. doi:10.1002/9781118784235

Li, T. (2009). *The verbal system of the Aramaic of Daniel: An explanation in the context of grammaticalization*. Leiden: Brill. doi:10.1163/ej.9789004175143.i-200

Llisterri, J. (1995). Relationships between speech production and speech perception in a second language. In *Proceedings of the 13th International Congress of Phonetic Sciences* (Vol. 4, pp. 92-99). Stockholm, Sweden: Royal Institute of Technology/Stockholm University.

Long, M. (1996). The role of the linguistic environment in second language acquisition. In Handbook of second language acquisition. San Diego, CA: Academic Press. doi:10.1016/B978-012589042-7/50015-3

Lothers, M. & Lothers, L. (2012). Mirpuri immigrants in England: A sociolinguistic survey. *SIL Electronic Survey Report, 2012* (12), 1-33

Lust, B. (2006). *Child language: Acquisition and growth.* Cambridge, UK: Cambridge University Press. doi:10.1017/CBO9780511803413

Lwin, S. M. (2010). *Narrative structures in Burmese folk tales.* Amherst, NY: Cambria Press.

Lwin, S. M. (2015). Using folktales for language teaching. *English Teaching, XLIV*(2), 74–83.

Lwin, S. M. (2016). Promoting language learners' cross-cultural awareness through comparative analysis of Asian folktales. *TEFLIN Journal, 27*(2), 166–181.

Lwin, S. M., & Teo, P. (2014). How do we use language to make meaning? In R. E. Silver & S. M. Lwin (Eds.), *Language in education: Social implications* (pp. 45–65). London: Bloomsbury.

Machin, D., & Maya, A. (2012). *How to do critical discourse analysis: A multimodal introduction.* London: Sage.

Major, R. C. (2008). Transfer in second language phonology: A review. In J. Hansen Edwards & M. Zampini (Eds.), *Phonology and second language acquisition* (pp. 65–94). Amsterdam: John Benjamins Publishing. doi:10.1075ibil.36.05maj

Marcus, G. F. (1993). Negative evidence in language acquisition. *Cognition, 46*(1), 53–85. doi:10.1016/0010-0277(93)90022-N PMID:8432090

Martin, K. C. (2018, October 3). New words notes for October 2018 [Web log post]. Retrieved from https://public.oed.com/blog/new-words-notes-september-2018/

McClelland, J. L., Fiez, J. A., & McCandliss, B. D. (2002). Teaching the /r/-/l/ discrimination to Japanese adults: Behavioral and neural aspects. *Physiology & Behavior, 77*(4–5), 657–662. doi:10.1016/S0031-9384(02)00916-2 PMID:12527015

McCulloch, G. (2014, June 9). *Ish: How a suffix became a word.* Retrieved from https://slate.com/human-interest/2014/06/ish-how-a-suffix-became-an-independent-word-even-though-it-s-not-in-all-the-dictionaries-yet.html

McGregor, A., & Reed, M. (2018). Integrating pronunciation into the English language curriculum: A framework for teachers. *The CATESOL Journal, 30*(1), 69–94.

McLellan, H. (n.d.). *Politeness is more than "please."* Retrieved from https://americanenglish.state.gov/files/ae/resource_files/howard.pdf

Mehan, H. (1979). "What time is it, Denise?": Asking known information questions in classroom discourse. *Theory into Practice, 18*(4), 285–294. doi:10.1080/00405847909542846

Meisel, J., Clahsen, H., & Pienemann, M. (1981). On determining developmental stages in natural second language acquisition. *Studies in Second Language Acquisition, 3*(2), 109–135. doi:10.1017/S0272263100004137

Milroy, L. (1980). *Language and social networks.* Oxford, UK: Blackwell.

Minami, M. (2008). Telling good stories in different languages: Bilingual children's styles of story construction and their linguistic and educational implication. *Narrative Inquiry, 18*(1), 83–110. doi:10.1075/ni.18.1.05min

Mochizuki, M. (1981). The identification of /l/ and /ɹ/ in natural and synthesized speech. *Journal of Phonetics, 9,* 283–303.

Montague, R. (1974). *Formal philosophy: Selected papers of Richard Montague* (R. H. Thomason, Ed.). New Haven, CT: Yale University Press.

Montrul, S. (2000). Transitivity alternations in L2 acquisition: Toward a modular view of transfer. *Studies in Second Language Acquisition*, 22(2), 229–273. doi:10.1017/S0272263100002047

Montrul, S. (2001). First-language-constrained variability in the second-language acquisition of argument-structure-changing morphology with causative verbs. *Second Language Research*, 17(2), 144–194. doi:10.1177/026765830101700202

Morgan, J. L., & Travis, L. L. (1989). Limits on negative information in language input. *Journal of Child Language*, 16(3), 531–552. doi:10.1017/S0305000900010709 PMID:2808572

Morris, C. H. (1938). *Foundations of the theory of signs*. Chicago: University of Chicago Press.

Morrison, G. S. (2002). Perception of English /i/ and /ɪ/ by Japanese and Spanish listeners: Longitudinal results. In G. S. Morrison, & L. Zsoldos (Eds.), *Proceedings of the North West Linguistics Conference 2002* (pp. 29-48). Burnaby, Canada: Simon Fraser University Linguistics Graduate Student Association.

Munro, M. J. (2018). How well can we predict second language learner's pronunciation difficulties? *The CATESOL Journal*, 30(1), 267–282.

Myles, F., Mitchell, R., & Hooper, J. (1999). Interrogative chunks in French L2: A basis for creative construction? *Studies in Second Language Acquisition*, 21(1), 49–80. doi:10.1017/S0272263199001023

Nagy, W., & Townsend, D. (2012). Words as tools: Learning academic vocabulary as language acquisition. *Reading Research Quarterly*, 47(1), 91–108. doi:10.1002/RRQ.011

Nahavandi, N., & Mukundan, J. (2013). Impact of textual enhancement and explicit rule presentation on Iranian elementary EFL learners' intake of simple past tense. *English Language Teaching*, 6, 1.

Nash, H., & Snowling, M. (2006). Teaching new words to children with poor existing vocabulary knowledge: A controlled evaluation of the definition and context methods. *International Journal of Language & Communication Disorders*, 41(3), 335–354. doi:10.1080/13682820600602295 PMID:16702097

National Center for Education Statistics. (2017). *The condition of education 2017*. Retrieved from https://nces.ed.gov/pubsearch/pubsinfo.asp?pubid=2017144

National Governors Association Center for Best Practices, Council of Chief State School Officers. (2010). *Common core state standards for English language arts & literacy in history/social studies, and technical subjects, Appendix A: Research supporting key elements of the standards*. Washington, DC: Author.

National Reading Panel (U.S.) & NICHD (National Institute of Child Health and Human Development). (2000). *Report of the National Reading Panel: Teaching children to read: An evidence-based assessment of the scientific research literature on reading and its implications for reading instruction: Reports of the subgroups*. Washington, DC: National Institute of Child Health and Human Development, National Institutes of Health.

Nattinger, J. R., & DeCarrico, J. S. (1992). *Lexical phrases and language teaching*. Oxford, UK: Oxford University Press.

O'Dell, M., & Port, R. (1983). Discrimination of word-final voicing in German. *The Journal of the Acoustical Society of America*, 73(S1), S31–S31. doi:10.1121/1.2020331

O'Grady, W. (2005). *How children learn language*. Cambridge, UK: Cambridge University Press. doi:10.1017/CBO9780511791192

O'Grady, W., Archibald, J., Aronoff, M., & Rees-Miller, J. (2017). *Contemporary linguistics: An introduction* (7th ed.). Boston: Bedford/St. Martin's Macmillan Learning.

O'Neal, G. (2010). The effects of the presence and absence of suprasegmentals on the intelligibility and assessment of an expanding-circle speaker according to other expanding-circle English listeners. *Niigata Studies in Foreign Language and Cultures, 15,* 65–87.

Odlin, T. (1989). *Language transfer: Cross-linguistic influence in language learning.* Cambridge, UK: Cambridge University Press. doi:10.1017/CBO9781139524537

Ogden, R. (2017). *An introduction to English phonetics.* Edinburgh University Press.

Ogiermann, E. (2009). Politeness and in-directness across cultures: A comparison of English, German, Polish and Russian requests. *Journal of Politeness Research, 5*(2), 189–216. doi:10.1515/JPLR.2009.011

Oller, D. K. (1974). *Towards a general theory of phonological processes in first and second language learning.* Paper presented at the Western Conference on Linguistics, Seattle, WA.

Orion, G. F. (2011). *Pronouncing American English: Sounds, stress, and intonation.* Boston, MA: Heinle Cengage Learning.

Oshita, H. (2001). The unaccusative trap in second language acquisition. *Studies in Second Language Acquisition, 23*(2), 279–304. doi:10.1017/S0272263101002078

Ota, M., Hartsuiker, R. J., & Haywood, S. L. (2009). The KEY to the ROCK: Near-homophony in nonnative visual word recognition. *Cognition, 111*(2), 263–269. doi:10.1016/j.cognition.2008.12.007 PMID:19230869

Painter, C. (2001). Understanding genre and register: Implications for language teaching. In A. Burns & C. Coffin (Eds.), *Analysing English in a global context: A reader* (pp. 167–180). London: Routledge.

Pallier, C., Bosch, L., & Sebastián-Gallés, N. (1997). A limit on behavioral plasticity in speech. *Cognition, 64*(3), B9–B17. doi:10.1016/S0010-0277(97)00030-9 PMID:9426508

Pallier, C., Colomé, A., & Sebastián-Gallés, N. (2001). The influence of native-language phonology on lexical access: Concrete exemplar-based vs. abstract lexical entries. *Psychological Science, 12*(6), 445–449. doi:10.1111/1467-9280.00383 PMID:11760129

Palmer, F. R. (2012). *Mood and modality.* Cambridge, UK: Cambridge University Press.

Pariona, A. (2018, July 9). *Language families of the world.* Retrieved from www.worldatlas.com/articles/language-families-with-the-highest-number-of-speakers.html

Peng, L. (2013). *Analyzing sound patterns: An introduction to phonology.* Cambridge, UK: Cambridge University Press. doi:10.1017/CBO9781139043168

Peperkamp, S., & Bouchon, C. (2011). The relation between perception and production in L2 phonological processing. *Proceedings of Interspeech, 2011,* 161–164.

Perlmutter, D. M. (1978). Impersonal passives and the unaccusative hypothesis. *Proceedings of the 4th Annual Meeting of the Berkeley Linguistics Society,* 157-190.

Perlmutter, D. M., & Postal, P. M. (1984). The 1-Advancement Exclusiveness Law. In D. M. Perlmutter & C. Rosen (Eds.), *Studies in Relational Grammar 2* (pp. 81–125). Chicago, IL: University of Chicago Press.

Pierrehumbert, J. B. (2006). The statistical basis of an unnatural alternation. *Laboratory Phonology, 8,* 81–107.

Pike, K. L. (1947). *Phonemics.* Ann Arbor, MI: The University of Michigan Press.

Pinker, S. (1984). *Language learnability and language development.* Cambridge, MA: Harvard University Press.

Pinker, S. (1989). *Learnability and cognition: The acquisition of argument structure.* Cambridge, MA: MIT Press.

Portner, P. (2018). *Mood.* Oxford, UK: Oxford University Press.

Pullum, G. K., & Scholz, B. C. (2002). Empirical assessment of stimulus poverty arguments. *Linguistic Review, 19,* 9–50.

Pustejovsky, J. (1995). *The generative lexicon.* Cambridge, MA: MIT Press.

Putnam, H. (1962). The analytic and the synthetic. In H. Feigh & G. Maxwell (Eds.), Minnesota studies in the philosophy of science, Vol. 3: Scientific explanation, space, and time (pp. 358–397). Minneapolis, MN: University of Minnesota Press.

Radford, A., Atkinson, M., Britain, D., Clahsen, H., & Spencer, A. (2009). *Linguistics: An introduction.* Cambridge, UK: Cambridge University Press. doi:10.1017/CBO9780511841613

Radford, A., Felser, C., & Boxell, O. (2012). Preposition copying and pruning in present-day English. *English Language and Linguistics, 16*(3), 403–426. doi:10.1017/S1360674312000172

Ramus, F., Peperkamp, S., Christophe, A., Jacquemot, C., Kouider, S., & Dupoux, E. (2010). A psycholinguistic perspective on the acquisition of phonology. In C. Fougeron, B. Kühnert, M. d'Imperio, & N. Vallée (Eds.), *Laboratory phonology 10: Variation, phonetic detail and phonological representation* (pp. 311–340). Berlin: Mouton de Gruyter.

Ranbom, L. J., & Connine, C. M. (2011). Silent letters are activated in spoken word recognition. *Language and Cognitive Processes, 26*(2), 236–261. doi:10.1080/01690965.2010.486578

Reynolds, M. (2002). Punjabi/Urdu in Sheffield: Language maintenance and loss and development of a mixed code. In P. Gubbins & M. Holt (Eds.), *Beyond boundaries: Language and identity in contemporary Europe* (pp. 145–162). Clevedon, UK: Multilingual Matters Ltd. doi:10.21832/9781853595578-012

Richards, J. C., & Schmidt, R. (2013). *Longman dictionary of language teaching and applied linguistics.* New York, NY: Routledge. doi:10.4324/9781315833835

Riggenbach, H. (1999). Discourse analysis in the language classroom: Vol. 1. *The spoken language.* Ann Arbor, MI: University of Michigan Press.

Rivero, M. L., & Arhonto, T. (1995). Imperatives, V-movement and logical mood. *Journal of Linguistics, 31*(2), 301–332. doi:10.1017/S0022226700015620

Rogers, H. (2013). *The sounds of language: An introduction to phonetics.* New York, NY: Routledge.

Rogerson-Revell, P. (2011). *English phonology and pronunciation teaching.* New York, NY: Continuum.

Rosch, E. (1978). Principles of categorization. In E. Rosch & B. Lloyd (Eds.), *Cognition and categorization* (pp. 27–48). Hillsdale, NJ: Lawrence Erlbaum.

Rose, K. R. (2000). Interlanguage pragmatic development in Hong Kong, phase 2. *Journal of Pragmatics, 41*(11), 2345–2364. doi:10.1016/j.pragma.2009.04.002

Rose, K. R. (2005). On the effects of instruction in second language pragmatics. *System, 33*(3), 385–399. doi:10.1016/j.system.2005.06.003

Rose, K. R., & Kasper, G. (Eds.). (2001). *Pragmatics in language teaching.* Cambridge, UK: Cambridge University Press. doi:10.1017/CBO9781139524797

Ruellot, V. (2011). Computer-assisted pronunciation learning of French /u/ and /y/ at the intermediate level. In J. Levis, & K. Le-Velle (Eds.), *Proceedings of the 2nd pronunciation in second language learning and teaching conference* (pp. 199-213). Ames, IA: Iowa State University.

Ruiz-Soto, A. G., Hooker, S., & Batalova, J. (2015). *Top languages spoken by English language learners nationally and by state*. Migration Policy Institute. Retrieved from https://www.migrationpolicy.org/research/top-languages-spoken-english-language-learners-nationally-and-state

Rutherford, W. (1983). Language typology and language transfer. In S. Gass & L. Selinker (Eds.), *Language transfer in language learning* (pp. 358–369). Rowley, MA: Newbury House.

Saeed, J. I. (2016). *Semantics* (4th ed.). Oxford, UK: Wiley Blackwell.

Saito, K. (2011). Examining the role of explicit phonetic instruction in native-like and comprehensible pronunciation development: An instructed SLA approach to L2 phonology. *Language Awareness*, *20*(1), 45–59. doi:10.1080/09658416.2010.540326

Sakai, M., & Moorman, C. (2018). Can perception training improve the production of second language phonemes? A meta-analytic review of 25 years of perception training research. *Applied Psycholinguistics*, *39*(1), 187–224. doi:10.1017/S0142716417000418

Sanchez, T. (2005). *Constraints on structural borrowing in a multilingual contact situation* (Doctoral dissertation). University of Pennsylvania.

Sato, C. (1984). Phonological process in second language acquisition: Another look at interlanguage syllable structure. *Language Learning*, *34*(4), 43–57. doi:10.1111/j.1467-1770.1984.tb00351.x

Schachter, J. (1974). An error in error analysis. *Language Learning*, *24*(2), 205–214. doi:10.1111/j.1467-1770.1974.tb00502.x

Schmidt, R. (1990). The role of consciousness is second language learning. *Applied Linguistics*, *11*(2), 129–158. doi:10.1093/applin/11.2.129

Schmidt, R. W. (1983). Interaction, acculturation, and the acquisition of communicative competence: A case study of an adult. In N. Wolfson & E. Judd (Eds.), *Sociolinguistics and language acquisition* (pp. 137–174). Newbury House.

Schmitz, J., Díaz, B., Fernández Rubio, K., & Sebastian-Galles, N. (2018). Exploring the relationship between speech perception and production across phonological processes, language familiarity, and sensory modalities. *Language, Cognition and Neuroscience*, *33*(5), 527–546. doi:10.1080/23273798.2017.1390142

Schwartz, B. D., & Sprouse, R. A. (1996). L2 cognitive states and the full transfer/full access model. *Second Language Research*, *12*(1), 40–72. doi:10.1177/026765839601200103

Searle, J. (1969). *Speech acts: An essay in the philosophy of language*. Cambridge, UK: Cambridge University Press. doi:10.1017/CBO9781139173438

Searle, J. R. (1975). *A taxonomy of illocutionary acts*. Minneapolis, MN: University of Minnesota Press.

Searle, J. R. (1975). Indirect speech acts. In P. Cole & J. L. Morgan (Eds.), Syntax and semantics: Vol. 3. *Speech acts* (pp. 59–82). New York: Academic Press.

Searle, J. R. (1976). A classification of illocutionary acts. *Language in Society*, *5*(1), 1–23. doi:10.1017/S0047404500006837

Selinker, L. (1972). Interlanguage. *International Journal of Applied Linguistics*, *10*, 209–230.

Senft, G. (2014). *Understanding pragmatics*. London: Routledge. doi:10.4324/9780203776476

Shannon, C., & Weaver, W. (1949). *The mathematical theory of communication*. Urbana-Champaign, IL: University of Illinois Press.

Sheldon, A., & Strange, W. (1982). The acquisition of /r/ and /l/ by Japanese learners of English: Evidence that speech production can precede speech perception. *Applied Psycholinguistics, 3*(3), 243–261. doi:10.1017/S0142716400001417

Shriberg, L. D., & Kent, R. D. (2012). *Clinical phonetics* (4th ed.). Boston, MA: Pearson.

Sibata, T. (1969). *Methods in linguistic geography.* Tokyo: Chikumashobo.

Simons, G. F., & Fennig, C. D. (Eds.). (2018). *Ethnologue: Languages of the world* (21st ed.). Dallas, TX: SIL International. Retrieved from https://www.ethnologue.com/guides/how-many-languages

Singler, J. V. (2001). Why you can't do a VARBRUL study of quotatives and what such a study can show us. *University of Pennsylvania Working Papers in Linguistics, 7,* 257–78.

Skehan, P. (1989). *Individual differences in second-language learning.* London: Edward Arnold.

Slabakova, R. (2016). *Second language acquisition.* Oxford, UK: Oxford University Press.

Slobin, D. I. (Ed.). (1985). *The crosslinguistic study of language acquisition.* Hillsdale, NJ: Lawrence Erlbaum Associates, Inc.

Snyder, W., & Lillo-Marin, D. (2011). Principles and parameters theory and language acquisition. In P. Colm Hogan (Ed.), *The Cambridge encyclopedia of language sciences* (pp. 670–673). Cambridge, UK: Cambridge University Press.

Sorace, A. (2005). Selective optionality in language development. In L. Cornips & K. P. Corrigan (Eds.), *Syntax and variation: Reconciling the biological and the social* (pp. 55–80). Amsterdam: John Benjamins. doi:10.1075/cilt.265.04sor

Speas, M. (1990). *Phrase structure in natural language.* Dordrecht: Kluwer. doi:10.1007/978-94-009-2045-3

Sperber, D., & Wilson, D. (1995). *Relevance: Communication and cognition.* Oxford, UK: Blackwell.

Sprouse, R. A. (2006). Full transfer and relexification: L2 acquisition and creole genesis. In C. Lefebvre, L. White, & C. Jourdan (Eds.), *L2 acquisition and creole genesis: Dialogues* (pp. 169–181). Amsterdam: John Benjamins. doi:10.1075/lald.42.11spr

Stahl, S. (2005). Four problems with teaching word meanings (and what to do to make vocabulary an integral part of instruction). In E. H. Hiebert & M. L. Kamil (Eds.), *Teaching and learning vocabulary: Bringing research to practice* (pp. 95–114). Mahwah, NJ: Lawrence Erlbaum.

Stanescu, O. (n.d.). *The subjunctive in that-clauses.* Retrieved from https://www.academia.edu/15279111/THE_SUBJUNCTIVE_IN_THAT_COMPLEMENTS_1._On_the_concept_of_modality

Stavans, A., & Webman Shafran, R. (2018). The pragmatics of requests and refusals in multilingual settings. *International Journal of Multilingualism, 15*(2), 149–168. doi:10.1080/14790718.2017.1338708

Stevens, K. N. (1998). *Acoustic phonetics.* Cambridge, MA: MIT Press.

Stringer, D. (2010). The gloss trap. In Z.-H. Han & T. Cadierno (Eds.), *Linguistic relativity in SLA: Thinking for speaking* (pp. 102–124). Clevedon, UK: Multilingual Matters. doi:10.21832/9781847692788-007

Stringer, D. (2012). The lexical interface in L1 acquisition: What children have to say about radical concept nativism. *First Language, 32*(1-2), 116–136. doi:10.1177/0142723711403879

Sullivan, K. P. H., & Lindgren, E. (2006). *Computer keystroke logging: Methods and applications.* Oxford, UK: Elsevier.

Swadesh, M. (1934). The phonemic principle. *Language, 10*(2), 117–129. doi:10.2307/409603

Swan, M., & Smith, B. (Eds.). (2014). *Learner English: A teacher's guide to interference and other problems*. Cambridge, UK: Cambridge University Press.

Swinney, D. (1979). Lexical access during sentence comprehension: (Re)consideration of context effects. *Journal of Verbal Learning and Verbal Behavior, 18*(6), 645–660. doi:10.1016/S0022-5371(79)90355-4

Tagliamonte, S., & D'Arcy, A. (2005). When people say, "I was like...": The quotative system in Canadian youth. *University of Pennsylvania Working Papers in Linguistics, 10*(2), 257-272.

Tagliamonte, S. (2012). *Variationist sociolinguistics: Change, observation, interpretation*. Malden, MA: Wiley-Blackwell.

Tagliamonte, S., & Hudson, R. (1999). Be like et al. beyond America: The quotative system in British and Canadian youth. *Journal of Sociolinguistics, 3*(2), 147–172. doi:10.1111/1467-9481.00070

Taguchi, N. (2006). Analysis of appropriateness in a speech act of request in L2 English. *Pragmatics, 16*(4), 513–533. doi:10.1075/prag.16.4.05tag

Talmy, L. (1985). Lexicalization patterns: Semantic structure in lexical forms. In T. Shopen (Ed.), Language typology and syntactic description, Vol.3: Grammatical categories and the lexicon (pp. 57-149). Cambridge, UK: Cambridge University Press.

Tanaka, K. (1997). Developing pragmatic competence: A learners-as-researchers approach. *TESOL Journal, 6*(3), 14–18.

Tarone, E. (1980). Some influence on the syllable structure of interlanguage phonology. *IRAL, 18*, 139–152.

Templeton, S., & Bear, D. R. (2011). Teaching phonemic awareness, spelling, and word recognition. In T. Rasinski (Ed.), *Rebuilding the foundation: Effective reading instruction for 21st century literacy* (pp. 153–178). Bloomington, IN: Solution Tree Press.

Thomas, J. (1995). *Meaning in interaction. An introduction to pragmatics*. London: Longman.

Thomson, R. I., & Derwing, T. M. (2014). The effectiveness of L2 pronunciation instruction: A narrative review. *Applied Linguistics, 36*(3), 326–344. doi:10.1093/applin/amu076

Thorum, A. R. (2013). *Phonetics: A contemporary approach*. Burlington, MA: Jones & Bartlett Learning.

Ting-Toomey, S., & Chung, L. (2012). *Understanding intercultural communication*. New York: Oxford University Press.

Tomasello, M. (2003). *Constructing a language: A usage-based theory of language acquisition*. Cambridge, MA: Harvard University Press.

Travis, L. de M. (2008). The role of features in syntactic theory and language variation. In J. M. Liceras, H. Zobl, & H. Goodluck (Eds.), *The role of formal features in second language acquisition* (pp. 22–47). New York: Lawrence Erlbaum Associates.

Tremblay, A. (2005). Theoretical and methodological perspectives on the use of grammaticality judgment tasks in linguistic theory. *Second Language Studies, 24*, 129–167.

Trier, J. (1931). *Der deutsche Wortschatz im Sinnbezirk des Verstandes* [German vocabulary in the 'sense district' of the mind]. Heidelberg, Germany: Winter.

Trnavac, R., & Taboada, M. (2016). Cataphora, backgrounding and accessibility in discourse. *Journal of Pragmatics, 93*, 68–84. doi:10.1016/j.pragma.2015.12.008

Tsimpli, I. M., & Dimitrakopoulou, M. (2007). The Interpretability Hypothesis: Evidence from *wh*-interrogatives in second language acquisition. *Second Language Research, 23*(2), 215–242. doi:10.1177/0267658307076546

United States Census. (1980). *General Population Characteristics: Michigan*. Retrieved from https://www2.census.gov/prod2/decennial/documents/1980/1980censusofpopu80124uns_bw.pdf

United States Census. (2010). *Profile of general population and housing characteristics: 2010*. Retrieved from https://factfinder.census.gov/faces/nav/jsf/pages/community_facts.xhtml

United States Department of State. (n.d.). *Teaching pragmatics*. Retrieved from: https://americanenglish.state.gov/resources/teaching-pragmatics

Unsworth, S. (2007). L1 and L2 acquisition between sentence and discourse: Comparing production and comprehension in child Dutch. *Lingua, 117*(11), 1930–1958. doi:10.1016/j.lingua.2006.11.009

upvote, v. (2019). In *OED Online* (3rd ed.). Retrieved from http://www.oed.com/view/Entry/74232793

Usó-Juan, E., & Martínez-Flor, A. (2008). Teaching learners to appropriately mitigate requests. *ELT Journal, 62*(4), 349–357. doi:10.1093/elt/ccm092

van Dijk, T. A. (1993). Principles of critical discourse analysis. *Discourse & Society, 4*(2), 249–283. doi:10.1177/0957926593004002006

Veltman, C. (1983). *Language shift in the United States*. Berlin: Mouton. doi:10.1515/9783110824001

Vendler, Z. (1967). *Linguistics in philosophy*. Ithaca, NY: Cornell University Press.

Vennard, W. (1968). *Singing, the mechanism and the technic*. New York: Carl Fischer.

Vinka, M., & Waldmann, C. (2013). Doing it in Swedish doesn't mean you've done it. In J. Iyer & L. Kusmer (Eds.), *NELS 44: Proceedings of the Forty-Fourth Annual Meeting of the North East Linguistic Society* (pp. 243–254). University of Massachusetts.

Vogt, M., & Echevarría, J. (2008). *99 Ideas and activities for teaching English learners with the SIOP Model*. Boston: Pearson.

von Fintel, K., & Iatridou, S. (2017). A modest proposal for the meaning of imperatives. In A. Arregui, M. L. Rivero, & A. Salanova (Eds.), *Modality across syntactic categories* (pp. 288–319). Oxford, UK: Oxford Scholarship Online.

Vygotsky, L. (1986). *Thought and language*. Cambridge, MA: MIT Press.

Waldmann, C., & Sullivan, K. P. H. (2019). How the materiality of mobile video chats shapes emergent language learning practices in early childhood. In T. Cerratto Pargman & I. Jahnke (Eds.), *Emergent practices and material conditions in learning and teaching with technologies* (pp. 217–229). Springer. doi:10.1007/978-3-030-10764-2_13

Walsh, S. (2011). *Exploring classroom discourse: Language in action*. London: Routledge. doi:10.4324/9780203827826

Wardhaugh, R. (1970). The contrastive analysis hypothesis. *TESOL Quarterly, 4*(2), 123–130. doi:10.2307/3586182

Waring, H. Z. (2018). *Discourse analysis: The questions discourse analysts ask and how they answer them*. New York, NY: Routledge.

Warriner, J. E. (1946). *Warriner's English grammar and composition*. New York: Harcourt.

Wayland, R., & Guion, S. (2003). Perceptual discrimination of Thai tones by naive and experienced learners of Thai. *Applied Psycholinguistics*, *24*(01), 113–129. doi:10.1017/S0142716403000067

Weber, A., & Cutler, A. (2004). Lexical competition in non-native spoken-word recognition. *Journal of Memory and Language*, *50*(1), 1–25. doi:10.1016/S0749-596X(03)00105-0

Wennerstrom, A. (2003). Discourse analysis in the language classroom: Vol. 2. *Genres of writing*. Ann Arbor, MI: University of Michigan Press.

Werker, J. F., & Tees, R. C. (1984). Cross-language speech perception: Evidence for perceptual reorganization during the first year of life. *Infant Behavior and Development*, *7*(1), 49–63. doi:10.1016/S0163-6383(84)80022-3

White, L. (2003). *Second language acquisition and universal grammar*. Cambridge, UK: Cambridge University Press. doi:10.1017/CBO9780511815065

Whitman, R., & Jackson, K. L. (1972). The unpredictability of contrastive analysis. *Language Learning*, *22*(1), 29–41. doi:10.1111/j.1467-1770.1972.tb00071.x

Wilson, D., & Sperber, D. (1988). Mood and the analysis of non-declarative sentences. In J. Dancy, J. M. Moravcsik, & C. C. W. Taylor (Eds.), *Human agency, language, duty and value. Philosophical essays in honor of J.O. Urmson* (pp. 77–101). Stanford, CA: Stanford University Press.

Wittgenstein, L. (1958). *Philosophical investigations* (2nd ed.). Oxford, UK: Blackwell.

Wolfram, W. (2004). The grammar of urban African American vernacular English. In B. Kormann & E. Schneider (Eds.), *Handbook of Varieties of English* (pp. 111–132). Berlin: Mouton de Gruyter.

Wolfram, W., & Johnson, R. (1982). *Phonological analysis: Focus on American English*. Englewood Cliffs, NJ: Prentice Hall Regents.

Wray, A. (2000). Formulaic sequences in second language teaching: Principle and practice. *Applied Linguistics*, *21*(4), 463–489. doi:10.1093/applin/21.4.463

Wray, A. (2008). *Formulaic language: Pushing the boundaries*. Oxford, UK: Oxford University Press.

Yang, W., & Sun, Y. (2012). The use of cohesive devices in argumentative writing by Chinese EFL learners at different proficiency levels. *Linguistics and Education*, *23*(1), 31–48. doi:10.1016/j.linged.2011.09.004

Yavas, M. S. (2011). *Applied English phonology*. Oxford, UK: Wiley-Blackwell. doi:10.1002/9781444392623

Yip, M. (1987). English vowel epenthesis. *Natural Language and Linguistic Theory*, *5*(4), 463–484. doi:10.1007/BF00138986

Yip, M. (2002). *Tone*. New York: Cambridge University Press. doi:10.1017/CBO9781139164559

Young, R., & Morgan, W. Sr. (1987). *The Navajo language: A grammar and colloquial dictionary*. Albuquerque, NM: University of New Mexico Press.

Yule, G. (2010). *The Study of Language* (4th ed.). Cambridge, UK: Cambridge University Press. doi:10.1017/CBO9780511757754

Yun, S. (2009). *The socializing role of codes and code-switching among Korean children in the U.S.* (Doctoral dissertation). Oklahoma State University.

Yu, V. Y., & Andruski, J. E. (2010). A cross-language study of perception of lexical stress in English. *Journal of Psycholinguistic Research*, *39*(4), 323–344. doi:10.100710936-009-9142-2 PMID:20033291

Zanuttini, R., Pak, M., & Portner, P. (2012). A syntactic analysis of interpretive restrictions on imperative, promissive, and exhortative subjects. *Natural Language and Linguistic Theory*, *30*(4), 1231–1274. doi:10.100711049-012-9176-2

Zappa, F. (1982). Valley Girl [Recorded by Frank Zappa]. On Ship Arriving too Late to Save a Drowning Witch. California: Barking Pumpkin Records.

Zobl, H. (1989). Canonical typological structures and ergativity in English L2 acquisition. In S. M. Gass & J. Schachter (Eds.), *Linguistic perspectives on second language acquisition* (pp. 203–221). New York: Cambridge University Press. doi:10.1017/CBO9781139524544.015

Zoski, J., & Erickson, K. (2016). Morpheme-based instruction in kindergarten. *The Reading Teacher*, *70*(4), 491–496. doi:10.1002/trtr.1542

Zsiga, E. C. (2013). *The sounds of language: An introduction to phonetics and phonology*. Malden, MA: Wiley-Blackwell.

About the Contributors

Nabat Erdogan, Ph.D., is an Assistant Professor and Coordinator of the MSE (Master of Science in Education) in ELL degree program in the School of Teaching and Learning at the University of Central Missouri. She earned her first Ph.D. in Linguistics from Azerbaijan University of Languages in 2008 and her second Interdisciplinary Ph.D. in TESOL and English from the University of Missouri - Kansas City in 2018. Dr. Erdogan has over twenty years of experience in the field of TESOL, as an elementary, middle, and high school EFL/ESL teacher, ESL program director, and university professor for undergraduate and graduate Linguistics and TESOL courses both in the United States and abroad. Her research interests include comparative typological linguistics, applied linguistics, syntax, phonetics, second language literacy, and reading development for ELLs. Her long-term goal is to contribute to research in the areas of Applied Linguistics and Second Language Teaching and Learning as well as to the education of English learners through the preparation of ESOL teachers and TESOL professionals.

Michael Wei, Ph.D. is Associate Professor and Program Director of TESOL program at School of Education, University of Missouri – Kansas City. His research interests include applied linguistics, reading/writing English as a second or foreign language, learning environments, early second language development, and second language acquisition. He is the 2019 recipient of the Chancellor's Award for Excellence in Teaching at University of Missouri – Kansas City.

* * *

Nikki Ashcraft, Ph.D., is an Associate Teaching Professor in the online M.Ed. TESOL program at the University of Missouri, where she enjoys working with teachers in classrooms around the world. Previously, she trained pre-service and in-service teachers in the United Arab Emirates and Chile. She is former chair of the TESOL International Association's Teacher Education Interest Section and the author of Lesson Planning (TESOL Press, 2014).

Gulsat Aygen has a BA in English Languages and Literature and an MA in Linguistics at Bogazici University in Istanbul, Turkey. She received her Ph.D. ('02) at Harvard University. She has taught English for almost thirty years abroad and in the US. She has taught English and Linguistics at Harvard University and Reed College. She is currently a professor of linguistics at the Department of English in Northern Illinois University where she teaches English Grammar, English Linguistics, Syntax, Morphology, and Phonology. She has won many teaching awards in her career, and she is a Distinguished Teaching Professor at NIU.

Jon Bakos is an Assistant Professor in Linguistics and TESL/Linguistics with primary interests in dialect acquisition and usage-based language theory. He completed his PhD at Oklahoma State University in 2013, and his dissertation work was on the dialects of Oklahoma and the speech attitudes of local residents. Much of his fieldwork currently is in Indiana, and he has additionally been examining the uses of dialect in country music. He is also studying online discourse, particularly how players of Star Citizen and World of Warcraft acquire the game's jargon.

Clara Vaz Bauler is an Assistant Professor of TESOL/Bilingual Education at Adelphi University, New York. She has a Ph.D. in Education with emphasis in Applied Linguistics and Cultural Perspectives and Comparative Education from the University of California, Santa Barbara. She draws from thirteen years of national and international classroom teaching and work with English Language Learners from preschool to adult levels to inform her practice. Her research focuses on academic language development among multilingual learners, integration of scaffolding principles and practices into content area instruction, co-teaching and collaboration between ESOL and content-area teachers, and the use of web-based collaborative tools to support multilingual learners' writing. She is the assistant editor for the NYSTESOL Journal. She has led workshops for New York City and Long Island teachers and teacher assistants/paraprofessionals in scaffolding instruction for ELLs and cultural diversity.

Timothy Hall received his Ed.D. in Second Language Acquisition from Teachers College, Columbia University. He currently coordinates and teaches in a grant-funded program for ESL / Bilingual teacher certification through The College of New Jersey. His interests include usage-based linguistics and the intersect between teacher preparation and the field of Instructed Second Language Acquisition.

Victoria Hasko is Associate Professor of TESOL and World Language Education in the Department of Language and Literacy education at the University of Georgia (Athens, GA, U.S.A.) Her scholarship focuses on advanced second language proficiency attainment and explores such topics as acquisition of culturally-mediated concepts by second, foreign, and heritage language learners (e.g., motion structures, expressive morphology, identity repertoire, affective talk.) She studies the dynamics of language development as it interrelates with students' learning histories and sociocultural milieus. Her current projects include studying embodied cognition via eyetracking in monolinguals and bilinguals; investigating digital telecollaboration for language education and the affordances that it creates for fostering learner self-expression, inquiry-based learning, democracy in language classrooms, and global citizenship; and raising trilingual children. She is the Director of the University of Georgia Russian Flagship program funded by the federal National Security Education Program (NSEP).

Sofia Ivanova is Program Coordinator for the Russian Flagship Program at the University of Georgia (Athens, GA, U.S.A). Prior to this, she held the positions of Limited-Term Clinical Assistant Professor in the Department of Language and Literacy Education at the University of Georgia; Instructor of Russian at the University of North Georgia; Instructor of English at Kennesaw State University; and Lecturer of Anthropology at the University of North Carolina, Greensboro. She holds a BA in English and Anthropology from the University of North Carolina at Greensboro, an MA in Biocultural Anthropology from the Ohio State University, and a PhD in Linguistics with a specialization in Second Language Acquisition, Phonetics, and Phonology from the University of Georgia. Her research interests include second language acquisition, the acquisition of sound systems by adult learners, cue weighting in the acquisition of novel vowel contrasts, and Russian linguistics. Her most recent work examines the acquisition of English vowel contrasts and interdental fricatives by native speakers of Russian.

Patricia Kilroe, since completing her master's degree in linguistics at Georgetown University and doctorate in Romance linguistics at The University of Texas at Austin, has pursued a career in university teaching, administration, and research. In her current position of Associate Professor in the Writing & Literature Program at California College of the Arts, Kilroe teaches composition, linguistics, dramatic literature, and professional writing to multilingual students majoring in fine arts, design, and architecture. She has written and presented on the teaching of grammar to multilingual college students, the use of visual images in writing pedagogy, the value of an ongoing writing practice among composition faculty, the effectiveness of content-based instruction in second-language composition courses, and the role of language and rhetoric in dream formation processes. Kilroe is the author of Write on Art: An Image-Based College Composition Course for Multilingual Writers (2017).

Anna Krulatz is Full Professor of English at the Faculty of Teacher Education at the Norwegian University of Science and Technology in Trondheim, Norway. She obtained her PhD in Applied Linguistics from the University of Utah (2012). Her research interests include multilingualism with English, dominant language constellations, pragmatic development in adult language learners, content-based instruction, and language teacher education. She has authored and co-authored peer-reviewed articles in journals such as Language Teaching Research, Journal of Linguistics and Language Teaching, and Reading in a Foreign Language, book chapters, and popular scientific articles. Some of her recent or forthcoming publications include "Enacting Multilingualism. From Research to Practice in the English Classroom" (co-authored with A. Dahl and M. E. Flognfeldt; Cappelen Damm Akademisk, 2018), and "Handbook of Research on Cultivating Literacy in Diverse and Multilingual Classrooms" (co-edited with G. Neokleous and R. Farrelly; IGI Global, under contract).

Charles X. Li (née Xingzhong Li) is Professor of English in the Department of English at Central Washington University, where he serves as Graduate Coordinator of the M.A. TESOL program and Founder/Adviser of the Linguistics Minor program. He earned an M.A. in English at University of Canterbury and a Ph.D. in English at University of Missouri-Columbia. His teaching and research interests are in linguistics, second language acquisition, TESOL, linguistic approaches to literature, and poetic metrics. He is co-editor, with Luis López and Tom Stroik, of "Papers from 1997 Mid-America Linguistics Conference," translator of three novels from English to Chinese, including "Raymond Carver: A Writer's Life," and author of numerous articles on linguistics, stylistics, TESOL, and historical poetic metrics.

Solange A. Lopes-Murphy is a teacher educator in the fields of English as a Second Language and Literacy at The College of New Jersey. She has experience teaching English as a Second Language and Spanish to PK-12 students as well as undergraduate and graduate students in teacher education programs. Her research focuses on areas of multiculturalism in teacher education, cultural competence, cultural intelligence, the Universal Design for Learning (UDL), and the representation of English learners in special education programs. Dr. Lopes Murphy has published in the International Journal of Teaching and Learning in Higher Education, Journal of Effective Teaching, Vida Hispanica, Journal of the Imagination in Language Learning and Teaching, Teacher Educator Journal, TESOL Case Studies Series, among others.

Soe Marlar Lwin has a PhD in Language Studies from the National University of Singapore. She is currently an Associate Professor (Applied Linguistics - TESOL) at Singapore University of Social Sciences. She teaches courses on TESOL Methods and Classroom Discourse in the MA Applied Linguistics (TESOL) program, and Text/Discourse Analysis in the BA English program. Prior to that, she was an Assistant Professor at the National Institute of Education, Nanyang Technological University, Singapore, and taught courses on Introduction to the Study of Language, Language in Context, Analyzing Language Use and Oracy Development and Research to pre/in-service teachers in the BA (Education) and MA (Applied Linguistics) programs. Her research on narrative structures, multimodal analysis of oral storytelling discourse, and the use of stories and storytelling in language and literacy education has been published in international refereed journals such as *Language and Literature, Literacy, Language and Education,* and *Narrative Inquiry.*

John Rothgerber is a PhD candidate in Second Language Studies at Indiana University. His primary research focuses on the representation of speech sounds in the mental lexicon of the second language learner, and the ways in which perception and other factors affect this. He is also interested in pronunciation instruction and how it can be adapted to task-based language teaching contexts. He has over 13 years of experience teaching ESL/EFL in the United States and Japan.

David Stringer received his PhD in Linguistics from the University of Durham (UK) and is an Associate Professor of Second Language Studies at Indiana University. His main research area is the acquisition of syntax and lexical semantics. Other areas of research interest include World Englishes, language attrition, and biocultural diversity (linking language revitalization in indigenous cultures to the conservation of ecosystems).

Kirk Sullivan is Professor of Linguistics at Umeå University, Sweden. After having taken his PhD in 1992 and working in higher education in New Zealand and Sweden, he realized that he had a growing interest in education and enrolled in the University of Bristol's EdD programme, taking his education doctorate in 2010. Today, Dr. Sullivan's research interests lie at the nexus of linguistics, education, and cognition, and frequently technology. He has held a number of research grants, heads Umeå University's postgraduate school within the field of the educational sciences, publishes in journals such as the British Journal of Education, Second Language Writing, and International Journal of Multilingualism, and has recently co-edited two anthologies, Indigenous Writing and Literacies, and Observing Writing: Insights from keystroke logging and handwriting.

Angelica Vanderbilt graduated Summa Cum Laude and Phi Beta Kappa from The College of New Jersey in May 2018 as an English and Urban Elementary Education dual major. She is set to complete her Master of Education in Teaching English as a Second Language (TESL) in May 2019. She has been working in schools for the past 5 years, including student teaching internationally in Rome, participating in a New York City Teaching Fellowship with adolescent, bilingual students, internships in two bilingual kindergarten settings, time as an assistant teacher in two, multi-age Montessori schools, and experience tutoring Spanish-dominant 5th graders in math. Her hope is to help cultivate a love of reading, writing, and literature in her future students, by integrating inquiry and student-centered learning into her approach. She is excited to embark on her first year of teaching this fall.

Christian Waldmann is Associate Professor of Scandinavian Languages at the Department of Swedish, Linnaeus University in Sweden. Christian completed his PhD at Lund University, Sweden, in 2008, focusing on first language acquisition of grammar. With a background in linguistics and language acquisition theory, his current research interests include (technology-enhanced) language teaching and learning in formal and informal learning contexts, and cognitive aspects of writing development in students with and without special needs. He currently works as a researcher in a project on writing in upper-secondary students with and without a history of reading difficulties in elementary school, financed by the Swedish Research Council (2019-2022). Since 2017, Christian has been the Vice President of the Swedish Association for Applied Linguistics (Association suédoise de linguistique appliquée).

Howard Williams is Senior Lecturer in the Program in Applied Linguistics & TESOL at Teachers College, Columbia University, where he has taught since 1998. A Ph.D. graduate in Applied Linguistics at UCLA, he is a major contributor to the second and third editions of Celce-Murcia & Larsen-Freeman (1999/2016), The Grammar Book. He has published articles in ELT Journal and the Journal of Pragmatics. His major interests are in general linguistic theory and pragmatics and their relation to language pedagogy; he has a special research interest in reported discourse and citation norms.

Caroline Wiltshire earned her PhD in Linguistics at the University of Chicago in 1992, with specializations in Phonology and Dravidian languages. She is now an Associate Professor in the Department of Linguistics at the University of Florida, which she chaired from 2005-2012. Dr. Wiltshire has published over 50 articles in peer-reviewed journals, books and conference proceedings, and co-edited three books. Her focus of research and teaching has been on theoretical phonology and its interactions with morphology, phonetics, and second language acquisition, and she is currently working on a series of articles on the phonology and phonetics of varieties of English spoken as a second language.

Index

P

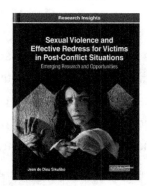

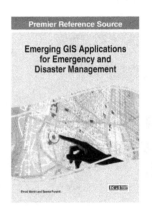
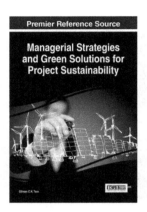

IGI Global's Transformative Open Access (OA) Model:
How to Turn Your University Library's Database Acquisitions Into a Source of OA Funding

In response to the OA movement and well in advance of Plan S, IGI Global, early last year, unveiled their OA Fee Waiver (Offset Model) Initiative.

Under this initiative, librarians who invest in IGI Global's InfoSci-Books (5,300+ reference books) and/or InfoSci-Journals (185+ scholarly journals) databases will be able to subsidize their patron's OA article processing charges (APC) when their work is submitted and accepted (after the peer review process) into an IGI Global journal.*

How Does it Work?

1. When a library subscribes or perpetually purchases IGI Global's InfoSci-Databases including InfoSci-Books (5,300+ e-books), InfoSci-Journals (185+ e-journals), and/or their discipline/subject-focused subsets, IGI Global will match the library's investment with a fund of equal value to go toward subsidizing the OA article processing charges (APCs) for their patrons.

   Researchers: Be sure to recommend the InfoSci-Books and InfoSci-Journals to take advantage of this initiative.

2. When a student, faculty, or staff member submits a paper and it is accepted (following the peer review) into one of IGI Global's 185+ scholarly journals, the author will have the option to have their paper published under a traditional publishing model or as OA.

3. When the author chooses to have their paper published under OA, IGI Global will notify them of the OA Fee Waiver (Offset Model) Initiative. If the author decides they would like to take advantage of this initiative, IGI Global will deduct the US$ 1,500 APC from the created fund.

4. This fund will be offered on an annual basis and will renew as the subscription is renewed for each year thereafter. IGI Global will manage the fund and award the APC waivers unless the librarian has a preference as to how the funds should be managed.

Hear From the Experts on This Initiative:

"I'm very happy to have been able to make one of my recent research contributions, 'Visualizing the Social Media Conversations of a National Information Technology Professional Association' featured in the *International Journal of Human Capital and Information Technology Professionals*, freely available along with having access to the valuable resources found within IGI Global's InfoSci-Journals database."

— **Prof. Stuart Palmer**,
Deakin University, Australia

For More Information, Visit: www.igi-global.com/publish/contributor-resources/open-access or
contact IGI Global's Database Team at eresources@igi-global.com.

CPSIA information can be obtained
at www.ICGtesting.com
Printed in the USA
BVHW011618120220
572078BV00020B/21